POPULAR LECTURES

ON

SCIENCE AND ART;

VOLUME I.

MÄDLER'S TELESCOPIC VIEW OF THE MOON.

G. & W. ENDICOTT LITH.

POPULAR LECTURES

ON

SCIENCE AND ART;

DELIVERED IN THE PRINCIPAL

CITIES AND TOWNS OF THE UNITED STATES.

BY

DIONYSIUS LARDNER,

DOCTOR OF CIVIL LAW, FELLOW OF THE ROYAL SOCIETIES OF LONDON AND EDINBURGH—OF THE ROYAL IRISH ACADEMY, MEMBER OF THE PRINCIPAL EUROPEAN SOCIETIES FOR THE ADVANCEMENT OF SCIENCE, AND FORMERLY PROFESSOR OF ASTRONOMY AND NATURAL PHILOSOPHY IN THE UNIVERSITY OF LONDON.

"The most obvious means of elevating the people, is to provide for them works on popular and practical science, freed from mathematical symbols and technical terms, written in simple and perspicuous language, and illustrated by facts and experiments which are level to the capacity of ordinary minds."

London Quarterly Review.

IN TWO VOLUMES.

VOL. I.

TWELFTH EDITION.

NEW YORK:

GREELEY & McELRATH, TRIBUNE BUILDINGS.

1850.

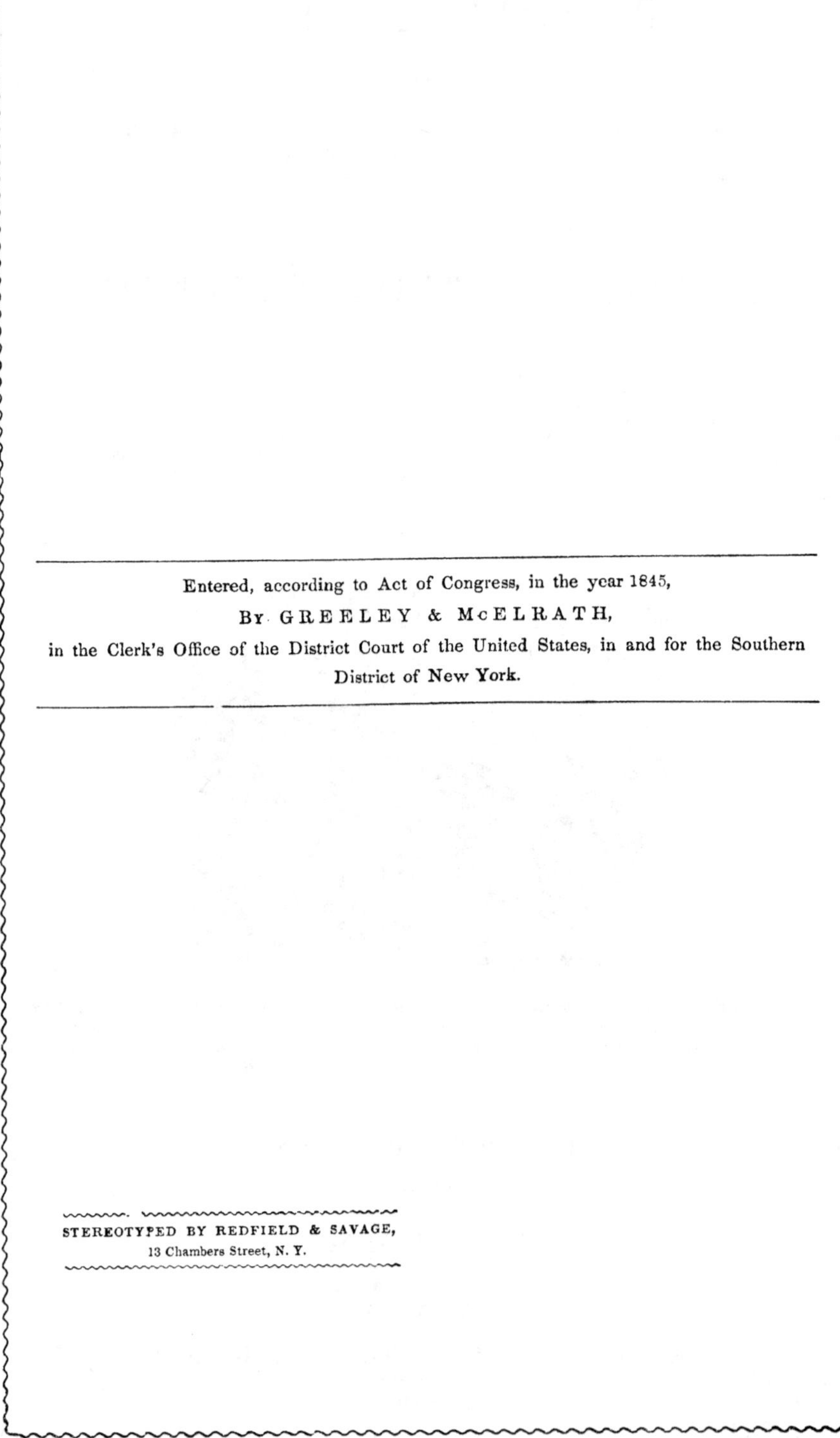

STEREOTYPED BY REDFIELD & SAVAGE,
13 Chambers Street, N. Y.

PUBLISHERS' ADVERTISEMENT.

The publishers announce that Dr. Lardner, having brought to a close his public lectures in this country, they have availed themselves of the opportunity thus presented to induce him to prepare for publication the present complete and authentic edition of these discourses. The general interest which they excited in every part of this country is universally felt and acknowledged. Probably no public lecturer ever continued for the same length of time to collect around him so numerous audiences. Nor has there been any exception to this favorable impression. Visit after visit has been made to all the chief cities; and, on every succeeding occasion, audiences amounting to thousands have assembled to hear again and again these lessons of useful knowledge. The same simplicity of language, perspicuity of reasoning, and felicity of illustration, which rendered the oral discourses so universally acceptable, are preserved in these miscellanies, which are, as nearly as possible, identical with the lectures as they were delivered.

The publishers feel that in these volumes they present to the American public a most agreeable offering, and an interesting and useful miscellany of general information, which will also afford that large class of persons, who have attended the lectures, an agreeable means of reviving the impressions from which they have already derived so much profit and pleasure.

GREELEY & McELRATH.

New York, *June*, 1846.

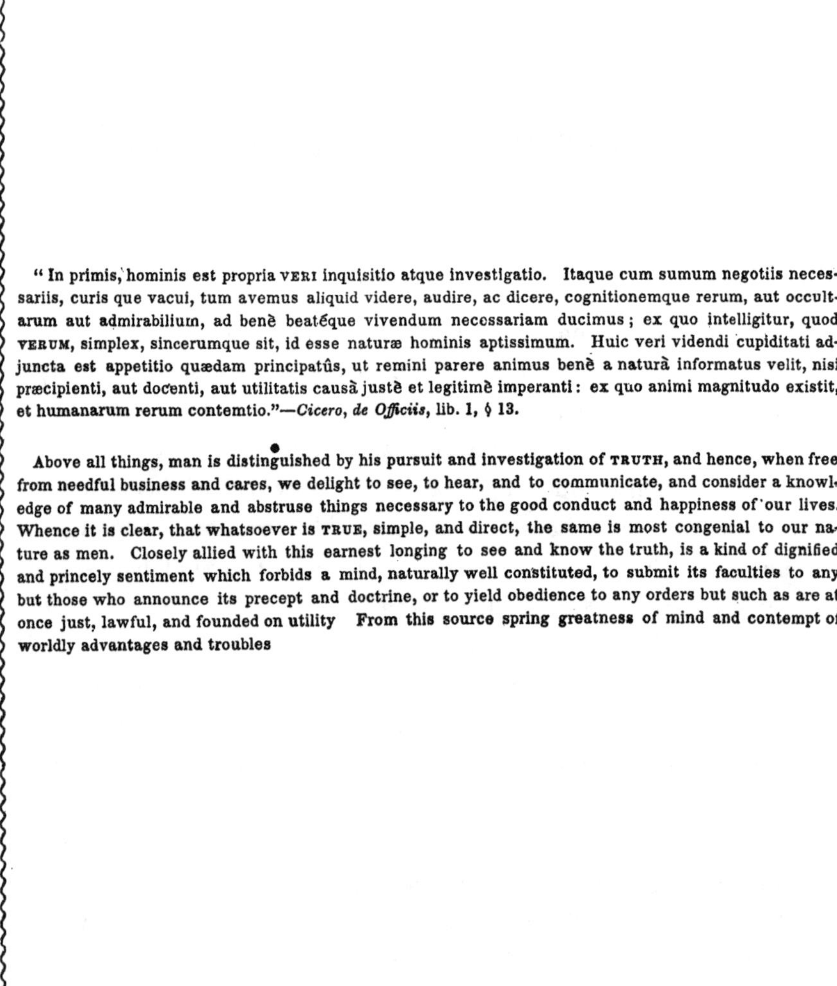

"In primis, hominis est propria VERI inquisitio atque investigatio. Itaque cum sumum negotiis necessariis, curis que vacui, tum avemus aliquid videre, audire, ac dicere, cognitionemque rerum, aut occultarum aut admirabilium, ad benè beatèque vivendum necessariam ducimus; ex quo intelligitur, quod VERUM, simplex, sincerumque sit, id esse naturæ hominis aptissimum. Huic veri videndi cupiditati adjuncta est appetitio quædam principatûs, ut remini parere animus benè a naturâ informatus velit, nisi præcipienti, aut docenti, aut utilitatis causâ justè et legitimè imperanti: ex quo animi magnitudo existit, et humanarum rerum contemtio."—*Cicero, de Officiis*, lib. 1, § 13.

Above all things, man is distinguished by his pursuit and investigation of TRUTH, and hence, when free from needful business and cares, we delight to see, to hear, and to communicate, and consider a knowledge of many admirable and abstruse things necessary to the good conduct and happiness of our lives. Whence it is clear, that whatsoever is TRUE, simple, and direct, the same is most congenial to our nature as men. Closely allied with this earnest longing to see and know the truth, is a kind of dignified and princely sentiment which forbids a mind, naturally well constituted, to submit its faculties to any but those who announce its precept and doctrine, or to yield obedience to any orders but such as are at once just, lawful, and founded on utility From this source spring greatness of mind and contempt of worldly advantages and troubles

PREFACE.

In presenting to the American public the collection of scientific miscellanies which forms the contents of these volumes, it may be proper to explain the circumstances which gave occasion to them in their original form of oral discourses, the character of the audiences to which they were addressed, and of the readers to whose information and amusement it is hoped they may contribute in their present more permanent state.

Engaged for a large portion of my life in the practical application of the physical sciences to the uses of life, and more especially to those scientific industries which derive their efficacy from the agency of steam, I had always looked forward with the liveliest interest to a time when I might be enabled to visit a country which had taken so prominent a part in the advancement of these arts, and which had formed from an early period so grand a theatre for their development, as the United States. To the claims which that country presented to the attention of every intelligent and inquiring tourist, arising from its important commercial relations with the old world, from its peculiar political institutions, and from the grandeur of its territorial extent and physical resources, I was as sensible as other travellers. But in addition to these, the enterprising character of its population, and the inventive spirit which so universally prevailed there in the mechanical and physical arts, rendered the country which had been the cradle of steam navigation more than commonly attractive to me. Had I, like most tourists, been contented to have made a short visit to America, flying through the states as fast as steamboats and railways could transport me, without remaining in any one place a sufficient time to see more than the external forms of things, and scarcely even that, I might easily have accomplished my purpose. But these travellers were beacons to warn, rather than examples to be followed. I knew that it were worse than useless to cross the Atlantic, until I could do so with the power of remaining in America for such a time as might enable me to acquire a knowledge of its population, their character and habits, the physical features and industrial resources of the country, and the practical working of its political institutions in all their various phases. The full attainment of such an object would require, not a summer's tour, or a winter's residence, but a sojourn of several years, to be judiciously distributed among different parts of that vast country in the proportion of their relative interest and importance.

Prepared to carry out these views, I departed for America in the autumn of 1840, and entered the splendid bay of New York on the evening of the 29th September. I determined to divide the first year of my residence between the two chief cities, New York and Philadelphia. After remaining for a few days in the former city, at the Globe hotel, I accordingly established myself in Philadelphia, where I remained for seven months; after which I removed to New York, where I resided about the same period. I now prepared to commence what might properly be called the grand tour of the states; and being accompanied by my family, the consequent expenses of travelling for so long a time, and through such distant countries, became a subject of consideration. Besides this view of my projected tour, another presented itself. Might I not render myself useful to the public, while gleaning information from them? and in the act of being useful to them, might I not multiply and enlarge the means of obtaining the information of which I was in quest? Since my arrival, I had often been solicited to deliver in one or other of the chief cities popular lectures on scientific subjects, such as I had occasionally given in England. I had already observed that the American public in New York and Philadelphia manifested more than ordinary taste for that species of oral instruction. Societies under various denominations existed in these cities and elsewhere, whose chief object was to get up weekly lectures on miscellaneous and unconnected subjects, delivered by various individuals invited for the purpose by the directors of such societies. These lectures, although for the most part since discontinued, were at that time popular and numerously attended. The success of these projects was the more encouraging when the quality of the article so greedily enjoyed by the public was considered. It is true, that among the numerous discourses thus brought together from all parts of the Union, some were found eminently possessing the qualities which such discourses ought to have, and which were well deserving of success. But these were like angels' visits, few and far between—

Apparent rari nantes in gurgite vasto.

In general, the history of such productions might be thus

traced: The committee of the ——— society of ———, in the state of ———, having determined to make up a course of weekly lectures to run through the ensuing season, send applications to all persons whose names they imagine will prove attractive to their subscribers. The real fitness of the individuals by their talents, acquirements, or habits, to fulfil the duty of a public instructor is little regarded. But the title of the Honorable A. B., senator from the state of C. D., or, if senators cannot be found, the Honorable E. F., member of the house of representatives, is regarded as a qualification of the first order. In any case an honorable is most important. The selection being made, a missive in due form is despatched by the president of the society, inviting the honorable legislator to deliver a lecture in the course of the ensuing season before the members of the ——— society, on such subject as the honorable legislator may please to select. To this an answer arrives in due time, graciously accepting the proffered invitation, and informing the committee that the subject on which the honorable legislator will descant for the edification of the members of the ——— society will, for example, be the life and character of Dr. Johnson. When the important evening, in the fulness of time, arrives, the lecturer is ushered in solemn form by the members of the committee to the pulpit, where a decanter of water, a glass goblet, and a pair of wax candles, are duly provided, and the members of the society are entertained for an hour and one half with selections from Boswell's Life of Johnson, in the formation of which the use of the scissors bears an unconscionable ratio to that of the pen.

Such was the process by which courses of lectures were usually got up. Now and then, however, these societies would obtain the aid of one of those self-styled professors who made a business of popular lecturing. In such cases, however, the instruction offered to the audience was but a shade better than that afforded by the amateurs to whom I have just referred. The information of these teachers is usually but skin deep. Their study, if so it can be called, is made expressly for their lectures, and the measure of their own information is strictly limited by the demands of their audience. They have learned for the occasion so much about the matter in hand as they shall have to say, and no more. Like certain storekeepers in Broadway and Chesnut-street, they exhibit their entire stock in their windows.

Although such was the general character of the popular lectures given in the chief cities at the time to which I refer, there were, nevertheless, occasional exceptions. Public teachers, eminently qualified, were from time to time induced to extend the benefits of their labors from the professional chairs of the universities, colleges, and public schools, to the more mixed and popular assemblies of the literary societies of the towns and cities of the Union, or to deliver courses to classes brought together by the talents and reputation of the lecturer. In such case, I observed that the superior value of the instruction offered was duly appreciated by the public, and that large and attentive audiences were collected, notwithstanding the unavoidable imposition of a much higher fee of admission.

Encouraged by all these circumstances, I proceeded to prepare the necessary means of illustration adapted for large and popular audiences, and commenced my proceedings by a public lecture given in the lecture-room of Clinton-Hall, in New York, in November, 1841. The result having proved to be successful, I removed to the theatre at Niblo's gardens, where an advantageous arrangement was made with the proprietor, and the lectures were continued every evening until Christmas. The months of January and February, 1842, were passed at Boston, where the lectures were given at the Melodeon and at the Tremont theatre. The unprecedented numbers collected in the latter building to attend the lectures will not be forgotten by those who were present on these occasions, and they afforded a satisfactory proof that the discourses delivered were adapted to the wants and the tastes of the population of that part of the Union.

The reputation which this species of entertainment had thus acquired now brought invitations from the other chief cities of the Union, and after having passed the months of January and February in Boston, I went to Philadelphia, where discourses were delivered in the Chesnut-street theatre on the alternate evenings during the month of March.

Between this time and the close of the year 1844, I visited every considerable city and town of the Union, from Boston to New Orleans and from New York to St. Louis. Most of the principal cities were twice visited, and several courses were given in Boston, New York, and Philadelphia. Nor did the appetite for this species of intellectual entertainment appear to flag by repetition. The audiences at Palmo's theatre, New York, in August, 1844, were even more crowded than they had been at Niblo's in 1841; those in the Melodeon at Boston, in October, 1844, were as numerous as they had been at the Tremont theatre in January, 1842; and the crowds assembled in the great saloon of the Philadelphia museum, in December, 1843, and January, 1844, were much greater than even the audiences of the Chesnut-street theatre, in March, 1842.

My purpose in mentioning these circumstances is not the gratification which such results might afford to my vanity, although I see no reason why I might not without impropriety express the pleasure which they afforded to me. I wish to produce them as affording a very striking characteristic of the American people. It was usual on each evening to deliver from two to four of the essays which compose the contents of the present volumes, and the duration of the entertainment was from two to three hours. On every occasion the most profound interest was evinced on the part of the audience, and the most unremitting and silent attention was given. These assemblies consisted of persons of both sexes of every age, from the elder class of pupils in the schools to their grandfathers and grandmothers. Frequently, as at the Tremont theatre, at the Chesnut-street theatre in 1842, and at Palmo's (New York) in 1844, the audiences amounted to twelve hundred, and sometimes, as at the Philadelphia museum in 1843, they exceeded two thousand. Nor was the manifestation of this interest confined, as might be imagined, to the northern Atlantic cities, where education is known to be attended to, and where, as in New England, the diffusion of useful knowledge is regarded as a paramount duty of the state. The same crowded assemblages were collected for a long succession of nights in the largest theatres of each of the southern and western cities—in the Charleston theatre; the Mobile theatre; the St. Charles theatre, New Orleans; the Vicksburg and Jackson theatres, Mississippi; the St. Louis theatre, Missouri; and in the theatres of Cincinnati, Pittsburg, and other western and central cities.

It cannot be denied, that such facts are symptomatic of a very remarkable condition of the public mind, more especially among a people who are admitted to be, more than any other nation, engrossed by money-getting and by the more material pursuits of life. The less pretension to eloquence and the attractive graces of oratory the lecturer can offer, the more surprising is the result, and the more creditable to the intelligence of the American people. It is certain that a similar intellectual entertainment, clogged, as it necessarily was, with a pecuniary condition of admission, would fail to attract an audience even in the most polished and enlightened cities of Europe.

It is proper to state here, that the lectures as orally given, though similar in substance with those which appear in the present volumes, differed considerably in form and expression. This must necessarily be the case. The oral discourses were strictly extemporaneous, in the only sense in which didactic discourses ever are so. They were delivered from the stage of the theatre without reference to any written notes or memoranda. The general outline of the subject, the leading arguments, and the most important illustrations and examples, alone were previously registered in the memory of the speaker. The language in which these were clothed, and the more minute details of the subjects, arguments, examples, and illustrations, were left to the suggestion and inspiration of the moment. Nor was this course adopted merely to save labor, or from any necessity arising from the over-pressure of business. It was pursued because it was found, from long practical experience in public lectures, to be the best. The style of the speaker is more animated than it could be when the discourse is uttered verbally from memory. The mastery which he has, or ought to have, over his subject, and the rich and various stores of illustration on which he draws, enables him to adapt his mode of reasoning and style of illustration to the varying character and capacity of his audience, and hence it will happen often that the same lecture, delivered on two different occasions and to two different audiences, will be given in different language, style, and with different illustrations. Those who have attended more than once the same lectures delivered by me, will recognise the truth of this observation.

But a written didactic discourse ought to differ materially from an oral discussion of the same subject. A reader and a hearer are placed under very different conditions. The one can proceed with such deliberation as the readiness or slowness of his capacity and the greater or less abstruseness of the subject may require. He may retrace his steps as often as he may find necessary, returning again and again on the same sentences. The other must catch the spirit and sense as fast as the words fall from the lips of the speaker. The style of a written essay is like that of a cabinet picture, that of an oral discourse like scene painting. The effect of the one is produced by elaborate finish, that of the other by bold and rough lines which seize the most inattentive and unskilled eye.

These distinctions, however true and important, are rarely attended to by those on whom the duty of public instruction devolves. Lectures accordingly, even when they proceed from those who by acquirement are most competent to instruct, are often either nothing more than demonstrations of scientific propositions and principles, or written discourses, generally read from the manuscript, or, as much more rarely happens, committed to memory, and delivered verbatim as written.

The qualifications of a good public lecturer for popular audiences are seldom found combined in the same person, although none of them can be regarded as very exalted intellectual gifts. Such a teacher must above all things possess a knowledge of his subject much more profound than that which he is required to impart. He must have a familiarity with all its details, such as can only be acquired by long experience in teaching. The same experience can alone make him know the difficulties of comprehension which his hearers will feel, and render him familiar with those means of illustration and exposition which will give him the easiest, surest, and most expeditious avenues to their understandings. He must possess such command of his subject, and such fluency of language,. as will render him altogether independent of written memoranda or notes, and enable him to speak directly from his thoughts and his understanding, and not merely repeat words which he has previously committed to memory. Clearness and order must be conspicuous in his reasonings, and his illustrations must not only be apposite, but adapted to the character, capacity, and acquirements of his audience. He must be endowed by nature with voice sufficiently powerful, and articulation sufficiently distinct, to render every syllable he utters easily and immediately audible to the most remote of his hearers, and his manner and appearance must be exempt from any peculiarities calculated to excite repugnance. Such a teacher will be sure to command success with a popular audience, and his labors will be beneficial to his hearers and profitable to himself.

That, in the delivery of the lectures comprised in these volumes, I was enabled to present this combination of qualifications I do not pretend; but I can state, with perfect truth, that ever since I commenced my duties as a public teacher, it has been my aim to acquire these qualifications to the utmost extent to which my natural gifts enabled me to attain them, and it is to the diligence with which these endeavors were directed, and the perseverance with which they were continued, that I ascribe the success which has attended my efforts as a popular lecturer, both in Europe and America. I may therefore be allowed to express a hope, that this statement may prove useful to others who may be induced to adopt a like course with the same public object.

The miscellaneous nature of the contents of the present volumes, and the absence of any logical connexion or arrangement among them, render some further explanation necessary respecting the mode in which the lectures were given. The audiences being composed, for the most part, of persons engaged in the pursuits of business, the exercise of professions, and the other active occupations of life, no regular cr consecutive attendance on any series of lectures could be looked for. Occasional attendances, as leisure, convenience, or inclination, might induce, were all that could be expected. It was, therefore, necessary that the discourses delivered on each evening should be, as far as possible, separate and independent, intelligible, useful, and entertaining of themselves, without reference to any others previously given, so that no one might be deterred from availing themselves of any one evening's lecture merely because they had not been enabled to attend the preceding ones. The same consideration rendered it unnecessary to observe any fixed order in the subjects of the lectures. It was usual to extend the evening's entertainment to a length not previously customary with public lectures. From two and one half to three hours was not an unusual length. This time, however, was not devoted to a single subject. A succession of two, three, and sometimes four subjects, would often be produced, having no connexion whatever with each other. Thus astronomy, electricity, and the steam-engine, would be successively noticed, short intervals of rest being left between them, as between the performances in a dramatic theatre. Unusual and unpromising as such a project may seem to have been, it was nevertheless perfectly successful, not in one, or in two, or in three cities, but in every part of the Union. This will explain much that might otherwise appear strange in the subject and contents of these volumes. The miscellaneous character of the subjects discussed—the rejection of all attempt at systematic arrangement—and the varying length of the articles—all correspond with the lectures as they were delivered to the public.

It is scarcely necessary to observe that the same series of discourses was not given in all places which I visited, nor was the entire collection contained in the present volumes given in any one place. Most of these essays were, however, on some one or other of my visits to New York, Philadelphia, and Boston, given in those cities.

A considerable number of these essays were prepared expressly for my lectures, among which may be mentioned all those on astronomical subjects, with one or two trifling exceptions, and several of those on steam. The substance of some have been incorporated in one or other of my former works, but in every case they have been more or less modified and adapted to their present purpose.

The object of this miscellany is not to enlighten those who devote themselves to the regularly-disciplined study of those sciences and arts which are here so slightly and popularly sketched. My purpose has been to instruct and inform, and at the same time rationally to amuse, those who have neither time, inclination, nor opportunity, to cultivate mathematics, by which alone a strict professional knowledge of astronomy, mechanics, and physics, can be acquired. To have attempted to adapt the work to both classes—to those who merely seek for general information on these subjects, without pursuing them through their strict scientific details, and to those whose object is to obtain a profound knowledge of them—would have assuredly led to the production of a work which would have been useless to both classes. It would have been unintelligible to the popular reader, and insufficient for the scientific student.

Mathematical reasoning and technical phraseology have, therefore, been almost if not altogether excluded from these essays. Instead of the rigid demonstrations of which the propositions and principles are susceptible by the aid of the language and symbols of the pure mathematics, other proofs are substituted, expressed in ordinary language, based on ordinary notions, and coming within ordinary comprehension. Illustrations which would be inadmissible in strictly scientific essays, are here freely used, and even profusely resorted to. The same position, where it presents any difficulty or abstruseness, is presented to the reader successively under different aspects, and elucidated by different illustrations; so that understanding, which may not be reached by one, will probably be struck by another. Subjects also are occasionally selected for discussion, such, for example, as the plurality of worlds, which, though quite admissible here, would scarcely find a fit place in a strictly scientific work.

Great pains have been taken by me, and no expense has been spared by the publishers, in supplying these volumes with instructive and useful diagrams. Those which I used in my public lectures, have been reduced in scale, and engraved for this purpose. The telescopic views of the planets have been taken from the drawings of the observers of highest reputation; and some of the views of the lunar surface, copied from Madler's drawings, now appear for the first time (so far as I am informed) in this country.

In the lectures on the steam-engine, I used large sectional models as illustrations. In lieu of these, the present volumes are illustrated with an extensive collection of plans and sections of steam-engines and their various parts, made on a scale as large as the size of these pages admitted. Among these, may be mentioned, as more especially deserving of attention, the series of eight large drawings of the locomotive-engines of Messrs. "Stephenson and Company."

It may be proper to observe here, that, as these discourses were designed for the use of the general reader, the practice I have found beneficial in my lectures, of using round numbers in preference to the exact numerical value, has been persevered in. Round numbers have the advantage of being easily impressed on the memory; and for the purposes of the readers for whose use these volumes are intended, they have all the necessary utility. Thus, for example, the distance of the earth from the sun is generally stated as a hundred millions of miles. This is easily remembered. Nor is it of any real importance for the objects of general information, that the real distance is more exactly ninety-five millions of miles. Again, the pressure of the atmosphere is a varying quantity, changing not only daily and hourly everywhere, but even at the same time differing in different places. It would be impossible to fix in the memory its average values at each season of the year, and at different places; but it is very useful and satisfactory to know that it may be assumed generally to be at the rate of about fifteen pounds on every square inch of surface exposed to its action.

These volumes have been designed for general information and amusement, rather than for the purposes of reference or systematic instruction. Nevertheless, the publishers have caused a copious index to be made for the work: the same facility of reference is afforded as if the usual order were observed in the arrangement and classification of the subjects.

DION. LARDNER.

MAY, 1846.

INTRODUCTION.

Several of the lectures delivered by Dr. Lardner in the city of New York were reported for "The New York Tribune," and were afterward published in pamphlet form. The last edition of these lectures was introduced by a "Sketch of the Progress of Physical Science," written by Dr. Thomas Thomson, of London. The publishers of this complete edition of Dr. Lardner's lectures deem the following extracts from that treatise, respecting the physical sciences of the ancients, an appropriate introduction to these volumes:—

The cradle of the human race was beyond dispute the southern portion of Asia—a delightful climate, where the original inhabitants of the earth first lived and multiplied. Chaldea and India had attained a high degree of civilization long before the Greeks and Romans had begun to emerge from a state of barbarism; but we know comparatively little of the attainments in science which these nations had reached. We are equally ignorant of the progress which mathematical and physical inquiries had made in China—not one of the treatises on mathematics, arithmetic, and astronomy, in the Chinese language, having been translated into any of the languages of modern Europe. But the resemblance between the Chinese and the ancient Egyptians is so very striking, and so complete, that it is difficult to avoid suspecting that they had a common origin. If this were so, China, from its contiguity to India and Chaldea, and from the delicious nature of its climate, must have been first furnished with inhabitants. And the Egyptians, if ever they were a colony of Chinese, must have been transplanted into Egypt long before the commencement of history. It was from Egypt that the Greeks drew the first rudiments of their mathematical and physical science; and the scientific acquisitions of that singular people constitute everything that we know respecting the progress which the ancients had made in the investigation of nature.

From the genial climate of the early inhabitants of the east, and the nature of the life which they led, it was natural to expect that the magnificent spectacle of the heavens would speedily attract their attention. We are certain that the Chaldeans made astronomical observations at least as early as the twenty-seventh and twenty-eighth years of the era of Nabonasser; that is to say, seven hundred and nineteen and seven hundred and twenty years before the commencement of the Christian era: for Ptolemy makes use of three observations of the eclipses of the moon, which took place during these years, and which he found in their records. Diogenes Laertius informs us that the Egyptians had preserved in their annals an account of three hundred and seventy-three eclipses of the sun, and eight hundred and thirty-two of the moon, which had happened before the arrival of Alexander the Great in their country. Now these eclipses required between twelve hundred and thirteen hundred years to happen. Alexander's visit to Egypt took place in the year 331 before the Christian era. If we add this number to the length of time during which the Egyptians continued to observe the eclipses of the sun and moon, we obtain sixteen hundred and thirty-one years before the commencement of the Christian era for the period at which the Egyptians began to record their observations. This period is rather more than a century after the death of Moses, and is about twenty-four years before the institution of the Olympic games; constituting but a small part of the forty-eight thousand, eight hundred and sixty-three years during which they boasted that they had been engaged in making astronomical observations; but this was obviously a fable, invented for the purpose of raising themselves in the opinion of the Macedonian conqueror.

What progress the Chaldeans and Egyptians had made in astronomy, it is hard to say. They certainly had become acquainted with the planets; but whether the Egyptians had discovered, as Macrobius assures us, that Mercury and Venus revolve round the sun, is not so clear. Their notions respecting the length of the solar year, and the mean length of the lunation, must have been a near approximation to the truth. This is evident from the famous Chaldean period called *Saros*. It consisted of two hundred and twenty-three lunar months, at the end of which the sun and moon were in the same situation with respect to each other as when the period began. This period includes a certain number of eclipses of each luminary, which are repeated every saros in the same order.

The Chaldeans appear to have divided the day into twelve hours, and to have constructed sun-dials for pointing out the hour. The sun-dial of Ahaz is mentioned in the Old Testament, on the occasion of the recovery of Hezekiah; but nothing is said about its construction. Undoubtedly, however, such sun-dials would require a certain knowledge of gnomonics—which, therefore, the Chaldeans must have possessed.

That the Egyptians had made some progress in mathematics admits of no doubt, as the Greeks inform us that they derived their first knowledge of that branch of science from the Egyptian priests. But that the mathematical knowledge of the people could not have been very extensive, is evident from the ecstasy into which Pythagoras was thrown when he discovered that the square of the hypotenuse of a right-angled triangle is equal to the square of the two sides: for ignorance of this very elementary, but important proposition, necessarily implies very little knowledge even of the most elementary parts of mathematics.

It was in Greece that pure mathematics first made decided progress. The works of three Greek mathematicians still remain, from which we have obtained information of all or almost all the mathematical knowledge attained by the Greeks. These are Euclid, Appolonius, and Archimedes.

Euclid lived in Alexandria during the reign of the first Ptolemy. Nothing whatever is known respecting the place of his nativity; though it is certain he lived in Greece, and that he died in Egypt, after the foundation of the celebrated Alexandrian school. He collected all the elementary facts known in mathematics before his time, and arranged them in such an admirable order—beginning with a few simple axioms, and deducing from them his demonstrations, every subsequent demonstration depending on and rigidly deduced from those that immediately precede it—that no subsequent writer has been able to produce anything superior or even equal. His "Elements" still continue to be taught in our schools, and could not be dispensed with, unless we were to give up somewhat of that rigor which has been always so much admired in the Greek geometricians. Perhaps, however, we carry this admiration a little too far. The geometrical axioms might be somewhat enlarged, without drawing too much upon the faith of beginners. And were the method followed, considerable progress might be made in mathematics without encountering some of those difficult demonstrations that are apt to damp the ardor of beginners.

The elements of Euclid consist of thirteen books. In the first four he treats of the properties of lines, parallel lines, angles, triangles, and circles. The fifth and sixth treat of proportions and ratios. The seventh, eighth, ninth, and tenth, treat of numbers. The eleventh and twelfth treat of solids; and the thirteenth of solids: also of certain preliminary propositions about cutting lines in extreme and mean ratio. It is the first four books of Euclid chiefly that are studied by modern geometricians. The rest have been, in a great measure, superseded by more modern improvements.

Appolonius was born at Perga in Pamphylia, about the middle of the second century before the Christian era. Like Euclid, he repaired to Alexandria, and acquired his mathematical knowledge from the successors of that geometrician. The writings of Appolonius were numerous and profound; but it is upon his "Treatise on the *Conic Sections*," in eight books, that his celebrity as a mathematician chiefly depends.

The conic sections, which, after the circle, are the most important of all curves, were discovered by the mathematicians of the Platonic school; though who the discoverer was is not known. A considerable number of the properties of these curves were gradually developed by the Greek geometricians. And the first four books of Appolonius are a collection of everything known respecting these curves before his time. The last four books contain his own discoveries. In the fifth book he treats of the greatest and smallest lines which can be drawn from each point of their circumference, and many other intricate questions, which required the greatest sagacity and the most unremitting attention to investigate. The sixth book is not very important nor difficult; but the seventh contains many very important problems, and points out the singular analogy that exists between the properties of the various conic sections. The eighth book has not come down to us. The fifth, sixth, and seventh books, were discovered by Borelli, in Arabic, in the library of the grand-duke of Tuscany. He got them translated, and published his translation, with notes and illustrations, in the year 1661. Dr. Halley published an edition of Appolonius in 1710, and has supplied the eighth book from the account given by Pappus of the nature of its contents.

Archimedes was, beyond dispute, the greatest mathematician that antiquity produced. He was born in Sicily, about the year 287 before the Christian era, and is said to have been a relation of Hiero, king of Syracuse. So ardent a cultivator was he of the mathematics, that he was accustomed to spend whole days in the deepest investigations, and was wont to neglect his food, and forget his ordinary meals, till his attention was called to them by the care of his domestics. His studies were particularly directed to the measurement of curvilinear spaces; and he invented a most ingenious method of performing such measurement, well known by the name of the "Method of Exhaustions."

When it is required to measure the space bounded by curve lines, the length of a curve, or the solid bounded by curve surfaces, the investigation does not fall within the range of elementary geometry. Rectilinear figures are compared on the same principle as superposition; but this principle can not be applied to curvilinear figures. It occurred to Archimedes, that, by inscribing a rectilinear figure within, and another without the figures, two limits would be obtained, the one greater and the other smaller than the area required. It was evident that, by increasing the number, and diminishing the sides of these figures, these two limits were made continually to approach each other. Thus they came nearer and nearer to the curve area which was intermediate between them. He observed, by thus increasing the number of sides for a great number of times successively, that he approached a certain assignable rectilinear area, and could come nearer to it than any difference how small soever. It was evident that this rectilinear area was the real size of the curvilinear area to be measured. It was in this way that he found that two thirds the rectangle under the abscissa and ordinate of a parabola, is equal to the area contained by the abscissa and ordinate, and that part of the circumference of the parabola lying between them. In the same way he obtained an approximate measure of the area of the circle, demonstrating that if the radius be unity, the circumference is less than $3\frac{10}{70}$, and greater than $3\frac{10}{71}$. His two books on the sphere and cylinder were conducted by a similar method of reasoning. He measures the surface and solidity of these bodies, and terminates his treatise by demonstrating that the sphere (both in surface and solidity) is two thirds of the circumscribed cylinder.

In the same spirit his "Treatise on Conoids and Spheroids" was conducted. These names he gave to solids formed by the revolutions of the conic sections round their axis. We pass over his researches on the "Spiral of Archimedes," as it is usually called, though in reality discovered by Conon, one of his friends; but must notice the treatise entitled "Psammites," or "Arenarius." Some persons had affirmed that no number, however great, was sufficient to express the number of grains of sand situated on the seashore. This induced Archimedes to write his treatise, in which he demonstrated that the fiftieth term of a ducuple increasing progression is more than sufficient to express all the grains of sand contained in a sphere, having for its diameter the distance between the earth and the sun, and totally filled with grains of sand. The treatise is short, but abstruse, in consequence of its imperfect method of expressing numbers employed by the Greeks. Were our figures substituted for the Greeks letters, the reasoning would be sufficiently simple and clear.

Archimedes did not confine himself to pure mathematics: he turned his attention likewise to mechanics, and may in some measure be considered as the founder of that important branch of physical science. He first laid down the true principles of *statics* and *hydrostatics*. The former he treats in his work entitled "Isorropica," or "De Equiponderantibus." His statics are founded on the ingenious idea of the *centre of gravity*, which he first conceived, and which has been so advantageously employed by modern writers on statics. By means of this principle, and a few simple axioms, he demonstrates the reciprocity of the weight, and the distance in the lever and in balances, with unequal arms. He determined the centre of gravity of various figures, particularly of the parabola, with great ingenuity.

His discoveries in hydrostatics were the consequence of a query put to him by King Hiero. This monarch had given a certain quantity of gold to a jeweller, to fabricate a crown, and he suspected that the artist had purloined a portion of the gold, and substituted silver in its place. Archimedes was requested to point out a method of determining how much gold had been purloined, and how much silver substituted. The method, it is said, occurred to him all at once, while in the bath; and he was so transported with joy, that he ran naked through the streets of Syracuse, crying out, εὕρηκα, εὕρηκα,—"I have found it! I have found it!" The discovery with which he was so deservedly delighted was this: "Every body plunged into a fluid loses as much of its weight as is equal to the weight of a quantity of the fluid equal in bulk to the body plunged in." This discovery furnished him with the method of determining the specific gravity of pure gold and pure silver. These being known, he had only to take the specific gravity of the crown, which (supposing no alteration in volume when the two metals are melted together) would enable him to discover how much gold and how much silver it contained.

The first principle being known, Archimedes deducted from it various other well-known hydrostatical principles, which he consigned in the first book of his treatise "de Incidentibus in Fluido." The second book of that treatise is occupied with various difficult questions respecting the situation and stability of certain bodies immersed in a fluid.

The ancients ascribe to him the invention of forty remarkable mechanical contrivances; but nothing more than some obscure notices of two or three of them have come down to us. His sphere, a machine by which he represented the movements of the stars and planets, is one of the most celebrated. It has been noticed by grave philosophers, and sung by poets, as may be seen in the following epigram of Claudian :—

> "Jupiter, in parvo cum cerneret æthera vitro,
> Risit, et ad superos talia verba dedit:
> Huccine mortalis progressa potentia curæ;
> Ecce Syracusii ludimur arte senis."

Archimedes wrote a description of this machine, under the name of "Sphæropœia;" but it is lost, and with it everything respecting the nature of the sphere has perished.

The burning mirrors, by which he is said to have set fire to the Roman vessels in the harbor of Syracuse, were long considered as fabulous. But Buffon showed how, by placing a number of small mirrors so that every one of them should reflect the image of the sun to the same point, heat enough might be produced to kindle wood at the distance of one hundred and forty feet.

The protracted defence of Syracuse against the Romans, chiefly in consequence of the wonderful mechanical inventions of Archimedes, is too well known to be enlarged on here.

If we except the discoveries of Archimedes in statics and hydrostatics, hardly any other branch of physical science was much cultivated by the ancients. They have made, indeed, considerable progress in the knowledge of acoustics, so far as music is concerned. In optics they can scarcely be said to have made any progress of consequence; and, in astronomy, very little till the time of Hipparchus, who may be considered as, in some measure, the founder of that sublime science.

Dr. Thomson lays down two methods by which the physical sciences are advanced: observation and experiment; and the application of mathematical reasoning to deduce new facts from principles already established. We give his remarks on observation and experiment, in which he exhibits an analysis of the theory of Bacon on this subject:—

It was not to be expected that mankind should at first make any rapid progress in investigating the laws which regulate the changes that take place in the material world. The objects were too numerous and too varied, and escaped his attention by their very regularity. Everywhere in the early ages of the world, we meet with descriptions of prodigies and wonders, while the regular operations of nature scarcely attracted attention. The method of investigating nature by observation and experiment was scarcely thought of, except by two individuals, who, by means of them, made some progress in mechanics and hydrostatics, and in astronomy: these were Archimedes and Hipparchus. The mechanical discoveries of Archimedes were slightly extended by Ctesibius and Hero, by Anthemius, and by Pappus; while the astronomical observations begun by Hipparchus were continued by Ptolemy.

But at the revival of letters, in the sixteenth century, a spirit of observation and inquiry awoke, which nothing could damp, and men began to pry into the secrets of nature, by the way of experiment. Galileo, in Italy, and Gilbert, in England, especially the former, constitute remarkable examples of the successful investigation by experiment. But it was Francis Bacon, Lord Verulam, who first investigated the laws according to which such experimental investigations should be conducted, who pointed out the necessity of following these laws in all attempts to extend the physical sciences, and who foretold the brilliant success that would one day repay those who should adopt the methods which he pointed out. This he did in his "Novum Organum," published in the early part of the seventeenth century.

Before laying down the rules to be followed in his new, or inductive process, Bacon enumerated the causes of error, which he divided into four sets, and distinguished, according to the fashion of the times, by the following fanciful but expressive names:—

Idols of the tribe;
Idols of the den;
Idols of the forum;
Idols of the theatre.

The *idols of the tribe* are the causes of error, founded on human nature in general. Thus all men have a propensity to find in nature a greater degree of order, simplicity, and regularity, than is actually indicated by observation. This propensity, usually distinguished by the title of *spirit of system*, is one of the greatest enemies to its progress that science has to struggle with.

The *idols of the den* are those that spring from the peculiar character of the individual. Each individual, according to Bacon, has his own dark cave or den, into which the light is imperfectly admitted, and in the obscurity of which an idol lurks, at whose shrine the truth is often sacrificed. Some minds are best adapted to catch the differences, others the resemblances of things. Some proceed too rapidly, others too slowly. Almost every person has acquired a partiality for some branch of science, to which he is prone to fashion and force every other.

The *idols of the forum* are those which arise out of the intercourse of society, and especially from language, by means of which men communicate with each other. It is well known that words, in some measure, govern thought, and that we cannot think accurately unless we are able to express ourselves accurately. The same word does not convey the same idea to different persons. Hence many disputes are merely verbal, though the disputants may not be aware of the circumstance.

The *idols of the theatre* are the deceptions which have taken their rise from the systems of different schools of philosophy. These errors affected the philosophy of the ancients more than that of the moderns. But they are not yet without their effect, and often act powerfully upon individuals without their being aware of their effect.

After an historical view of science from its dawn among the Greeks to his own time, and pointing out the little progress which it had made, in consequence of the improper way in which it had been cultivated, Bacon proceeds, in his second book, to point out the true way of advancing science by *induction*.

The first object ought to be, to prepare a history of the phenomena to be explained, in all their modifications and varieties. This history is to comprehend not only all such facts as spontaneously offer themselves, but all the experiments instituted for the sake of discovery, or for any of the purposes of the useful arts. It ought to be composed with great care ; the facts should be accurately related and distinctly arranged—their authenticity carefully ascertained, and those that are doubtful should be marked as uncertain, with the grounds for the judgment formed. This record of facts Bacon calls *natural history*.

The next object is, a comparison of the different facts, to find out the cause of the *phenomenon*.

The method of induction here laid down is applicable to all investigations where experience is the guide, whether in the moral or natural world.

It is obvious that all facts, even supposing them truly and accurately recorded, are not of equal value in the discovery of truth. Some of them show the thing sought for in its highest degree, others in its lowest; some show it simple and uncombined, while others are confused with a variety of circumstances. Some facts are easily interpreted, others are very obscure, and are understood only in consequence of the light thrown on them by the former. This led Bacon to consider the comparative value of facts as means of discovery. He enumerates twenty-seven different species ; but we shall satisfy ourselves here with noticing a few of the most important of them :—

1. *Instantiæ solitariæ* are examples of the same quality existing in two bodies, which have nothing else in common ; or of a quality differing in two bodies, which are in all other respects the same.

2. The *instantiæ migrantes* exhibit some nature or property of bodies passing from one condition to another, either from less to greater, or from greater to less. Thus, glass while entire is colorless, but becomes white when reduced to powder.

3. The *instantiæ ostensivæ* show some particular nature in its highest state of power or energy. In this way the thermometer shows the expansive power of heat, and the barometer the weight of air.

4. The *instantia analogicæ* consist of facts between which an analogy or resemblance is visible in some particulars, notwithstanding great diversity in all the rest. Such are the telescope and microscope in works of art, compared with the eye in the works of nature.

5. The *instantiæ crucis* is the division of this experimental logic which is the most frequently resorted to in the practice of inductive investigation. When, in such an investigation, the understanding is, as it were, placed in equilibrio between two or more causes, each of which accounts equally well for the appearances, so far as they are known, nothing remains but to look out for a fact which can be explained by the one of these causes, and not by the other. If such a fact can be found, the uncertainty is removed, and the true cause becomes apparent. Such

facts perform the office of a *cross*, erected at the meeting of two roads, to direct the traveller which way he is to go. On this account, Bacon gave them the name of *instantiæ crucis*. Suppose it were inquired into why metals become heavier when calcined, various explanations might be conceived. But the *experimentum crucis* of Lavoisier removed the ambiguity. He enclosed a quantity of tin in a large glass vessel, which was hermetically sealed. Heat being then applied, the tin melted and was partly calcined. The process being finished, the weight of the glass and its contents were found unchanged. But the glass being opened, a quantity of air rushed in, amounting in weight to ten grains; and the tin was found to have increased in weight to ten grains. It was obvious from this, that by the calcination of the tin a portion of the air had been absorbed, which had occasioned the increase of the weight.

In cases where an *experimentum crucis* cannot be resorted to, there is often a great want of conclusive evidence. This is the case in agriculture, in medicine, in political economy, &c. To make one experiment similar to another in all respects but one, is what the *experimentum crucis* and the principle of induction in general requires. But this, in the sciences just named, can seldom be accomplished. Hence the great difficulty of separating the causes, and allotting to each its due proportion of the effect. Men deceive themselves in consequence of this continually, and think they are reasoning from fact and experience, when in reality they are drawing their conclusions from a mixture of truth and falsehood. Facts so incorrectly apprehended only serve to render error more incorrigible.

Of the twenty-seven classes into which *instantiæ* are arranged by Bacon, fifteen address themselves immediately to the understanding; five serve to correct or inform the senses; and seven to direct the hand in raising the superstructure of art on the foundation of science. The examples which we have selected are from the first of these divisions. The other two are of inferior importance, and may be omitted in this imperfect summary.

Such are the rules laid down by Bacon for prosecuting the sciences by induction. The effects which were ultimately produced by the "Novum Organum" must have been very great. It may be questioned, indeed, whether those who have contributed most effectually to the advancement of the sciences, have rigidly adhered to Bacon's rules. And, in general, such a rigid adherence is unnecessary ; because so much assistance can, in general, be derived from what knowledge has been already acquired, that a rigid natural historical detail of all the phenomena becomes unnecessary. It was only in the infancy of science that such details were requisite. Boyle often draws them up in his inquiries into the cause of various phenomena, and his investigations were of considerable use in forwarding those branches of science which he cultivated. Bacon also was mistaken in conceiving that, by investigation, mankind may become acquainted with the *essences* of the powers and qualities residing in bodies. So far as science has hitherto advanced, no one essence has been discovered, either as to matter or as to any of its more extensive modifications. Thus we are still in doubt whether heat and electricity be qualities or substances. Yet we have discovered many important properties or laws, by means of which heat and electricity, whether properties or substances, are regulated. And from this knowledge, probably, we derive as much advantage as could be obtained from a complete knowledge of their essence.

By *experiment* or *observation* all the new facts in every science are acquired. By the application of mathematical reasoning to these facts, they are reduced to the requisite simplicity, and the general principles which regulate every particular science determined.

ANALYTICAL INDEX.

[NOTE.—The volumes are indicated by the numeral letters i., ii., and the page by the figures.]

B.

C.

D.

E.

M.

N.

O.

P.

Q.

R.

S.

T.

U.

V.

W.

Y.

Z.

THE PLURALITY OF WORLDS.

Contemplation of the Firmament.—Reflections thereby suggested.—Limited Powers of the Telescope.—What it can do for us.—Its effect on the Appearances of the Planets.—Are the Planets inhabited?—Circumstantial Evidence.—Analogies of the Planets to the Earth.—Plan of the Solar System.—Uniform Supply of Light and Warmth.—Expedient for securing it.—Different Distances of the Planets do not necessarily infer different Temperatures—nor different Degrees of Light.—Admirable Adaptation of the Rotation of the Earth to the Organization of its Inhabitants.—The same Provision exists on the Planets.—Minor and Major Planets.—Short Days on the latter.—The Seasons.—Similar Arrangement on the Planets.—The Atmosphere.—Similar Appendage to the Planets.—Many uses of the Atmosphere.—Clouds.—Rain, Hail, and Snow.—Mountains on the Planets.—Land and Water.—Weights of Bodies on the Planets analogous to Weight on the Earth.—Appearances of the Sun.—Conclusion.

"The Heavens declare the glory of God:
And the Firmament showeth his handy-work."

Ps. xix. 1.

THE PLURALITY OF WORLDS.

WHEN we walk forth on a serene night and direct our view to the aspect of the heavens, there are certain reflections which will present themselves to every mind gifted with the slightest power of contemplation. Are those shining orbs which so richly decorate the firmament peopled with creatures endowed like ourselves with reason to discover, with sense to love, and with imagination to expand toward their limitless perfection the attributes of Him of "whose fingers the heavens are the work?" Has He who "made man lower than the angels to crown him," with the glory of discovering that light in which he has "decked himself as with a garment," also made other creatures with like powers and like destinies; with dominion over the works of his hands, and having all things "put in subjection under their feet?" And are those resplendent globes which roll in silent majesty through the measureless abysses of space, the dwellings of such beings? These are questions which will be asked, and which will be answered. These are inquiries against which neither the urgency of business nor the allurements of pleasure can block up the avenues of the mind. These are questions that have been asked, and that will continue to be asked, by all who view the earth as an individual of that little cluster of worlds called the solar system.

Those whose information on topics of this nature is limited, would be prompted, in seeking the satisfaction of such inquiries, to look immediately for direct evidence; and consequently to appeal to the telescope. Such an appeal would, however, be fruitless. Vast as are the powers of that instrument, and great the improvements which have been conferred upon it, it still falls infinitely short of the ability to give direct evidence on such inquiries. What will a telescope do for us in regard to the examination of the heavenly bodies, or indeed of any distant object? It will accomplish this, and nothing more: it will place us at a less distance from the object to which we direct our view; it will enable us to approach it within a certain limit of distance, and to behold it as we should do without a telescope at the lesser distances. But, strictly speaking, it cannot accomplish even this; for to suppose it did, would be to imagine it to possess all the admirable optical perfection of the eye. That instrument, however nearly it approaches the organ of vision in its qualities, is still deficient in some of the attributes which have been conferred upon the eye by its Maker. It is found that in proportion as we augment the magnifying power of the telescope, we diminish both the quantity of light upon the object we behold, and also the distinctness of its features and outlines. These and some other circumstances peculiar to the telescope, which need not be particularly detailed now, impose a limit on the magnifying powers that are practically available in inquiries of this kind.

Let us, however, suppose that we could resort to the use of a telescope having the magnifying power of a thousand in examining any of the heavenly bodies: what would such an instrument do for us? It would in fact place us a thousand times nearer to the object that we are desirous to examine, and thus enable us to see that object as we should see it at that diminished distance without a telescope at all. Such is the extent of the aid which we should derive from the telescope. Now, let us see what this aid would effect. Take the case of the moon, the nearest body in the universe to the earth. The distance of that object is about 240,000 miles; the telescope would then place us about 240 miles from it. Could we at the distance of 240 miles distinctly, or even indistinctly, see a man, a horse, an elephant, or any other natural object? Could we discern any artificial structure? Assuredly not! But take the case of one of the planets. When Mars is nearest to the earth, its distance is about 50,000,000 of miles. Such a telescope would place us at a distance of 50,000 miles from it. What object could we expect to see at 50,000 miles' distance? The planet Venus, when nearest the earth, is at a distance something less than 30,000,000 of miles, but at that distance her dark hemisphere is turned toward us; and when a considerable portion of her enlightened hemisphere is visible, her distance is not less than that of Mars. All the other planets, when nearest to the earth, are at much greater distances. As the stars lie infinitely more remote than the most remote planet, it is needless here to add anything respecting them.

It is plain, then, that the telescope cannot afford any direct evidence on the question whether the planets, like the earth, are inhabited globes. Yet, although science has not given direct answers to these questions, it has supplied a body of circumstantial evidence bearing upon them of an extremely interesting nature. Modern discovery has collected together a mass of facts connected with the position and motions, the physical character and conditions, and the parts played in the solar system by the several globes of which that system is composed, which forms a body of analogies bearing on this inquiry, even more cogent and convincing than the proofs on the strength of which we daily dispose of the property and lives of our fellow-citizens, and hazard our own.

In considering the earth as a dwelling-place suited to man and to the creatures which it has pleased his Maker to place in subjection to him, there is a mutual fitness and adaptation observable among a multitude of arrangements which cannot be traced to, and which indeed obviously cannot arise from, any general mechanical law by which the motions and changes of mere material masses are observed to be governed. It is in these conveniences and luxuries with which our dwelling has been so considerately furnished, that we see the beneficent intentions of its Creator more immediately manifested, than by any great physical or mechanical laws, however imposing or important. If—having a due knowledge of our natural necessities—of our appetites and passions—of our susceptibilities of pleasure and pain—in fine, of our physical organization—

we were for the first time introduced to this glorious earth with its balmy atmosphere—its pure and translucent waters—the life and beauty of its animal and vegetable kingdoms—with its attraction upon the matter of our own bodies just sufficiently great to give them the requisite stability, and yet not so great as to deprive them of the power of free and rapid motion—with its intervals of light and darkness, giving an alternation of labor and rest nicely corresponding with our muscular power—with its grateful succession of seasons, and its moderate extremes of temperature, so justly suited to our organization: with all this fitness before us, could we hesitate to infer that such a place must have been provided expressly for our habitation? If, then, the discoveries of modern science disclose to us in each planet, which, like our own, rolls in regulated periods round the sun, provisions in all respects similar—if they are proved to be habitations similarly built, ventilated, warmed, illuminated, and furnished—supplied with the same alternations of light and darkness by the same expedient—with the same pleasant succession of seasons—the same geographical diversity of climates—the same agreeable distribution of land and water—can we doubt that such structures have been provided as the abodes of beings in all respects resembling ourselves? The strong presumption raised by such proofs is converted into a moral certainty, when it is shown from physical analogies of irresistible force that such bodies are the creation of the same Hand that raised the round world and launched it into space. Such, then, is the nature of the evidence which science offers on this interesting question. Let us endeavor to strip it of such technical forms of language and reasoning as are intelligible only to the scientific, and to present it so as to be easily and agreeably comprehended.

If we look at a plan of the solar system, the first glance will impress us with an idea that the earth is an individual of a class; that that class is the planets; that the sun is an object provided for different purposes, and the same may be said of the satellites. We take this impression from the simple fact that the planets, including the earth among the number, move round the sun as a centre in circles all in the same direction, and nearly in the same plane; while the satellites or moons (in a manner which we shall hereafter notice) revolve respectively round the planets. The impression is irresistible that the planets, including the earth, form a class; but let us see the purposes in the economy of nature which are fulfilled by this common character given to the motion of the planets and the position of the sun. We find, upon considering the qualities of organized bodies, and especially the species of the animals and vegetables upon the earth, that the maintenance of their physical well-being is essentially dependant on the uniformity and regularity with which they are supplied with the two great physical principles of light and heat. Should these, or either of them, be subject to any extreme variations, such vicissitudes would be incompatible with the organization of the species. There is a cold on one hand and a heat on the other, under which no organized body could continue to exist, and there are still narrower limits within which it is necessary to confine the temperatures they are exposed to in order to secure the perfection of their physical health. There are also degrees of light, the intensity of which would be incompatible with the continued perfection of the organs of vision.

We see, then, how essential to the well-being of the infinite varieties of creatures that people this globe, a uniform regulation of light and heat is. How, then, is this great and important end attained? If we had a fire which at once supplied light and heat in our neighborhood, and that circumstances obliged us continually to shift our position in regard to it, but at the same time so to order our movements as to receive from it a uniform intensity of light and heat, how should we move? Should we not take care to keep always at the same distance from it? And to accomplish this, should we move in any other path than that of a circle, having the fire in the centre? This, however, is precisely what is accomplished by the annual motion of the earth. It traverses its course round the central fire of the system, keeping always nearly at the same distance from the inexhaustible fountain of light and warmth. By this simple expedient of observing a circular path, with the sun in the centre, this necessary object is attained.

Now, in examining the movements of all the other planets, we find that the same expedient is provided: that they severally, in their periodical courses, like the earth, preserve uniform distances from the sun—moving round that body in circles, of which it is the common centre.

Seeing, then, that this motion in the case of the earth is a means whereby an important end is attained, analogy justifies the conclusion that it is to be regarded likewise as a means for the attainment of a similar end in each of the planets. But it will probably be said that the planets are at different distances from the sun; that the most remote of them is nearly twenty times farther from that luminary than the earth, while the nearest of them is little more than one third the earth's distance; therefore, that although it must be admitted that each planet (considered *per se*) is supplied uniformly with light and warmth by this circular motion; yet the intensity of these principles to which the several planets are exposed, comparing one with another, is so extremely different as to destroy all analogy between them.

In answer to this, we are, however, to consider that the influence of light and heat upon a planet does not depend solely on its distance from the sun. The heat, as is well known, produced by the solar rays, depends on the density of the air which surrounds the objects affected by it. Thus we find the temperature, at great elevations in our own atmosphere, considerably lower than at the mean surface of our globe; because at these elevations the air becomes so thin as to be incapable of collecting and retaining the sun's heat. We can therefore easily imagine, provided the existence of their atmospheres be conceded, that their density has been so regulated, that the nearest planets to the sun, which receive the greatest intensity of its rays, may not, after all, be more heated than the most remote ones, which are exposed to the least intensity of its rays: just as we find that the temperature of the summits of lofty mountains at the tropics is as low as the temperature of some of the polar latitudes. It is plain, then, how the effects of the various distances of the planet from the sun may be equalized and compensated. The means of accomplishing this are provided in the form of atmospheres, as we shall presently see.

But let us turn to the consideration of the solar light. The intensity of the sun's light varies with his distance exactly in the same proportion as that of his heat; and the brightness of a day in the most remote planet would be less than that of a day in the nearest in the same proportion as the sun's heat would be less. It may therefore be objected that there might be scarcely daylight enough in the planet Herschel to serve the purposes of social and civil life. Such might undoubtedly be the case if we were to deny the possibility of any variation, however minute, in the organs of vision; but without denying this, let us consider how the matter would stand. The perception which the eye of any creature acquires of light, depends (*cæteris paribus*) upon the magnitude of the circular aperture or *foramen*, in front of the eye, called the *pupil*, which has, externally, the appearance of a circular black spot; but which is, in reality, a circular hole through which the light is admitted to the interior of the chamber of vision, there to affect the membranous coating which transmits its influence to the brain and causes the sensation. It must be evident, even to the least informed, that the brightness of light will then depend upon the magnitude of this *foramen*. Granting that there are two eyes, in one of which the pupil is twice as large as it is in the other, the organ being in all other respects the same, then it is evident that one would admit twice as much light as the other. If, then, the large pupil was exposed to light of only one half the intensity or brightness of that to which the smaller one is exposed, then the two lights would appear to these eyes of the same brilliancy, although in fact, one would be only half as bright as the other. What, then, shall we say of the planets? Grant that the pupils of the eyes of all creatures endowed with vision upon them are enlarged in their opening according as the planets are more removed from the sun and diminished as they are nearer to that luminary, and the whole difficulty arising from the varying intensity of light will vanish. The inhabitants of all the planets will, in fact, enjoy days of the same brightness, notwithstanding the extreme difference of their distances from the sun.

In considering closely the physical powers of locomotion and strength conferred upon animals on the surface of the earth, we find that they have certain limitations; that animals are capable of exercising the powers of locomotion for certain periods of time, varying, it is true, among individuals, but still in the main comprised within certain narrow limits. We find that after the lapse of certain intervals, bodily repose is wanted. But besides the disposition to activity and locomotion and the alternate want of rest, animals in general have also other physical wants and capabilities of enjoyment which are periodical. Thus they are capable of wakefulness for certain periods, after which recurs the physical want of sleep.

Now upon a general survey of the creation, it is found that the average periods which must regulate the intervals of labor and rest, of wakefulness and sleep, corresponds in the main with those which regulate the alternations of light and darkness. In the vegetable kingdom we find prevailing also periodical functions, certainly not so obvious and apparent, but not on that account the less interesting, which are ascertained to have the same close alliance with the period that regulates the returns of light and darkness.

Plants undergo certain changes and suffer certain effects, in the presence of solar light, which are different from, and in some respects contrary to, those which they undergo in its absence. These changes are essential to the vegetable health of the creature; without them the tribes of plants would be extinct. The duration of these operations is just as essential as their alternations. Light must be present a certain time and neither more nor less; and its absence must be equally regulated by limits, otherwise the plant must perish. There is, then, it is evident, an essential relation between the functions and qualities of the vegetable kingdom—between the power of activity, the susceptibility of enjoyment and the physical wants of animals, and the periods which separate light from darkness; but what are those periods? What is the mechanical expedient to which He has resorted to accomplish his inscrutable purposes, who divided the light from the darkness, and "*saw that it was good*." Nothing can be more simple. Nothing can be more beautiful. Nothing can be more admirably perfect. While the globe of the earth makes its annual course round the sun, it has at the same time a spinning motion, on a certain diameter, as an axis, in virtue of which it successively exposes all parts of its surface to the light and warmth of the sun. Each complete rotation is accomplished in the space which we call twenty-four hours; subject to a variation which we shall notice hereafter. All points on our earth are alternately exposed to and withdrawn from the solar light; the average intervals being twelve hours.

Now when we reflect on the close, the exact correspondence between these intervals and the indispensable wants of all organized creatures, can we for a moment doubt that the earth was made to turn upon its axis in that particular time rather than any other, because it was more conducive than otherwise to the well being of the countless myriads of species, the production of the Divine hand, for whose enjoyment the earth was made? Had the time of rotation been materially less than it is, our periods of activity and labor would be too short to prepare us for the return of darkness, and had the time of rotation been greater, we should have needed rest before the return of the natural epoch designed for it. As it is, the natural vicissitudes are nicely adapted to our wants; and yet our organization is in no way connected physically with the rotation of the earth, by any relation of the nature of cause and effect, and to suppose such an adaptation fortuitous, would be an outrage upon all principles of probability. This mutual fitness is, then, another of the many proofs which offer themselves that the earth as a dwelling, and man as a dweller, has been each expressly designed for the other.

Many practical examples may be given of this correspondence between the time of rotation of the earth upon its axis and the periodical functions of the organized world. Thus, Linnæus proposed the use of what he termed a *floral clock*, which was to consist of plants which opened and closed their blossoms at particular hours of the day. Thus, the day-lily opens at five in the morning, the common dandelion at six, the hawkweed at seven, the marigold at nine, and so on; the closing of the blossoms marking corresponding hours in the afternoon. Nor was this to be regarded as a specific effect of light upon the plants, for when the flowers were introduced into a dark chamber they were found to open and close their blossoms at the same times.

The necessity of observing a correspondence between the intervals of activity and repose, the taking of food, &c., and the period of light and darkness, was practically shown in the case of voyages made to the north pole, where navigators attained those latitudes in which the sun never rises for several weeks, in which cases it was found necessary to make the crews of the ships adhere with the utmost punctuality to the habit of retiring at nine o'clock and rising at a quarter before six. Under these circumstances they enjoyed a state of salubrity very remarkable, notwithstanding the trying severity of climate to which they were exposed.

Seeing then,—that the expedient of making the globe of the earth turn upon its axis in twenty-four hours is one productive of such multifarious benefits, and so intimately related to the organized species of our globe, that were it to turn otherwise than it does, in a greater or less time, an entire derangement of the animal or vegetable economy would ensue,—it becomes an interesting question to ascertain whether the other planets are provided with a similar expedient; and if so, to what extent the application of such expedient corresponds with the case of the earth. We accordingly find that all the planets without exception have a motion of rotation on certain diameters as an axis while they make their periodical revolutions round the sun, and that the diameter in which they so rotate has been selected in such a manner as to secure to each of them regular alternations of light and darkness in every part of their surfaces; in fact, they, like the earth, have days and nights. But are those days and nights regulated by the same intervals as ours? for that is an important question; such intervals being, as we have shown, a key to the organizations and functions of the creatures upon them respectively.

We shall on another occasion show that the planets consist of two groups which, although characterized by common qualities, are still distinct in several particulars. The inner group consists of *Mercury*, *Venus*, *Mars*, and the *Earth;* the outer group consists of *Jupiter*, *Saturn*, and *Herschel*. There are circumstances which prepare us to expect some discrepancies in the provisions made in these two groups; but everything leads us to anticipate a uniformity in each of them respectively. We shall on another occasion show that the three planets, *Mercury*, *Venus*, and *Mars*, which with our own form the inner group, do all turn on their axes; that they have all a diurnal motion completed in the same time, or very nearly so, as that of the earth. Thus these several planets not only have days and nights, but have days and nights precisely similar to our own. They are regulated by the same average duration; and He that gave them those alternations has seen it good to "divide the light from the darkness" after the same fashion.

If, then, the duration of our days and nights be evidently regulated with a view to the accommodation and well-being of the organized creatures to which the earth has been appropriated, we are surely warranted by all analogy in concluding that the adaptation of the same expedients in the planets, *Mercury*, *Venus*, and *Mars*, have been directed to the same beneficent purposes, and that the creatures upon them, as upon the earth, are so organized as to require the same intervals of labor and rest, of activity and repose, of wakefulness and sleep.

In the outer group the times of rotation are different, yet among them a similar uniformity prevails. *Jupiter* and *Saturn* revolve on their axes in about ten hours. The telescope has not informed us of the time of rotation of *Herschel;* but it is probably not different from the two cognate planets. It appears then that the intervals of light and darkness in these remote bodies, instead of being regulated by intervals of twelve hours, is determined by average intervals of five hours. A corresponding difference of organization and functions may of course be inferred to prevail upon them; but still it will be observed that the difference between them and the inner group, lies merely in the duration of intervals of light and darkness; those intervals being in the main preserved. There is no planet, then, in which are not provided days and nights.

In considering the expedient by which days and nights are secured to the planets, it is interesting to contemplate the particular position of the diameters on which they have been made to turn. There are a great variety of different diameters upon which the earth might have spun while it revolves round the sun. It might, for example, have turned on a diameter at right angles to its annual orbit. If it had been so we should have had equal days and nights throughout the entire year, and at every part of the earth. It might again have turned upon a diameter lying in the plane of its annual orbit. In such a case we should not have had alternations of days and nights at all; we should have had the sun constantly visible for six months, and absent for other six months, modified in a very complex manner, however, by other vicissitudes; in fact we should have had changes of light and darkness utterly unfit for our wants. In the first case we should have been deprived of seasons and of the means of maintaining any convenient chronology. Thus, in either case, we should be stripped of many of the benefits and utilities arising from the present arrangement. Again, the earth might have turned upon an axis nearly perpendicular to the plane of its annual orbit; or in nearly that plane; it might, in fact, be inclined in any position, between those extremes. Had it stooped down nearly to the ecliptic, consequences would have ensued almost as fatal as those which any position in the plane of the ecliptic would have inferred. We find, however, in fact, that a position has been given to this axis slightly inclined from the perpendicular. In virtue of this inclination the northern hemisphere leans toward the sun during one half of the year, and the southern hemisphere during the other. We enjoy the grateful succession of seasons; it is thus that spring, summer, autumn, and winter, follow each other with pleasant variety, marking in their progress by obvious phenomena the course of time. Yet this inclination or stooping of the axis is so regulated that the extremes of the seasons are confined within such moderate limits as are necessary and conducive to the physical well-being of the numerous tribes which people the earth.

It is true that this succession of seasons was not indispensably necessary to the continuance of the races that inhabit the earth, for had the axis been perpendicular to the orbit so as to render days and nights perpetually and everywhere equal, the organized world would still have continued to exist. Thus we see that the seasons are a provision received from the Divine hand, partaking more of the character of a luxury than of an absolute physical want. We could have done without them, but not so well. We are therefore prepared on examining the other planets to expect a greater difference to prevail among them in this respect than in regard to the other provisions, such as days and nights, without which the organized world could not have continued.

On examining the position of axes on which the several planets revolve, we find them to be such as might be anticipated. Some of them correspond almost minutely with that of the earth. Thus the seasons in *Mars* are regulated by exactly the same extremes as those upon the earth; the summer and winter ranging between similar limits of heat and cold. The same is true of the planet *Saturn*. In the case of *Jupiter*, on the other hand, we find the axis nearly perpendicular to the orbit, so as to produce scarcely any perceptible effect in the form of seasons. Great difficulties have been encountered in ascertaining the position of the axes of the planets Mercury and Venus. There appears reason for believing that they are inclined at very great angles from the perpendicular, and consequently that the extremes of the seasons are proportionally great; in short, if the position of the axes of these planets be rightly determined a very complicated succession of seasons would prevail upon their surfaces; however, until observations of a most decisive character shall be obtained, it is vain to speculate upon these bodies.

The atmosphere which surrounds our globe is an appendage which does not arise from any known physical law, yet it is one which has an obvious and important relation to the animal and vegetable kingdoms. That respiratory beings depend upon it for the maintenance of vitality is obvious. The mechanical and chemical apparatus of the breathing organs is expressly constructed to be the object of its operation. Its relation to vegetable life is no less important. But besides these qualities, without which life would become extinct on the surface of the globe, the atmosphere administers to our convenience and pleasures in other ways. It is the medium by which sound is transmitted; and as the apparatus of the lungs is adapted to operate chemically upon it, so as to impart to the blood the principle by which that fluid sustains life, so the exquisite mechanism of the ear is constituted to receive the effects of its pulsations and convey them to the *sensorium* to produce the perception of sound. Again, the mechanism of the organs of voice is adapted to impress on the atmosphere those pulsations, and thereby to convey its intonations to the correspondingly susceptible organization of the ear. Without the atmosphere, therefore, even supposing we could live in its absence, however perfect might be our organs of speech and hearing, we should possess them in vain. Voice we might have, but no word could we utter; listeners we might be, but no sound could we hear; endowed with the full powers of hearing and speaking, we should nevertheless be deaf and dumb.

Another important manner in which the atmosphere administers to our convenience, is by diffusing in an agreeable manner the solar light, and mitigating its intensity. In this respect, the atmosphere may be considered as performing in regard to the sun what the imperfect transparency of a ground-glass shade performs for the glare of the lamp. In the absence of an atmosphere, the light of the sun would only illuminate objects on which its direct rays would fall; we should have no other degrees of light but the glare of intense sunshine, or the most impenetrable darkness. Shade, there would be none; the apartment whose casement did not face the sun, at the mid-day would be as at midnight. The presence of a mass of air extending from the surface of the earth upward to a height of from thirty to forty miles, becomes strongly illuminated by the sun. This air reflects the solar light on every object exposed to it, and as it spreads over every part of the earth's surface, it conveys with it the reflected, but greatly mitigated light of the sun.

When the evening sun withdraws its light, the atmosphere continuing to be illuminated by its beams, supplies the gradual declining twilight which terminates in the shade of night. Before it rises, in like manner, the atmosphere is the herald of its coming, and prepares us for its splendor by the gray dawn and increasing intensity of morning twilight. In the absence of an atmosphere, the moment of sunset would be marked by an abrupt and instantaneous transition from the blaze of solar light to the most impenetrable darkness; and for the same reason, the morning would be characterized by an equally abrupt change from absolute darkness to broad, unmitigated sunshine.

In the absence of an atmosphere we could have no clouds; day would be one unvaried wearisome glare of the sun. The bright azure sky, so grateful to the sight, is nothing more than the natural color of the air reflected to the eye. The air which fills a room is not perceived to be blue only because it is not present in sufficient quantity to excite in the eye any perception of its color; just as a glass of sea-water seems translucent and colorless, while the same water viewed through a considerable depth, appears with its proper hue of green.

When we look up, therefore, through forty miles of atmosphere, we behold it of its proper tint of blue. In the absence of the atmosphere the great vault of the heavens would present one unvaried and eternal black, the stars dimly twinkling here and there, the whole forming a most funereal contrast with the bright orb which would be seen holding its solitary course through this eternal expanse of darkness.

The atmosphere produces effects on the temperature of our habitation which are not less important. It retains and diffuses warmth, whether proceeding from the sun above, or from sources of internal heat within the globe itself. What situation with respect to temperature we should be placed in by its absence, or even by a considerable diminution of its quantity or density, may be easily inferred by considering the state of those parts of the earth which are placed at such an altitude as to leave below them a large portion of the atmosphere. The summits of lofty ridges, such as those of the Alps, the Andes, and the Himalaya, are examples of this. No intensity of direct solar heat can compensate for the absence of a sufficiently dense atmosphere, and even within the tropics water can not exist in a liquid form at elevations above 14,000 feet. The summits of the Andes are clothed in everlasting snow.

Had we, therefore, been unprovided with an atmosphere, or even had our atmosphere been so rare and attenuated as it is at an elevation of three miles (scarcely one tenth of its whole height), the waters of our oceans would have been solid. Vegetation could never have existed, and in spite of the light and genial warmth of the sun—in spite of the grateful changes of season—in spite of the beautiful and simple provision by which spring succeeds winter, and is followed by summer and autumn, the earth would have been a barren and arid waste, enveloped in a shell of eternal ice, devoid of life, motion, form, and beauty.

Seeing, then, how necessary to the existence of an animal and vegetable world an atmosphere is—how indispensable its presence is to a society of creatures whose means of intercommunication is sound—and yet bearing in mind at the same time that this atmosphere is not essential to any of the great mechanical functions of the earth in the economy of the solar system—considering also that without its presence the part which that earth, as a whole, performs in the society of the planets, would be the same as it now is—can we come to any other conclusion than that this atmosphere was cast around the earth expressly with a view of the well-being of its occupants—to afford them a genial warmth—to give them diffused and gentle light—to convey the varieties of sound—to promote and facilitate social felicity, by supplying the means of intercommunication by language—to preserve the seas liquid—and supplying propitious winds to stimulate the intercourse of nations and knit together the races of beings who occupy its most distant points by the kindly bonds of reciprocal beneficence? If then such, and such only, be admitted to be the purposes and uses of our atmosphere, the question whether other planets, in situations resembling ours, are occupied by similar beings, must be materially influenced by the result of an investigation as to whether or not these planets are supplied with like atmospheres.

Telescopic observations have most clearly and satisfactorily answered this question. The atmosphere around the planets are as palpable to sight as the clouds which float on our own. *Venus* and *Mercury* are enveloped in thick atmospheres: in the former the air is especially conspicuous, nay, we can even see the morning and evening twilight in that distant world. The atmosphere of *Mars* is likewise apparent. We see the clouds floating on it. *Jupiter* and *Saturn* afford not less unequivocal manifestations of atmospheres; and if we have not the same clear and satisfactory evidence in the case of *Herschel*, we have abundant reason for the want of it, in its enormous distance and the hitherto deficiency of telescopic power.

The ascertained existence of clouds in the planets proves more than the mere presence of atmospheres upon them. An atmosphere is necessary to support clouds, but must not be identified with them. Clouds are no more parts of the atmosphere than the mud and sand which float in a turbid river are parts of its waters. Water is converted into vapors by the agency of the sun and wind. This vapor, when it escapes from the surface of the liquid, is generally lighter, bulk for bulk, than that part of the atmosphere contiguous to it. It rises into more exalted regions, where, by the agency of cold, and by electricity, it is made to resume its liquid state, but in such minute particles that it floats and forms those semi-opaque masses called clouds. Clouds are, then, in fact, water existing in a very minute state of mechanical division, and affected in peculiar ways by electricity.

When these particles are caused to coalesce into drops or spherules of water—an effect which may arise from temperature or electricity, or both combined—their weight renders their further suspension impossible, and they descend to the surface in the form of rain; or if the cold be so great as to congeal the particles before they coalesce into globules, they descend in the form of snow; or, finally, if by the sudden evolution of heat caused by electrical influences their solidification is effected into drops, they come down in the form of hail.

Thus wherever the existence of clouds is made manifest, *there* WATER must exist; *there* EVAPORATION must go on; *there* ELECTRICITY, with its train of kindred phenomena, must reign; *there* RAINS must fall; *there* HAIL and SNOW must descend.

That healthful and refreshing winds agitate the atmospheres of the group of worlds in the centre of which our sun presides, and of which he is the common band—that showers refresh their surfaces—that their climates and seasons are modified by evaporation—that their continents are bounded by seas and oceans —that intercourse is facilitated by winds which convert the surfaces of their waters into highroads for nations—these and a thousand other consequences of what has been here explained, all tending to one conclusion—that these various globes are placed in the system for the same purpose as the earth—that they are in fact, the dwellings of beings in all respects, even from their lowest physical wants to their highest social advantages, like ourselves, crowd upon the mind so thickly that we can scarcely give them expression in a clear and intelligible order.

It may be asked whether by immediate observation we may not perceive the geographical surfaces of the planets, so as to declare by direct survey their divisions of land and water, mountain and valley, and other varieties of surface.

Even the most superficial view of the subject will render apparent some great difficulties which must obstruct such an inquiry with respect to most of the planets. The very presence of those atmospheres and the clouds with which they are loaded, offers a serious obstruction to any observations having for their object to ascertain the geographical character of their surfaces. The great distance of some of them is a formidable obstacle to such an inquiry; still, where some peculiar circumstances favor the observation, something has been done in this investigation.

Venus and Mars, the two planets in the system which come nearest to the path of the earth, are evidently the most eligible objects for such an inquiry, and sufficient has been ascertained, especially with regard to the latter planet, to draw very closely indeed the ties of analogy by which the planets are associated with the earth.

Notwithstanding the dense atmosphere and thick clouds with which Venus and Mercury are constantly enveloped, the existence of mountains of great elevation upon them has been discovered; but it is upon the planet Mars that the most surprising advances have been made in this department of telescopic inquiry. The Prussian astronomers, Beer and Madler, have devoted their labors for many years back to the examination of Mars, and the result has put us in possession of a map of the geography of that planet, almost as exact and well defined as that which we possess of our own. In fact, the geographical outlines of land and water have been made apparent upon it. Thus we see that in the other planets on which the clouds clear away sufficiently to disclose to our view their geographical nature, the surface is the same as our own; and analogy justifies the conclusion that, if we could get an equally clear view of the surfaces of the other planets, we should find upon them the same characteristics.

Connected with the observations of these Prussian astronomers, as well as those of the younger Herschel on the planet Mars, there is a circumstance too interesting to be passed without noticing it here. They have discovered, on the polar regions of that planet, an extensive deposition of snow, which is found, in a great degree, to melt away during the summer, and to be reproduced during the winter.

In tracing the analogies whieh prove the suitableness of the planets for inhabitable globes, and which connect them by ties of kindred with the earth, one of the most important and interesting is dependant upon the quantity of matter composing these planets, compared with their volumes or bulks. Let us see how this affects the condition of the organized creatures that dwell upon them.

All organized beings, whether animal or vegetable, are endowed with a certain limited amount of bodily strength. In the case of animals, which have powers of locomotion, this strength is regulated with reference to their weight, and the extent and quantity of motion necessary for their well-being on the surface of the globe. The structure of every animal is such, in the first place, as to give it strength to support and move its own body; but this is not enough; it must have a further amount of disposable force, to enable it to supply its own wants by the pursuit of its prey; by the collection of its food; by the erection of its dwelling; and, in general, by its labor in the supply of its physical wants. In the case of vegetables, the strength must be sufficient to support its weight, and resist those external disturbances to which it is exposed—such as the action of winds and other natural effects. But what, let us ask, regulates this necessary quantity of strength? What is the chief resistance which it has to overcome? We answer, mainly the weight of the creature itself. But again; what is this weight? It is a force produced by what? By the combined attractions of the whole mass of matter composing the globe of the earth, exercised upon the matter composing the creature itself; thus the weight of a man is merely the amount of the attraction of the globe of the earth exercised upon the matter composing the body of the man. The amount of this attraction, therefore, depends upon the quantity of matter in the earth; but not on that alone: it is a universal law of nature, that the energy of the attraction exerted by matter, is increased with the proximity of the attracted body to the centre of the attracted mass. Now if the matter composing the globe of the earth were condensed into half its present bulk, all bodies placed upon the surface, being proportionally nearer the centre, would be attracted with greater energy; and, on the other hand, if the matter of the earth were swelled into a larger bulk, the distance of objects on the surface from the centre being proportionally increased, the energy of the attraction would be diminished. In the one case the weights of all bodies would be augmented, and in the other they would be diminished. The weights, then, of bodies placed on the surface of the earth, depend conjointly in the mass of matter composing the earth, and on its density.

It is evident, then, that the adaptation which we see usually to prevail between the strength of animals and plants and their weights, is, in reality, an exquisite harmony which is maintained between the strength of these infinitely various tribes of organized creatures, and the mass and density of the globe upon which they are placed; the slightest disturbance or change in this relation would utterly derange the fitness of things, and would render the globe unfit for its creatures, and its creatures unfit for the globe. The amount of attraction, or, to use the more familiar term, the weight of the body on the surface of the globe, is, then, an index, so to speak, to the organization of the creatures placed upon the globe. If we would, then, inquire respecting the probable organization of the dwellers upon the planets, one of the means of our inquiry would be to ascertain what would be the weights of bodies upon their surfaces. Physical science enables us perfectly to accomplish this. The masses of matter composing all the planets have been discovered with a great degree of precision. Their magnitudes have also been measured. Now, to ascertain the weights of bodies placed upon the surface of any of them, it is only necessary to consider their masses and their magnitudes. The weight of a body placed upon any planet is greater or less, *cæteris paribus*, than the weight of a body placed upon the earth, just in proportion as the mass of matter in the planet is greater or less than the mass of matter in the earth. If the distance from the surface to the centre of the planet be double the corresponding distance in the case of the earth, then the weight of bodies upon its surface would, on that account alone, be four times less than in the case of the earth. But if, at the same time, the mass of matter in the planet were sixteen times greater than the mass of matter in the earth, then the weight of bodies on the planet, on that account alone, would be sixteen times greater. The weight, then, on the one score, would be sixteen times greater, and on the other, four times less ; the result being that the actual weight under such circumstances, would be four times greater than upon the earth. Such are the principles by which may be calculated the weights of bodies upon the surfaces of the different planets. It has been found that the weights of bodies on the surfaces of Mercury, Venus, and Saturn, are nearly the same as upon the earth; that upon Mercury they are one half less, and on Jupiter three times more. Thus it is apparent that there are no very extreme deviations in weight, comparing the surface of one planet with another, and hence we are led to infer the probability of an organization not very different upon the several planets.

We have already explained by how easy means the great variety of light and warmth conveyed to the different planets by the sun may be practically equalized, by the adaptation of the organization of the eye, and the regulation of the density of the atmosphere. Since, however, this difference in the physical condition of the planets excites usually much attention, it may be well here, before closing this discourse, to enlarge somewhat further on this point.

The principles of optics prove that the sun's light will be less upon the planet Mars than upon the earth, in the proportion of *one* to *two*. Jupiter will receive about twenty-five times, and Saturn about one hundred times less warmth than the earth does, while the diminution in the case of the most remote planet, Herschel, will be nearly four hundred fold; on the other hand, Venus and Mercury, being nearer to the sun than the earth, the one will receive twice, and the other seven times, as much light and warmth as the earth does. The apparent magnitude of the sun to these planets will be in the same proportion. To Jupiter it will have an apparent diameter five times less than to the earth. To Saturn the diameter will be ten times less, and to the planet Herschel nearly twenty times less.

The apparent magnitude of the sun as we behold it is measured by an angle of about thirty minutes; consequently, to the inhabitants of the planet Herschel it will appear under an angle less than two minutes, or about three times the size of Jupiter when that planet appears the largest and brightest. We should, however, form a very erroneous estimate of the actual light of the sun under these circumstanes by these comparisons. It shines by its own light, whereas the objects with which it is attempted to be compared shine with reflected light. The full moon has the same apparent magnitude as the sun, the difference being that the one shines with direct, and the other with reflected light; how much is lost in splendor on this score may be judged, when we state that the light of the full moon is three hundred thousand times less than that of the sun; we may also form some guess at the effect of the sun's light, even at the most remote planet, Herschel, when it is stated that it gives a light equal nearly to that of a thousand full moons.

If we could actually behold the day of Saturn and Herschel on the one hand, and of Mercury and Venus on the other, we should be surprised how disproportionate to their numerical representation their apparent splendor would be. The eye is a bad *photometer*. In a solar eclipse, in which half the sun's disk is covered, we are scarcely sensible of diminished light; and even when the eclipse is nearly total—when only a thin crescent of the sun remains uncovered—there is still the broad light of day, though very sensibly diminished in splendor. A thick covering of clouds upon the firmament produces an immense numerical diminution of the light of day, yet we suffer no inconvenience in being exposed to all the varying degrees of splendor between that and the unclouded radiance of a summer's sun.

How various may be the circumstances of climate and temperature in places receiving exactly the same influences from the sun's rays, will be apparent by a reference to the tropical regions of our own globe. There under the same influences of the same solar heat, we have in different elevations every variety of climate and temperature. On the general surface, near the elevation of the sea, we have the fierce climate of the torrid zone; we have only to ascend the mountains to a certain height, to behold the trees, fruits, and flowers, of the temperate zone; while at a still greater elevation, we encounter all the atmospheric phenomena and vegetable productions of the frigid zone. In the low valleys of the Andes are rich bananas and palms, while the elevated parts of the range produce oaks, firs, and the tribes common to the north of Europe. The oak flourishes on them at elevations varying from six to ten thousand feet. At fifteen thousand feet of height vegetation disappears, save the lichens, and then we enter the solitude of everlasting snow, in which every living thing disappears.

How easy, then, and how natural, is it not, to conceive that atmospheric arrangements like those which, under a tropical sun, produce at certain elevations the moderate temperature of our own climate—at others, less or greater, the fierce heat of the line, or the rigor of the poles—may be the means of modifying the varieties of effect which would be produced in different planets by their different distances from the sun!

Such is, then, the brief view which we offer of that vast body of analogy which leads the intelligent and reflecting mind, that loves to see the most exalted attributes of Divine power manifested throughout all parts of creation, to the conclusion that the planets are worlds, fulfilling in the economy of the universe the same functions, and are created by the same Divine hand, for the same moral purposes, and with the same destinies, as the earth.

THE SUN.

The most Interesting Object in the Firmament.—Its Distance.—How Measured.—Its Magnitude.—How Ascertained.—Its Bulk and Weight.—Its Density.—Form.—Time of Rotation.—Spots.—Its Physical Constitution.—Nature of the Spots.—Luminous Coating.—Its Thickness.—Probable Temperature of the Surface of the Sun.—Nature of its Luminous Matter.

THE SUN.

Although perhaps the moon is the object among the heavenly bodies which presents the subject of most interesting inquiry to the world in general, yet, to the thoughtful and contemplative mind, the Sun is undoubtedly one of vastly superior interest. The sun—the fountain of light and life to a family of circumvolving worlds—the inexhaustible store of genial warmth by which the countless tribes of organized beings that people these globes are sustained—the physical bond whose predominating attraction gives stability, uniformity, and harmony, to the movements of the entire planetary system: to collect together in a brief compass the information which modern scientific research has supplied relating to this body, cannot be otherwise than an interesting and agreeable task.

DISTANCE OF THE SUN.

When we direct our inquiries to any object in the heavens, the first questions which present themselves naturally to us are, "What is its distance, magnitude, motion, and position?" When we say that the distances of the bodies composing the solar system can be measured with the same degree of relative accuracy with which we ascertain the distances of bodies on the surface of the earth, those who are unaccustomed to investigations of this kind usually receive the statement with a certain degree of doubt and incredulity; they cannot conceive how such spaces can be accurately measured, or indeed measured at all. Thus, when they are told that the sun is at a distance from the earth amounting to nearly 100,000,000 of miles, the mind instantly revolts from the idea that such a space could be exactly ascertained and estimated. Yet, let us ask, why this difficulty? whence this incredulity? Is it because the distance thus measured is enormously great? Greater transcendently than any distance we are accustumed to contemplate upon our own globe? To this we reply that the magnitude of a distance or space does not constitute of itself any difficulty in its admeasurement. Nay, on the contrary, it is often the case that we are able to measure large distances with greater accuracy than small ones ; this is frequently so in the surveys conducted on the surface of our own globe. If, then, the greatness of the magnitudes does not constitute of itself any difficulty, to what are we to ascribe the doubt entertained by the popular mind in regard to such measurement? It will, perhaps, be replied that the object, whose distance we claim to have measured, is inaccessible to us ; that we cannot travel over the intermediate space, and therefore cannot be conceived to measure it. But again, let us ask whether this circumstance of being inaccessible constitutes any real difficulty in the measurement of the distance of an object? The military engineer, who directs his projectiles against the buildings within a town which is besieged, can, as we well know, level them so as to cause a shell to drop on any individual building which may have been chosen. To do this, he must know the exact distance of the building from the mortar. Yet the building is inaccessible to him ; the walls of the town, the fortifications, and perhaps a river, intervene. Yet he finds no difficulty in measuring the distance of this inaccessible building. To accomplish this, he lays down a space upon the ground he occupies, called the *base* line, from the extremities of which he takes the bearings or directions of the building in question. From these bearings, and from the length of the base line, he is enabled to calculate by the most simple principles of geometry and arithmetic the distance of the building in question. Now imagine the building in question to be the sun, and the base line to be the whole diameter of the globe of the earth. in what respect would the problem be altered? The building within the town is inaccessible—so is the sun ; the base line of the engineer is exactly known—so is the diameter of the earth ; the bearings of the building from the ends of the base line are known—so are the bearings of the sun's centre from the extremes of the earth's diameter. The problems are, in fact, identical ; they differ in nothing except the accidental and unimportant circumstance of the magnitudes of the lines and angles that enter the question. In short, the measurement of distances of objects in the heavens is effected upon principles in all respects similar to those which govern the measurement of distances upon the earth ; nor are they attended with a greater difficulty, or more extensive sources of error.

By such means, then, it has been ascertained that the distance of the sun from the earth is about 100,000,000 of miles. The distance is more exactly 95,000,000 of miles ; but let me counsel those, who for the mere purpose of general information, and without any strictly or scientific object, study subjects of this nature, to be content to confine themselves generally to round numbers—they are more easily remembered, and answer all purposes as well ; for this reason I shall, in the course of these discourses, generally adopt, in the expression of distances, magnitudes, motions, and times, the nearest round numbers.

MAGNITUDE OF THE SUN.

Having explained the distance of the sun, let us now see how its magnitude can be ascertained. There is one general principle by which the magnitudes of all the heavenly bodies can be ascertained when their distance is known. This is, in fact, accomplished by the device of comparing them with some object of known magnitude and which at any known distance will have the same apparent size. As this is important, considered as a general principle applied to all objects in the heavens, it may not be uninteresting to develop it somewhat fully in its application to the present object, the sun.

The common observation of every one who directs his view to the heavens, will inform him of the fact that the sun and full moon appear to be of the same size. The mere effect of ordinary visual observation is, perhaps, enough to establish this; but if more be desired, instruments expressly adapted to measure the apparent magnitudes of objects may be applied. We are also confirmed in the fact by the consideration of the well-known phenomena of solar eclipses. A solar eclipse is produced by the interposition of the globe of the moon between the eye and the globe of the sun. The eclipse is said to be central when the centre of the moon is directly in line between the eye and the centre of the sun. When this takes place we find that the globe of the moon generally covers, pretty exactly that of the sun. Owing, however, to a slight variation in the apparent size of these bodies, from a cause that we shall explain on another occasion, the moon at one time a little more than covers the sun and at another time a little less. In short, the average apparent magnitude of these bodies are the same, the one exactly covering or concealing the other.

But we have already stated that the distance of the moon is only a quarter of a million of miles. It appears, then, that the distance of the sun is four hundred times greater than that of the moon; yet these two globes appear to the eye to be of the same magnitude. The sun, notwithstanding its being four hundred times farther off, appears just as large as the moon. What, then, are we to infer respecting its real magnitude? If the sun were really equal in magnitude to the moon, it would assuredly appear four hundred times less at four hundred times a greater distance: but as at that greater distance it does not appear less or greater, but of the same magnitude, the irresistible conclusion level to the apprehension of any understanding, is, that the sun must in reality be four hundred times greater in its diameter than the moon. If it were less, at four hundred times the moon's distance, it would appear less than that of the moon; if it were greater, at that distance it would appear greater. It follows, then, that whatever be the magnitude of the diameter of the moon, the diameter of the sun must assuredly be four hundred times greater. Now it has been ascertained by absolute measurement that the diameter of the moon measures about two thousand miles. If we multiply this by four hundred we shall obtain eight hundred thousand miles, which is, therefore, the diameter of the sun.

These calculations have been made roughly and in round numbers; more accurately, the diameter of the sun measures 888,000 miles, but as we recommend the adoption of round numbers, we shall call the sun's diameter 900,000 miles. Such is the stupendous mass placed in the centre of the system which, by its attraction, coerces the movements of the planets.

Such magnitudes are so far beyond all the ordinary standards with which we are familiar, that the imagination is confounded in its efforts to form to itself any distinct conception of them. Let us see whether we may not find some illustration which will aid the understanding in conceiving the dimensions of this immense globe. We know that the earth is a globe whose diameter is eight thousand miles, and that the moon holds its monthly course around it at the distance of about a quarter of a million of miles. Let us suppose the centre of the earth at E., placed at the centre of the sun. Let the moon, M., hold its monthly course around it, the distance from M. to E. will then be about two hundred and fifty thousand miles, but the surface of the sun, S., is at a distance from its centre E. a little less than four hundred and fifty thousand miles. Consequently it follows that the earth and its moons would thus be not only continued within the globe of the sun, but the surface of the sun would even then be two hundred thousand miles outside the monthly orbit of the moon. The sun would, in fact, contain the moon and earth within it, and have a couple of hundred thousand miles to spare!

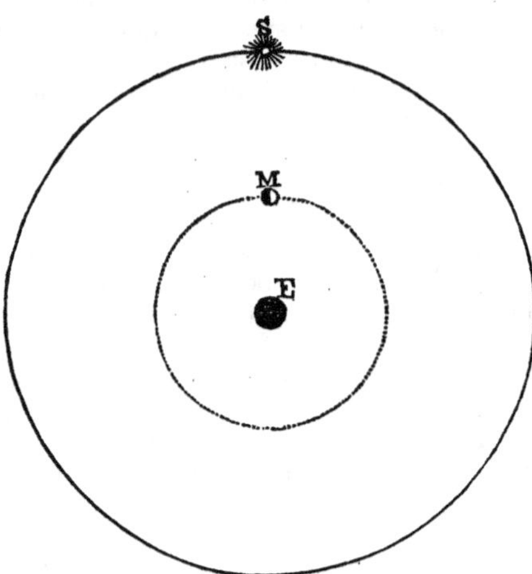

VOLUME OF THE SUN.

But we have hitherto only spoken of the diameter of the sun ; let us now consider its bulk. When we know the diameters of two globes we can always, by an easy operation of arithmetic, estimate their bulks. Thus, if one globe have a diameter double another, the bulk of the former will be eight times that of the latter. If the diameter be ten times greater, the bulk will be a thousand fold greater, and so on. Now we know that the diameter of the sun is about one hundred and twelve times greater than that of the earth, from which we infer, by the same principles of arithmetic, that the bulk of the sun must be very nearly one million four hundred thousand times the bulk of the earth. To make a globe like the sun, it would then be necessary to roll one million four hundred thousand globes like the earth into one ! It is found by considering the bulks of the different planets, that if all the planets and satellites in the solar system were moulded into a single globe, that globe would still not exceed the five hundredth part the globe of the sun : in other words, the bulk of the sun is five hundred times greater than the aggregate bulk of all the rest of the bodies of the system.

WEIGHT OF THE SUN.

The astronomer, however, is called upon to execute processes more difficult and yet no less indispensable, than the mere measurement of distances and magnitudes. If we desire to know the quantities of matter composing those distant orbs, we must not merely measure their magnitudes and fathom their distances, but we must wing our flight, in imagination, across those vast distances which separate us from them and *weigh* their stupendous masses. If the popular student finds it difficult to believe and comprehend how we can measure distances and magnitudes such as those of the heavenly bodies, how much more will he be confounded when he is assured that we have at our disposal a balance of the most unerring exactitude in which we can place those vast orbs and poise them ! The globe of the sun itself, transcendently greater than the earth and all the planets put together, is weighed with as great relative precision, as that with which the chemist in his analysis, estimates the weights of the constituents of the bodies which pass under his hands. As the general principles by which the weights of the bodies of the universe are ascertained is in spirit the same for all, it may be worth while here to explain the method, once for all, in its application to the sun.

When a body revolves in a circle, we know from common and familiar experiments that it has a tendency to fly from the centre of the circle, which tendency is greater the more rapidly the body revolves and the greater its distance from the centre. The boy who whirls a stone in a sling is conscious of this physical truth. The stone, as it revolves, stretches the string with a certain definite force; this force is not in the gravity of the stone, for it would be equally manifested if the stone revolved in a horizontal plane. It is that tendency which we have just adverted to, and which is technically called centrifugal force. If you increase the velocity with which the stone is whirled round, you will find the string will be more and more tightly stretched, and you may augment the velocity to such an extent as to break the string. If you lengthen or shorten the string, preserving the same velocity of rotation, you will find that the tendency to stretch the string will be proportionally increased or diminished; in short, a fixed rule or *law*, as it is called, will be easily discovered by a series of simple experiments which will enable us to predict how much the string will be stretched, provided we know the distance of the revolving weight from the centre of the circle and the time it takes to make each revolution.

To apply this general principle, then, to the case before us, let it be considered that the moon in its monthly course revolves in a circle round the centre of the earth. We know its distance and we know the time which it takes to make each revolution, we are therefore in a condition to declare with what force it would stretch a string, tying it to the centre of the earth. That the moon exercises such a force cannot then be doubted. But on what, it will be asked, is that force expended? There is no string, rod, or any other material or tangible connection between the moon and the centre of the earth. And yet the moon is held as firmly and steadily in its circular course round the earth, as if it were tied to the centre by a string. In the absence of the string there must then be some physical agency which plays its part; there must be something to resist that tendency which the string, if there, would have resisted. That *something* was discovered by Newton to be the attraction of the earth's GRAVITATION exercised upon the moon and holding the moon in its circular orbit, in the same manner that it would be held by the string which has been just described. As we know, by the simple mechanical law above explained, the force with which that string would be stretched by the moon in this case, we are enabled by the same principle to say what is the amount of attractive force which the earth exercises upon the moon to keep it in its monthly orbit.

In this manner, in general, we are enabled to estimate the force of attraction which a central mass exercises upon another body revolving in a circle round it at a known distance, and in a known time.

While, on the one hand, we know the distance and time of the moon's revolution round the earth, we also know the distance and time of the earth's revolution round the sun. We are thus, allowing for the difference of the two distances, in a condition to compare the actual amount of attraction which the earth and the sun respectively exercise upon bodies revolving round them, and we find, accordingly, that the attraction exercised by the sun upon any body is greater than the attraction that would be exercised by the earth upon the same body in a like position, in the proportion of three hundred and fifty thousand to one. But as these attractions are, in fact, produced by the respective masses of matter composing the sun and the earth, it follows that the weight of the sun, or what is the same, the mass of matter composing it, is three hundred and fifty thousand times greater than the the mass of matter or weight of the earth.

To make a globe as heavy as the sun, it would then be necessary to agglommerate into one three hundred and fifty thousand globes like the earth

DENSITY OF THE SUN.

Having ascertained the weights and bulks of the bodies of the universe, we are in a condition to determine their densities, and thus to obtain some clue to a knowledge of their constituent materials. We have seen that while the bulk of the sun is about one million and four hundred thousand times greater than that of the earth, its weight is greater in the much less proportion of three hundred and fifty thousand to one. Let us see to what inference this leads in regard to the nature of the matter that composes the sun. If the materials of the sun were similar to those of the earth, its weight would necessarily be greater than that of the earth in the same proportion as its bulk, and in that case, of course, the weight of the sun would be one million and four hundred thousand times that of the earth. But it is not nearly so great as this; on the contrary, it is much less. Consequently, it follows that the constituent materials of the sun are lighter than those of the earth in the proportion of about four to one. The density of the sun is, therefore, very nearly equal to that of water, and, consequently, the weight of the solar orb is equal to the weight of a globe of the same magnitude composed altogether of water.

FORM AND ROTATION OF THE SUN.

Although to minds unaccustomed to the rigor of scientific research, it might appear sufficiently evident, without further demonstration, that the sun is globular in its form, yet the more exact methods pursued in the investigation of physics demand that we should find more conclusive proof of the sphericity of the solar orb than the mere fact that the disk of the sun is always circular. It is barely possible, however improbable, that a flat circular disk of matter, the face of which should always be presented to the earth, might be the form of the sun; and indeed there are a great variety of other forms which, by a particular arrangement of their motions, might present to the eye a circular appearance as well as a globe or sphere. To prove, then, that a body is globular, something more is necessary than the mere fact that it always appears circular.

When a telescope is directed to the sun, we discover upon it certain marks or spots, of which we shall speak more fully presently. We observe that these marks, while they preserve the same relative position with respect to each other, move regularly from one side of the sun to the other. They disappear, and continue to be invisible for a certain time, come into view again on the other side, and so once more pass over the sun's disk. This is an effect which would evidently be produced by marks on the surface of a globe, the globe itself revolving on an axis, and carrying these marks upon it. That this is, in fact, the case, is abundantly proved by the fact that the periods of rotation for all these marks are found to be exactly the same, viz., about twenty-five and a half days. Such is, then, the time of rotation of the sun upon its axis, and that it is a globe remains no longer doubtful, since the globe is the only body which, while it revolves with a motion of rotation, could always present the circular appearance to the eye. The axis on which the sun revolves is very nearly perpendicular to the plane of the earth's orbit, and the motion of rotation of the sun upon the axis is in the same direction as the motion of the planets round the sun, that is to say, from west to east.

SPOTS ON THE SUN.

One of the earliest fruits of the invention of the telescope was the discovery of the spots upon the sun, and the examination of these has gradually led to a knowledge of the physical constitution of the centre of our system.

When we submit a solar spot to telescopical examination, we discover its appearance to be that of an intensely black irregularly-shaped patch, edged with a penumbral fringe, the brightness of the general surface of the sun gradually fading away into the blackness of the spot. When a spot is watched for a considerable time, it is found to undergo a gradual change in its form and magnitude; at first increasing gradually in size, until it attains some definite limit of magnitude, when it ceases to increase, and soon begins, on the contrary, to diminish; and its diminution goes on gradually, until at length the bright sides closing in upon the dark patch, it dwindles first to a mere point, and finally disappears altogether. The period which elapses between the formation of the spot, its gradual enlargement, subsequent diminution, and final disappearance, is very various. Some spots appear and disappear very rapidly, while others have lasted for weeks and even for months. The magnitudes of the spots are in proportion to the magnitude of the sun itself. At the distance of the sun, a spot, the magnitude of which would be barely visible, must have a diameter of four hundred and sixty miles, and an area of one hundred and sixty-six thousand square miles, which is, therefore, the smallest space on the surface of the sun which would be distinctly seen. Among the many spots which have been recorded, one was observed by Mayer, the area of which was about fifteen hundred millions of miles square, or about thirty times the surface of the earth.

Spots have been occasionally seen on all parts of the sun, but that region on which they are found generally to prevail, is one which corresponds with the tropical parts of the earth, that is, a space extending about thirty degrees on either side of the solar equator.

PHYSICAL CONSTITUTION OF THE SUN.

What are the spots? Two, and only two, suppositions have been proposed to explain them. One supposes them to be scoriæ, or dark scales of incombustible matter floating on the general surface of the sun. The other supposes them to be excavations in the luminous matter which coats the sun, the dark part of the spot being a part of the solid non-luminous nucleus of the sun. In this latter supposition it is assumed that the physical constitution of the sun is a solid non-luminous globe, covered with a coating of a certain thickness of luminous matter. This latter supposition has been in a great measure demonstrated by continued and accurate observations on the spots.

That the spots are excavations, and not mere black patches on the surface, is proved by the following observations: If we select a spot which is at the centre of the sun's disk, having some definite form, such as that of a circle, and watch the appearance of the same spot when, by the motion of the sun upon its axis it is carried toward the edge, we find, first, that the circle becomes an oval. This, however, is what would be expected even if the spot were a circular patch, inasmuch as a circle seen obliquely is foreshortened into an oval. But we find that as the spot moves toward the side of the sun's limb, the black patch gradually disappears, the penumbral fringe on the inside of the spot becomes invisible, while the penumbral fringe on the outside of the spot increases in apparent breadth, so that when the spot approaches the edge of the sun, the only part that is visible is the external penumbral fringe. Now this is exactly what would occur if the spot were an excavation. The penumbral fringe is produced by the shelving of the sides of the excavation, sloping down to its dark basis. As the spot is carried toward the edge of the sun, the height of the inner side is interposed between the eye and the bottom of the excavation, so as to conceal the latter from view. The surface of the inner shelving side also takes the direction of the line of vision or very nearly, diminishes in apparent breadth, and ceases to be visible, while the surface of the shelving side next the edge of the sun becomes nearly perpendicular to the line of vision, and, consequently, appears of its full breadth.

In short, all the variations of appearance which the spots undergo, as they move across the sun's disk, changing their distances and positions with regard to the sun's centre, are exactly those changes of appearance which would be produced by an excavation, and not at all those which a dark patch on the solar surface would undergo.

It may be considered then as proved, that the spots on the sun are excavations; and that the apparent blackness is produced by the fact that the part constituting the dark portion of the spot is either a surface totally destitute of light or by comparison so much less luminous than the general surface of the sun as to appear black. This fact combined with the appearance of the penumbral edges of the spots have led to the supposition, which appears scarcely to admit of doubt, that the solid, opaque nucleus, or globe of the sun, is invested with two atmospheres, that which is next the sun being like our own, non-luminous, and the superior one being that in which alone light and heat are evolved; at all events, whether these strata be in the gaseous state or not, the existence of two such, one placed above the other, the superior one, being luminous, seems to be exempt from doubt.

By observing the magnitude of the spots, and the rate at which they increase and diminish, the velocity of their edges has been ascertained, and this velocity has been found to be such as can scarcely be attributed to matter except in the gaseous form.

We are not warranted in assuming that the black portion of the spots are really surfaces deprived of light, for the most intense artificial light which can be produced, such, for example, as that of a piece of quick-lime exposed to the action of the compound blow-pipe, when seen projected on the sun's disk, appears as dark as the spots themselves; an effect which must be ascribed to the infinitely superior splendor of the sun's light. All that can be legitimately inferred respecting the spots, then, is, not that they are destitute of light, but that they are incomparably less brilliant than the general surface of the sun.

The thickness of the luminous coating which covers the sun, was attempted to be measured by Sir William Herschel, by means of observations made on the spots, and the result of his inquiry was that its depth varied from two to three thousand miles. The under and non-luminous stratum, by reflecting a considerable portion of the rays which fall upon it from the luminous stratum above, not only increases the light which the luminous stratum disperses through space, but serves as a canopy to screen the solid body of the sun from the overpowering effects of the light and heat of the superior stratum. Herschel even supposed that the density of the lower stratum might be such as to maintain a temperature on the actual surface of the solid globe of the sun not higher than that upon our earth. However this may be, there seems to be little doubt that the actual temperature at the visible surface of the sun, that is to say, upon its luminous coating, must be much more elevated than any artificial heat we are able to produce.

According to Sir John Herschel, we have various indications of this.

First, from the law of the decrease of radiant heat and light, which being in the inverse proportion of the squares of the distances, it follows that the heat received on a given area exposed at the distance of the earth, and on an equal area at the visible surface of the sun, must be in the proportion of the apparent magnitude of the sun to the whole extent of the firmament, that is, in the proportion of about one to three hundred thousand. A far less intensity of solar radiation collected in the focus of a burning-glass, is sufficient to evaporate gold or platinum.

Secondly, from the facility with which the sun's heat passes through glass, a property possessed by artificial heat in a very small degree, and always in the direct proportion of its intensity.

Thirdly, from the fact that the most vivid flames and intense artificial light appear, as we have already stated, only as black spots when held between the disk of the sun and the eye.

The idea that the heat of the sun arises from any process analogous to that of common combustion, seems to be beset with insuperable difficulties. How can we suppose the inexhaustible supply of the materials necessary to support so enormous and interminable a conflagration? There are two other sources of heat which may be imagined, that are not subject to the same difficulty. Bodies submitted to friction evolve heat without any change in the condition of their constituent parts. Also when a galvanic current is transmitted through certain conducting substances, they become heated with more or less intensity and sometimes to such a degree as to emit light of the most intense brilliancy, and yet in this process they suffer no other physical change than that of temperature. It is therefore possible to suppose either of these causes, but especially the latter, to be in constant operation on the sun, with sufficient energy to educe the light and heat which it affords.

The actual physical character of the luminous matter which coats the sun had not been ascertained until a recent period. According to the report of the astronomical lectures of Arago, lately delivered in Paris, it would seem that that philosopher has succeeded in solving this problem. As we have not had access to the original papers containing this investigation, we can only speak of it from the imperfect information supplied by that report. It would seem from it that Arago reasons in the following manner: There are two states in which light is capable of existing; the ordinary state, and the state of polarization. It has been proved by Fourier, that all bodies rendered incandescent by heat, which are in the solid or liquid state, emit polarized light; while bodies which are gaseous, when rendered incandescent, invariably emit light in its ordinary state. Thus the physical condition of a body may be distinguished when it is incandescent, by examining the light which it affords. There are polariscopic instruments by which we are enabled to distinguish these different states of light. On applying these tests to the direct light of the sun, it has been found to be in the unpolarized, or ordinary condition. Hence it has been inferred by Arago, that the matter from which this light proceeds must be in the gaseous state. It will doubtless be readily understood that gas, when incandescent, is that which is commonly called *flame.* If Arago's reasoning, then, be rightly reported, and his observations correct, it follows that the globe of the sun is a solid, opaque, non-luminous orb, invested with an ocean of flame.

Certain observations made by Bouguer, led that astronomer to suppose that the sun is surrounded by an atmosphere of considerable extent above the surface of the luminous coating. The ground of this supposition was the impression that the splendor of the sun's light near the borders of the disk was less than near the centre; an effect which could not be produced if the luminous coating had nothing above it imperfectly transparent. On the contrary, the brightness toward the borders, owing to the obliquity of the direction of the surface to the line of vision would be greater, inasmuch as a greater extent of luminous, surface would be comprised within the same visual angle. The more accurate observations, however, of Arago, made with delicate polariscopic instruments disprove this by showing that the brightness is the same on all parts of the sun's disk

ECLIPSES.

Lunar and Solar Eclipses.—Their Causes.—Shadow of the Earth.—And Moon.—Magnitude of Eclipses.—When they can happen.—Central Solar Eclipse.—Great Solar Eclipse described by Halley.—Ecliptic Limits.

ECLIPSES.

Of all the occasional astrononomical phenomena, those which have attracted most popular attention are LUNAR and SOLAR ECLIPSES. We shall on the present occasion explain the principal circumstances attending them.

When a luminous body, radiating light in all directions around it, throws these rays upon an opaque body, that body prevents a portion of the rays from penetrating into the space behind it. That portion of the space from which the light is thus excluded by the interposition of the opaque body, is called in astronomy the SHADOW of that body.

The shape, magnitude, and extent, of the shadow of an opaque body, will depend partly on the shape and magnitude of the opaque body itself, and partly on that of the body from which the light proceeds.

In the cases before us, the form of the bodies are globes. If the globe of the SUN were equal in magnitude to the globe of the earth, the shadow of the latter would be a cylinder, the base of which would be equal to a great circle of the earth, and such shadow would be interminable, since its sides would be parallel. This will be evident by an inspection of the annexed figure, 1, in which *S.* represents the sun, and *E.* the earth; the rays *S. E.* forming the sides of the shadow, being parallel, could never meet, and consequently the shadow would be infinite, since light can never penetrate into the space between them. If, on the other hand, the sun were a globe less in magnitude than the earth, then the shadow of the latter would have diverging sides as represented in the annexed figure, 2, which would widen as they proceed from the earth, and would be interminable; but the sun having in reality a diameter about one hundred and twelve times greater than that of the earth, the rays which proceed from the upper and lower limb of the sun, and which touch the earth at *a* and *b*, fig. 3, will converge to certain point at *f*, behind the earth, and will form a conical space, whose base will be at *a b*, and whose apex will be at *f*. From the space enclosed by this cone the light of the sun is entirely excluded, and it is therefore properly the shadow of the earth. But there is also a certain space behind the earth from which the sun's light is only partially excluded, and which

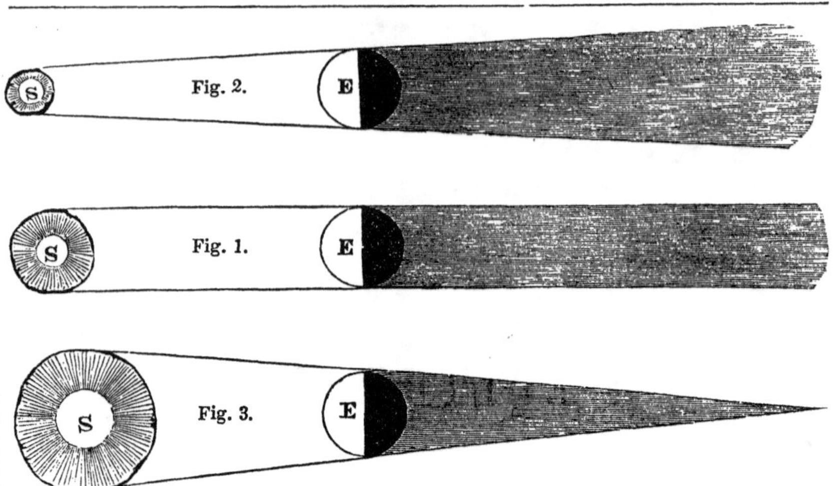

forms what is called the earth's penumbra. The ray *m a*, fig. 4, from the top of the sun's disk passes to the point *f*, while the ray *n a* from the lowest point of the sun's disk passes to the point *c*. The space between *a f* and *a c* will be partially illuminated by the sun. If a spectator were placed anywhere in that space, he would see a portion of the upper limb of the sun, and would see more of it the nearer he might be to *c*, and less of it the nearer he might be to *f*.

As he would see the sun, he would of course receive a portion of its light. Thus that part of the space included between *a f*, and *a c*, which is near *a f*, receives light from a small portion of the upper limb of the sun, while that part which is near *a c* receives light from nearly the whole of the sun ; and in short, proceeding from *a f* to *a c*, the light received from the sun will be gradually increased.

Fig. 4.

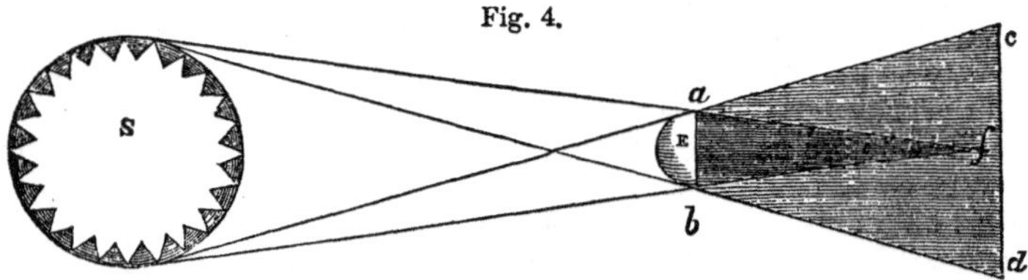

In like manner, the ray *m b* proceeding from the upper limb of the sun and continued to *d*, will include between it and the ray *b f* a space which is only partially illuminated, and will be subject to the same observations as we have made respecting the space between *a f* and *a c*.

When any object which receives its light from the sun passes between the lines *a c* and *b d*, it will be either wholly or partially deprived of the sun's light. If it be outside the limits *b f* and *a f*, it will be only partially obscured ; but if it be within these limits, it will be altogether darkened.

The length of the line *a f* being incomparably less than the distance of any body in the universe from the earth except the moon, but being on the contrary considerably greater than the distance of the moon, it follows that the only body in the system which can be deprived of light by the earth's shadow is the moon, and that whenever that object is in opposition to the sun, and at the same time so near the ecliptic as to be included between the lines *a c* and *b d*, it will be partially deprived of the sun's light; but if it be so much nearer as to be included between the lines *a f* and *b f*, it will be wholly deprived of the sun's light. Thus the causes of a partial or total eclipse of the moon are explained.

If the plane of the moon's orbit coincided with that of the ecliptic, the moon would pass behind the centre of the earth in the direction of the line *E f* forming the axis of the shadow, every revolution, and consequently there would be a total lunar eclipse every month; but as the moon's orbit is inclined at an angle of five degrees to the plane of the ecliptic, the distance of the moon from that plane is greater than the distance of lines of *a c* and *b d* from *E f*, except when the moon is near to that point where its orbit crosses the ecliptic, which is called the moon's *node*.

No lunar eclipses happen, therefore, except when either of the moon's nodes is nearly in opposition to the sun.

When a lunar eclipse does happen, the moon will first enter the penumbra at *a c*, and will be very slightly obscured. As it approaches *a f*, it is more and more deprived of the sun's light, until finally it enters the shadow *a f b*, where it is altogether obscured. At the end of the eclipse, as it must pass through the penumbra, it will recover the sun's light by slow degrees.

The length of the line *E f* being about 800,000 miles, and the distance of the moon from the earth being less than 250,000, the moon when it passes through the shadow will be about 500,000 miles within the point *f*, and will consequently pass through the shadow at a part of considerable breadth.

In expressing the magnitude of the eclipse, whether of the sun or of the moon, it is customary to suppose the diameters of these bodies divided into twelve equal parts, called *digits*, and the magnitude of the eclipse is expressed by stating the proportion of the diameter of the disk which is obscured. Thus when half the disk is obscured, we say that the eclipse measures six digits, and so on.

From what has been stated, it is evident that an eclipse of the moon will not be affected in its appearance by the position of the observer on the surface of the earth. Wherever he may be, the eclipse will appear to him the same; but if it should happen that while the moon is passing through the shadow, the person desirous to observe it is in a portion of the earth which at that time is turned toward the sun, the eclipse will, of course, be invisible to him. In short, it will only be visible from that hemisphere of the earth that is turned from the sun at the time of its occurrence.

The moon, like the earth, receiving the sun's light, projects behind it a conical shadow and a diverging penumbra: if this shadow or penumbra fall upon any portion of the earth's surface, they will deprive such portion wholly or partially of the sun's light, and there will be a solar eclipse of a corresponding species. When the moon is between the sun and earth, the length of its shadow is about equal to its distance from the earth, and consequently the point of the shadow would just reach the surface of the earth; but as the moon's distance is subject to a slight variation, it sometimes happens that the length of the moon's shadow is a little more and sometimes a little less than its distance from the earth. If the length of the shadow be greater than its distance from the earth, then the shadow will cover a small portion of the earth's surface, to all places within which there will be a total solar eclipse. The circumstances affecting a solar eclipse are represented in the annexed figure, where S is the centre of the sun's disk, W is its upper limb, and V its lower limb; *c d* is the moon, and *e* the point of its shadow; *d h* and *c g* are the sides of its penumbra, and *a b* is the portion of the earth on which the penumbra falls. An observer placed between *e* and *g*, will see the upper limb of the sun only, the lower limb being

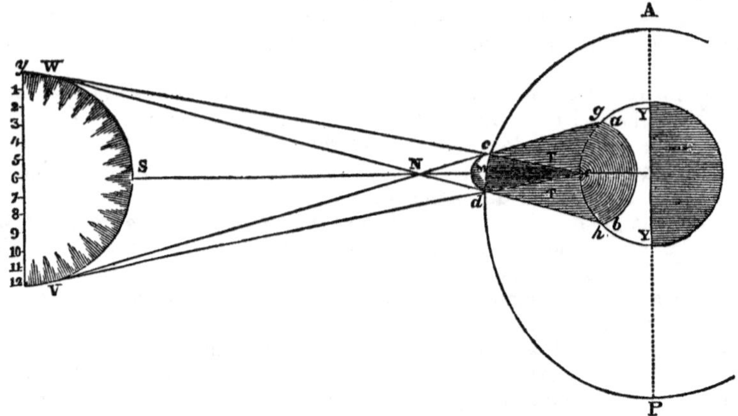

eclipsed. An observer, on the other hand, between *d e* and *d h*, would see the lower limb only, the upper limb being eclipsed; and the eclipse would be greater to each of these observers the nearer their position would be to the point *e*. To observers between *h* and Y or *g* and Y, there would be no eclipse, for no part of the moon would be interposed between them and any part of the sun.

If the vertex of the cone of the moon's shadow is farther from the moon than the surface of the earth, then there will be a small portion of the earth's surface at *e* within the shadow; and to an observer within any portion of that surface, the sun will be totally eclipsed; but if the vertex of the shadow do not reach the earth, then an observer at *e* will see a ring of the sun, not covered by the moon, surrounding the globe of the moon, and the phenomenon will be what is called an annular eclipse.

These circumstances will render easily intelligible all the ordinary circumstances of solar eclipses. It will be readily understood, that while a lunar eclipse is the same to all observers on the earth, a solar eclipse will vary in its magnitude and character with the position of the observer; the same solar eclipse which at one part of the earth is total or annular, at other parts of the earth is partial in various degrees, and at other parts again is not exhibited at all.

A natural consequence of the diffusion of knowledge is, that while it lessens the vague sense of wonder, with which singular phenomena in nature are beheld, it increases the feeling of admiration at the harmonious laws, the development of which renders effects apparently strange and unaccountable easily intelligible. It will be easily imagined what a sense of astonishment, and even terror, the sudden disappearance of an object like the sun or moon must have produced in an age when the causes of eclipses were known only to the learned. Such phenomena were regarded as precursors of divine vengeance. History informs us that in ancient times armies have been destroyed by the effects of the consternation spread among them by the sudden occurrence of an eclipse of the sun. Commanders who happened to possess some scientific knowledge, have taken advantage of it to work upon the credulity of those around them by menacing them with prodigies the near approach of which they were well aware of, illustrating thus, in a singular and perverted manner, the maxim that knowledge is power. Happily, in the present day information is too generally diffused to permit the bulk of mankind to be thus played upon.

Of all the various phenomena presented by eclipses, that which is transcendantly the most remarkable and interesting is a central eclipse of the sun. If it be total, the spectacle it offers is most imposing: the light of day is gradually withdrawn to such a degree that the brighter planets, such as Venus and Jupiter, and the stars of the first magnitude, become visible to the naked eye. We see, however, a faint light of the sun behind the disk of the moon. Sometimes, as has been stated, when the apparent magnitude of the moon is a little less than that of the sun, the disk of the moon conceals the entire disk of the sun, except only a thin luminous ring surrounding it. This is a phenomenon of very rare occurrence, and only to be seen at particular places on the earth. An instance of it occurred on the 7th of September, 1820. It commenced to be visible at the north latitude of 80°, in Hudson's bay, near the eastern coast of New North Wales. It was visible next in the direction of the northeast of Greenland, at the mouth of the Wesel, at Bremen, in the gulf of Venice, and in Arabia deserta, and ceased near the Persian gulf. While this eclipse was produced in these different places, the observers who were on the same meridians, but further south, saw only a partial eclipse, and others, still further south, saw no eclipse at all, the contrary took place with observers on the same meridians farther north, to all of whom the eclipse was annular.

It was during a phenomenon of this kind that Schröter imagined he saw the solar light coming through an immense opening in the moon. Other observers, however, who saw, or imagined they saw, luminous spots on the dark hemisphere of the moon, in a solar eclipse, ascribed them to lunar volcanoes. As to the existence of these luminous spots on the dark hemisphere of the moon, rendered manifest in a total eclipse of the sun, we have the testimony of so many astronomers, among whom, besides Schröter, may be mentioned Sir William Herschel and Kater, that we can scarcely doubt their reality. The causes which may produce them have only been explained in the two ways above mentioned, namely, either by the supposed existence of active volcanoes, on the moon, or perforations through the moon, through which the sun's light passes.

The following description of a total eclipse of the sun, given by Halley, who observed it, is quoted by Arago, and will be read with interest:—

"I send you, according to promise, my observations of the solar eclipse, though I fear they will not be of much use to you. Not being furnished with the necessary instruments for measuring time, I confined my views to examining the spectacle presented by nature under such extraordinary circumstances, a spectacle which has hitherto been neglected or imperfectly studied. I chose for my point of observation a place called Haradowhill, two miles from Amesbury, and east of the avenue of Stonehenge, of which it closes the vista. In front is that celebrated edifice upon which I knew that the eclipse would be directed. I had, moreover, the advantage of a very extensive prospect in every direction, being on the loftiest hill in the neighborhood, and that nearest to the centre of the shadow. To the west, beyond Stonehenge, is another rather steep hill, rising like the summit of a cone above the horizon. This is Clay hill, adjoining Westminster, (?) and situated near the central line of darkness which was to set out from this point, so that I could be aware in time of its approach. I had with me Abraham Sturges and Stephen Evans, both natives of the country, and able men. The sky, though overcast, gave out some straggling rays of the sun, that enabled me to see around us. My two companions looked through the blackened glasses, while I made some reconnaissance of the country. It was half-past five by my watch when they informed me that the eclipse was begun. We watched its progress, therefore, with the naked eye, as the clouds performed for us the service of colored glasses. At the moment when the sun was half obscured, a very evident circular rainbow formed at its circumference, with perfect colors. As the darkness increased, we saw the shepherds on all sides hastening to fold their flocks, for they expected a total eclipse of an hour and a quarter duration.

"When the sun assumed the appearance of the new moon, the sky was tolerably clear, but it was soon covered with deeper clouds. The rainbow then vanished, the steep hill I have named became very obscure, and on each side, that is, north and south, the horizon exhibited a blue tint, like that which it possesses in summer toward the close of day. Scarcely had we time to count ten, when Salisbury spire, six miles to the south, was enveloped in darkness. The hill disappeared entirely, and the deepest night spread around us. We lost sight of the sun, whose place till then we had been able to distinguish in the clouds, but whose trace we could now no more discover than if it had never existed.

"By my watch, which I could scarcely discern by some light that reached us from the north, it was thirty-five minutes past six. Shortly before, the sky and the earth had assumed, literally speaking, a livid tint, for it was a mixture of black and blue, only the latter predominated on the earth and at the horizon. There was also much black diffused through the clouds, so that the whole picture presented an awful aspect, that seemed to announce the death of nature.

"We were now enveloped in a total and palpable darkness, if I may be allowed the expression. It came on rapidly, but I watched so attentively, that I could perceive its progress. It came upon us like rain, falling on our left shoulders (we were looking to the west), or like a great black cloak thrown over us, or like a curtain drawn from that side. The horses we held by the bridle seemed deeply struck by it, and pressed to us with marks of extreme surprise. As well as I could perceive, the countenances of my friends wore a horrible aspect. It was not without an involuntary exclamation of wonder I looked around me at this moment. I distinguished colors in the sun, but the earth had lost all its blue, and was entirely black. A few rays shot through the clouds for a moment, but immediately afterward the earth and the sky appeared totally black. It was the most awful sight I had ever beheld in my life.

"Northwest of the point whence the eclipse came on, it was impossible for me to distinguish in the least degree the earth from the sky, for a breadth of sixty degrees or more. We looked in vain for the town of Amesbury, situated below us; scarcely could we see the ground under our feet. I turned frequently during the total darkness, and observed that, at a considerable distance to the west, the horizon was perfect on both sides, that is, to the north and to the south; the earth was black, and the lower part of the sky clear; the obscurity, which extended to the horizon in those points, seemed like a canopy over our heads, adorned with fringes of a lighter color, so that the upper edges of all the hills, which I recognised perfectly by their outlines, formed a black line. I saw perfectly that the interval between light and darkness, observable in the earth, was between Mortinsol (?) and St. Anne; but to the south it was less distinctly marked.

"I do not mean to say that the line of shadow passed between these two hills, which were twelve miles distant from us; but as far as I could distinguish the horizon, there was none behind, and for this reason: My elevated position enabled me to see the light of the sky behind the shadow; still, that yellowish green line of light I saw was broader toward the north than toward the south, where it was of a tan color. At this period it was too black behind us, that is, to the east, looking toward London, to enable me to see the hills beyond Andover, for the anterior extremity of the shadow lay beyond that place. The horizon was then divided into four parts, differing in extent, in light, and in darkness. The broadest and least black was to the northwest, and the longest and brightest to the southwest. The only change I could perceive during the whole time the phenomenon lasted, was that the horizon divided into two parts—one clear, the other obscure. The northern hemisphere then acquired more length, brightness, and breadth, and the two opposite parts coalesced.

"Like the shadow in the beginning of the eclipse, the light approached from the north, and fell on our right shoulders. I could not, indeed, distinguish on that side either defined light or shadow upon the earth, which I watched attentively; but it was evident that the light returned but gradually, and with oscillation: it receded a little, advanced rapidly, till at last, with the first brilliant point that appeared in the sky, I saw plainly enough an edge of light that grazed our sides for a considerable time, or brushed our elbows from west to east. Having good reason, therefore, to suppose the eclipse ended for us, I looked at my watch, and found that the hand had traversed three minutes and a half. The hill-tops then resumed their natural color, and I saw a horizon at the point previously occupied by the centre of the shadow. My companions cried out that they again saw the steep hill toward which they had been looking attentively. It still, indeed, remained black to the southeast, but I will not say that the horizon was difficult to discover. Presently we heard the song of the larks hailing the return of light, after the profound and universal silence in which everything had been plunged. The earth and sky appeared then as they do in the morning before sunrise. The latter was of a grayish tint, inclining to blue; the former, as far as my eye could reach, was deep green or russet.

"As soon as the sun appeared, the clouds grew denser, and for several minutes the light did not increase, just as happens at a cloudy sunrise. The instant the eclipse became total, till the emersion of the sun, we saw Venus, but no other stars. We perceived at this moment the spire of Salisbury cathedral. The clouds not dispersing, we could not push our observations further: they cleared up, however, considerably toward evening. I have hastened home to write this letter. So deep an impression has this spectacle made upon my mind, that I shall long be able to recount all the circumstances of it with as much precision as now. After supper, I made a sketch of it from memory, on the same paper on which I had previously drawn a view of the country.

"I will own to you I was, methinks, the only person in England who did not regret the presence of clouds: they added much to the solemnity of the spectacle—incomparably superior, in my opinion, to that of 1715 which I saw perfectly from the top of the belfrey of Boston, in Lincolnshire, where the sky was very clear. There, indeed, I saw the two sides of the shadow coming from afar, and passing to a great distance behind us; but this eclipse exhibited great variety, and was more awfully imposing; so that I cannot but congratulate myself on having had opportunities of seeing, under such different circumstances, these two rare accidents of nature."

The Ecliptic derives its name from the fact, that the shadow of the earth always lying in it, no object can be *eclipsed* unless it be very near to it. If we imagine a line drawn from the centre of the sun through the centre of the earth, and continued beyond the earth, that line will be the axis of the earth's shadow, and the diameter of the conical shadow must be everywhere less than the diameter of the earth. The moon can not touch the shadow, if the distance of its nearer limb from the ecliptic be greater than the diameter of the earth.

The *ecliptic limits*, is a term expressing the greatest distances of the moon from its node at which it is possible that an eclipse, either lunar or solar, can happen. This distance for eclipses of the moon is twelve degrees, and for eclipses of the sun seventeen degrees.

Whenever the moon is less than seventeen degrees from its node at a time when it is in conjunction with the sun, there *must* be a solar eclipse; and whenever it is less than twelve degrees from its node at the time of full moon, there *must* be a lunar eclipse. Within these limits the less the distance of the moon from its node, the greater will be the number of digits eclipsed, whether of the sun or moon.

THE AURORA BOREALIS.

Origin of the Name.—Produced by Electricity.—General Phenomena of Auroras.—Various Examples of this Meteor.—Biot's Excursion to the Shetland Isles to observe the Aurora.—Lottin's Observations in 1838-'9.—Various Auroras seen by him.—Theory of Biot to explain these Meteors.—Objections to it.—Hypothesis of Faraday.—Auroras seen on the Polar Voyage of Captain Franklin.

THE AURORA BOREALIS.

The aurora borealis is a luminous phenomenon, which appears in the heavens, and is seen in high latitudes in both hemispheres. The term aurora borealis, or northern lights, has been applied to it because the opportunities of witnessing it are, from the geographical character of the globe, much more frequent in the northern than in the southern hemisphere. The term aurora polaris would be a more proper designation.

This phenomenon consists of luminous rays of various colors, issuing from every direction, but converging to the same point, which appear after sunset generally toward the north, occasionally toward the west, and sometimes, but rarely, toward the south. It frequently appears near the horizon, as a vague and diffuse light, something like the faint streaks which harbinger the rising sun and form the dawn. Hence the phenomenon has derived its name, the northern morning. Sometimes, however, it is presented under the form of a sombre cloud, from which luminous jets issue, which are often variously colored, and illuminate the entire atmosphere.

A meteor so striking as the aurora could not fail at an early period to attract the attention of scientific inquirers, and to give rise to various theories. Some supposed it to be the refraction of the solar rays; others ascribed it to the effects of the magnetic fluid. Euler identified it with the tails of comets. Mairan supposed it to proceed from the intermixture of the far-extending atmosphere of the sun with that of the earth. When, however, the luminous effects of artificial electricity were shown—when the electric light transmitted through rarefied air was exhibited—and when the identity of lightning with electricity was established, these various hypotheses were by common consent abandoned; and the explanation proposed by Eberhart, of Halle, and Paul Frisi, of Pisa, which ascribed the phenomenon to electricity transmitted through regions in which the atmosphere is in a highly rarefied state, was adopted. Any doubt which might have hung round this explanation was dispelled when the relations between magnetism and electricity were demonstrated; and although the complete explanation of the details of the aurora has not been accomplished, the electricity and magnetism of the earth and its atmosphere must now be regarded as its source.

In his treatise on these meteors, Mairan describes their appearance and the succession of changes to which they are subject with great minuteness and precision. The more conspicuous auroras commence to be formed soon after the close of twilight. At first a dark mist or foggy cloud is perceived in the north, and a little more brightness toward the west than in the other parts of the heavens. The mist gradually takes the form of a circular segment, resting at each corner on the horizon. The visible part of the arc soon becomes surrounded with a pale light, which is followed by the formation of one or several luminous arcs. Then come jets and rays of light variously colored, which issue from the dark part of the segment, the continuity of which is broken by bright emanations, which indicate a movement of the mass, which seems agitated by internal shocks, during the formation of these luminous radiations, which issue from it as flames do from a conflagration. When this species of fire has ceased, and the aurora has become extended, a crown is formed at the zenith, to which these rays converge. From this time the phenomenon diminishes in its intensity, exhibiting, nevertheless, from time to time—sometimes on one side of the heavens and sometimes on another—jets of light, a crown and colors more or less vivid. Finally the motion ceases, the light approaches gradually to the horizon; the cloud, quitting the other parts of the firmament, settles in the north. The dark part of the segment becomes luminous, its brightness being greatest near the horizon, and becoming more feeble as the altitude augments, until it loses its light altogether.

The aurora is sometimes composed of two luminous segments, which are concentric, and separated from each other by one dark space, and from the earth by another. Sometimes, though rarely, there is only one dark segment, which is symmetrically pierced round its border by openings, through which light or fire is seen, as represented in fig. 1. A meteor of this kind was ob-

Fig. 1.

served by Mairan himself at Breuille-Pont, on the 19th of October, 1726. This meteor was seen at the same time in distant parts of Europe, such as Warsaw, Moscow, St. Petersburg, Rome, Naples, Lisbon, and Cadiz. The least height which is compatible with its observed position in these places would be about fifty leagues above the surface of the earth.

In the year 1817, M. Biot made a voyage to the Shetland isles, where he had frequent and favorable opportunities of observing these phenomena; and the known habits of accuracy and skill in experimental investigation of that philosopher must confer great value on the results of his observations. A remarkable aurora was seen by him on the 27th of August, 1817.

Several thin jets of light were first seen to rise at the northeast to a small height. Having played for some time, they were extinguished; but, after an hour and a half, they reappeared, with increased extent and brilliancy, in the same part of the sky. They soon began to form above the horizon a regular arc, like a rainbow, which was not complete at first, but by degrees increased its amplitude, and, after some moments, was completed, by the sudden formation of the remainder, which rose in a moment, accompanied by a multitude of jets of light, which issued from all points of the northern horizon. The vertex of the bow then reached very nearly to the zenith. This bow was at first fleeting and undecided in its character, as if the matter of which it was composed had not yet taken a stable arrangement; but all this agitation quickly subsided, and then it remained hanging in the heavens in all its beauty for more than an hour, having a progressive motion barely sensible toward the southeast, where it seemed to be carried by a light wind which was then felt from the northeast. M. Biot had thus full time to contemplate it; and he observed its position with the instruments he had provided for astronomical purposes. He found that it embraced an extent upon the horizon of 128° 42′, and that its centre was placed precisely in the direction of the magnetic meridian. The whole extent of the firmament traversed by this grand arc, on the northwestern side, was continually intersected, in every direction, by jets of light, the forms, motions, colors, and continuance of which, strongly attracted his attention. Each of these jets, when it first appeared, was a simple line of whitish light: its magnitude and splendor were augmented rapidly, presenting sometimes singular variations of direction and curvature. When it attained its entire development, it was contracted to a thin straight thread, the light of which was extremely vivid and brilliant, and of a decided red tint. After this it grew gradually fainter, and became extinct frequently at the same place precisely where it commenced its appearance. This permanence of a great number of jets, each in the same apparent place, while their brightness exhibited an infinite variety of degrees, renders it probable, in the opinion of Biot, that their light is not reflected, but direct, and that it is developed in the place where it is seen. This inference is further confirmed by the circumstance that no trace of polarization could be discovered in it. All these meteors, and the bow within which their play was confined, must have occupied a region above the clouds, since the latter occasionally intercepted their light.

One of the most recent and detailed descriptions of the aurora borealis is due to M. Lottin, an officer of the French navy, and a member of the scientific commission sent some years ago to the north seas.

During the winter of 1838–'9, M. Lottin observed the auroras at Bossekop, in the bay of Alten, on the coast of West Finmark, in the latitude of 70° N. Between September, 1838, and April, 1839, being an interval of two hundred and six days, he observed one hundred and forty-three auroras: they were most frequent during the period which the sun remained below the horizon, that is, from the 17th of November to the 25th of January. During this night of seventy times twenty-four hours, there were sixty-four auroras visible, without counting those which were rendered invisible by a clouded sky, but the presence of which was indicated by the disturbance they produced on the magnetic needle.

Without entering into the details of the individual appearances of these meteors, we shall here briefly describe the appearances and the succession of changes which they usually presented.

Between the hours of four and eight o'clock in the afternoon, a light sea-fog, which almost constantly prevailed, extending to the altitude of from four to six degrees, became colored on its upper border, or rather was fringed with the light of the aurora, which was then behind it; this border became gradually more regular, and took the form of an arc of a pale yellow color, the edges of which were diffuse, and the extremities rested on the horizon. This bow swelled upward more or less slowly, its vertex being constantly on the magnetic meridian, or very nearly so. It was not easy to determine this with precision, because of the motion of the bow, and the great magnitude of the circle, of which it formed but a small segment: blackish streaks divided regularly the luminous matter of the arc, and resolved it into a system of rays; these rays were alternately extended and contracted; sometimes slowly, sometimes instantaneously; sometimes they would dart out, increasing and diminishing suddenly in splendor. The inferior parts, or the feet of the rays, presented always the most vivid light, and formed an arc more or less regular. The length of these rays was very various, but they all converged to that point of the heavens indicated by the direction of the southern pole of the dipping needle, as indicated in fig. 2. Sometimes they were prolonged to the point where their

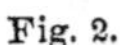

Fig. 2.

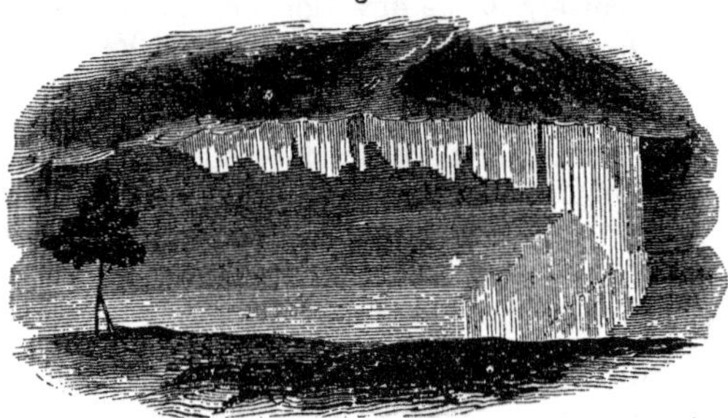

directions intersected, and formed the summit of an enormous dome of light, as represented in fig. 3.

Fig. 3.

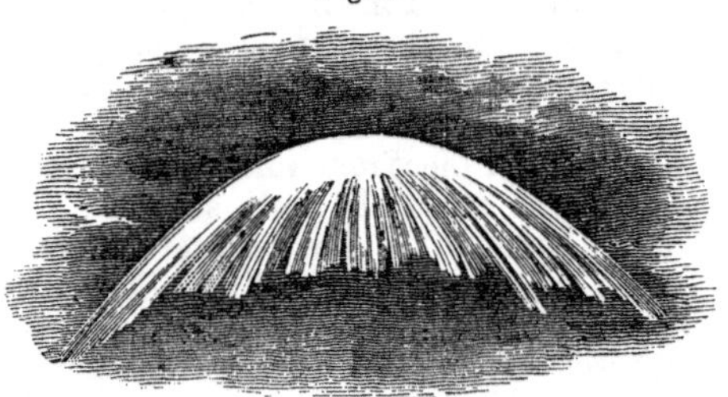

The bow then would continue to ascend toward the zenith: it would suffer an undulatory motion in its light—that is to say, that from one extremity to the other the brightness of the rays would increase successively in intensity. This luminous current would appear several times in quick succession, and it would pass much more frequently from west to east than in the opposite direction. Sometimes, but rarely, a retrograde motion would take place immediately afterward; and as soon as this wave of light would run successively over all the rays of the aurora from west to east, it would return, in the contrary direction, to the point of its departure, producing such an effect that it was impossible to say whether the rays themselves were actually affected by a motion of translation in a direction nearly horizontal, or if this more vivid light was transferred from ray to ray, the system of rays themselves suffering no change of position.

The bow, thus presenting the appearance of an alternate motion in a direction nearly horizontal, had usually the appearance of the undulations or folds of a riband or flag agitated by the wind, as represented in fig. 4. Sometimes

Fig. 4.

one and sometimes both of its extremities would desert the horizon, and then its folds would become more numerous and marked, the bow would change its character, and assume the form of a long sheet of rays returning into itself, and consisting of several parts forming graceful curves, as represented in fig. 5.

Fig. 5.

The brightness of the rays would vary suddenly, sometimes surpassing in splendor stars of the first magnitude ; these rays would rapidly dart out, and curves would be formed and developed like the folds of a serpent ; then the rays would effect various colors, the base would be red, the middle green, and the remainder would preserve its clear yellow hue. Such was the arrangement which the colors always preserved ; they were of admirable transparency, the base exhibiting blood-red, and the green of the middle being that of the pale emerald ; the brightness would diminish, the colors disappear, and all be extinguished, sometimes suddenly, and sometimes by slow degrees. After this disappearance, fragments of the bow would be reproduced, would continue their upward movement, and approach the zenith ; the rays, by the effect of perspective, would be gradually shortened ; the thickness of the arc, which presented then the appearance of a large zone of parallel rays (fig. 6), would be estimated ; then the vertex of the bow would reach the magnetic zenith, or the point to which the south pole of the dipping needle is directed. At that moment the rays would be seen in the direction of their feet. If they were colored, they would appear as a large red band, through which the green tints of their superior parts could be distinguished ; and if the wave of light above mentioned passed along them, their feet would form a long sinuous undulating zone, while, throughout all these changes, the rays would never suffer any oscillation in the direction of their axis, and would constantly preserve their mutual parallelisms.

While these appearances are manifested, new bows are formed, either commencing in the same diffuse manner, or with vivid and ready-formed rays : they succeed each other, passing through nearly the same phases, and arrange themselves at certain distances from each other. As many as nine have been

Fig. 6.

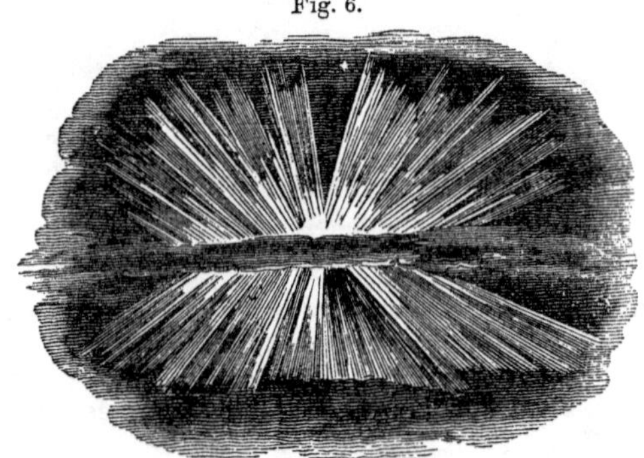

counted, forming as many bows, having their ends supported on the earth, and, in their arrangement, resembling the short curtains suspended one behind the other over the scene of a theatre, and intended to represent the sky. Sometimes the intervals between these bows diminish, and two or more of them close upon each other, forming one large zone, traversing the heavens, and disappearing toward the south, becoming rapidly feeble after passing the zenith. But sometimes, also, when this zone extends over the summit of the firmament from east to west, the mass of rays which have already passed beyond the magnetic zenith appear suddenly to come from the south, and to form with those from the north the real boreal corona, all the rays of which converge to the zenith. This appearance of a crown, therefore, is doubtless the mere effect of perspective; and an observer, placed at the same instant at a certain distance to the north or to the south, would perceive only an arc.

The total zone, measuring less in the direction north and south than in the direction east and west, since it often leans upon the earth, the corona would be expected to have an elliptical form; but that does not always happen: it has been seen circular, the unequal rays not extending to a greater distance than from eight to twelve degrees from the zenith, while at other times they reach the horizon.

Let it, then, be imagined, that all these vivid rays of light issue forth with splendor, subject to continual and sudden variations in their length and brightness; that these beautiful red and green tints color them at intervals; that waves of light undulate over them; that currents of light succeed each other; and, in fine, that the vast firmament presents one immense and magnificent dome of light, reposing on the snow-covered base supplied by the ground—which itself serves as a dazzling frame for a sea, calm and black as a pitchy lake—and some idea, though an imperfect one, may be obtained of the splendid spectacle which presents itself to him who witnesses the aurora from the bay of Alten.

The corona, when it is formed, only lasts for some minutes: it sometimes forms suddenly, without any previous bow. There are rarely more than two on the same night; and many of the auroras are attended with no crown at all.

The corona becomes gradually faint, the whole phenomenon being to the south of the zenith, forming bows gradually paler, and generally disappearing before they reach the southern horizon. All this most commonly takes place in the first half of the night, after which the aurora appears to have lost its intensity: the pencils of rays, the bands and the fragments of bows, appear and disappear at intervals; then the rays become more and more diffused, and ultimately merge into the vague and feeble light which is spread over the heavens grouped like little clouds, and designated by the name of *auroral plates* (*plaques aurorales*). Their milky light frequently undergoes striking changes in its brightness, like motions of dilatation and contraction, which are propagated reciprocally between the centre and the circumference, like those which are observed in marine animals called Medusæ. The phenomena become gradually more faint, and generally disappear altogether on the appearance of twilight. Sometimes, however, the aurora continues after the commencement of daybreak, when the light is so strong that a printed book may be read. It then disappears, sometimes suddenly; but it often happens that, as the daylight augments, the aurora becomes gradually vague and undefined, takes a whitish color, and is ultimately so mingled with the cirrho-stratus clouds that it is impossible to distinguish it from them.

Among the various theories and hypotheses which have been proposed to explain auroras, that which appears most entitled to attention has been suggested by M. Biot.

The first question which naturally urges itself upon the consideration of the scientific inquirer is, whether the phenomenon is to be regarded as meteorological or astronomical; in other words, whether it takes place within the limits of our atmosphere, and partakes in common with that fluid in the diurnal motion of the earth, or is situate in a region beyond the limits of the atmosphere, being seen through it, like the stars, planets, comets, and other celestial objects. The relation which the form of aurora invariably bears to the direction of the magnetic meridian raises a *primâ facie* presumption in favor of the phenomenon being atmospheric; but all doubt on this question has been removed by the observations of M. Biot, from which it appears that the apparent place of the aurora in relation to celestial objects is not fixed; that its altitude and azimuth do not undergo those hourly changes to which celestial objects are subject; and that they undergo no motion, in reference to the zenith or horizon, such as would be produced by the diurnal rotation of the earth. It must then be taken as demonstrated, that the aurora borealis is a phenomenon placed within the limits of our atmosphere, and that it is connected with the atmosphere or with some matter suspended in it, partaking of the diurnal motion common to the atmosphere and the globe.

The fact that the rays or columns of light are always paralled to the dipping needle, and that the bows, coronæ, and other visible forms which the phenomena affect, are always symmetrically placed with respect to the magnetic meridian, demonstrate that the cause of the phenomena, whatever it may be, has an intimate relation with that of terrestrial magnetism.

M. Biot conceives that the luminous columns composing the aurora have not in reality the position or form which they appear to the eye to have; but that their apparent form is merely the result of perspective. He considers that the phenomenon is produced by an infinite number of luminous columns, parallel to the dipping needle and to each other, arranged side by side at nearly the same height from the surface of the earth; these systems of columns being placed at unequal distances from the eye, and seen under different angles of obliquity, are projected into various figures, which are subject to variation arising from the varying splendor of their component rays.

It has been attempted, on various occasions, to determine the height of auroras by the same method which has been applied with such accurate results to the determination of the distances of the sun, moon, and other celestial objects. This method consists in the comparison of two observations of the exact apparent place in the heavens observed at the same moment in distant parts of the earth. Many causes, however, conspire to render this method inapplicable to auroras; among which may be mentioned the difficulty of making the two observations at the same instant of time, and the total impossibility of the two observers being certain of directing their observations to precisely the same point of the aurora. To such causes must be ascribed the widely-varying estimates of the height of auroras; obtained in this manner—estimates which vary from fifty to three hundred miles from the surface of the earth. Meanwhile, whatever be their height, it is evidently subject to continual variation, even in the same aurora, as is rendered apparent by the sudden changes which the phenomenon undergoes, and by the progressive motion of its arcs.

Great differences have existed among meteorologists respecting the sounds which are said to proceed from auroras. The inhabitants of the northern regions, where these appearances most prevail, are unanimous in declaring that they are frequently accompanied by hissing and cracking noises in the air, like those produced by artificial fireworks. Persons engaged in the whale-fisheries make the same statements. M. Biot found the inhabitants of the Shetland islands unanimous on the question; and M. Lottin found the same impression among the far-distant inhabitants of Siberia. On the other hand, during the sojourn of M. Biot in the Shetland isles, he witnessed several great auroras, but heard no sound. During M. Lottin's expedition, he witnessed one hundred and forty-three auroras, in not one of which was he sensible of any sound. The only strictly scientific observer who appears to have personally experienced such sounds is Cavallo, who states that he has distinctly heard them on several occasions, but limits his testimony to this general form, assigning neither time nor place. Such discordancy of evidence can only be reconciled by the supposition that such sounds are audible on rare occasions, when the region in which the aurora is developed is within a very limited distance of the observer; and if the existence of such sounds be thus admitted, it must be also admitted that the height of the aurora is, at least in such cases, infinitely less than is commonly estimated; and if, in particular cases, its height be so small, it is probably in all others proportionally under the highest estimates which have been made of it.

From a comparison of all the observed effects, it may then be assumed as nearly, if not conclusively, proved, that the aurora borealis is composed of real clouds, proceeding generally from the north, and formed of extremely attenuated and luminous matter floating in the atmosphere, which frequently arrange themselves in series of lines or columns parallel to the dipping needle. What the nature of the matter is composing such clouds must, in the present state of science, rest upon mere conjecture. The following is the substance of the theory of M. Biot on this subject already referred to:—

Among material substances, certain metals alone are susceptible of magnetism. Since, then, the luminous matter composing the aurora obeys the magnetic influence of the earth, it is very probable that the luminous clouds of which it consists are composed of metallic particles reduced to an extremely minute and subtile form. This being admitted, another consequence will immediately ensue. Such metallic clouds, if the expression be allowed, will be conductors of electricity, more or less perfect, according to the degree of proximity of their constituent particles. When such clouds arrange themselves in columnar forms, and connect strata of the atmosphere at different elevations, if such strata be unequally charged with electricity, the electrical equilibrium will be re-established through the intervention of the metallic columns, and light and sound will be evolved in proportion to the imperfect conductability of the metallic clouds arising from the extremely rarefied state of the metallic vapor, or fine dust, of which they are constituted. All the results of electrical experiments countenance these suppositions, when the phenomena are produced in the more elevated regions, where the air is highly rarefied, little resistance being opposed to the motion of the electric fluid: light alone is evolved without sensible sound, as is observed when electricity is transmitted through exhausted tubes; but when the aurora is developed in the lower strata of the atmosphere, it would produce the hissing and cracking noise which appears to be heard on some occasions. If the metallic cloud possess the conducting power in a high degree, the electric current may pass through it without the evolution of either light or sound; and thus the magnetic needle may be affected as it would be by an aurora at a time when no aurora is visible. If any cause alters the conductability of those columnar clouds suddenly or gradually, a sudden or gradual change in the splendor of the aurora would ensue.

According as those clouds advance over more southern countries, the direction of their columns being constantly parallel to the dipping needle, they take gradually a more horizontal position, and consequently the strata of atmosphere at their extremities become gradually less distant, and consequently more nearly in a state of electrical equilibrium; hence it follows, that as the latitude diminishes, the appearance of aurora becomes more and more rare, until, in the lower latitudes, where the columns are nearly parallel to the horizon, such phenomena are never observed.

This ingenious and beautiful theory still, however, requires, before its validity can be admitted by the rigid canons of modern physics, that the main fact on which it rests should be proved: it is necessary that it should be shown that such metallic clouds as are here supposed, and on the agency of which the whole theory is based, should be accounted for. This demand is accordingly answered by M. Biot.

The magnetic pole, or its vicinity, is evidently the point from which these columnar masses of meteoric light proceed. Therefore, the extremely minute rays composing these columns must issue from the earth in that region. Now it is well known that that part of the globe is, and always has been, characterized by the prevalence of frequent and violent volcanic eruptions, and several volcanoes have been, and still are, in activity round the place where the magnetic pole is situate. These eruptions are always accompanied by electric phenomena. Thunder issues from the volcanic clouds ejected by the craters; and these clouds of volcanic dust, thus charged with electricity, are projected to great heights, and carried to considerable distances through the air, carrying with them all the electricity taken from the crater.

These vast eruptions, issuing from depths so unfathomable that they seem almost to penetrate the globe, and issuing with such violence from the gulfs by which they are projected into the atmosphere, must necessarily produce strong vertical currents of air, by which the volcanic dust will be carried to an elevation exceeding that of common clouds. Travellers who have visited Iceland have often seen suspended over it, during eruptions, a species of volcanic fog. Such clouds are known to be of a sulphureous and metallic nature, painfully irritating the eyes, mouth, and nostrils. Moreover, the existence of dry fogs, diffusing a fetid and sulphureous odor, was ascertained in 1783, when all Europe was enveloped in a fog of that description.

To this it may be added, that more recent observations have rendered it highly probable, if not certain, that metallic matter, and more particularly iron in a pure and uncombined state, is frequently precipitated from the clouds in thunder-storms.

To the theory of M. Biot it is objected by M. Becquerel, that the existence of metal in that uncombined form, in which alone it has the conducting power, in volcanic eruptions, has not been proved; that the matter ejected from volcanoes consists of vitrified substances, silicates, aluminates, and other substances, which are non-conductors, but that pure metal is never found.

At the time when M. Biot promulgated his theory, it was necessary for him to assign an adequate source whence the electricity was derived, to which he ascribed the aurora; and he accordingly supposed it to proceed from the polar volcanoes. In the progress of electrical discovery, so many new sources of electricity have, however, been since disclosed, that this part of his hypothesis has become needless.

The following hypothesis has been suggested by Professor Faraday (*Exp. Research.* 192):—

"I hardly dare venture, even in the most hypothetical form, to ask whether the aurora borealis and australis may not be the discharge of electricity, thus urged toward the poles of the earth, whence it is endeavoring to return by natural and appointed means above the earth to the equatorial regions. The non-occurrence of it in very high latitudes is not at all against the supposition; and it is remarkable that Mr. Fox, who observed the deflections of the magnetic needle at Falmouth, by the aurora borealis, gave that direction of it which perfectly agrees with the present view." The manner in which the electricity above alluded to is urged toward the poles, belongs to another division of our subject, "Magneto Electricity." If the above view is correct, may it not help us in the difficult question of atmospheric electricity?

The mode adopted to illustrate the electrical nature of the aurora, is to exhaust a tall glass tube by means of the air-pump, and then to pass a succession of electric sparks down the interior of the tube, from the prime conductor of the machine. The effects produced by a powerful machine are most brilliant; a close inspection shows that the whole tube is at times filled with a mass of miniature flashes of lightning; the color varies from the usual bright electrical light to a vivid violet. The most exalted effects have been produced by means of the hydro-electric machine. The tension of this machine is equal to a spark of twelve or fourteen inches in the atmosphere, and therefore of power to pass readily through four or five feet of partial vacuum, and its quantity is equivalent to a charge of eighty feet of coated surface in ten seconds. A peculiar effect attending this powerful discharge is, that sometimes the aurora appears with a bright line of light proceeding from each end of the tube, and a revolving spiral embracing the lower part.

The falling star is an experiment of the auroral character often introduced in books on electricity. Cavallo says (vol. ii., p. 101), "When the receiver is not exhausted, the discharge of a jar through some part of it will appear like a *small globule* exceedingly bright." Whence we often hear it said, that the discharge of a battery will produce a ball of light passing from one end to the other of the exhausted receiver. If this really were the case, it would be a most important experiment; for if the ball were *seen to pass* from one end to the other, it would follow that its *direction* had been actually seen; and, if so, the one-fluid theory would have been *demonstrated.* But very little reflection will suffice to show the impossibility of such an appearance; for, admitting the actual existence of a ball, though we are more inclined to suppose that any such thing would be like an oblong spheroid, the extreme velocity of electricity would take it to the end of its course before the impression of its first appearance on the retina had subsided; just, indeed, as the rotating wheel, having red radii, appears entirely red during the period of rapid rotation; and so, instead of seeing a ball, if such really were there, the eye would recognise a continuous line of light. And this is actually the case. We have ourselves repeated the experiment under very favorable circumstances, and in the presence of very competent witnesses, and one and all agreed in perceiving in every case a distinct continuous line of light, but no appearance of a ball or falling star.

An extraordinary experiment, illustrative of the theory of the aurora similar to that suggested by Faraday, with the addition that "electricity is radiated in a peculiar manner from magnetized bodies," was introduced by Mr. Nott at the meeting of the British Association at Cork (1843). He rotated a steel globe, and passed magnets from the equator to the poles, till the globe was perfectly magnetized. He then insulated the globe, and placed an insulated ring around its equatorial regions. He connected the ring with the prime conductor of the resinous plate of his "rheo-electric machine," and one pole of the globe with the conductor of the vitreous plate. It is necessary to mention, that the machine alluded to consists of two parallel plates, one glass, the other resin, rotating on the same axis, and provided with separate rubbers. The circuit, including the rubbers and conductors, is completed in various ways; the machine is described as producing a current of electricity of tension analogous to that of the pile. In the present experiment, when the machine is rotated, a truly beautiful and luminous discharge takes place between the unconnected pole of the globe and the ring. A dense atmosphere is more favorable to the success of the experiment than a dry one. It had then the appearance of a ring of light, the upper part of which was brilliant, and the under dark: above the ring, all around the axis were foliated diverging flames, one behind the other.

In Captain Franklin's narrative, the auroras observed at Fort Enterprise, in North America, are described by Lieutenant Wood as follows:—

They rise with their centres sometimes in the magnetic meridian, and sometimes several degrees to the eastward or westward of it. The number visible seldom exceeds five, and is seldom limited to one. The altitude of the lowest, when first seen, is never less than four degrees. As they advance toward the zenith, their centres (or the parts most elevated) preserve a course in the magnetic meridian, or near to it; but the eastern and western extremities vary their respective distances, and the arches become irregularly broad streams in the zenith, each dividing the sky into two unequal parts, but never crossing one another until they separate into parts. Those parts which were bright at the horizon, increase their brilliancy in the zenith, and discover the beams of which they are composed, where the interior motion is rapid. This interior motion is a sudden glow, not proceeding from any visible concentration of matter, but bursting out in several parts of the arch, as if an ignition of combustible matter had taken place, and spreading itself rapidly toward each extremity. In this motion the beams are formed. They have two motions: one at right angles to their length, or sidewise, and the other a tremulous and short vibration, in which they do not exactly preserve their parallelism to each other. The wreaths, when in the zenith, present the appearance of coronæ boreales. The second motion is always accompanied by colors; for it must be observed that beams are often formed without any exhibition of colors, and I have not in that case perceived the vibratory motion.

The northern lights are sometimes tinged with the various prismatic colors, among which orange and green, but more frequently the different shades of red, predominate. Maupertius describes one seen by him in Lapland, by which an extensive region of the heavens toward the south appeared tinged with so lively a red, that the whole constellation of Orion seemed as if dyed in blood. Some observers of this meteor have affirmed that they have heard a rustling or crackling sound proceed from it; doubts have, however, been entertained on this point, from the circumstance that no such noises were heard by Scoresby, Richardson, Franklin, Parry, and Hood, who observed the polar lights with great care, under the most favorable circumstances, in very high latitudes. But the testimony of other observers is so positive a kind, as to leave no reasonable doubt that the phenomenon has, at least in particular instances, been accompanied by sounds.

From the accounts which have been collected of the polar lights, it would seem that the phenomenon was less frequent in former ages than it is now ; but it must be kept in mind that meteoric observations have not always been so much attended to as at present. Aristotle describes the phenomenon with sufficient accuracy in his book of meteors. Allusions are also made to it by Pliny, Cicero, and Seneca ; so that it must have been witnessed by the ancients, even in the climates of Greece and Italy. The descriptions of armies fighting in the air, and similar observations, in the dark ages, doubtless owed their origin to the striking and fantastic appearances of the northern lights. It is remarkable, however, that no mention is made by any English writer of an aurora borealis having been observed in England from the year 1621 to 1707. Celsius says expressly that the oldest inhabitants of Upsala considered the phenomenon a great rarity before 1716. In the month of March in that year, a very splendid one appeared in England, and by reason of its brilliancy attracted universal attention. It has been described by Dr. Halley in the Philosophical Transactions, No. 347. Since then the meteor has been much more common. A complete account of all the appearances of auroras recorded previous to 1754 may be found in the work of Mairan, " Traité de l'Aurore Boraele."

The aurora is not confined to the northern hemisphere, similar appearances being observed in high southern latitudes. An aurora was observed by Don Antonio d'Ulloa at Cape Horn in 1745 ; one appeared at Cuzco, in 1744 ; and another is described by Mr. Forster (who accompanied Captain Cook in his last voyage round the world), which was seen by him in 1773, in latitude 58° south, and resembled entirely those of the northern hemisphere, excepting that the light exhibited no tints, but was of a clear white. Similar testimony is given by subsequent navigators.

There is great difficulty in determining the exact height of the aurora borealis above the earth, and accordingly the opinions given on this subject by different observers are widely discordant. Mairan supposed the mean height to be one hundred and seventy-five French leagues ; Bergman says four hundred and sixty, and Euler several thousand miles. From the comparison of a number of observations of an aurora that appeared in March, 1826, made at different places in the north of England and south of Scotland, Dr. Dalton, in a paper presented to the Royal Society, computed its height to be about one hundred miles. But a calculation of this sort, in which it is of necessity supposed that the meteor is seen in exactly the same place by the different observers, is subject to very great uncertainty. The observations of Dr. Richardson, Franklin, Hood, Parry, and others, seem to prove that the place of the aurora is far within the limits of the atmosphere, and scarcely above the region of the clouds ; in fact, as the diurnal rotation of the earth produces no change in its apparent position, it must necessarily partake of that motion, and consequently be regarded as an atmospherical phenomenon.

ELECTRICITY.

Electric Phenomena observed by the Ancients.—Thales.—Gilbert de Magnete.—Otto Guericke's Electric Machine.—Hawkesbee's Experiments.—Stephen Grey's Discoveries on Electrics and Non-Electrics.—Wheeler and Grey's Experiments.—Dufaye discovers the Resinous and Vitreous Electricities.—Invention of the Leyden Phial.—Singular Effects of the first Electric Shocks.—Experiments of Watson and Bevis.—Experiments on Conductors.—Franklin's Experiments and Letters.—His Celebrated Theory of Positive and Negative Electricity.—His Experiments on the Leyden Phial.—His Discovery of the Identity of Lightning and Electricity.—Reception of his Suggestions by the Royal Society.—His Kite Experiment.—His Right to this Discovery denied by Arago.—His Claim vindicated.—Invention of Conductors.—Death of Richmann.—Beccaria's Observations.—Canton's Experiments.—Discovery of Induction.—Invention of the Condenser.—Works of Æpinus.—Theory of Symmer.—Experiments of Coulomb.—Balance of Torsion.—Electricity of the Atmosphere.—Effects of Flame.—Experiments of Volta.—Lavoisier and Laplace.—Analytical Work of Poisson.

ELECTRICITY.

Although it has been reserved for modern times to bring to perfection the methods of investigation pursued in physical researches, these great divisions of human knowledge have nevertheless been always progressive. If the labors of the ancients were obstructed, their advancement retarded, and their productions disfigured by fantastical theories ; the facts they accumulated, the phenomena they described, and the observations they recorded, have formed a bequest of the highest value to the better disciplined inquirers and observers of later days. Astronomy, the mechanics of solid and fluid bodies, and the physics of the imponderable agents, light and heat, received severally more or less attention at an early epoch of the progress of human knowledge ; and the results of ancient researches in some of these branches of science, astronomy for example, form an important element of the knowledge we now possess. Electricity, however, is a remarkable exception to this state of progressive movement. To that particular division of physics antiquity has contributed absolutely nothing. The vast discoveries which have accumulated respecting this extraordinary agent, by which its connexion with and influence upon the whole material universe, its relations to the phenomena of organized bodies, the part it plays in the functions of animal and vegetable vitality, its subservience to the uses of man as a mechanical power, its intimate connexion with the chemical constitution of material substances, in fine, its application in almost every division of the sciences, and every department of the arts, have been severally demonstrated, are exclusively and peculiarly due to the spirit of modern research, and in a great degree to the labors of the present age.

The beginnings of science have often the appearance of chance. A felicitous accident throws a certain natural fact under the notice of an inquiring and philosophic mind. Attention is awakened and investigation provoked. Similar phenomena under varied circumstances are eagerly sought for ; and if in the natural course of events they do not present themselves, circumstances are designedly arranged so as to bring about their production. The seeds of science are thus sown, and soon begin to germinate: Whether such primary facts are really fortuitous, or ought not rather to be viewed as the prompting of HIM, whose will is that intellectual progression shall be incessant, it is certain that they not only give the first impetus to science, but their occasional and timely occurrence in its progress produces frequently greater effects on the celerity of its advancement than the most exalted powers of the human mind, unsupported by such aid, have ever accomplished. It may then be imagined that if any such hints were offered by ordinary phenomena, an agent so all-pervading as electricity could scarcely have eluded notice, or failed to command attention, during a succession of ages which witnessed the growth and extension of so many other parts of natural knowledge. On the contrary, the class of effects in which electricity originated was observed by and well known to the early philosophers of Greece. THALES, six centuries before the Christian era, was acquainted with the property of amber, from which electricity derives its name;* and Theophrastus and Pliny, as well as other writers, Greek and Roman, mention the property of this and certain other substances, in virtue of which, when submitted to friction, they acquire the power to attract straws, and other light bodies, as a magnet attracts iron. In the spirit which characterized the times, such effects were regarded with feelings of superstition. A soul was ascribed to amber, and it was held sacred.

Nor were these the only phenomena which presented themselves to the ancients, and afforded them a clue to the foundation of this part of physics. Various other scattered facts are recorded, which prove that nature did not conceal her secrets with more than usual coyness in this case. The luminous appearance attending the friction of those substances which exhibited electrical effects was observed. The Roman historians record the frequent appearance of a flame at the points of the soldiers' javelins, at the summits of the masts of ships, and sometimes even on the heads of the seamen.† The effects of the torpedo and electrical fishes are referred to by Aristotle, Galen and Oppian; and at a period less remote, Eustathius, in his Commentary on the Iliad of Homer, mentions the case of Walimer, a Gothic chief, the father of Theodoric, who used to eject sparks from his body; and further refers to a certain ancient philosopher, who relates of himself that on one occasion, when changing his dress, sudden sparks were emitted from his person on drawing off his clothes, and that flames occasionally issued from him, accompanied by a crackling noise.‡

Such phenomena attracted little attention, and provoked no scientific research. Vacant wonder was the most exalted sentiment they raised; and they accordingly remained, while twenty centuries rolled away, barren and isolated facts upon the surface of human knowledge. The vein whence these precious fragments were detached, and which, as we have shown, *cropped out* sufficiently often to challenge the notice of the miner, continued unexplored and undiscovered; and its splendid treasures were reserved to reward the toil and crown the enterprise of our generation.

The work of classification and generalization was first commenced upon the phenomena of electricity by Gilbert, an English physician, in a work entitled *De Magnete*, published in the beginning of the seventeenth century. In this treatise, the substances then known to be susceptible of electrical excitement were enumerated, and several of the circumstances which affect the production of electrical phenomena, such as the hygrometric state of the atmosphere, were explained. Between that period and the earlier part of the last century

* Ἤλεκτρον, amber.
† Cæsar, de Bell. Afr. cap. vi. Liv. cap. xxxii. Plut. Vita Lys. Plin. sec. Hist. Mun. lib. ii.
‡ Eustath. in Iliad, E.

the science was not advanced by any capital discoveries. In that interval, however, Otto Guericke, celebrated as the inventor of the air-pump, contrived the first electrical machine. This apparatus consisted of a globe of sulphur, mounted upon a horizontal axis, from which it received a motion of rotation, by means of a common handle or winch. The operator turned this handle with one hand, while with the other he applied a cloth to the globe, the friction of which produced the electrical state.

Aided by such apparatus, this philosopher discovered, that after a light substance has been attracted by and brought into contact with an electrified body, it will not be again attracted, but, on the contrary, will be repelled by the same body; but that after it has been touched by the hand, its primitive condition is restored, and it is again attracted. He also showed that a body becomes electric by being brought near to an electrified body without touching it; but offered no explanation of this fact, which, as will be seen hereafter, indicated one of the most important principles of electrical science.

Whether it was that all his attention was altogether engrossed by the researches which he prosecuted with such splendid results in astronomy, the higher mechanics, and optics, or that facts had not yet accumulated in sufficient number and variety to impress him with a just notion of the importance of electricity as a general physical agent, Newton bestowed on it no attention. One experiment only proceeding from him is recorded, in which he shows that when one surface of a plate of glass is electrified, the attraction will be transmitted through the glass, and will be manifested by its effect on any light substances placed on the other side of it.

In the beginning of the eighteenth century, Hawkesbee made a series of experiments on electrical light produced in rarefied air; but as no consequences were deduced from them affecting the progress of the science, we shall not further notice them. In the construction of the apparatus for producing electricity, he substituted a glass sphere for the globe of sulphur proposed by Otto Guericke. This was a considerable improvement; and yet the experimentalists who followed abandoned it, and used no more convenient apparatus than glass tubes, which were held in one hand, and rubbed with the other. To this circumstance Dr. Priestley ascribes in a great degree, the slow progress made by the immediate successors of Hawkesbee in electrical discoveries.

About the year 1730 commenced that splendid series of discoveries which has proceeded with accelerated speed to the present day, and now forms the body of electrical science. Mr. Stephen Grey, a pensioner of the Charter House, impelled by a passionate enthusiasm, engaged in a course of experimental researches, in which were developed some general principles, which produced important effects on subsequent investigations.

The most considerable discovery of Mr. Grey was, that all material substances might be reduced, in reference to electrical phenomena, to two classes, *electrics* and *non-electrics;* the former, including all bodies then supposed to be capable of electric excitation by friction; and the other, those which were incapable of it. He also discovered that non-electrics were capable of acquiring the electric state by contact with excited electrics. As the experiments which led to these conclusions were of the highest interest, we shall here state them.

Desiring to make some experiments with an excited glass tube, he procured one about three feet and a half long, and an inch and a quarter in diameter. To keep the interior free from dust, he stopped it at the ends with corks. When this tube was excited, he happened to present one of the corks to a feather, and was surprised to observe that the feather was first attracted, and then repelled by the cork, in the way it was wont to be by the glass tube itself. He concluded from this, that the electric virtue conferred on the tube by friction passed spontaneously to the cork.

It then occurred to him to inquire whether this transmission of electricity would be made to other substances besides cork. With this view he obtained a deal rod about four inches in length, to one end of which he attached an ivory ball, and inserted the other in the cork, by which the glass tube was stopped. On exciting the tube, he found that the ivory ball attracted and repelled the feather even more vigorously than the cork. He then tried longer rods of deal; next rods of brass and iron wire, with like results. He then attached to one end of the tube a piece of common packthread, and suspended from the lower end of this thread the ivory ball and various other bodies, all of which he found capable of acquiring the electric state when the tube was excited. Experiments of this kind were made from the balconies of his house and other elevated stations.

With a true philosophic spirit, he now determined to inquire what circumstances attending the *manner* of experimenting produced any real effect upon the results; and, first, whether the *position* or *direction* of the rods, wires, or cords, by which the electricity was transmitted from the excited tube, affected the phenomena. For this purpose he extended a piece of packthread in a horizontal direction, supporting it at different points by other pieces of similar cord, which were attached to nails driven into a wooden beam, and which were therefore in a vertical position. To one end of the horizontal cord he attached the ivory ball, and to the other he tied the end of the glass tube. On exciting the tube he found that no electricity was transmitted to the ball, a circumstance which he rightly ascribed to its escape by the vertical cords, the nails supporting them and the wooden beam.

Soon after this, Grey was engaged in repeating his experiments at the house of Mr. Wheeler, who was afterward associated with him in these investigations, when that gentleman suggested that threads of silk should be used to support the horizontal line of cord instead of pieces of packthread. It does not appear that this suggestion of Wheeler proceeded from any knowledge or suspicion of the electric properties of silk; and still less does it appear that Grey was acquainted with them; for, in assenting to the proposition of Wheeler, he observed, that "silk might do better than packthread on account of its smallness, as less of the virtue would probably pass off by it than by the thickness of the hempen line which had been previously used."

They accordingly extended a packthread through a distance of about eighty feet in a horizontal direction, supporting it in that position by threads of silk. To one end of this packthread they attached the ivory ball, and to the other the glass tube. When the latter was excited, the ball immediately became electric, as was manifested by its attraction upon metallic leaf held near it. After this, they extended their experiments to lines of packthread still longer when the silk threads used for its support were found to be too weak, and were broken. Being under the erroneous impression that the escape of the electricity was prevented by the fineness of the silk, they now substituted for it thin brass wire, which they expected, being still smaller than the silk, would more effectually intercept the electricity; and which, from its nature, would have all the necessary strength. The experiment, however, completely failed. No electricity was conveyed to the ivory ball, the whole having escaped by the brass wire, notwithstanding its fineness. They now saw that the silk threads intercepted the electricity, because they were *silk*, and not because they were *small*.

Having thus accidentally discovered the insulating property of silk, they proceeded to investigate its generalization, and found that the same property was enjoyed by resin, hair, glass, and some other substances. In fact, it soon became apparent that this property belonged in a greater or less degree to all those substances which were then known to be capable of being rendered electrical by friction, and which were denominated *electrics*.

Grey now extended his inquiry to fluids and animal bodies. Having at that time no other test of the electrical state of a body than its attraction for light substances placed on a stand under it, the application of such a test to liquids presented at first some difficulty. This was soon surmounted by the expedient of blowing a soap-bubble from the bole of a tobacco-pipe. The bubble was held suspended over some leaf metal, and on bringing the excited tube to the small end of the pipe, the bubble immediately became electrical.

It was in the prosecution of these experiments that he discovered that, when the electrified tube was brought near to any part of a non-electric body, without touching it, the part most remote from the tube became electrified. He thus fell upon the fact which afterward led to the principle of INDUCTION. The science, however, was not yet ripe for that great discovery, and Grey accordingly continued to apply the principle of inductive electricity, without the most remote suspicion of the rich mine whose treasures lay beneath his feet.

In another series of experiments, Grey was also unfortunate in missing a subsequent discovery on which he just touched. He found that certain electric bodies were capable of becoming permanently excited without the previous process of attrition. He took nineteen different substances, among which were resin, gum-lac, shell-lac, sulphur, and pitch, and the remainder of which were various compounds of these. The sulphur he melted in a glass vessel, the others in a spherical iron ladle. When they became solid, and cooled, and were removed from the moulds in which they were, in this manner, cast, he found them to be electrified, and that, on preserving them from exposure to the air, by wrapping them in paper or wool, this electrified state continued for an indefinite time. In the case of sulphur, he found that not only the sulphur was electrical, but also the glass from which it was removed. Had he carried these inquiries further, and looked carefully into the circumstances of the attraction exhibited by the sulphur and the glass, he could not have failed in discovering the existence of the two opposite electricities, and would probably have also found the reason why the iron ladle did not exhibit electrical signs as well as the glass. This, however, escaped him, and the honor of the discovery was reserved for a contemporary philosopher.

In his investigations respecting the power of liquids to receive electricity from excited glass, Grey exhibited, in a manner which at that period appeared striking, the attraction of the glass tube for liquids. We shall, however, pass over these and some other experiments of less importance, since they did not conduce to the development of any general principle.

Contemporary with Grey was the celebrated Dufaye, who, though not impelled by the same enthusiasm, nor exhibiting the same unwearied activity in multiplying experiments, was endowed with mental powers of a much higher order, and consequently was not slow to perceive some important consequences flowing from the experiments of Grey, which had eluded the notice of that philosopher. Dufaye, in the first place, extended the class of substances called electrics—showing that all substances whatever, except the metals and bodies in the soft or liquid state, were capable of being electrified by friction with any sort of cloth, and that, to secure the result, it was only necessary to warm the body previously. He also showed that the property of receiving electricity by contact with an excited electric was much more general than was supposed by Grey, and that most substances exhibited that property in a greater or less degree, when supported by glass well warmed and dried. Dufaye also showed that the conducting power of the packthread used in the experiments of Grey depended on the moisture contained in it, and that the conducting power was considerably increased by wetting it. By this expedient he transmitted electricity along a cord to the distance of about thirteen hundred feet.

It had been previously ascertained that when any substance charged with electricity communicated the electric principle to another body near it, but not in contact with it, the electricity passed from the one body to the other in the form of a spark, accompanied by a snapping or cracking noise, like that of a slight explosion. It had also been discovered by Grey and Wheeler that the bodies of men and animals would become charged with electricity if placed in the usual manner in contact with an excited glass tube, provided they were suspended by silk cords, so as to prevent the escape of the electricity. Dufaye, therefore, reasoned that a man being so suspended by silk cords, the electricity imparted to his person could not escape; and being charged by the excited glass tube, sparks of fire ought to issue from his body, if any body capable of receiving the electricity were presented to it. To reduce this to the immediate test of experiment, Dufaye suspended his own person by silk lines; and being electrified, the Abbé Nollet, who assisted him in these experiments, presented his hand to his body, when immediately a spark of fire issued from the person of the one philosopher and entered the body of the other. Although such a result had been predicted as a consequence of the arrangement, the astonishment was not the less great at its occurrence. Nollet states that he can never forget the surprise of both Dufaye and himself when they witnessed the first explosion from the body of the former.

The celebrity of Dufaye rests, however, not on his experiments, but on the sagacity which led him to evolve natural laws of a high degree of generality from his own experiments, and from those of the philosophers who preceded him. He reproduced in a more definite form the principles of attraction and subsequent repulsion, which had previously been announced by Otto Guericke. "I discovered," says Dufaye, "a very simple principle, which accounts for a great part of the irregularities, and, if I may use the term, the caprices, that seem to accompany most of the experiments in electricity." This principle was, first, that excited electrics attract all bodies in their natural state; second, that after a body is so attracted, and has touched the excited electric, then such body is repelled by the excited electric; third, that if, after being so repelled, such body touches any other, it will be again attracted, and again repelled by the excited electric, and so on.

But a discovery of a much higher order was due to Dufaye. "Chance," says he, "threw in my way another principle more universal and remarkable than the preceding one, and which casts a new light upon the subject of electricity. The principle is, that there are two distinct kinds of electricity, very different from one another; one of which I shall call *vitreous*, and the other *resinous* electricity. The first is that of glass, rock-crystal, precious stones, hair of animals, wool, and many other bodies. The second is that of amber, copal, gum-lac, silk-thread, paper, and a vast number of other substances. The characteristic of these two electricities is, that they repel themselves and attract each other. Thus a body of the vitreous electricity repels all other bodies possessed of the vitreous, and, on the contrary, attracts all those of the resinous electricity. The resinous also repels the resinous, and attracts the vitreous. From this principle one may easily deduce the explanation of a great number of other phenomena, and it is probable that this truth will lead us to the discovery of many other things."

This was a discovery of the highest order, and in its consequences fully justified the anticipation that "it would lead to the discovery of many other things." It is the basis of the only theory of electricity which has been found sufficient to explain all the phenomena of the science, and with the subsequent hypothesis of Symmer, and the laws of attraction developed by the researches of Coulomb, it has brought the most subtle and incontrollable of all physical agents under the subjection of the rigorous canons of mathematical calculation.

A new question now arose respecting any body which has been rendered electrical, whether by immediate excitation, or by contact with another body already excited. It was not enough to ascertain that it was electrified ; but it was necessary to know with which of the two kinds of electricity it was invested. The test of this proposed by Dufaye was the same which has ever since his time been adhered to. He electrified a light substance freely suspended with a known species of electricity ; say, for example, with resinous electricity. If this substance was repelled on bringing it near another electrified body, then the electricity of that body was known to be resinous ; but if, on the contrary, it was attracted, then the electricity of the other body was known to be vitreous.

Dr. Desaguliers, whose works in other parts of physical science are well known, devoted some attention to electricity from the close of the labors of Grey till the year 1742, but the researches of this philosopher contributed nothing to the extension of the science. He methodized the elements which had already accumulated, and improved in some important instances the nomenclature. He denominated all substances in which electricity may be excited *electrics per se*, and defined in a distinct manner their characters. He also first applied the term *conductor* to bodies which freely transmitted electricity, and showed that animal substances owed this property to the fluids which they contain. He however failed to discover that moisture was the conducting agent in many other bodies which at that time were used to propagate electricity to a distance.

The subject of electricity now began to attract the attention of the Germans, and the first consequence was considerable improvement in the power and efficiency of electrical apparatus. The globe of glass revolving on a horizontal axis, which had originated with Hawkesbee, but had, ever since that time, greatly to the detriment of the science, been abandoned in favor of the glass tube, was now resumed by Professor Boze of Wittemburg, who added, for the first time, the *prime conductor* to the machine. This conductor consisted of an oblong cylinder, or tube, of iron or tin. It was at first supported by a man, who was insulated by standing on cakes of rosin ; but it was subsequently suspended by silken cords.

The method of exciting the globe or tube hitherto generally practised, and, indeed, long afterward persevered in, was to rub them with the hand, taking care that it was dry and warm. Winkler, a professor in the university of Leipsic, substituted the more convenient expedient of a *cushion* fixed in contact with the globe, and gently pressed upon its surface by springs, or any similar means. Gordon, a Scottish Benedictine monk, who was professor of philosophy at Erfurt, abandoned the use of the *globe*, and substituted for it a *cylinder* of glass, having its geometrical axis horizontal, and supported on pivots so as to revolve on that axis. The cylinders he used were eight inches long, and four inches in diameter. Thus the electrical machine assumed a form very nearly identical with the cylindrical machines of the present day.

The effects produced by these improved and powerful apparatus are related to have been extraordinary. Various inflammable substances, such as spirits, heated oil, pitch, and wax, were fired. Appearances of electrical light issuing from points, and the experiment since known as the *electrical bells*, were the productions of this epoch. The spark drawn from the conductor by the finger is described as being so intense as to burst the skin, draw blood, and produce a wound. Other effects on the animal system are related, in which there is probably some exaggeration.

The year 1746 forms a remarkable epoch in the history of electricity, being signalized by the invention of the LEYDEN PHIAL. The merit of this discovery is disputed, being claimed for Professor Muschenbroek, Cuneus, a native of Leyden, and Kleist, a monk of that place. Probably all these individuals were engaged in the proceedings in which the discovery originated. Dr. Priestley, a contemporary writer, gives an account of this invention, apparently obtained by personal inquiry, of which the following is the substance :—

Professor Muschenbroek and his associates having observed that electrified bodies exposed to the atmosphere speedily lost their electric virtue, which was supposed to be abstracted by the air itself, and by vapor and effluvia suspended in it, imagined that if they could surround them with any insulating substance, so as to exclude the contact of the atmosphere, they could communicate a more intense electrical power, and could preserve that power for a longer time. Water appeared one of the most convenient recipients for the electrical influence, and glass the most effectual and easy insulating envelop. It appeared, therefore, very obvious, that water enclosed in a glass bottle must retain the electricity given to it, and that by such means, a greater charge or accumulation of electric force might be obtained than by any expedient before resorted to.

In the first experiments made in conformity with these views, no remarkable results were obtained. But it happened on one occasion that the operator held the glass bottle in his right hand, while the water contained in it communicated by a wire with the prime conductor of a powerful machine. When he considered that it had received a sufficient charge, he applied his left hand to the wire to disengage it from the conductor. He was instantly struck with the convulsive shock with which electricians are now so familiar, and which has been since, and is at present, so frequently suffered from motives of curiosity or amusement.

It is curious to observe how much effects on the organs of sense depend on the previous knowledge of them, which may or may not occupy the minds of those who sustain them. Those who now think so lightly of the shock, produced even by a powerful Leyden phial, would be surprised at the letter in which Muschenbroek gave Réaumer an account of the effect produced upon him by the first experiment. He states, that "he felt himself struck in his arms, shoulders, and breast, so that he lost his breath, and *was two days before he recovered from the effects of the blow and the terror.*" He declared, that "he would not take a second shock for the whole kingdom of France."

Nor was Muschenbroek singular in his extraordinary estimate of the effects of the shock. M. Allamand, who made the experiment with a common beer glass, stated that he lost the use of his breath for some moments, and then felt so intense a pain along his right arm that he feared permanent injury from it. Professor Winkler, of Leipsic, stated, that the first time he underwent the experiment he suffered great convulsions through his body; that it put his blood into agitation; that he feared an ardent fever, and was obliged to have recourse to cooling medicines! That he also felt a heaviness in his head, as if a stone were laid upon it. Twice it gave him bleeding at the nose, to which he was not subject. The lady of this professor, who appears to have been as little wanting in the curiosity which is ascribed to her own, as in the courage assumed for the other sex, took the shock twice, and was rendered so weak by it that she could hardly walk. In a week, nevertheless, her curiosity again got the better of her discretion, and she took a third shock, which immediately produced bleeding at the nose.

No sooner were these experiments made known, than the amazement of all classes of people of every age, sex, and rank, was excited at what was regarded as "a prodigy of nature and philosophy." Philosophers everywhere repeated the experiment, but none succeeded in explaining its effects. After the first emotions of astonishment had abated, the circumstances which influenced the force of the shock were examined. Muschenbroek observed that if the glass were wet on the outer surface the success of the experiment was impaired; and Dr. Watson proved that the force of the shock was increased by the thinness of the glass of which the bottle containing the water was made. He also observed, that the force of the charge did not depend on the power of the electrical machine by which the phial was charged. Dr. Watson also showed that the shock could be transmitted, undiminished, through the bodies of several men touching each other.

By further repeating and varying the experiment, Watson found that the force of the charge depended on the extent of the external surface of the glass in contact with the hand of the operator; and it occurred to Dr. Bevis that the hand might be efficient merely as a conductor of electricity, and in that case the object might be more effectually and conveniently attained by coating the exterior of the phial with sheet-lead or tin-foil. This expedient was completely successful; and the phial, so far as related to its external surface, assumed its present form.

Another important step in the improvement of the Leyden jar was also due to the suggestion of Dr. Bevis. It appeared that the force of the charge increased with the magnitude of the jar, but not in proportion to the quantity of water it contained. It was conjectured that it might depend on the extent of the surface of glass in contact with water; and that as water was considered to play the part merely of a conductor in the experiment, metal, which was a better conductor, would be at least equally effectual. Three phials were therefore procured and filled to the usual height with shot instead of water. A metallic communication was made between the shot contained in them respectively. The result was a charge of greatly augmented force. This was, in fact, the first electric battery.

Dr. Bevis now saw that the seat of the electric influence was the surface of contact of the metal and the glass, and rightly inferred that the form of a bottle or jar was not in any way connected with the principle of the experiment. He therefore took a common pane of glass, and having coated the opposite faces with tin-foil, extending on each surface within about an inch of the edge, he was able to obtain as strong a charge as from a phial having the same extent of coated surface. Dr. Watson being informed of this, coated large jars made of thin glass both on the inside and outside surface with silver leaf, extending nearly to the top of the jars, the effects of which fully corroborated the anticipations of Dr. Bevis, and established the principle that the force of the charge was in proportion to the quantity of coated surface.

The results of all these experiments led to the inference that, in the discharge of the phial, the electricity passed through the circle of conducting matter which was extended between the inside and the outside coating of the jar. If that circle were anywhere interrupted by the presence of non-conducting matter, or *electrics per se*, as they were then called, no discharge took place. Also, if any portion of the circle were formed of living animals, each animal sustained the shock. To carry the demonstration of this further, Dr. Watson placed, at several points in the circuit, spoons filled with spirits between the extremities of iron bars, but not in contact with them. In such cases the spirits in all the spoons were inflamed apparently at the instant of the discharge.

Many of these properties were simultaneously discovered by Mr. Wilson, who experimented in Dublin. He coated the external surface of the jar in the first experiments by plunging it in water. He also made several experiments with a view to affect by a shock one part of the human body without affecting the other parts. But the most remarkable discovery of this electrician was the *lateral* shock. He observed, that a person standing near the circuit through which the shock is transmitted, would sustain a shock if he were only in contact with any part of the circuit, or *even placed very near it.*

Those who are conversant with the science, and aware of the important principle of induction, will see, with much interest, how nearly many of the philosophers engaged in these researches touched, from time to time, on that property, and yet missed the honor of its discovery. Without it, the explication of the phenomenon of the charge and discharge of the Leyden phial was impossible. The lateral shock just adverted to, and observed by Wilson, was almost a *glaring instance* of it; but a still more striking manifestation of the theory of the Leyden phial was afforded by an experiment of Mr. Canton, who showed that if a charged phial be insulated, the internal and external coatings would give alternate sparks, and then, by continuing the process, the phial might be gradually discharged. Canton just touched on the discovery of dissimulated electricity.

While these investigations were proceeding in England, the philosophers of France were not wanting in that zeal and activity which they have always manifested for the advancement of physical science. The Abbé Nollet, M. de Monnier, and others, prosecuted similar experimental researches, and arrived at the knowledge of several of the important circumstances developed in England. Nollet showed that a phial containing rarefied air admitted of being charged as readily as one which contained water, and stated that the water in the Leyden experiment served no purpose except to conduct the electricity to the glass.

From this time to the period at which Dr. Franklin commenced his researches, no important progress was made in the science, although at no former period were experiments on so grand a scale projected and executed; nor was public attention ever before so powerfully attracted to any scientific subject. Numerous and extensive experiments were made, both in England and France, to determine the distance through which the electric shock could be transmitted, the nature of the substances through which it could be propagated, and the rate at which it moved. At Paris, M. Nollet transmitted it through a chain of 180 soldiers; and at the convent of the Carthusians he formed a chain measuring 5,400 feet, by means of iron wires extending between every two persons, and the whole company gave a sudden spring, and sustained the shock at the same instant.

But it was in England that the experiments on this subject were made on the most magnificent scale. Mr. Martin Folkes, then president of the Royal Society, Lord Charles Cavendish, Dr. Bevis, and several other fellows of the Society, formed a committee to witness these experiments, the chief direction and management of them being undertaken by Dr. Watson. A circuit was first formed by a wire carried from one side of the Thames to the other over Westminster bridge. One extremity of this wire communicated with the interior of a charged jar; the other was held by a person on the opposite bank of the river. This person held in his other hand an iron rod, which he dipped into the river. On the other side, near the jar, stood another person, holding in one hand a wire communicating with the exterior coating of the jar, and in the other hand an iron rod. This rod he dipped into the river, when instantly the shock was received by both persons, the electric fluid having passed over the bridge, through the body of the person on the other side, through the water across the river, through the rod held by the other person, and through his body to the exterior coating of the jar. Familiar as such a fact may now appear, it is impossible to convey an adequate idea of the amazement, bordering on incredulity, with which it was at that time witnessed.

The next experiment was made at Stoke Newington, near London, where a circuit of about two miles in length was formed, consisting, as in the former case, partly of water and partly of wire. In one case there were about 2,800 feet of wire, and 8,000 feet of water. The result was the same as in the case of the experiment at Westminster bridge. In this case, on repeating the experiment, the rods, instead of being dipped in the water, were merely fixed in the soil at about twenty feet from the water's edge, when it was found that the shock was equally transmitted. This created a doubt whether, in the former case, the shock might not have been conveyed through the ground between the two rods, instead of passing through the water, and subsequent experiments proved that such was the case.

The same experiments were repeated at Highbury, and finally at Shooter's Hill, in August, 1747. At the latter place the wire from the inside of the jar was 6,732 feet, and that which touched the outside coating was 3,868 feet long. The observers placed at the extremity of these wires, were two miles distant from each other. The circuit, therefore, consisted of two miles of wire, and two miles of soil or ground, the latter being the space between the two observers. The result of the experiment proved that no observable interval elapsed between the moments at which each observer sustained the shock. In this experiment the wires were insulated by being supported on rods of baked wood.

We shall here pass over a variety of experiments made in England, France, and Germany, on the effects of electricity on organized bodies, and on some proposed medical applications of that agent; such researches not having led to any general principles affecting the real advancement of the science.

Passing from the analysis of the confused experimental labors of his immediate predecessors, labors which contributed so little to the development of the nature and laws of electrical phenomena, to the researches of Franklin, is like the transition from the mists and obscurity of morning twilight to the unclouded splendor of the noontide sun. It was in the summer of the year 1747, that a fortuitous circumstance, happily for the progress of knowledge, first drew the attention of this truly great and good man, and (as he afterward proved) acute philosopher, to the subject of electricity. Mr. Peter Collinson, a fellow of the Royal Society of London, and a gentleman who took much interest in scientific affairs, made a communication to the Literary Society of Philadelphia, explaining what had been recently done in England in electrical experiments, and with his letter he sent a present of one of the glass tubes then commonly used to excite electricity, with directions for its use. Previous to this time, Franklin does not appear to have ever given his attention to physical science. Nevertheless, he now commenced repeating the European experiments with all the ardor of an enthusiast, and extending, varying, and adapting them to the development of great general laws, with all the skill and sagacity of a practised experimental philosopher. Within the brief period of four months after the arrival of the tube, he commenced a series of letters to Mr. Collinson, in which are related a body of discoveries, which for the high generality of the laws they unfolded, the surpassing beauty and clearness of the experimental demonstrations on which they were based, and their intimate connexion with the uses of ife, are well worthy to be put in juxtaposition with the discoveries of Newton respecting the analysis and properties of light. How different, however, was the position of these two great discoverers and benefactors of the human race! One brought to bear on the subject of his inquiry a mind early disciplined in scientific investigation, a memory stored with profound mathematical erudition, faculties rendered more acute and strong by the severe studies exacted from all aspirants to academical honor and office in the universities of the old countries, zeal awakened, emulation stimulated, and enthusiasm kindled by associates, among whom were included all that was most distinguished in the physical sciences; the other, first a tallow-chandler's apprentice, and next a poor printer's boy, unschooled, undisciplined, self-informed, having nothing to aid him but the inborn energy of his mind, separated by an ocean three thousand miles wide from the countries which alone were the seats of the sciences, and where alone those aids and encouragements derivable from the society of others engaged in like inquiries could be obtained. Such was the individual whose researches we must now briefly notice. The series of letters in which he embodied the details of his experiments, and developed the laws which resulted from them, were continued from 1747 to 1754, and were subsequently collected and published.

"Nothing," says Priestley, "was ever written upon the subject of electricity which was more generally read and admired in all parts of Europe than these letters. There is hardly any European language into which they have not been translated; and, as if this were not sufficient to make them properly known, a translation of them has lately been made into Latin. It is not easy to say whether we are most pleased with the simplicity and perspicuity with which these letters are written, the modesty with which the author proposes every hypothesis of his own, or the noble frankness with which he relates his mistakes when they were corrected by subsequent experiments."*

In the analysis of Franklin's discoveries, it is necessary to distinguish carefully fact from hypothesis, and to separate the great natural laws which he brought to light, the truth and reality of which can never be shaken, based, as they are, on innumerable observed phenomena, from the theory by which these phenomena and their laws are attempted to be explained by him; which latter, though marked by great sagacity and ingenuity, and adequate to the explication of most of the ordinary effects of electricity, has been found insufficient to represent the results of subsequent researches, and has been generally superseded by another theory, which will be noticed hereafter.

The first step made by this philosopher in the brilliant series of discoveries by which he rendered his name so memorable, was one which produced a material influence on his subsequent proceedings, since it formed the foundation of his celebrated hypothesis of positive and negative electricity, which served him as the link by which many scattered facts might be grouped and connected, and as a clue to the development of new and unobserved phenomena. To reduce to the most brief, simple, and general terms, the expression of the first fruit of his observations, it may be said to consist in the establishment of the general principle, that when electricity is excited by the mutual friction or attrition of any two bodies, both these bodies become electrified; and if both are insulated they will continue to be so electrified. They will, however, be in different electrical states, since, if moveable, they would *attract* and not repel each other; but, nevertheless, each of them will exhibit in relation to other bodies not electrified, the same properties. Thus sparks may be drawn indifferently from either; and each of them may be *de-electrised*,

* History of Electricity, per. ix., sect. i.

or discharged of their electricity, by being put in metallic communication with the ground. These general facts he proved by direct experiment.

He placed two persons, A. and B., on insulating supports. In the hand of A. he put a glass tube, which being rubbed by A. became electrified. This tube was then touched at every part of the rubbed surface by B.; after which the same process was several times repeated, the tube being deprived of its electricity as often as it was touched by B. A third person, C., not insulated, now presented his finger or a metallic sphere to B., from whom a spark was drawn; and by repeating this, or by touching the person of B., the latter was deprived of the electricity he had received from the tube. This was no more than was expected. But on subjecting A. to the same process, the very same effects were produced. It appeared, therefore, that both A. and B. were electrified.

Being again electrified, as before, by the friction of the tube, instead of A. and B. being successively touched by C., they were made to touch each other, both remaining insulated. After this both were found to be as completely *de-electrised* and restored to their ordinary state as when they had been touched by C.

A cork ball, suspended by a silk thread, being electrified by contact with the excited glass tube, was repelled when brought near the person of B., but it was attracted when brought near the person of A.

From these experiments it appeared the electrical states of A. and B. were different. Franklin called the state of B., and consequently that of the glass tube from which he drew the electricity, *positive* and that of A. *negative.* The one was said to be *positively*, the other *negatively electrified.* The cloth with which A. rubbed the glass tube was, like A., negatively electrified—it attracted the cork ball; and the glass tube, like B., was positively electrified—it repelled the cork ball.

The generality of this result was established by a great variety of experiments. In all cases it appeared that the opposite electrical charges of the two bodies submitted to friction, or of any insulated bodies in communication with them, had the same reciprocally neutralizing power; in virtue of which, when brought into contact, or when a metallic communication was established between them, all signs of electricity would disappear.

Such is a strict statement of the facts as evolved in the experiments. The hypothesis proposed by Franklin for their explication was as follows: All bodies in their natural state are charged with a certain quantity of electricity, in each body this quantity being of definite amount. This quantity of electricity is maintained in equilibrium upon the body by an attraction which the particles of the body have for it, and does not therefore exert any attraction for other bodies. But a body may be invested with more or less electricity than satisfies its attraction. If it possess more, it is ready to give up the surplus to any body which has less, or to share it with any body in its natural state; if it have less, it is ready to take from any body in its natural state a part of its electricity, so that each will have less than their natural amount. A body having more than its natural quantity is electrified positively or *plus*, and one which has less is electrified negatively or *minus*.

When two bodies are submitted to mutual attrition and become electrified, one parts with a portion of its proper electricity, which is received by the other. The latter then has *more* than its natural amount, and is *positively* electrified; the former has *less*, and is *negatively* electrified.

In the instance above stated, when A. rubs the glass tube, he loses a portion of his natural electricity, and is negatively electrified; while the tube receives what he loses, and becomes *positively* electrified. When B. touches the tube, he takes from it nearly all the electricity with which it is charged over and above its natural amount; for his body being of so much greater magnitude than the tube, the proportion which will remain on the tube will be insignificant.

If when A. rubs the tube he were not insulated, he would not be electrified, because, as fast as his body would lose its proper amount of electricity, the deficiency would be made up from the earth, with which he is in free electrical communication; whereas in the former case being insulated, this supply could not be obtained. Hence, in this theory, the earth is regarded as the common reservoir of electricity, from which bodies negatively electrified receive what they want, and to which bodies positively electrified give up their surplus, except in the case in which the one or the other are insulated.

Such, in general, was the Franklinian theory; which, however, will be more fully developed hereafter.

Assuming these hypothetical principles, Franklin next proceeded to analyze the phenomena of the Leyden jar. His first experiments were directed to establish the fact, that when the jar is charged, the inside is electrified positively, and the outside negatively. A charged jar was placed on an insulating support, and a metallic wire bent into the form of a circular arc was then placed with one end in contact with the outer coating. The other end was capable of being brought into contact with the hook of the wire inserted through the cork, and thereby put in metallic communication with the water contained in the jar. This bent wire being supported by a handle of sealing-wax was itself insulated, and no electricity could pass in the experiment, otherwise than between the inside of the jar and the coating on the outside. On bringing the upper extremity of the bent wire into contact with the hook, the jar was instantly discharged, both the inside and the outside being restored to their natural state. Franklin inferred from this, that before the discharge the interior of the jar was *positively* electrified, and the exterior coating negatively electrified, in an equal degree; that is to say, that the interior of the jar contained an excess of electricity over and above its natural amount, and the exterior coating fell short of its natural amount by a quantity equal to that excess.

Various other experiments were made to verify this doctrine. Two metallic knobs were placed near each other, one communicating with the external coating, and the other with the water within the jar. A small cork ball suspended by a silk thread was placed between those two knobs. The ball was alternately attracted and repelled, "playing incessantly from one to the other, till the bottle was no longer electrised; that is, it fetched and carried fire from the top (inside) to the bottom (outside) of the bottle, till equilibrium was restored."*

It had been observed by electricians in Europe, that a jar could not be charged if its external coating were insulated; that, in fact, it was a necessary condition that a communication between that coating and the ground should be provided and maintained by some conducting matter, such as a metallic wire. Franklin assumes, that no electricity can be conveyed to the inside without causing the expulsion of an equal quantity from the outside; but if the jar be insulated, no means of escape being left for the electricity on the outside, no accumulation can take place on the inside.†

In these experiments, we find also a description of the method of charging a series of jars, now called the charge *by cascade*. "Suspend two or more phials on the prime conductor, one hanging on the tail of another, and a wire from the last to the floor. An equal number of turns of the wheel will charge them all equally, and every one as much as one alone would have been; what

* Franklin's Works (Letters), vol. v., p. 192. Boston, 1837. † Letters, p. 190.

is drawn out of the tail of the first serving to charge (the inside of) the second; what is driven out of the second charging the third, and so on."*

In this way he constructed an electrical battery. After charging a series of jars he separated them, putting the insides in metallic communication with each other, and the outsides, in like manner, in metallic communication. By such means he obtained discharges sufficiently powerful to kill the smaller animals.

But the experiment which appeared to be most conclusive in the support it gave to his hypothesis of the transfer of the electricity from the exterior to the interior of the jar in the process of charging it, was the following: A jar was suspended by its hook on the prime conductor of the machine, so that a metallic communication was maintained between the conductor and the inside of the jar. Meanwhile, the rubber was insulated. On working the machine, the jar was found to receive no charge. A metallic wire was now rolled round the outer coating of the jar, and carried thence to the rubber, so as to make a communication between them, both being still, in other respects, insulated. The jar was now charged with ease, which was explained by the supposition that the electric fluid passed from the outside coating by the wire to the rubber, and thence by the glass globe and prime conductor to the inside of the jar.†

According to the hypothesis above stated, there is no essential distinction, so far as relates to the charge, between the external coating and the internal contents of the jar; the one ought to be as easily charged as the other. This was accordingly found to be the case. A jar was placed on an insulating support, and while the external coating was put in communication with the prime conductor of the machine, the wire extending from the interior was put in communication with the rubber. The electricity of the outer coating was now positive, and that of the inside negative; and the jar was discharged, and produced the same effects as before.

The next important investigation was as to the place in which the electricity of the jar was contained. To determine this, Franklin charged a jar, and insulated it. He then removed the cork, and the wire by which the electricity was conveyed from the machine to the inside of the jar. On examining these, he found them free from electricity. He next carefully decanted the water from the charged jar into another insulated vessel. On examining this it was found to be free from electricity. Other water in its natural state was now introduced into the charged jar to replace that which had been decanted; and on placing one hand on the outside coating, and the other in the water, he received the shock as forcibly as if no change had been made in the jar since it was first charged.‡

A piece of glass was then placed between two plates of lead extending nearly to its edge on every side. One of these plates of lead being touched by the hand, the other was charged with electricity as usual. The plates were then removed from the glass, and, being examined, were found to be in their natural state. On presenting the finger to the glass where the lead had covered it, little sparks were received; and on displacing the lead and touching it at both surfaces, a violent shock was received.

From this he inferred that the glass was the substance in which the electricity was deposited; and the metallic coating, or the water, or other conductor, applied to it, "served only, like the armature of the loadstone, to unite the forces of the several parts, and bring them at once to any point desired; it being the property of a non-electric [conductor], that the whole body instantly receives, or gives, what electrical fire is given to, or taken from any one of its parts."‖

From a very early period of the progress of electrical observations, the anal

* Letters, p. 199. † Letters, p. 253. ‡ Letters, p. 201. ‖ Letters, p. 202.

ogy between electricity and lightning had been noticed, and conjectures as to their identity were expressed; and in some cases distinct predictions hazarded, that the time would arrive which would fully establish their identity. Dr. Wall, in a paper published in the "Philosophical Transactions," speaking of the electricity of amber, said that he had no doubt, "that by using a longer and larger piece of amber, both the cracklings and the light would be much greater. This light and crackling seems in some degree to represent thunder and lightning."*

Mr. Grey, whose experiments have been already referred to, says, speaking of electrical effects: "These are at present but in *minimis*. It is probable that, in time, there may be found out a way to collect a greater quantity of electric fire, and consequently to increase the force of that power, which, by several of these experiments, *si licet magnis componere parva*, seems to be of *the same nature* with that of *thunder and lightning*."

But of all the anticipations which are pretended to of the grand discovery of the philosopher of Philadelphia, that which is by far the most remarkable proceeded from his contemporary and competitor, the Abbé Nollet. Immediately after the first exhibition of the experiments proving the identity of electricity and lightning, the abbé urged his claim to a share of the merit of having suggested them. In a paper, dated Paris, June 6, 1752, the abbé, after noticing the experiments, observes that he "is more interested than any one to come at the facts, which prove a true analogy between lightning and electricity, since these experiments establish incontestably a truth which he had conceived, and which he ventured to lay before the public more than four years ago."

In the fourth volume of his *Leçons de Physique* is found the following passage: "If any one should undertake to prove, as a clear consequence of the phenomenon, that thunder is, in the hands of nature, what electricity is in ours—that those wonders which we dispose at our pleasure are only imitations on a small scale of those grand effects which terrify us, and that both depend on the same mechanical agents—if it were made manifest that a cloud prepared by the effects of the wind, by heat, by a mixture of exhalations, &c., is in relation to a terrestrial object, what an electrified body is in relation to a body near it not electrified, I confess that this idea, well supported, would please me much; and to support it, how numerous and specious are the reasons which present themselves to a mind conversant with electricity. The universality of the electric matter, the readiness of its action, its instrumentality, and its activity in giving fire to other bodies; its property of striking bodies externally and internally, even to their smallest parts (the remarkable example we have of this effect even in the Leyden jar experiment, the idea which we might truly adopt in supposing a greater degree of electric power); all these points of analogy which I have been for some time meditating, begin to make me believe that one might, by taking electricity for the model, form to oneself, in regard to thunder and lightning, more perfect and more probable ideas than any hitherto proposed."†

The volume containing this passage was printed and published toward the close of the year 1748, as appears by the register of the Academy of Sciences, in which the order to print it bears date on the 9th of August in that year. It will presently appear that Franklin's first publication of the same views was in a letter addressed to Mr. Collinson, despatched in 1749. So far, therefore, as relates to these speculations, the priority of publication must be conceded to Nollet. It seems, however, improbable that Franklin, residing in Philadelphia, could have seen Nollet's volume between the date of its publication and

* Priestley, History of Electricity, p. 11.
† Nollet, Leçons de Physique, tom iv., p. 315, 8me. edition.

the despatch of his letter, an interval not exceeding a few months; and the probability is, therefore, that these views occurred simultaneously to the American and the French philosopher.

From the moment that Franklin first engaged in electrical inquiries, his views were constantly bent on the discovery of some useful purpose to which the science could be applied. *Cui bono?* was a question never absent from his thoughts.* This craving after *utility* was the great characteristic of his mind, and might be regarded as being carried almost to a fault. To bring the properties of matter and the phenomena of nature into subjection to the uses of civilized life, is undoubtedly *one* of the great incentives to the investigation of the laws of the material world; but it is assuredly a great error to regard it as either the only or the principal motive to such inquiries. There is in the perception of truth itself—in the contemplation of connected propositions, leading by the mere operation of the intellectual faculties, exercised on individual physical facts, to the development of those great general laws by which the universe is maintained—an exalted pleasure, compared with which the mere attainment of convenience and utility in the economy of life is poor and mean. There is a nobleness in the power which the natural philosopher derives from the discovery of these laws, of raising the curtain of futurity, and displaying the decrees of nature, so far as they affect the physical universe for countless ages to come, which is independent of all utility. There is a lofty and disinterested pleasure in the mere contemplation of the harmony and order of nature, which is above and beyond mere utility. While, however, we thus claim for truth and knowledge all the consideration to which, on their own account, they are entitled, let us not be misunderstood as disparaging the great benefactors of the human race, who have drawn from them those benefits which so much tend to the wellbeing of man. When we express the enjoyment which arises from the beauty and fragrance of the flower, we do not the less prize the honey which is extracted from it, or the medicinal virtues it yields. That Franklin was accessible to such feelings, the enthusiasm with which he expresses himself throughout his writings in regard to natural phenomena abundantly proves. Nevertheless, *useful application* was, undoubtedly, ever uppermost in his thoughts; and he probably never witnessed any physical fact, or considered for a moment any law of nature, without inwardly proposing to himself the question, "In what way can this be made beneficial in the economy of life?"

The analogy and probable identity of lightning and electricity were first suggested and demonstrated by Franklin in a letter addressed to Collinson, which appears without a date, and which has by some been referred to the date (1750) of that which immediately follows it in the published collection of letters. It appears, however, by a subsequent letter,† addressed to the same gentleman in 1753, that he was occupied in the investigation of this question from 1747 to

* After he had succeeded in making the discoveries which have been already explained, and besides inventing a little moving power, which he called an *electrical jack*, he expressed to Mr. Collinson, in his usual playful manner, his disappointment at being unable to find any application of the science beneficial to mankind. "Chagrined a little that we have hitherto been able to produce nothing in this way of use to mankind, and the hot weather coming on when electrical experiments are not so agreeable, it is proposed to put an end to them for this season, somewhat humorously, in a party of pleasure on the banks of the Schuylkill. Spirits, at the same time, are to be fired by a spark sent from side to side through the river without any other conductor than the water; an experiment which we some time since performed to the amazement of many. A turkey is to be killed for dinner by the *electrical shock*, and roasted by the *electrical jack*, before a fire kindled by the *electrified bottle*, when the healths of all the famous electricians of England, Holland, France, and Germany, are to be drunk in *electrified bumpers*, under the discharge of guns from the *electrical battery*." —*Letters*, p. 210.

† "In my former paper on this subject, written first in 1747, enlarged and sent to England in 1749, I considered the sea as the great source of lightning," &c.—*Letters*, p. 300.

1749; that the paper now referred to was first written in the former year, but that it was enlarged and improved and sent to England in 1749, which must, therefore, be taken as its date. In this letter he enters very fully into his reasons for considering the cause of electricity and lightning to be the same physical agent, differing in nothing save the intensity of its action; and he truly observes, that the difference in degree, however enormous, is no argument against the identity of the agents, but that, on the contrary, an almost infinite difference might be naturally looked for. "When a gun-barrel in electrical experiments has but little electrical fire in it, you must approach it very near with your knuckle before you can draw a spark. Give it more fire, and it will give a spark at greater distance. Two gun-barrels united, and as highly electrified, will give a spark at a still greater distance. But if two gun-barrels electrified will strike at two inches distance, and make a loud snap, to what a great distance may ten thousand acres of electrified cloud strike and give its fire, and how loud must be that crack!"*

The analogies which he stated as affording presumptive evidence of the identity of lightning and electricity may be briefly enumerated. The electrical spark is zigzag, and not straight; so is lightning. Pointed bodies attract electricity; lightning strikes mountains, trees, spires, masts, and chimneys. When different paths are offered to the escape of electricity, it chooses the best conductor; so does lightning. Electricity fires combustibles; so does lightning. Electricity fuses metals; so does lightning. Lightning rends bad conductors when it strikes them; so does electricity when rendered sufficiently strong. Lightning reverses the poles of a magnet; he proved by direct experiment that electricity had the same effect. A stroke of lightning when it does not kill, often produces blindness; he rendered a pigeon blind by a shock of electricity intended to kill it. Lightning destroys animal life; he killed a hen and a turkey by electrical shocks.

Having ascertained by experiment the property of points in attracting and discharging electricity, Franklin, acknowledging his inability to give a satisfactory theory of this effect, set himself to inquire how "this power of points might possibly be of some use to mankind." To discover this, he suspended a large conductor, by silk lines, from the ceiling, and charged it with electricity, so as to enable it to give a spark at the distance of two inches, "strong enough to make one's knuckle ache." Under these circumstances, he found that if a person presented the point of a needle to the conductor at more than a foot distance, no electricity could be retained upon it, all passing off by the needle as fast as it was supplied. He also found, that if, after it was strongly electrified, the needle was presented at the same distance, the conductor would instantly lose its electricity. That the electricity, in this case, really passed off by the point, he ascertained by observing that, in the dark, the light was visible on the point of the needle; and also because, when the person presenting the needle was himself insulated, or stuck the needle in a bundle of sealing wax, the electricity no longer escaped.

The next experiment is so remarkable in itself, and so characteristic of the mind of Franklin, that we shall give it in his own words:—

"Take a pair of large brass scales, of two or more feet beam, the cords of the scales being silk. Suspend the beam by a packthread from the ceiling, so that the bottom of the scales may be about a foot from the floor; the scales will move round in a circle by the untwisting of the packthread. Let an iron punch (a silversmith's iron punch, an inch thick, is what I use) be put on the end upon the floor, in such a place as that the scales may pass over it in making their circle; then electrify one scale by applying the wire of a charged

* Letters, p. 218.

phial to it. As they move round, you see that scale draw nigher to the floor, and dip more when it comes over the punch; and, if that be placed at a proper distance, the scale will snap, and discharge its fire into it. But if a needle be stuck on the end of the punch, its point upward, the scale, instead of drawing nigh to the punch and snapping, discharges its fire silently through the point, and rises higher from the punch. Nay, even if the needle be placed upon the floor near the punch, its point upward, the end of the punch, though so much higher than the needle, will not attract the scale and receive its fire; for the needle will get it, and convey it away, before it comes nigh enough for the punch to act.

"Now, if electricity and lightning be the same, the conductor and scales may represent electrified clouds. If a tube (conductor) of only ten feet long will strike and discharge its fire on the punch at two or three inches distance, and electrified cloud of perhaps ten thousand acres may strike and discharge on the earth at a proportionally greater distance. The horizontal motion of the scales over the floor may represent the motion of the clouds over the earth, and the erect iron punch a hill or high building; and then we see how electrified clouds, passing over hills or high buildings at too great a height to strike, may be attracted lower till within their striking distance. And, lastly, if a needle fixed on the punch with its point upright, or even on the floor below the punch, will draw the fire from the scale silently at a much greater than the striking distance, and so prevent its descending toward the punch; or if in its course it would have come nigh enough to strike, yet, being first deprived of its fire, it cannot, and the punch is thereby secured from the stroke: *I say, if these things are so, may not the knowledge of this power of points be of use to mankind in preserving houses, churches, ships, &c., from the stroke of lightning, by directing us to fix, on the highest parts of those edifices, upright rods of iron, made sharp as a needle, and gilt to prevent rusting; and, from the foot of those rods, a wire down the outside of the building into the ground, or down round one of the shrouds of a ship, and down her side till it reaches the water? Would not these pointed rods probably draw the electrical fire silently out of a cloud before it came nigh enough to strike, and thereby secure us from that most sudden and terrible mischief?*

"To determine this question, whether the clouds that contain lightning be electrified or not, I would propose an experiment to be tried, where it may be done conveniently. On the top of some high tower or steeple, place a kind of sentry-box, big enough to contain a man and an electrical stand. From the middle of the stand let an iron rod rise, and pass, bending, out of the door, and then upright twenty or thirty feet, pointed very sharp at the end. If the electrical stand be kept clear and dry, a man standing on it, when such clouds are passing low, might be electrified, and afford sparks, the rod drawing fire to him from a cloud. If any danger to the man be apprehended, let him stand on the floor of his box, and now and then bring near to the rod the loop of a wire that has one end fastened to the leads, he holding it by a wax handle; so the sparks, if the rod is electrified, will strike from the rod to the wire, and not affect him."*

When this and other papers by Franklin, illustrating similar views, were sent to London, and read before the Royal Society, they are said to have been considered so wild and absurd that they were received with laughter, and were not considered worthy of so much notice as to be admitted to a place in the "Philosophical Transactions."† They were, however, shown to Dr. Fothergill, who considered them of too much value to be thus stifled; and he wrote a

* Letters, p. 235.

† Franklin's works (memoirs), vol. i., p. 299.

preface to them, and published them in London. They subsequently went through five editions.

After the publication of these remarkable letters, and when public opinion in all parts of Europe had been expressed upon them, an abridgment or abstract of them was read to the society on the 6th of June, 1751. It is a remarkable circumstance that, in this notice, no mention whatever occurs of Franklin's project of drawing lightning from the clouds. Possibly this was the part which had before excited laughter, and was omitted to avoid ridicule.

Franklin was under an impression that a pointed rod could not be expected to attract the lightning, unless it were placed at a very great height in the atmosphere; and to render the result of his projected experiment more certain, he determined to wait for the completion of a spire then being erected in Philadelphia. Meanwhile, however, a different and more promising expedient occurred to him; which was, to send up the pointed wire upon a kite, by the string of which the lightning might be brought within his reach. He soon succeeded in realizing this, the most bold and grand conception which ever presented itself to the imagination of an experimental philosopher.

He prepared his kite by making a small cross of two light strips of cedar, the arms of sufficient length to extend to the four corners of a large silk handkerchief stretched upon them. To the extremities of the arms of the cross he tied the corners of the handkerchief. This being properly supplied with a tail, loop, and string, could be raised in the air like a common paper kite, and, being made of silk, was more capable of bearing rain and wind. To the upright arm of the cross was attached an iron point, the lower end of which was in contact with the string by which the kite was raised, which was a hempen cord. At the lower extremity of this cord, near the observer, a key was fastened; and, in order to intercept the electricity in its descent, and prevent it from reaching the person who held the kite, a silk riband was tied to the ring of the key, and continued to the hand by which the kite was held.

Furnished with this apparatus, on the approach of a storm, he went out upon the commons near Philadelphia, accompanied by his son, to whom alone he communicated his intentions, well knowing the ridicule which would have attended the report of such an attempt, should it prove to be unsuccessful. Having raised the kite, he placed himself under a shed, that the riband by which it was held might be kept dry, as it would become a conductor of electricity when wetted by rain, and so fail to afford that protection for which it was provided. A cloud, apparently charged with thunder, soon passed directly over the kite. He observed the hempen cord, but no bristling of its fibres was apparent, such as was wont to take place when it was electrified. He presented his knuckle to the key, but not the smallest spark was perceptible. The agony of his expectation and suspense can be adequately felt by those only who have entered into the spirit of such experimental researches. After the lapse of some time, he saw that the fibres of the cord near the key bristled, and stood on end. He presented his knuckle to the key, and received a strong bright spark. It was lightning. The discovery was complete, and Franklin felt that he was immortal.

A shower now fell, and, wetting the cord of the kite, improved its conducting power. Sparks in rapid succession were drawn from the key, a Leyden jar was charged by it, and a shock given; and, in fine, all the experiments which were wont to be made by electricity were reproduced identical in all their concomitant circumstances.

This experiment was performed in the month of June, 1752. It will be remembered that Franklin's letters to Mr. Collinson had been previously published, translated, and widely circulated in different languages throughout Europe ; and in these letters, not only the object of the experiment and the principle it was designed to establish were fully explained, but minute and circumstantial directions were given as to the manner of executing it. Persons engaged in physical inquiries in different parts of Europe were invited, and prepared to submit it to a trial when convenient opportunities offered. Among these was a French electrician, M. Dalibard, who, in the spring of 1752, prepared means of making the experiment at Marly-la-Ville, a place situate about six leagues from Paris. He succeeded on the 10th of May, about a month before the experiment of Franklin, and made a report of his proceedings to the Academy of Sciences at Paris on the 13th, in which he states that the experiment had been made at the suggestion and according to the method laid down by Franklin.* The experiment of Franklin, in June, was made before he could have been informed of that of Dalibard. The same experiment was repeated on the 18th of May by M. de Lor, at his house in the Estrapade, at Paris ; and an account of it, as well as that of M. Dalibard, was communicated to the Royal Society of London by the Abbé Mazeas, in a letter dated 20th May, two days after the latter experiment, in which the abbé ascribes all the credit of the experiment to Franklin.†

The right of Franklin to the credit of having established the identity of lightning and electricity has been denied, and the honor claimed for the French philosophers Nollet and Dalibard. This claim was advanced, not when Europe from east to west, and from north to south, was filled with amazement and admiration at the philosophic boldness of the "Philadelphian experiment" (as it was universally called), or the profound sagacity with which it was conceived, with which its minute details were prescribed, and its results foretold —not when its illustrious author was elected by acclamation a member of the learned societies of Europe, and received the academical degree from the most ancient and honored of universities—but after the lapse of nearly a century, after the story of Franklin's kite had passed from the transactions of philosophical societies, and the memoirs of institutes of sciences, into the primers of children. In short, it was so recently as the year 1831, that, in his admirable *Eloge* of Volta, M. Arago, taking a retrospect of electrical discovery, maintained that after the conjecture of Nollet, on the identity of lightning and electricity, an experiment to ascertain the fact was *almost useless*. And the reasons he assigned for such inutility were, that the experiment had been first made when flame appeared on the spears of soldiers, and the masts of ships ;‡ but that, if any credit be claimed for the actual exhibition of the fact by immediate experiment, that credit is due to M. Dalibard.

If such a statement, supported by such a reason, had proceeded from a quarter less entitled to respect than the "perpetual secretary of the Academy of

* "En suivant la route que M. Franklin nous a tracée, j'ai obtenu une satisfaction complète."—*Mémoir de M. Dalibard,* quoted in Franklin's works, vol. v., p. 288.

† See Phil. Trans., vol. xvii. 1752.

‡ "Les premières vues de Franklin sur l'analogie de l'électricité et du tonnerre n'étaient, comme les idées antérieures de Nollet que de simples conjectures. Toute la différence, entre les deux physiciens, se réduisait alors à un projet d'expérience, dont Nollet n'avait pas parler. . . . . . Sans porter atteint à la gloire de Franklin, je dois remarquer que l'expérience proposée était presque inutile. Les soldats de la cinquième légion Romaine l'avaient déja faite pendant la guerre d'Afrique, le jour où, comme César le rapporte, le fer de tous les javelots parut en feu à la suite d'un orage. Il en est de même des nombreux navigateurs à qui *Castor et Pollux* s'étaient montrés, soit aux pointes métalliques des mâts ou des vergues, soit sur d'autres parties saillantes de leurs navires. . . . . Au reste, soit que plusieurs de ces circonstances fussent ignorées, soit qu'on ne les trouvât pas démonstratives, des essais directs semblèrent nécessaires, et c'est à Dalibard, notre compatriote, que la science en a étéredevable. Le 10 Mai, 1752, pendant un orage, la grande tige de métal pointue qu'il avait établie dans un jardin de Marly-la-Ville donnait de petites étincelles, comme le fait le conducteur de la machine électrique ordinaire, quand on en approche un fil de fer. Franklin ne réalisa cette même expérience aux Etats-Unis, à l'aide d'un cerf volant, qu'un mois plus tard."—*Eloge de Volta*, p. 12.

Sciences," the astronomer royal of France, the man who stands, if not first, incontestably in the first rank of living meteorologists—in a word, than M. Arago—no one would think it entitled to a serious answer. It would be classed among those strange obliquities of historic vision which have led some persons to see in Richard and Macbeth, not tyrants and murderers, but mild and virtuous princes, cruelly wronged by the calumnies of tradition.

Nollet conjectured the probable identity of lightning and electricity, but gave not the most distant hint of any possible method by which the probability could be experimentally tested. Franklin boldly maintained the identity of these agents, gave numerous and cogent reasons to support that position, and moreover prescribed with minute details two distinct methods by which lightning could be brought into the hands of the observer, and submitted to the same experimental examination as electricity had undergone. One of these two methods was, in scrupulous accordance with his directions, applied in France; and the other, within a few weeks, was adopted by himself in America. The results of both were precisely what Franklin had foretold. Both were completely successful.

But, rejoins M. Arago, the whole affair of the experiment was useless, for it had already been effected. The flame on the javelins of the Roman sentinels of the fifth legion was sufficient as an experiment, not to mention *Castor* and *Pollux*, so often seen by sailors on their mast-tops! What would so severe a reasoner as M. Arago say to another who should maintain, without further experiment, that either of these luminous appearances was identical with lightning?—and if that were conceded, where would have been found the proof that these meteors, and the lightning with which they would be granted to be identified, were due to the same physical agent as that manifested by the friction of glass and resin?

If however, says M. Arago again, the experiment *were* necessary or useful, science owes it to M. Dalibard, who executed it at Marly-la-Ville a month before Franklin, with his kite, made it at Philadelphia. This statement is not attended with the circumstantial accuracy whieh M. Arago is accustomed to observe. The fact, as stated by M. Dalibard himself, was, that he took Franklin's printed directions as to the manner of performing his (Franklin's) projected experiment, and followed them to the letter in preparing his apparatus at Marly-la-Ville. Having accomplished this, he put the directions for making the observations into the hands of one Coiffier, an old retired soldier, who followed the trade of a carpenter, and who probably also erected the apparatus itself, and desired Coiffier to make the experiment in the manner prescribed by Franklin, if a storm should occur at a time when he (Dalibard) was absent. The first storm did occur when Dalibard was at Paris. Coiffier presented a piece of metal to the rod, and received several sparks. He then ran for the curé, who, with him, repeated the experiment, and immediately wrote a full description of it, with which he despatched Coiffier himself to Paris to M. Dalibard.

Thus it appears that so far from science being indebted to M. Dalibard for the earliest exhibition of this capital experiment, that philosopher had no other share in it, save that of having caused the erection of the conducting rod and other apparatus according to Franklin's directions. In the actual performance of the first experiment, he had no share whatever.

Let us now see how the account of credit stands on the score of this memorable discovery:—

In 1708, Dr. Wall mentions a *resemblance* of electricity to thunder and lightning.

In 1735, Mr. Grey *conjectures* their *identity*, and that they differ only in *degree*.

In 1748, the Abbé Nollet reproduces the conjecture of Grey, attended with more circumstantial reasons.

In 1749, Franklin strongly maintains their *identity*, and accurately describes two ways of experimentally testing it, and sends his instructions to Europe, to enable others with better local opportunities than he possessed to try it.

In 1752, MM. Dalibard and Delor, in France, make the preparations prescribed according to one of Franklin's methods; and Franklin makes in Philadelphia preparations according to the other method.

On 10th May, 1752, Coiffier and the curate make the experiment as directed by Franklin, and obtain the results foretold by Franklin.

In June, 1752, Franklin makes the same experiment in Philadelphia, according to the other method, with like results.

If the credit of the discovery is due to him who first *conjectured* the identity of lightning and electricity, then it is due to Mr. Stephen Gray.

If it be due to him who showed the method of making the capital experiment by which the identity must be either established or refuted, it belongs to Franklin.

If it be due to the persons at whose expense Franklin's apparatus was first constructed, then it must be shared between Franklin, Dalibard, and Delor.

If it be due to him who first, in person, *performed* the experiment proposed by Franklin, it must be accorded to the carpenter and dragoon Coiffier.

We shall now dismiss this matter, to which more space has been allotted than it is entitled to, merely observing, that much as living philosophers must be surprised at the claim advanced in favor of M. Dalibard, that electrician himself, could he rise from his tomb, would see with infinitely more astonishment an honor sought for him to which he never himself aspired, or supposed he had the slightest title.

Franklin having established, beyond the possibility of dispute, the identity of lightning and electricity, proceeded, in accordance with that characteristic attribute of his mind already noticed, to turn this discovery to the benefit of mankind, and proposed the general adoption of those pointed metallic rods now so commonly erected at the summits of buildings to protect them from the effects of lightning. The principle of this apparatus, as now constructed for edifices and ships, differs in nothing essential from that proposed by its celebrated inventor.

This part of the labors of Franklin in electricity cannot be dismissed without a passing notice of the dispute which was maintained in England respecting the comparative advantages of conductors with pointed ends as proposed by Franklin, or with round or blunted ends as suggested by some others. It were for the honor of science that this discreditable controversy had never taken place. It forms a rare, if not a solitary example, of the prostitution of philosophy to gratify the meanest passions of an obstinate and imbecile prince. The persevering tenacity with which the British monarch fastened his last grasp on his American subjects about to wrest themselves from his power, and assert their independence, is well known. By his pursuit of that object, after all reasonable hope of securing it had expired, the treasures of his kingdom were lavished, and the blood of his people flowed in mutual slaughter. Bad as were these consequences, they were nevertheless the ordinary consequences of war. But the vindictive spirit of the court passed from the field and council-board to the peaceful halls of science; and because Franklin, the agent, representative, and counsellor of the American people, had proposed the use of *pointed* conductors, a party of parasites was found, who, to gratify George III., advocated *blunt* conductors; and to crown this most egregious absurdity, *blunt conductors* were actually erected upon the royal palace! *

Franklin next directed his inquiries to the quantity and nature of the electricity with which the clouds in various states of the atmosphere were charged. To facilitate his experimental inquiries on this subject, he erected in his house in Philadelphia a pointed iron rod, which he was enabled to insulate at pleasure. This rod was put in communication with a system of bells, which alternately attracted and repelled their hammers when electrified. Whenever a cloud charged with electricity passed over the house within such a distance as to affect the conductor, these bells would ring and inform him of the opportunity of prosecuting his experiments.

Having satisfied himself that the clouds were frequently in an electrified state when there was no thunder or lightning, his next inquiry was, whether they were electrified positively or negatively. This was a question of more interest to him, because, according to his theory, if their electricity were negative, the earth, " in thunder-strokes, would strike into the clouds, and not the clouds into the earth." To determine this, he " took two phials and charged one of them with lightning from the iron rod, and gave the other an equal charge (of electricity) from the prime conductor. When charged he placed them on a table within three or four inches of each other, a small cork ball being suspended by a fine silk thread from the ceiling, so as to play between the wires. If both bottles then were electrified *positively*, the ball being attracted and then repelled by the one must be repelled by the other. If the one *positively* and the other *negatively*, then the ball would be attracted and repelled by each, and continue to play between them, so long as any considerable charge remained."†

From experiments with this apparatus, he concluded that clouds were sometimes *positively* and sometimes *negatively* electrified, but oftener *negatively*. Electrical instruments had not yet, however, advanced to such a state of improvement as to enable a mind, even acute as his, to make much further discovery in atmospheric electricity; and although the details of his experiments and his theoretical speculations regarding them must always be read with profound interest, yet no further principles of importance appear to have been evolved from them.

If it be true that the Royal Society laughed at his speculations and refused to them a place in their Transactions, they were not slow to retract and repair their error. They conferred upon him their highest honor (the Copley medal), and unanimously elected him an honorary member of their society, in 1753.

An experiment so remarkable as the attraction of lightning from the clouds, could not fail to be verified and repeated by many enthusiastic lovers of science. One of the first instances of this zeal was rendered memorable by its fatal result. Professor George William Richmann, of St. Petersburg, was preparing an essay on electricity; and in order to obtain the most certain and accurate knowledge of the phenomena, he placed a conductor on his house, making a metallic communication between it and his study, where he provided means for repeating Franklin's experiments. On the 6th of August, 1753, while Richmann attended a meeting of the Petersburg Academy of Science, distant thunder was heard, on which he went to his house, accompanied by Sokolow, the engraver, who being engaged to illustrate his work, desired to see those elec-

* " The king's changing his *pointed* conductors for *blunt* ones is a matter of small importance to me. If I had a wish about them, it would be, that he would reject them altogether as ineffectual. For it is only since he thought himself and his family safe from the thunder of heaven that he has dared to use his own thunder in destroying his innocent subjects."—*Franklin's Works,* viii. 227.

† Letters, p. 302.

trical appearances which he would have to represent in the plates. While Richmann was describing to Sokolow the nature of the apparatus, a thunder-clap was heard louder and more violent than any which had been remembered at St. Petersburg. Richmann stooped toward the electrometer of the apparatus to observe the force of the electricity, and "as he stood in that posture, a great white and bluish fire appeared between the rod of the electrometer and his head. At the same time a sort of steam or vapor arose, which entirely benumbed the engraver, and made him sink on the ground." Several parts of the apparatus were broken in pieces and scattered about. The doors of the room were torn from their hinges, and the house shaken in every part. The wife of the professor, alarmed by the shock, ran to the room, and found her husband sitting on a chest, which happened to be behind him when he was struck, and leaning against the wall. He appeared to have been instantly struck dead.*

During 1752 and the succeeding years the subject of atmospheric electricity engaged the attention of persons devoted to physical science in different parts of Europe. The climate of England being less favorable to such researches than more southern latitudes, fewer opportunities of observation were offered; nevertheless, Canton, Wilson, and Bevis, soon repeated and verified the Philadelphia experiments. Canton showed that the clouds were electrified, sometimes negatively and sometimes positively, and carried such observations further than Franklin.

But the most acute and indefatigable follower of Franklin at this time, in atmospheric electricity, was Beccaria, who, in 1753, published a treatise on electricity at Turin, and a series of letters on the same subject, at Bologna, in 1758. He erected numerous conducting rods in different places of observation, and elevated kites according to Franklin's method. By raising these to various heights, he observed the electricity of different atmospheric strata, and he improved this mode of observation by interlacing the strings with metallic wire. To keep his kites constantly insulated, and at the same time to give them more or less string, he rolled the string upon a reel, which was supported by pillars of glass, and his conductors were placed in metallic communication with this reel.

This profound philosopher, and acute and accurate observer, has left in the history of electricity traces of his genius second only to those with which Franklin and Volta impressed it. Beccaria was the first who diligently studied and recorded the circumstances attending the phenomena of a thunder-storm. He observes that the first appearance of a thunder-storm (which generally happens when there is little or no wind) is one dense cloud or more, increasing rapidly in magnitude, and ascending into the higher regions of the atmosphere. The lower edge is black and nearly horizontal, but the upper is finely arched and well defined. Many of these clouds often seem piled one upon the other, all arched in the same manner; but they keep constantly uniting, swelling, and extending their arches. When such clouds rise, the firmament is usually sprinkled over with a great number of separate clouds of odd and bizarre forms, which keep quite motionless. When the thunder-cloud ascends, these are drawn toward it; and as they approach they become more uniform and regular in their shapes, till, coming close to the thunder-cloud, their limbs stretch mutually toward one another, finally coalesce, and form one uniform mass. But sometimes the thunder-cloud will swell and increase without the addition of these smaller adscititious clouds. Some of the latter appear like white fringes at the skirts of the thunder-cloud or under the body of it, but they continually grow darker and darker as they approach it.

* Phil. Trans., vol. xlix., p. 61.

When the thunder-cloud, thus augmented, has attained a great magnitude, its lower surface is often ragged, particular parts being detached toward the earth, but still connected with the rest. Sometimes the lower surface swells into large protuberances, tending uniformly toward the earth; and sometimes one whole side of the cloud will have an inclination to the earth, which the extremity of it will nearly touch. When the observer is under the thunder-cloud after it has grown large and is well formed, it is seen to sink lower and to darken prodigiously, and, at the same time, a great number of small clouds are observed in rapid motion, driven about in irregular directions below it. While these clouds are agitated with the most rapid motions, the rain generally falls in abundance; and if the agitation be very great, it hails.

While the thunder-cloud is swelling and extending itself over a large tract of country, the lightning is seen to dart from one part of it to another, and often to illuminate its whole mass. When the cloud has acquired a sufficient extent, the lightning strikes between the cloud and the earth in two opposite places, the path of the lightning lying through the whole body of the cloud and its branches. The longer this lightning continues, the rarer does the cloud grow, and the less dark in its appearance, till it breaks in different places and shows a clear sky. When the thunder is thus dispersed, those parts which occupy the upper regions of the atmosphere are spread thinly and equally, and those that are beneath are black and thin also, but they vanish gradually without being driven away by the wind.

The instruments for electrical observation used by Beccaria never failed to give indications corresponding to the successive changes in progress in the atmosphere above his observatory. The stream of fire from his conductor was generally uninterrupted while the thunder-cloud was directly above it. The same cloud in its passage electrified his conductor alternately with positive and negative electricity. The electricity of the conductor continued to be of the same kind so long as the thunder-cloud was simple and uniform in its direction; but when the lightning changed its place, a change in the species of electricity ensued. A sudden change of this kind would also happen after a violent flash of lightning; but the change would be gradual when the lightning was moderate, and the progress of the thunder-cloud slow.*

But among the labors of this philosopher, that rendered by modern discoveries most memorable was one which by his contemporaries and their immediate successors was regarded as an ingenious and over-refined conjecture, rather than what it afterward proved to be, the distant shadow of a coming discovery detected by the far-sighted mind of this acute and extraordinary man. Franklin had been the first to magnetize fine sewing-needles by the electric spark. Dalibard observed that the extremity of the needle at which the spark from the excited glass entered had northern polarity, and both Franklin and Dalibard discovered that a spark of equal force given to the other end of the needle deprived it of the magnetic virtue. From these and from similar experiments made by himself, Beccaria inferred that the polarity of the magnetic needle was determined by the direction in which the electric current had passed through it. He assumed the magnetic polarity acquired by ferruginous bodies which had been struck by lightning, as a test of the direction of the electric current in passing through them, and thence inferred the species of electricity with which the thunder-cloud had been charged.†

Extending this analogy to the earth itself, Beccaria conjectured that terrestrial magnetism was, like that of the needle magnetized by Franklin and Dali-

* Beccaria, Lettere dell' Elettricismo. Bologna, 1758: p. 146, *et seq.*

† "I poli del mattone teste descritto, provano che anche in certi corpi che abbiano certa porzione di ferro, *il fulmine imprime un segno permanente della sua direzione.*"—*Beccaria, Lettere,* p. 261.

bard, the mere effect of permanent currents of natural electricity, established and maintained upon its surface by various physical causes ; that, as a violent current, like that which attends the exhibition of lightning, produces instantaneous and powerful magnetism in substances capable of receiving that quality, so may a more gentle, regular, and constant circulation of the electric fluid upon the earth impress the same virtue on all such bodies as are capable of it. Observation proves that a vast quantity of this fluid circulates between different parts of the atmosphere in storms ; that a quantity not inconsiderable circulates in the time of ordinary rain ; and that even when the weather is serene and the heavens unclouded, some quantity is still observable. "Of such fluid, thus ever present," observes Beccaria, "I think that some portion is constantly passing through all bodies situate on the earth, especially those which are metallic and ferruginous ; and I imagine it must be those currents which impress on fire-irons, and other similar things, the power which they are known to acquire of directing themselves according to the magnetic meridian when they are properly balanced."*

He observed, that to say we are insensible to this current around us, is no good argument against its existence ; for that its uniformity, constancy, and universality, would necessarily render it imperceptible, since all bodies must partake of it in common. His hypothesis to account for the *variation* and *dip* is not the least remarkable part of this extraordinary anticipation. He considers that the electro-magnetic currents have not all a common centre, but may have several situate in our northern hemisphere. The aberration of their common centre from the true terrestrial pole may probably be the cause of the variation of the compass. The periodical change to which the position of this common centre is subject would correspond with and cause the periodical change of that variation, and the obliquity of these currents may be the cause of the dip.†

That the anticipation of the fundamental principle of electro-magnetism, and terrestrial magnetism, should have been complete in all its details, could scarcely have happened at that epoch without something approaching to inspiration ; but it will be readily admitted that these guesses of Beccaria, when compared with the discovery of Orested and the theory of Ampère, form one of the most striking episodes in the history of science.

The analogy between lightning and the electric spark, arising from the peculiar noise or explosion with which each was attended, had been noticed by many electricians. Beccaria, however, investigated and demonstrated its cause, by showing that it proceeded from a pulsation produced in the air by the sudden displacement of that portion of it through which the electric fluid passes. This displacement being transmitted through the atmosphere in exactly the same manner as vibrations are produced by a sonorous body, the sound accompanying an electric discharge, and the thunder which attends the atmospheric elec-

* "Di tale fuoco, io penso che alcuna parte perpetuamente discorra per tutti i corpi situati sopra la terra, massimamente per i metallici e ferigni. Penso che esso sia, il quale attraversando le padelle, le molle, le palette ed altri si fatti bislunghi ferri, i quali d'ordinario pendono o posano verticalmente, imprima loro la virtù di situarsi nella meridiana magnetica, allora che sono convenientemente bilicati."—*Lettere*, p. 266.

† "Questa sistematica elettrico-magnetica circolazione, secondo me, non procederebbe da un solo punto settentrionale, ma avrebbe infinite sorgenti in diversi punti del nostro settentrionale emisfero, forse successivamente, più folte nè luoghi più vicini ad alcun punto settentrionale ; e la frequenza, la posizione, o piuttosto la direzione del corso loro mi si rappresenterebbono dalla posizione, frequenza, e diverzione, con che si dispongono intorno alli emisferi di una sferica calamita le ordinatissime filze della limitura di ferro. E giusta una tale ipotesi, l'aberrazione del centro comune di tutte le varie sorgenti, che estenderebbono la loro azione ad una data ragione, dal vero punto settentrionale mi spiegherebbe l'aberrazione della calamita ; il periodo di quella aberrazione mi spiegherebbe il periodo di questa declinazione ; l'obbliquità, con che quelle sorgenti spiccierebbono da terra, e si direggerebbono verso mezzo dì, mi spiegherebbe e la inclinazione degli aghi, e la particolare facilità con che si calamitano i ferri si fattamente inclinati."—*Lettere*, p. 268.

tricity, ensue. Beccaria verified this hypothesis by experiment. He constructed a glass siphon, in one leg of which air was enclosed above a column of mercury, and compressed by the column in the other leg of the siphon. On discharging a Leyden jar through the air thus enclosed, the column of mercury in the other leg was suddenly elevated, and recovered its position after several oscillations.* This fact was also noticed by Kinnersley, the friend and associate of Franklin, but not until a later period.

This was afterward corroborated by Bouguer and De la Condamine, when they encountered a violent thunder-storm on one of the highest mountains of Peru. The cloud from which the thunder proceeded was placed at but a small distance above their heads. The thunder heard by them consisted only of single cracks, or explosions, like those which attend the discharge of electric batteries; an effect manifestly produced by the proximity of the cause of the sound, and the highly rarefied state of the air at that great elevation.

Contemporaneously with Beccaria, Franklin, and Canton, the subject of atmospheric electricity engaged the attention of Lemonnier, who erected an apparatus according to Franklin's method at St. Germain-en-Laye, with which he showed that sparks were received from the conductor not only in times of storm, but also when the heavens were cloudless. He also first showed that the electricity of the air underwent every twenty-four hours periodical variations of intensity.

Beccaria determined the law of these variations, and was the first who demonstrated that at all seasons, at all heights, and in every state of the wind, the electricity of an unclouded atmosphere is positive. He found no indications of electricity in the air in high winds, when the firmament was covered with black and scattered clouds, having a slow motion in a humid state of the air; but in the absence of actual rain, he found that in changeable squally weather, attended with occasional showers of snow, hail, or rain, the electricity was very variable, both as to its quantity and quality, being sometimes feeble and sometimes intense, sometimes positive and sometimes negative.

Contemporaneously with Beccaria in Italy, Canton prosecuted inquiries in many respects similar in England, and in various matters of minor importance these philosophers arrived at the same results. The most considerable discovery due to Canton was, that the electricity developed in the friction of the same substance is not always of the same kind. It will be remembered that Dufaye gave the names *vitreous* and *resinous* to the two fluids, on the supposition that each was invariably produced by the friction of the classes of bodies signified by these terms. Canton, however, showed that glass itself was capable of being electrified negatively, and would be always so electrified, if the rubber used were the fur of a cat. Canton also (as well as Beccaria) proved that a volume of air in a quiescent state might be charged with electricity. To Canton is also due the discovery of the virtue of the amalgam of tin and mercury, still used with so much effect to augment the development of electricity on glass.

The progress of the science had now attained a point at which the great principle of induction could scarcely fail to force itself upon the notice of those engaged in electrical researches. A natural law of the highest order, embracing within the range of its application nearly the whole domain of electrical phenomena, its discovery and development, forms an epoch in the history of the science, scarcely second in importance even to that by which Franklin brought meteorology within the legislation of electricity. How much, then, will the veneration in which the memory of the philosopher of the West is

* Beccaria, Elettricismo Artificiale. Turin, 1753: p. 227.

held be increased, if it can be demonstrated, contrary to what has been generally maintained by the historians of the science, that to him is justly owing the honor of the discovery of this physical principle!

Some of the more obvious phenomena of induction were noticed so early in the progress of electrical science as the researches of Mr. Grey; and many other effects proceeding from it presented themselves to subsequent experimental inquiries, but attracted no attention, and led to no consequences. The first series of experiments, conducted so as to develop in an unequivocal manner this principle, were laid before the Royal Society by Canton, on the 6th of December, 1753.* They consisted chiefly in rendering insulated conductors electrical, by bringing near to one end an excited glass tube, or stick of wax, and exhibiting the varying state of cork-balls suspended on the conductor by the alternate approach and removal of the excited electric.

These experiments having been communicated to Franklin, he pursued the inquiry, and succeeded in expressing, in clear and unequivocal terms, the principle of induction; that is to say, in demonstrating that a body charged with either kind of electricity will, on approaching a conductor in its natural state, render that part of such conductor which is nearest to it electrical; that its electricity will be contrary to that of the approaching electrified body; that on removing the electrified body, the conductor would be restored to its natural state: all which effects Franklin showed would follow from his theory, by assuming that the electric fluid is self-repulsive, and attracted by the matter of the conductor.

The experiments and reasoning which appear to establish Franklin's right to the honor of this discovery are so concise, that they may be stated here nearly in his own words.

Let a metallic conductor, about five feet long and four inches in diameter, be suspended by dry silk lines, so as to be insulated. From one end of it suspend a tassel consisting of fifteen or twenty threads in a damp state, so as to give them a conducting power. Present an electrified glass tube within five or six inches of the opposite end, and keep it in that position for a few seconds. The threads of the tassel will diverge, and when the tube is withdrawn they will collapse.

While the tube is held near the opposite end of the conductor and the threads are divergent, present the finger to the end of the conductor at which the tassel is suspended. A spark will be received, and the threads of the tassel will collapse.

Let the tube be then removed. The threads of the tassel will again diverge.

Let the tube be again presented as before. The threads will again collapse, and so on.

Finally, let the tube be presented to the tassel. The divergence of the threads will immediately increase, and continue to increase, as the tube is brought nearer to the tassel.

These phenomena are accounted for by Franklin in the following manner: "By taking the spark from the end of the conductor, you rob it of part of its natural quantity of electrical matter, which part so taken away is not supplied by the glass tube, and the conductor remains *negatively* electrified. On withdrawing the tube, the electric matter on the conductor recovers its equilibrium, or equal diffusion; and the conductor having lost some of its natural electricity, the threads connected with it lose part of theirs, and so are electrified negatively, and repel each other.

* Phil. Trans., vol. xlviii., p. 350.

"When the tube is again presented to the opposite end of the conductor, the part of the natural electricity which the threads had lost is again restored to them by the repulsion of the tube forcing the electric fluid toward them from other parts of the conductor, and thus restoring them to their natural state. When the tube is once more withdrawn, the fluid is again equally diffused, and the threads, as before, are negatively electrified.

"Finally, when the tube is presented to the threads already diverging with negative electricity, still more of their natural electricity is repelled by the excited tube, and the threads are more strongly negative than before, and their divergence is consequently augmented."

Pursuing the principle thus developed still further, Franklin now having restored the conductor to its natural state, presented the excited glass tube to the tassel. The threads immediately diverged.

Maintaining the tube in that position with one hand, he presented the finger of the other to the tassel. The threads receded from the finger as if repelled by it.

This was explained on the same principle. When the excited tube is presented to the tassel, part of the natural electricity of the threads is driven out of them into the conductor, and they are negatively electrified, and therefore repel each other. When the finger is presented to the tassel (being then close to the glass tube), part of its natural electricity is driven back through the hand and body, and the finger becomes, as well as the threads, negatively electrified, and so repels, and is repelled by them. To confirm this, hold a slender light lock of cotton, two or three inches long, near a conductor positively electrified. You will see the cotton stretch itself out toward the conductor. Attempt to touch it with the finger of the other hand, and it will be repelled by the finger. Approach it with a positively-charged wire of a bottle, and it will fly to the wire. Bring it near a negatively-charged wire of a bottle, it will recede from that wire in the same manner that it did from the finger, which demonstrates that the finger was negatively electrified as well as the cotton.*

The great principle thus thrown before the scientific world by Franklin, was immediately taken up and pursued through its consequences by Wilke and Æpinus, who carried on their researches together at Berlin. The most important result of their combined labors was the invention of the instrument, which, as subsequently improved under the hands of Volta, became the CONDENSER now so useful in electroscopical investigations.

In applying the principle of induction to the phenomena of the Leyden jar, and to the same effects as exhibited by the oppositely electrified surfaces of a coated plate of glass, these philosophers saw that the negative state of one surface of the glass was, according to the Franklinian theory, the necessary consequence of the positive state of the other. This contrary state of the electricities could only be maintained on the supposition that glass was impermeable by the electric fluid; and Wilke and Æpinus reasoned, that to whatever extent air or any other body might be similarly impermeable, to the same extent might it be charged on its opposite surfaces. To realize this conception with a plate of air, they coated two large boards of equal size with tin-foil, and suspended them one over the other, leaving a space of about an inch in thickness between them. This space was, in fact, a plate of air, of which the upper and lower surfaces were in contact with the metallic coating of the boards. The lower board communicated with the ground, and a charge of positive electricity was given to the upper one. The lower one then became charged with negative electricity; and when a person touched at the same time the

* Letters, p. 341. Also see Phil. Trans., vol. xlix., p. 300.

coating of the two boards, the equilibrium was re-established, and he received the shock produced by the passage of the electric fluid from the one to the other.

Many curious experiments were exhibited with this apparatus. They found that the two boards, when electrified, strongly attracted each other, and would have rushed together if they had not been prevented by the strings. Sometimes, when the charge was strong, the intervening plate of air was not sufficiently impermeable to resist the mutual attraction of the opposite electricities, and a spontaneous discharge would take place through it. They considered these two plates to represent the state of the clouds and the earth during a thunder-storm; the clouds being always charged with one kind of electricity, and the earth with the other, while the body of atmosphere between them was analogous to the stratum of air between the two boards. When the charges of the earth and clouds become so strong that the air can no longer resist the passage of the electric fluid through it, a spontaneous discharge ensues, the fluid is seen in its passage by the light it evolves, and the violent displacement of the air produced in its passage causes the thunder.

From these experiments, Æpinus inferred that the phenomena of the Leyden jar was not owing, as Franklin supposed, to any peculiar attraction of the glass for the electric fluid; for, since a plate of air might be charged as well as a plate of glass, that property must be common to them, and was not peculiar to the glass. He inferred, therefore, that this impermeability was a property of all non-conductors; and, since they can all receive electricity to a certain degree, it must consist in the difficulty and slowness with which the electric fluid moves in their pores, whereas, in perfect conductors, it meets with no obstruction at all.*

Æpinus brought to the investigation of the Franklinian theory of electricity those mathematical attainments in which its illustrious founder was deficient. The manner in which that theory had been assailed by its opponents, and defended by its partisans, was such as might have allowed interminable controversy. Æpinus first reduced its principles to exact mathematical statement, with a view to ascertain whether the consequences deducible from them, by rigorous calculation, should be in accordance with the observed phenomena, not only in their general character, but in their numerical quantity. He assumed, according to Franklin's hypothesis, that the molecules of the electric fluid were self-repulsive, and that they were attracted by those of the bodies on which they were diffused. He found, however, that the phenomena could not be explained on these suppositions, unless it were also assumed that between the matter composing the masses of different bodies there existed a mutually repulsive force, acting at sensible distances. At first he recoiled from an assumption in direct opposition to the known properties of matter; but the necessity of its admission, in order to give consistency and validity to the Franklinian theory, appears at length to have reconciled him to it.

The investigation of the physical relation between the principle of heat and that of electricity, had attracted the attention of experimental philosophers at a very early period in the history of electrical research. Beccaria suspected that heat might itself be an immediate means for the development of electricity, and made some experiments to illustrate this. He soon, however, relinquished the inquiry, concluding that, in cases where the appearance of electricity followed the application of heat, the effect was due to evaporation, or other physical agents, which ensued. Priestley observed that heat had some relation to the conducting power of bodies, since, by the elevation of temperature, that quality was improved.

* Æpini Tentamen, &c. Petersburg, 1759, p. 82, 83.

A mineral substance, brought from the east by the Dutch navigators, called by the natives of Ceylon, where chiefly it was found, *Tournamal*, and since known as *Tourmaline*, exhibited, under certain circumstances, a property similar to that of amber, and other electrics. But the power was excited in it by mere elevation of temperature. Lemery, the Duc de Noia, Wilson, Priestley, and others, made experiments on this mineral, and published results, in which there were much discordance and contradiction. Æpinus first showed that the attraction and repulsion exerted by this gem when exposed to heat were owing to the development of electricity upon it; and that, when so excited, its opposite sides or ends had contrary kinds of electricity, one being always negative and the other positive. This was the first case of the distinct exhibition of electrical polarity. Canton observed that the development of the electric fluid upon it was produced only by change of temperature, and that whenever the gem was broken each fragment exhibited the same electrical polarity.

At this period effects were observed, which, if chemical science had attained a sufficiently advanced state, could not fail to have led to the discovery of electro-chemistry. Beccaria, by the electric spark, decomposed the sulphuret of mercury, and recovered the metals, in some instances, from their oxides.* Watson found that an electric discharge passing through fine wire rendered it incandescent, and that it was even fused and burned. Canton, repeating these experiments with brass wire, found that, after the fusion by electricity, drops of copper only were found, the zinc having apparently evaporated. Beccaria observed that when the electric spark was transmitted through water, bubbles of gas rose from the liquid, the nature or origin of which he was unable to determine. Had he suspected that water was not what it was then supposed to be, a simple elementary substance, the discovery of its composition could scarcely have eluded his sagacity.

After general laws have once been developed, and their application to particular phenomena has become familiar, it appears wonderful that even quick-sighted and acute observers should have had such effects continually reproduced under their eyes, without even making an approach to the discovery of their causes. Franklin found that the frequent application of the electric spark had eaten away iron; on which Priestley observed, that it must be the effect of some acid, and suggested the inquiry, whether electricity might not probably *redden vegetable blues?* Priestley also observed that in transmitting electricity through a copper chain, a black dust was left on the paper which supported the chain at the points where the links touched it; and, on examining this dust, he found it to contain copper.

Some years after the invention of the Leyden jar, when the necessity of some sufficient indicator of the presence of electricity, and some visible measure of its power became apparent, the invention of electrometers engaged the attention of electricians. After several abortive attempts on the part of others, the Abbé Nollet proposed the simple expedient of suspending two threads, which, when electrified, would separate by their mutual repulsion. Cavallo afterward improved upon this, by substituting two pith balls, suspended in contact by fine metallic wires—an apparatus still used. After this, various forms of electroscopic instruments were suggested and constructed by Volta, Saussure, and others, all depending on the principle that the intensity of the electric fluid was manifested by the force of its attraction or repulsion exerted upon light substances to which it was imparted.

The principle of induction applied to the *air-condenser* by Wilke and Æpinus, was taken up by Volta, and applied, first, to the construction of the ELEC-

* Lettere del Elettricismo, § 341, p. 282.

TROPHORUS, and subsequently to the common CONDENSER, which, combined with the electroscope, became in electricity an instrument of investigation analogous in its character and importance to the compound microscope in optics.

The manner in which the electrified fluid is distributed upon insulated electrified conductors next became the subject of inquiry. Beccaria showed that its distribution is superficial, and that the internal parts of the electrified body are in their natural state. It was shown that, whether the electrified conductor were hollow or solid, the electricity contained on it was the same. Lemonnier first showed that the form of the conductor had an influence on the quantity and the distribution of the fluids.

In 1778 Volta published a memoir on this subject, in which he proved, that of two cylinders of equal superficial dimensions, that which had the greater length would receive, *cæteris paribus*, the stronger charge, and inferred that great advantage would arise from the substitution of a system of small cylinders for the large conductors of electrical machines. About the same period, he showed how inflammable gases could be ignited in close glass receivers by the electric spark, the apparatus for which purpose soon grew into his *eudiometer*, for the analysis of gases. Soon after this, the same apparatus supplied the means of inflaming a mixture of oxygen and hydrogen gas, which led to the discovery of the composition of water.

In the year 1759 appeared, in the "Philosophical Transactions," a series of papers by Mr. Robert Symmer, which are entitled to be recorded in the history of electricity; not so much on account of what they describe, as for the theoretical views developed in them. The experiments of Symmer consisted chiefly in exhibiting, by striking examples, the effect of the mutual attraction of bodies electrified by opposite kinds of electricity. These results led him to doubt the sufficiency of the Franklinian theory, then and long afterward universally received, to explain satisfactorily the phenomena; and he was led to consider whether the hypothesis of Dufaye might not be so modified as to explain them more adequately. Dufaye, as has been already stated, assumed the existence of two independent electric fluids, which he supposed to be latent in two distinct classes of bodies, the one in bodies of a vitreous, and the other in bodies of a resinous nature; and that these fluids, while they were each self-repulsive, were mutually attractive of each other.

It was obvious that such an hypothesis was quite inconsistent with the known phenomena of electricity, even limited as they were in variety at the period now referred to. Symmer retained the supposition of Dufaye so far as regarded the assumed existence of two distinct fluids mutually attractive, but he maintained that these fluids were *not* independent of each other. On the contrary, he assumed that they were always co-existent in bodies not electrified; that, by their natural attraction, they held each other in subjection; that every body in its natural state contained equal quantities of these fluids, each molecule of the vitreous fluid being combined with a molecule of the resinous fluid, the compound molecule thus formed exciting neither attraction nor repulsion on the other parts of the natural fluid.

This theory of two fluids was left by its author unsupported by any extensive application to the phenomena which could be expected to shake the confidence then generally given to the hypothesis of Franklin; and although it is noticed at some length in his history of electricity by Dr. Priestley, it obtained no countenance or support until further advances in electrical experiments rendered apparent the defects of the theory of a single fluid. It may be here observed, that the French writers generally ascribe the theory of two fluids to Dufaye, and are silent as to Symmer's share in it; with what justice will be apparent from what has been above stated.

In the year 1770, Dr. Priestley published his works on electricity. This philosopher did not contribute materially to the advancement of the science by the development of any new facts; but in his History of Electricity he collected and arranged much useful information respecting the progress of the science. At this period the Honorable Henry Cavendish, whose name has been distinguished in other departments of physics, engaged in some original investigations respecting electricity. The discovery of the composition of water, by transmitting an electric spark through a mixture of oxygen and hydrogen gases, has been generally ascribed to him.* Cavendish conceived the notion of reducing the phenomena of electricity to mathematical analysis, and had proceeded with a memoir on that subject, which was completed before he learned that Æpinus had produced a work with the same object. On comparing his own paper with the *Tentamen* of Æpinus, he found that they were nearly similar. Nevertheless, Cavendish published his memoir.

The year 1785 formed an important epoch in the history of electrical science, marking, as it did, the commencement of those labors by which Coulomb laid the foundations of ELECTRO-STATICS. This great experimental philosopher was the first who really brought the phenomena of electricity within the reach of numerical calculation, and thereby prepared the way for his followers in the same field to reduce this most subtle of all physical agents to the rigorous sway of mathematics. It is to Coulomb we owe it that statical electricity is now a branch of mathematical physics.

The immediate instrument by which this vast object was attained was the *balance of torsion*, which he had already used with signal success in other delicate physical inquiries. This apparatus, which will be fully explained in the following pages, consisted of a needle suspended in a horizontal position by an exceedingly fine wire or filament of silk attached to its centre of gravity. The attraction, or other force of which the intensity is to be measured, is made to act on one end of this needle, so as to twist the filament by which it is suspended; and it is resisted in its effort to effect this by the reaction proceeding from the torsion so produced. This reaction, and therefore the force which produces it, and is in equilibrium with it, was proved by Coulomb to be proportionate to the angle described by the needle round its centre of motion. Such was the sensibility of this exquisite instrument, that it was found to be perceptibly affected by a force not exceeding the twenty-millionth part of a grain.

With this instrument Coulomb measured the force with which electrified bodies attract and repel each other; and the first result of this investigation was the discovery, that the law of this attraction and repulsion was the same which Newton showed to prevail among the great bodies of the universe. In fact, he showed that two bodies, oppositely electrified, attract each other with a force which, *cæteris paribus*, is the same at equal distances, and which augments in the same proportion as that in which the square of the distance is diminished. Also if two bodies be similarly electrified, they will repel each other by a force which increases according to the same proportion when the distance between them is diminished.

By attaching a very small circular disk of paper coated with metallic foil to an insulating handle, Coulomb found that by touching with the face of the disk an electrified surface, and then submitting the disk itself thus electrified by contact to the test of the balance of torsion, he could determine the depth of the electric fluid on the surface touched by the disk. In this manner was he enabled to *gauge* or *sound* the electricity on the surface of bodies, so as to com-

* This claim has been recently called in question.—See Lardner on the Steam-Engine. Seventh Edition, p. 303.

pare numerically its depth on different bodies, or on different parts of the same body.

With this instrument he measured the proportion in which electricity was shared between insulated conductors when brought into contact, and also the law according to which its depth varied on different parts of the same insulated conductor. These results acquired, at a later period, still greater importance, supplying, as they did, tests by which the mathematical analysis of the science could be tried.

The same apparatus supplied the means of investigating the law according to which an insulated electrified conductor had its charge gradually diminished by dissipation in the surrounding air, and by the escape of the fluid by the imperfect insulation of the supports.

The results of the observations of Coulomb on the distribution of the electric fluid on the surfaces of conductors illustrated satisfactorily the doctrine of points, which formed so prominent a part of Franklin's researches. The theoretical solution of this problem was not, however, effected till a later period.

The demonstration of the identity of lightning and electricity naturally directed the attention of philosophers to the solution of other meteorological phenomena by means of the same agency. The explanation of the *aurora borealis* had long exercised the sagacity and baffled the attempts of those devoted to physical researches. Some ascribed this appearance to solar light refracted in the higher regions of the air, others assigned it to the agency of the magnetic fluid. Euler imagined it to proceed from the same ether which formed the tails of comets; Mairan conceived it to arise from the mixture of the atmosphere of the sun with that of the earth; but when the properties of electric light became known, and when its appearance in rarefied air had been observed, all these hypotheses were by common consent abandoned, and no doubt was entertained that, whatever might be the details of the natural process by which it was produced, the *aurora borealis* was an effect of atmospheric electricity. Eberhart, professor at Halle, and Paul Frisi at Pisa, were the first who proposed an explanation of it, founded on the following facts: "1. Electricity transmitted through rarefied air exhibits a luminous appearance, precisely similar to that of the aurora borealis."—"2. The strata of atmospheric air become rarefied as their altitude above the surface of the earth is increased." Hence they argued that the aurora is nothing more than electrical discharges transmitted through parts of the upper regions of the atmosphere, so rarefied as to produce that peculiar luminous appearance which they exhibit. This theory, which was embraced and improved in its details by Canton, Beccaria, Wilke, Franklin, and other contemporary electricians, has received further countenance from more recent researches.

Attempts were also made to explain on electrical principles other meteorological effects; such as waterspouts, whirlwinds, rain, fogs, hail, &c., but no satisfactory conclusions resulted from these investigations, and the discussion of such phenomena forms a part of the meteorological inquiry of the present time.

While the series of experimental researches which have just been related were in progress, many attempts were made to trace electricity in the phenomena of vegetable and animal life, and more especially to apply it as a medical agent in cases of organic disease in the animal system. None of these attempts, however, led to any consequences sufficiently important to entitle them to attention in this brief sketch.

After electroscopes had been much improved, and in their application to atmospheric electricity had derived great power from the addition of a long pointed conductor, extending from the diverging balls to a height of several feet, Volta engaged in the investigation of the electric state of the air. He substituted for the suspended balls two blades of dry straw, hanging in contact and communicating with the lower end of the conducting rod. In addition to this, he had recourse to another apparently strange and unusual expedient. He placed on the point of the rod a taper, so as to cause this conductor to terminate in a flame. He contended that the flame attracted to the point of the conductor three or four times as much electricity as would be collected in its absence. This was explained by the effect of the vertical current of air which the flame maintained directly over it, which established a better communication between the metallic conductor and the strata of air above it.

Assuming this property of flame, Volta argued, that since fires robbed the atmosphere above them of electricity faster and more effectually than metallic points, it must follow that, to prevent coming storms, or to mitigate their force, the best expedient would be to light enormous fires in the middle of extensive plains, or, better still, on elevated stations. If the effects of the lamp on the atmospheric electrometer were admitted, there would be nothing unreasonable in the supposition that large fires may, in a short interval of time, rob immense volumes of air and vapor of their electricity.

Volta wished to submit this theory to an experiment on a large scale, but was not able to carry the design into effect. M. Arago suggested, that by making suitable meteorological observations in those parts of Staffordshire and other English counties which abound in vast iron furnaces, where fires of extraordinary magnitude are maintained night and day, and comparing the results with similar observations made in adjoining agricultural districts, the conjecture of Volta might be tested.*

Observations of this kind have accordingly been recently made both in England and in certain parts of Italy, the results of which will be explained at the proper place in this volume.

It has been already stated, that direct observations proved that the atmosphere, in its ordinary condition, is always charged with positive electricity. The beginning of the year 1780 was signalized by a capital experiment, by which it was proved that the source whence this vast amount of the electric fluid was derived, or, to speak more correctly, the cause of the disturbance of the general equilibrium of the globe, which gives a surplus of the positive fluid to the air, and leaves the earth surcharged with negative fluid, and which, in its effects, assumes all the terrific forms of the tempest and the hurricane, and probably of many other violent convulsions which are occasionally exhibited in the war of the elements, is to be found in the process of natural evaporation, which continually maintains its silent and imperceptible progress upon the surfaces of ocean, lake, and river, and even upon those of organized bodies. That heat passes off in a latent form by such means, and equalizes and moderates the general temperature around us, was well known; but it was not suspected that the elements of the storm, the coruscations of meteoric light, and the splendors of he aurora, were due to the same cause.

Volta states, that in the year 1778 this idea occurred to him, and that he conceived the notion of an experiment by which it might be brought to an immediate trial. Let a metallic dish filled with water be placed on an insulating support, and exposed in the open air until it evaporates, the dish being maintained in communication with a sufficiently sensible condensing electroscope. If, in evaporating, the positive fluid be carried off, the dish will, after the evaporation, be negatively electrical, and the electroscope will show it; if not, the electroscope will give no sign. Various circumstances prevented Volta from trying this experiment until the month of March, 1780, when, being in Paris,

* Eloge de Volta, p. 18.

he succeeded, *in company with* some members of the Academy of Sciences. There appears, nevertheless, to remain some doubt as to the share which Volta really had in this famous experiment, since, in the account of it published by Lavoisier and Laplace, it is related as performed by them, and Volta is mentioned incidentally as being present on the occasion.*

After the phenomena of electricity had, by the labors of Coulomb, been reduced to exact numerical estimation, this branch of physics was in a state to permit its being brought within the pale of mixed mathematics. To accomplish this it was necessary to express, by mathematical formulæ, the intensity of the electric fluid on different parts of insulated conductors of given forms, placed either separately, or in such a position as to exercise an electrical influence upon each other without contact, or, finally, when placed in actual contact. To establish such formulæ, it was necessary to assume some definite hypothesis as the law of electrical action. The Franklinian theory of a single fluid appeared to be incapable of affording the means of explaining, with numerical precision, the state of such bodies. It is true that this long-received hypothesis was sufficient to account, in a general way, for the electrical state of bodies under the ordinary circumstances of their mutual action; but when rigorous numerical accuracy was demanded—when not merely the general circumstances of the dense accumulation of electricity in one part of the surface, its more feeble intensity at another, its total abstinence from a third place, or the presence of negative electricity on a certain side of a conductor, and positive electricity on another, were severally demanded; but when it was required to determine the *exact numerical measure of the depth of the fluid at each particular spot on a given insulated conductor*, placed under given conditions with reference to others, so that such numerical measure, so obtained by calculation, might be compared with the actual depth observed by the instruments invented and applied by Coulomb, then this theory appeared to fail; at least, none of its advocates produced any such calculations. Laplace investigated, on mathematical principles, the distribution of electricity on ellipsoids of revolution, assuming, as the basis of his reasoning, the hypothesis of two fluids. Biot also investigated the same problem applied to spheroids of small eccentricity; but the general subjugation of this portion of electrical science to mathematical analysis is due to Poisson.

This illustrious analyst took as the basis of his investigations the theory of two fluids proposed by Symmer and Dufaye, with such modifications and additions as were suggested by the researches of Coulomb. He regarded the mutual attractions and repulsions exhibited by electrified bodies, not as real forces exercised by those bodies, but as altogether due to the electric fluids with which they are charged. The laws of attraction and repulsion developed by Coulomb are therefore assumed as those of the electric fluids. The particles of each of these fluids are assumed to repel each other with a force varying according to that law, while the particles of each fluid attract those of the contrary fluid by a force governed by the same law. These conditions are sufficient to supply the mathematical formulæ necessary to the determination of the depth and quality of the electric fluid on every part of the surface of a body of given figure placed under any given electrical conditions. The electric fluids of either kind would, by virtue of their self-expansive property, escape from the surface of the body on which they rest; but this is prevented by the pressure of the surrounding air, which retains them in their position so long as their expansive force is less than that pressure. On bodies of elongated forms, or those which have edges, corners, or points, it is shown, as a consequence of this theory, that the electric fluid accumulates in greater depths

* Eloge de Volta, p. 21.

about the ends, edges, corners, or points, than in other places. Its expansive force at such parts is therefore greater than elsewhere, and will exceed the atmospheric pressure, and escape when at other parts of the surface it is retained.

This theory will be explained in the present work, as far as its development is consistent with the object of this volume. It will not, therefore, be needful to enlarge upon it further in this place. It may, however, be asked why it is, seeing that the theory of two fluids is sufficient for the explanation of all the phenomena to which it has yet been applied, and that, on the other hand, the theory of a single fluid fails to afford any satisfactory or accurate explanation of so many phenomena, the latter theory, nevertheless, still has followers, and that even among electricians, whose opinions cannot be regarded otherwise than with sentiments of respect, it is still clung to as the hypothesis best entitled to reception and confidence? It is not easy to assign any sufficient reason for this, unless one can be found in the profound and abstruse nature of the mathematical principles by the aid of which alone the effects are capable of being expressed. When it is remembered that, until very recently, electricity was regarded as exclusively a part of experimental physics; that researches in it were chiefly carried on by persons engaged in chemical investigations; that, from the nature of their studies and pursuits, such persons rarely cultivated even the elements of mathematics, and almost never pursued analytical science into those more profound parts which are now indispensable for the solution of the class of problems which electricity has presented—it cannot be matter of much surprise that reasoning which is incapable of being expressed save by symbols of which the force and import must be unintelligible to the great mass of such persons, should fail to carry conviction to their understanding. To arrive at such conviction, they must either commence their education anew, or be content to receive those new doctrines on their faith in the assurance of those who are capable of investigating them. Either side of such an alternative is never very willingly embraced.

Having now followed the progress of discovery in this part of electrical science to that point at which all subsequent researches must be regarded as the labor of our contemporaries, the province of the historian ceases. Whatever has been effected more recently will properly form a part of the subject matter of the volume here presented to the reader, of which it is hoped that a brief exposition and analysis of the researches of contemporary philosophers will form not the least interesting and useful portion.

THE MINOR PLANETS.

Classification of the Planets.—Mercury.—Transit over the Sun.—Relative Position with regard to the Sun.—Difficulty of observing it.—Venus.—Diurnal Motion of Venus and Mercury indicated by the Shadows of Mountains.—Direction of the Axis of Rotation.—Seasons, Climates, and Zones.—Orbits and Transits of Mercury and Venus.—Mountains on Mercury and Venus.—Influence of the Sun at Mercury and Venus.—Twilight on Mercury and Venus.—Mars.—Atmosphere of Mars.—Physical Constitution of Mars.—Has Mars a Satellite ?—Appearance of the Sun at Mars.—Its Close Analogy to the Earth.

THE MINOR PLANETS.

THERE is no subject of inquiry to which the improved powers of the telescope have been directed with greater effect than the investigation of the physical condition of the several planets composing the solar system. We shall on the present occasion take a review of some of these bodies, and shall state the chief circumstances which have been discovered respecting them.

In a general survey of the system, the planets composing it will naturally be classed in three distinct groups, the *first* of which we shall call the *minor planets*, the *second* the *new planets*, and the *third* the *major planets*.

Proceeding from the sun outward in the system, the four planets which are nearest to that luminary are *Mercury*, *Venus*, the *Earth*, and *Mars*. Between these bodies there prevails a striking analogy. We find that they are not very different in magnitude; that they correspond closely, so far as we can discover, in their geographical character; that they receive in not very different proportions the influence of the sun. The close alliance between them has also occurred to other astronomical writers, inasmuch as they are sometimes called the *terrestrial planets*, from their analogy to the earth.

OF THE PLANET MERCURY.

The planet *Mercury* revolves at a distance from the sun of about thirty-six millions of miles, completing his periodical revolution in about eighty-eight days, or something less than three of our months. The diameter of this planet is about three thousand two hundred miles, or four tenths of that of the earth, and consequently its volume or bulk is about a sixteenth of that of our globe. As Mercury revolves round the sun in an orbit enclosed within that of the earth, it follows that his illuminated hemisphere, which is always presented to the sun in the course of each revolution, must assume every possible variety of position in regard to the earth. Thus when Mercury is between the sun and earth as at A, in what is called *inferior conjunction*, his dark hemisphere is turned toward us, and he is invisible, except in the case which sometimes occurs, in which he is so exactly in line of the direction of the sun as to be between the eye and some portion of the solar disk. In that case the planet is seen as a circular black spot on the disk of the sun, and the appearance of its motion upon that disk is called a *transit of Mercury.*

When the planet, on the other hand, is on the opposite side of the sun, at B, its illuminated hemisphere is presented directly in the line of vision; but in that case, the planet being in exactly the same quarter of the heavens as the sun is, would necessarily rise and set with the sun, and its appearance being obscured by the immeasurably superior splendor of the sun, it would not be seen. When the planet is in an intermediate position on either side of the sun in its periodical course, its illuminated hemisphere being presented as it always is, directly to the sun, will only be partially turned to the earth, and the planet

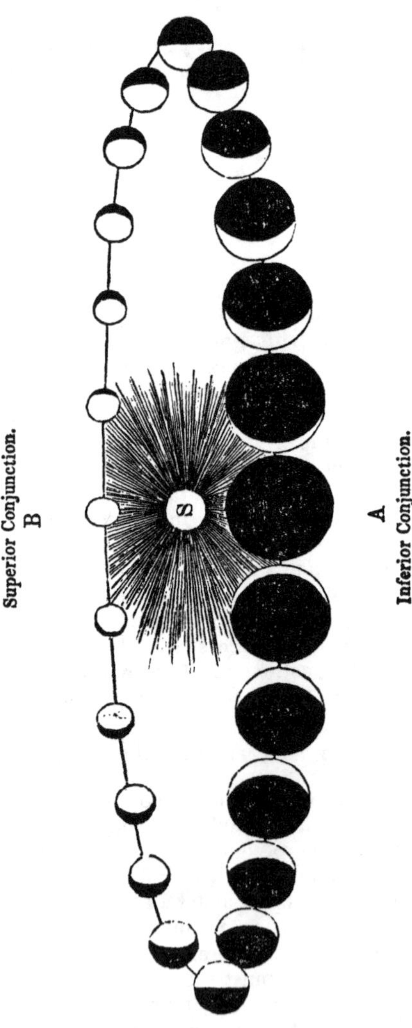

will be seen under a corresponding variety of phases, in short, it will undergo all the changes which the moon presents in its monthly course round the earth, as represented in the figure.

When near the point behind the sun, it will be nearly full, or gibbous; and when near the point where its dark hemisphere is turned to the earth, it will be a crescent. In a certain intermediate position it will be halved, and will pass through all the other phases.

In making its circuit round the sun, it will be seen alternately at the east and at the west of that luminary, separating from it in each direction to an extent limited by the magnitude of its orbit round the sun. When it is at the west of the sun, it sets before the sun, and rises before the sun. It cannot, in that case, be seen in the evening; but if it be separated from the sun by a sufficient distance, it will rise so early as to anticipate the light of the morning which precedes the sun's rays, and may then be seen as a morning star. On the other hand, when it is at the east of the sun, it rises after the sun, and sets after it. It cannot, therefore, be seen in the morning; but provided it be sufficiently distant from the sun to remain above the horizon until the darkness is sufficient to render it visible, it will be seen as an evening star.

The orbit of Mercury is so limited in its breadth, compared with the distance of the earth from the sun, that even when that planet is at its greatest apparent distance from the sun, it sets in the evening long before the end of twilight; and when it rises before the sun, the latter luminary rises so soon after it that it is never free from the presence of so much solar light as to render it extremely difficult to see the planet with the naked eye. In short, Mercury is seldom seen at all, except with a telescope. It is said that Copernicus himself never saw this planet.

OF THE PLANET VENUS.

The planet VENUS is, on many accounts, more favorably circumstanced for telescopic observation than Mercury. Its diameter is nearly equal to that of the earth, and nearly three times as great as that of Mercury. Its distance from the sun being about seventy millions of miles, it separates itself in its periodical course so widely from the sun, that when it is east of the sun it remains above the horizon in the evening after night-fall; and when it is west of the sun it rises in the morning so long before the hour of sunrise that it is distinctly visible. Owing to the absence of the solar light, it forms, therefore, the object with which every one is familiar, under the names of the morning and evening star. It is subject, by the operation of the same causes, to the same variety of appearances as Mercury. When it is nearly between the earth and the sun it appears a thin crescent, and when beyond the sun it appears full; and in the intermediate positions exhibits, like Mercury, all the variety of phases of the moon.

DIURNAL MOTION OF VENUS AND MERCURY.

One of the most interesting objects of telescopic inquiry regarding the condition of the planets is, the question as to their diurnal rotation. In general, the manner in which we should seek to ascertain this fact would be, by examining with powerful telescopes the marks observable upon the disk of the planet. If the planet revolves upon an axis, these marks, being carried round with it, would appear to move across the disk from one side to the other; they would disappear on one side, and, remaining for a certain time invisible, would reappear on the other, passing, as before, across the visible disk. Let any one stand at a distance from a common terrestrial globe, and let it be made to revolve upon its axis: the spectator will see the geographical marks delineated on it pass across the hemisphere which is turned toward him. They will successively disappear and reappear. The same effects must, of course, be expected to be seen upon the several planets, if they have a motion of rotation resembling the diurnal motion of our globe. If this species of observation be attempted with respect to the planets MERCURY and VENUS, we shall immediately find the investigation obstructed by an unexpected difficulty. Their disks present no permanent marks or characteristics. They are, it is true, diversified more or less by lights and shadows, but we soon discover that these varieties of feature are not of a permanent kind; but, on the contrary, that they are continually shifting and changing, like the clouds that float in an atmosphere. It has, in fact, been ascertained, that these appearances in the inferior planets are produced by *clouds*, with which the thick atmosphere that invest them are continually loaded. These clouds are so continuous that they never permit us to see the geographical character of the planets Mercury and Venus at all.

For a long period this circumstance seemed to render futile all attempts to ascertain the rotation of these planets accurately. At length, however, a circumstance, apparently accidental, led CASSINI and SCHRÖTER to the discovery of the fact of the rotation of VENUS on its axis.

This discovery was effected by observing that the points of the horns of the crescent of Venus were at certain moments cut off square, and after a certain time would recover their sharpness. This was found to take place nearly at the same time each successive evening and morning. The cause was soon ascertained. In a certain part of the surface of the planet a lofty mountain flung its shadow across the region which formed a point to the horn. The diurnal rotation of the planet soon carried this point into another position, so that the shadow disappeared and allowed the horn of the crescent to recover its sharpness. Each time that the horn became thus blunted, it was ascertained that the mountain had returned to the same position, and consequently that the planet must have completed one revolution on its axis.

It is a remarkable fact, that the same circumstance was found to take place in the instance of the planet MERCURY, and the result has been, that these two planets have been ascertained to have a diurnal rotation; that of MERCURY being completed in 24 hours, 5 minutes, 28 seconds, and that of VENUS in 23 hours, 21 minutes, 7 seconds. Thus it appears the alternations of day and night in these planets are regulated by the same intervals as the earth.

DIRECTION OF THE AXIS OF ROTATION.—SEASONS, CLIMATES, AND ZONES.

The position of the axis on which a planet revolves, is ascertained by observing the direction of the apparent motion of the permanent marks upon its disk—the axis being necessarily perpendicular to such motion. Since, however, the rotation of MERCURY and VENUS, as we have just explained, do not show the apparent motion of any of these permanent marks, the circumstances which led to the discovery of their rotation, did not indicate the position of the axes on which they turned. It is said, however, that observations have been made which justify the conclusion that the axis on which the planet VENUS turns, has a position in reference to its orbit very different indeed from that of the earth. Let it be remembered, that the axis of the earth leans from the perpendicular through an angle of $23\frac{1}{2}°$, in consequence of which the polar circles and tropics have corresponding limits. It is this arrangement which divides the surface of our globe into the temperate and frigid zones; the temperate being those which lie between the tropics and the polar circles, in which the sun is never vertical, on the one hand, nor, on the other hand, is ever absent for twenty-four successive hours. How different must be the circumstances attending the planet Venus, if it be true, as there seems reason to believe, that the axis of that planet, instead of being inclined $23\frac{1}{2}^{\circ}$ from the perpendicular, is inclined 75° from it. The polar circles would include a portion of each hemisphere, the extent of which would be five sixths of its entire breadth. Thus the greater portion of such a globe would be subject to vicissitudes somewhat similar to those which are incidental to our frigid zone, but the changes would be much more complicated. Within a certain space of such a planet, the sun would at one season of the year pass through the zenith, and the circumstances of the day would resemble those between our own tropics; while at another period of the year, the sun would never rise for twenty-four hours. In fact, the polar circle would overlay the tropics, and the phenomena of each zone would alternately prevail at different seasons.

The position of the axis of Mercury is not ascertained, but there is reason to believe that, like that of Venus, it is inclined at a very large angle from the perpendicular.

ORBITS AND TRANSITS OF MERCURY AND VENUS.

The motion of the planets Mercury and Venus, like that of the other bodies of the system, is very nearly in the plane of the ecliptic. The orbit of Mercury makes with the plane of the ecliptic an angle of 7°, and that of Venus an angle of less than 4°; the consequence of which is, that these planets are never seen much above or below the ecliptic. The apparent diameter of the sun is about half a degree; consequently the greatest distance to which Venus can depart from the ecliptic, will be less than eight diameters of the sun; and the greatest distance of the planet Mercury from it will be fourteen diameters of the sun. The points at which these planets are seen upon the ecliptic are called the NODES of the orbits; and if at the time they pass near these nodes they happen to be in inferior conjunction, they may be directly between the eye of the observer on the earth and the sun's disk. In that case, they would be seen as a black spot moving in the sun's disk. In order that this remarkable phenomenon, which is called a *transit*, should take place, it is obviously necessary that the distance of the disk of the planet from the place of the sun's centre should be less than half the sun's apparent diameter; that is, less than fifteen minutes of a degree. If, then, the distance of either of the inferior planets from the ecliptic at the time they are in inferior conjunction be less than fifteen minutes, there must be a transit; and the less that distance is, the greater the extent of the sun's disk over which the planet will be seen moving. If the planet be exactly in its node at the time of the inferior conjunction, then it will be passing directly across the centre of the sun.

It will be evident that the part of the sun's disk in which the planet is seen projected in a transit, will also depend on the position of the observer upon the earth. It may happen that, from some parts of the earth, the planet would not be projected upon the solar disk at all; and, in short, at different parts of the earth, the line of its projected course will necessarily be different. These effects will depend on the extent of the earth, and its distance from the sun and the planet.

These phenomena have, therefore, supplied a very happy expedient by which the distance of the sun from the earth may be exactly ascertained. The transit of Venus is especially applicable to this investigation, and has been used with signal success. When the transit of the planet occurred in 1769, observers were sent by different European governments to the most favorable parts of the earth for observing it: some to Otaheite, some to Cajaneburgh in Swedish Lapland, and elsewhere. The result of their observations proved that the distance of the sun from the earth is ninety-five millions of miles.

The intervals between the successive transits at each node are 8 and 113 years. The following are the series of transits to take place for the next four centuries :—

		h. m.
1874	Dec. 9	4 8 A. M.
1882	Dec. 6	4 16 P. M.
2004	June 8	8 51 A. M.
2012	June 6	1 17 A. M.
2117	Dec. 11	2 57 A. M.
2125	Dec. 18	3 9 P. M.
2247	June 11	0 21 P. M.
2255	June 9	4 44 A. M.

The duration of a transit depends on the part of the sun's disk on which the planet is projected. It may last so long as seven hours, if the planet pass across the centre of the disk of the sun.

The last transit of Mercury took place on the 7th of November, 1835. It was visible in this country but not in Europe, the sun having set there before its commencement. The next transit will happen in the present year, 1845, on the 8th of May: it will commence at nineteen minutes past four in the afternoon, and will terminate at nine minutes before eleven at night, Greenwich time. At New York it will begin and end four hours and fifty-six minutes earlier; it will therefore begin at twenty-three minutes past eleven in the forenoon, and will terminate at five minutes before six in the afternoon. The entire transit will therefore be visible in the United States.

The transits of Mercury during the present century will be as follows :—

		h. m.
1845	May 8	7 54 P. M.
1848	Nov. 9	1 38 P. M.
1861	Nov. 12	7 20 P. M.
1868	Nov. 5	6 44 A. M.
1878	May 6	6 38 P. M.
1881	Nov. 8	0 40 A. M.
1891	May 10	2 45 A. M.
1894	Nov. 10	6 17 P. M.

The times here given are the mean times at Greenwich of the middle of the transit.

MOUNTAINS ON MERCURY AND VENUS.

It is supposed that mountains of extraordinary elevation prevail both in Mercury and Venus. Those upon Venus are estimated to be about four times higher than upon the earth.

Sir William Herschel was unable to distinguish any permanent marks on Mercury. Schroter, however, has been more successful. This astronomer has discovered mountains on the surface of the planet, and has even succeeded in ascertaining the height of some of them. One of them he found to rise to an altitude of 5,600 feet, and another to the scarcely credible height of nearly eleven miles, being nearly four times the height of Ætna or the peak of Teneriffe, and more than double the height of the loftiest mountain on the earth. It is remarkable that the highest mountains in Mercury are situated in the southern hemisphere of the planet.

Schroter, to whose observations we are indebted for much of the knowledge that we possess of the planet Venus, showed the existence of several mountains on that planet, the height of some of which he estimated to amount to twenty-two miles. There were three which he estimated: the first at nineteen miles, or five times the height of Chimborazo; the second at eleven and a half miles; and the third at ten and three quarters miles.

INFLUENCE OF THE SUN AT MERCURY AND VENUS.

The distance of the earth from the sun being greater than that of Mercury in the ratio of 100 to 39, or nearly 5 to 2, the apparent diameter of the sun as seen from Mercury will be greater than as seen from the earth in the same ratio. If E represent the apparent magnitude of the sun as seen from the earth, M will represent it as seen from Mercury.

The intensity of the sun's light being in the proportion of the area of its apparent disk, will be greater at Mercury than at the earth in the ratio of 25 to 4, or nearly as 6 to 1. If the heat depended solely on the sun's rays, it would be in the same proportion greater than at the earth, but this may be modified by many causes in operation on the planet and in its atmosphere.

The distance of the earth from the sun is greater than that of Venus in the ratio of 10 to 7 nearly, and consequently the apparent diameter of the sun as seen from Venus will be greater in the same ratio than as seen from the earth. If E represent the apparent magnitude of the sun as seen from the earth, V will represent its apparent magnitude as seen from Venus.

The intensity of the sun's light at Venus will be about twice its intensity at the earth.

TWILIGHT ON VENUS AND MERCURY.

The existence of an extensive twilight in these planets has been well ascertained. By observing the concave edge of the crescent which corresponds to the boundary of the illuminated and dark hemispheres of the planets, it is found that the enlightened portion does not terminate suddenly, but there is a gradual fading away of the light into the darkness, produced by the band of atmosphere illuminated by the sun which overhangs a part of the dark hemisphere, and produces upon it the phenomena of twilight.

When we examine the dark hemisphere of the planet *Venus*, there is observed upon occasions a faint reddish and grayish light, which is visible on parts too distant from the illuminated hemisphere to be produced by the light of the sun. It is supposed that these effects are indications of the play of some atmospheric phenomena in this planet similar to the *aurora borealis*.

OF THE PLANET MARS.

Proceeding outward in the solar system from the sun, the first planet which we find revolving beyond the earth and including the annual path of the earth within its periodical course is the planet MARS. This body makes its revolution round the sun at a distance of nearly one hundred and fifty millions of miles from that luminary, and completes its revolution in six hundred and eighty-six days, or a little less than two years.

When the earth is between Mars and the sun, the distance of the planet from the earth is less than fifty millions of miles, and as it is then seen in the meridian at midnight, the circumstances are extremely favorable to telescopic observation. Although its distance from the earth at that epoch is greater than that of Venus when near inferior conjunction, yet as Venus in that position has her dark hemisphere turned to the earth, while the enlightened hemisphere of Mars is turned fully toward us, the observations made on the latter are more satisfactory.

The diameter of Mars is about half that of our globe, and it has been found by the observations of Arago that its polar diameter is little less than its equatorial, and that consequently, like the earth, it is an oblate spheroid.

As the planet includes the orbit of the earth within its periodical course round the sun, the hemisphere which it presents to the sun is always very nearly, although not exactly, presented to the earth ; the consequence of which is that Mars is always seen with a full phase, or very slightly gibbous. It has the appearance of a reddish star

DIURNAL ROTATION OF MARS.

On examining with a sufficiently powerful telescope the disk of Mars, it is found to be characterized by features of lights and shadows, like those which prevail on the other planets. These were observed at a very early period in the progress of astronomical discovery. There are diagrams given in the first volume of the "*Philosophical Transactions*," showing telescopic views of this planet.

By attentively watching these marks, they have been observed to move in parallel lines east and west—to disappear at one side of the disk, and to reappear after equal intervals at the other side. Hence it was discovered at a very early epoch by CASSINI that Mars has a diurnal motion upon its axis in a time very little different from that of the earth. Cassini's estimation of the time of rotation of this planet was twenty-four hours and forty minutes. A more accurate estimate proves it to be twenty-four hours, thirty-nine minutes, and twenty-one seconds. The axis on which it turns, and which is perpendicular to the lines in which the marks on the disk move, is at an angle of about thirty degrees from the perpendicular to its orbit. When it is remembered that the earth's axis is inclined at an angle of twenty-three and a half degrees, and that it is this inclination which produces the succession of seasons, and which divides the earth into zones and climates, it will be easily inferred that the same phenomena prevails in Mars—the limits of the seasons being little more extreme than those which prevail in the earth.

ATMOSPHERE OF MARS.

The existence of an atmosphere upon Mars is proved by the gradual diminution which the light of a star suffers as his disk approaches it, and by the variable character of the lights and shadows apparent upon the disk. The ruddy appearance of the planet has been explained by the supposition of an atmosphere of great density around it; but more accurate telescopic observations have led Herschel and others rather to incline to the opinion that this redness must be ascribed to a peculiar color prevailing on the surface of the planet, like that of the red sandstone districts upon the earth. A slight appearance of belts has always been noticed on this planet, which affords another indication of an atmosphere, as will be more clearly understood when the belts of Jupiter and Saturn shall be explained.

PHYSICAL CONSTITUTION OF MARS.

Telescopic inquiry has been directed to determine the physical condition of this planet, and with a degree of success greater perhaps than that which has attended similar inquiries respecting any other body in the solar system, except the sun and moon. Sir William Herschel, and after him his son, Sir John Herschel, ascertained the form and position of a variety of the features of light and color on the disk; but it has been reserved for the Prussian astronomers, BEER and MADLER, to carry this inquiry to a much greater degree of detailed accuracy.

Sir John Herschel made a series of observations on Mars within the last fourteen years, and supplied a telescopic drawing of one hemisphere of the planet. We annex a figure exhibiting this sketch.

He stated that the outlines here exhibited were found to be permanent and unvariable, and must therefore be regarded as geographical and not atmospheric features. It is true that they were not always visible, being sometimes obscured, or varied by what seems to be clouds; but when visible they were always the same. Some portions appeared of a reddish color, while others had a greenish tint. He supposes the red portions to be land whose geological character im-

parts to them that peculiar color. The greenish portions he inferred to be seas.

Among the features apparent on this planet, what attracted most attention are certain white spots seen around the polar regions. These were among the very first permanent marks discovered on the planet, and are represented even in the first rude drawing given of its telescopic appearances in the proceedings of the Royal Society. In the observations of Herschel—both father and son—they have, however, been more rigorously examined and described; and still more so in the investigations of Beer and Mädler.

It has been ascertained from the changes they undergo that they must be produced by deposites of snow in the polar regions. Herschel observed that when the pole had been turned from the sun during the winter, and first reappeared in the spring of the planet, the whiteness was most extensive and vivid; and that when the same pole was exposed to the influence of the sun during the summer, which is double the length of the summer upon the earth, this whiteness gradually diminished, and always disappeared. Such indications cannot be mistaken, and admit of no other explanations save what I have now adverted to.

The elaborate observations of Beer and Mädler have supplied various telescopic views of this planet. In their work upon this subject they have published forty views of hemispheres made by planes passing nearly through the poles, which is the only view presented to the observer by the planet. Having, by combining together many observations, made as it were a survey of the entire surface of the globe of Mars, they have given two views, one of its northern and the other of its southern hemisphere.

We have obtained copies of these views, and have affixed them here. Two of the views of this planet, bounded by a circle passing nearly through its poles, are annexed. The views of the hemispheres are given on page 12.

HAS MARS A SATELLITE?

Analogy naturally suggests the probability that the planet Mars might have a moon. These attendants appear to be supplied to the planets in augmented numbers as they recede from the sun; and if this analogy were complete, it would justify the inference that Mars must at least have one, being more remote from the sun than the earth, which is supplied with a satellite. No moon has ever been discovered in connexion with Mars. It has, however, been contended that we are not therefore to conclude that the planet is destitute of such an appendage; for as all secondary planets are much less than their primaries, and as Mars is by far the smallest of the superior planets, its satellite, if such existed, must be extremely small. The second satellite of Jupiter is only the forty-third part of the diameter of the planet; and a satellite which would only be the forty-third part of the diameter of Mars, would be under one hundred miles in diameter. Such an object could scarcely be dis-

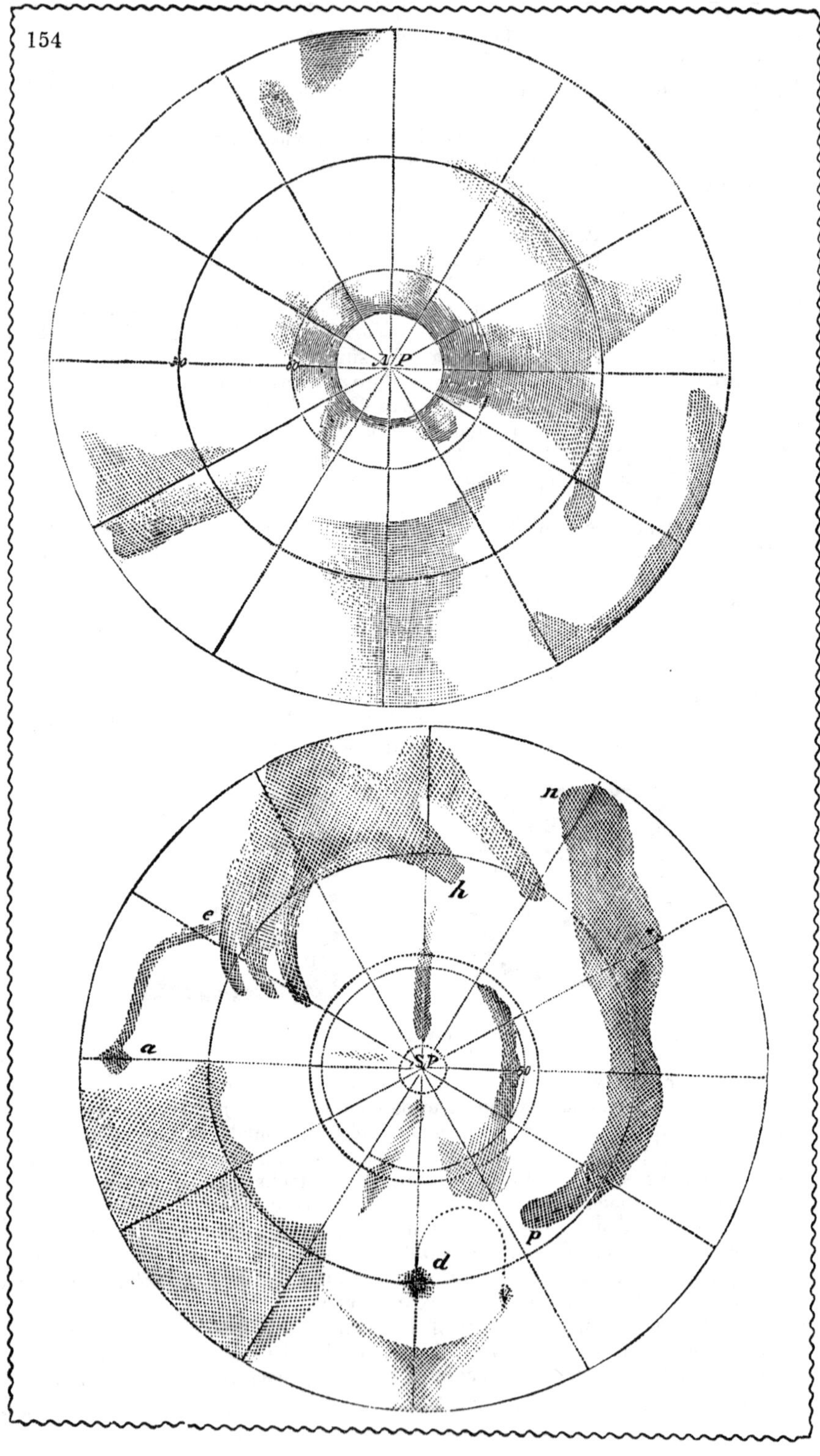
N P
S P
h
n
a
p
d

covered, even by powerful telescopes, especially if it did not recede far from the disk of the planet.

APPEARANCE OF THE SUN AT MARS.

The distance of Mars from the sun being greater than that of the earth in the proportion of three to two, it follows that the apparent magnitude of the sun to the inhabitants of Mars will be less than to the inhabitants of the earth in the same proportion. In the annexed diagram, if E represents the appearance of the sun to the earth, M will represent its appearance at Mars.

The light which it affords will be in the same proportion as its apparent magnitude; and as the superficial magnitude of the disk will be about half that which it presents to the earth, it follows that the intensity of the sun's light at Mars will be less in the same proportion. But, for the reasons which have been elsewhere stated, no safe inference can be made respecting the effect of the sun on the temperature of the planets.

The close analogy in which this planet stands to the earth will be apparent to those who have considered the facts and phenomena now described. It is a globe whose diurnal motion is such as to give it days of the same length ; its seasons succeeding each other in the same manner, and are limited by the same extremes of temperature. Its latitudes are diversified by the same torrid, temperate, and frigid zones, and the same varieties of climate. Its surface is characterized by a like distribution of land and water ; and, like the earth, it has its continents, islands, and seas. It is invested with an atmosphere, supplying doubtless all the interesting objects and advantages which result from our own.

WEATHER ALMANACS.

Merits of Weather Almanacs.—Excitability of the London Public.—Fright produced by Biela's Comet.—London Water Panic.—London Air Panic.—London Bread Panic.—Rage for Weather Almanacs.—Patrick Murphy's Pretensions.—Examination of the Predictions of the Weather Almanac.—Their Absurdity.—Comparison of the Predictions with the Event—Morrison's Weather Almanac—Charlatanism of these Publications.—Great Frost of 1838 in London.—Other Visitations of Cold.

WEATHER ALMANACS.

NOTE.—The subject of weather almanacs having occasionally been introduced in an abridged form in my lectures, I have thought it best to give it here in the form in which I originally presented it in London, when a rage for this sort of scientific charlatanism prevailed in an extraordinary degree. The following appeared in the spring of 1838.

IF the weather almanacs presented no other claims to our attention than those which rest upon their intrinsic importance, they would assuredly never have been noticed by us. We should as soon think of discussing their merits among our scientific discourses, as of reviewing the performances of the penny theatres, or the buffoonery of the booths at Bartholomew fair. When, however, we are told that the circulation of some of these publications is reckoned by hundreds of thousands, and that at a price which would impose a narrow limit on the sale on any ordinary *brochure* of equal bulk—and when we know, as we do, that this enormous circulation is not either exclusively or principally confined to the lower and less-informed classes, but extends to those who are, or ought to be, the best educated and most enlightened—we feel that, however much beneath scientific criticism such productions may be, they have acquired some claims to attention from the success with which they have wrought upon the credulity of the "most thinking people" in the world.

It is astonishing, in this age of the diffusion of knowledge, how susceptible the public mind is of excitement on any topic, the principles of which do not lie absolutely on the surface of the most ordinary course of elementary education. It was only in the year 1832 that a general alarm spread throughout France, lest Biela's comet, in its progress through the solar system, should strike the earth; and the authorities in that country, with a view to tranquillize the public, induced M. Arago, the astronomer royal, to publish an essay on comets, written in a familiar and intelligible style, to show the impossibility of such an event.

Several panics in England, connected with physical questions, have occurred within our memory. There prevailed in London a "water panic," during which the public was persuaded that the water supplied to the metropolis was destructive to health and life. While this lasted, the papers teemed with announcements of patent filtering machines; solar-microscope makers displayed to the terrified Londoners troops of thousand-legged animals disporting in their daily beverage; publishers were busy with popular treatises on entomology; and the public was seized with a general hydrophobia. It was in vain that Brande analyzed the water at the Royal Institute, and Faraday attempted to reason London into its senses. Knowledge ceased to be power; philosophy lost its authority. Time was, however, more efficacious than science; and the paroxysms of the disease having passed through their appointed phases, the people were convalescent. There was at another time a panic against atmospheric air, during which the inhabitants of the great metropolis (in a literal sense) scarcely dared to breathe. The combustion of coal was denounced as the great evil in this case. Calculations were circulated of the number of cubic feet of sulphurous gas taken into the lungs of each adult inhabitant per annum; the properties of carbonic acid were discussed behind counters; patent furnaces were plentifully invented and advertised for sale; and parliament was urged to pass a bill for the purification of the atmosphere, and to compel all who used fires to consume their own smoke.

A few years ago, the people of London were seized with a persuasion that bakers used a poisonous substance to *bleach* the necessary article of food which they manufactured, and forthwith a *bread panic* arose. A joint-stock-digestive-brown-bread company was immediately formed. "Fancy baker," a title previously assumed as a recommendation to their customers' favor, was painted over; brown loaves usurped the place of French rolls; and the lacquey, whose master adhered to his old taste in defiance of poison, as he sought for white loaves, hummed—

"Tell me where is fancy *bread*."

In 1838, the public turned its attention to meteorology, and the causes which govern the changes of weather was the all-absorbing topic. Some of the intelligent conductors of the daily and weekly press seriously descanted on the great advantages which would accrue to the farmer, the gardener, the manufacturer, the mariner, and others, from the certain prediction of the weather, and looked forward, evidently not without hope, to an early period when, by a new principle of science discovered by a Mr. Murphy, and he said, "probably known only to himself"—

"Careful observers may foretell the hour,
By sure prognostics, when to dread a shower."

Among the gifted individuals to whom it has been vouchsafed to see the shadows which coming events cast before them, and who have conferred on the public the inestimable benefit of their knowledge, the most conspicuous was a gentleman who took the appellation and appendages of P. Murphy, Esquire, M. N. S. What prænomen is indicated by P., we are not certainly informed, but we believe it to be that of the patron saint of the Emerald isle, of which this weather-seer is said to be a native. Indeed, there is abundant proof of his country, in the prevalence throughout his writings of that peculiar species of modesty which is generally considered characteristic of the "Land of Song." We have, however, looked in vain among the many combinations of letters expressing the various learned societies in this and other countries for the signification of M. N. S. We have found societies designated by every letter in the alphabet, from the Astronomical to the Zoological, the letter N alone excepted.

After all, the name of Patrick Murphy may be unwarrantably assumed. Francis Moore, physician, has long been so; and a table, miscalled Herschel's weather-table, obtained confidence from its unauthorized adoption of the name of that eminent astronomer. Perhaps the weather almanac has as little relation to the veritable Patrick Murphy as Herschel's weather-table had to the great telescopic observer; and as it was beneath the dignity of Sir William even to disavow such trash as the weather-table, so Sir Patrick may possibly rely on the dignity of his station, and his reputation among the numerous members of the N—— Society, as a sufficient refutation of this imposture.

Until the appearance of the weather almanac, the pretenders to prediction confined their forebodings to the general character of the weather at particular epochs. In the weather almanac there was, however, a distinct prediction for every successive day of the year. Every possible variety of weather was reduced under one or other of three denominations—*fair*, *rain*, and *changeable*; one or other of these words being affixed to each day of the year. For some days there was added one or other of the words *frost*, *wind*, *storm*, or *thunder*.

A precaution was taken in the preface to explain the meaning in which these several terms are intended to be received.

Fair, means a day in which drought is expected to predominate.

Rain, a day in which rain is expected to predominate.

Changeable, a day in which it is uncertain whether drought or rain will predominate.

To be enabled fairly to compare the predictions with the facts, it is necessary that these explanations of the terms *fair*, *rain*, and *changeable*, be clearly understood.

Does *rain*, we would ask, include snow, hail, and sleet? We must presume that it does, since these vicissitudes are not otherwise expressed in the almanac.

Does *drought* signify anything more than the absence of rain, snow, or sleet? We shall presume that it does, because otherwise this very common state of the weather would have no designation in the nomenclature of the weather almanac, and we should have a prediction of a severe frost in January, without any prediction of the thaw which follows it.

The term "predominate," used in these explanations, we take to refer to *duration*. Thus, if in twenty-fours, rain fall for less than twelve hours, the day is to be designated *fair*, since drought *predominates;* and if rain fall for more than twelve hours, then the day is to be designated *rain*, since rain *predominates*.

The causes which govern the phenomena of weather being physical agencies independent of the will or interference of any being save of Him "who rules the storm," are as fixed and as certain in their operation, and as regular in the production of their effects, as those which maintain and regulate the motions of the solar system. The moment of the rising or setting of the sun on any given day of the ensuing year is therefore, *in the nature of things*, not more certain than the atmospheric phenomena which will take place on that day. The doubt and uncertainty which attend these events belong altogether to our anticipations of them, and not to the things themselves. If our knowledge of meteorology were as advanced as our knowledge of astronomy, we should be in a condition to declare the time, duration, and intensity, of every shower which shall fall during the ensuing year, with as much certainty and precision as we are able to foretell the rising, setting, and southing, of the sun and moon, or the rise and fall of the tides of the ocean. When it is said, therefore, that drought or rain is *expected* to predominate, the uncertainty implied by the term *expected* must be understood to belong to the knowledge, or rather ignorance, of him who makes the prediction, and not to the event, which, as we have shown, is *necessary*, and not *contingent*.

But the most absurd of these explanations is that of the word *changeable*, which is here used in a most novel sense. Changeable weather, in the ordinary use of the word, is applied to weather which changes frequently and suddenly at short intervals, from fair and clear to cloudy and wet. But the weather-almanac sense of this term is, weather *in which it is uncertain whether drought or rain will predominate*. Now, as we have already shown that no uncertainty can attend the weather itself, but that the uncertainty belongs only to the mind of the author of the weather almanac, it will be necessary to remember that changeable weather is weather about which the said author confesses that he has no foreknowledge; thus, though for a week the face of the heavens continue clear and cloudless, the temperature of the air mild and uniform, and the atmosphere calm and still, yet the weather during such week might be *changeable*, according to the weather almanac, and its author would claim the credit of a prediction fulfilled. In fact, every day in the year to which he has annexed the word changeable, *must* fulfil his prediction, whatever be the state of the weather; since, happen what will, no one can doubt the uncertainty of the author's own mind as to the event, when that uncertainty is itself the essence of his prediction.

The author states, that by *wind* he means *a gale*, excluding from this term light winds; also, that by *storm* he means *a more violent gale;* and that *thunder* and *storm* are to be considered to a certain extent synonymous, it being not always possible to decide in which way these phenomena will develop themselves.

To these explanations we have nothing to object, and have only to say, that it were better for the author's reputation for honesty or sanity, if he had carried his *indecision* to a much greater extent. We are told in the preface, that—

"When it is taken into account that, as connected with the principles and laws of movement, of temperature, &c., in the sun and planets—a totally new class of proofs—*never, perhaps, so much as supposed to exist by the immortal Newton, nor by any other, is proposed by the present work;* and which, if found, to a certain extent, correct, will have the effect of placing these departments of science a century in advance; it will be allowed that, independent of its utility in other respects, this should be sufficient to secure it a favorable reception from an enlightened public.

"In regard to the principles themselves on which the calculations of the weather are founded, it will be sufficient to say that, as, according to any principles hitherto known or recognised, calculations of the kind could not be made, the circumstances necessarily presupposes the discovery of others; and as showing the connexion of the latter with, it may be said every department of the physical sciences, and, consequently, with the interests of every class of society—a *scientific notice* is subjoined by the editor, in order that such of the patrons of the almanac as may feel disposed to obtain information on the subject, may have the opportunity to consult his views."

On reading this, we turned with strong feelings of curiosity to the *scientific notice*, in the hope of being informed of the "totally new class of proofs, never supposed to exist by the immortal Newton, *nor by any other*." But alas! so imperfect was our intellectual vision, that we looked in vain, and we forced ourselves *with those others* who, in common with "the immortal Newton," not only never supposed such proofs to exist, but cannot persuade ourselves even now of their existence. In truth, were it not for the high scientific reputation of

Mr. Murphy, and the respect we entertain for the discrimination of the members of the N—— society, who elected him into their body, we would pronounce the said scientific notice to be as sheer and unmitigated nonsense as it has ever been our fortune to encounter. As matters stand, however, we must ascribe all to the feebleness of our own powers compared to those of Mr. Murphy.

Having thus candidly acknowledged our inability to comprehend the author's theory of meteoric action, the sublimity of which we shall not be so presumptuous as to doubt, much less to dispute, we must be content with the more humble office of comparing the predictions of the Weather Almanac with the actual phenomena, so far as time has converted the future into the past. We have the less hesitation in adopting this test of the validity of the author's principles, as it is one which he has himself courted.

"The event in reference to these predictions being thus admitted to be in some degree *contingent*, it may be asked—If *certainty* cannot be attached to the prediction, of what use can it be? To this we answer, that the exceptions in reference to the predictions as marked in the tables, will, it is anticipated, be found to bear but a small proportion to the remainder; and in our turn we shall demand, if, in nine cases out of ten, the event be found to correspond with the prediction, does it follow, because *one* of the anticipated effects, as set down in the table, does not take place, that the public is to remain ignorant of the remaining nine? For if an objection such as this were valid, it were the same to say, because the quadrature of the circle cannot be found, that the practical parts of mathematics should be abandoned: such exceptions, as in other cases, serve but the more fully to prove the rule, as to the correctness of the principles of calculation on which the predictions in the tables are founded."

Undoubtedly nothing could be more unreasonable or unphilosophical; nay, we will go further, and will admit that the author must be classed among the great lights of the age, if his predictions be fulfilled even in a much smaller ratio than that which he proposes. Nothing can be more true than the observation with which he concludes his preface:—

"It may not, however, be amiss to add, in regard to these principles of calculation, that, though by *chance* the state of the weather at any particular time might *possibly* be predicted, that it is quite different as refers to a *number of facts:* as to attempt to follow the sinuosities of the weather (as in the present almanac) from fair to rain and from rain to fair, even for *seven days consecutively*, without the aid of correct principles, were about the same as to attempt a discourse in an unknown tongue; the thing never having been done before, and for a sufficiently simple reason, because it was utterly impossible."

Let us see whether the author has "followed the sinuosities of the weather" even for three days successively.

We have before us, on the one hand, the predictions of the Weather Almanac for the first forty-eight days of the present year, and on the other, the Meteorological Journal, kept by order of the council of the Royal Society during that time. We shall resolve these forty-eight days into three classes: 1st, Those on which the weather *fulfilled* the prediction; 2d, Those on which the weather *did not fulfil* the prediction; and, 3d, Those for which no prediction was made, which, as we have already shown, is the case of all those days to which changeable is annexed.

In deciding whether the prediction has been fulfilled or not, we have been careful to follow those explanations of his terms which the author has very properly given in his preface; and when the character of the day, as recorded in the journal of the Royal Society, has been doubtful, as compared with the prediction, we have given the author the benefit of it:—

Prediction fulfilled—Jan. 7, 8, 12, 13, 19, 20, 26, 27, 28; Feb. 1, 6, 9, 10, 13. Number of days, 14.

Prediction not fulfilled—Jan. 1, 2, 3, 9, 10, 11, 15, 16, 17, 18, 24, 25, 30, 31; Feb. 3, 8, 12, 14, 16, 17. Number of days, 20.

No prediction made—Jan. 4, 5, 6, 14, 21, 22, 23, 29; Feb. 2, 4, 5, 7, 11, 15. Number of days, 14.

Thus it appears that, of forty-eight days, the weather corresponded with the prediction on fourteen; it did not correspond with it on twenty; and on the fourteen remaining days no prediction was made.

Now, we will ask, if any person of common observation acquainted with the climate of the country, were to annex to each of the first forty-eight successive days of the year at hazard, the characters of weather generally found to prevail at that season, whether he would not, according to all probability, be right in a greater number of cases than fourteen in forty-eight, that is, one case in three and a half?

The predictions of the Weather Almanac, then, fail in seventeen cases out of twenty-four! yet this is the production which the public bought, at a high price, by the hundred thousand! This is the production for which the demand was so urgent, and for which the public impatience was so irrepressible, that the shop of the bookseller, like those of bakers in a famine, was obliged to be protected by the police, so violent was the demand of the thousands who flocked to obtain it!

By reference to the above table it will be seen, that there is no case in which the predictions have been fulfilled, even for three successive days, except from the 26th to the 28th of January inclusive. Even in that case, the prediction for the 26th agrees but imperfectly with the event; the prediction being *fair*, without mention of wind or frost, while the Meteorological Journal says overcast; brisk wind the whole day; sharp frost. Much of the attention this publication received has been ascribed to the supposed fulfilment of the prediction for the 20th of January, which is marked in the Weather Almanac as the lowest winter temperature. This was a fortuitous coincidence, such as happens frequently in other cases, as in the fulfilment of dreams, &c. We shall not insist here on the fact, that the 20th was *not* the day of the greatest cold by the diary of the Royal Society, since the thermometer fell a little lower on the 16th, because we think it really unimportant.*

But it may be said, that, although the prediction has failed as to the exact time at which the several changes took place, yet, in the main, the changes predicted *did* take place, and that the prediction "followed the sinuosities of the weather."

Let us, then, see how far the predictions in the Weather Almanac will bear a comparison with the actual succession of changes.

Actual succession of changes.		Succession of changes predicted.	
Number of days.		*Number of days.*	
6	Mild and warm.	3	Frost.
14	Frost.	3	Changeable.
3	Thaw.	7	Frost.
4	Frost.	1	Changeable.
4	Thaw.	6	Frost.
6	Frost.	3	Changeable.
3	Thaw.	2	Rain.

* The thermometer at the Horticultural Society is said to have been four degrees below zero on the night of the 19th and 20th. This is so much at variance with the journal of the Royal Society, that we doubt the accuracy of the observation.

8 Frost.	3 Frost.
—	1 Changeable.
48	1 Rain.
	2 Frost.
	1 Changeable.
	1 Rain.
	2 Changeable.
	1 Fair.
	1 Changeable.
	2 Rain.
	1 Fair.
	1 Changeable.
	1 Rain and wind.
	1 Fair.
	1 Rain and wind.
	1 Changeable.
	1 Rain.
	1 Fair and frost.
	—
	48

We shall leave it to the skill of our readers to discover where the correspondence lies between "the sinuosities of the weather," and the sinuosities of Mr. Murphy's predictions. Dismissing this very absurd publication, to which we have given more space than it deserves, we shall merely add, that it is not the only production of the kind which public credulity fostered into life. Besides the eternal Francis Moore, physician, we had also the Meteorological Almanac, and Farmers' and Shipmasters' Guide, containing the general character of the weather all through the year 1838, by Lieutenant Morrison, R.N., Member of the London Meteorological Society, and numerous others.

Without further discussing the prognostications of such persons, or comparing them with facts, we shall merely ask those who appear to afford them so easy faith, to consider the nature of the physical questions pretended to be solved, and the qualifications of those who profess to have solved them. The investigation of the causes which affect the atmosphere and produce the vicissitudes of temperature and of drought, is a problem of transcendent difficulty, to the solution of which even the most extensive powers of modern science are inadequate. It is a problem to which, hitherto, scarcely an approximation has been made, even by the most eminent natural philosophers ; and, as it is one of the details of which the public in general cannot be expected to understand, they can only regulate the confidence which they will place in its pretended solutions by the reputation and authority of those who propound them.

Who, then, it may be asked, are the persons that put forth those predictions ; and on what grounds do they ask the faith of the public ? Among these prognosticators, is any name found holding a respectable rank in the community of science ? What have the labors and researches of these persons contributed to the actual advancement of our knowledge of nature ? What are the works on which their reputations are founded ? Do these weather-prophets possess any of the recognised qualifications, founded on education and previous attainments which would fit them for encountering such a problem ? What learned societies in Europe have these pretenders enriched by their labors ? Where are the transactions in which their investigations and discoveries have appeared ? These questions would be answered by a mere enumeration of their names—names utterly unknown in philosophy or letters. It would be answered that among them there is found not one individual whose presence would be tolerated in any scientific reunion in Europe. Such are the class of persons to whom the public, in the contemptuous silence of the great leaders and guides of science in every part of the world, surrendered their faith.

As the subject of this article has given us occasion to notice the late visitation of cold, it may be not uninteresting to compare the particulars of that part of the season with similar events in former years.

The weather in London, from last Christmas until the seventh of January, was remarkably fine and mild. During the first four days of January, the thermometer was never lower than 40 degrees, and ranged between that and 50 degrees. On the 6th it fell to 32 degrees, between which and 38 degrees it ranged on that day. On the 7th the severe frost commenced, the thermometer, however, being rather higher on that than on the preceding day. But on the following day (the 8th) the frost became rigorous, the thermometer falling more than four degrees below the freezing point. The temperature continued to fall until the 16th, when it attained the minimum—the thermometer then having descended to 11·4 degrees, which is twenty degrees and a half below the freezing point. A very slight increase of temperature succeeded for the next three days, when, on the 20th, the temperature again fell to 11½ degrees of the thermometer. On that day the thermometer ranged between that temperature and 21 degrees (eleven degrees below the freezing point). This was the day of greatest average cold, though, strictly speaking, it was not the day on which the temperature was lowest. On the 22d and 23d, the thermometer rose to above 40 degrees, and a rapid thaw ensued; which, however, was succeeded by a return of frost—the thermometer again falling seven or eight degrees below the freezing point. On the 29th commenced a rapid thaw, the thermometer rising to 44 degrees on the 30th. Frost succeeded this on the 1st of February, which continued until the 6th, when it was succeeded by a thaw, which continued through the 7th, 8th, and 9th. On the 10th the frost recommenced, and has continued to the moment of writing these observations (the 17th).

Thus between the 7th of January and the 17th of February, the lowest point to which the temperature fell was 11½ degrees, which it attained twice—namely, on the 16th and 20th. The average of the lowest daily temperature throughout this periods was 25⅓; the average of the highest daily temperature was 36¾.

Throughout this frost there was so little snow that the face of the ground was not covered and protected, and vegetables were, consequently, exposed to a temperature so rigorous as to occasion extensive destruction of the products of the garden.

The last severe frost with which this can be compared occurred in January, 1826. On the 8th of that month the thermometer fell one degree below the freezing point, and on the 16th it stood at 17 degrees at 9 in the morning—being fifteen degrees below the freezing point, the lowest temperature recorded since that day to the present time. The frost terminated on the 18th, the thermometer then rising to 36 degrees.

This frost of 1826 can only be compared to the recent cold in the extreme of its temperature, its duration having been only ten days.

A severe frost took place in January, 1814, which continued throughout that month, and did not terminate until the 6th of February. The lowest temperature recorded during this frost is 17 degrees, which was the temperature at 8 in the morning on the 10th. The greatest height of the thermometer throughout the month of January was 40 degrees, and the mean temperature of the month was 28·08. This frost, therefore, in its duration, was less than the late frost; the lowest and mean temperatures were also lower in the present year than in 1814.

In January, 1795, there occurred a frost which, for rigor and continuance, exceeded the present. The mean temperature during that month was about 26 degrees, and on the 25th of the month the thermometer stood at 7 degrees—being 25 degrees below the freezing point. The mean temperature during the frost was about the same as during the present, but the extreme temperature was four degrees lower. Since 1795 till the present time—a period of forty-two years—there has been no cold of intensity and duration equal to the present.

Since the preceding observations were sent to press, we have received a journal of the state of the weather during the last month in Paris, the particulars of which may not be uninteresting to compare with the corresponding phenomena in London. As in London, the first days of the month were mild and fair, the thermometer ranging from the first to the sixth between 33½ degrees and 29 degrees. On the seventh, as in London, the frost commenced, and the thermometer gradually fell until the fourteenth, on which day the maximum temperature was 13 degrees, and the minimum 4 degrees.

The thermometer rose on the fifteenth, but afterward gradually fell until the twentieth, when it attained the lowest temperature of the month. On that day the highest temperature was 21 degrees below the freezing point, and the lowest was 34 degrees below it.

The mean maximum temperature from the first to the tenth was 33½ degrees, and the mean minimum was 27 degrees.

The mean maximum temperature from the eleventh to the twentieth was 19 degrees, and the mean minimum temperature was 8 degrees.

The mean maximum temperature from the twenty-first to the thirty-first was 35 degrees, and the mean minimum temperature was 21 degrees.

The mean maximum temperature throughout the month was 35 degrees, and the mean minimum temperature was 18 degrees.

The absolute mean temperature of the month was a little under 24 degrees.

The fourth and fifth of the month were attended with a thick fog, followed by a clouded sky on the sixth and seventh. Between the seventh and twelfth there occurred a fall of snow, followed by almost continuous fair weather till the twenty-fifth. The last six days of the month were cloudy.

From a comparison of these particulars with those of the weather in London, it will be perceived that the day of the greatest cold was the twentieth in both places, but that the minimum temperature was much lower in Paris. In London the thermometer fell on the twentieth 20 degrees below the freezing point, but in Paris it fell on the same day 34 degrees below it. In London, the highest temperature on the twentieth was 11 degrees below the freezing point; in Paris the highest temperature on the same day was 31 degrees below it. In London the mean temperature of the month was 1 degree above the freezing point; in Paris it was 8 degrees below it.

It will be perceived that the severity of cold in Paris was in every point of view greater than that in London.

It is remarkable, also, that the frost not only commenced on the same day in Paris as in London, but the cold varied in very nearly the same manner, though in different degrees. The increase of temperature perceptible in London on the sixteenth, commenced in Paris on the fifteenth, and was of the same duration. On the twenty-second and twenty-third in London, the thermometer rose to above 40 degrees; and on the same day in Paris it likewise rose to above 40 degrees. This increase of temperature was in like manner followed by a return of frost, which continued till the twenty-ninth, when the thermometer rose to 44 degrees in both places.

The subject of the weather, and the influences which are supposed to affect it, will be noticed on another occasion, when I shall examine in all the necessary detail the question of the supposed influence exerted by the phases of the moon upon the changes of the weather.

HALLEY'S COMET.

Predictions of Science.—Structure of the Solar System.—Motion of Comets.—How to identify them.—Intervals of their Appearance.—Halley's Comet.—Its History.—Newton's Conjectures.—Sagacity of Voltaire.—Halley's Researches.—Foretells the Reappearance of the Comet in 1759.—Principle of Gravitation applied to its Motion by Clairaut.—Researches of that Mathematician.—Anecdotes of Lalande and Madame Lepaute.—Minute and circumstantial Prediction of the Reappearance of Halley's Comet.—Discovery of the Planet Herschel anticipated by Clairaut.—Reappearance of the Comet at the predicted Time.—Second Prediction of its Return in 1835.—Prediction fulfilled.—Observations on its Appearance in 1835.

HALLEY'S COMET.

For the civil and political historian the past alone has existence—the present he rarely apprehends, the future never. To the historian of science it is permitted, however, to penetrate the depths of past and future with equal clearness and certainty; facts to come are to him as present, and not unfrequently more assured than facts which are passed. Although this clear perception of causes and consequences characterizes the whole domain of physical science, and clothes the natural philosopher with powers denied to the political and moral inquirer, yet foreknowledge is eminently the privilege of the astronomer. Nature has raised the curtain of futurity, and displayed before him the succession of her decrees, so far as they effect the physical universe, for countless ages to come; and the revelations of which she has made him the instrument, are supported and verified by a never-ceasing train of predictions fulfilled. He "shows us the things which will be hereafter," not obscurely shadowed out in figures and in parables, as must necessarily be the case with other revelations, but attended with the most minute precision of time, place, and circumstance. He converts the hours as they roll into an ever-present miracle, in attestation of those laws which his Creator through him has unfolded; the sun cannot rise—the moon cannot wane—a star cannot twinkle in the firmament, without bearing witness to the truth of his prophetic records. It has pleased the "Lord and Governor" of the world, in his inscrutable wisdom, to baffle our inquiries into the nature and proximate cause of that wonderful faculty of intellect—that image of his own essence which he has conferred upon us; nay, the springs and wheelwork of animal and vegetable vitality are concealed from our view by an impenetrable veil, and the pride of philosophy is humbled by the spectacle of the physiologist bending in fruitless ardor over the dissection

Note.—A portion of the matter which forms my lectures on Comets, was formerly contributed by me, on various occasions, to the Edinburgh Review, and other leading periodicals in England; and a part was included among the additions to the late edition of Arago's Lectures, edited by me in America

of the human brain, and peering in equally unproductive inquiry over the gambols of an animalcule. But how nobly is the darkness which envelopes metaphysical inquiries compensated by the flood of light which is shed upon the physical creation! *There* all is harmony, and order, and majesty, and beauty. From the chaos of social and political phenomena exhibited in human records—phenomena unconnected to our imperfect vision by any discoverable law, a war of passions and prejudices, governed by no apparent purpose, tending to no apparent end, and setting all intelligible order at defiance—how soothing and yet how elevating it is to turn to the splendid spectacle which offers itself to the habitual contemplation of the astronomer! How favorable to the development of all the best and highest feelings of the soul are such objects! The only passion they inspire being the love of truth, and the chiefest pleasure of their votaries arising from excursions through the imposing scenery of the universe—scenery on a scale of grandeur and magnificence, compared with which whatever we are accustomed to call sublimity on our planet, dwindles into ridiculous insignificancy. Most justly has it been said, that nature has implanted in our bosoms a craving after the discovery of truth, and assuredly that glorious instinct is never more irresistibly awakened then when our notice is directed to what is going on in the heavens. "Quoniam eadem Natura cupiditatem ingenuit hominibus veri inveniendi, quod facillime apparet, cum vacui curis, etiam quid in cœlo fiat, scire avemus; his initiis inducti omnia vera diligimus; id est, fidelia, simplicia, constantia; tum vana, falsa, fallentia odimus." *

Among the multitude of appearances which succeed each other in their appointed order, and of the times and manner of which the perfect knowledge of the astronomer enables him to advertise us, there are some which more powerfully seize upon the popular mind, as well by reason of their infrequency and the extraordinary circumstances which attend them, as by the imaginary consequences with which ignorance and superstition have, in times past and present, invested them. Among these, Solar Eclipses had a prominent place; but a still more interesting position must be assigned to Comets.

It is well known that the solar system, of which our planet forms a part, consists of a number of smaller bodies revolving in paths, which are very nearly circular, round the great mass of the sun placed in the centre. These paths, or orbits, are very nearly in the same plane; that is to say, if the earth, for example, be conceived to be moving on a flat surface, extended as well beyond its orbit as within it, then the other planets never depart much above or below this plane. A spectator placed upon the earth keeps within his view each of the other planets of the system throughout nearly the whole of its course. Indeed, there is no part of the orbit of any planet in which, *at some time or other*, it may not be seen from the earth. Every point of the path of each planet can therefore be observed; and although without waiting for such observation its course might be determined, yet it is material here to attend to the fact, that the whole orbit may be submitted to direct observation. The different planets also present peculiar features by which each may be distinguished. Thus they are observed to be spherical bodies of various magnitudes. The surfaces of some are marked by peculiar modes of light and shade, which, although variable and shifting, still, in each case, possess some prevailing and permanent characters by which the identity of the object may be established, even were there no other means of determining it. The sun is the common centre of attraction, the physical bond by which this planetary family are united, and prevented from wandering independently through the abyss of space. Each planet thus revolving in a circle, has the same tendency to fly from the centre that a

* Cic. de Fin. Bon. et Mal. ii. 14.

stone has when whirled in a sling. Why, then, it will be asked, do not the planets yield to this natural tendency? What enables them to resist it? To this question no satisfactory answer can be given; but the fact that the tendency *is* resisted, being certain, the existence of some physical principle in which the means of such resistance resides, is proved. As the tendency to fly off is directed from the centre of the sun, the opposing physical influence must consequently be directed toward that centre. This central influence is what has been called gravitation. Although we are still ignorant of the nature or proximate cause of this force, and of its *modus operandi*, we have obtained a perfect knowledge of the laws by which it acts; and this is all that is necessary or material to enable us to follow out its consequences. By virtue of this force of gravitation, then, the planetary masses receive a tendency to drop toward the sun, which tendency equilibrates with the opposite tendency to fly away, produced by their orbitual motion. On the exact equilibrium of these two opposite physical principles, depends the stability of the system. If the centrifugal tendency proceeding from the orbitual motion were in excess, the planets would fall off from the central body, and depart for ever into the depths of space; if, on the other hand, the central influence, or gravitation toward the sun, existed in excess, these bodies would gradually approach that luminary, and finally coalesce with his mass.

Besides these bodies, the greater part of which have been long known, and the motions of most of which have been in some degree understood, even from remote antiquity, there is a still more numerous class of objects, whose appearances in the system were of such a nature as to defy the powers of philosophical inquiry, until these powers received that prodigious accession of force which was conferred upon them by the discoveries of Newton. Unlike planets, comets do not present to us those individual characters above mentioned, by which their identity may be determined. None of them have been satisfactorily ascertained to be spherical bodies, nor indeed to have any definite shape. It is certain that many of them possess no solid matter, but are masses consisting entirely of aeriform or vaporous substances; others are so surrounded with this vaporous matter, that it is impossible, by any means of observation which we possess, to discover whether this vapor enshrouds within it any solid mass. The same vapor which thus envelopes the body (if such there be within it), also conceals from us its features and individual character. Even the limits of the vapor itself are subject to great change in each individual comet. Within a few days they are sometimes observed to increase or diminish some hundred fold. A comet appearing at distant intervals, presents, therefore, no very obvious means of recognition. A like extent of surrounding vapor would evidently be a fallible test of identity; and not less inconclusive would it be to infer diversity from a different extent of nebulosity.

If a comet, like a planet, revolved round the sun in an orbit nearly circular, it might be seen in every part of its path, and its identity might thus be established independently of any peculiar characters in its appearance. But such is not the course which comets are observed to take. These bodies usually are observed to rush into our system suddenly and unexpectedly, from some particular quarter of the universe. They first follow in a straight line, or nearly so, the course by which they entered; and this course is commonly directed to some point not far removed from the sun. As they approach that luminary, their path becomes curved; at first slightly, but afterward more and more; the curve being concave toward the sun. Having arrived at a certain least distance from the centre of our system, they again begin to recede from the sun, and as their distance increases, their path becomes less and less curved; until at length they shoot off in a straight course, and make their exit from our system toward some quarter of the universe wholly different from that from which they came.

We have stated that none of the planets depart much above or below the plane of the earth's orbit; it is quite otherwise with comets, which follow no certain law in this respect. Some of them sweep the system nearly in the plane in which the planets move; others rush through it in curves, oblique in various degrees to this plane; while some move in planes perpendicular to it. The planets also move round the sun all in one direction. Comets, on the other hand, rebel against this law, and move, some in one direction and some in another.

So far then as observation informs us, we are left to decide between two suppositions: 1. That the comet has entered the system for the first time; and that having swept behind the sun, it has emerged in a different direction, never to return: 2. That it moves in a large orbit, of which the sun is not the centre, but, on the contrary, is placed very near the path of the body itself; that the comet is visible only in that part of its orbit which is in the immediate neighborhood of the sun, but is invisible throughout that large part, which perhaps extends, through depths of space, far beyond our most remote planet. If the latter supposition be adopted, it would follow that the same comet, after emerging from our system, would, after the lapse of a certain time, return to it, and pursue the same path, or nearly the same path, round the sun as before. If then we find, after the lapse of a certain time, a comet following the same path while visible, as a former comet was observed to follow, we infer that they also followed the same path during that much longer period in which they were beyond the sphere of our observation, and consequently we infer, with a high degree of probability, that the comets which thus follow precisely the same track, must be the same comet. We say with probability, because there is a possibility, although it be a bare possibility, that two different comets should move precisely in the same orbit.

Now, let us suppose that, during the appearance of a comet, its path from day to day, or perhaps from hour to hour, is so carefully observed, that we could delineate it with a corresponding degree of accuracy in any plan or model of the system. This path would, as we have seen, form a very small fragment of its entire orbit; but if the nature of that orbit were known, the principles of geometry would also enable us to complete the curve. Thus, if a small arc of a large circle be traced upon paper, every one conversant with geometry will be able to complete the circle, even though he be not told with what centre the small arc was described, or with what length of radius. It is the same with other curves. Newton has proved that every mass of matter which is moved through the system, under the attracting influence of the sun, must, by its motion, trace one or other of those curves called *conic sections;* and that the curve must be so placed, that the centre of the sun shall be in that point which is called its *focus*. Now, conic sections are of three kinds; the *ellipse*, which is a curve of oval form, such that a point moving on it would retrace the same course every revolution. But the other two species (called the *parabola* and *hyperbola*), consist of two branches diverging from their point of connexion in two different directions, and proceeding in those directions without ever again reuniting. If a body (as it might do by the established law of gravitation) entered our system by one branch of such a curve, it would, after sweeping behind the sun, emerge by the other branch never to return. Thus it appears, that either of the two suppositions which we have just made, would be compatible with the law of gravitation; and it is possible that some comets might move in ellipses, returning continually over the same path at stated intervals, while others, moving in parabolas, or hyperbolas, entering our system for the first and only time, would emerge from it in another direction, and quit it for ever. It will perhaps be asked, if the orbits must be conic sections, with the sun in the focus, how is it that the planetary orbits are considered as circles? The fact is, the planetary orbits are not strictly circular, though very nearly so; they are *ellipses*, which are so slightly oval, that, when exhibited in a drawing, they would not be perceived to be so, unless their length and breadth were accurately measured. The centre of the sun, also, is in their focus, and not in their centre; but owing to their slightly oval form, the distance of the focus from the centre is very inconsiderable compared with their whole magnitude.

To obtain a correct notion of the form of an ellipse, let a flexible string be attached to two points, such as A and B, and let a pencil be looped in it so that when the string is stretched the pencil will be at D; the string extending from A to D, and from D to B. Let the pencil be moved, carrying the loop

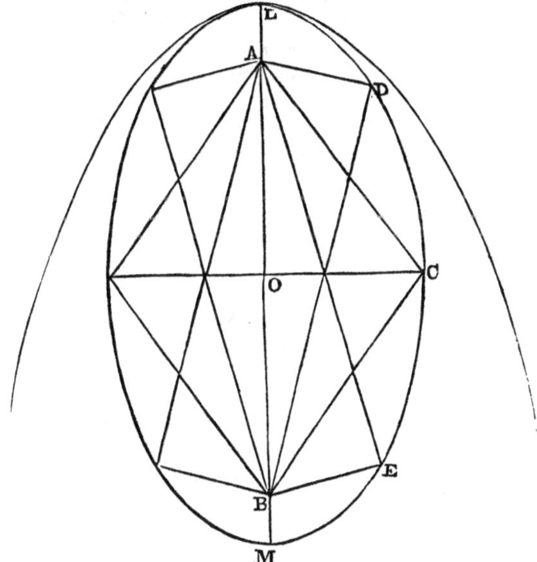

with it. It will pass successively to the points C, E, M, &c., &c., describing the oval curve, D, C, E, M, L. This curve is called an *ellipse*. The points A and B are called its *foci*, and the point O, at the middle of the distance A B, is called its *centre*. The ellipse will be more or less oval as the string is less or greater than the distance A B.

Such is the general form of the curves in which the comets move. If the entire ellipse except the part D, L, G, were blotted out, it would be very difficult to distinguish the arc D, L, G, from that of a parabola or hyperbola.

On the appearance of a comet then, the first question which presents itself to the astronomical inquirer is, whether the same comet has ever appeared before? and the only means which he possesses of answering this inquiry is, by ascertaining, from such observations as may be made during its appearance, the exact path it follows; and this being known, to discover, by the principles of geometry, the nature of its orbit. If the orbit be found to be an ellipse, then the return of the comet would be certain, and the time of the return would be known by the magnitude of the ellipse. If the path, on the other hand, should appear to be either a parabola or hyperbola, then it would be equally certain that the comet had never been before in our system, and would never return to it.

But a difficulty of a peculiar nature obstructs the solution of this question. It so happens that the only part of the course of a comet which ever can be visible, is a portion such as D, L, G, throughout which the ellipse, the parabola, and hyperbola so closely resemble one another, that no observations can be obtained with sufficient accuracy to enable us to distinguish one from the other. In fact, the observed path of any comet, while visible, may indifferently belong to an ellipse, parabola, or hyperbola.

There is, nevertheless, a certain degree of definiteness in the observed course of the body, which, although insufficient to enable us to say what the nature of the entire orbit may be, is still sufficiently exact to enable us to recognise *any other comet*, which moves, while visible, nearly in the same course. If then, after the lapse of a certain time, a comet should be found following that course, there would be a strong presumption that it is the same comet returning again to our system, after having traversed the invisible part of its orbit. This probability would be strengthened, if, on the two occasions, the body should present a similar appearance; although this is not essential to the identity, since, as has been stated, the same comet is observed to undergo considerable changes, even during a single appearance.

The time between the appearances of comets following nearly the same path being noted, the interval—the identity of the bodies being assumed—must either consist of a single period, or of two or more complete periods. The epoch which is usually taken as the commencement of a new revolution being the instant of time at which the comet is at its least distance from the sun, the place of the comet at that moment is called its *perihelion*. The *period* of a comet may, therefore, be defined to be the interval of time between two successive arrivals at its perihelion.

Having succeeded in identifying the path of any two comets, we are then in a condition to predict with some degree of probability the time at which the next appearance may be expected. It is *certain*—providing that it be the same comet—that it will arrive at its perihelion after the same interval nearly; also that it *may* arrive at half the interval, or a third of the interval, or any other fraction corresponding to the possible number of unobserved appearances which may have taken place in the interval between those appearances from which its return has been predicted. The times, therefore, at which the comet may be looked for with a probability of finding it, may without difficulty be predicted; and if it has been a conspicuous body in the heavens on the occasion of its former appearances, there is a probability that the whole interval between these appearances constituted but one period, and that no return of the comet had escaped observation.

Such are the circumstances which may have been conceived to have presented themselves when the idea first occurred of attempting to ascertain the identity of former comets, and to discover the means of predicting their future return. The *Principia* of Newton, which laid the foundation of all sound astronomical science, had appeared soon after the middle of the seventeenth century; and Halley, the contemporary and friend of Newton, had his attention naturally directed to the physical inquiries which that immortal book suggested.

One of the most curious and interesting of these questions was that to which we now allude. Halley, referring to the records of all former observers, with a view to obtain means of determining, so far as possible, the course of former comets, succeeded in identifying one which he had himself observed in 1682, with comets which had appeared on several former occasions; and found, that the interval between its successive returns was from 75 to 76 years. This discovery has since been fully confirmed, and the comet has received the name of *Halley's comet*. We now propose to lay before the reader the history of this celebrated comet.

In retracing the history of a body of this nature so far as we can collect it from ancient chroniclers and historians, it is necessary to bear in mind that the terror which the appearance of comets inspired, had a tendency to produce an exaggeration of their effects. The propensity to ascribe to supernatural causes, effects which the understanding fails to account for, has rendered comets peculiarly objects of superstitious terror. They have been accordingly regarded in past ages as the harbingers of war, pestilence, and famine, and of all the greatest scourges which have visited the human race. But more especially they have presided at the birth and death of the most celebrated heroes. Thus, a conspicuous body of this kind appeared for several days succeeding the death of Julius Cæsar, and was regarded as the soul of that illustrious person transferred to the heavens. Another was seen at Constantinople in the year of the birth of Mohammed. It is obvious, that under the influence of such powerful prejudices, the circumstances attending these appearances would naturally be amplified and exaggerated; and the probability of exaggeration is increased by the fact that since science has shed its light upon the civilized world, these terrible objects have, in a great degree, disappeared, and comets have dwindled for the most part into very insignificant appearances. One of the ill consequences of this exaggeration is, that it greatly increases the difficulty of identifying the bodies which have been described with those which have appeared in more recent times. In fact, we have little more to guide us than the epochs of the respective appearances; and, antecedently to the fifteenth century, we possess absolutely no other evidence of the identity of these bodies except the record of their appearance at the times at which we know, from their ascertained periods, they ought to have appeared. Adopting this test of identity, it would seem at least probable that the first recorded appearance of Halley's comet was that which was supposed to signalize the birth of Christ. It is said to have appeared for twenty-four days; its light is described to have surpassed that of the sun; its magnitude to have extended over a fourth part of the firmament; and it is stated to have occupied consequently about four hours in rising and setting.

In the year 323, a comet appeared in the sign Virgo. Another, according to the historians of the Lower Empire, appeared in the year 399, seventy five years after the last; this last interval being the period of Halley's comet.

The interval between the birth of Mithridates and the year 323 was four hundred and fifty-three years, which would be equivalent to six periods of seventy-five and a half years. Thus, it would seem, that in the interim there were five returns of this comet unobserved, or at least unrecorded. The appearance in the year 399 was attended with extraordinary circumstances. In the *Theatrum Cometarum* of Lobienietski, it is described as *cometa prodigiosæ magnitudinis, horribilis aspectu, comam, ad terram usque demittere visus.* The next recorded appearance of a comet agreeing with the ascertained period, marks the taking of Rome by Totila in the year 550; an interval of one hundred and fifty-one years, or two periods of seventy-five and a half years, having elapsed. One unrecorded term must, therefore, have taken place in this interim. The next appearance of a comet coinciding with the assigned period is three hundred and eighty years afterward, viz., in the year 930, five revolutions having been completed in the interval. The next appearance is recorded in the year 1005, after an interval of a single period of seventy-five years. Three revolutions would now seem to have passed unrecorded, when the comet again makes its appearance in 1230. In this, as well as in former appearances, it is right to state once more, that the sole test of identity of these comets with that of Halley, is the coincidence of the times of their appearances, as nearly as historical records enable us to ascertain, with the epochs at which the comet of Halley might have been expected to appear. That such evidence, however, must needs be imperfect will be evident, if the frequency of cometary appearances be considered; and if it be remembered that hitherto we find no recorded observations which could enable us to trace even with the rudest degree of approximation the paths of those comets, the times of whose appearances raise a presumption of their identity with that of Halley. We now, however, descend to times in which more satisfactory evidence may be expected.

In the year 1305, one of those in which the comet of Halley may have been expected, a comet is recorded of remarkable appearance: *Cometa horrendæ magnitudinis visus est circà ferias Paschatis, quem secuta est pestilentia maxima.* Had the horrid appearance of this body alone been recorded, this description might have passed without the charge of great exaggeration; but when we find the Great Plague connected with it as a consequence, it is impossible not to conclude that the comet was seen by its historians through the magnifying medium of the calamity which followed it. Another appearance is recorded in the year 1380, unaccompanied by any other circumstance than its mere date. This, however, is in strict accordance with the ascertained period of Halley's comet.

We now arrive at the first appearance at which observations were taken, possessing sufficient accuracy to enable subsequent investigators to determine the path of the comet: and this is accordingly the first comet, the identity of which with the comet of Halley can be said to be conclusively established. In the year 1456, a comet is stated to have appeared, of "unheard-of magnitude;" it was accompanied by a tail of extraordinary length, which extended over sixty degrees (a third of the heavens), and continued to be seen during the whole of the month of June. The influence which was attributed to this appearance renders it probable that in the record there exists more or less of exaggeration. It was considered as the celestial indication of the rapid success of Mohammed II., who had taken Constantinople, and struck terror into the whole Christian world. Pope Calixtus II. levelled the thunders of the church against the enemies of his faith, terrestrial and celestial, and in the same bull exorcised the Turks and the comets; and in order that the memory of this manifestation of his power should be for ever preserved, he ordained that the bells of all the churches should be rung at midday—a custom which is preserved in those countries to our times. It must be admitted that, notwithstanding the terrors of the church, the comet pursued its course with as much ease and security as those with which Mohammed converted the church of St. Sophia into his principal mosque.

The extraordinary length and brilliancy which was ascribed to the tail upon this occasion, have led astronomers to investigate the circumstances under which its brightness and magnitude would be the greatest possible; and, upon tracing back the motion of the comet to the year 1456, it has been found that it was then actually under the circumstances of position with respect to the earth and sun most favorable to magnitude and splendor. So far, therefore, the results of astronomical calculation corroborate the records of history.

The next return took place in the year 1531. Pierre Appian, who first ascertained the fact that the tails of comets are usually turned from the sun, examined this comet, with a view to verify his statement, and to ascertain the true direction of its tail. He made accordingly numerous observations upon its position, which, though, compared with the present standard of accuracy, they must be regarded as of a rude nature, were still sufficiently exact to enable Halley to identify this comet with that observed by himself in 1682.

The next return took place in 1607, when the comet was observed by the celebrated Kepler. This astronomer, on his return from a convivial party, first saw it on the evening of the 26th of September; it had the appearance of a star of the first magnitude, and, to his vision, was without a tail; but the friends who accompanied him, having better sight, distinguished the tail. Before three o'clock the following morning, the tail had become clearly visible, and had acquired great magnitude. Two days afterward the comet was observed by Longomontanus; he describes its appearance, to the naked eye, to be like Jupiter, but of a paler and more obscure light; that its tail was of considerable length, of a paler light than that of the head, and more dense than the tails of ordinary comets. He states that on the 24th of September following, the comet was not apparent; that on the 24th of October it was seen obscurely, and some days afterward disappeared altogether.

The next appearance, and that which was observed by Halley himself, took place in 1682, a little before the publication of the *Principia*. A comet of frightful magnitude had appeared in 1680, and had so terrified all Europe, that the subject of our present inquiry, though of such immense astronomical importance, excited comparatively little popular notice. In the interval, however, between 1607 and 1682, practical astronomy had made great advances; instruments of observations had been brought to a state of comparative perfection; numerous observatories had been established, and the management of them had been confided to the most eminent astronomers of Europe. In 1682, the scientific world was, therefore, prepared to examine this visiter of our system with a degree of care and accuracy before unknown. It was observed at Paris by Lahire, Picard, and Dominique Cassini; at Dantzic, by Hevelius; at Padua, by Montonari; and in England, by Halley and Flamstead.

In 1686, about four years afterward, Newton published his *Principia*, in which he applied to the comet of 1680 the general principles of physical investigation first promulgated in that work. He explained the means of determining, by geometrical construction, the visible portion of the path of a body of this kind, and invited astronomers to apply these principles to the various recorded comets—to discover whether some among them might not have appeared at different epochs, the future returns of which might consequently be predicted. Such was the effect of the force of analogy upon the mind of Newton, that, without awaiting the discovery of a periodic comet, he boldly assumed these bodies to be analogous to planets in their revolution round the sun.

In the third book of his *Principia*, he calls them a species of planets revolving in elliptic orbits, of a very oval form, and even remarks an analogy observable between the order of their magnitudes and those of the planets. He says, "As among planets without tails, those which revolve in less orbits, and nearer to the sun, are of less magnitude, so comets which in their perihelia approach still nearer to the sun than the planets, are much less than the planets, that their attraction may not act too strongly on the sun. But," he continues, "I leave to be determined by others the transverse diameters and periods, by comparing comets which return after long intervals of time to the same orbits."

It is interesting to observe the avidity with which minds of a certain order snatch at generalizations, even when but slenderly founded upon facts. These conjectures of Newton were soon after adopted by Voltaire: "Il y a quelque apparence," says he, in an essay on comets, "qu'on connaitra un jour un certain nombre de ces autres planetes qui sous le nom de comêtes tournent comme nous autour du soleil, mais il ne faut pas espérer qu'on les connaissent toutes."

And again, elsewhere, on the same subject:—

"Comêtes, que l'on craint à l'egal du tonnere,
Cessez d'epouvanter les peuples de la terre;
Dans une ellipse immense achevez votre cours,
Remontez, descendez pres de l'astre des jours."

Extraordinary as these conjectures must have appeared at the time, they were soon strictly realized. Halley undertook the labor of examining the circumstances attending all the comets previously recorded, with a view to discover whether any and which of them, appeared to follow the same path. Antecedently to the year 1700, four hundred and twenty-five of these bodies had been recorded in history; but those which had appeared before the fourteenth century had not been submitted to any observations by which their paths could be ascertained—at least not with a sufficient degree of precision to afford any hope of identifying them with those of other comets. Subsequently to the year 1300, however, Halley found twenty-four comets on which observations had been made and recorded, with a degree of precision sufficient to enable him to calculate the actual paths which these bodies followed while they were visible. He examined with the most elaborate care the courses of each of these twenty-four bodies; he found the exact points at which each of them penetrated the plane of the earth's orbit; also the angle which the direction of their motion made with that plane; he also calculated the nearest distance at which each of them approached the sun, and the exact place of the body when at that nearest distance. In a word, he determined all the circumstances which were necessary to enable him to lay down, with sufficient precision, the path which these comets must have followed while they continued to be visible.

On comparing their paths, Halley found that one which appeared in 1661, followed nearly the same path as one which had appeared in 1532. Supposing, then, these to be two successive appearances of the same comet, it would follow that its period would be one hundred and twenty-nine years; and Halley accordingly conjectured that its next appearance might be expected after the lapse of one hundred and twenty-nine years, reckoning from 1661. Had this conjecture been well founded, the comet must have appeared about the year 1790. No comet, however, appeared at or near that time following a similar path.

In his second conjecture, Halley was more fortunate, as indeed might be expected, since it was formed upon more conclusive grounds. He found that the paths of comets which had appeared in 1531 and 1606, were very nearly identical, and that they were in fact the same as the path followed by the comet observed by himself in 1682. He suspected, therefore, that the appearances at these three epochs were produced by three successive returns of the same comet, and that consequently its period in its orbit must be about seventy-five and a half years.

So little was the scientific world at this time prepared for such an announcement, that Halley himself only ventured at first to express his opinion in the form of conjecture; but after some further investigation of the circumstances of the recorded comets, he found three others which at least in point of time agreed with the period assigned to the comet of 1682, viz., those of 1305, 1380, and 1456.* Collecting confidence from these circumstances, he announced his discovery as the result of combined observation and calculation, and entitled to as much confidence as any other consequence of an established physical law.

There were nevertheless two circumstances, which to the fastidious skeptic

* The path of the comet of 1456 was afterward fully identified with that of 1682.

might be supposed to offer some difficulty. These were, first, that the intervals between the supposed successive returns to perihelion were not precisely equal; and, secondly, that the inclination of the comet's path to the plane of the earth's orbit was not exactly the same in each case. Halley, however, with a degree of sagacity which, considering the state of knowledge at the time, cannot fail to excite unqualified admiration, observed that it was natural to suppose that the same causes which disturbed the planetary motions must likewise act upon comets; and that their influence would be so much the more sensible upon these bodies because of their great distances from the sun. Thus, as the attraction of Jupiter upon Saturn was known to affect the velocity of the latter planet, sometimes retarding and sometimes accelerating it, according to their relative position, so as to affect its period to the extent of thirteen days, it might well be supposed that the comet might suffer by a similar attraction, an effect sufficiently great to account for the inequality observed in the interval between its successive returns; and also for the variation to which the direction of its path upon the plane of the ecliptic was found to be subject. He observed, in fine, that as in the interval between 1607 and 1682 the comet passed so near Jupiter that its velocity must have been augmented, and consequently its period shortened by the action of that planet, this period, therefore, having been only seventy-five years, he inferred that the following period would probably be seventy-six years or upward; and consequently that the comet ought not to be expected to appear until the end of 1758, or the beginning of 1759. It is impossible to imagine any quality of mind more enviable than that which, in the existing state of mathematical physics, could have led to such a prediction. The imperfect state of mathematical science rendered it impossible for Halley to offer to the world a demonstration of the event which he foretold. "He therefore," says M. de Pontecoulant, "could only announce these felicitous conceptions of a sagacious mind as mere intuitive perceptions, which must be received as uncertain by the world, however he might have felt them himself, until they could be verified by the process of a rigorous analysis."

The theory of gravitation, which was in its cradle at the time of Halley's investigations, had grown to comparative maturity before the period at which his prediction could be fulfilled. The exigencies of that theory gave birth to new and more powerful instruments of mathematical inquiry: the differential and integral calculus was its first and greatest offspring. This branch of science was cultivated with an ardor and success by which it was enabled to answer all the demands of physics, and consequently mechanical science advanced, *pari passu*. Newton's discoveries having obtained reception throughout the scientific world, his inquiries and his theories were followed up; and the consequences of the great principle of universal gravitation were rapidly developed. Among these inquiries one problem was eminently conspicuous for the order of minds whose powers were brought to bear upon it. One of the first and simplest results of the theory of gravitation was, that if a single planet attended the sun (its mass being insignificant compared with that of the sun), that planet must revolve in an ellipse, the focus of which must be occupied by the centre of the sun; but, if a second planet be admitted into the system, then the elliptic form of their paths round the sun can be preserved only by the supposition that the two planets have no attraction for each other, and that no physical influence is in operation, except the attraction of the solar mass for each of them. But the law of universal gravitation is founded upon the principle that *every body in nature must attract and be attracted by every other body.* Thus, the elliptic character of the orbit is effaced the moment a second planet is introduced. But let us remember that in this case each of the two supposed planets are in mass absolutely insignificant compared with the sun. The amount of attraction depending on the greatness of the attracting body, the intensity of the solar attraction of each of the planets must predominate enormously over the comparatively feeble influence of their diminutive masses on each other. The tendency of the solar attraction to impress the elliptic form on the paths of those planets, must therefore prevail *in the main;* and although their mutual attraction, however feeble, cannot be wholly ineffective, their orbits will, in obedience to the solar mandate, preserve a general elliptic form, subject to those very slight deviations, or *disturbances*, due to their reciprocal attraction. The problem to discover the nature and amount of these disturbances is one of paramount importance in astronomy, and has been called the "problem of three bodies;" and its extension embraces the effects of the mutual gravitation of all the planets of the system upon each other. This celebrated problem presented enormous mathematical difficulties. A particular case of it, which, from the comparative smallness of the third body considered, was attended with greater facility, was solved by Euler, D'Alembert, and Clairaut. This was the case in which the single planet, revolving round the sun, was the earth, and the third body the moon.

Clairaut undertook the difficult application of this problem to the case of the comet of 1682, with a view to calculate the effects which would be produced upon it by the attraction of the different planets of the system; and by such means to convert the conjecture of Halley into a distinct astronomical prediction, attended with all the circumstances of time and place. The exact verification of the prediction would, it was obvious, furnish the most complete demonstration of the principle of universal gravitation; which, though generally received, was not yet considered so completely demonstrated as to be independent of so remarkable a body of evidence as the fulfilment of such a calculation would afford.

To attain completely the end proposed, it was necessary to solve two very different classes of problems, requiring different powers of mind, and different habits of thought and application. The mathematical part of the inquiry, strictly speaking, consisted in the discovery of certain general analytical formulæ, applicable to the case in question; which, when translated into ordinary language, would become a set of rules expressing certain arithmetical processes, to be effected upon certain given numbers; and when so effected would give as the final results, numbers which would determine the place of the comet, under all the circumstances influencing it from hour to hour. The *actual place* of the body being thus determined, it became a simple question of practical astronomy to ascertain its *apparent place* in the firmament, at corresponding times. A table exhibiting its apparent place thus determined in the firmament for stated intervals of time, is called its *Ephemeris;* it is the final result to which the whole investigation must tend, and is that whose verification by observation would ultimately decide the validity of the reasoning, and the accuracy of the computations. Clairaut, a mathematician and natural philosopher, was eminently qualified to conduct such an investigation, as far as the attainment of those general analytical formulæ which embodied the rules by which the practical astronomer and arithmetician might work out the final results; but beyond this point neither his habits nor his powers would conduct him. Lalande, a practical astronomer, no less eminent in his own department, and who, indeed, first urged Clairaut to this inquiry, accordingly undertook the management of the astronomical and arithmetical part of the calculation. In this prodigious labor (for it was one of most appalling magnitude) he was assisted by the wife of an eminent watchmaker in Paris, named Lepaute, whose exertions on this occasion have deservedly registered her name in astronomical history.

It is difficult to convey to one who is not conversant with such investigations, an adequate notion of the labor which such an inquiry involved. The calculation of the influence of any one planet of the system upon any other, is itself a problem of some complexity and difficulty; but still, one general computation, depending upon the calculation of the terms of a certain series, is sufficient for its solution. This comparative simplicity arises entirely from two circumstances which characterize the planetary orbits. These are, that though they are ellipses, they differ very slightly from circles; and though the planets do not move in the plane of the ecliptic, yet none of them deviate considerably from that plane. But these characters do not, as we have already stated, belong to the orbits of comets, which, on the contrary, are highly eccentric, and depart from the ecliptic at all possible angles. The consequence of this is, that the calculation of the disturbances produced in the cometary orbit by the action of the planets, must be conducted, not like the planets, in one general calculation applicable to the whole orbit, but in a vast number of separate calculations, in which the orbit is considered, as it were, bit by bit, each bit requiring a calculation similar to that of the whole orbit of the planet. In fact, for a very small part of its course, we treat the comet as we would a planet; making our calculations, and completing them, nearly in the same manner; but for the next part we are obliged to enter upon a new calculation, starting with a different set of numbers, but performing over again similar arithmetical operations upon them. When it is considered that the period of Halley's comet is about seventy-five years, and that every portion of its course, for two successive periods, was necessary to be calculated separately in this way, some notion may be formed of the labor encountered by Lalande and Madame Lepaute. "During six months," says Lalande, "we calculated from morning till night, sometimes even at meals, the consequence of which was, that I contracted an illness which changed my constitution for the remainder of my life. The assistance rendered by Madame Lepaute was such, that without her we never could have dared to undertake this enormous labor, in which it was necessary to calculate the distance of each of the two planets, Jupiter and Saturn, from the comet, and their attraction upon that body, separately, for every successive degree, and for 150 years."*

These elaborate calculations having been completed, Clairaut, fearing that the comet would anticipate his announcement, presented his first memoir to the Academy on the 14th of November, 1758. In this memoir he was compelled to adopt the path of the comet upon its former appearance, as determined by the observations of Appian. These, however, were made at a time when little attention was paid to comets; and were made, moreover, without that consciousness on the part of the observer of their future importance, which would doubtless have produced greater accuracy. In calculating the effect of the attraction of Jupiter and Saturn upon the comet, in its two periods between 1707 and 1682, and between the latter period and the expected return, Clairaut proceeded upon the supposition that the masses of these planets were each what they were then supposed to be. It has, however, since appeared, that the estimates of these masses were incorrect, more especially that of Saturn. The planet Herschel being then unknown, its influence upon the comet was, of

* The name of Madame Lepaute does not appear in Clairaut's memoir; a suppression which Lalande attributes to the influence exercised by another lady to whom Clairaut was attached. Lalande, however, quotes letters of Clairaut, in which he speaks in terms of high admiration of "la savante calculatrice." The labors of this lady in the work of calculation (for she also assisted Lalande in constructing his *Ephemerides*) at length so weakened her sight, that she was compelled to desist. She died in 1788, while attending on her husband, who had become insane. See the articles on comets, written with considerable ability, in the *Companion to the British Almanac* for the year 1833. They are understood to be the production of Mr. De Morgan, secretary of the Astronomical Society.

course, wholly omitted. Neither did Clairaut take into account the action of the earth. Encumbered with the disadvantages of precision in his data, he predicted, in his first memoir, that the comet would arrive at its nearest point to the sun on the 18th of April, 1759; but he stated at the same time that the imperfection of some of the methods of calculation he was compelled to adopt, was such as to leave a possibility of his prediction being erroneous to the extent of a month. After presenting this memoir he resumed his calculations, and completed some which he had not time to execute previously. He then announced that the 4th of April would be the day of the comet's arrival at the nearest distance to the sun.

This wonderful astronomical prediction was accompanied by a circumstance still more remarkable and interesting than that which we have noticed in the conjectures of Halley as to the disturbing effects of the planets upon the comet's period. Clairaut stated that there might be very many circumstances which, independently of any error either in the methods or process of calculation, might cause the event to deviate more or less from its predicted occurrence; one of which was the probability of *an undiscovered planet of our system revolving beyond the orbit of Saturn*, and acting by its gravitation upon the comet. In twenty-two years after this time this conjecture was accurately fulfilled by the discovery of the planet Herschel, by the late Sir William Herschel, revolving round the sun one thousand millions of miles beyond the orbit of Saturn!

In the successive appearances of the comet subsequent to 1456, it was found to have gradually decreased in magnitude and splendor. While in 1456 it occupied two thirds of the firmament, and spread terror over Europe, in 1607 its appearance, when observed by Kepler and Longomontanus, was that of a star of the first magnitude; and so trifling was its tail, that Kepler himself, when he first saw it, doubted if it had any. In 1682 it excited little attention except among astronomers. Supposing this decrease of magnitude and brilliancy to be progressive, Lalande entertained serious apprehensions that on its expected return it might escape the observation even of astronomers; and thus that, this splendid example of the power of science, and unanswerable proof of the principle of gravitation, would be lost to the world. It is not uninteresting to observe the misgivings of this distinguished astronomer with respect to the appearance of the body, mixed up with his unshaken faith in the result of the astronomical inquiry. "We cannot doubt," says he, "that it will return; and even if astronomers cannot see it, they will not therefore be the less convinced of its presence; they know that the faintness of its light, its great distance, and perhaps even bad weather, may keep it from our view; but the world will find it difficult to believe us; they will place this discovery, which has done so much honor to modern philosophy, among the number of chance predictions. We shall see discussions spring up again in the colleges, contempt among the ignorant, terror among the people, and seventy-six years will roll away before there will be another opportunity of removing all doubt."

Fortunately for science, the arrival of the expected visiter did not take place under such untoward circumstances. As the commencement of the year 1759 approached, "Les Astronomes," says Voltaire, "ne se couchèrent pas."

The honor, however, of the first glimpse of the stranger was not reserved for the possessors of scientific rank, nor the members of academies or universities. On the night of Christmas day, 1758, George Palitzch of Prolitz, near Dresden, "a peasant," says Sir John Herschel, "by station, an astronomer by nature," first saw the comet. He possessed an eight-foot telescope, with which he made the discovery; and the next day communicated the fact to Dr. Hoffman, who immediately went to his cottage, and saw the comet on the evenings of the 27th and 28th of December. An astronomer of Leipzic observed it immediately afterward; "but," says M. de Pontecoulant, "jealous of his discovery, as a lover of his mistress, or a miser of his treasure, he would not share it, and gave himself up to the solitary pleasure of following the body in its course from day to day, while his contemporaries throughout Europe were vainly directing their anxious search after it to other quarters of the heavens." At this time Delisle, a French astronomer, and his assistant, Messier, who, from his unwearied assiduity in the pursuit of comets, received from Louis the Fifteenth the appellation of *La Furet de Comètes* (the *comet-ferret*), had been constantly engaged for eighteen months in watching for the return of Halley's comet. It would seem that La Caille, and other French astronomers at that time, considering that Delisle and Messier, from the attention which they had given to such objects, and more especially from the ardor and indefatigable perseverance of the latter, could not fail to detect the expected body the moment it came within view, did not occupy themselves in looking for it. Delisle computed an Ephemeris, and made a chart of its supposed course in the heavens, and placed it in the hands of Meisser to guide him in his search. This chart was erroneous, and diverted the attention of Meisser to a quarter of the firmament through which the comet did not pass, and thus, most probably, deprived that zealous and assiduous observer of the honor of first discovering its return to our system. He succeeded, nevertheless, in observing it on the 21st of January, 1759; nearly a month after it had been seen by Palitzch and Hoffman, but without knowing that it had been already observed.* The comet was now observed in various places. It continued to be seen at Dresden, also at Leipzic, Boulogne, Brussels, Lisbon, Cadiz, &c. Its course being observed, it was found that it arrived at its perihelion, or at its nearest point to the sun, on the 13th of March, between three and four o'clock in the morning; exactly thirty-seven days before the epoch first assigned by Clairaut, but only twenty-three days previous to his corrected prediction. The comet on this occasion appeared very round, with a brilliant nucleus, well distinguished from the surrounding nebulosity. It had, however, no appearance of a tail. About the middle of the latter month, it became lost in the rays of the sun while approaching its perihelion; it afterward emerged from them on its departure from the sun, and was visible before sunrise in the morning on the 1st of April. On this day it was observed by Messier, who states that he was able to distinguish the tail by his telescope. It was again observed by him on the 3d, 15th, and 17th of May. Lalande, however, who observed it on the same occasions, was not able to discover any trace of the tail.

Although it is certain that the splendor and magnitude of the comet in 1759 were considerably less than those with which it had previously appeared, yet we must not lay too much stress upon the probability of its really diminished magnitude. In 1759 it was seen under the most disadvantageous circumstances—it was almost always obscured by the effect of twilight, and was in situations the most unfavorable possible for European observers. It had been observed, however, in the southern hemisphere at Pondicherry by Pere Cœur-Doux, and at the isle of Bourbon by La Caille, under more favorable circum-

* An interesting memoir of Messier may be found in the *Histoire de l'Astronomie au dixhuitième Siècle*, by Delambre. La Harpe (*Correspondence Litteraire*, Paris, 1801, tom. i., p. 97) says, that "he passed his life in search of comets. The *ne plus ultra* of his ambition was to be made a member of the Academy of Petersburgh. He was an excellent man, but had the simplicity of a child. At a time when he was in expectation of discovering a comet, his wife took ill and died. While attending upon her, being withdrawn from his observatory, Montagne de Limoges anticipated him by discovering the comet. Messier was in despair. A friend visiting him began to offer some consolation for the recent affliction he had suffered: Messier, thinking only of his comet exclaimed: '*I had discovered twelve. Alas, that I should be robbed of the thirteenth by Montagne!*' and his eyes filled with tears. Then, remembering that it was necessary to mourn for his wife, whose remains were still in the house, he exclaimed, '*Ah! cette pauvre femme,*' and again wept for his comet."

stances; and both of these astronomers agree in stating that the tail was distinctly visible by the naked eye, and varied in length at different periods from ten degrees to forty-seven degrees.* These circumstances are obviously in perfect accordance with the former appearances of the same body.

On its departure from the sun it continued to be observed until the middle of April, when its southern position caused the time of its rising to follow that of the sun; consequently it ceased to be visible in the morning. By a further change in its position, however, it again appeared after sunset on the 29th, and Messier then describes it as having the appearance of a star of the first magnitude. But here again unfortunately another circumstance interposed a difficulty—the light of the moon was at that time so strong as in a great degree to overcome the effect of the comet. The body disappeared altogether in the beginning of June.

The comet had now commenced a new period under circumstances far more favorable than had ever before occurred. An interval of seventy-six years would throw its return into the year 1835. But during that interval, the science of analysis, more especially in its application to physical astronomy, has made prodigious advances. The methods of investigation have acquired greater simplicity, and have likewise become more general and comprehensive; and mechanical science, in the large sense of that term, now embraces in its formularies the most complicated motions and the most minute effects of the mutual influences of the various members of our system. These formulæ exhibit to the eye of the mathematician a *tableau* of all the evolutions of these bodies in ages past, and of all the changes they must undergo (the laws of nature remaining unchanged) in ages to come. Such has been the result of the combination of transcendent mathematical genius and unexampled labor and perseverance for the last century. The learned societies established in the various centres of civilization, have more especially directed their attention to the advancement of physical astronomy: and have stimulated the spirit of inquiry by a succession of prizes offered for the solution of problems arising out of the difficulties which were progressively developed by the advancement of astronomical knowledge. Among these questions the determination of the return of comets, and the disturbances which they experience in their course, by the action of the planets near which they happen to pass, hold a prominent place. The French Academy of Sciences, in the year 1778, offered a high mathematical prize for an essay on this subject, which was the means of calling forth the splendid Memoir of Lagrange, which formed at once a complete solution and a model for all future investigations of the same kind. Lagrange's investigation was, however, of a general nature, and it remained to apply it to the particular case of Halley's comet, the only one then known to be periodic. In 1820, the Academy of Sciences at Turin offered a prize for this application of Lagrange's formula, which was awarded to M. Damoiseau. In 1826, the French Institute proposed a similar prize, having twice before offered it without calling forth any claimant. On this occasion M. de Pontecoulant aspired to the honor. "After calculations," says he, "of which those alone who have engaged in such researches can estimate the extent and appreciate the fatigueing monotony, I arrived at a result which satisfied all the conditions proposed by the Institute. I determined the perturbations of Halley's comet by taking into account the simultaneous actions of Jupiter, Saturn, Uranus (Herschel), and the earth; the comet having passed in 1759 sufficiently near our planet to produce in it (the comet) sensible disturbances; and I then fixed its return to its nearest point to the sun for the 7th of November, 1835." Subsequently to this, however, M. de Pontecoulant made some further researches, which have

* Memoires de l'Académie des Sciences, 1760.

led him to correct the former result; and he has since announced that the time of its arrival at its nearest point to the sun will be on the morning of the 14th November.

The comet appeared in the heavens in August, 1835, exactly in the position it was predicted to have, and passed its perihelion, on the 16th November, within 48 hours of the predicted epoch.

The drawing of this comet usually given is here subjoined.

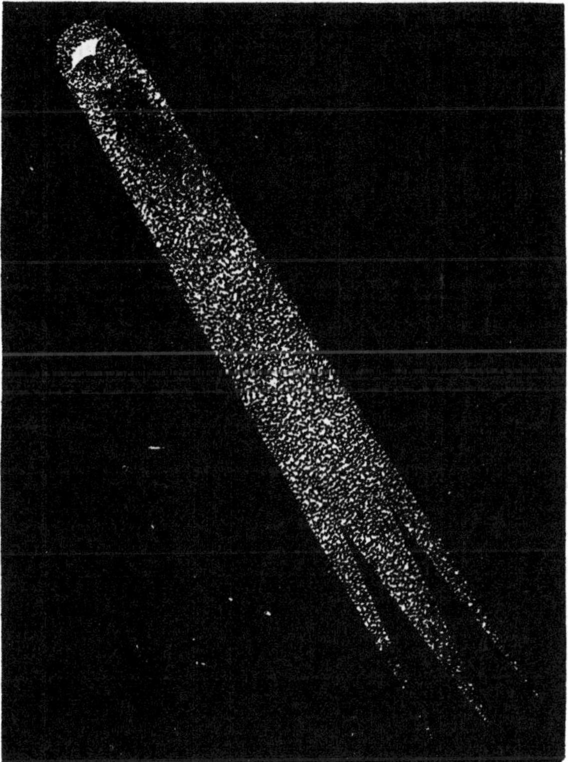

One of the circumstances, not the least surprising, connected with this comet, is the magnitude of its orbit. It is a very oblong oval, the total length of which is about thirty-six times the earth's distance from the sun; and the greatest breadth about ten times that distance. The nearer extremity of the oval is at a distance from the sun equal to about half the earth's distance; and the more remote extremity at a distance equal to thirty-five and a half times the earth's distance from the sun. The earth's distance from the sun, is, in round numbers, one hundred millions of miles; the comet's least distance then will be fifty millions of miles, and its greatest distance three thousand five hundred and fifty millions of miles. Also, since the heat and light supplied by the sun to bodies which surround it, diminish in the same proportion as the square of the distance increases, it follows, that at the nearest distance of the comet, the heat and light of the sun will be four times the heat and light at the earth, and at the greatest distance they will be about twelve hundred times less. Also the heat and light at the more remote extremity of the orbit, will be nearly five thousand times less than at the nearer extremity; so that while the sun seen from the comet will appear four times as large as it appears at the earth at the nearer extremity, it will be reduced to the magnitude of a star at the more remote extremity. The vicissitudes of temperature, not to mention those of light, consequent upon this change of position, will be sufficiently obvious. If the earth were transported to the more remote extremity of the comet's orbit, every liquid substance would become solid by congelation; and it is extremely probable that atmospheric air and other permanant gases might become liquids. If the earth was, on the other hand, transferred to the nearer extremity of the comet's orbit, all the liquids upon it would be converted into vapor, would form permanent gases, and would either by their mixture constitute atmospheric air, or would arrange themselves into strata, one above the other, according to their specific gravities. All the less refractory solids would be fused, and would form in the cavities of the nucleus, oceans of liquid metal.

The following observations of Dick on this comet will be read with interest:—

"Soon after the middle of September, as I was taking a sweep with a two-feet telescope over the northeastern quarter of the heavens, near the point where I expected its appearance, I happened to fix my eye on this long-expected visiter, which appeared very small and obscure. I immediately directed an excellent three and a half feet achromatic telescope, with a diagonal eye piece, magnifying about thirty-four times, to the comet, when it was distinctly seen, and appeared of a considerable diameter, but still somewhat hazy and obscure. I afterward applied a power of forty-five, and another of ninety-five; but it was seen most distinctly with the lower power. With ninety-five it appeared extremely obscure, and nearly of the apparent size of the moon.*

"There appeared at this time nothing like a tail, but the central part was much more luminous than the other portions of the comet, and presented something like the appearance of a star of the third or fourth magnitude, surrounded with a haze. In some of the views I took of this object, the luminous part, or nucleus, appeared to be considerably nearer one side than another. At this period, and for a week or ten days afterward, the comet was altogether invisible to the naked eye. Many subsequent observations were made and published in the provincial newspapers, but which my present limits prevent me from inserting.

"After the comet became visible to the naked eye, the tail began to appear, and increased in length as it approached its perihelion, and at its utmost extent was estimated to be above thirty degrees in length. On the 13th of October, according to the observations of Arago, a luminous sector was visible in its head; on the day following, this sector had disappeared, and a more brilliant one, and of greater longitudinal extent, was formed in another place. This second sector was observed on the 17th, when it appeared less bright; and on the 18th its weakness had decidedly increased. This comet was concealed till the 21st, but on that day three distinct sectors were visible in the nebulosity. On the 23d, all traces of these sectors had disappeared, the nucleus, which had previously been brilliant and well defined, having become so large and diffuse that the observer could scarcely believe in the reality of such a sudden and important alteration, till he satisfied himself that the appearance was not occasioned by moisture on the glasses of his instrument. It appears, likewise, that one of these luminous fans or sectors was observed by Sir J. Herschel, at the Cape of Good Hope, after the comet had passed its perihelion. The nebulosity of this comet appears to have increased in magnitude as it approached

* In viewing comets, telescopes with large apertures, and comparatively low magnifying powers, should generally be used, as the faint light emitted by comets, whether it be inherent or reflected, will not permit the use of so high magnifying powers as may be applied to the planets.

the sun, but its changes were sometimes unaccountably rapid: on one occasion it was observed to become obscure and enlarged in the course of a few hours, though a little before, its nucleus was clear and well defined. On the 11th of October, the Rev. T. W. Webb and two other observers remarked coruscations in the tail. On that evening, at seven hours and thirty minutes, the tail was very conspicuous, extending between χ and γ Draconis, and evidently fluctuated, or rather coruscated, in length, being occasionally short, and then stretching in the twinkling of an eye to its full extent, which was at least equal to ten degrees. Its changes were extremely similar to the kindling and fading of a very faint streamer of the aurora borealis.

"The influence of the ethereal medium on the motion of Halley's comet will be known after another revolution, and future astronomers will learn, by the accuracy of its returns, whether it has met with any unknown cause of disturbance in its distant journey. Undiscovered planets beyond the visible boundary of our system may change its path and the period of its revolution, and thus may indirectly reveal to us their existence, and even their physical nature and orbit. The secrets of the yet more distant heavens may be disclosed to future generations by comets which penetrate still further into space, such as that of 1763, which, if any faith may be placed in the computation, goes nearly forty-three times further from the sun than Halley's does, and shows that the sun's attraction is powerful enough at the distance of 144,600,000,000 of miles to recall the comet to its perihelion. The periods of some comets are said to be many thousand years, and even the average time of the revolution of comets generally is about a thousand years; which proves that the sun's gravitating force extends very far. La Place estimates that the solar attraction is felt throughout a sphere whose radius is a hundred millions of times greater than the distance of the earth from the sun."

"The orbit of Halley's comet is four times longer than it is broad; its length is about three thousand four hundred and twenty millions of miles—about thirty-six times the mean distance of the earth from the sun. At this perihelion it comes within fifty-seven millions of miles of the sun, and at its aphelion it is sixty times more distant. On account of this extensive range, it must experience three thousand six hundred times more light when nearest to the sun than in the most remote point of its orbit. In the one position the sun will seem to be four times larger than he appears to us, and at the other he will not be apparently larger than a star." *

The appearance of this comet so near the time predicted by astronomers, and in positions so nearly agreeing with those which were previously calculated, is a clear proof of the astonishing accuracy which has been introduced into astronomical calculations, and of the soundness of those principles on which the astronomy of comets is founded. It likewise shows that comets in general are *permanent* bodies connected with the solar system, and that no very considerable change in their constitution takes place while traversing the distant parts of their orbits.†

* Mrs. Somerville's "Connexion of the Physical Sciences," a work which, though written in a popular style, would do honor to the first philosophers of Europe. Of this lady's profound mathematical work on the "Mechanism of the Heavens," the Edinburgh Reviewers remark: "It is unquestionably one of the most remarkable works that female intellect ever produced in any age or country; and with respect to the present day, we hazard little in saying, that Mrs. Somerville is the only individual of her sex in the world who could have written it."

† The most particular observations on Halley's comet, during its appearance in 1835, which I have seen, are those which were made by the Rev. T. W. Webb, of Tretire, near Ross, an account of which, with deductions and remarks, was read to the Worcestershire Natural History Society. The observations were made with an excellent achromatic telescope, by Tulley, of 5 feet 6 inches focal length, and 37·10 inches aperture. Through the kindness of this gentleman, I was favored with a manuscript copy of these observations, and would have availed myself of many of his judicious remarks, had my limits permitted.

Among the circumstances attached to the comet of Halley, which will attract attention, is the fact of its gradually decreasing brightness. We have seen that on some occasions of its recorded visits at remote periods, it presented an appearance which filled the people with terror. Every one knows how insignificant an object it was on its return in 1835. If it be true that comets thus waste themselves away, new data will be afforded to aid in forming a physical theory for their explanation. On another occasion, I shall show that this comet may be regarded as a *feeler* which the solar system throws out into space to ascertain if there be any considerable masses of matter occupying the space which immediately surrounds it.

THE ATMOSPHERE.

Atmospheric Air is Material.—Its Color.—Cause of the Blue Sky.—Cause of the Green Sea.—Air has Weight.—Experimental Proofs.—Air has Inertia.—Examples of its Resistance.—It acquires Moving Force.—Examples of its Impact.—Air is Impenetrable.—Experimental Proofs.—Elastic and compressing Forces equal.—Limited Height of the Atmosphere.—Elasticity proportioned to the Density.—Experimental Proofs.—Internal and External Pressure on close Vessels containing Air.

THE ATMOSPHERE.

The Atmosphere is the thin transparent fluid which surrounds the earth to a considerable height above its surface and which, in virtue of one of its constituent elements, supports animal life by respiration, and is necessary, also, to the due exercise of the vegetable functions. This substance is generally, but erroneously regarded as invisible. That it is not invisible may be proved by turning our view to the firmament: that, in the presence of light, appears a vault of an azure or blue color. This color belongs not to anything which occupies the space in which the stars and other celestial objects are placed, but to the mass of air through which these bodies are seen. It may probably be asked, if the air be an azure-colored body, why is not that which immediately surrounds us perceived to have this azure color, in the same manner as a blue liquid contained in a bottle exhibits its proper hue? The question is easily answered.

There are certain bodies which reflect color so faintly, that when they exist in limited quantities, the portion of colored light which they reflect to the eye is insufficient to produce sensation; that is, to excite in the mind a perception of the color. Almost all semi-transparent bodies are examples of this. Let a champagne glass be filled with sherry, or other wine of that color. At the thickest part, near the top of the glass, the wine will strongly exhibit its peculiar color, but as the glass tapers, and its thickness is diminished, this color will become more faint and, at the lowest point, it will almost disappear, seeming nearly as transparent as water.

Now let a glass tube, of very small bore, be dipped in the same wine, and the finger being applied to the upper end, let it be raised from the liquid, the wine will remain suspended in the tube, and if it be looked at through the tube it will be found to have all the appearance of water and to be colorless. In this case there can be no doubt that the wine in the tube has actually the same color as the liquid of which it originally formed a part, but existing only in a small quantity, that color is transmitted to the eye so faintly as to be inefficient in producing perception.

The water of the sea exhibits another remarkable example of this effect. If we look into the sea where the water has considerable depth, we find that its color is a peculiar tint of green; but if we take up a glass of the water which thus appears green, we shall find it perfectly limpid and colorless. The reason is, that the quantity of the color is too small to be perceivable; while the great mass of water, viewed when we look into the deep sea, throws up the color in such abundance as to produce a strong and decided perception of it.

The atmosphere is in the same circumstances; the color, from even a considerable portion of it, is too faint to be perceptible. Hence the air which fills an apartment, or which immediately surrounds us when abroad appears colorless and transparent. But when we behold the immense mass of atmosphere through which we view the firmament, the color is reflected with sufficient force to produce distinct perception. But it is not necessary for this that so great an extent of air should be exhibited to us as that which forms the whole depth or thickness of the atmosphere. Distant mountains appear blue, not because that is their color, but because it is the color of the medium through which they are seen.

Although the preceding observations belong more properly to optics than to our present subject, yet still, since the exhibition of color is one of the manifestations of the presence of body, they may not be considered as foreign to an investigation of the mechanical properties of atmospheric air. The mind unaccustomed to physical inquiries finds it difficult to admit that a thing so light, attenuated, impalpable, and apparently spiritual as air, should be composed of parts whose leading properties are identical with those of the most solid and adamantine masses. The knowledge that we *see* the air must, at least, prepare the mind for the admission of the truth of this proposition that "air is a body."

WEIGHT OF AIR.

Among the properties which are observed to appertain to matter, and which as far as we know are inseparable from it, in whatever form, and under whatever circumstances it exists, weight and inertia hold a conspicuous place. To be convinced, therefore, that air is material, we ought to ascertain whether it possesses those properties. We shall have frequent and numerous proofs of this; but it will at present be convenient to demonstrate it in such a manner that we shall be warranted in assuming it in some of the explanations which we shall have to offer.

The most direct proof that air has weight, is the fact that if a quantity of it be suspended from one arm of a balance, it will require a definite weight to counterpoise it in the opposite scale. By the aid of certain pneumatical engines, the nature of which will be explained hereafter, but the operation and effects of which will for the present be assumed, this may be experimentally established.

Let a vessel containing about two quarts, be formed of thin copper, with a narrow neck, in which is placed a stop-cock, by turning which the vessel may be opened or closed at pleasure. Let two instruments be provided called syringes; one, the exhausting syringe, and the other the condensing syringe. Let the exhausting syringe be screwed upon the neck of the vessel and let the stop-cock be opened so that the interior of the vessel shall have free communication with the bottom of the syringe; if the syringe be now worked, a large portion of the air contained in the vessel may be withdrawn from it. When this has been done, let the stop-cock be closed to prevent the re-admission of air, and let the vessel be detached from the syringe. Let it then be placed in the dish of a well-constructed balance and accurately counterpoised by weights in the opposite scale. The weight which is thus counterpoised is that of the vessel, and the small portion of air which remains in it, if the latter have any weight. Let the stop-cock be now opened and the external air will be immediately heard rushing into the vessel.

When a small quantity has been thus admitted let the stop-cock be again closed. It will be found that the copper vessel is now heavier, in a small degree, than it was before the air was admitted, for the arm of the balance from which it is suspended will be observed to preponderate. Let such additional weights be placed in the opposite scale as will restore equilibrium, the stop-cock being now once more opened, the air will be observed to rush in as before, and will continue to do so until as much has passed into the vessel as it contained before the exhausting syringe was applied. The weight of the vessel will now be observed to be further increased, the end of the beam from which it is suspended preponderating.

These facts are, perhaps, sufficient proofs that air has weight; but the experiment may be carried further. Let the condensing syringe be now attached to the neck of the vessel, and let the stop-cock in the neck be opened so as to leave a free communication between the vessel and the bottom of the syringe. The construction of this instrument is such that by working it an increased quantity of air may be forced into the vessel to any extent which the strength of the vessel is capable of bearing. A considerably increased quantity of air being thus deposited in the vessel, let the stop-cock be closed so as to prevent its escape. The vessel being detached from the syringe, is restored to the dish of the balance: the weights which counterpoised it before the increased quantity of air was forced in still remaining unchanged in the opposite scale. The vessel will now no longer remain counterpoised, but will preponderate, and will require an increased weight in the opposite scale to restore it to equilibrium.

In this experiment, we see that every increase which is given to the quantity of air contained in a vessel produces a corresponding increase in its weight, and that every diminution of the quantity of air it contains produces a corresponding diminution in its weight. Hence we infer that the air which is introduced into or withdrawn from the vessel has weight, and that it is by the amount of its weight that the weight of the vessel is increased or diminished.

We shall hereafter have many other instances of the gravitation of atmospheric air, but we shall for the present assume the principle that air has weight, founded on the experimental proof just given.

INERTIA OF AIR.

That air, in common with all other bodies, possesses the quality of inertia, numerous familiar effects make manifest. Among the effects which betray this quality in solid bodies, is the fact that when one solid body puts another in motion, the former loses as much force as the latter receives. This loss of force is called resistance, and is attributed to the quality of inertia, or inability in either the striking or struck body to call into existence more force in a given direction than previously existed. When the atmosphere is calm and free from wind, the particles of air maintain their position, and are in a state of rest. If a solid body, presenting a broad surface, be moved through the air in this state, it must, as it moves, drive before it and put in motion those parts of the air which lie in the space through which it passes. Now, if the air had no inertia, it would require no force to impart this motion to them, and to drive them before the moving solid; and as no force would in that case be imparted to the air, so no force would be lost by the solid; in other words, the solid would suffer no resistance to its motion.

But every one's experience proves this not to be the case. Open an umbrella and attempt to carry it along swiftly with its concave side presented forward—it will immediately be felt to be opposed by a very considerable resistance, and to require a great force to draw it along. Yet this force is nothing more than what is necessary to push the air before the umbrella.

On the deck of a steamboat propelled with any considerable speed, we feel on the calmest day a breeze directed from the stem to the stern. This arises from the sensation produced by our body displacing the air as we are carried through it.

It is the inertia of the atmosphere which gives effect to the wings of birds. Were it possible for a bird to live without respiration, and in a space void of air, it would no longer have the power of flight. The plumage of the wings being spread, beating with a broad surface on the atmosphere beneath them, is resisted by the inertia of the atmosphere, so that the air forms a fulcrum, as it were, on which the bird rises by the leverage of its wings.

As a body at rest manifests its inertia by the resistance which it offers when put in motion, so a body in motion exhibits the same quality by the force with which it strikes a body at rest. We have seen examples of the resistance which the atmosphere at rest offers to a body in motion; but the force with which the atmosphere in motion acts upon a body at rest is exhibited by examples far more numerous and striking. Wind is nothing more than moving air; and its force, like that of every other body, depends on the quantity moved, and the speed of the motion. Every example, therefore, of the effects of the power of wind, is an example of the inertia of atmospheric air. In a windmill, the moving force of all the heavy parts of the machinery is derived from the moving force of the wind acting upon the sails, and the resistance of the work to which the mill is applied is overcome by the same power. A ship is propelled through the deep, and the deep itself is agitated and raised in waves by the inertia of the atmosphere in motion. As the velocity increases, the force becomes more irresistible, and we find buildings totter, trees torn from the roots, and even the solid earth itself yield before the force of the hurricane.

IMPENETRABILITY OF AIR.

Since air may be *seen* and *felt*—since it has color and weight—and since it opposes resistance when acted upon, and strikes with a force proportionate to the speed of its motion—we can scarcely hesitate to admit that it has qualities which entitle it to be classed among material substances; but one other quality still remains to be noticed, which perhaps decides its title to materiality more unanswerably than any of the others. Air is impenetrable; it enjoys that peculiar property of matter by which it refuses admission to any other body to the space it occupies, until it quit that space. This property air possesses as positively as adamant. The difficulty which is commonly felt in conceiving the impenetrability of substances of this nature arises partly from confounding the quality of impenetrability with that of hardness, and partly from not attending to the fact that, when a body moves through the air, it drives the air before it in the same manner as a vessel moving through the water propels the fluid.

Let a bladder be filled with air, and tied at the mouth: we shall then be able to feel the air it contains as distinctly as if the bladder were filled with a solid body. We shall find it impossible, so long as the air is prevented from escaping, to press the sides of the bladder together; and if the bladder be submitted to such severe pressure as may be produced by mechanical means, it will burst before the air will allow it to collapse.

That air will not allow the entrance of another body into the space where it is present, may also be proved by the following experiment:—

Let A B, fig. 1, be a glass vessel open at the end A, and having a short tube from the bottom, furnished with a stopcock C. Let D E, fig. 2, be another glass vessel containing water. On the surface of this water let a small piece of cork F float. Let the vessel A B, having the stopcock C closed, be now inverted; let its mouth A be placed over the cork F, and let it thus be pressed to any depth in the reservoir D E. If the air in A B were capable of permitting the entrance of another body into the space in which it is present, the water in the reservoir D E would now enter at the mouth of the vessel A, and rising in it, would stand at the same level within the vessel A B as that which it has without it. But this is not found to be the case. When the vessel A B is pressed into the reservoir, the surface of the water within A B will be observed still near the mouth A, as will be indicated by the position of the cork which floats upon it, and as is represented in fig. 3. It appears, there-

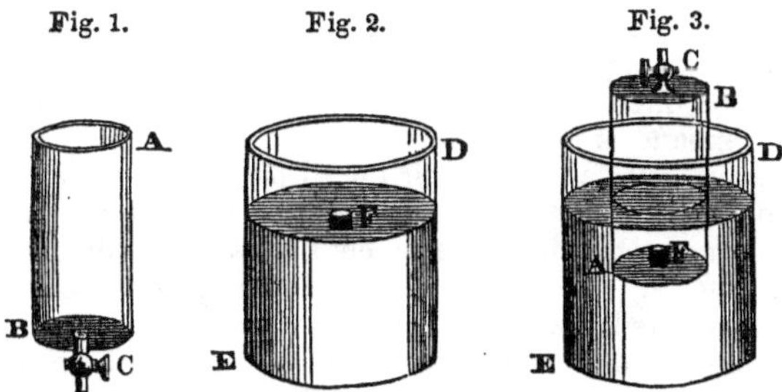

fore, manifestly, that whatever be the cause, the water is excluded from the vessel A B. That this cause is the presence of the air included in the vessel, is proved by opening the stopcock C, and allowing the air to escape. By the established principles of hydrostatics, the surface of the water within the vessel A B exerts an upward pressure proportionate to the depth of that surface below the surface of the water exterior to the vessel A B. This pressure acting upon the air enclosed in the vessel A B, forces it out the moment the stopcock C is opened, and immediately the surface of the water within A B rises to the level of the surface without it.

We have stated that the surface of the water within A B remains nearly at the mouth of that vessel when it is plunged in the reservoir. It would remain exactly at the mouth if air were incompressible; but, on the contrary, this fluid is highly compressible, allowing itself to be forced into reduced dimensions by the application of adequate mechanical force. It is necessary, however, not to confound compressibility with penetrability. So far from these qualities being identical, the one implies the absence of the other. A body is compressible when the forcible intrusion of another body into the space within which it is confined causes its particles to retreat and to accommodate their arrangement to the more limited space within which they are compelled to exist.

The very fact of their thus retreating before the intruding body is a distinct manifestation of their impenetrability. If they were penetrable, the body would enter the space in which they were confined, without driving them before it, or otherwise disturbing their arrangement.

ELASTICITY AND COMPRESSIBILITY OF AIR.

It will be evident, upon the slightest reflection, that the elasticity of air must be equal to the force which is necessary to confine it within the space it occupies. Let us suppose that A B, fig. 4, is a cylinder, having a piston P fitting

Fig. 4.

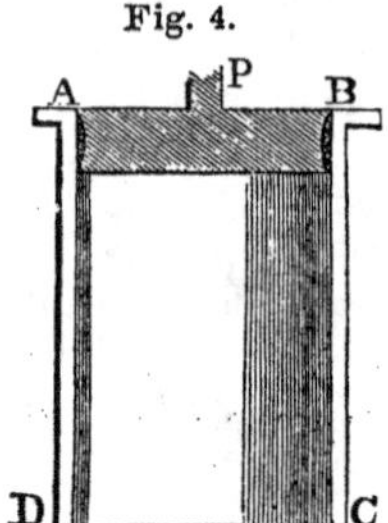

air-tight at the top; and let us imagine that this piston P is not acted upon by any external force having a tendency to keep it in its place. If the cylinder below the piston be filled with air, this air will have a tendency, by virtue of its elasticity, to expand into a wider space, and this tendency will be manifested by a pressure exerted by the air on all parts of the surfaces which confine it. The piston P will therefore be subject to a force tending to displace it and drive it from the cylinder, the amount of which will be the measure of the elasticity of the air beneath it. Now, if this piston be not subject to the action of a force directed inward, exactly equal in amount to the pressure thus exerted by the elastic force of the air, it cannot maintain its position. If it be subject to an inward force of less amount than the elastic pressure, then the latter will prevail, and the piston be forced out. If it be subject to an inward force greater in amount than the elastic pressure, then the former will prevail, and the piston will be forced in, the air being compelled to retreat within a more confined space. In no case, therefore, can the piston maintain its position, except when it is subject to an inward pressure exactly equal to the elastic force of the air enclosed in the cylinder.

The property of elasticity renders it necessary that, in whatever state air exist, it shall be restrained by adequate forces of some definite amount, and which serve as antagonist principles to the unlimited power of dilatation which the elastic property implies. In all cases which fall under common observation, air is either restrained by the resistance of solid surfaces, or it is pressed by the incumbent weight of the mass of atmosphere placed above it. It may be asked, however, whether it will not follow from this, that the extent of our atmosphere is infinite: for that, as we ascend in it, the weight of the superior mass of air must be gradually and unceasingly lessened, and therefore the force which resists the expansive principle being removed by degrees, the fluid will spread through dimensions which are subject to no limitation. Although it is undoubtedly true that these considerations lead us justly to conclude that our atmosphere extends to a great distance from the surface, and that the higher strata of it are attenuated to a degree which not only exceeds the powers of art to imitate, but even outstrips the powers of imagination to conceive; yet still the understanding can suggest a definite limit to this expansion. Numerous physical analogies favor the conclusion that the divisibility of matter has a limit, or that all material substances consist of ultimate constituent particles or atoms, which admit of no further subdivision, and on the mutual relations of which the form and properties of the various species of bodies depend.

Now those ultimate particles of the air are endued with a certain definite weight, because it is the aggregate of their weights which form the weight of any mass of air. It is a fact, established by experiment, that in proportion as air expands, its elastic force is diminished; and therefore, if it continue to expand, it will at length attain a state of attenuation in which the disposition of its constituent particles to separate by their elasticity is so far diminished as not to exceed the gravity of those constituent particles themselves. In this state the two forces will be in equilibrium, and the elastic force being neutralized, the particles will no longer be dilated.

In these observations we have assumed a principle which is of the last importance in pneumatics, and which, indeed, may be regarded as forming the basis of this part of physical science, in the same manner as the power of transmitting pressure is the fundamental principle of hydrostatics. This latter principle, indeed, also extends to elastic fluids; and all the consequences of the free transmission of pressure which do not also involve the supposition of incompressibility, are applicable to elastic fluids with as much truth as to liquids. But the principle to which we now more especially refer, and which may be looked upon as the chief characteristic of this form of body, and necessary to render definite the notion of their elasticity, may be announced as follows:—

"The elastic force of any given portion of air is augmented in exactly the same proportion as the space within which it is enclosed is diminished; and its elastic force is diminished in exactly the same proportion as the space through which it is allowed to expand is augmented."

Fig. 5.

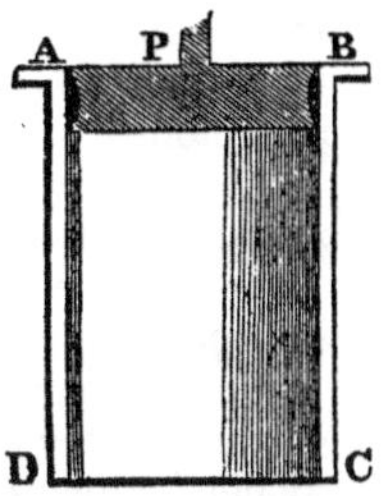

Fig. 6.

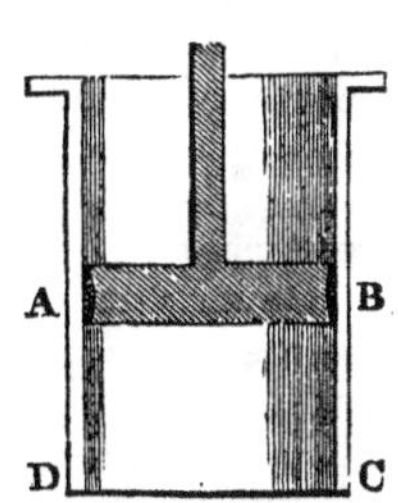

To explain this, let A B C D, fig. 5, be conceived to be a cylinder, in which a piston, A B, moves air tight, and without friction, and let us suppose the distance of the lower surface, A B, of the piston, from the bottom, D C, of the cylinder, to be 12 inches. Let air be imagined to be enclosed below the piston, and let us suppose that the elastic force of this air is such as to press the piston with a force of 16 ozs. From what has already been stated, it is clear that, to maintain the piston in its place, it is necessary that it should be pressed downward with an equivalent force of 16 ozs. Now let the force upon the piston be doubled, or let the piston be loaded with a pressure of 32 ounces. The inward pressure prevailing over the elasticity, the piston will immediately be forced toward D C, but will cease to move at a certain distance, A B, fig. 6, from the bottom. Now, if this distance A D be measured, it will be found to be exactly 6 inches. The air has, therefore, contracted itself into half its former dimensions.

Since the piston is sustained in the position represented in fig. 6, it follows that the elasticity of the air beneath it is equivalent to the weight of the piston, A B; and, therefore, that the air included in the cylinder acquires double its original elasticity when it is compressed into half its original bulk.

Let the piston be now loaded with three times its original weight, or 48 ounces; it will be observed to descend into the cylinder, and further to compress the air, until its distance from the bottom is reduced to 4 inches. At that distance it will rest, being balanced by the increased elasticity of the air: this air is now compressed into one third of its original bulk, and it has three times its original elastic force.

In the same manner, in whatever proportion the weight of the piston be augmented, in the same proportion will the distance from the bottom at which it will rest in equilibrium be diminished, and, consequently, the elastic force of the air is increased in the same proportion as the space into which it is compressed is diminished.

Let us, again, suppose the piston to be loaded with sixteen ounces, and to be balanced, as in fig. 5, by the resistance of the air at 12 inches from the bottom of the cylinder. But let us also suppose the cylinder continued upward to a height exceeding 24 inches; let the weight upon the piston be now reduced to eight ounces. Since the elasticity of the air beneath the piston was capable of supporting sixteen ounces, it will now prevail against the diminished pressure of eight ounces. The piston will continue to rise in the cylinder until the elasticity of the air is so far diminished by expansion that it is capable of supporting no more than eight ounces; the piston will then remain in equilibrium. If the height of the piston above the bottom be now measured, it will be found to be 24 inches, that is, double its former height; the air has, therefore, expanded to double its former dimensions, and is reduced to half its former elasticity.

In like manner it may be shown that if the weight upon the piston were reduced to four ounces, or a fourth of its original amount, the piston would rise to four times its original height, or 48 inches, before it would be capable of balancing the reduced elasticity of the air. Thus, by expanding to four times its primitive dimensions, the elasticity of the air is reduced to one fourth of its primitive amount.

By like experiments, it is easy to see how the general law may be established. In whatever proportion the weight of the piston may be increased or diminished, in the same proportion exactly will the space filled by the air which balances it be diminished or increased.

The preceding illustration has been selected with a view rather to make the property itself intelligible, than as a practical experimental proof of it. The use of pistons moveable in cylinders is attended with inconvenience in cases of this kind, arising from the effects of friction, and the difficulties of making due allowance for them. There is, however, another method of bringing the law to the test of experiment, which is not less direct, and is more satisfactory.

Let A B C D, fig. 7, be a glass tube curved at one end, B C, and having the short leg, C D, furnished with a stop-cock at its extremity; let the leg B A be more than 60 inches in length. The stop-cock D being opened so as to allow a free communication with the air, and the mouth A of the longer leg being also open, let as much mercury be poured into the tube as will fill the curved part B C, and rise to a small height in each leg. By the principles of hydrostatics, the surfaces of the mercury E and F will stand at the same level. Let the stop-cock D be now closed, the levels E F will still remain undisturbed. When the stop-cock D was opened, the surface F sustained a pressure equal to the weight of a column of air continued from F upward as far as the atmosphere extends. But the stop-cock D being closed, the effect of the weight of all the air above that point is intercepted; and, consequently, the surface F can sustain no pressure arising from weight, except the amount of the weight of the small quantity of air included between F and D, which is altogether insignificant. But the air thus included presses on the surface F by its elasticity; and the amount of this pressure is equal to the force which confined the air within the space F D before the stop-cock was closed: but this force was the weight of the column of atmosphere above D; and hence it appears, that the elastic force of the air confined in the space D F is equal to the atmospheric pressure.

Now the other surface, E, the end A of the tube being open, is subject to the atmospheric pressure. Thus the two surfaces, F and E, of the mercury, are each subject to a pressure arising from a different quality of atmosphere; the one F, being pressed by its elasticity, and the other, E, being pressed by its weight. These pressures being equal, the surfaces F and E continue at the same level.

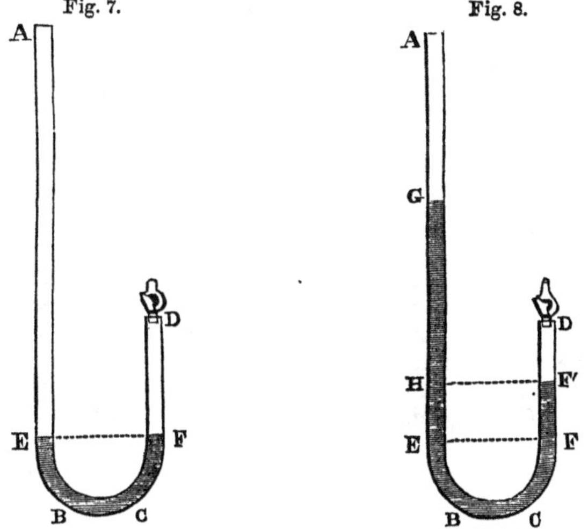

The method of ascertaining experimentally, the pressure arising from the weight of the atmosphere, will be fully explained hereafter; meanwhile, it is necessary for our present purpose to assume this pressure as known.

Let us suppose, then, that the atmospheric pressure acting upon the surface E is the same as would be produced by a column of mercury 30 inches in height resting on the surface E: the force with which the elasticity of the air confined in D F presses on the surface F is therefore equal to the weight of a a column of thirty inches of mercury. The pressure of the atmosphere acting on the surface E is transmitted by the mercury to the surface F and balances the elastic force just mentioned. Let the position of the surface F be marked upon the tube, and let mercury be poured into the longer leg at A. The increased pressure produced by the weight of this mercury will be transmitted to the surface F, and will prevail over the elasticity of the confined air; this surface will therefore rise toward D, compressing the air into a smaller space. Let the mercury continue to be poured in at A, until the surface F rise to F′, fig. 8, the middle point between the end D of the tube, and its first position F. The air included is thus compressed into half its former dimensions, and its elasticity will be measured by the amount of the force with which the surface A is pressed upward against it: this force is the weight of the column of mercury in the leg B A above the level of F together with the height of the atmosphere pressing on the top G of the column. Let a horizontal line be drawn from the surface F′, to the leg B A, and let the column G H be measured; its height will be found to be accurately 30 inches, and its weight is, therefore, equal to the atmospheric pressure. The force with which F is pressed upward is, therefore, equal to twice the atmospheric pressure, or to double the force with which F, in fig. 7, was pressed upward. Hence it appears that the elasticity of the air confined in the space D F, fig. 8, is double its former elasticity when filling the space D F′, fig. 7. Thus, when the air is compressed into half its volume its elasticity is doubled.

In like manner, if mercury be poured into the tube A until the air included in the shorter leg is reduced to a third of its bulk, the compressing force will be found to be three times the atmospheric pressure, and so on.

That the elasticity of the air which surrounds us is equal to the weight of the incumbent atmosphere, has been proved incidentally in the preceding experiment. Indeed, this is a proposition the truth of which must appear evident upon the slightest consideration, and which is manifested by innumerable familiar effects. If the elastic force of the air around us were less than the weight of the incumbent atmosphere, it would yield and suffer itself to be compressed until it acquired an elastic force equal to that weight. If it were greater in amount than the weight of the incumbent atmosphere, it would overcome that weight, and would press the atmosphere upward until, by expanding, its elasticity were reduced to equality with the weight of the atmosphere, and these effects are continually going forward.

The incumbent atmosphere is subject to continual fluctuations in weight, as will hereafter be proved, and the lowest stratum of air which surrounds us is continually undergoing corresponding contractions and expansions, ever accommodating its elasticity to the pressure which it sustains. Also this stratum of air is itself subject to changes of elasticity from vicissitudes of temperature proceeding from the earth to which it is contiguous. These changes produce a necessity for expansion and contraction in it, even while the weight of the incumbent atmosphere remains unchanged; but the full development of this last consideration belongs to the theory of heat rather than to our present subject.

An open vessel which is commonly said to be empty, is, in fact, filled with air; and when any solid or liquid is placed in it, so much of the air is expelled as occupied the space into which the solid or liquid entered. If such a vessel be closed by a lid or stopper, the pressure of the external atmosphere will act upon every part of the exterior surface with an intensity proportionate to its weight. The air which is enclosed in the vessel will, however, act on the interior surface with an intensity proportionate to its elasticity. According to what has already been explained, this elasticity is equal to the pressure; and, therefore, there is a force tending to press the sides of the vessel outward exactly equal to the pressure acting on the exterior surface, and tending to press them inward. These two forces neutralize each other, and the vessel is circumstanced exactly as if neither of them acted upon it.

When the operation and properties of some pneumatical instruments have been explained, we shall have occasion to notice many other effects of the elasticity of air.

THE NEW PLANETS.

Indications of a Gap in the Solar System.—Bode's Analogy.—Prediction founded upon it.—Piazzi discovers Ceres.—Dr. Olbers discovers Pallas.—Harding discovers Juno.—Dr. Olbers discovers Vesta.—Indications afforded by these Bodies of the Truth of Bode's Predictions.—Fragments of a Broken Planet.—Others probably still undiscovered.—Their Ultra-Zodiacal Motions.—Their Eccentricities.—They are probably not Globular.—Other Singularities of their Appearance.

THE NEW PLANETS.

At a very early period of astronomical inquiry it was observed that the spaces which intervene in the solar system between planet and planet augment in a double proportion as the planets recede from the sun. Thus the space between Mercury and Venus is only half that which intervenes between Venus and the earth. The latter, again, is only half that which separates this planet from Mars. In like manner, the space between Jupiter and Saturn is only half the space between Saturn and Herschel. To this remarkable law, however, a conspicuous exception was noticed by Kepler, and was more emphatically insisted upon and more strictly demonstrated in the latter part of the last century, by Bode of Berlin. While the spaces which successively intervene between the planets Mercury, Venus, the earth, and Mars, are continually in the proportion of one to two, that which intervenes between Mars and Jupiter, instead of being as it ought to be, in accordance with the law thus indicated—double the space between Mars and the earth—is, in fact, nearly six times that space. A planet, therefore, which would move between Mars and Jupiter, at a distance beyond Mars equal to twice the distance of Mars from the earth, would complete the system; for then there would be between such a planet and Jupiter twice the space which would intervene between it and Mars. The presence of such a planet would then remove all exception in the system to this law of increasing distance. Professor Bode ventured to predict that a planet would at some future period be discovered revolving in that position; and even if no such planet were discovered, he maintained that we should be justified in the inference that, at some former epoch, a planet did exist in such a position.

There is an instinctive faith in the harmony and universality of nature's laws; and when we behold in any of them a glaring exception, we are led at once to anticipate that such exception is only apparent, and that by increased knowledge we shall discover that the law is in reality universal.

This remarkable prediction, as may be easily imagined, attracted the attention of astronomers to those quarters of the firmament where the suspected planets ought to be seen; and on the first day of the present century, PIAZZI, an Italian astronomer, had his attention engaged by a small star of the fifth magnitude, which he thought presented peculiar appearances. He observed it accordingly from night to night, and soon found that it had a motion among the fixed stars, which was incompatible with the supposition that it could be a body of that class. In short, he soon discovered that this object was a true planet, and afterward applying to the observations made upon it the usual methods of calculation, he found that it moved in the solar system round the sun in the space between Mars and Jupiter, in such a position that its distance from the latter was double its distance from the former. In short, it appeared that this planet filled the vacant place.

On the 28th of March, in the following year, Dr. OLBERS, of Bremen, discovered the planet PALLAS, moving nearly at the same distance. In September, 1803, HARDING, also at BREMEN, discovered JUNO; and finally, on the 29th of March, 1807, Dr. OLBERS discovered the fourth new planet, VESTA. Thus within the first five years of the present century, four new members of the solar system were discovered, presenting, among other anomalous circumstances, the spectacle of four planets equidistant from the sun, and therefore all equally filling the vacant place declared to exist in the system by Kepler and Bode. As these four planets move nearly at the same distance from the sun, they also have nearly equal periods.

The analogy prevailing between the distances of the planets, indicated by Bode and Kepler, justified the expectation of the discovery of a single planet: how, then, are we to reconcile the principle indicated by this analogy with the known existence of four such bodies? This difficulty has been attempted to be removed by the hypothesis that the four new planets are, in fact, fragments of a single planet which has been broken! But how, it may be asked, could such a catastrophe as the fracture of a planet be brought about? To this it is answered that there are two causes—the possibility and reality of which are not disputed—either of which might produce such an effect. The volcanic phenomena developed on our own globe indicate to us the existence of internal causes which may easily be supposed to acquire sufficient energy to cause the explosion of the planet. The intersection, on the other hand, of the solar system, by innumerable comets rushing among the planets constantly and in every direction, renders the collision of such a body with a planet a possible occurrence. Either of these causes, then, being sufficient to produce the supposed catastrophe, and both being possible, the next question to be settled is, whether the circumstances attending the appearance, condition, and motion, of the new planets, are such as would attend the fragments of a single planet exploded or broken by either of these causes.

In the first place, then, it is evident that the magnitude of these four bodies recently discovered afford a strong presumption in favor of such a supposition. Their magnitudes are so minute, that astronomical observers as yet have been unable to agree as to their dimensions; but it seems certain that their diameters do not amount to more than a few hundred miles. They are therefore not only incomparably smaller than any of the other planets, but even smaller than the satellites. It is estimated that the bulk of VESTA does not exceed the twenty-five thousandth part of the earth. HERSCHEL states that the diameter of CERES cannot much exceed a hundred and fifty miles, and that that of JUNO is under one hundred miles. It is calculated that the aggregate of the volumes of all these four planets united would not exceed the twenty-fifth part of the bulk of our globe.

This minuteness of size is evidently a circumstance that might naturally be expected in the fragments of a single planet; and as from their smallness it is difficult to observe these planets even by the aid of telescopes, it seems probable there may be other fragments revolving round the sun too minute to be discovered.

If a planet were broken into fragments, whether by external collision or by internal explosion, it is demonstrable that the fragments into which it would be resolved would severally revolve round the sun as independent planets. Their orbits would be all nearly at the same distance from the sun as the orbit of the original planet. These orbits, however, would be likely to differ from that of the original planet in some respects. It is consistent with mechanical laws that these orbits should some of them be inclined at a considerable angle to the general plane of the solar system. It is also probable that these orbits or some of them, might be more eccentric in their elliptical character than the planetary orbits generally are. Now we find on examining the orbits of the four new planets, that they partake of these characters. They are inclined to the ecliptic at angles so considerable that they are the only planets which transcend the limits of the zodiac, and are thence called *ultra-zodiacal planets*. The eccentricities of some of their orbits are three or four times greater than those of the planets generally.

It is also demonstrable that if a planet were broken by any cause the orbits of its fragments which would form independent planets would all pass through a common point. Now this is a character which is also found to attach to the four new planets generally.

These circumstances would themselves afford a presumption so strong in support of the supposition that the new planets are in fact fragments of a single planet that has been broken as to amount almost to a moral certainty —but they are not the only ones that favor this hypothesis.

Appearances have been observed upon these planets which render it extremely probable if not certain that they are not like the other bodies of the system globular but that they are irregular in their form, having corners and angular extremities. This fact has been indicated by the sudden diminution of their light when the angular points pass the line of vision.

It is remarkable that VESTA, which is the smallest of the four in its absolute magnitude, appears, nevertheless, the most brilliant, having the lustre of a star of the fifth or sixth magnitude. SCHRÖTER, for this reason, was led to the supposition that VESTA was a self-luminous body. The three other planets, which are greater in magnitude than Vesta, have the appearance, nevertheless, of stars of the ninth and tenth magnitude. CERES would seem to be extremely irregular in its shape, since its light is very variable; sometimes it is reddish and vivid, sometimes whitish and pale.

The atmospheric circumstances attending these bodies are very remarkable. CERES and PALLAS, especially, seem to be enveloped in very dense atmospheres, which extend to a height from their surface from twelve to fifteen times greater than ours.

The light of Vesta is more intense and white than that of any other of the new planets. It also differs from them in not being surrounded by any nebulosity. Schröter affirms that he saw it several times with the naked eye, a circumstance which must have arisen from the brilliant light reflected from its surface not being obscured by any nebulous envelope.

The planet Juno subtends to the eye, when nearest to the earth, an angle of three seconds. It is of a reddish color; and Schröter discovered around it an atmosphere which he considered to be more dense than any of the atmospheres of the old planets. Remarkable and sudden changes were observed in the light of this planet, which Schröter first attributed to atmospheric phenomena upon it, but which have been since ascribed to great irregularity in its form. He imagined also that its appearance afforded indications of a diurnal rotation in twenty-seven hours: this, however, has not been confirmed by subsequent observation.

The apparent magnitude of Ceres is about six seconds: it is an object of a ruddy color, appears about the size of a star of the eighth or ninth magnitude, and is invisible to the naked eye. It is surrounded with a dense atmosphere, and shows an ill-defined disk. Schröter found, by a great number of observations, that the height of its atmosphere amounted to nearly seven hundred miles—that it was very dense near the surface of the planet, and more attenuated at greater heights—and that it was subject to changes which produced great variations in the apparent size of the planet.

Sir William Herschel, about the year 1802, immediately after the discovery of Ceres and Pallas, undertook a series of observations with his powerful reflecting telescopes, with a view of ascertaining whether either of these planets were attended by satellites. Many minute stars appeared near the disk of Ceres, but none exhibited that change of position which could be supposed to belong to a satellite. His observations fully corroborated those of Schröter. He says that when viewed with a power of 550, Ceres is surrounded with a strong haziness; the breadth of the coma beyond the disk may amount to the extent of a diameter of the disk, which is not very sharply defined. Were the whole coma and star taken together, they would be at least three times as large as the star. The coma was very dense near the nucleus, but lost itself pretty abruptly on the outside, though a gradual diminution was still very perceptible.

The planet Pallas has a ruddy appearance, but not so much so as Ceres. It is surrounded also by a nebulosity, but not so extensive. The height of its atmosphere, according to Schröter, is about 450 miles, being two thirds of that of Ceres. The light of the planet is eminently subject to those sudden variations which have been taken to indicate irregularity of form.

Sir William Herschel says, in speaking of Pallas: "I cannot, with the utmost attention, and under the most favorable circumstances, perceive any sharp termination which might denote a disk; it is, rather, what I would call a nucleus. The appearance of Pallas is cometary, the disk, if it has any, being ill-defined. When I see it to the best advantage, it appears like a much-compressed, extremely-small, but ill-defined, planetary nebula. With a twenty-foot reflector, power 477, I see Pallas well. I perceive a very small disk, with a coma of some extent about it, the diameter of which may amount to six or seven times that of the disk alone." These observations were made in 1802.

Great diversity of opinion has prevailed respecting the actual diameter of the new planets, Herschel estimating all of them to be considerably under 200 miles, while Schröter maintains that some of them are as large as our moon. This diversity is doubtless produced by the extreme smallness of the planets, their great distance, and the undefined appearance they have, owing to the nebulosity which surrounds them.

We shall have occasion again to notice the theory which explains them by the supposition that they are fragments of a broken planet, when we shall refer to the subject of meteoric stones.

THE TIDES.

Correspondence between the Tides and Phases of the Moon shown by Kepler.—Erroneous popular Notion of the Moon's Influence.—Actual Manner in which the Moon operates.—Influence of the Sun.—Combined Action of the Sun and Moon.—Spring Tides.—Counter-action of the Sun and Moon.—Neap Tides.—Priming and Lagging of the Tides.—Discussions at the British Association.—Whewell's Researches.—Effect of Continents and Islands on the Tides.—General Progress of the Great Tidal Wave.—Velocity of the Tidal Wave.—Range of the Tide.

14

THE TIDES.

The phenomena of the tides of the ocean are too remarkable and important to the social and commercial interests of mankind, not to have attracted notice at an early period in the progress of knowledge. The intervals between the epochs of high and low water everywhere corresponding with the intervals between the passage of the moon over the meridian above and below the horizon, suggested naturally the physical connexion between these two effects, and indicated the probability of the cause of the tides being found in the motion of the moon.

Kepler developed this idea, and demonstrated the close connexion of these phenomena; but it was not until the theory of gravitation was established by Newton, and its laws fully developed, that all the circumstances of the tides were clearly explained, and shown incontestably to depend on the influence of the sun and moon.

There are few subjects in physical science about which there prevail more erroneous notions among those who are but a little informed, than with respect to the tides. A common idea is, that the attraction of the moon draws the waters of the earth toward that side of the globe on which the moon happens to be placed, and that consequently they are heaped up on that side, so that the oceans and seas acquire there a greater depth than elsewhere; and thus it is attempted to be established that high water will take place under, or nearly under, the moon. But this neither corresponds with the fact, nor, if it did, would it explain it. High water is not produced merely under the moon, but is equally produced upon those parts most removed from the moon. Suppose a meridian of the earth so selected, that, if it were continued beyond the earth, its plane would pass through the moon; then we find that, subject to certain modifications, a great tidal wave, or what is called *high water*, will be formed on both sides of this meridian; that is to say, on the side next the moon, and on the side remote from the moon. As the moon moves in her monthly course round the earth, these two great tidal waves follow her. They are, of course, separated from each other by half the circumference of the globe. As the globe revolves with its diurnal motion upon its axis, every part of its surface passes successively under these tidal waves; and at all such parts as they pass under them, there is the phenomenon of high water. Hence it is that in all places there are two tides daily, having an interval of about twelve hours between them. Now if the common notion of the cause of the tides were well founded, there would be only one tide daily; viz., that which would take place when the moon is at or near the meridian.

That the moon's attraction upon the earth simply considered would not explain the tides, is easily shown. Let us suppose that the whole mass of matter on the earth, including the waters which partially cover it, were attracted equally by the moon; they would then be equally drawn toward that body, and no reason would exist why they should be heaped up under the moon; for if they were drawn with the same force as that with which the solid globe of the earth under them is drawn, there would be no reason for supposing that the waters would have a greater tendency to collect toward the moon than the solid bottom of the ocean on which they rest. In short, the whole mass of the earth, solid and fluid, being drawn with the same force, would equally tend toward the moon; and its parts, whether solid or fluid, would preserve among themselves the same relative position as if they were not attracted at all.

When we observe, however, in a mass composed of various particles of matter, that the relative arrangement of these particles is disturbed, some being driven in certain directions more than others, the inference is, that the component parts of such a mass must be placed under the operation of different forces; those which tend more than others in a certain direction being driven with a proportionally greater force. Such is, in fact, the case with the earth, placed under the attraction of the moon. NEWTON showed that the law of gravitation is such, that its attraction increases as the distance of the attracted object diminishes, and diminishes as the distance of the attracted object increases. The exact proportion of this change of energy of the attractive force, is technically expressed by stating that it is the inverse proportion of the square of the distance; the meaning of which is, that the attraction which any body like the moon would exercise at any proposed distance, is four times that which it would exercise at twice the distance; nine times that which it would exert at three times the distance; one fourth of that which it would exercise at half the distance, and one ninth of that which it would exercise at one third the distance, and so on. Thus we have an arithmetical rule, by which we can with certainty and precision say how the attraction of the moon will vary with any change of its distance from the attracted object. Let us see how this will be brought to bear upon the explanation of the effect of the moon's attraction upon the earth.

Let A, B, C, D, E, F, G, H, represent the globe of the earth, and, to simplify the explanation, let us first suppose the entire surface of the globe to be covered with water. Let M, the moon, be placed at the distance K L from the nearest point of the surface of the earth. Now it will be very apparent that the various points of the earth's surface are at different distances from the moon, M. A and G are more remote than H; B F still more remote; C and E more distant again, and D more remote than all. The attraction which the moon exercises at H is, therefore, greater than that which it exercises at A and G, and still greater than that which it produces at B and F; and the attraction which it exercises at D is least of all. Now this attraction equally affects matter in every state and condition. It affects the particles of fluid as well as solid matter, but there is this difference between these effects; that where it acts upon solid matter, the component parts of which are at different distances from it, and therefore

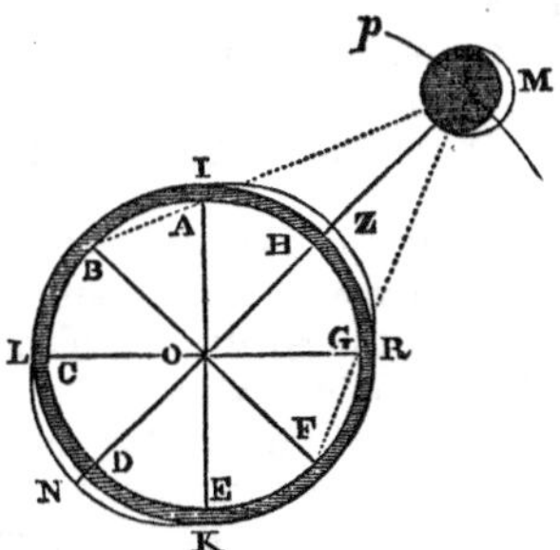

subject to different attractions, it will not disturb the relative arrangement of these particles, since such disturbances or disarrangements are prevented by the cohesion which characterizes a solid body; but this is not the case with fluid, the particles of which are mobile, and which, when solicited by different forces, will have their relative arrangements disturbed in a corresponding manner.

The attraction which the moon exercises upon the shell of water which is collected immediately under it near the point Z, is greater than that which it exercises upon the solid mass of the globe at H and D; consequently there will be a greater tendency of this attraction to draw the fluid which rests upon the surface at H toward the moon, than to draw the solid mass of the earth which is more distant.

As the fluid, by its nature, is free to obey this excess of attraction, it will necessarily heap itself up in a pile or wave at H, forming a more convex protuberance, as represented in the figure between R and I. Thus high water will take place at H, immediately under the moon. The water which thus collects at H, will necessarily flow from the regions B and F, where, therefore, there will be a diminished quantity of water in the same proportion.

But let us now consider what happens to that part of the earth, D, most remote from the moon. Here the waters being more remote from the moon than the solid mass of the earth under them, will be less attracted; and consequently will have a less tendency to gravitate toward the moon. The solid mass of the earth, D H, will, as it were, recede from the waters at N, in virtue of the excess of attraction, leaving these waters behind it, which will thus be heaped up at N, so as to form a convex protuberance between L and K, similar, exactly to that which we have already described between R and I. As the difference between the attraction of the moon on the waters at Z and the solid earth under the waters, is nearly the same as the difference between its attraction on the latter and upon the waters at N, it follows that the height of the fluid protuberances at Z and N are equal. In other words, the height of the tides on opposite sides of the earth, the one being under the moon and the other most remote from it, are equal.

Now from this explanation, it will, we trust, be apparent, that the cause of the tides, so far as the action of the moon is concerned, is not, as is vulgarly supposed, due to the mere attraction of the earth; since, if that attraction were equal in all the component parts of the earth, there would assuredly be no tides. We are to look for the cause, then, not in the attraction of the moon, but in the *inequality* of its attraction on different parts of the earth. The greater this inequality is, the greater will be the tides. Hence, as the moon is subject to a slight variation of distance from the earth, it will follow, that when it is at its least distance, or at the point called *perigee*, the tides will be greatest; and when it is the greatest distance, or at the point called *apogee*, the tides will be least; not because the entire attraction of the moon in the former case is greater than in the latter, but because the diameter of the globe bearing a greater proportion to the lesser distance than the greater, there will be a greater *inequality* of attraction.

It will doubtless occur to those who bestow on these observations a little reflection, that all which we have stated in reference to the effect produced by the attraction of the moon upon the earth, will also be applicable to the attraction of the sun. This is undoubtedly true; but in the case of the sun the effects are modified, in some very important respects, as will readily be seen. The sun is at four hundred times a greater distance than the moon, and the actual amount of its attraction on the earth would, on that account, be one hundred and sixty thousand times less than that of the moon; but the mass of the sun exceeds that of the moon in a much greater ratio than that of one hundred and sixty thousand to one. It therefore possesses a much greater attracting power in virtue of its mass, compared with the moon, than it loses by its increased distance. The effect is, that it exercises upon the earth an attraction enormously greater than the moon exercises. Now, if the simple amount of its attraction were, as is commonly supposed, the cause of the tides, the sun ought to produce a vastly greater tide than the moon. The reverse is, however, the case, and the cause is easily explained. Let it be remembered that the tides are due solely to the inequality of the attraction on different sides of the earth; and the greater that inequality is, the greater will be the tides, and the less that inequality is, the less will be the tides.

Now in the case of the sun, its total distance from the earth is one hundred millions of miles, and the difference between its distance from one side of the earth, and from the other, is only eight thousand miles, or about one hundred and twenty thousandth part of the whole distance. The inequality of the attraction of the sun, therefore, on different sides of the earth will be in the proportion of the square of the numbers one hundred and twenty thousand and one hundred and twenty thousand and one to each other, a proportion which it will be evident, is extremely small. But in the case of the moon, the distance of that object being about two hundred and forty thousand miles, or thirty diameters of the earth, the difference between its distance from one side to

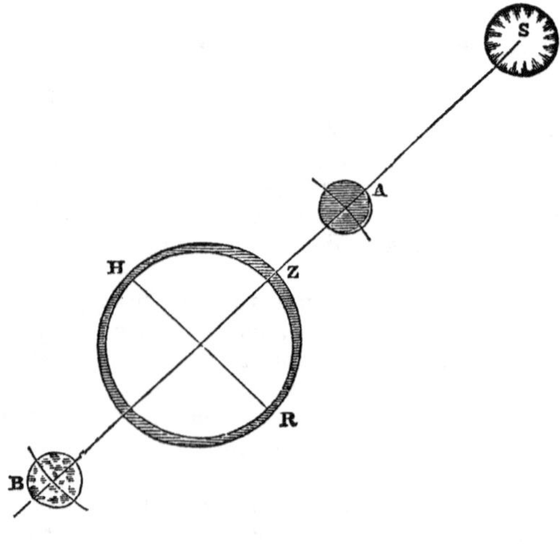

the other will be in the proportion of thirty to thirty-one; and the difference of the attraction will be in the proportion of the squares of those numbers. In the case, therefore, of the sun, the difference of the distances to the whole, then, is in proportion of one to one hundred and twenty thousand; whereas, in the case of the moon it is in the proportion of one to thirty.

Still, although the difference of the attractions of the sun on different sides of the earth is infinitely less than those of the moon, it is not imperceptible; and the sun does actually produce sensible tides on opposite sides of the earth, as the moon does. When the sun and moon, therefore, are either on the same side of the earth, or on the opposite sides of the earth; in other words, when it is new or full moon, then their effects in producing tides are combined, and the spring tide is produced; the height of which is equal to the solar and lunar tides taken together. These positions are represented in the preceding diagram, where S is the sun, A the moon when new, and B the moon when full. Hence it is that, at the epochs of new and full moons, we have tides of extraordinary elevation, called *spring tides*.

On the other hand, when the sun and moon are separated from each other by a distance of one fourth of the heavens, that is, when the moon is in the quarters, the effect of the solar tide has a tendency to diminish that of the lunar tide. This position is represented in the annexed diagram.

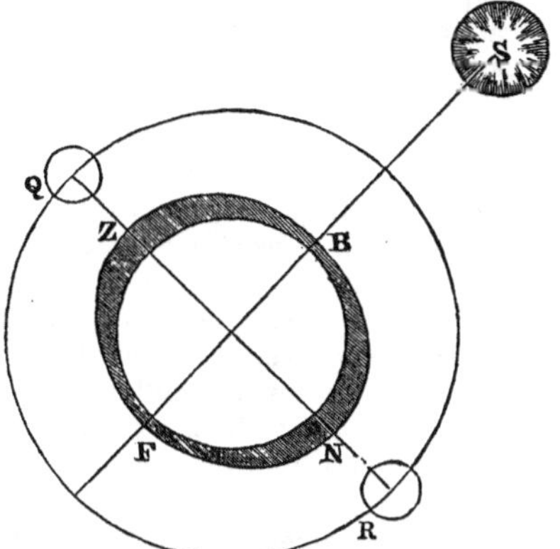

If *Q* and R represent positions of the moon, and *S* that of the sun at the epochs of the quarters, then the lunar tides would cause the waters to be collected at *Z* and *N;* whereas the solar tides would take place at *B* and *F*. The tendency, therefore, of the sun, would be to draw the water from *Z* and *N* toward *B* and *F;* and to the same extent would diminish the effect of the moon's attraction. The lunar tides would be less, under these circumstances, than in other positions of the moon. These have, therefore, been called the *neap tides*.

If physical effects followed immediately, without any appreciable interval of time, the operation of their causes, then the tidal wave produced by the moon would be on the meridian of the earth directly under and opposite to that luminary; and the same would be true of the solar tides. But the waters of the globe have, in common with all other matter, the property of inertia, and it takes a certain interval of time to impress upon them a certain change of position. Hence it follows that the tidal wave produced by the moon is not formed immediately under that body but follows it at a certain distance. In consequence of this, the tide raised by the moon does not take place for 2 or 3 hours after the moon passes the meridian; and as the action of the sun is still more feeble, there is a still greater interval between the transit of the sun and occurrence of the solar tide.

But besides these circumstances, the tide is affected by other causes. It is not the separate effect of either of these bodies, but to the combined effect of both, and at every period of the month, the time of actual high water is either accelerated or retarded by the sun. In the first and third quarters of the moon, the solar tide is westward of the lunar one; and, consequently, the actual high water which is the result of the combination of the two waves will be to the westward of the place it would have if the moon acted alone, and the time of high water will therefore be accelerated. In the second and fourth quarters the general effect of the sun is, for a similar reason, to produce a retardation in the time of high water. This effect produced by the sun and moon combined, is what is commonly called the *priming* and *lagging* of the tides.

The highest spring tides occur when the moon passes the meridian about an hour after the sun; for then the maximum effect of the two bodies coincides.

The subject of the tides has of late years received much attention from several scientific investigators in Europe. The discussions held at the annual meetings of the British association for the advancement of science, on this subject, have led to the development of much useful information. The labors of Professor Whewell have been especially valuable on these questions. Sir John Lubbock has also published a valuable treatise upon it. To trace the results of these investigations in all the details which would render them clear and intelligible, would greatly transcend the necessary limits of this discourse. We shall, however, briefly advert to a few of the most remarkable points connected with these questions.

The apparent time of high water at any port in the afternoon of the day of new or full moon, is what is usually called the *establishment of the port*. Professor Whewell calls this the vulgar establishment, and he calls the *corrected establishment* the mean of all the intervals of the tides and transit of half a month. This corrected establishment is consequently the luni-tidal interval corresponding to the day on which the moon passes the meridian at noon or midnight.

The two tides immediately following another, or the tides of the day and night, vary, both in height and time of high water, at any particular place with the distance of the sun and moon from the equator. As the vertex of the tide wave always tends to place itself vertically under the luminary which produces it, it is evident that of two consecutive tides that which happens when the moon is nearest the zenith or nadir will be greater than the other; and, consequently, when the moon's declination is of the same denomination as the latitude of the place, the tide which corresponds to the upper transit will be greater than the opposite one, and *vice versa*, the differences being greatest when the sun and moon are in opposition, and in opposite tropics. This is called the diurnal inequality, because its cycle is one day; but it varies greatly at different places, and its laws, which appear to be governed by local circumstances, are very imperfectly known.

We have now described the principal phenomena that would take place were the earth a sphere, and covered entirely with a fluid of uniform depth. But the actual phenomena of the tides are infinitely more complicated. From the interruption of the land, and the irregular form and depth of the ocean, combined with many other disturbing circumstances, among which are the inertia of the waters, the friction on the bottom and sides, the narrowness and length of the channels, the action of the wind, currents, difference of atmospheric pressure, &c., &c., great variation takes place in the mean times and heights of high water at places differently situated; and the inequalities above alluded to, as depending on the parallax of the moon, her position with respect to the sun, and the declination of the two bodies, are in many cases altogether obliterated by the effects of the disturbing influences, or can only be detected by the calculation and comparison of long series of observations.

By reason of these disturbing causes, it becomes a matter of great difficulty to trace the propagation of the tide wave, and the connexion of the tides in different parts of the world. In the *Philosophical Transactions* for 1832, Sir John Lubbock published a map of the world, in which he inserted the times of high water at new and full moon at a great number of places on the globe, collected from various sources, as works on navigation, voyages, sailing directions, &c., and in order that the march of the tide wave might be traced more readily, the times were expressed in Greenwich time, as well as the time of the place. In the same *Transactions* for 1833, Mr. Whewell prosecuted this subject at greater length, and availing himself of *à-priori* considerations, as well as of a mass of information collected in the hydrographer's office at the admiralty, inserted in the map a series of *cotidal lines*, or lines along which high water takes place at the same instant of time. But these cotidal lines, as Sir John Lubbock remarks, are entirely hypothetical; for we have few opportunities of determining the time of high water at a distance from the coast, though this is sometimes possible by means of a solitary island, such as St. Helena.—*Lubbock's Elementary Treatise on the Tides*, 1839.

According to Mr. Whewell's deduction, the general progress of the great tide wave may be thus described; it is only in the Southern ocean, between the latitudes of 30° and 70°, that a zone of water exists of sufficient extent to allow of the tide-wave being formed. Suppose, then, a line of contemporary tides, or *cotidal line*, to be formed in the Indian ocean, as the theory supposes, that is to say, in the direction of the meridian, and at a certain distance to the eastward of the meridian in which the moon is. As this tide-wave passes the Cape of Good Hope, it sends off a derivative undulation, which advances northward up the Atlantic ocean, preserving always a certain proportion of its original magnitude and velocity. In travelling along this ocean the wave assumes a curved form, the convex part keeping near the middle of the ocean, and ahead of the branches, which, owing to the shallower waters, lag behind on the American and African coasts, so that the cotidal lines have always a tendency to make very oblique angles with the shore, and, in fact, run parallel to it for great distances. The main tide, Mr. Whewell conceives, after reaching the Orkneys, will move forward in the sea bounded by the shores of Norway and Siberia on one side and those of Greenland and America on the other, will pass the pole of the earth and finally end its course on the shores in the neighborhood of Behring's straits. It may even propagate its influence through the straits, and modify the tides of the North Pacific. But a branch tide is sent off from this main tide into the German ocean; and this, entering between the Orkneys and the coast of Norway, brings the tide to the east coast of England and to the coasts of Holland, Denmark, and Germany. Continuing its course, part of it passes through the strait of Dover and meets in the British channel the tide from the Atlantic, which arrives on the coast of Europe twelve hours later; but in passing along the English coast, another part of it is reflected from the projecting land of Norfolk upon the north coast of Germany, and again meets the tide wave on the shores of Denmark. Owing to this interference of different tide-waves, the tides are almost entirely obliterated on the coast of Jutland, where their place is supplied by continual high water.

In the Pacific ocean the tides are very small; but there are not sufficient observations to determine the forms and progress of the cotidal lines. Off Cape

Horn, and round the whole shore of Terra-del-Fuego, from the western extremity of Magellan's strait to Staten Island, it is very remarkable that the tidal wave, instead of following the moon in its diurnal course, travels to the *eastward*. This, however, is a partial phenomenon; and a little farther to the north of the last-named places, the tides set to the north and west. In the Mediterranean and Baltic seas the tides are inconsiderable, but exhibit irregularities for which it is difficult to account. The Indian ocean appears to have high water on all sides at once, though not in the central parts at the same time.

Since the tides on our coast are derived from the oscillations produced under the direct agency of the sun and moon in the Southern ocean, and require a certain interval of time for their transfer, it follows that, in general, the tide is not due to the moon's transit immediately preceding, but is regulated by the position which the sun and the moon had when they determined the primary tide. The time elapsed between the original formation of the tide and its appearance at any place is called the *age* of the tide, and sometimes, after Bernoulli, the *retard*. On the shores of Spain and North America, the tide is a day and a half old; in the port of London, it appears to be two days and a half old when it arrives.

VELOCITY OF THE TIDE WAVES.

In the open ocean the crest of tide travels with enormous velocity. If the whole surface were uniformly covered with water, the summit of the tide wave, being mainly governed by the moon, would everywhere follow the moon's transit at the same interval of time, and consequently travel round the earth in a little more than twenty-four hours. But the circumference of the earth at the equator being about 25,000 miles, the velocity of propagation would therefore be about 1,000 miles per hour. The actual velocity is, perhaps, nowhere equal to this and is very different at different places. In latitude 60° south, where there is no interruption from land (excepting the narrow promontory of Patagonia), the tide wave will complete a revolution in a lunar day, and consequently travel at the rate of 670 miles an hour. On examining Mr. Whewell's map of cotidal lines, it will be seen that the great tide wave from the Southern ocean travels from the Cape of Good Hope to the Azores in about twelve hours, and from the Azores to the southernmost part of Ireland in about three hours more. In the Atlantic, the hourly velocity in some cases appears to be 10° latitude, or near 700 miles, which is almost equal to the velocity of sound through the air. From the south point of Ireland to the north point of Scotland, the time is eight hours, and the velocity about 160 miles an hour along the shore. On the eastern coast of Britain, and in shallower water, the velocity is less. From Buchanness to Sunderland it is about sixty miles an hour; from Scarborough to Cromer, thirty-five miles; from the north Foreland to London, thirty miles; from London to Richmond, thirteen miles an hour in that part of the river. (Whewell, *Phil. Trans.* 1833 and 1836.) It is scarcely necessary to remind the reader that the above velocities refer to the transmission of the undulation, and are entirely different from the velocity of the current to which the tide gives rise in shallow water.

RANGE OF THE TIDE.

The difference of level between high and low water is affected by various causes, but chiefly by the configuration of the land, and is very different at different places. In deep inbends of the shore, open in the direction of the tide wave and gradually contracting like a funnel, the convergence of water causes a very great increase of the range. Hence the very high tides in the Bristol channel, the bay of St. Malo, and the bay of Fundy, where the tide is said to rise sometimes to the height of one hundred feet. Promontories, under certain circumstances, exert an opposite influence, and diminish the magnitude of the tide. The observed ranges are also very anomalous. At certain places on the southeast coast of Ireland, the range is not more than three feet, while at a little distance on each side it becomes twelve or thirteen feet; and it is remarkable that these low tides occur directly opposite the Bristol channel, where (at Chepstow) the difference between high and low water amounts to sixty feet. In the middle of the Pacific it amounts to only two or three feet. At the London docks, the average range is about 22 feet; at Liverpool, 15.5 feet; at Portsmouth, 12.5 feet; at Plymouth, also 12.5 feet; at Bristol, 33 feet.

A great number of observations of the tides at the port of Brest during the last century were discussed by Laplace in the *Mécanique Céleste;* but in order to determine the motion of the tide wave, and separate the general laws of the phenomena from local irregularities, it is necessary to have regular series of observations made at different parts of the ocean. Until very recently, theory may be said to have been in advance of observation; but of late years the subject has received great attention, and at the present time a more perfect theory of hydrodynamics appears to be necessary for the physical explanation of the phenomena. In 1829, Sir John Lubbock undertook the discussion of the tide observations which are made at the London docks, with the view of obtaining correct tables for predicting the time and height of the tides for the *British Almanac.* The results, which were published in the *Philosophical Transactions* for 1831, are deduced from a series of upward of thirteen thousand observations during a period of nineteen years, and are of great importance, both as affording materials for the construction of tide-tables, and as pointing out the defects of the equilibrium theory, with which they were accurately compared. In some of the subsequent volumes of the *Transactions* the author has continued his investigations, and has also published separately an account of Bernoulli's *Traité sur le Flux et Reflux,* and an elementary treatise which appeared in 1839. In the *Philosophical Transactions* for 1833, Mr. Whewell gave an *Essay toward a first Approximation to a Map of Cotidal Lines,* which has been followed by a series of interesting papers in the subsequent volumes. Mr Whewell's researches have been chiefly directed to the determination of the following points: First, the motion of the tide wave at different parts of the ocean; secondly, the comparison of the observed laws at different places with the theory; and lastly, the laws of diurnal inequality. In 1834 the British Association procured an extensive series of observations to be made on the coasts of Britain and Ireland at five hundred and thirty-nine stations of the coast guard. These were repeated at the same places in June, 1835; and at the request of the British government, simultaneous observations were made by the other maritime powers of Europe and the United States. The number of stations in America was twenty-eight, extending from the mouth of the Mississippi to Nova Scotia; and the number on the continent of Europe one hundred and one, between the straits of Gibraltar and the North cape of Norway. The results of these observations reduced under Mr. Whewell's superintendence were published in the *Philosophical Transactions* for 1836; and they are of great importance, not only as affording a far more precise determination of the progress of the tide wave and the forms of the cotidal line on the coasts of Europe and North America than previously existed, but as furnishing more correct data for the construction of the tide-tables.

Besides the numerous causes of irregularity depending on the local circumstances, the tides are also affected by the state of the atmosphere. At Brest, the height of high water varies inversely, as the height of the barometer, and rises more than eight inches for a fall of about half an inch of the barometer. At Liverpool, a fall of one tenth of an inch in the barometer corresponds to a rise in the river Mersey of about an inch; and at the London docks, a fall of one tenth of an inch corresponds to a rise in the Thames of about seven tenths of an inch. With a low barometer, therefore, the tide may be expected to be high, and *vice versa*. The tide is also liable to be disturbed by winds. Sir John Lubbock states, that, in the violent hurricane of January 8, 1839, there was no tide at Gainsborough, which is twenty-five miles up the Trent—a circumstance unknown before. At Saltmarsh, only five miles up the Ouse from the Humber, the tide went on ebbing, and never flowed until the river was dry in some places; while at Ostend, toward which the wind was blowing, contrary effects were observed. During strong northwesterly gales the tide marks high water earlier in the Thames than otherwise, and does not give so much water, while the ebb tide runs out late, and marks lower; but upon the gales abating and weather moderating, the tides put in and rise much higher, while they also run longer before high water is marked, and with more velocity of current: nor do they run out so long or so low.

LIGHT.

Structure of the Eye.—Manner in which distant Objects become Visible.—Corpuscular Theory.—Undulatory Theory.—Its general Reception.—Velocity of Light.—Account of its Discovery by Roemer.—Measurement of the Waves of Light by Newton.—Color produced by Waves of different Magnitudes.—Magnitudes of Waves of different Color.—Summary View of the Corpuscular Theory.—Summary View of the Undulatory Theory.—These Theories compared.—Discoveries of Dr. Young.—Discoveries of Malus, Arago, Poisson, Herschel, and Airy.—Relations of Light and Heat.

LIGHT.

Among the many marvellous results of the labors of the human mind directed to the discovery of the laws of the physical creation, there is perhaps none which strike us with more astonishment than the knowledge which has been obtained relating to the qualities and laws of LIGHT. The principles which govern its reflection from opaque surfaces, and its transmission through transparent bodies, we shall examine on another occasion. I propose for the present to bring before you the facts which have been disclosed regarding its physical nature and its motion through space, as well as the manner in which it affects the organ of vision, so as to produce the perception of external and distinct objects.

Between the eye and any distant object, there intervenes a space of greater or less extent, and often, as in the instance of the stars, so great as to be scarcely capable of being clearly and adequately expressed by any standard or modolus of magnitude with which we are familiar. Yet objects, at these immense distances, are rendered visible to us by some physical effects which they are capable of producing and which in fact they do produce upon our organs of vision.

We shall see that the interior of the eye-ball is lined with a membrane highly susceptible of mechanical vibration and connected by a continuity of nerves with the brain; and to this membrane admission is given for light by an opening in front of the eye called the *pupil.* The light then proceeding from any distant object must be supposed to pass over the space intervening between the object and the eye, to enter the pupil and to produce upon the membrane within the eye a specific mechanical effect, which being propagated to the brain, is the means of producing in the mind a perception of the distant object.

How then are we to conceive that an object placed at any distance, for example, say one hundrod millions of miles, from the eye, can transmit over and through that space a mechanical effect which shall be impressed on the eye?

We answer that there are two and only two ways in which it is possible to conceive such an action to take place. These two are the following:—

First.—The distant object thus visible to us, may emit particles of matter from its surface, which particles of matter may pass over the intervening space, may enter the pupil of the eye, may strike upon the nervous membrane, and so affect it as to produce vision.

Secondly.—There may be in the space between the distant visible object and the eye, *a medium possessing elasticity*, so as to be capable of receiving and transmitting pulsations or undulations like those imparted to the air by a sounding body. If this be admitted, the distant visible object may, without emitting any particles of matter from its surface affect such a medium surrounding it with pulsations or undulations, in the same manner as a bell affects the air around it. These pulsations or undulations may pass along the space intervening between the visible object and the eye, in the same manner as the pulsations or undulations produced by a bell pass along the air between the bell and the ear. In this manner the pulsations transmitted from the visible object, and propagated by the medium, we have referred to, may reach the eye and affect the membrane which lines it, in the same manner exactly as the pulsations in the air affect the tympanum of the ear.

These are the two, and the only two modes, in which any human mind ever yet conceived that a distant object could become visible to the eye.

In the first, there is an analogy between the eye and the organs of smelling. Odorous objects do actually emit material effluvia, which must be supposed to form part of their own substance. These effluvia reach the organ of smelling, and produce upon it a specific effect, which impresses the mind with a corresponding perception. According to the first supposition, a visible object at any distance would act in the same way, and would eject continual particles of light, which particles of light would move to the eye and produce vision, acting mechanically on its membrane in the same manner as the effluvia of a rose produce a physical effect upon the organs of smelling.

The second method places the eye in analogy with the ear. So close is this analogy that all the mathematical formulæ by which the effects of sound are expressed in acoustics, will, with very slight changes, be capable of expressing the effects of vision, according to the latter hypothesis. It is evident, however, that as the first hypothesis requires us to admit that distant visible objects are continually ejecting matter from their surfaces to produce vision; so the second hypothesis as peremptorily requires the admission of the existence of some physical medium pervading the universe,—some subtle ethereal fluid endowed with a property of propagating the pulsations or undulations of distant visible objects and transmitting them to the eye. This hypothetical fluid has been called the *luminiferous ether*. The first of these two celebrated theories of light has been called the CORPUSCULAR THEORY, and the second the UNDULATORY THEORY.

Newton, although he did not identify his investigations in optics with any hypothesis, but in the spirit of the inductive philosophy founded by Bacon, based his conclusions on experiments and observations only, adopted nevertheless the nomenclature and language of the corpuscular theory, and, probably, from veneration for his authority, English philosophers, until recently, have very generally given the preference to that theory.

The undulating theory, on the other hand, was adopted by Huygens, and after him by most continental philosophers.

The researches in the phenomena of optics within the last hundred years have been marked by singular diligence and success. A vast variety of phenomena previously unknown, have been accurately investigated, new laws have been developed, and the general result has been that the undulatory theory has prevailed over the corpuscular. It is perhaps not an unfair statement of the actual condition of these two celebrated hypotheses, to say that while the corpuscular system is found sufficient to explain most of the common and obvious phenomena of optics, it totally fails in explaining many of the most remarkable effects brought to light by modern observations and experiments. On the other hand, the undulatory theory in general offers a satisfactory explanation for all. This circumstance has very properly and legitimately enlisted under that hypothesis almost all the leading scientific men of the present day.

Although the principal facts which we shall have now to explain are in fact independent of either of these two hypotheses, and incontestably true, whichever may be adopted, yet in their exposition, it will be necessary to adopt the language of one or the other of these theories. We shall, for the reason just stated, use the nomenclature of the undulatory theory.

We are then to imagine light to consist of undulations propagated through the universal ether, in the same manner as the waves or undulations of sound are propagated through the air.

The first question then that arises is, what is the velocity with which these waves move? At what rate does light come from a distant star to the eye? Is it propagated instantaneously? Would a fire suddenly lighted at a point one hundred millions of miles from the eye be seen at the moment the light was produced?—or would an interval of time be necessary to allow the light to reach the eye? and if so, what would be the interval of time in relation to the distance of the luminous object?

In tracing the progress of human knowledge, we frequently have occasions to behold with surprise, and not without a due sense of humility, the important part which accident plays in the advancement of science. Often are we with diligent zeal in search of things, which, if found, would be of trifling or no value, when we stumble on inestimable treasures of truth. The frequency of this, strongly impresses the mind with the persuasion that there is in secret operation a power whose will it is that knowledge and the human mind should be constantly progressive. It is in physics as in morals. We ignorantly seek that which is worthless and often find what is inestimable.

In the pursuit of knowledge we might well say that which we are taught to express in the pursuit of what is moral and good. We might say that the power which governs its progress knows better than what we do, "our necessities before we ask, and our ignorance in asking." We shall see a striking example of this in the narrative which I shall now offer of the celebrated discovery of the motion of light.

Soon after the invention of the telescope, and the consequent discovery of Jupiter's satellites, Roemer, an eminent Danish astronomer, engaged in a series of observations, the object of which was the discovery of the exact time of the revolution of one of these bodies around Jupiter. The mode in which he proposed to investigate this, was by observing the successive eclipses of the satellite, and noticing the time between them.

Let S represent the sun and A B C D E F G H the successive positions of the earth. Let J be Jupiter projecting behind him his conical shadow, and let M N O, represent the orbit of one of his satellites. After each revolution the satellite will enter the shadow at M, and emerge from it at N.

Now if it were possible to observe accurately the moment at which the satellite would, after each revolution, either enter the shadow, or emerge from it, the interval of time between these events would enable us to calculate exactly the velocity and motion of the satellite. But by attentively watching the satellite we can note the time it enters the shadow, for at that moment it is de-

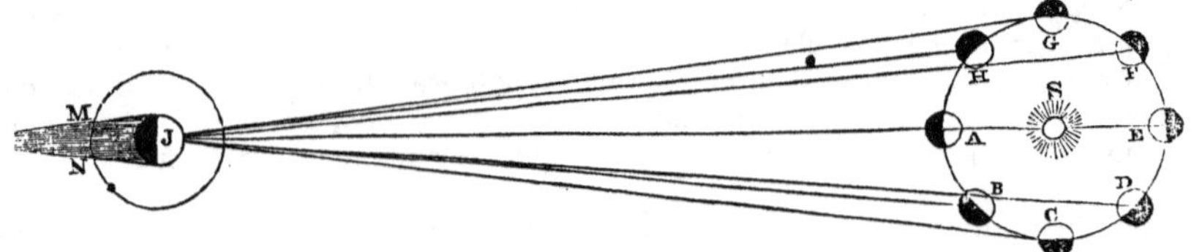

prived of the sun's light and becomes invisible. We can also note the moment of its emergence, because then escaping from the edge of the shadow it comes into the sun's light and becomes visible. It was, then, in this manner that Roemer proposed to ascertain the motion of the satellite. But in order to obtain this estimate with the greatest possible precision, he proposed to continue his observations for several months.

Let us, then, suppose that we have observed the time which has elapsed between two successive eclipses, and that this time is, for example, forty-three hours. We ought to expect that the eclipse would recur after the lapse of every successive period of forty-three hours.

Imagine, then, a table to be computed in which we shall calculate and register before hand the moment at which every successive eclipse of the satellite for twelve months to come shall occur, and let us conceive that the earth is at A, at the commencement of our observations, we shall then, as Roemer did, observe the moments at which the eclipses occur and compare them with the moments registered in the table.

Let the earth, be supposed at A, at the commencement of these observations, where it is nearest to Jupiter. When the earth has moved to B, which it will do in about six weeks, it will be found that the occurrence of the eclipse is *a little later* than the time registered in the table. When the earth arrives at C, which it will do at the end of three months, they will occur *still later* than the registered time. In fact at C, the eclipses will occur about eight minutes later than the registered time. At D they will be twelve minutes later, and at E sixteen minutes later.

By observations such as these Roemer was struck with the fact that his predictions of the eclipses proved in every case to be wrong. It would at first occur to him that this discrepancy might arise from some errors of his observations, but if such were the case, it might be expected that the result would betray that kind of irregularity which is always the character of such errors. Thus it would be expected that the predicted time would sometimes be later, and sometimes earlier than the observed time, and that it would be later and earlier to an irregular extent. On the contrary, it was observed during the six months which the earth took to move from A to E, that the observed time was continually later than the predicted time, and moreover, that the interval by which it was later continually and regularly increased. This was an effect, then, too regular and consistent to be supposed to arise from the casual errors of observation; it must have its origin in some physical cause of a regular kind.

The attention of Roemer being thus attracted to the question, he determined to pursue the investigation by continuing to observe the eclipses for another half year. Time accordingly rolled on, and the earth transporting the astronomer with it, moved from E to F. On arriving at F and comparing the observed with the predicted eclipse, it was found that the observed time was now only twelve minutes later than the predicted time. At the end of the ninth month when the earth arrived at G, the observed time was found to be only eight minutes later; at H it was only four minutes later, and finally, when the earth returned to the same relative position with the planet, the observed time corresponded precisely with the predicted time.*

From this course of observation and inquiry it became apparent that the lateness of the eclipse depended altogether on the increased distance of the earth from Jupiter. The greater that distance, the later was the occurrence of the eclipse as apparent to the observers, and on calculating the change of distance, it was found that the delay of the eclipse was exactly proportional to the increase of the earth's distance from the place where the eclipse occurred. Thus when the earth was at E, the eclipse was observed 16 minutes, or about 1,000 seconds later than when the earth was at A. The diameter of the orbit of the earth, A E, measuring about two hundred millions of miles, it appeared that that distance produced a delay of a thousand seconds, which was at the rate of two hundred thousand miles per second. It appeared, then, that for every two hundred thousand miles that the earth's distance from Jupiter was increased, the observation of the eclipse was delayed one second.

Such were the facts which presented themselves to Roemer. How were they to be explained? It would be absurd to suppose that the actual occurrence of the eclipses was delayed by the increased distance of the earth from Jupiter. These phenomena depend only on the motion of the satellite and the position of Jupiter's shadow, and have nothing to do with, and can have no dependance on the position or motion of the earth, yet unquestionably the time they *appear* to occur to an observer upon the earth, has a dependance on the distance of the earth from Jupiter.

To solve this difficulty, the happy idea occurred to Roemer that the moment at which we see the extinction of the satellite by its entrance into the shadow is not, in any case, the very moment at which that event takes place, but sometime afterward, viz.: such an interval as is sufficient for the light which left the satellite just before its extinction to reach the eye. Viewing the matter thus, it will be apparent that the more distant the earth is from the satellite, the longer will be the interval between the extinction of the satellite and the arrival of the last portion of light which left it, at the earth; but the moment of the extinction of the satellite is that of the commencement of the eclipse, and the moment of the arrival of the light at the earth is the moment the commencement of the eclipsed is observed.

Thus Roemer with the greatest facility and success explained the discrepancy between the calculated and the observed times of the eclipses; but he saw that these circumstances placed a great discovery at his hand. In short, it was apparent that light is propagated through space with a certain definite speed, and that the circumstances we have just explained supply the means of measuring that velocity.

We have shown that the eclipse of the satellite is delayed one second more for every two hundred thousand miles that the earth's distance from Jupiter is increased, the reason of which, obviously is, that light takes one second to move over that space; hence it is apparent that the velocity of light is at the rate, in round numbers, of two hundred thousand miles per second.

Such was the discovery which has conferred immortality upon the name of Roemer; a discovery to which, as we have shown, he was accidentally led when seeking to determine the velocity of one of the moons of Jupiter. The velocity thus determined would, in the corpuscular theory, be regarded as that with which the particles of light issuing from the surface of a visible object move

* Strictly speaking, the interval is longer than twelve months, but the circumstance is not important here.

through space. In the undulatory theory, however, which is more generally received, this velocity must be regarded as that with which the waves or undulations of light are propagated through space in the same sense as waves appear to move on the surface of water if a pebble be dropped in to form a centre round which they are propagated. It is necessary to remember when considering any system of undulations, no matter through what medium they may be propagated, that the progressive motion which belongs to them is a motion of form merely, and not of matter. The waves which are propagated round a centre when a pebble is dropped into calm water, present an appearance to the eye as though the water which formed the wave really moved outward from the centre of the undulations. Such is, however, not the case. No particle of the fluid has any progressive motion whatever, of which many proofs may be offered. If any floating body be placed on the surface of the water, it will not be carried along by the waves, and if similar waves be formed, as they might be, by giving a peculiar motion to a sheet or cloth, they would have the same appearance of progressive motion, although the parts of the sheet or cloth, as is evident, would have no other motion than the up-and-down motion that would form the apparent undulations. We are then to remember that when light is propagated through space with the astonishing velocity of two hundred thousand miles per second, there is no material substance which really has this progressive velocity; it belongs merely to the form of the pulsations, or undulations. The same observations, exactly, are applicable to the transmission of the waves of sound through the air.

In order to submit the phenomena of light to a strict physical analysis, it is not enough to measure the motion of its waves. We require also to know the amplitude or breadth of these waves, just as in the case of the waves of the sea we should require to know not only the rate at which they are propagated over the surface of the water, but also the space which intervenes between the hollow or crest of each successive wave and the hollow or crest of the succeeding one.

For the solution of this refined problem in the analysis of light, we are indebted to Newton himself. To render clearly intelligible the mode in which he solved it, let us imagine a flat plate of glass, such as A B, placed upon a convex lens of glass, such as C D, but let it be imagined that the degree of convexity is much less than that represented in the figure.

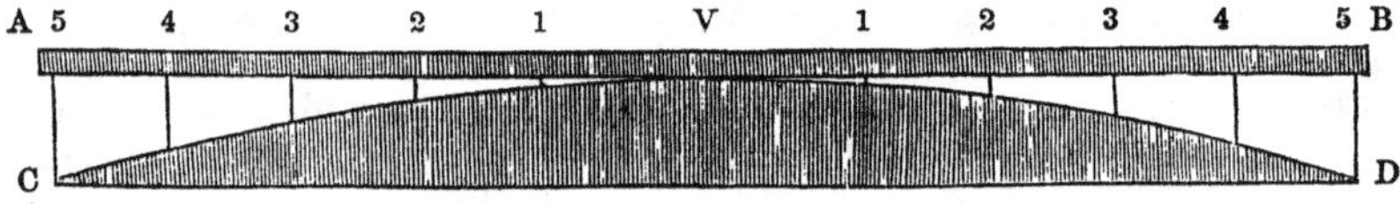

The under surface of the flat plate will touch the vertext of the convexity at V, and the further any point on the under surface is from V, the greater will be the distance between the surfaces of the two glasses. Thus the distance between them at 1 is less than at 2, and the distance at 2 is less than at O, and so on. The distance at the surfaces gradually increasing, in fact, from V outward.

If looking down on the plate A B, we consider the point V as a centre, and a circle be described round it, at all points of that circle the surfaces of the glasses will have the same distances between them, and the greater that circle is, the greater will be the distances between the surfaces of glass.

Having the glasses thus arranged, Newton let a beam of light of some particular color, produced by a prism, as red, for example, fall on the surface of the glass, A B. He found that the effect produced was that a black spot appeared at the centre, V, where the glasses touched; that immediately around this spot there appeared a circle of red light; that beyond that circle appeared a dark ring; that outside of that dark ring there was another circle of red light, still having the point V as its centre. Outside this second circle appeared another dark ring, beyond which there was another circle of red light, and so on, a series of circles of red light, alternated with dark rings being formed, all having the point V as their common centre.

The distances between the surfaces of glass at which the successive circles of red light were found, were too minute to be directly measured, but they were easily calculated by measuring the diameters of the circles of light; and knowing the diameters of the convex surface C V D, this was a simple problem of geometry, easily solved, and admitting the greatest accuracy.

On making these calculations, Newton found that the distance between the glass surfaces where the second red circle was formed was double the distance corresponding to the first; that at the third red circle the distance was triple that of the first, and so on. • It followed, of course, that wherever the dark rings were formed, the distance between the glass surfaces were not an exact number of times the space corresponding to the first red circle.

Thus if we express the space between the glasses at the first red circle by 1, the space between them within that circle, toward the centre V, would be a fraction. The space corresponding to the first dark ring outside the first red circle, would be expressed by 1 and a fraction; the space at the second red circle would be expressed by 2; the space at the second dark ring would be expressed by 2 and a fraction, and so on.

Newton was not slow to see that these phenomena were the direct manifestation of those effects which, in the corpuscular theory whose nomenclature he used, corresponded to the amplitude of the waves of light in the undulatory theory. The space between the surfaces of glass at the first red ring was the amplitude of a single wave, the space at the second red circle the amplitude of two waves, and so on. Within the first red circle, the space between the glasses being less than the amplitude of a wave, the propagation of the undulation was stopped, and darkness ensued; in like manner, in the space corresponding to the second dark ring, the distance between the glasses being greater than the amplitude of one wave, but less than the amplitude of two, the propagation was again stopped, and darkness produced. But at the second red circle, the space being equal to the amplitude of two waves, the undulations were reflected and the red ring produced, and so on.

It was evident, then, that to measure the amplitude of the luminous waves, it was only necessary to calculate the distance between the glasses at the first red ring.

When light of other colors was thrown upon the glass, a similar system of luminous rings was produced, but it was found in each case that the first ring varied in its diameter according to the color of the light, and consequently that the amplitude of the waves of lights of different colors are different. It appeared that the waves of red light were the largest; orange came next to them; then yellow, green, blue, indigo, and violet, succeeded each other, the waves of each being less than those of the preceding. But the most astonishing part of this most celebrated investigation was the minuteness of these waves. It appeared that the waves of red light were so minute, that forty thousand of them would be comprised within an inch, while the waves of violet light, forming the other extreme of the series, were so small, that sixty thousand spread over an inch, and the waves of light of other colors were of intermediate magnitudes.

Thus was discovered the physical cause of the splendor and variety of colors, and a singular and mysterious alliance was developed between color and sound. Lights are of various hues, according to the magnitude of the pulsations that produce them, exactly as musical sounds vary their tone and pitch according to the magnitude of the aerial pulsations from which they result.

But this is not all. The alliance between sound and light does not terminate here. We have only spoken of the amplitude of the luminous waves, and have shown that it determines the tints of colors. What are we to say for the altitudes of the waves? Here, again, is another link of kindred between the eye and the ear. As the altitude of sonorous waves determines the loudness of the sounds, so the altitude of luminous waves determines the intensity or brightness of the color.

There is one step more in the series of wondrous results which these memorable investigations have unfolded. As the perception of sound is produced by the tympanum of the ear vibrating in sympathetic accordance with the pulsations of the air produced by the sounding body, so the perception of light and color is produced by similar pulsations of the membrane of the eye vibrating in accordance with ethereal pulsations propagated from the visible object. As in the case of the ear, the rigor of scientific investigation requires us to estimate the rate of the pulsation of the tympanum corresponding to each particular note, so in the case of light are we required to count the vibrations of the retina of the eye corresponding to every tint and color. It may well be asked, in some spirit of incredulity, how the solution of such a problem could be hoped for; yet, as we shall now see, nothing can be more simple and obvious.

Let us suppose an object of any particular color, as a red star, for example, placed at a distance and seen by the eye. From the star to the eye there proceeds a continuous line of waves; these waves enter the pupil and impinge upon the retina; for each wave which thus strikes the retina, there will be a separate pulsation of that membrane. Its rate of pulsation, or the number of vibrations which it makes per second, will therefore be known, if we can ascertain how many luminous waves enter the eye per second.

It has been already shown that light moves at the rate of about two hundred thousand miles per second; it follows, therefore, that a length of ray amounting to two hundred thousand miles must enter the pupil each second; the number of times, therefore, per second, which the retina will vibrate, will be the same as the number of the luminous waves contained in a ray two hundred thousand miles long.

Let us take the case of red light. In two hundred thousand miles there are in round numbers a thousand millions of feet, and therefore twelve thousand millions of inches. In each of these twelve thousand millions of inches there are forty thousand waves of red light. In the whole length of the ray, therefore, there are four hundred and eighty millions of millions of waves. Since this ray, however, enters the eye in one second, the retina must pulsate once for each of these waves; and thus we arrive at the astounding conclusion, that when we behold a red object, the membrane of the eye trembles at the rate of four hundred and eighty millions of millions of times between every two ticks of a common clock!

In the same manner, the rate of pulsation of the retina corresponding to other tints of colors is determined; and it is found that when violet light is perceived, it trembles at the rate of seven hundred and twenty millions of millions of times per second.

In the annexed table are given the magnitudes of the luminous waves of each color, the number of them which measure an inch, and the number of undulations per second which strike the eye:—

Colors.	Length of undulation in parts of an inch.	Number of undulations in an inch.	Number of undulations per second.
Extreme Red...............	0·0000266	37640	458,000000,000000
Red.....................	0·0000256	39180	477,000000,000000
Orange..................	0·0000240	41610	506,000000,000000
Yellow..................	0·0000227	44000	535,000000,000000
Green...................	0·0000211	47460	577,000000,000000
Blue....................	0·0000196	51110	622,000000,000000
Indigo..................	0·0000185	54070	658,000000,000000
Violet..................	0·0000174	57490	699,000000,000000
Extreme Violet............	0·0000167	59750	727,000000,000000

The preceding calculations are, as will be easily perceived, made only in round numbers, with a view of rendering the principles of the investigation intelligible. In the table the exact results of the physical investigations which have been carried on, on this subject, are given.

In considering the two theories of light, each of which has been rendered memorable by the eminent philosophers who have favored them respectively, it is necessary that we should distinguish in each of them that which is purely hypothetical, and which remains yet to be established as a matter of fact, from that which expresses real and ascertained phenomena.

In explaining these points, we cannot do better than adopt the clear and candid language and reasoning of Sir John Herschel. In explaining generally the postulates of these theories, he says that in the corpuscular hypothesis the following assumptions are made.

1. That light consists of particles of matter possessed of inertia, and endued with attractive and repulsive forces, and projected or emitted from all luminous bodies with nearly the same velocity, of about two hundred thousand miles per second.

2. That these particles differ from each other by the intensity of the attractive and repulsive forces which reside in them, and in their relations to the material world, and also in their actual masses, or inertia.

3. That these particles, impinging on the retina, stimulate and excite vision; the particles whose inertia is greatest producing the sensation of red, those of the least inertia, violet, and those in which it is intermediate, the intermediate colors.

4. That the molecules of material bodies and those of light exert a mutual action on each other, which consists in attraction and repulsion, according to some law or function of the distance between them; that this law is such as to admit perhaps of several alternations or changes from repulsive to attractive force, but that when the distance is below a certain very small limit, it is always attracted up to actual contact; and that beyond this limit resides at least one sphere of repulsion. This repulsive force is that which causes the reflection of light at the external surfaces of dense media, and the interior attraction that which produces the refraction and interior reflection of light.

5. That these forces have different absolute values or intensities, not only for all different material bodies, but for every different species of the luminous molecules, being of a nature analogous to chemical affinities or elective attractions; and that hence arises the different refrangibilities of the rays of light.

6. That the motion of a particle of light, under the influence of these forces and its own velocity, is regulated by the same mechanical laws which govern the motions of ordinary matter; and that therefore each particle describes a trajectory, capable of strict calculation, as soon as the forces which act on it are assigned.

7. That the distance between the molecules of material bodies is exceedingly small in comparison with the extent of their spheres of attraction and repulsion on the particles of light.

8. That the forces which produce the reflection and refraction of light are, nevertheless, absolutely insensible at all measurable or appreciable distances from the molecules which exert them.

9. That every luminous molecule, during the whole of its progress through space, is continually passing through certain periodically recurring states, called by Newton fits of easy reflection and easy transmission, in virtue of which they are more disposed, when in the former states or phases of their periods, to obey the influence of the repulsive or reflective forces of the molecules of a medium; and when in the latter, of the attractive.

Such are the principles necessary to be admitted in the corpuscular theory. Herschel states those of the undulatory theory as follows:—

1. That an excessively rare, subtle, and elastic medium, or *ether*, fills all space, and pervades all material bodies, occupying the intervals between their molecules; and either by passing freely among them, or by its extreme rarity, offering no resistance to the motion of the earth, the planets, or comets, in their orbits, appreciable by the most delicate astronomical observations; and having inertia, but not gravity.

2. That the molecules of the ether are susceptible of being set in motion by the agitation of the particles of ponderable matter; that when any one is thus set in motion, it communicates a similar motion to those adjacent to it; and that the motion is propagated farther and farther in all directions, according to the same mechanical laws which regulate the propagation of undulations in other elastic media, as air, water, or solids, according to their respective constitutions.

3. That in the interior of refracting media the ether exists in a state of less elasticity, compared with its density, than in vacuo (that is, space empty of all other matter); and that the more refractive the medium, the greater, relatively speaking, is the elasticity of the ether in its interior.

4. That vibrations communicated to the ether in free space are propagated through refractive media by means of the ether in their interior, but with a velocity corresponding to its inferior degree of elasticity.

5. That when regular vibratory motions of a proper kind are propagated through the ether, and, passing through our eyes, reach and agitate the nerves of our retina, they produce in us the sensation of light, in a manner bearing a more or less close analogy to that in which the vibrations of the air affect our auditory nerves with that of sound.

6. That as, in the doctrine of sound, the frequency of the aerial pulses, or the number of excursions to and fro from the point of rest made by each molecule of the air, determines the pitch or note; so, in the theory of light, the frequency of the pulses, or number of impulses made on our nerves in a given time by the ethereal molecules next in contact with them, determines the *color* of the light; and that as the absolute extent of the motion to and fro of the particles of air, determines the *loudness* of the sound, so the *amplitude* or extent of the excursions of the ethereal molecules from their points of rest determines the brightness or intensity of the light.

Whichever theory we adopt to explain the phenomena of light, we are led to conclusions that strike the mind with astonishment. According to the corpuscular theory, the molecules of light are supposed to be endowed with attractive and repulsive forces, to have poles to balance themselves about their centres of gravity, and to possess other physical properties which we can only ascribe to ponderable matter. In speaking of these properties, it is difficult to divest oneself of the idea of sensible magnitude, or by any strain of the imagination to conceive that particles to which they belong can be so amazingly small as those of light demonstrably are. If a molecule of light weighed a single grain, its momentum (by reason of the enormous velocity with which it moves) would be such that its effect would be equal to that of a cannon-ball of one hundred and fifty pounds, projected with a velocity of one thousand feet per second. How inconceivably small must they therefore be, when millions of molecules, collected by lenses or mirrors, have never been found to produce the slightest effect on the most delicate apparatus contrived expressly for the purpose of rendering their materiality sensible!

If the corpuscular theory astonishes us by the extreme minuteness and prodigious velocity of the luminous molecules, the numerical results deduced from the undulatory theory are not less overwhelming. The extreme smallness of the amplitude of the vibrations, and the almost inconceivable but still measurable rapidity with which they succeed each other, were computed by Doctor Young, and are exhibited in the table previously shown.

On a cursory view, it must appear singular that two hypotheses, founded on assumptions so essentially different, should concur in affording the means of explaining so great a number of facts with equal precision and almost equal facility. This, however, is the case with respect to the corpuscular and undulatory theories of light, from both of which the mathematical laws to which the phenomena are subject may be deduced, though not in all cases with the same degree of facility. So far as the corpuscular doctrine is available for the purposes of deductive explanation, it possesses all the characteristics of a good theory. It supposes the operation of a force with which we are in some measure familiar. We are accustomed to contemplate the effects of attraction in the grand phenomena of astronomy; we perceive them at every instant in the downward tendency of all heavy bodies; and, though they disappear in the small bodies of nature, they are reproduced in the phenomena of electricity, magnetism, capillary attraction, and various chemical actions, where they can be not only distinctly traced, but reduced to mathematical formulæ, and submitted to accurate calculation. The undulatory hypothesis is not seized by the mind with the same facility; yet it also possesses some of the least equivocal characteristics of philosophical truth. No phenomenon has yet been discovered decidedly at variance with any of its principles. On the contrary, most of the phenomena follow from those principles with remarkable ease; and in numerous instances, consequences deduced from the theory by a long and intricate analysis, and where no sagacity could possibly have divined the result, have been found to be accurately true when brought to the test of experiment. Hence this hypothesis begins to be generally adopted by philosophers, and, in recent times, by far the most illustrious names in the annals of optical discovery are included in the list of its supporters.

That the sensation of light is produced by the vibrations of an extremely rare and subtle fluid, is an idea that was maintained by Descartes, Hooke, and some others; but it is to Huygens that the honor solely belongs of having reduced the hypothesis to a definite shape, and rendered it available to the purposes of mechanical explanation. Owing to the great success of Newton in applying the corpuscular theory to his splendid discoveries, the speculations of Huygens were long neglected; indeed, the theory remained in the same state in which it was left by him till it was taken up by our countryman, the late Dr. Young. By a train of mechanical reasoning, which in point of ingenuity has seldom been equalled, Dr. Young was conducted to some very remarkable numerical relations among some of the apparently most dissimilar phenomena of optics to the general laws of diffraction, and to the two principles of coloration of crystallized substances. Malus, so late as 1810, made the important discovery of the polarization of light by reflection, and successfully explained the phenomenon by the hypothesis of an undulatory propagation. The theory subsequently received a great extension from the ingenious labors of Fresnel; and the still more recent researches of Arago, Poisson, Herschel, Airy, and others, have conferred on it so great a degree of probability, that it may almost be regarded as ranking in the class of demonstrated truths. "It is a theory," says Herschel, "which, if not founded in nature, is certainly one of the happiest fictions that the genius of man has yet invented to group together natural phenomena, as well as the most fortunate in the support it has received from whole classes of new phenomena, which at their discovery seemed in irreconcilable opposition to it. It is, in fact, in all its applications and details, one succession of *felicities*; inasmuch as that we may almost be induced to say, if it be not true, it deserves to be."

Light and heat are so intimately related to each other, that philosophers have doubted whether they are identical principles, or merely coexistent in the luminous rays. They possess numerous properties in common: being reflected, refracted, and polarized, according to the same optical laws, and even exhibit the same phenomena of interference. Most substances during combustion give out both light and heat; and all bodies, except the gases, when heated to a high temperature, become incandescent. Nevertheless, there are many circumstances in which they appear to differ.

A thin plate of transparent glass interposed between the face and a blazing fire intercepts no sensible portion of the light, but most sensibly diminishes the heat. Light and heat are therefore not intercepted alike by the same substances. Heat is also combined in different degrees with the different rays of the solar spectrum. A very remarkable discovery on this subject was made by Sir William Herschel, which would seem to establish the independence of the heating and illuminating effects of the solar rays. Having placed thermometers in the several prismatic colors of the solar spectrum, he found the heating power of the rays gradually increased from the violet (where it was least) to the extreme red, and that the maximum temperature existed some distance beyond the red, out of the visible part of the spectrum. The experiment was soon after repeated with great care by Berard, who confirmed Herschel's conclusions relative to the augmentation of the calorific power from the violet to the red, and not beyond the spectrum. This discovery of the inequality of the heating power of the different rays led to the inquiry whether the chemical action produced by light upon certain bodies was merely the effect of the heat accompanying it, or owing to some other cause. By a series of delicate experiments, Berard found that this action is not only independent of the heating power, but follows entirely a different law; its intensity being greater in the violet ray, where the heating power is the least, and least in the red ray, where the heating power is the greatest. We are thus led to the conclusion that the solar rays possess at least three distinct powers—those of heating, illuminating, and effecting chemical combinations and decompositions; and these powers are distributed among the different refrangible rays in such a manner as to show their complete independence of each other.

I shall dismiss this subject, however, for the present, as I shall have another opportunity of more fully developing the relations of heat and light.

THE MAJOR PLANETS.

Space between MARS and JUPITER.—Jupiter's Distance and Period.—His Magnitude and Weight.—His Velocity.—Appearance of his Disk.—Day and Night on Jupiter.—Position of his Axis.—Absence of Seasons.—His Telescopic Appearance.—His Belts.—Causes of his Belts.—Currents in his Atmosphere.—Madler's Telescopic Views of Jupiter.—Appearance of the Sun as seen from Jupiter.—His Satellites.—The Variety of his Months.—Magnificent Appearance of the Moons as seen from Jupiter.—Their Eclipses.—SATURN.—His diurnal Rotation.—Appearance of the Sun as seen from him.—His Atmosphere.—His Rings.—Their Dimensions.—Biot's Explanation of their Stability.—Herschel's Theory of the same.—Appearances and Disappearances of the Rings.—Various Phases of the Rings.—Saturn's Satellites.—HERSCHEL or URANUS.—His Distance and Magnitude.—His Moons.—Reasons why there is no Planet beyond his Orbit.

THE MAJOR PLANETS.

Passing across the wide space which intervenes between the minor planets which, with the earth, circulate under the immediate wing of the sun, in the midst of which space we encounter the strange spectacle of the ruins of a shattered world, we arrive at the region of the system in which roll in silent majesty the stupendous orbs of Jupiter, Saturn, and Herschel, accompanied by their gorgeous apparatus of multiplied moons, rings, and belts. The mind is prepared to expect here another order of worlds, and it is not disappointed. The first of these sublime globes which attracts our attention is that of Jupiter, whose diameter is eighty-eight thousand miles, and whose bulk is fifteen hundred times that of our own globe. The distance of this planet from the sun is nearly five hundred millions of miles, and when our globe is nearest to it, it is nearly four times more distant from us than the sun. Nevertheless, such is its stupendous size that it subtends to the eye an angle of forty-five seconds, and is, next to the sun and moon, the most brilliant object in the heavens. It has in this respect the advantage over Venus, that when nearest to us its illuminated hemisphere is presented directly to the line of vision, and it is seen in the meridian at midnight, when the entire absence of the sun's light so much favors its apparent splendor. The orbit of the earth, which is included in that of Jupiter, is so small, compared with that of the planet, that its illuminated hemisphere, which is presented precisely to the sun, is always presented very nearly to the earth. Jupiter, therefore, does not appear sensibly gibbous, and, consequently, is always seen with a full face.

The time which Jupiter takes to make his complete revolution round the sun, is 4,333 days, being something less than twelve years. Such is the length of the *year* of Jupiter.

The weight or mass of the planet Jupiter is 316 times greater than that of the earth; but its bulk, being greater than that of the earth, in the higher proportion of about fifteen hundred to one, it follows that its density is about four times less than that of the earth; being nearly equal to the density of the sun.

The globe of Jupiter is therefore about as heavy as if it was composed of water from its surface to its centre.

There is nothing connected with the motion of the planets more surprising than their enormous velocities, which, to our observation, are nevertheless scarcely perceptible, owing to the fact that their distances from us are proportionally great. Jupiter, when nearest to us, is at a distance of four hundred millions of miles. A cannon-ball which moves at the rate of five hundred miles an hour, would require nearly a hundred years to come from Jupiter to us, and if a steam-engine on a railway, moving at twenty miles an hour, were to take its departure for Jupiter, it would not arrive at its destination until the expiration of two thousand three hundred years.

Taking the diameter of Jupiter's orbit at a thousand millions of miles, its circumference is more than three thousand millions of miles, which is traversed in less than twelve years. The space moved over annually by Jupiter is, then, two hundred and fifty millions of miles; and the space moved over monthly about twenty millions of miles; and the space moved over daily about seven hundred thousand miles; and the space moved over hourly about thirty thousand miles; being at the rate of about five hundred miles a minute; a velocity sixty times greater than that of a cannon-ball.

DIURNAL ROTATION OF JUPITER.

Although the varieties of light and shade which characterize the disk of Jupiter are subject to variations which show, as will be seen hereafter, that they are principally produced by clouds in his atmosphere, yet permanent marks were discovered upon it at an early epoch, by which the fact was established that the planet has a diurnal rotation. In the years 1664–'5, Hook and Cassini observed a spot on one of the belts which was permanent in its position, and was observed to move across the disk of the planet. It contracted in its breadth as it approached the edge of the disk; a circumstance which obviously arose from its being fore-shortened by the position in which it was there presented to the eye, that portion of the surface of the planet being seen very obliquely, the spot disappeared at one side, and after being invisible for a time reappeared at the other. This spot continued to be seen for more than a year, and fully proved the fact that Jupiter completes his rotation on an axis very slightly inclined to his orbit in nine hours and fifty-six minutes.

The alternations of light and darkness on Jupiter are therefore regulated by intervals much shorter than those which govern the days and nights of the minor planets, and we shall presently see that this is a character which probably prevails among all the major planets. The average interval of the days and nights must be a little under five terrestrial hours.

This rapid motion, considered with reference to the great magnitude of Jupiter, leads to the inference that the velocity of that part of his surface which is near his equator must be exceedingly great. The circumference of Jupiter at his equator must be about two hundred and seventy thousand miles, and as this revolves in ten hours, the motion of any point upon it must be at the enormous rate of twenty-seven thousand miles an hour, or a little less than five hundred miles a minute. Thus it appears that the velocity which the equatorial regions have, in virtue of the diurnal motion, is very little less than the orbitual motion of the planet round the sun.

This rapid diurnal rotation would produce a considerable variation in the weights of bodies at different latitudes on the surface of Jupiter, since the centrifugal force near the equator would counteract the weight in a very sensible manner, while toward the poles its effects would cease to be perceptible.

The great length of Jupiter's year compared with its rapid diurnal rotation, will resolve the year into a much greater number of days than its proportional length compared with the terrestrial year would infer. While Jupiter makes one complete revolution round the sun, it will make ten thousand four hundred and seventy revolutions on its axis. Such, therefore, is the number of days in Jupiter's year.

The axis of Jupiter is inclined to its orbit at an angle of about three degrees, and as this inclination determines the limits of the seasons, it follows that there can be scarcely any perceptible change of season upon the planet during one half of his year. The sun will, during one half year, gradually pass to three degrees north of his equator, and during the other half year to three degrees south of it. The extreme change of the sun's meridional altitude would therefore not exceed six degrees. This perhaps might be sufficient for the purposes of chronology, but could scarcely produce any effects on the organized world, nor would the temperature of the seasons undergo any observable change. The range of the tropics would be three degrees on each side of the equator of the planet, and within these regions the sun would pass near the zenith daily.

The sun would rise and set daily throughout the year, to every part of the planet except a small circle extending three degrees round the poles.

The diameter of Jupiter being eleven times that of the earth, his surface will be greater than that of our planet in the proportion of a hundred and twenty to one, and if the distribution of land and water be similar, it will afford accommodation for a population a hundred and twenty times more numerous.

The actual bulk of the globe of Jupiter, which is the largest body of the system next to the sun, is fourteen hundred times greater than that of the earth. In other words, to make a globe equal to that of Jupiter, we should roll into one fourteen hundred globes like that of the earth.

TELESCOPIC APPEARANCE OF JUPITER.

The spectacle presented to the observer who enjoys the use of a powerful telescope by the planet Jupiter, is magnificent indeed. The surface of the planet appears as large and distinct as the full moon to the naked eye. His disk is marked with certain features of light and shadow, which are in general variable. They are, therefore, produced by clouds floating in his atmosphere, the presence of which is indeed rendered quite evident by the telescope. Although these lights and shadows in general are variable, yet they are found to be characterized by a certain regularity of arrangement. Their streaks are generally parallel, as in the annexed figures, which exhibit views of Jupiter seen on different occasions.

These streaks, which are called the belts of Jupiter, were observed before the middle of the 17th century, and are visible to telescopes of no very considerable power. They are variable not only in their breadth and form, but in their number. Sometimes not more than one can be discovered; at other times two or more, and sometimes as many as eight. Sometimes they have continued without sensible variation for nearly three months, and sometimes a new belt has appeared in an hour or two. The annexed diagrams have been given by different authors as representing the appearances of these belts at different times. They have, sometimes, though rarely, been seen broken up and distributed over the whole surface of the planet as represented in fig. D. Fig. B gives a view taken at an early period by Dr. Hook. Fig. A is a view taken in the year 1832. Fig. C is in 1837. It is, however, extremely difficult to obtain sketches of this kind executed with tolerable fidelity.

Mr. Thomas Dick states that he has had frequently an opportunity of view-

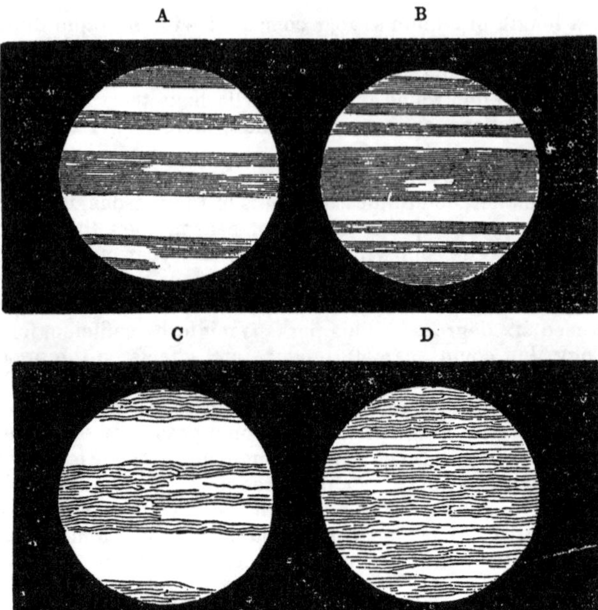

ing Jupiter with good telescopes, both reflecting and refracting, for twenty or thirty years past; and among several hundreds of observations, has never seen above four or five belts at one time. The most common appearance observed, is that of two belts distinctly marked, one on each side of the planet's equator, and one at each pole, generally broader, but much fainter than the others. He has never perceived much change in the form or position of the belts during the same season, but in successive years a slight degree of change has been perceptible, some of the belts having either disappeared, or turned much fainter than they were before, or shifted somewhat their relative positions, but has never seen Jupiter without at least two or three belts. Some of the largest of these belts being at least the one eighth part of the diameter of the planet in breadth, must occupy a space at least 11,000 miles broad, and 270,000 miles in circumference; for they run along the whole circumference of the planet, and appear of the same shape during every period of its rotation. It is probable that the smallest belts we can distinctly perceive by our telescopes are not much less than a thousand miles in breadth.

CAUSES OF THE BELTS.

It is well known that the diurnal motion of the earth, combined with the heat of the sun acting directly on the intertropical regions, produces those atmospheric currents which blow with a constancy and regularity so singular from east to west in the lower latitudes of both hemispheres. These currents are attended with others in a contrary direction, which constitute their reaction, blowing almost as constantly and regularly from west to east in the higher latitudes. Thus the atmosphere covering the surface of the earth is continually swept by systems of currents blowing in either direction parallel to the line—and these currents will have a tendency, in proportion to their force and regularity, to produce corresponding arrangements parallel to the line, in the clouds which float upon our atmosphere. It is evident that such an effect would be more strongly marked in proportion as the energy of the causes producing it would be increased.

In the case of the earth, the surface at the equator is moved by the diurnal motion at the rate of about a thousand miles an hour; and the sun, at different seasons of the year, departs from the equator on either side to a distance of twenty-three and a half degrees. If the velocity of the surface of the equator were to become ten or twenty times greater, and the sun, instead of departing from it twenty-three degrees, were constantly vertical to it, then we might expect to have atmospheric currents parallel to the line much more energetic, constant, and regular.

But in the case of JUPITER, it will be easily seen that the causes producing such currents are far more energetic than on the earth. Instead of revolving in twenty-four hours, Jupiter revolves in ten hours. If, then, the globe of Jupiter were equal to that of the earth, the velocity of his surface at the line would be greater than in the case of the earth in the proportion of two and a half to one. The velocity of his surface would, in fact, be about two thousand five hundred miles an hour. But the diameter of Jupiter, and therefore also the circumference, is eleven times greater than that of the earth; and therefore, on that account alone, even though he revolved in the same time, the velocity of his surface would be eleven times greater than that of the earth. From these two causes combined, it follows that the velocity of the surface of Jupiter at the equator is about twenty-seven and a half times greater than that of the earth, and is, in fact, twenty-seven thousand five hundred miles an hour.

It is evident, then, that the velocity of the surface of Jupiter produced by his diurnal revolution being nearly twenty-eight times greater than that of the earth, and the sun appearing always vertical to his equator, or nearly so, the causes which produce a system of atmospheric currents parallel to his equator, act with infinitely more energy than upon the earth. We accordingly see the effects of such currents exhibited in the decided arrangements of the strata of his clouds parallel to his equator. Thus we see that there prevail in Jupiter atmospheric currents similar to those which prevail on the earth, blowing constantly from east to west in some latitudes, and from west to east in others. As we cannot doubt that they were intended to fulfil that purpose in the social intercourse of the people of the globe which they actually do fulfill, we are supplied with one analogy more to support the conclusion that the planets are inhabited globes like the earth.

Annexed are two views of Jupiter, showing the appearance of the belts, taken from original drawings by Madler, made from observations taken so recently as 1841.

APPEARANCE OF THE SUN AT JUPITER.

If E in the annexed figure represent the appearance of the sun to the inhabitants of the earth, J will represent its appearance to those of Jupiter.

The distance of Jupiter from the sun being nearly five times that of the

earth, the apparent diameter of the sun as seen from Jupiter will be one fifth of its apparent diameter from the earth. It will, therefore, measure about six minutes, since the diameter of the earth measures about thirty minutes. The apparent magnitude of the sun as we see it, is very nearly that which a cent piece would have if seen at the distance of one hundred and twenty feet from the eye. The apparent magnitude of the sun as seen from Jupiter would then be the same, or nearly so, as that of a cent piece seen at six hundred feet distance.

It is proved in those branches of physics in which the laws of heat and light are developed, that the density of these principles is diminished in proportion as the square of the distance from the body from which they emanate is increased. It follows, therefore, that the heat and light of the sun at Jupiter will be about twenty-five times less than at the earth.

JUPITER'S SATELLITES.

When Galileo directed the first telescope to the examination of Jupiter, he observed four minute stars, which appeared in the line of the equator of the planet. He took these at first to be fixed stars; but he was soon undeceived. He saw them alternately approach and recede from the planet. He observed them pass behind it and before it; and, in fact, to oscillate, as it were, to the right and the left of the planet, to certain limited distances: each of the four stars receding to equal distances east and west of the planet. He soon arrived at the obvious conclusion that these objects were not fixed stars, but that they were bodies which revolved round Jupiter in circular orbits, at limited distances; and that each successive body included the orbit of the others within it. In short, that they formed a miniature of the solar system, in which, however, Jupiter himself played the part of the sun. As the telescope improved, it became apparent that these bodies were small globes, related to Jupiter in the same manner exactly as the moon is related to the earth; that, in fine, they were a *cortege* of four moons, attending Jupiter round the sun in the same manner, and subserving the same purpose, as our moon does in reference to the earth.

Thus, then, it seems that the population of Jupiter are favored by four moons in their firmament. Since the examination of the motion of these bodies has been carried to a greater extent of accuracy, it has been found that there is a singular law prevailing among their motions, in virtue of which it is impossible that the four satellites can ever be at the same time on the same side of Jupiter; one, at least, must be on the contrary side from the other three. Thus it follows that there must always be one moon full, or nearly so; for if three of the four satellites be on the same side of Jupiter with the sun, and therefore in the condition of new or waning moons, the fourth must be on the opposite side, and therefore nearly a full moon.

But, connected with these appendages to Jupiter, there is perhaps nothing more remarkable than the period of their revolutions round him. That moon which is nearest to Jupiter completes its revolution in forty-two hours. In that brief space of time it goes through all its various phases; it is a thin crescent; it is halved, gibbous, and full. It must be remembered, however, that the day of Jupiter, instead of being twenty-four hours, is about ten nours. This moon, therefore, has a month equal to a little more than four of Jupiter's days. In each day it passes through one complete quarter; thus the first day of the month it passes from the thinnest crescent to the half moon; in the second day, from the half moon to the full moon; on the third day, from the full moon to the last quarter; and on the fourth day returns to conjunction with the sun.

So rapid are these changes that we can conceive the gradual changes of the phases of the moon to be actually visible as they proceed. The next satellite makes its complete revolution in about eighty-five hours, or in about eight of Jupiter's days and a half. Such is the month of the second satellite. The third satellite completes his revolution in one hundred and seventy hours, or in about seventeen days of Jupiter. The fourth and most distant satellite, requires about four hundred hours, to complete its revolution, and therefore has a month of about forty of Jupiter's days.

It appears, then, that upon Jupiter there are four different months, corresponding to the four different moons; one of about four days' duration, another about eight days, a third about seventeen days, and the fourth about forty days. What a complicated system of reckoning time is thus supplied!

The magnitude of the nearest of Jupiter's moons is about a quarter greater than that of our own; that of the second is equal to ours; the diameter of the third, however, is nearly double to that of our moon, and it is nearly equal to the planet Mercury; the diameter of the fourth satellite is about one half greater than that of our moon.

The distance of the nearest moon from the surface of Jupiter is somewhat less than the distance of ours from the surface of the earth. Its apparent magnitude, therefore, seen from Jupiter, will be greater than ours. The distance of the second moon from Jupiter is about one half greater than the distance of our moon, and as its diameter is nearly equal to that of our moon, its apparent magnitude will be proportionally less. The distance of the third moon is more than double the distance of ours, but as its magnitude is a little less than double, its appearance to the inhabitants of Jupiter will be nearly the same as that of ours. The appearance of the fourth moon will be somewhat less.

Thus it appears that the four moons which attend Jupiter vary very little in the apparent magnitude they present to its inhabitants from that which ours presents to the inhabitants of the earth.

One of the peculiarities in the motion of our moon which distinguishes it in a remarkable manner from the planets, is its revolution upon its axis. It will be remembered, that the planets generally rotate on their axes in times somewhat analogous to that of the earth. Now, on the contrary, the moon revolves on its axis in the same time that it takes to revolve round the earth; in consequence of which adjustment of its motions it turns the same hemisphere continually toward the earth. It would seem that this is a general characteristic of all satellites; for the observations of Sir William Herschel on those of Jupiter, show that the same motion prevails among them; that they, as they revolve round their primary, turn constantly the same hemisphere toward Jupiter.

The globe of Jupiter, though of considerable magnitude, is small compared with that of the sun. In consequence of this, it throws in the direction opposite to that of the sun a conical shadow of considerable length, the thickness of which, at Jupiter, is equal to the diameter of the planet, but which diminishes until it is reduced to a point in receding from Jupiter. As the satellites move round Jupiter, in the plane of his equator, and as the plane of his equator is very nearly coincident with that of his orbit round the sun, it follows that the satellites, every revolution, as they pass behind him, must move through his shadow. The only exception to this is presented by the fourth, or most distant satellite, which, owing to its great distance from the planet, and the obliquity of its orbit, sometimes, in passing behind the planet, goes above or below its shadow. When the satellites get into the shadow of Jupiter they become invisible to us; and hence we know that they are opaque bodies, which shine, like the moon, by the reflected light of the sun. All the circumstances connected with their eclipses are visible to us. We see them enter the shadow and leave it, and we can estimate the duration of each eclipse, and observe exactly its beginning and ending. These eclipses, as we shall show on another occasion, have been instrumental, not only to useful purposes in art, but also to great discoveries in science. It is by them, among other means, that the longitude of places on the surface of the earth is determined; but by far the most important discovery connected with these bodies, is that of the motion and velocity of light. How this was accomplished we shall also explain on another occasion. It was shown, however, by these means, that the velocity of reflected light was the same as that of direct light.

SATURN.

Beyond the orbit of Jupiter, a space equal in extent to the distance of Jupiter from the sun, is unoccupied by any planetary body. At a distance little short of a thousand millions of miles from the sun, the SATURNIAN SYSTEM revolves, in a period of twenty-nine years and a half, consisting of a globe little less than Jupiter, begirt with two (and probably more) stupendous rings, and a cortege of no less than seven moons.

The diameter of SATURN is eighty thousand miles, and its bulk is, consequently, a thousand times greater than that of the earth.

DIURNAL ROTATION OF SATURN.

The distance of Saturn is so great that it requires the most powerful telescopes to render the marks on his disk visible, so as to discover his diurnal motion. From purely theoretical views, Laplace conjectured that it was performed in about ten hours. Sir William Herschel, by the aid of the large instruments constructed by him, inferred that it revolves in ten hours, sixteen minutes, and nineteen seconds. Sir John Herschel estimates the time of its rotation to be ten hours, twenty-nine minutes, and seventeen seconds.

The axis on which it turns is, like that of Jupiter, at right angles to the direction of the belts, but unlike Jupiter, Saturn inclines his axis to the plane of his orbit in a manner similar to the earth and Mars. The consequence of this arrangement is that the year of Saturn is varied by the same succession of seasons subject to the same range of temperature as those which prevail on our globe.

The alternation of light and darkness is the same as upon Jupiter. This rapid return of day, after an interval of five hours night, seems to assume the character of a *law* among the major planets, as the interval of twelve hours certainly does among the minor planets.

The year of Saturn is equal in duration to 10,759 terrestrial days, or to 258,192 hours. But as the rotation of the planet is completed in less than ten hours and a half, the number of Saturnian days in the planet's year must be 24,592.

The distance of Saturn from the sun being above nine times that of the earth, the sun's apparent diameter at that planet will be less than at the earth in a like proportion. If in the annexed figure E represent the appearance of the sun at the earth, S will exhibit its appearance at Saturn.

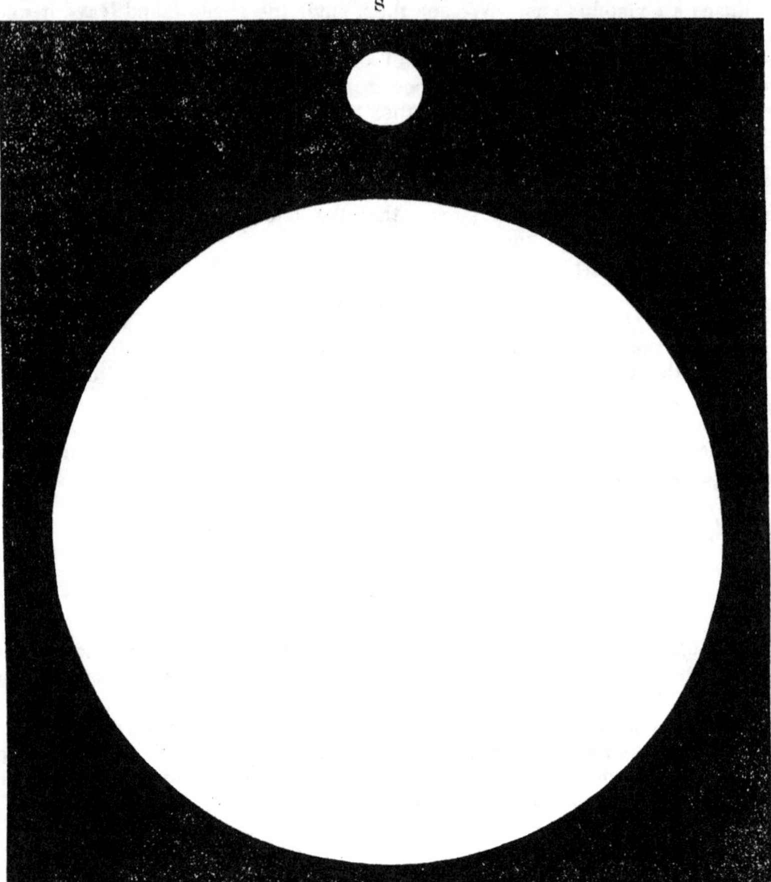

ATMOSPHERE OF SATURN.

The planet Saturn has been found to be invested with an atmosphere similar to that of Jupiter, and attended in all respects with the same phenomena. The belts are effects of the same kind, and produced by the same causes, and all that we have said regarding the atmospheric currents, clouds, and other meteorological phenomena, in JUPITER, will be equally applicable in SATURN.

RINGS OF SATURN.

At a very early epoch in the history of the telescope, the application of that instrument to the examination of SATURN led to the supposition that the planet was not globular, but oval. Further observation created the impression that *ears* or *handles* were attached to each side of the disk. But as the means of observation were farther improved, the astonishing discovery was made that Saturn is surrounded by a stupendous ring of solid matter lying in the plane of his equator, the inner edge being at a distance from his surface of about twenty thousand miles. More recent observations made by Sir William Herschel establish the fact that this ring is not, as was first supposed, a single annular plate of matter, but has a division by which it is separated into two independent rings, one outside the other, which have no mutual point of contact or connexion. This separation appeared at first, as a dark streak upon the surface of the ring running parallel to its edges. Sir William Herschel, however, succeeded in seeing stars which were behind the ring through this apparent streak, and consequently arrived at the conclusion that it was an opening or separation between two independent rings. It was found also that the surface of the ring was marked by parallel streaks or bands, like the belts of the planet.

Very recent observations made at Rome upon this planet, appear to countenance the supposition that the ring, instead of being double, is quintuple, and that there are *four* divisions instead of *one*, as supposed by Sir William Herschel. It is even said that six divisions have been observed, and therefore there are seven independent rings, one within another, all being concentric with the planet and in the plane of its equator.

One of the most striking discoveries of Sir William Herschel respecting Saturn, was the revolution of the rings around the planet. He found that they revolve round their own centre and that of the planet in their own plane, and that they complete a revolution in the same time that a satellite would revolve in, at the same distance. Their motion, therefore, is conformable to the laws of gravitation which would govern that of satellites or moons. The dimensions of the rings, as observed by Sir William Herschel, are as follows:—

	Miles.
Exterior diameter of exterior ring	176,418
Interior diameter of exterior ring	155,272
Breadth of exterior ring	10,573
Exterior diameter of interior ring	151,690
Interior diameter of interior ring	117,339
Breadth of the interior ring	17,175
Equatorial diameter of the planet	79,160
Interval between the planet and the interior ring	19,090
Interval of the rings	1,791
Thickness of the rings not exceeding	100

It appears then that the thickness of the rings is incomparably smaller than their breadth; the thickness being not more than the three hundredth part of the breadth.

One of the circumstances attending the contemplation of the planet Saturn which excites most surprise, is the fact that the planet and the two rings should be capable of maintaining their relative position with the prodigious velocity with which they move round the sun, without either overtaking the other or any collision taking place. Let it be remembered that the circumference of Saturn's orbit round the sun measures about six thousand millions of miles, and that the planet completes this circuit in less than thirty years, so that he moves at the rate of about seven millions and three quarter miles per day, or three hundred and twenty-five thousand miles an hour. This is a velocity six hundred and fifty times greater than that of a cannon-ball. Yet with this prodigious celerity of motion continued for countless ages, neither of the rings has ever overtaken the planet or the planet overtaken them, and still more wonderful, the two rings, separated only by a space of about eighteen hundred miles, which they would move over with their orbitual motion in about three minutes, have never overtaken each other. This astonishing precision of movement would become still more surprising if it be true, as it is suspected to be, that there are five or more independent rings, one included within the other.

This apparent mystery has however been most clearly and beautifully explained by Biot, to whom the happy idea occurred that the rings could be brought under the same laws of motion as moons. To make this explanation clearly understood, let us first imagine a globe like the moon moving periodically round the planet like the earth. The manner in which the attraction of gravitation combined with centrifugal force causes it to keep revolving round the earth without falling down upon it by its gravity on the one hand, or receding indefinitely from it by the centrifugal force on the other is well understood. In virtue of the equality of these forces, the moon keeps continually at the same distance from the earth while it accompanies the earth round the sun. Now it would be easy to suppose another moon revolving by the same law of attraction at the same distance from the earth. It would revolve in the same time, and with the same velocity, as the first. We may extend the supposition with equal facility to three, four, or a hundred moons, at the same distance. Nay, we may suppose as many moons placed at the same distance round the earth as would complete the circle, so as to form a ring of moons touching each other. They would still move in the mame manner and with the same velocity as the single moon. Nor will the circumstances be altered if this ring of moons be supposed to be beaten out into a thin flat ring like those of Saturn. It is plain, then, that if the ring of Saturn revolve in its own plane round the planet in the same time as that in which a single satellite placed at the same distance would revolve, the stability of the ring with reference to the planet is explicable exactly upon the same principles as those by which we explain the motion of a satellite. But Sir William Herschel, as has been already stated, discovered the important fact that the rings do move round their own centre and that of the planet in the same time that a satellite placed at the same distance would do. Biot, therefore, has, with a happy adroitness, adopted this as the key to the explanation of the stability of the ring.

The following observations of Sir John Herschel on the rings indicated another cause of their stability:—

Although the rings are, as we have said, very nearly concentric with the body of Saturn, yet recent micrometical measurements of extreme delicacy have demonstrated that the coincidence is not mathematically exact, but that the centre of gravity of the rings oscillates round that of the body describing a very minute orbit, probably under laws of much complexity. Trifling as this remark may appear, it is of the utmost importance to the stability of the system of the rings. Supposing them mathematically perfect in their circular form, and exactly concentric with the planet, it is demonstrable that they would form (in spite of their centrifugal force) a system in a state of *unstable equilibrium*, which the slightest external power would subvert—not by causing a rupture in the substance of the rings—but by precipitating them, *unbroken*, on the surface of the planet. For the attraction of such a ring or rings on a point or sphere eccentrically situate within them, is not the same in all directions, but tends to draw the point or sphere toward the nearest part of the ring, or away from the centre. Hence, supposing the body to become, from any cause, ever so little eccentric to the ring, the tendency of their mutual gravity is, not to correct but to increase this eccentricity, and to bring the nearest parts of them together. Now, external powers, capable of producing such eccentricity, exist in the attractions of the satellites; and in order that the system may be *stable*, and possess within itself a power of resisting the first inroads of such a tendency, while yet nascent and feeble, and opposing them by an opposite or maintaining power, it has been shown that it is sufficient to admit the rings to be *loaded* in some part of their circumference, either by some minute inequality of thickness, or by some portions being denser than others. Such a load would give to the whole ring to which it was attached somewhat of the character of a heavy and sluggish satellite, maintaining itself in an orbit with a certain energy sufficient to overcome minute causes of disturbance, and establish an average bearing on its centre. But even without supposing the existence of any such load—of which, after all, we have no proof—and granting, therefore, in its full extent, the general instability of the equilibrium, we think we perceive, in the periodicity of all the causes of disturbance, a sufficient guarantee of its preservation. However homely be the illustration, we can conceive nothing more apt in every way to give a general conception of this maintenance of equilibrium under a constant tendency to subversion, than the mode in which a practised hand will sustain a long pole in a perpendicular position resting on the finger, by a continual and almost imperceptible variation of the point of support. Be that, however, as it may, the observed oscillation of the centres of the rings about that of the planet is in itself the evidence of a perpetual contest between conservative and destructive powers—both extremely feeble, but so antagonizing one another, as to prevent the latter from ever acquiring an uncontrollable ascendency, and rushing to a catastrophe.

Since the plane of the rings coincides with that of Saturn's equator, and since the sun is during one half of Saturn's year north, and during the other half south of his equator, it follows that the northern side of the ring is illuminated, and the southern side dark, during the summer half year of his northern hemisphere, and that the southern side is illuminated and the northern side dark during the winter half year of his northern hemisphere. At his equinoxes the edge of the ring is presented to the sun, and neither side of it is illuminated. Since the half year of Saturn is equal to fifteen terrestrial years, it follows that the northern and southern sides of the rings are alternately illuminated by the sun during intervals of fifteen years.

It is evident that the rings can only be seen from the earth when the sun and earth are at the same side of Saturn's equator. From the great magnitude of Saturn's orbit, compared with that of the earth, this must be generally the case. In order that the sun and earth should be at opposite sides of the plane of the ring, that plane must be so placed that its edge is directed to some point between the sun and earth. This will be the case for a short time before and after it is directed to the sun, that is to say, a little before and after Saturn's equinox.

If we suppose two lines touching the earth's annual orbit, and parallel to the *line of nodes* of Saturn's ring, to be drawn and continued in both directions to Saturn, it will be only when Saturn is between these lines that the earth and sun can be at different sides of the ring. These lines will include a length of the orbit of Saturn equal to the diameter of the orbit of the earth, and since Saturn will move over such a space in his periodical course round the sun in one year, it follows that the sun and earth must be always at the same side of Saturn's ring, except for six months before and six months after each of Saturn's equinoxes, at which times it may happen that the sun and earth may be on opposite sides of the rings.

Saturn's rings may become invisible from the earth by any of three causes.

1. When the edge of the rings be presented to the sun, the edge being then the only illuminated part, and being too thin to be seen even by telescopes at so great a distance, the ring is invisible. This will happen once every fifteen years.

2. When the edge of the ring is presented to the earth, it is invisible because of its minuteness and distance. This will happen once every fifteen years.

3. When the sun and earth are on opposite sides of the ring. This will also happen once every fifteen years.

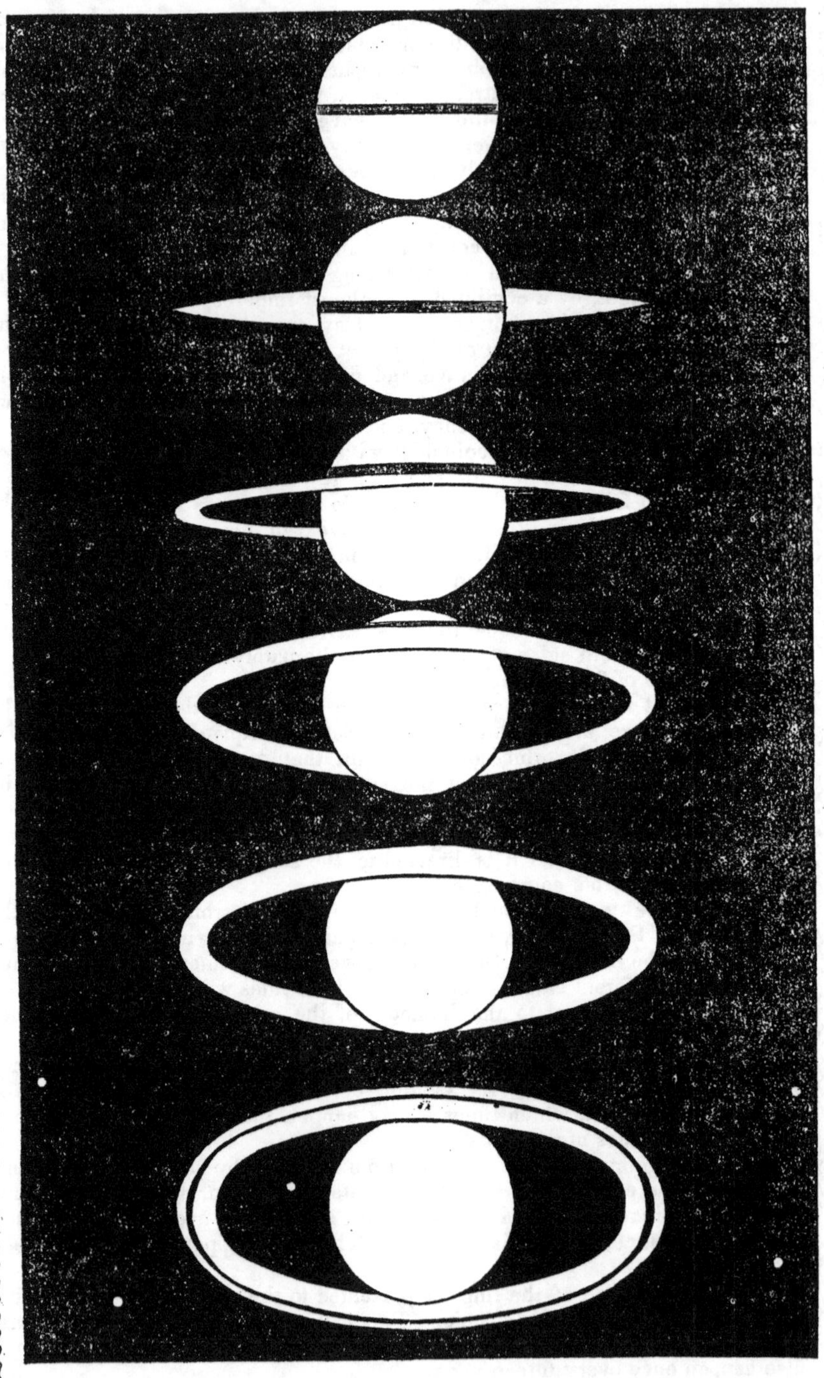

Except therefore for an interval of a few months every fifteen years, the rings of Saturn are always in a position to be seen from the earth. These circumstances occur when the planet passes through the twentieth degrees of the signs Virgo and Pisces. They took place in the year 1832–'33, and will recur again in 1847–'48.

The angle at which the plane of the rings is inclined to that of the ecliptic being about 30°, the rings must always be seen obliquely from the earth, more or less so, as the earth is more or less distant from the plane of the rings, but the obliquity of the view can never be less than 30°. Now, since a circle seen obliquely is always foreshortened into an oval, the appearance of the rings, even in the most favorable position must be elliptical. If a circle be viewed at an angle of 30°, it will be seen as an ellipse whose lesser axis is half its greater. Such is the form of the ring as seen at intervals of seven years and a half from Saturn's equinoxes, or when the planet is in the signs Scorpio and Gemini, which takes place at the middle of the intervals of the disappearances of the rings. This occurred last in 1839–'40, and will occur again in 1854–'55. Between the epochs at which the ring is in its most open state, and the times of its disappearances it undergoes all the intermediate phases.

In the annexed figures the appearances it presented between 1832 and 1840 are given from the observations of William Dick.

In October, November, and December, 1832, the ring appeared as in fig. 1. In the beginning of January, it appeared like a pure thread of light on each side of the planet as in fig. 2. It began to appear a little larger during the months of January, February, and March, 1833; but in April it again disappeared as the earth was then in the plane of the ring, and it continued invisible till near the end of June; after which it again appeared as represented in fig. 2. In about a year after its second disappearance, it appeared as in fig. 3, and a year and a half afterward was seen as in fig. 4. In 1837 it appeared as in fig. 5, and finally assumed its most open form, as represented in fig. 6.

From 1838 to 1847, the ring gradually passes through similar phases in a contrary order.

SATELLITES OF SATURN

On examining Saturn with powerful telescopes, it is found to be attended by objects revolving round it similar in all respects to the satellites of Jupiter, but amounting to seven in number. These revolve nearly in the plane of the ring and beyond that body. The times of revolution are such as to present various and interesting appearances to the inhabitants of the planet. The nearest satellite, makes its complete revolution in 22½ hours, which is equivalent to about two of Saturn's days. This moon, therefore, exhibits all its various changes within that time. It passes from the crescent to the first quarter in half of one of Saturn's days; from the first quarter to the full moon in another half day, and from the full to the new moon in another half day; so rapid is the succession of its phases. The next in the order of distance, makes its revolutions in thirty-three hours, or in about three of Saturn's days, which constitutes another sort of month; within which it passes through all its various phases. The third revolves in forty-five hours, or about four of Saturn's days; the fourth in seventy-five hours, or about seven and a half of Saturn's days; the fifth in one hundred and eight hours, or nearly eleven of Saturn's days; the sixth in about three hundred and eighty hours, or in about thirty-eight of Saturn's days; the seventh in about nineteen hundred hours, or one hundred and eighty of Saturn's days. Such are the seven different months prevalent upon SATURN.

The magnitudes of the satellites of Saturn have not been certainly ascertained; their distances from the earth are too great to enable us hitherto, actually to measure their diameters.

Sir John Herschel estimates the diameter of the most remote satellite to be little less than that of Mars, which is 4,200 miles. The next to it cannot be much less, being the most conspicuous in its appearance. As to the magnitudes of the four minor satellites, we are left to conjecture.

It is usual to designate these bodies in the order of their discovery, and not in the order of their distances from Saturn. If the following figures represent the succession of their distances, the order of their discovery is that expressed above the figures respectively:—

Seventh,	Sixth,	First,	Second,	Third,	Fourth,	Fifth.
1	2	3	4	5	6	7

The distance of the nearest satellite from the surface of Saturn does not exceed 80,000 miles, a space equal to one diameter of the planet. Its distance beyond the edge of the ring is only 18,000 miles.

This moon completes its revolution round Saturn in 22½ hours, or a little more than two Saturnian days. In one of the planet's days it passes therefore from new to full moon, and in the next from full to new moon. Its change of phase from hour to hour must be distinctly perceivable.

It is probable, from analogy, that its magnitude is greater than that of our moon, and since its distance from the surface of Saturn is three times less than that of our moon, its apparent diameter at Saturn must be more than three times greater. It will therefore appear with a disk at least ten times as great as that of our moon.

The next moon is at a distance of 160,000 miles from the centre, and 120,000 miles from the surface of Saturn, which being half the distance of our moon from the earth, shows that if, as is probable, this satellite be equal in magnitude to our moon, it will appear with a disk four times as great. It completes its revolution in three of Saturn's days, within which time it exhibits all its phases.

The moon next in order is at a distance of 200,000 miles from the centre and 160,000 from the surface of the planet. It appears a little less than four times larger than our moon and goes through all its phases in less than five of Saturn's days.

The next satellite is at a distance of 260,000 miles from the centre and 220,000 miles from the surface of Saturn, and therefore appears larger at Saturn than our moon does at the earth. It passes through all its phases in six and a half of Saturn's days.

Thus it appears that Saturn is supplied with four moons, all moving nearer to his surface than ours is to the earth, and appearing from twice to ten times as large, and passing through all their phases in from two to seven of Saturn's days.

The fifth moon from Saturn, completing its month in eleven and a half of Saturn's days, is at a distance a little greater than that of our moon, and probably appears of the same magnitude seen from Saturn. The sixth moon, completing its month in forty of Saturn's days, is at more than three times the distance of our moon, but is twice its diameter. It appears from Saturn but little less than ours. The most remote of this system of moons completes its revolution in two hundred Saturnian days, and its distance from Saturn is ten times that of our moon from the earth. This is the largest moon of the system, but still, owing to its great distance, must appear smaller at Saturn than ours does at the earth.

The orbits of the six inner satellites are nearly in the plane of the ring, but that of the most remote one is inclined to it at the rather large angle of 30°.

Owing to the great obliquity of the orbits of the satellites to that of Saturn, they are seldom eclipsed. The frequency of the eclipses of the satellites of Jupiter, is a consequence of the fact that their orbits are nearly in the plane of that of the planet.

The most remote of Saturn's moons (commonly called the fifth satellite) exhibits variations of brilliancy which have given ground for the conjecture that those moons, like our own and those of Jupiter, revolve on their axes in the time they take to revolve in their orbits.

The two innermost satellites were the latest discovered, and are by far the most difficult to be seen. It is only by means of telescopes of the most powerful kind, and under circumstances most favorable to observation, that they can be detected at all. Those who have been so fortunate as to possess instruments capable of observing them, say that at the equinoxes of Saturn, when his ring becomes invisible, they have been seen threading like beads the almost infinitely thin filament of light to which the ring is then reduced, and for a short time moving off it at either end, speedily to return, and hastening again to their habitual concealment.

OF HERSCHEL, OR URANUS.

The planet of the solar system which is the most remote from the sun, and which, there are strong reasons for believing to be the extreme limit of the system, is called Uranus, and sometimes, from its distinguished discoverer, Herschel. This body is a globe 35,000 miles in diameter, the bulk of which is about eighty times that of the earth; and it revolves at a distance from the sun of eighteen hundred millions of miles; being double the distance of Saturn. The great distance of this object from the earth and the consequent minuteness of its appearance, has rendered our knowledge of its physical condition much less distinct and satisfactory than those of the nearer planets.

It has been hitherto unascertained whether it has a diurnal rotation; but analogy favors the conjecture that it revolves rapidly upon its axis like the cognate planets, Jupiter and Saturn. The disk has not been seen with sufficient distinctness to detect upon it those indications which would decide the question, whether it is invested with an atmosphere.

The period for this planet going round the sun is eighty-four terrestrial years, and as the date of its discovery was 1781, it has not yet made a complete revolution since astronomical observation was first directed to it. It is a striking example of the power of science, that we are nevertheless as certainly assured of its periodical path round the sun, as if it had been observed for a long succession of its periods like other planets.

Being nearly twenty times farther from the sun than the earth, the diameter of the sun will appear to it proportionally less; and as the sun's apparent diameter at the earth is thirty minutes, it will subtend at Herschel at an angle of only a minute and a half. We subjoin here a diagram in which, if we suppose the larger circle E, to represent the appearance of the sun as seen from the earth; the smaller one H, will represent its appearance as seen from Herschel.

As the intensity of solar light diminishes in the same proportion as the superficial magnitude of the sun's disk diminishes, it will follow that the brightness of day at the planet Herschel must be between three and four hundred times less than at the earth! We might be led, however, from such a numerical estimate to form a very incorrect estimate of what the solar light under

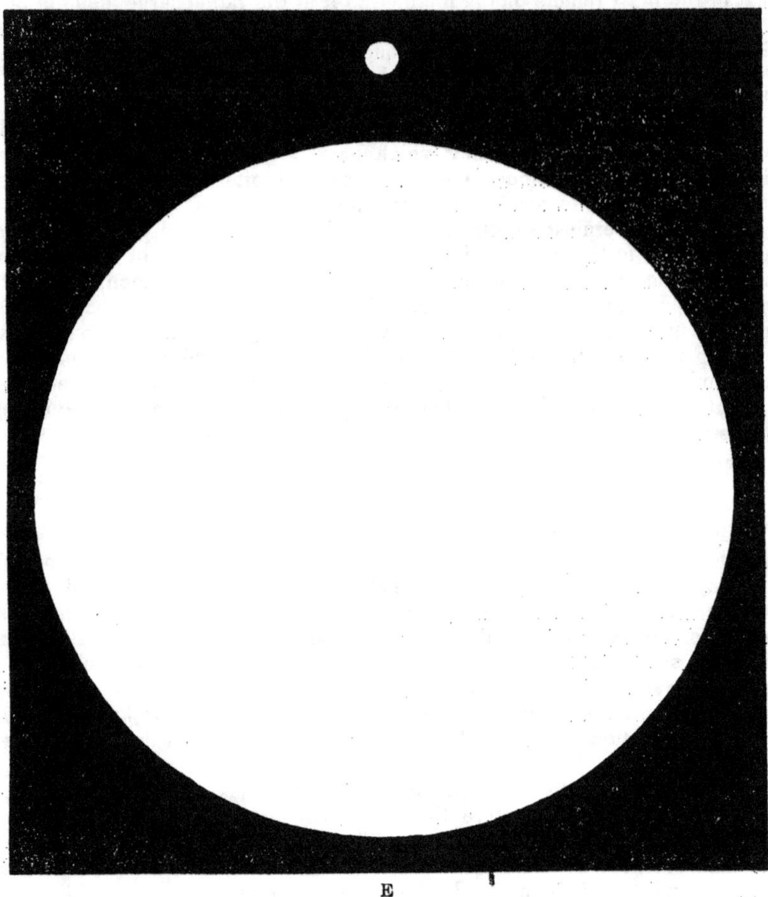

such circumstances must really be. The light of the full moon is about three hundred thousand times less than that of the sun ; consequently it follows that the light of day at Herschel will be equal to the light of more than one thousand full moons.

Independent of this consideration, however it will be remembered, as we have urged on another occasion, that the *perception* of the brightness of light, does not depend only upon the density of the light itself ; but also, upon the magnitude of the pupil of the eye and the sensibility of the *retina*. Nothing can be more easy to imagine than a very small alteration of the proportions of the eye, without even the necessity of admitting any in its structure, which would render the light of the sun at Herschel as efficient for the purpose of vision as at the earth.

It has been, in various popular works, and even in some strictly scientific treatises, urged that the cold which prevails at this and other remote planets, must be so intense that the liquids of our globe could not exist there ; and, on the other hand, that at the planet Mercury, a degree of heat must exist equally incompatible with the existence of physical arrangements similar to those which prevail upon the earth; such inferences are, as we conceive, premature and unfounded. They are based upon the supposition that the temperature depends solely upon the density of the solar rays. Now we have noticed elsewhere the fact that other agencies are concerned in the production of temperature, and have given as an example all the varieties of temperature which prevail between the tropics at different elevations.

In the valleys and planes of these regions, we find their proper climate; ascending the tropical ranges, at great elevations we encounter all the vegetable phenomena of temperate climates, and at still greater elevations we arrive at a temperature as rigorous as that at the poles. How easy is it, then, to conceive atmospheres and geographical arrangements provided on other planets, which, combined with the peculiar intensity of solar light and heat, shall produce a result which will fix the general temperature of any of the planets within the same limits that restrain it on the surface of the earth.

We have thus taken a general survey of the planetary system; but it may be asked how we know that this survey is completed, or that future telescopic observations may not bring to light another planet revolving round the sun, 2,000,000,000 of miles beyond the planet Herschel, and 4,000,000,000 of miles from the sun. The existence of a body such as Herschel, would have been regarded before its discovery, just as chimerical as another planet would now be considered, revolving beyond it.

We have, however, direct proofs of a very cogent character in favor of the position that Herschel is the last and most remote member of the solar system. Physical astronomy has been pushed in these, our days, to so great a degree of perfection that we are enabled to calculate beforehand the most minute effects which attend the reciprocal gravitation of the bodies of the solar system. Thus we can plainly discern in the movement of each planet, not only the effect produced upon it by the preponderating influence of the sun's gravity, but also the more minute and less perceptible effects of the gravitation of each of the other planets.

If, then, a planet exist beyond the limits of Herschel, unless it were of an extremely small mass, we could scarcely fail to discover its disturbing influence upon the general movement of the system. The great masses of the more remote planets compared with the nearer ones, render it improbable, if such a planet existed, that its mass could be small.

But we are not left to depend on this proof alone; the comets are bodies whose masses are incomparably less, even, than the smallest of the satellites, and they are therefore highly susceptible of receiving the effects of the gravitation of the bodies in their neighborhood. They may be regarded in astronomy as what electroscopical instruments are in physics; tests by which the existence of the smallest gravitating power may be ascertained.

One of these bodies, called Halley's comet, makes a periodical excursion which is completed in seventy-five years, issuing to a distance beyond the orbit of Herschel, amounting to very nearly 4,000,000,000 of miles from the sun. If, in its excursion, that body came within the gravitating influence of any mass of matter not known to astronomers, its motion would be affected by such influence, so that it would be accelerated or retarded, and the epoch of its return to the solar system would be sooner or later than that predicted by astronomers, upon the supposition that it is subject only to the attraction of the known bodies of the solar system. Now the comet of Halley has twice returned since its periodic motion was discovered, and in both cases the time and place of its return corresponded so exactly with that which would happen supposing it to be subject to no other attractions but those of the solar system, as to raise a presumption amounting to moral certainty, that it suffers in its long course, no disturbing influences, and consequently, that beyond the orbit of Herschel there exists no mass of matter attached to the solar system, sufficiently great to produce any effect upon so light a body as Halley's comet.

REFLECTION OF LIGHT.

Ray of Light.—Pencil of Light.—Reflection.—Irregular Reflection.—Regular Reflection.—Different Powers of Reflection in different Bodies.—Reflection at plane Surfaces.—Its Laws.—Image of an Object in a plane Reflector.—Reflection of curved Surfaces.—Concave Reflectors.—Convex Reflectors.—Images in spherical Reflectors.—Illusion of the air-drawn Dagger.—Effects of common Looking-Glasses analyzed.—A flattering Glass explained.—Metallic Specula.—Reflection in Liquids.—Image of the Banks of a Lake or River.

REFLECTION OF LIGHT.

THE physical theories by which the phenomena connected with the propagation of light are explained, have been given with some details on another occasion. We shall now notice some of the more simple and elementary laws of optics, which must stand undisturbed, whatever theory of light may be adopted.

Whether light consists of undulations, or of corpuscles of matter, *sui generis*, it is invariably propagated in straight lines so long as it passes through the same medium ; the straight line along which the light holds its course is called a *ray of light*, and any collection of such lines of definite thickness is called a *pencil of light*.

If the rays composing the pencil be parallel to each other, the pencil is called a parallel pencil ; if the rays intersect each other at a point, the pencil is said to diverge from or converge to that point according to the direction in which the light is conceived to move, and the pencil is accordingly called a converging or diverging pencil.

If rays of light, after passing in straight lines through any uniform medium, encounter the boundary or surface of another medium of a different kind, they will either turn back and take other directions in the medium from which they came, or they will enter the new medium, and will in general take new directions in it. In the former case the second medium is said to be opaque, and the rays are said to be reflected from its surface ; in the latter case it is said to be transparent, and the rays are said to be refracted by it.

Reflection and refraction are then two very important effects to which light is subject, and it will be both interesting and profitable briefly to notice the leading principles that govern these phenomena.

REFLECTION OF LIGHT.

The surfaces of opaque bodies reflect the light incident upon them in various ways, and produce a corresponding variety of effects thereby on the sense of sight.

All ordinary surfaces are more or less rough. The light which falls upon them is irregularly reflected by them ; each point upon them being illuminated, disperses the light which strikes upon it in every direction around it, and it is thus that the point itself becomes visible to an eye placed anywhere within view of it. The surfaces of bodies in general are by this means seen from every quarter around.

But as the light of the sun is of one uniform color and quality, it will be asked how it happens that the surfaces of different bodies and different parts of the surface of the same body produce different effects upon vision, appearing to have a variety of colors and tints of colors. If they reflect to the eye no light except that which falls upon them, and if that which falls upon them be all of a uniform quality, how, it may be asked, does it happen that the light reflected by different surfaces impresses the eye with the perception of different colors ? In answer to this it is necessary to explain that although the light of the sun is, in a certain sense, of a uniform quality and color, it is nevertheless not simple and homogeneous ; it is, in fact, a compound principle, produced by the mixture of lights of different colors in different proportions. It is this mixture which produces the white light of the sun.

Now, the surfaces of opaque bodies are endowed with various properties of reflecting light. Some possess the virtue of reflecting light of one color, while they absorb or extinguish light of another. One, for example, will have a strong power of reflecting red light, but will be altogether incapable of reflecting blue light; in short, various surfaces have infinitely various powers of reflecting lights of different colors.

Why, then, does one opaque object appear to the eye red, while another appears blue ? Because in the compound light of the sun, which equally falls on both of these objects, there is contained both red and blue light ; the surface of the object which appears red absorbs or extinguishes all the elements of the solar light except the red rays which it reflects ; and the object which appears blue, on the other hand, absorbs all the elements of the solar light except the blue rays, which alone are reflected by it.

Thus it appears that all objects, whether natural or artificial, derive their peculiar tints of color from the property which they possess of decomposing solar light. Such elementary colors as they have the power of reflecting blended together produce the peculiar tints which characterize them, the other constituents of the solar light being stopped.

But besides the colors presented by visible objects, they exhibit various degrees of illumination, or, what is familiarly called, various degrees of light and shade. This arises from the more or less favorable position which different parts of their surfaces have with respect to the light which falls upon them, and it is by this means that the form and shape of bodies are perceivable by the eye.

But if the surface of an opaque body, instead of being more or less rough, so as to render each of its points separately a centre of reflected light, could be rendered perfectly smooth and polished, then the light would not be reflected from it in the manner now described. The various points upon it would not then become centres from which light would be dispersed in every direction ; on the contrary, the rays of light falling on such a surface would be reflected by peculiar laws.

REFLECTION AT PLANE SURFACES.

Let us suppose that A B, fig. 1, is such a surface, and that a ray of light proceeding from the sun at S illuminates a point I, placed upon this surface. In the

Fig. 1.

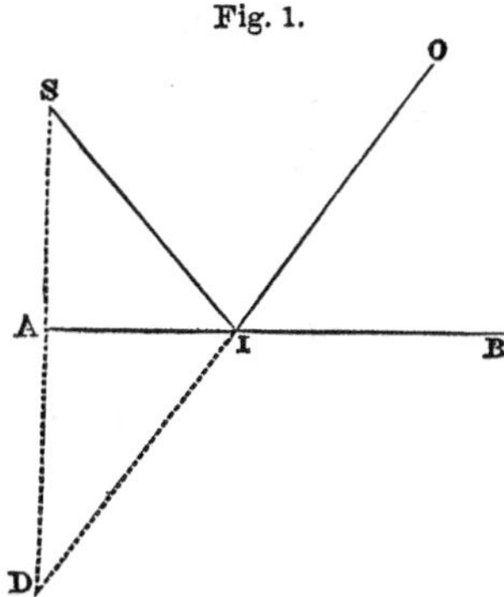

former case, the light striking at I or a part of it, would be dispersed in every direction above the surface A B, so as to render the point I visible to an eye placed anywhere in the space above A B. But such is not the case when the surface A B is perfectly smooth and polished. In that case, the light proceeding from S and striking on I, will be reflected only in one direction, viz., as if it came from a point D as far behind A B as S is before it. Thus if we draw S A at right angles to A B, and continue it until A D is equal to A S, then the light will be reflected along I O as if it came from D.

As a consequence of this, it follows that the incident light S I and the reflected light I O make equal angles with the reflecting surface A B.

This is a universal and very important law of optics, and is usually expressed thus :—

When a ray of light falls on a perfectly polished, reflecting surface, it is so reflected that the angle of reflection shall be equal to the angle of incidence. In the diagram, A I S is the angle of incidence, and O I B is the angle of reflection.

But if a surface such as A B, fig. 2, be exposed to a source of light, it is not one

Fig. 2.

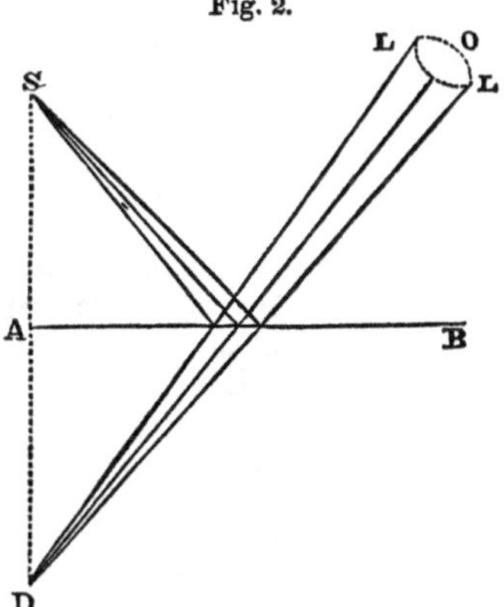

point, but every point of it, that will be illuminated. Rays in fact will diverge from S, and will strike upon all points of A B. From what has been already stated, it will be apparent that, after reflection, they will each of them proceed as if they had originally diverged from D. The effect, therefore, of the reflecting surface A B will be to convert a pencil of rays, which diverges from the point F, into another which will have the effect of diverging from the point D.

Now let us suppose a visible object, such as S S′, fig. 3, placed in front of a plane mirror, such as A B. Each point of that object will be a separate source of light of the peculiar tint which may characterize the object. The light which proceeds from each of these points falling on the surface A B, will be reflected as if it came from a corresponding point behind the mirror; and an eye placed anywhere before the mirror, as at O, will receive that light exactly as it would receive it if the body which is at S S′ were really at D D′. Consequently, the eye will see an object at D D′ exactly similar to S S′.

Fig. 3.

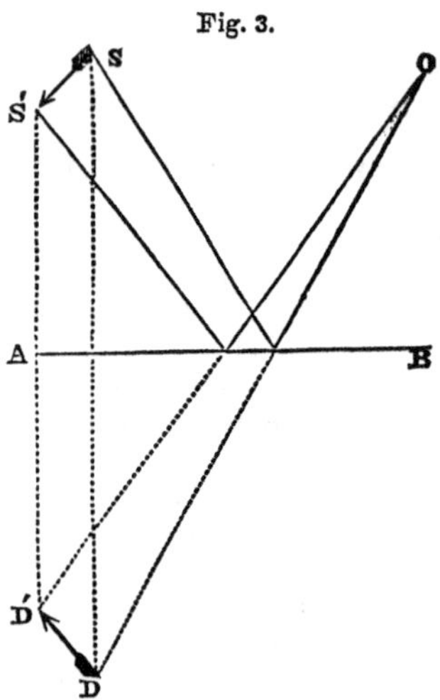

Such is the simple explanation of the effects of common plane mirrors. If we stand before a mirror, each point of our persons emits light of a peculiar color, which, diverging, falls on the surface of the mirror, and is reflected by that surface as if it came from a person exactly resembling ourselves in form and color, facing us, and standing at the same distance behind the mirror that we are before it

The form of an object thus rendered optically visible by a mirror is technically called its image.

It is evident, from what has been stated, that if I stand before a mirror and see my person in it, the image of my right arm being immediately opposite to that arm and behind the mirror, will be the left arm of the image; and in like manner, the image of my left arm will be the right arm of the image. It is the same with the images of all objects formed by plane reflectors: right becomes left, and left right; in other words, the image is reversed laterally.

In some cases, as will be seen hereafter, optical images are not merely reversed laterally, but inverted vertically, so as to be seen upside down. This is, however, not the case with plane mirrors; for the head and the feet of the image being on the other side of the mirror merely at the same distance behind it as the head and the feet of the object are before it, the head will be at the top and the feet at the bottom of the image. Objects are therefore seen erect in plane mirrors.

In cases where the arrangement from right to left is essential, the images produced by plane mirrors become defective for the ordinary purposes of exhibition. Thus a printed word, or an inscription, when held before a mirror, will be altogether deranged; it will have the same appearance to the eye as the types have from which it is printed.

REFLECTION AT CURVED SURFACES.

Whatever be the form of a curved surface, it may be conceived to consist of separate parts of such small dimensions that each of them may be considered as a portion of a sphere or globe; and therefore if the principles which regulate the reflection of light from a spherical surface be known, the effects of curved surfaces of other forms may be easily investigated. We shall therefore confine our observations here to the reflection of light from perfectly smooth spherical surfaces.

CONCAVE REFLECTORS.

Let M A M′, fig. 4, represent a portion of a concave spherical reflecting surface, and let S represent a point from which light diverges; let C be the centre of the spherical surface. A ray of light falling from S upon the point I, will be reflected in the direction I R, so as to make the angle R I C equal to the angle S I C. If the point S be very near to or in the line A C, and at a very great distance from the reflector, then the point R will be at the middle of the distance C A, so that it will divide the radius C A into two equal parts.

Fig. 4.

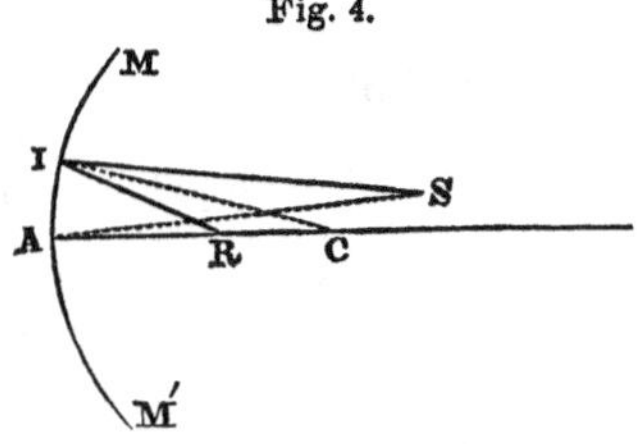

If the point S be in any object, the corresponding point R will be its image, and in like manner the images of all the other points will be formed.

When a concave speculum is presented to a very distant object, an image of that object will be formed in front of the speculum, and at a distance from it equal to half its radius. This image, however, will be inverted.

If the object be not at a very great distance from the reflector, its image will be formed at a point farther from the surface than half the radius, and will still be inverted.

In a convex reflecting surface, the image of an object placed in front will be formed behind the reflecting surface; as in the case of a plane mirror, it will be erect and smaller than the object.

The positions assumed by the images of objects formed by concave and convex reflectors, have rendered this species of mirrors amusing means of occasional optical exhibition.

If an object be placed in front of a convex mirror, its image will be formed behind the mirror at a distance something less than half the radius of the convexity. This image will be always erect, but will be smaller than the object; and the more distant the object is from the mirror, the smaller will be the image.

Whatever be the form of the object, the image will have a tendency to a convex form, and consequently such mirrors always produce distortion.

If an object be placed before a concave mirror at a distance from it greater than that of the geometric centre of its curvature, an image will be formed of this object in front of the mirror at a distance from its surface greater than half its radius.

This image will be inverted, and will be less than the object; as the object approaches the centre of the curvature of the mirror, the image will also approach that point, and thus the object and image will approach each other; the image will at the same time be increased in magnitude. If the object be placed within the centre of curvature of the mirror, but farther from its surface than half its radius, a magnified image will be formed at a distance more or less considerable in front of the mirror. Thus, let us suppose that a mirror formed with a curvature having a radius of four feet, has an object in front of it at a distance of three feet from its surface · an image of that object will be formed at six feet in front of the mirror, and this image will be double the height or length of the object.

In this manner, a mirror placed out of sight of a person may be made to throw the image of an object close to him; thus a dagger may be presented to one's bosom, which, however, is literally an air-drawn dagger.

The only form of reflecting surface which presents an object in its natural position and proportions is the plane mirror commonly used for domestic purposes; and even this, as already explained, reverses the object laterally—making right left, and left right. For the purposes, however, to which it is usually applied, this derangement does not impair its utility.

The perfection with which a mirror presents the image of an object placed before it depends upon its form and material. It is, above all things, essential that its surface should be perfectly plain and even: any deficiency in this quality will produce a corresponding distortion of the image. Cheap looking-glasses are often striated and streaked with inequalities and ridges, which render them nearly useless. Whatever be the substance used to form a mirror, a part only of the light which falls upon it will be instrumental in forming the image. The entire quantity of light which falls on the mirror may be accounted for as follows:—

1. A part will be *regularly reflected* according to the laws above explained and it is by this part the image will be formed.

2. Another part will be *irregularly reflected*—that is to say, it will be scattered in every direction around from every part of the surface. It is this portion of the light which renders the surface of the mirror visible.

3. A part will be absorbed upon the reflecting surface and lost.

The more highly polished and even the reflecting surface is, the less will be the part irregularly reflected, and the brighter will be the image. The part of the light absorbed or stopped will depend on the physical quality of the matter of which the reflector is formed.

Since art cannot produce a perfect reflecting surface, there will always be a portion of the incident light irregularly reflected and absorbed. It follows, therefore, that light is always lost in reflection; and in the case of plane mirrors, where the magnitude of the image is equal to that of the object, the brightness of the image must always be less than that of the object.

There is no substance which reflects with equal facility all tints of color. It generally happens that lights of one tint are more absorbed than the lights of another. Mirrors, therefore, will produce a change more or less according to their degree of imperfection in the tints which characterize the object before them; in other words, the color or tints of the image will not correspond exactly with those of the object.

It is therefore a fact true in science, although sometimes ridiculed, that different looking-glasses will present a more or less agreeable representation of the person who uses them, according to the colors which they may happen to absorb. Thus, if a mirror has a tendency to absorb the red tints, it will give a pallid tint to the complexion; whereas, if it absorb the blue tints, it will throw a blush over the appearance, and may be called a flattering glass.

Glass is the most convenient material for mirrors intended for domestic use, because it is the cheapest and most durable; but it is far from being the best. Its defects will become apparent by considering the mode in which its effects are produced. A coating of metallic foil is attached to the hinder surface of the glass, and by the mode of its adhesion a smooth metallic surface is thus formed under or behind the glass. It is this surface, and not the front of the glass, which is the real mirror: it is by it that the images of objects in front of the looking-glass are produced. The light has to pass through the thickness of the glass to reach this surface, and after being reflected by it, has again to pass through its thickness in order to reach the eye and produce a perception of the image. There are here three successive stages in which light is lost. A part only of the light which strikes upon the front surface of the glass penetrates it, and a part of what does penetrate it is lost upon the hinder surface; and again, after reflection, in issuing through the front surface, another portion is lost.

But the loss of light is not the only defect: in passing through the glass, partial absorption of color takes place; and hence, as has been already stated, the tints of the image will be different from those of the object.

A portion of the light which falls on the front surface of the glass is regularly reflected, and produces a faint image of the object, which, by careful observation, may be easily distinguished a little in front of the stronger image produced by the silvered surface. The distance of this faint image in front of the other will be equal to the thickness of the glass.

It is evident, from what has been just observed, that the thinner the glass is, the better will be the mirror.

The defects which have been just explained have rendered glass reflectors inapplicable to telescopes or any of the class of superior optical instruments used for scientific purposes. In these instruments metallic reflectors alone are used. An alloy of metals is selected for this purpose as white as possible in color, and susceptible of a high polish. A very accurate figure is imparted to it and a very perfect polish by various processes known in the arts. Although with such reflectors incomparably less light is lost than in common looking-glasses, still a much greater loss of light takes place than in transmission through transparent media; hence the received maxim in optics, that more light is lost in reflection than in refraction. Liquid surfaces afford in general, when at rest, good plane reflectors. If the liquid be opaque, the reflection is very perfect. This will be rendered apparent by pouring some clear quicksilver on a plate; to exhibit this effect, the quicksilver should be strained through a piece of chamois leather: it would otherwise have a film upon it composed of foreign matter, which would destroy its reflecting power.

The objects on the banks of a calm river or a tranquil lake will be seen reflected in its surface; but it is worthy of notice that the observer can only see this reflection when he looks very obliquely at the surface of the water: the reason of which is, that the rays which strike nearly at right angles to the water penetrate it in virtue of its transparency. It is only those which glance obliquely on it that are reflected; just as a stone which, thrown perpendicularly on the water, would immediately sink, will, if projected at a small angle with the surface, be reflected from the water, leaping from point to point of the surface, and affording the sport which boys call "duck and drake."

The laws which govern the refraction of light through transparent media show that when a ray strikes the transparent surface of a medium more rare than that through which it has passed, it cannot penetrate that surface, but will be reflected, unless its angle of obliquity exceed a certain magnitude. This mode of reflection is the most perfect with which we are acquainted, and is resorted to with great advantage in some optical instruments.

PROSPECTS OF STEAM-NAVIGATION.

Retrospect of Atlantic Steamers.—Origin of the Great Western.—Cunard Steamers.—Can Steam Packet-Ships be Successful?—Difficulties attending their Operation.—In a commercial Sense.—In a mechanical and nautical Sense.—Great Expedition must be given up.—Defects of Common Paddle-Wheels—Defects of the present Steam-Vessels as applicable to War.—Difficulty of long Ocean-Voyages.—Ericsson's Propeller.—Loper's Propeller.—Advantages of Submerged Propeller.—Method of raising the Propeller out of the Water.—Fuel.—Form and Arrangement of the proposed Steam Packet-Ships.—War Steamers.—The Princeton.—Effects to ensue from the New Steamships.—Conclusion.

PROSPECTS OF STEAM-NAVIGATION.

TEN years have now rolled away since the project was first announced to the world to supersede the far-famed NEW YORK AND LIVERPOOL PACKET-SHIPS by a magnificent establishment of STEAM-LINERS. These vessels were to sustain a constant, regular, and rapid communication between the New and Old World. They were to be the great channel for commerce, intelligence, and social intercourse, between the metropolis of the West and the vast marts of the United Kingdom; they were, in a word, to fulfil, not only all the functions which for half a century had been so admirably discharged by the packets, but to do so with expedition increased in a threefold proportion at the least. Such an announcement could not fail to captivate the great body of the public. The results to be anticipated were so obvious, so grand, and must be attended with effects so widely spread, that all persons of every civilized nation at once felt and acknowledged their importance. The announcement of the project was accordingly hailed with one general shout of acclamation. There were some, who, being conversant with the actual condition of the art of steam-engineering as applied to navigation, and aware of various commercial conditions which must affect the problem, were enabled to estimate calmly and dispassionately the difficulties and drawbacks, as well as the advantages, of the undertaking. These persons entertained doubts which clouded the brightness of their hopes, and warned the commercial world against the indulgence of too sanguine anticipations of the immediate and unqualified realization of the project They counselled caution and reserve against an improvident investment of extensive capital in schemes which could still be only regarded as experimental, and which might prove its grave. But the voice of remonstrance was drowned amid the loud shouts of public enthusiasm excited by the promise of an immediate practical realization of a scheme so grand. The keel of the Great Western was laid; an assurance was given that the seasons would not twice run through their changes before she would be followed by a splendid line of vessels, which should consign the packet-ships to the care of the historian as "things that were."

The Great Western progressed and was launched, and the enterprise has now had a fair trial during ten years—a sufficiently long time, it is presumed, to test it. The packet-ships, however, have not been swept from the face of the ocean. On the contrary, they have been improved in efficiency, increased in magnitude, and multiplied in number. Capital, instead of being drawn from them, allured by the prospective advantages of the STEAM-LINERS, has only collected round them in augmented amount—obeying, as it always does, that irresistible attraction which profitable results invariably exercise in commerce. On the other hand, the steam project, which was to prove their doom, has made its flash and disappeared, leaving the Great Western—

————————"alone in her glory"—

to establish at once the abstract practicability of the scheme in a mechanical sense, and the utter inadequacy of its organization and execution in a commercial sense. This fine ship has for several years maintained an occasional intercourse during the summer months between New York and one or other of the British ports.

The Great Western, it must be confessed, was established under most favorable auspices. Mr. Field, of the firm of Maudslay and Field, planned and executed her machinery, although the merit of it has been attempted to be filched from him by others. It combined all the perfection which the most consummate skill in practical engineering at that time could confer upon it. The vessel has accordingly proved the practicability of maintaining this line of steam communication, provided the traffic would bear its expense in that particular way of working it. If any experiment of that kind could encourage the investment of capital in the enterprise, this would have done so. Yet, with the practical monopoly of the line in their hands, the owners of this splendid ship have more than once offered her for public sale. That she now remains in their hands and still plies across the Atlantic, is owing to the fact that no buyers on equitable terms could be obtained. Meanwhile, the less ambitious but more manageable project to establish a line of *mail-steamers*, sustained by the liberal subsidy of the British postoffice, plying between Liverpool and Boston, has been, as all the world knows, successfully realized.

How, then, it will be rationally asked, are these things to be explained? Are we to relinquish the hope of uniting the great mart of the West with the ports of Europe by the agency of steam in such a manner as to serve the ends of commerce, and insure to the projectors that reasonable profit without which permanence cannot be obtained? Is that mighty power which for the last century has wielded its giant arm over the destinies of the human race—which has raised from the bowels of the earth those inestimable mineral treasures that, without its aid, would have been inaccessible—which has superseded human labor at the spindle and the loom, and supplied their products in unbounded quantity at a price little exceeding that of the raw material—which has invaded the waters of the Ganges and Mississippi, and poured the blessings of civilization even to the innermost recesses of the great continents of Asia and America—which has superseded the weary hand of human labor at the printing-press, and become the instrument of the diffusion of knowledge among the entire human race at a price which has rendered it accessible to all—which has unharnessed the horse from the car, and, taking its place, has given the speed of the wind to the social intercourse of distant centres of population—is the mighty arm of this omnipotent agent suddenly enfeebled and paralyzed, and are we, in the middle of the nineteenth century, destined to be the witnesses of this its first signal failure?—or is it rather that those whom chance has thrown into the management and guidance of this vast enterprise have wanted the skill to devise proper and adequate means of applying the power placed at their disposal? These are questions to which it were rash in any individual, however high his attainments, to give a dogmatical answer. Nor, indeed, would such an answer now be otherwise useful than as illustrating the history of the progress of steam-machinery.

The condition under which the problem presented itself ten years ago has been gradually and insensibly modified by the progressive improvements which each successive year, nay, even every revolving month, has developed in the art of steam-navigation. That which might have been impracticable and hopeless in 1837, was less so in 1838—was divested of still more of its difficulties and obstacles in 1839—became in some degree feasible in 1840; and thus, by the progress of invention and the improvement of art, presents itself now under much more cheering prospects.

Having attended with much interest to the growth of the Atlantic steam project from its earliest suggestion up to the present hour, and having, by my course of study and professional avocations, been informed of the condition of that branch of the useful arts on which its successful issue must depend—and having regarded it, moreover, not merely as a great *mechanical* experiment, but as a *commercial* project, the issue of which must depend on the permanent and certain advantage to be derived from it—I formed early opinions respecting it, and did not hesitate publicly to express them. It was apparent, as I conceived, that an establishment of STEAM-LINERS between New York and the ports of England must depend for their success upon their fitness and capability to serve those commercial purposes which were so well fulfilled hitherto by the packet-ships. It was well known that a line of post-office steamers, controlled and subsidized by the British government, and serving the colonial objects of that nation would be established, and would necessarily enjoy the monopoly of the mails, and receive a preference from those classes of voyagers to whom expedition was everything and expense nothing. Against such a line it was evidently hopeless to oppose one directed to similar objects, subject to equal expense, and not sustained by the same munificent subsidies. The New York and Liverpool line, then, if established at all, must direct itself to the fulfilment of objects not aimed at by the British postoffice line of steamers.

Such vessels, to be profitable to their owners and beneficial to the public, must aim at the acquisition of powers and capabilities which will enable them to perform the service of the packet-ships. They must, in a word, be packet-ships, in which sufficient steam-power shall be supplied as may give them that increased expedition, regularity, and punctuality, which, in the existing state of the arts, can only be obtained through that agency; but it is also important that they accomplish this without robbing these ships to any injurious extent of their present capability of satisfying the wants of commerce.

Now it appears evident that these ends can only be obtained by a material modification in the form and position of the propelling apparatus. A great reduction in the dimensions of the machinery, and the surrender to the uses of commerce of that invaluable space which it now occupies within the vessel, are also essential. It is incumbent on the engineer who assumes the high responsibility of the superintendence of such a project, to leave the present packet-ship in the full and unimpaired enjoyment of its functions as a sailing-vessel. Let him combine, in short, the agency of Steam with the undiminished nautical power of the Ship. Let him celebrate the marriage of the steam-engine with the sailing vessel. If he accomplish this with the skill and success of which the project is susceptible, he may fairly hope that his name will go down to posterity as a benefactor of mankind, united with those of Fulton and Watt.

When these reflections pass through the mind, it is cheering to think that they are neither visionary nor hopeless. It is pleasant to reflect that the day is most probably fast approaching, if not already at hand, when such ideas will be realized—when we shall behold a great highway cut across the wide Atlantic, not as now, subserving to those limited ends, the attainment of which will bear a high expense, but answering all the vast and varied demands of general commerce. But, to secure advantages so extensive, we shall doubtless be called on to compromise something on the score of extreme speed. It is probable, if not certain, that ships which would serve the purposes we have here shadowed out can never compete in mere speed with vessels in which cargo is nothing, expense disregarded, and expedition everything. Be it so. Leave to such vessels their proper functions; let them still enjoy to some extent the monopoly of the most costly branches of traffic, subsidized as they are by the British treasury. Let the New York Steam-Liner, securing to commerce equal regularity and punctuality, and probably more frequent despatch, be content with somewhat less expedition. Such is consistent with all the analogies of commerce.

There is another consideration which, in commencing such a project, ought not to be omitted. In all great advances in the arts of life, extensive improvements are at first attended with individual loss of greater or lesser amount. The displacement of capital is almost inevitably attended with this disadvantage. It is the duty, therefore, of the scientific engineer, in the arrangement and adoption of his measures, to consider how these objects may be best attained with the least possible injury to existing interests. To accomplish this will not only be a benefit to the public, but will materially facilitate the realization of his own objects, by conciliating in their favor those large and powerful interests whose destruction would be otherwise menaced by them. If, then, in the present case, it is found practicable with advantage to introduce into the present packet-ships, more especially into those most recently constructed, the agency of steam, a very important advantage will be gained for the public, and the almost unanimous support and countenance of the commercial community will be secured.

To attain the objects here developed, it will be evidently indispensable to remove those impediments which at once disfigure the appearance and destroy the efficiency of the sailing qualities of the ship by the enormous and unsightly excrescences projecting from the sides in the shape of paddle-wheels and the wheel-houses, or paddle-boxes, as they are called. These appendages are attended with many evils, the least of which is perhaps the impediment which they present to the progress of the ship. Few are aware of the amount of the resistance which the air offers to the passage of a large body moving with a considerable velocity. This was, however, proved in a striking manner by an extensive series of experiments made under my superintendence in the years 1838 and 1839 upon the English railways. The result of these conclusively proved that at high speeds the resistance of the air forms the main obstacle against which the moving power has to act. Now, although it be true that no speed yet attained on the ocean by steamships bears any comparison to the rate of transport on the English railways, yet it cannot be doubted that when steamships work under their greatest advantages, their speed is sufficient to render the atmosphere a formidable source of resistance, and that even at their average speed it robs the moving power of no inconsiderable portion of its efficacy. It is therefore apparent that no means should be neglected to remove from the ship everything which can augment the amount of this resistance, and it is obvious that the magnitude of the paddle-boxes and paddle-wheels must in this respect form one of the greatest obstructions.

But independently of this, and admitting for a moment that the propelling machinery of steamships is not obnoxious to this objection, it would still be subject to other even more serious objections. In order that a paddle-wheel of the common form should act with complete efficiency, it is found in practice (and this is countenanced by theory) that its immersion should not exceed the depth of the lowest paddle-board. If the immersion become greater than this, a portion more or less considerable of the moving power is lost in the mere elevation and depression of the water. If the immersion be less, the wheel whirls round without laying sufficient hold of the water to obtain a reaction sufficient for the propulsion of the vessel. It is therefore apparent that so long as the propelling power is conveyed through a pair of paddle-wheels at the sides of the vessel, having the form and structure of the wheels now in general use, a due economy of the moving power cannot be realized, except when the vessel moves as it does in inland navigation, on smooth water, and in a perfectly upright position. If the vessel leans to either side, one wheel becomes too much and the other too little immersed, and a loss of power is entailed upon both. If the surface of the water be rough and undulating, even though the vessel should be kept strictly in an upright position, both wheels will be momentarily varied in their immersion—now being too deeply and now not deeply enough immersed—and will on both accounts entail on the vessel a proportional waste of the moving power.

Such is the inevitable condition to which a steam-vessel of the present construction is exposed in navigating the ocean. Scarcely an hour throughout its entire voyage can the impelling power work with full and unimpaired efficiency. The swell of the ocean is incessant, nor does it even cease in the intervals of the abatement of the winds. The principles of this reasoning appear so evident, that it would be a slight upon the understanding to enlarge upon them. It will be easily perceived that the conclusion is inevitable, that when steam-vessels of the present form are applied to ocean-voyages, a large proportion of the moving power must be lost.

Among persons who have not devoted much time to the investigation of this question, it is a favorite argument to urge the immense speed obtained by the steam-vessels working with these propelling-wheels upon the extensive inland waters of this great continent. But there is no analogy whatever between the cases. Let it be remembered that the condition upon which this extraordinary efficiency depends can never be fulfilled in sea-going steamers. That efficiency depends essentially on the smooth and unruffled surface of the water on which the vessel moves, and the power of the vessel to maintain itself in a constantly perpendicular position.

When these observations are duly considered, it will be readily admitted that the attainment of perfect efficiency in ocean-steamers with the present propelling apparatus is hopeless.

But the form, magnitude, and position, of the propelling machinery, is far from being the only obstacle to the full success of the present steam-vessels when directed to the general purposes of commerce. The engines themselves, and the boilers, from which the moving power proceeds, and the fuel by which they are worked, occupy the very centre of the vessel, and engross the most valuable part of the tonnage. The chimney, which gives efficacy to the furnaces, is also an unsightly excrescence, and no inconsiderable obstruction.

If the present form and structure of steam-vessels be obnoxious to these many serious objections when considered with reference to the purposes of general commerce, they are still more exceptionable when considered with reference to the purposes of national defence. It is undoubtedly a great power with which to invest a vessel-of-war, to confer upon it the faculty of proceeding at will and immediately, in spite of the opposition of wind or tide, in any direction which may seem most fit to its commander. Such a power would surpass the wildest dreams of the most romantic and imaginative naval commander of the last century. To confer upon the vessels of a fleet the power immediately at the bidding of the commander to take any position that may be assigned to them relatively to the enemy, or to run in and out of a hostile port at pleasure, or fly with the rapidity of the wind past the guns of formidable forts before giving them time to take effect upon them—are capabilities which must totally revolutionize all the established principles of naval tactics. But these powers at present are not conferred upon steamships without important qualifications and serious drawbacks. The instruments and machinery from which these powers are immediately derived are unfortunately exposed in such a manner as to render the exercise of the powers themselves hazardous in the extreme. It needs no profound engineering knowledge to perceive that the paddle-wheels are eminently exposed to shot, which, taking effect, would altogether disable the vessel, and leave her at the mercy of the enemy; and the chimney is even more exposed, the destruction of which would render the vessel a prey to the enemy within itself in the shape of fire. But besides these most obvious sources of exposure in vessels of the present form intended as a national defence, the engines and boilers themselves, being more or less above the water-line, are exposed so as to be liable to be disabled by shot.

Such are a few of the many defects incidental to the present form of steamships as applied to the purposes of national defence.

When long ocean-voyages are contemplated, such as those between New York and the ports of England, there is another serious obstacle, which is especially felt in the westward trip, because of the prevalence of adverse winds. When the vessel starts on its long voyage, it is necessarily laden with a large stock of fuel, which is calculated to meet, not merely the average exigencies of the voyage, but the utmost extremity of adverse circumstances of wind and weather to which it can by possibility be exposed. This fuel is gradually consumed upon the voyage; the vessel is proportionally lightened, and its immersion diminished. If its trim be so regulated that the immersion of its wheels at starting be such as to give them complete efficiency, they may, before the end of the voyage, be almost if not altogether raised out of the water. If, on the other hand, the efficiency of propulsion in the latter part of the voyage be aimed at, they must have such a depth at its commencement as to impair in a serious degree their propelling effect, and to rob the vessel of its proper speed. Under such circumstances, there is no expedient left but compromise. The vessel must start with too great and arrive with too little immersion. There is no alternative, save to abandon altogether the form and structure of the present machinery, and to awaken the inventive genius of the age to supply other mechanical expedients, which shall not be obnoxious to these objections.

Although no one who has lived as long and witnessed so many disappointed hopes and fallacious anticipations in the progress of improvement as I have, will be very forward to commit themselves as to the results of projects which still exist in a state but partially tested by experience, I cannot refrain from giving expression to a strong hope and confident anticipation that the epoch is at hand which will witness a great advance in ocean-navigation, and a gift conferred by science upon the arts not equalled since the invention of the steamboat and the safety-lamp.

It is generally known that within the last seven years a form of sub-aqueous propeller placed at the stern of the vessel as a substitute for the paddle-wheels, has been invented and patented by Captain Ericsson. This contrivance has now been in practical operation for so long a time, and in so great a number and variety of vessels, that we must cease to regard it as an experiment. Its efficiency has been tested on an extensive scale. The propelling-wheel is fixed upon an axis which is placed parallel to the keel, and which issues from the stern of the vessel; the wheel therefore revolves with its face sternward. In wheels of this form and construction, the principle of action is in general similar to that of the common smoke-jack. The propelling surfaces have been usually placed at an oblique angle to the course of the vessel, and have extended from the axle or nave to the outer edge of the wheel. Now, it will be apparent, even to those who are least familiar with mechanical inquiries, that those parts of the blades which are near to the nave moving with the least velocity, are the most inefficient for propulsion; and were it worth while, it would be no very difficult matter to demonstrate that they are often an absolute obstruction. The outer ends of the blades, moving with greater velocity, act with proportionately greater efficiency.

These circumstances led Captain Ericsson to construct his wheel in such a manner as to remove altogether those parts of the blades nearest to the nave, and which were inefficient for propulsion, retaining only those which were most remote and most effective. This he accomplished by forming a hoop of metal concentric with the nave, and connected with it by two or more spokes, to enable which to pass through the water with the least possible resistance, he gave them a twisted or spiral form, regulated with such mathematical precision, that, by the progressive motion of the vessel, combined with their own rotation, they must always encounter the water edgewise.

Drawings of this propeller, as applied to the Princeton, are given in figs. 1, 2, and 3. A section parallel to the face of the wheel is given in fig. 1; a horizontal view is shown in fig. 2; and a section of the axle and hoop in fig. 3. The nave in which the axle is inserted is at N, from which proceed six twisted spokes R R, attached to and supporting the hoop H H H, bolted on to which are six spiral propelling surfaces P P, &c. The axis inserted in the nave is represented at A, fig. 2, where the obliquity and spiral form of the surfaces are also shown, as well as the manner in which they are bolted on the hoop.

In order to give to this wheel all the possible strength, six spiral spokes were supplied, one for each propelling blade. The material of the wheel is composition-metal, which resists oxydation.

A propeller has been also supplied by Captain Ericsson for the United States revenue-cutters Legaré and Jefferson, represented in figs. 4, 5, and 6. The corresponding parts are represented in the same manner as in the former diagrams, and are marked by the same letters. In this wheel, the same strength not being necessary, there are only four twisted arms supporting the hoop, and the material of the propeller is wrought iron.

Stern-propellers have been invented and patented of very various forms, which, however, all agree in certain properties. When they are totally submerged, with the face of the wheel presented backward, their revolution causes a current of water to be projected backward from the stern, the reaction of which is in fact the moving power. This effect is produced in all of them by placing the surfaces of the radiating arms or plates in a position inclined to the course of the vessel. If these surfaces were placed at right angles to the keel, the revolution of the wheel would make them cut the water edgewise, and no reaction would be obtained. If, on the contrary, they were parallel to the keel, with their edges in the direction of the vessel's course, they would drive

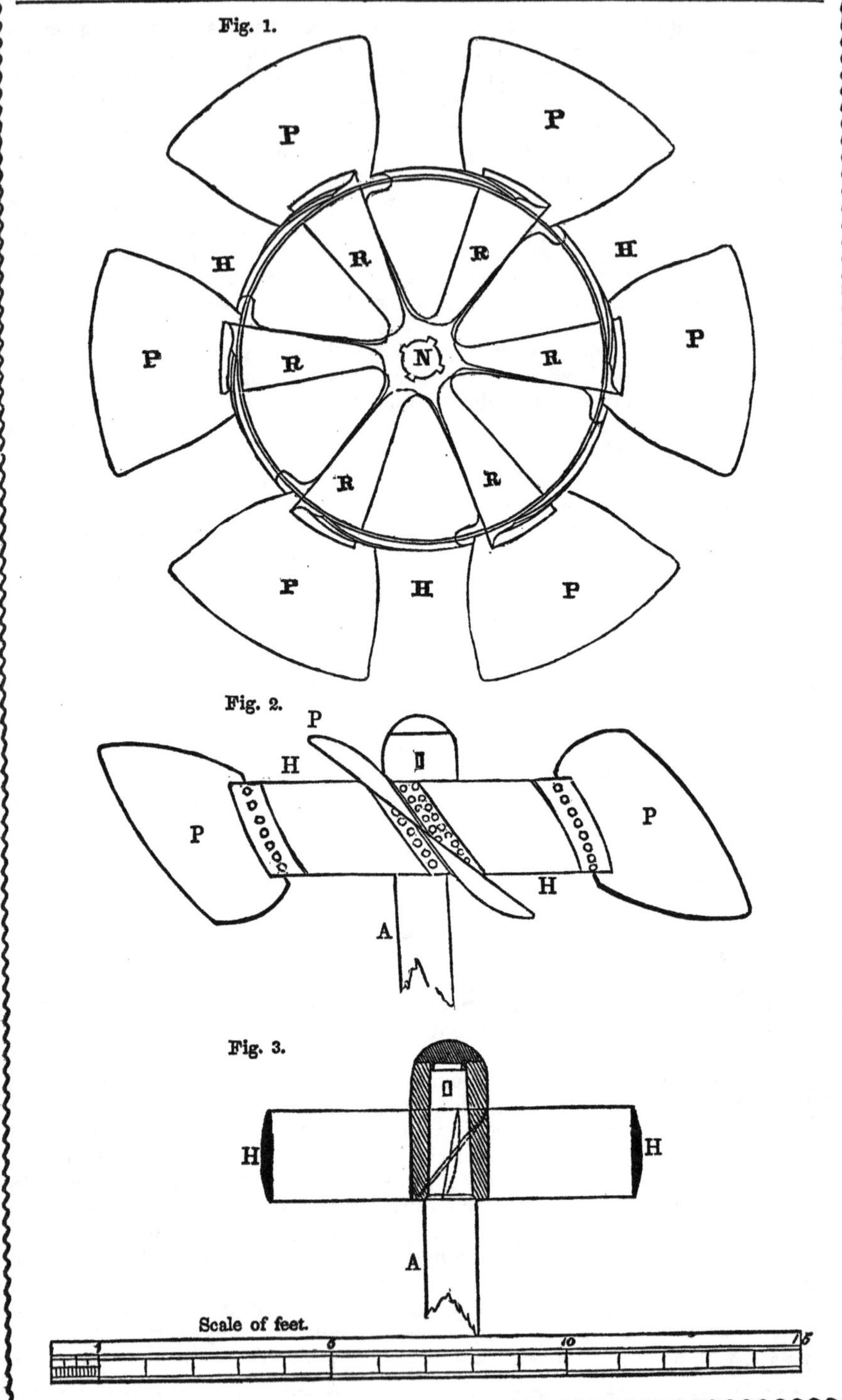

Fig. 1.
P
P
H
R
R
H
P
R
N
R
P
R
R
P
H
P
Fig. 2.
P
H
P
P
H
A
Fig. 3.
H
H
A
Scale of feet.
5
10
15

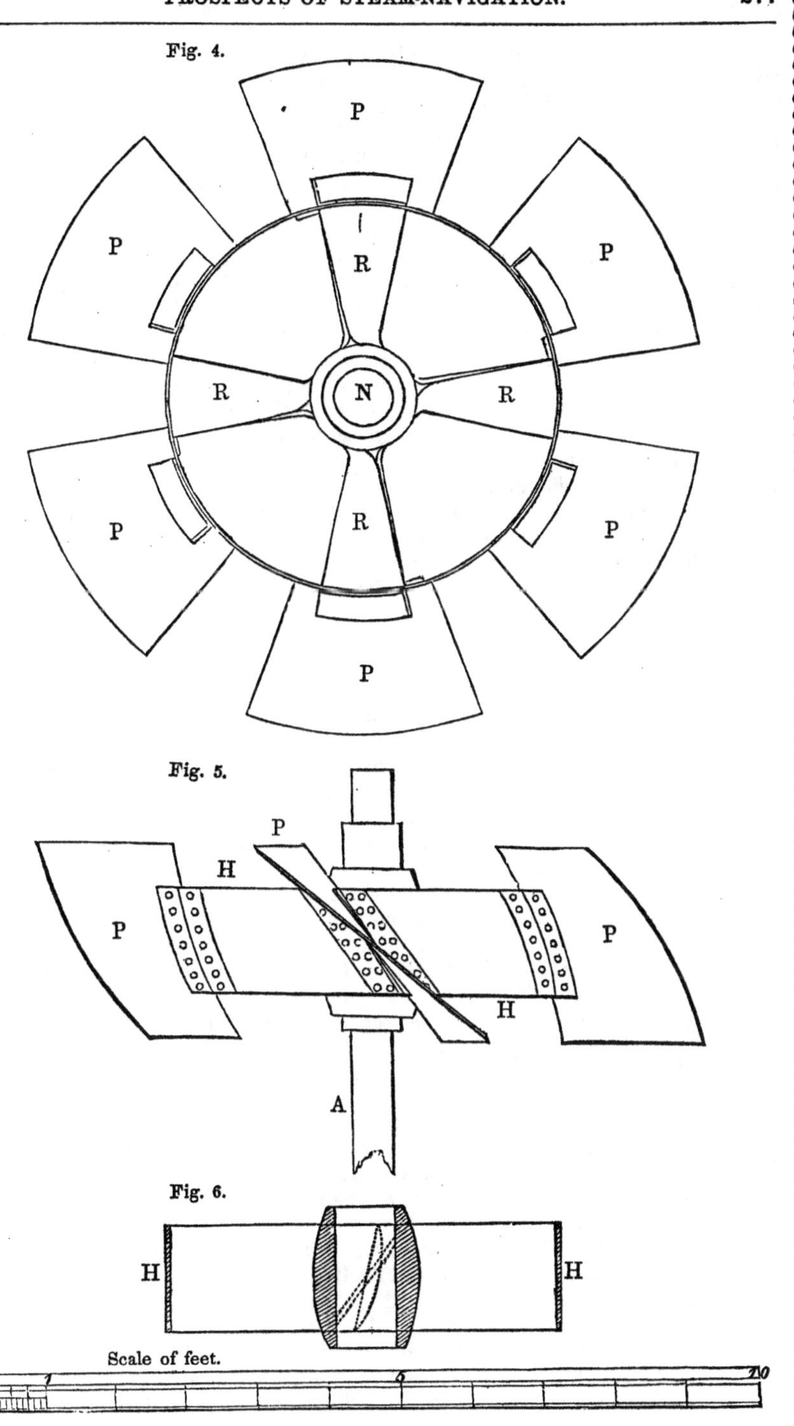
Fig. 4.
P
P
R
P
R
N
R
P
R
P
P
Fig. 5.
P
H
P
P
H
A
Fig. 6.
H
H
Scale of feet.
1
5
10

the water everywhere at right angles to that course, and no backward current would be produced; but by giving them a position between these two extremes —that is to say, inclined at some oblique angle to the course of the vessel— the revolution of the wheel will cause them to exert a certain portion of their force on the water in producing a backward current: and that particular obliquity should be given to them which will make that backward current most effective.

The calculation of this obliquity requires the application of the principles of mathematical science, and admits of a clear and definite solution. It is found, however, that the most effective obliquity for the propelling surface is not the same for all distances from the centre of the wheel, and consequently if the best possible form be given to the propelling blades, they must be shaped according to a certain spiral to be determined by conditions depending upon a variety of circumstances connected with the propeller and the vessel itself.

Some projectors, ignorant of these scientific principles, have constructed these propellers with plane surfaces, without the spiral form. Such is the patented contrivance called Loper's propeller. They are consequently and most obviously inefficient.

But besides the proper adjustment of the obliquity of the propelling surfaces, the experience of Captain Ericsson soon proved that the parts of the blades near the centre of the wheel were not only inefficient for propulsion, but formed an impediment to the progress of the vessel. It was for this reason, among others, that he cut away those parts of the blades near the centre, retaining only the more remote portions, and supported these by bolting them on to the hoop already described.

Such being the general character of this propelling instrument, it will be apparent that in every position which it can assume in the water, it must produce nearly the same propelling effect. However the ship may pitch or roll, or however unequal the surface of the sea may be, it will always produce the backward current, without any great variation of effect.

The circumstances which prevent the co-operation of the power of steam with that of the sails in the steam-vessels now in use, will not operate with a propeller of this form, inasmuch as its efficacy will be altogether independent of the careening of the ship; but although this defect is removed, the submerged stern-propellers are still subject to objections from which even the common paddle-wheels are free. Being permanently submerged and liable to accidental fracture and derangement from various causes, they are inaccessible, and cannot be repaired at sea; but besides this, when the object in view is to take full advantage of the power of the sails, that of the machinery being suspended, the submerged propeller becomes an obstruction, more or less considerable, to the progress of the vessel.

An invention, however, recently patented by Captain Ericsson, has finally removed this difficulty, and placed it in the power of the commander at any time within the space of five minutes to raise the propeller out of the water, or to submerge it, so as to convert for all intents and purposes a steamer into a sailing-vessel, or a sailing-vessel into a steamer, as he may see fit.

The shaft on which the propelling-wheel is fixed is provided with a simple mechanism within the vessel by which it may be easily at any time drawn out of the nave of the wheel. The wheel itself is sustained by a powerful vertical arm, the upper end of which is attached to a strong axis, which enters the vessel parallel to the main axis of the wheel and above the summit of the wheel. To this axis within the vessel is attached a piece of mechanism by which it may be turned through half a revolution by the power of two men with such force that the propeller will be made to perform half a revolution round the upper end of the vertical arm which supports it, by which that arm will be presented upward instead of downward. The wheel, therefore, instead of being submerged, will be supported at the stern of the vessel at the place where a boat is usually suspended.

The vessel will thus be free from all obstruction in passing through the water, and will acquire all the efficiency which any mere sailing-vessel can have, besides which the propeller is placed in such a situation that it may be repaired if necessary.

The main shaft which drives the propeller when submerged is at a depth of seven or eight feet under the lower deck. The cylinders by which it is impelled are supported in a slanting position on the timbers of the vessel, their piston-rods being presented toward the crank on the shaft, which they drive in the usual manner by connecting-rods. The boilers and the fuel occupy the space immediately forward of the cylinders. The entire machinery, including the boilers and fuel, are below the second deck of the vessel.

Such are the general features of the arrangements projected by Captain Ericsson,* and proposed to be adopted in a line of steam packet-ships to ply between New York and Liverpool. The first of these vessels is now in an advanced state at Boston, and the machinery is in progress in New York. It is expected that this ship will make her first voyage in August, 1845.

The fuel to be used is hard coal, and the furnaces will be ventilated by blowers, worked by the engine. There will be no smoke, nor any need of the draught produced by a chimney, and therefore that appendage will have no other use than as an exit for the gases evolved in the combustion. A square tunnel designed for this purpose is carried from the machinery upward through the two decks, terminating on the poop-deck, where a sliding tube, having a motion like a telescope-joint, by which a short discharge-pipe for the hot air and offensive gases can be elevated when the machinery is worked, and which can be lowered when the vessel is under sail.

Such a vessel, then, presents none of the appearances, internal or external, of a steamer. There is no visible machinery, no noise, heat, smoke, or perceptible vibration. The main-deck, clear of machinery from stem to stern, is occupied by the cabins, saloons, library, state-room, and the various other ac-

* The triumphs of genius, like all sublunary pleasures, are not unattended with alloy. The moment that any invention proves to be successful in practice, a swarm of vermin are fostered into being to devour the legitimate profits of the inventor, and to rob genius of its fair reward. Captain Ericsson, so long as his submerged propeller retained the character of a mere experiment, was left in undisturbed possession of it; but when it had forced its way into extensive practical use—when it was adopted in the United States navy, and in the revenue service—when the coast of this country witnessed its application in numerous commercial vessels—when it was known that in France and England its adoption was decided upon—then the discovery was made for the first time that this invention of Captain Ericsson's was no invention at all—that it had been applied since the earliest dates in steam-navigation. Old patents, some of which had been stillborn, and others which had been for years dead and buried, were dug from their graves, and their dust brought into courts of law, to overturn this invention, and wrest from Captain Ericsson his justly-earned reward. But this was not all: every mechanical expedient has about it accidents and essentials. It is the same with genius and art. Imitators, incapable of realizing the spirit or producing the essentials, are nevertheless capable of copying the accidents and mere forms. The success of Ericsson's inventions produced the usual swarm of imitators of this kind: and the smoke-jack was accordingly patented by a so-called inventor at Philadelphia, in which, with a singular obliquity of ingenuity, he stripped Ericsson's contrivance of everything that was good about it, and carefully combined all the bad features which could possibly attach to the common wheel of oblique action.

It is painful to be compelled to state that these base and contemptible proceedings have not failed in some instances to obtain countenance in high quarters. Will it be believed that the steamship Princeton, the performance of whose machinery was attended with complete success, has had its propeller removed, and another substituted, which is in fact a feeble and inefficient copy of the original—omitting, however, one or two of its best features? It is pretended, also—erroneously, as will be proved—that this inferior instrument has been more efficient in operation than the original wheel. No engineer or machinist, properly informed, can examine the wheel which has been thus substituted, without being convinced that the change must have been prompted by motives entirely unconnected with those of the improvement of the vessel.

commodations for passengers. Under that, the second or freight deck, also clear of machinery from stem to stern, is occupied by the cargo; and beneath this again, buried in the very bottom of the vessel, is the mechanical power of propulsion—occupying, however, only about one fifth of the space below the freight-deck. The square tunnel we have referred to for the discharge of the gases, and the ventilation of the engine-room, is carried up through the decks and stands in one of the saloons, but presents no other appearance to the eye than that of a pillar five feet square, handsomely empannelled and decorated, and adorned with mirrors. The freight-deck being interposed between the cabins and the machinery, intercepts all noise and vibration.

When this mode of propulsion is applied to vessels-of-war, as in the case of the Princeton, there is still another object to be accomplished. It is desirable that the whole of the machinery should be below the water-line, so as to be effectually protected from shot. This is accomplished by engines of a peculiar construction, invented and patented by Captain Ericsson, which have been worked with complete success in the Princeton. A representation of these, in transverse vertical section, is given in fig. 7. It consists of two semi-cylinders, presenting their semicircular sides downward, and being flat at the top. They are placed beside each other above the main shaft, having their axes parallel to it and to the keel. The ends of the axes are represented at A B. To these axes are attached vibrating rectangular planes, which move alternately from left to right, and right to left, within the semi-cylinders, and in steam-tight contact with them. These planes are attached to the axes of the cylinders, the ends of which appear at A and B, so that the vibrating motion of the planes will impart a corresponding motion to the arms A E and B F, attached to the ends of the axes A and B. The ends of these arms E and F are attached to two connecting-rods, E D and F D, which are both attached to the crank S D, which drives the main shaft.

The steam is admitted alternately to each side of the vibrating planes within the semi-cylinders, being at the same time withdrawn from the other side by a condenser.

The action of the connecting-rods on the crank will be best understood by following them successively through their various positions. In fig. 8, the rod F D is in the position in which it has no power on the crank: but the rod E D, being at right angles with the crank, has full effect upon it. The crank therefore moves from the position represented in fig. 8, to the position represented in fig. 9, where the rod E D becomes powerless. The crank is then driven to the position represented in fig. 10, where the rod D F becomes again powerless, and E D is effective. The crank is then moved to the position represented in fig. 11, where E D is powerless and F D effective, and so on.

Thus it appears by this arrangement that the relative positions of the crank and connecting-rods are such as to exercise a uniform action on the main shaft.

The space occupied by the machinery in the lower part of the stern of the vessel, is surrounded by fuel, as represented in figure 7, and the whole is considerably below the water-line W.

This machinery is designed only for war-vessels. Its construction and operation are somewhat too expensive to be used for the mere purposes of commerce, where the advantages of its being placed below the water-line are of no account.

The steam packet-ships to which we have referred are calculated to make an average speed of nine statute miles per hour when in full operation. It is computed that they can maintain the communication between New York and Liverpool with regularity and despatch—the average western passage being

Fig. 7.

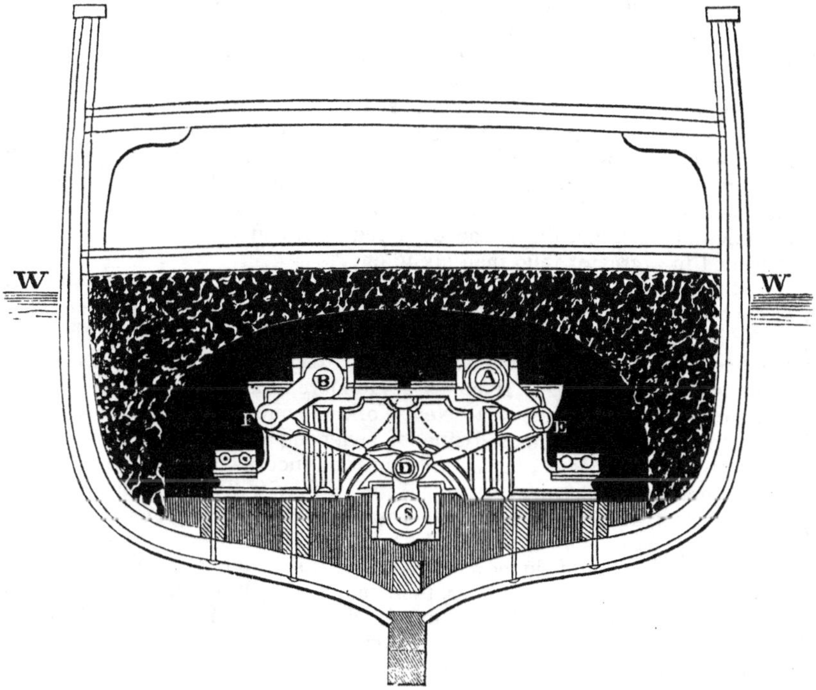

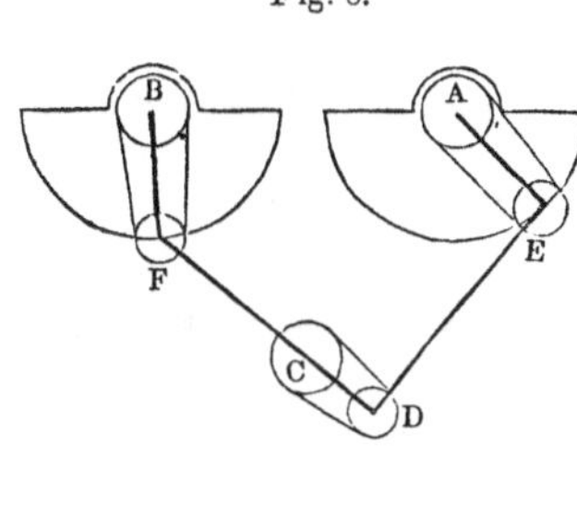

Fig. 8.

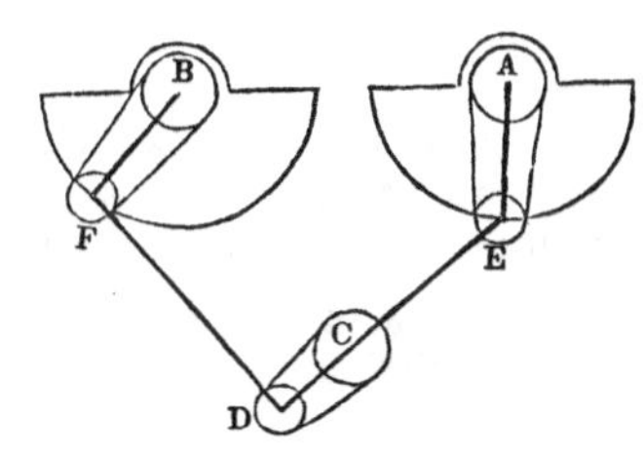

Fig. 9.

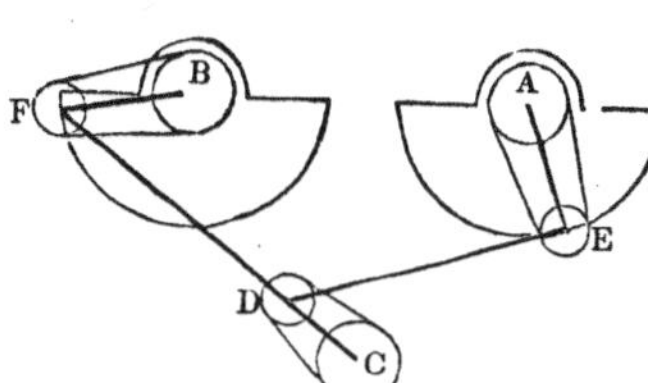

Fig. 10.

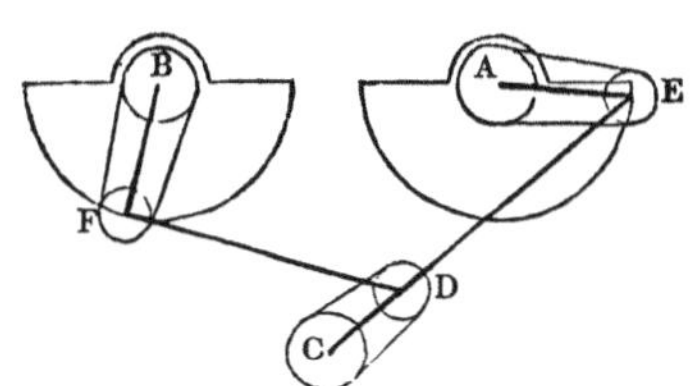

Fig. 11.

about twenty and the eastern sixteen days—their steam-machinery working for about one third the time of the voyage.

On comparing these vessels with the Great Western, it is to be considered that, in order to enable the latter vessel to make an average speed of ten miles, she is provided with four-hundred-horse power; while the power proposed to be given to the ship now in preparation being only that of one hundred and seventy-three horses, would give a speed of seven and a half knots per hour, which is equivalent to nine statute miles. Such is the result of a calculation made on the ordinary and admitted principles of mechanics. It appears, then, that by the small sacrifice of twenty-five per cent. of the speed, the power of the machinery is reduced in the proportion of forty to seventeen; and the consumption of fuel, and the space occupied by it and by the machinery, are diminished in a greater ratio than six to one.*

Let us consider for a moment the effect which the successful establishment of such a line of steamships would have upon the intercourse between this continent and Europe. The average passage of the Great Western to New York has been fifteen days and nineteen hours. That of the Cunard ships to Boston has been thirteen days. It appears, therefore, that these vessels at present bring occasional intelligence to New York, the one in sixteen and the other in fourteen days. The proposed line of steamships will accomplish the same passage in twenty days; but as they must, if successful at all, be as numerous as the present London and Liverpool liners, they will be continually dropping into this port, keeping up a never-ceasing stream of intelligence, not more than twenty days later from Europe. Instead, therefore, of the present mail-steamers, bringing, as they do now, intelligence in winter often thirty days later, and in summer fifteen days later, their functions will be limited to the conveyance of news occasionally five or six days later. In a word, it is evident that the line of packet-ships now contemplated will to a great extent strip the present mail-steamers of their great importance, not merely as respects intelligence, but also correspondence. A great epoch is indubitably at hand.

One of the numerous advantages attending these arrangements is, that the machinery is capable of being applied to any of the present packet-ships without any serious suspension of their operation, or any injurious expenditure. If the experiment about to be made shall therefore be attended with that success which we confidently anticipate, a brief period will be sufficient to convert the entire fleet of packet-ships between New York and Britain into steam-liners—uniting the expedition, certainty, and regularity, with all their present capabilities for commerce and cargo.

* This great reduction of bulk of fuel is realized chiefly by using the expansive principle to a considerable extent.

THE BAROMETER.

Maxim of the Ancients.—Abhorrence of a Vacuum.—Suction.—Galileo's Investigations.—Torricelli discovers the Atmospheric Pressure.—The Barometer.—Pascal's Experiment.—Requisites for a good Barometer.—Means of securing them.—Diagonal Barometer.—Wheel Barometer—Vernier.—Uses of the Barometer.—Variation of Atmospheric Pressure.—Weather-Glass.—Rules in common Use absurd.—Correct Rules.—Measurement of Heights.—Pressure on Bodies.—Why not apparent.—Effect of a Leather Sucker.—How Flies adhere to Ceilings and Fishes to Rocks.—Breathing.—Common Bellows.—Forge Bellows.—Vent Peg.—Tea-Pot.—Kettle.—Ink Bottles.—Pneumatic Trough.—Gurgling Noise in decanting Wine.

THE BAROMETER.

In the history of human discovery, there are few more impressive lessons of humility than that which is to be collected from the records of the progress by which the pressure of the atmosphere which surrounds us, and the manner in which it is instrumental in producing some most ordinary phenomena, became known. Looking back from the point to which we have now attained, and observing the numerous and obvious indications of this effect which present themselves at all times, and on all occasions, nature seems almost to have courted the philosopher to the discovery. With every allowance for the feebleness of the human understanding, and for the disadvantages which the ancients labored under, as compared with more recent investigators, still one is inclined to attribute the lateness of the discovery of the atmospheric pressure and its effects, not altogether to the weakness and inadequacy of the mental powers applied to the investigation. There seems to be something of wilful perverseness and obstinacy instigating men to step aside from that course, and to turn their minds from those instances which nature herself continually forces upon them.

The ancient philosophers observed that, in the instances which commonly fell under their notice, space was always filled by a material substance. The moment a solid or a liquid was by any means removed, immediately the surrounding air rushed in and filled the place which it deserted; hence they adopted the physical dogma that *nature abhors a vacuum*. Such a proposition must be regarded as a figurative or poetical expression of a supposed law of physics, declaring it to be impossible that space could exist unoccupied by matter.

Probably one of the first ways in which the atmospheric pressure presented itself was by the effect of suction with the mouth. One end of a tube being immersed in a liquid, and the other placed between the lips, the air was drawn from the tube by the ordinary process of inhaling; the water was immediately observed to fill the tube as the air retreated. This phenomenon was accounted for by declaring, that "nature abhorred a vacuum," and that she, therefore, compelled the water to fill the space deserted by the air.

The effects of suction by the mouth led, by a natural analogy, to suction by artificial means. If a cylinder be open at both ends, and a piston playing in it air-tight be moved to the lower end, upon immersing this lower end in water, and then drawing up the piston, an unoccupied space would remain between the piston and the water. "But nature abhors such a space," said the ancients, "and therefore the water will not allow such a space to remain unoccupied: we find, accordingly, that as the piston rises the water follows it." By such poetical reasoning pumps of various kinds were constructed.

The antipathy entertained by nature against an empty space served the purposes of philosophy for a couple of thousand years, when it so happened that some engineers employed at Florence in sinking pumps, had occasion to construct one to raise water from an unusually great depth. Upon working it, they found that the water would rise no higher than about thirty-two feet above the well. Galileo, the most celebrated philosopher of that day, was consulted in this difficulty, and it is said that his answer was, that "nature's abhorrence of a vacuum extended only to the height of thirty-two feet, but that beyond this her disinclination to an empty space did not extend." Some writers deny the fact of his having given this answer; others admit it, but take it to have been ironical. It has been more generally taken as a solution seriously intended. It appears, however, that Galileo, having his attention thus directed to the point, soon saw the absurdity of the maxim that "nature abhors a vacuum," and sought to account for the phenomenon in other ways.

He attributed the elevation of the water to an attraction exerted upon that liquid by the piston. This attraction he conceived to have a determinate intensity, and when such a column of water was raised as was equal in weight to the whole amount of the attraction, then any farther elevation of the water by the piston became impossible.

At a very remote period air was known to possess the quality of weight. Aristotle and other ancient philosophers expressly speak of the weight of air. The process of respiration is attributed by an ancient writer to the pressure of the atmosphere forcing air into the lungs. Galileo was therefore fully aware that the atmosphere possessed this property, and it is not a little surprising that when his attention was so immediately directed to one of the most striking effects of it, he was unable to perceive the connexion.

Some writers affirm, we know not upon what authority, that Galileo, at the time he was interrogated respecting the limited elevation of water in a common pump, was aware of the true cause of the effect; but that, not having thoroughly investigated the subject, he evaded the question of the engineers, with a view to conceal his knowledge of the principle until he had carried his inquiry to a more satisfactory result. It does not, however, appear that he published his solution of the problem. After his death, Torricelli, his pupil, directed his attention to the same problem. He argued that whatever be the cause which sustained a column of water in a common pump, the measure and the energy of that power must be the weight of the column of water; and, consequently, if another liquid be used, heavier or lighter, bulk for bulk, than water, then the same force must sustain a lesser or greater column of such liquid. By using a much heavier liquid, the column sustained would necessarily be much shorter, and the experiment in every way more manageable.

He therefore selected for the experiment mercury, the heaviest known liquid. The weight of mercury, bulk for bulk, being about 13½ times that of water, it follows that the height of a column of that liquid which would be sustained by a vacuum must be 13½ times less that the height of a column of water thus sustained.

Hence he computed that the height of the column of mercury would be about 28 inches. He procured a glass tube, A B (fig. 1), more than 30 inches in length, open at one end, A, and closed at the other end, B. Placing this tube in an upright position, with the open end upward, he filled it with mercury, and applying his finger to the end A, so as to prevent the escape of the mercury, he inverted the tube, plunging the end A into a cistern, C D (fig. 2), containing mercury, the open end A being below the surface F of the mercury in the cistern, and no air having been allowed to communicate with it.

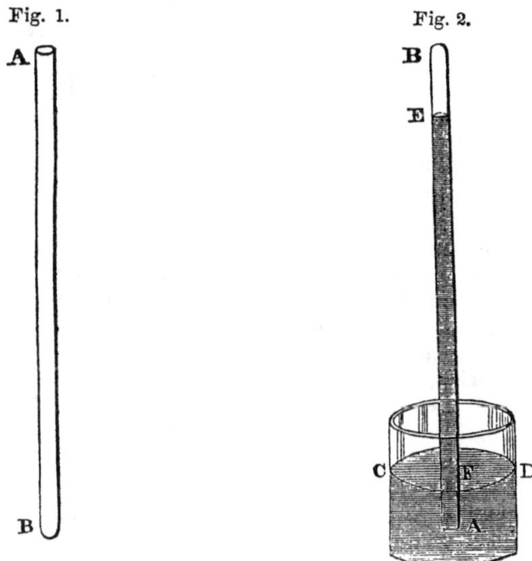

Fig. 1. Fig. 2.

Upon removing the finger, therefore, the mercury in the cistern came in immediate contact with the mercury in the tube. Immediately the mercury was observed to subside from the top of the tube, and its surface gradually to descend to the level E, about 28 inches above the mercury in the cistern. This result was what Torricelli anticipated, and clearly showed the absurdity of the supposition that nature's abhorrence of a vacuum extended to the height of 32 feet. Torricelli soon perceived the true cause of this phenomenon. The atmospheric pressure acting upon the surface F, while the surface E was protected from this pressure by the closed end B, of the tube, supported the weight of the column E F. This pressure was transmitted by the liquid mercury in the cistern from the external surface F, to the base of the column contained in the tube.

This experiment and its explanation soon became known to philosophers in every part of Europe, and, among others, it attracted the notice of the celebrated Pascal. In order to subject the explanation of Galileo to the most severe test, Pascal proposed to transport a tube of this kind to a great elevation upon a mountain, and argued that, if the cause which sustained the column in the tube were the weight of the atmosphere acting upon the external surface of the mercury in the cistern, then it must be expected that if the tube was elevated, having a less and a less quantity of atmosphere above it, the column sustained by the weight of this incumbent atmosphere must suffer a corresponding diminution in height. He accordingly directed a friend residing in the neighborhood of a mountain called Pays de Dome, near Auvergne, to ascend that mountain, carrying with him the apparatus already described. This was accordingly done, and the height of the column noted during the ascent. Conformably to the principle explained by Torricelli, the column was observed gradually to diminish in height, as the elevation of the apparatus was increased. The same experiment was repeated by Pascal himself, with similar success, upon a high tower in the city of Paris.

Meanwhile other effects were manifested which not less unequivocally proved the truth of Torricelli's solution. The apparatus being kept for a length of time in a fixed position, the height of the column was observed to fluctuate from day to day between certain small limits. This effect was, of course, to be attributed to the variation of the weight of the incumbent atmosphere, arising from various meteorological causes.

The apparatus which we have just described is, in fact, the common barometer. By the principles of hydrostatics it appears that the height of the column E F, sustained by the atmospheric pressure, will be the same, whatever be the magnitude of the bore of the tube. If we suppose the section of the bore to be equal to a square inch, then the column E F will be pressed upward, and held in equilibrium by the weight of a column of atmosphere pressing upon a square inch of the external surface F; consequently the weight of the column E F, must be equal to the weight of a column of the atmosphere whose base is a square inch, and which extends from the surface of the mercury in the cistern to the top of the atmosphere. If there be another tube whose bore is only half a square inch, then the pressure which will support the column in it will be that of a similar column of atmosphere, whose base is half a square inch; such pressure, then, will only be half the amount of the former, and therefore will only sustain half the weight of mercury. But a column of mercury of half the weight, having a base of half the magnitude, must necessarily have the same height. Hence it appears that so long as the atmosphere presses upon a given magnitude of the surface F, with the same intensity, the column of mercury sustained in the tube will have the same height, whatever be the magnitude of its bore.

In adapting such an apparatus as this to indicate minute changes in the pressure of the atmosphere, there are many circumstances to be attended to, which I propose to explain, so far as they are necessary to render intelligible the general principles and use of the barometer.

It is, in the first place, necessary to have the means of measuring exactly the height of the column E F, fig. 2. If the surface F were fixed, and the tube B A maintained in its position, it would be sufficient to mark a graduated scale upon the tube, indicating the number of inches and fractions of an inch of any part upon it, from the surface F. But it is obvious that this will not be the case when the pressure of the atmosphere is increased, as an additional quantity of mercury is forced into the tube, and consequently an equal quantity is forced out of the cistern. While the surface E rises toward B, the surface F therefore descends, and the distance of E from that surface is increased by both causes.

A graduated scale marked upon the tube would then only indicate the change in the position of the surface E, but would not show the change in the length of the column E F, so far as that change is affected by the fall of the surface F. There are several ways in which this defect may be remedied.

If the instrument be not required to give extremely accurate indications, it will be sufficient to use a tube the bore of which is small compared with the magnitude of the cistern. In this case, a small change in the height of the column will make but a very inconsiderable change in the whole quantity of mercury in the cistern, and therefore will produce a very minute effect upon the position of the surface F. If such a change in the level F, be so small as to affect the indications of the instruments in a degree which is unimportant for the purposes to which it is intended to be applied, the surface F may be regarded as fixed, and the whole change in the height of the column may be taken to be represented by the change in the position of the level E. All ordinary barometers are constructed in this manner. But it is not difficult to adjust a scale upon a tube which will give with accuracy the actual variation in the length of the column by means of the change in the level of the surface E. Let us suppose that the cistern P D has a flat, horizontal bottom and perpendicular sides, and that the magnitude of the bottom bears a certain known proportion to the bore of the tube. Suppose this proportion to be that of a hundred to one. If the pressure of the atmosphere increase, so as to cause the column of mercury sustained in the tube to be increased in height by one inch, then as much mercury as fills one inch of the tube will be withdrawn from the cistern; but as the base of the cistern is one hundred times greater than the bore of the tube, it is evident that this inch of mercury in the tube would only cause a fall of the hundredth of an inch in depth of the mercury in the vessel. Consequently it follows that the increased elevation of an inch in the column produces a depression of a hundredth of an inch in the surface F. Thus it appears that the increased length of the column E F, is produced by the surface F, falling through the one hundredth of an inch, while the surface E rises through ninety-nine hundredths parts of an inch. The same will be true whatever change takes place in the height of the column. We may therefore infer generally, that whatever variation may be produced in the surface E, the consequent variation produced in the height of the column is greater by a ninety-ninth part.

If, then, the top be so graduated that a portion of it, the length of which is one hundredth part less than an inch, be marked as an inch, and all other divisions and subdivisions marked according to the same proportion, then the indications will be as accurate as if the surface F were fixed, the tube being divided accurately into inches and parts of an inch.

Fig. 3.

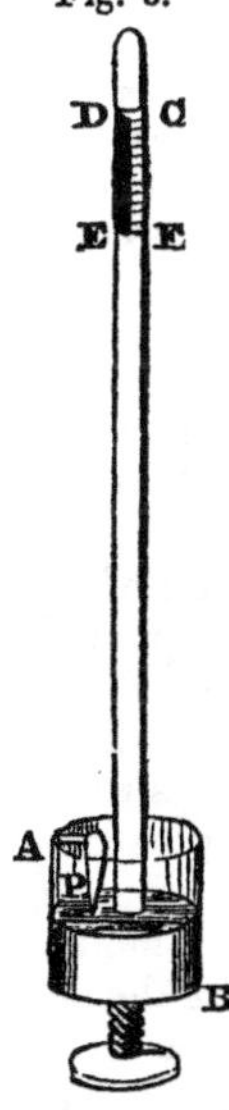

The barometer is represented mounted and furnished with a scale, in fig. 3. The glass tube is surrounded by one of brass in which there is an aperture cut at D E, of such a length and at such a height above the cistern, as to include all that space through which the level of the mercury in the tube usually varies in the place in which the barometer is intended to be used. In these countries the level of the mercury never falls below twenty-eight inches, nor rises above thirty-one inches; consequently a space somewhat exceeding these limits will be sufficient for the opening D E. The tube is permanently connected with the cistern A B, and a scale is engraved upon the brass tube, near the aperture D E, to indicate the fractions of the height of the mercury in the tube.

There is another method of avoiding the difficulty arising from the change in the level of the surface of the mercury in the cistern, used in the barometer here represented. The bottom of the cistern moves within it in such a manner as to prevent the mercury from escaping, and a screw is inserted at B, by turning which the bottom of the cylinder is slowly elevated or depressed. An ivory index is attached to the top of the cylinder, which is presented downward and brought to a fine point, so as to mark a fixed level. When an observation is made with the barometer, the screw V is turned until the surface is brought accurately to the point of the index, by raising or lowering the bottom according as the surface is below or above that point. It follows, therefore, that whenever an observation is made with this instrument, the surface of the mercury always stands at the same level, and therefore the divisions upon the scale C F, represent the actual change of height in the barometric column.

Since the column of mercury sustained in the barometric tube is taken to represent the pressure of the atmosphere, it is clear that no air or other elastic fluid should occupy the part of the tube above the mercury. To avoid such a cause of error is not so easy or obvious as may at first appear. Mercury, as it exists in the ordinary state, frequently contains air or other elastic fluids combined with it, and which are maintained in it by the atmospheric pressure, to which it is usually subject.

When it has subsided, however, in the barometric tube, it is relieved from that pressure, and the elastic force of such air as may be lodged in the mercury, being relieved from the pressure which confined it there, it will make its escape and rise to the surface, finally occupying the upper part of the tube, and exerting a pressure upon the surface of the column by means of its elasticity. Such a pressure will, then, assist the weight of the column of mercury in balancing the atmospheric pressure, and consequently a column of less height will balance the atmosphere than if the upper part of the tube were free from air. To remove this cause of error it is necessary to adopt means of purifying the mercury used in the barometer from all elastic fluids which may be combined with it.

The fact that the application of heat gives energy to the elastic force of gases, enables us easily to accomplish this. For if the mercury be heated, the particles of air or other elastic fluids which are combined with it acquire such a degree of elasticity that they dilate and rise to the surface, and there escape in bubbles. The same process of heating serves to expel any liquid impurities with which the mercury may be combined. These are converted into vapor and escape at the surface.

The presence of an elastic fluid at the top of the tube is thus removed so far as such fluid can proceed from the mercury. But it is also found that small particles of air and moisture are liable to adhere to the interior surface of the glass; and when the mercury is introduced, and a vacuum produced at the top of the tube, these particles of air dilate, and rising, lodge at the top and vitiate the vacuum which ought to be there; the particles of moisture also evaporate and rise likewise, both producing an aeriform fluid in the chamber above the surface of the mercury, which presses upon that surface with an elastic force and produces a corresponding diminution in the height of the column of quicksilver, sustained by the atmosphere as already explained. This imperfection may be avoided by previously heating the tube. The particles of air which adhere to its inner surface being thus expanded by heat, will fly off by their elastic force, and the particles of moisture will be converted into vapor, and likewise disengaged from the surface.

All the effects now explained may be produced by filling the tube with mercury in the first instance and then boiling the liquid in it, which may be easily accomplished. The heat will not only expel all liquid and gaseous impurities from the mercury itself, but also will disengage them from the inner surface of the tube. These precautions being taken, the column of mercury sustained in the tube will indicate by its weight the true amount of the atmospheric pressure. But in order to be able to compare the result of any one barometer with any other, it is necessary that the weights of equal bulks of the liquid mercury used in both cases should be the same ; and for this purpose we must be assured that the mercury used is pure, and not combined with other substances.

We have just seen how all substances in the liquid or gaseous form may be extracted from it. Impurities may still, however, be suspended in it in a solid form.

To remove these it is only necessary to enclose the mercury in a small bag of chamois leather : upon pressing this bag the quicksilver will pass freely through its pores, and any minute solid impurities which may be contained in the mercury will remain in the bag. Pure and homogeneous mercury being thus obtained, we have advanced another step toward the certainty that the indications of different barometers may correspond ; but there is still one other cause of discordancy to be attended to. Suppose a barometer to be used in Paris, and another in London, at a time when the pressure of the atmosphere in both places is the same, but the temperature of the air at Paris is higher than the temperature of London. The mercury in the one barometer will have a higher temperature than the mercury in the other. Now it is well known that when mercury or any other body is heated, its dimensions increase. In other words, bulk for bulk, it becomes slighter. Consequently, if two columns be equal in weight, that which has the higher temperature will have the greater altitude. Hence it appears, that under the circumstances supposed, at a time when the atmospheric pressure is the same in London as at Paris, the barometer at the latter place will be higher than at the former. To guard against this source of error, it is necessary, in making barometric observations, to note at the same time the contemporaneous indications of the thermometer. Tables are computed, showing the changes in the height of the mercury corresponding to given differences of temperature. It is evident that in comparing the results of the same barometer observed at different times, it is equally necessary to note the difference of temperature, and to allow for its effects. This, however, is a refinement of accuracy which is not attended to, except in observations made for philosophical purposes.

One of the difficulties attending barometric observations arises from the very minute changes produced in the height of the column by slight variations in the atmospheric pressure. The whole play of the upper surface of the column, in the most extreme cases, does not exceed three or four inches in a given place ; and mercury being a very heavy fluid, a variation in the pressure of the atmosphere, of sensible amount, may produce scarcely any perceptible change in the height of the column. One of the most obvious remedies, at first view, would seem to be the use of a fluid lighter than mercury. In the same proportion as the fluid is lighter, will the change in the height of the column, by a given change in the pressure of the atmosphere, be greater; but there are difficulties of a different kind which altogether preclude the use of other fluids. The lighter liquids are much more susceptible of evaporation, and the surface of the liquid in the tube being relieved from the atmospheric pressure, offers no resistance to the process of evaporation. The consequence is, that any liquid, except mercury, would produce a vapor, which, occupying the top of the tube, would press by its elastic force upon the surface, and co-operate with the weight of the suspended column in balancing the atmospheric pressure. Even from mercury we have reason to know that a vapor rises, which is present in the upper part of the tube; but this pressure exerts no power which can introduce inaccuracy to any sensible extent into our conclusions.

A form is sometimes adopted called the diagonal barometer, for the purpose of increasing the range of the mercury in the tube. This is represented in fig. 4, where A C B represents the barometer tube.

C is a point at a distance above the surface of the mercury in the cylinder less than the height of twenty-eight inches. The space C D includes the range which the mercury would have if the tube were vertical; but at C the tube is bent obliquely in the direction C B, having a sufficient length to bring the extremity B to the same level as D. The mercury, which, had the tube been vertical, would range between C and D, will now have its play extended through the greater space C B; consequently the magnitude of any part, however small, will be increased in the proportion of the line C D to the line C B. Thus, if C D be four inches, and C B twelve inches, then every change in the position of the surface of the mercury produced by a change in the atmospheric pressure, will be three times as great in the diagonal barometer as it would be in the vertical one.

Fig. 4.

Fig. 5.

Another contrivance for enlarging the scale, which is more frequently used, and for common domestic purposes attended with some convenience, is represented in fig. 5. This is called the *wheel barometer*. The barometric tube is here bent at its lower extremity B, and turned upward toward C. The atmospheric pressure acts upon the surface F, and sustains a column of mercury in the tube B A, which is above the level of F. The bore of the tube being in this case equal in every part of its length, it is clear that, through whatever space the surface E falls, the surface F will rise, and *vice-versa*. Hence it is obvious that the variation in the height of the barometric column will always be double the change in the height of either surface E or F; for if the surface F fall, the surface E must rise through the same space. They are thus receding from each other at the same rate, and therefore their mutual distance will be increased by the space through which each moves, or by double the space through which one of them moves.

In the same manner, if F rise, E must fall, the two points mutually approaching each other at the same rate; so that the distance between them will be diminished by the space through which each moves, or by double the space through which one of them moves. The change, therefore, in the height of the barometric column will always be double the change in the position of the level F.

Upon the surface at F floats a small ball of iron, suspended by a string, which is carried over a pulley or small wheel at P, and counterpoised by the weight at W, less in amount than the weight of the iron ball. When the surface F rises, the iron ball being buoyant, will be raised with it, and the counterpoise W will fall; and when the surface F falls, the weight of the iron ball being greater than the weight of the counterpoise W, will cause it to descend with the descending surface, and to draw the counterpoise W up. It is evident that, through whatever space the iron ball thus moves in ascending or descending, an equal length of the string will pass over the wheel P. Now this string rests in a groove of the wheel in such a manner that by its friction it causes the wheel to revolve, and consequently the revolution of this wheel indicates the length of string which passes over its groove, which length is equal to the change in the level of the surface F. Upon the centre of this wheel P an index H is placed, which, like the hand of a watch, plays upon a graduated circular plate. Let us suppose that the circumference of the wheel P is two inches: then one complete revolution of the wheel will correspond to a change of two inches in the level F, and therefore to a change of four inches in the barometric column. But in one revolution of the wheel P, the hand or index H moves completely round the circle; hence the circumference of this circle corresponds to a change of four inches in the barometric column. Now, the circular plate may easily be made so that its circumference shall measure forty inches; consequently ten inches of this circumference will correspond to one inch of the column, and one inch of the circumference will correspond to the tenth of an inch of the column. In this way variations in the height of the column amounting to the tenth of an inch are indicated by a motion of the hand H over one inch of the circumference of the plate. By further subdivision, a still greater accuracy may be obtained.

In this form of the barometer it is evident that the preponderance of the iron ball assists the atmospheric pressure in sustaining the column. This cause of error, however, may be diminished almost indefinitely by making the preponderance of the ball over the counterpoise W barely sufficient to overcome the friction of the wheel P.

Again, when the atmosphere is diminished in weight, and when the surface F has a tendency to rise, it is compelled to raise the ball; and there is this obvious limit to the indications of the instrument, namely, that a change so slight that the difference of pressure will not exceed the force necessary to elevate the ball, will fail to be indicated.

For scientific purposes, the vertical barometer is preferable to every other form of that instrument. In the oblique barometer the termination of the mercurial column is subject to some uncertainty, arising from the level of the mercury not being perpendicular to the direction of the tube. In the wheel barometer there are several sources of error, which, though so small in amount as not to injure it for domestic or popular use, yet are such as to render it altogether unfit for scientific inquiry.

A contrivance called a vernier, for noting extremely small changes, is usually applied to the vertical barometer, and supplies the place of an enlarged scale. It consists of a small graduated plate, which is moveable by a screw or otherwise, and which slides on the divided scale of the barometer. By means of this subsidiary scale, we are enabled to estimate magnitudes on the principal scale amounting to very small fractions of its smallest divisions.

The principle of the vernier is easily explained. Let B A, fig. 6, represent

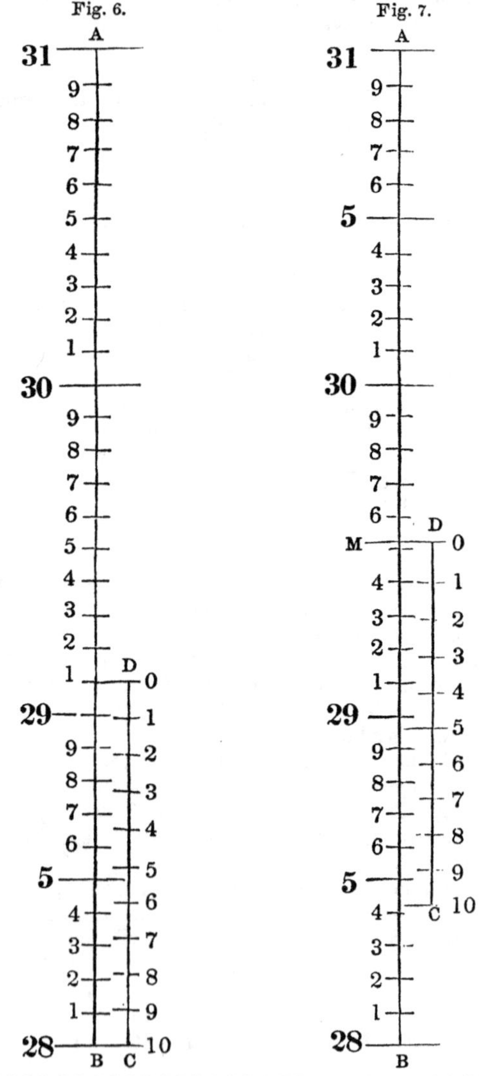

Fig. 6.

Fig. 7.

the scale of the barometer, extending through three inches, and divided to tenths of an inch. Let C D be the sliding scale of the vernier, equal in length to eleven divisions of the principal scale, and divided into ten equal parts.

Thus each division of the vernier will be the tenth of eleven divisions of the instrument; that is, it will be the tenth part of 11 tenths of an inch, but 11 tenths of an inch [illegible] the same as 110 hundredths, and the tenth part of this is 11 hundredths. Thus it appears that one division on the vernier is in this case the 11 hundredth part of an inch. Now, one division on the instrument being a tenth of an inch, or 10 hundredths of an inch, it is evident that a division on the vernier will exceed a division on the instrument by the hundredth part of an inch; for if we take 10 hundredths from 11 hundredths, the remainder will be 1 hundredth. Let us suppose that the vernier is placed so that its lowest division, marked 10, shall coincide with the lowest division on the instrument, marked 28; then the first division of the vernier, marked 0, will coincide with the division of the instrument next above the 29th. The division marked 1 on the vernier will then be a little below the division marked 29 on the scale, and the distance between these will be the hundredth of an inch, as already explained. The division marked 2 of the vernier will be a little below the division marked 9 on the scale, and the distance below it will be 2 hundredth parts of an inch, because two divisions of the vernier exceed two divisions of the scale by that amount. In like manner, the division marked 3 on the vernier will be below the division marked 8 on the scale by 3 hundredths of an inch, and so on.

Let us suppose that the mercury is observed to stand at a height greater than 29 inches and 5 tenths, but less than 29 inches and 6 tenths. Its level being expressed by the line M, figure 7, let the vernier now be moved on the scale until its highest division 0 exactly coincides with the level of the mercury. On comparing the several divisions of the vernier with those of the instrument, let us suppose that we find that the division marked 4 on the vernier coincides with that marked 1 on the instrument; then the distance from the level of the mercury M to the next division below it, marked 5, will be 4 hundredth parts of an inch, for the distance of the division marked 3 on the vernier above the division marked 2 on the instrument is 1 hundredth of an inch, because it is the difference between a division of the vernier and a division of the instrument. Again, the distance of the division of the vernier marked 2, above the division of the instrument marked 3, is 2 hundredths of an inch, and the distance of the division of the vernier marked 1, above the division of the instrument marked 4, is 3 hundredths of an inch. In like manner, the division of the vernier marked 0 is distant from the division of the instrument marked 5 by 4 hundredths of an inch. This will be manifest by considering what has already been explained. In general, we are to observe what division of the vernier coincides most nearly with any division of the instrument, and the figure which marks that division of the vernier will express the number of hundredths of an inch in the distance of the level of the mercury from the next division of the instrument below it.

The most immediate use of the barometer for scientific purposes is to indicate the amount and variation of the atmospheric pressure. These variations being compared with other meteorological phenomena, form the scientific data from which various atmospheric appearances and effects are to be deduced.

The fluctuations in the pressure of the atmosphere being observed in connexion with changes in the state of the weather, a general correspondence is supposed to prevail between these effects. Hence the barometer has been called a *weather-glass*. Rules are attempted to be established, by which, from the height of the mercury, the coming state of the weather may be predicted;

and we accordingly find the words "rain," "fair," "changeable," "frost," &c., engraved on the scale attached to common domestic barometers, as if, when the mercury stands at the height marked by these words, the weather is always subject to the vicissitudes expressed by them. These marks are, however, entitled to no attention; and it is only surprising to find their use continued in the present times, when knowledge is so widely diffused. They are, in fact, to be ranked scarcely above the *vox stellarum*, or astrological almanac.

It has been already explained, that in the same state of the atmosphere the height of the mercury in the barometer will be different, according to the elevation of the place in which the barometer is situated. Thus two barometers, one near the level of the Hudson and the other on the heights of West Point, will differ by half an inch; the latter being half an inch lower than the former. If the words, therefore, engraved upon the plates, are to be relied upon, similar changes of weather could never happen at these two situations. But what is even more absurd, such a scale would inform us that the weather at the top of a high building, such as Trinity church, New York, must always be different from the weather in Wall street, at its foot.

The variation in the altitude of the barometer in a given place, together with the corresponding vicissitudes of the weather, have been regularly recorded for very long periods. It is only by the exact comparison of such results that any general rule can be found. The rules best established by such observations are far from being either general or certain. It is observed that the changes of weather are indicated, not by the actual height of the mercury, but by its *change* of height. One of the most general, though not absolutely invariable rules is, that when the mercury is very low, and therefore the atmosphere very light, high winds and storms may be expected.

The following rules may generally be relied upon, at least to a certain extent:—

1. *Generally* the rising of the mercury indicates the approach of fair weather: the falling of it shows the approach of foul weather.

2. In sultry weather the fall of the mercury indicates coming thunder. In winter the rise of the mercury indicates frost. In frost its fall indicates thaw: and its rise indicates snow.

3. Whatever change of weather suddenly follows a change in the barometer may be expected to last but a short time. Thus, if fair weather follow immediately the rise of the mercury, there will be very little of it; and in the same way, if foul weather follow the fall of mercury it will last but a short time.

4. If fair weather continue for several days, during which the mercury continually falls, a long succession of foul weather will probably ensue; and again, if foul weather continue for several days, while the mercury continually rises, a long succession of fair weather will probably succeed.

5. A fluctuating and unsettled state in the mercurial column indicates changeable weather.

The domestic barometer would become a much more useful instrument if instead of the words usually engraved on the plate, a short list of the best established rules, such as the above, accompanied it, which might be either engraved on the plate, or printed on a card. It would be right, however, to express the rules only with that degree of probability which observation of past phenomena has justified. There is no rule respecting these effects which will hold good with perfect certainty in every case.

One of the most important scientific uses to which the barometer has been applied, is the measuring of heights. If the atmosphere, like a liquid, were incompressible, this problem would be very simple. The pressure on the mercury in the cistern would be equally diminished in ascending through equal heights. Thus, if the pressure produced by an ascent of 10 feet were equivalent to the weight of one inch of mercury, then the column would fall one inch in ascending that height. It would fall two inches in ascending 20 feet, three in ascending 30 feet, and so on. To find, therefore, the perpendicular height of the barometer at any time above its position, at any other time, it would be only necessary to observe the difference between the altitude of the mercury in both cases, and to allow 10 feet for every inch of mercury in that difference; and a similar process would be applicable if an inch of mercury corresponded to any other number of feet.

But this explanation proceeds on the supposition that in ascending through equal heights, the barometer leaves equal weights of air below it. Suppose in ascending 10 feet the mercury is observed to fall the hundredth of an inch, then it follows, that the air left below the barometer in such an ascent has a weight equal to the one hundredth of an inch of mercury. Now, in ascending the next ten feet, the air which occupies that space having a less weight above it will be less compressed, and, consequently, within that height of 10 feet there will be contained a less quantity of air than was contained in the first 10 feet immediately below it. In this second ascent the mercury will, therefore, fall, not the hundredth of an inch, but a quantity as much less than the hundredth of an inch as the quantity of air contained in the second 10 feet of height is less than the quantity of air that is contained in the first 10 feet of height. In like manner, in ascending the next ten feet a still less quantity of air will be left below the instrument, and the mercury will fall in a proportionally less degree. If the only cause affecting density of the air were compression produced by the weight of the incumbent atmosphere, it would be easy to find the rule by which a change of altitude might be inferred from an observed change of pressure. Such a rule has been determined, and is capable of being expressed in the language of mathematics, although it is not of a nature which admits of explanation in a more elementary and popular form. But there are other causes affecting the relation of the pressure to the altitude which must be taken into account. The density of any stratum of air is not only affected by the weight of the incumbent atmosphere, but also by the temperature of the stratum itself. If any cause increase this temperature the stratum will expand, and, with a less density, will support the same incumbent pressure. If, on the contrary, any cause produce a diminution of temperature, the stratum will contract, and acquire a greater density under the same pressure. In the one case, therefore, a change of elevation which would be necessary to produce a given change in the height of the barometer, would be greater than that computed on theoretical principles, and in the other case the change would be less. The temperature, therefore, forms an essential element in the calculation of heights by the barometer.

A rule or formulary has been deduced, partly from established theory, and partly from observed effects, by which the change of elevation may be deduced from observations made on the barometer and thermometer. To apply that rule, it is necessary to know, 1st, the latitude of the places of observation; 2d, the height of the barometer and thermometer at the higher station. By arithmetical computation the difference of the levels of the two stations may then be calculated. The formulary does not admit of being explained without the use of mathematical language.

It has been already stated, that the atmospheric pressure at the surface of the earth is capable of supporting a column of water 34 feet in height. It follows, therefore, that if our atmosphere were condensed to such a degree that its specific gravity would be equal to that of water, its height would be 34 feet. Now the specific gravity of a stratum of atmosphere contiguous to the surface is about 840 times less than the specific gravity of water; that is, a cubic inch of water weighs 840 times more than a cubic inch of air. If as we ascend in the atmosphere it continued to have the same density, then its height would be evidently 840 times the height of 34 feet, which would amount to 28,560 feet, or 5 miles and a quarter. It is obvious, therefore, that since even at a small elevation the density of the atmosphere is reduced to half its density at the surface, the whole height must be many times greater than this. The barometer in the balloon in which De Luc ascended, fell to the height of 12 inches. Supposing the barometer at the surface to have stood at that time at 30 inches, it follows that he must have left three fifths of the whole atmosphere below him. His elevation was upward of 20,000 feet.

A column of pure mercury, whose base is a square inch, and whose height is 30 inches, weighs about 15 lbs. avoirdupois. It follows, therefore, that when the barometer stands at 30 inches the atmosphere exerts a pressure on each square inch of the surface of the mercury on the cistern, amounting to 15 lbs. Now it is the nature of a fluid to transmit pressure equally in every direction, and if the surface on which the atmosphere acts were presented to it laterally, obliquely, or downward, still the pressure will be the same. Taking, therefore, the medium height of the barometric column at 30 inches, it follows that the pressure sustained by all bodies which exist at the surface of the earth, exposed to our atmosphere, are continually under this pressure, and that every square inch on their surface constantly sustains a force of about 15 pounds. Thus the body of a man the surface of which amounts to 2,000 square inches, will sustain a pressure from the surrounding air to the enormous amount of 30,000 pounds.

It might at first view be expected that this great force to which all bodies are subject, would produce manifest effects, so as to crush, compress, or break them, whereas we find bodies of most delicate texture unaffected by it. Thus a close bag, made of the finest silver paper, and partially filled with air, is apparently subject to no external force. Its sides do not collapse. This arises partly from the circumstance of the pressure on every side and in every direction being equal, and, therefore, producing mechanical equilibrium. It is obvious that a body which is driven in every possible direction, upward and downward, laterally and obliquely, with equal forces, will not move in any one direction, for to suppose such a motion would be to assume that the quantity of pressure in that direction exceeds the quantity of pressure in other directions. But still, though a body may not be driven in any direction by the atmospheric pressure, it may happen that its parts are crushed and compressed.

We do not, however, find this to happen. This arises from the fact, that the elastic force of the air is equal to its pressure; and since the internal cavities of a body, such as the thin bag above-mentioned, are filled with air, which is confined within them, that air has precisely the same tendency to swell the bag, and to keep the parts asunder, as the external pressure of the atmosphere has to make them collapse.

In the same manner we may account for the fact that animals move freely in the air without being sensible of the enormous pressure to which their bodies are subjected. The internal parts of their bodies are filled with fluids, both in the liquid and gaseous states, which offer a pressure from within exactly equivalent to the external pressure of the air. This may be easily rendered manifest by applying to the skin the mouth of a close vessel to which an exhausting syringe is attached. By this instrument, which will be described hereafter, the air may be rarefied in the vessel, and the atmospheric pressure consequently partially removed from the skin. Immediately the force of the fluid from within will swell the skin and cause it to be sucked into the glass. This experiment may be performed by the mouth on the flesh of the hand or arm. If the lips be applied to the flesh, and the breath drawn in so as to produce a partial vacuum in the mouth, the skin will be drawn or sucked into the mouth. This effect is owing, not to any force resident in the lips or the mouth drawing the skin in, but to the fact that the usual external pressure is removed, and that the pressure from within is suffered to prevail.

All cases of that class of effects which are commonly expressed by the word suction are accounted for in the same manner.

If a flat piece of moist leather be put in close contact with a heavy body, as a stone, it will be found to adhere to it with considerable force, and if a cord of sufficient length be attached to the centre of the leather, the stone may be raised by the cord. This effect arises from the exclusion of the air between the leather and the stone. The weight of the atmosphere presses their surfaces together with a force amounting to fifteen pounds on every square inch of those surfaces in contact. If the weight of the stone be less than the number of pounds which would be expressed by multiplying the number of square inches on the surfaces of contact by fifteen, then the stone may be raised by the leather; but if the stone exceed this weight, it will not suffer itself to be elevated by these means.

The power of flies and other insects to walk on ceilings and surfaces presented downward, or upon smooth panes of glass in an upright position, is said to depend on the formation of their feet. This is such that they act in the manner above described respecting the leather attached to a stone; the feet, in fact, act as suckers, excluding the air between them and the surface with which they are in contact, and the atmospheric pressure keeps the animal in its position. In the same manner the hydrostatic pressure attaches fishes to rocks.

The pressure and elasticity of the air are both exercised in the act of breathing. When we draw in the breath we first make an enlarged space in the chest. The pressure of the external atmosphere then forces air into this space so as to fill it. By a muscular action the lungs are next compressed so as to give this air a greater elasticity than the pressure of the external atmosphere. By the excess of this elasticity it is propelled, and escapes by the mouth and nose. It is obvious, therefore, that the air enters the lungs not by any direct act of these upon it, but by the weight of the atmosphere forcing it into an empty space, and that it is expired by the action of the lungs in compressing it.

The action of common bellows is precisely similar, except that the aperture at which the air is drawn in is different from that at which it is expelled. In the lower board of the bellows is a hole covered by a valve, consisting of a flat piece of stiff leather, moveable on a hinge, and which lies on the hole, but is capable of being raised by a slight pressure. When the upper board of the bellows is raised, the internal cavity is suddenly enlarged, and the air contained in it is considerably rarefied. The pressure of the atmosphere forces in air at the nozzle, but this being too small to allow its admission with sufficient ease and speed, the valve covering the hole is acted upon by the atmosphere and raised, and air rushes in through the large aperture under it. When the space between the boards is filled with air in its common state, the upper board is depressed, and the air confined in the bellows is suddenly condensed. The valve covering the hole is thus kept firmly closed, and the air has no escape except through the nozzle, from which it issues with a force proportioned to the pressure exerted on the upper board. A bellows, such as that in common domestic use, thus simply constructed, has an intermitting action and blows by fits, its action being suspended while the upper board is being raised. In forges and large factories in which fires are extensively used, it is found necessary to command a constant and unremitting stream of air, which may be conducted through the fuel so as to keep it in vivid combustion. This is effected by bellows with three boards, the centre board being fixed and furnished with a valve opening upward, the lower board being moveable with a valve also opening upward, and the upper board being under a continual pressure by weights acting upon it. When the lower board is let down, so that the chamber between it and the middle board is enlarged, the air included between these boards being rarefied, the external pressure of the atmosphere will open the valve in the lower board, and the chamber between the lower and middle boards will be filled with air in its common state. The lower board is now raised by the power which works the bellows, and the air between it and the middle board is condensed. It cannot escape through the lower valve, because it opens upward. It acts, therefore, with a pressure proportional to the working power on the valve in the middle board, and it forces open this valve, which opens upward. The air is driven from between the lower and middle boards into the chamber between the middle and upper boards. It cannot return from this chamber, because the valve in the middle board opens upward. The upper board being loaded with weights, it will be condensed while included in this chamber, and will issue from the nozzle with a force proportionate to the weights. While the air is thus rushing from the nozzle the lower board is let down and again drawn up, and a fresh supply of air is brought into the chamber between the upper and middle board. This air is introduced between the middle and upper boards before the former supply has been exhausted, and by working the bellows with sufficient speed, a large quantity of air will be collected in the upper chamber, so that the weights on the upper board will force a continual stream of air through the nozzle.

The effect produced by a vent-peg in a cask of liquid depends on the atmospheric pressure. If the vent-peg stop the hole in the top while the liquid is discharged by the cock below, a space will remain at the top of the barrel in which the air originally confined is allowed to expand and become rarefied; its pressure on the surface of the liquid above will, therefore, be less than the atmospheric pressure resisting the escape of the liquid at the cock; but still the weight of the liquid itself, pressing downward toward the cock, will cause the discharge to continue until the rarefaction of the air becomes so great, that the excess of the atmospheric pressure is more than sufficient to resist the escape of the liquid; the flow from the cock will therefore be stopped. If the vent-peg be now removed from the hole, air will be heard to rush in with considerable force and fill the space above the liquid. The atmospheric pressure on the surface above and on the mouth of the cock being now equal, the liquid will escape from the cock by the effect of the pressure of the superior column, according to the principles established in hydrostatics. If the vent-plug be again placed in the hole, the flow from the cock will be gradually diminished, and will at length cease. Upon the removal of the vent-peg, the same effect will be observed as before.

If the lid of a teapot be perfectly close, and fit the mouth air tight, or if the interstices, as frequently happens, be stopped by the liquid which lies round the edge of the mouth, then all communication between the surface of the liquid in the vessel and the external air is cut off. If we now attempt to pour liquid from the teapot it will flow at first, but will immediately cease. In this case the air under the lid becomes rarefied, and the pressure on the surface of the liquid in the teapot is so far diminished, that the atmospheric pressure resists its discharge at the spout.

To remedy this inconvenience, it is usual to make a small hole somewhere in the lid of the teapot for the admission of air; this hole serves the same purpose as the hole for the vent-peg in the cask.

Although it is not usually practised, a small hole should be made in the lid of a kettle, but for a different reason. If the lid of a kettle fit it closely, so as stop all communication between the external air and the interior of the vessel, when the water contained in it becomes heated, steam will rise from its surface, and the air enclosed in the space between the surface and the lid being heated, will acquire an increased elastic force. From these causes, the pressure which acts on the surface of the water in the kettle will continually increase so long as the lid maintains its position; this pressure, transmitted by the water in the kettle, will overcome the pressure of the atmosphere acting on the water in the spout, and the effect will be that the water will be raised in the spout, and flow from it, or, if the lid be not firmly enough fixed to withstand the pressure of the steam, it will be blown off the kettle. Such effects fall within every one's experience. If a small hole were made in the lid these effects would be prevented.

Ink-bottles constructed so as to prevent the inconvenience of the ink thickening and drying, owe their efficacy to the atmospheric pressure. The quantity of evaporation which takes place in the liquid, other circumstances being the same, is proportional to the quantity of surface exposed to the external air. To diminish this quantity of surface without inconveniently diminishing the quantity of ink in the bottle, bottles have been constructed of the shape represented in figure 8.

Fig. 8.

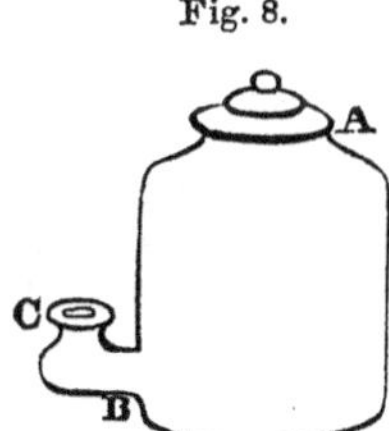

A B is a close glass vessel, from the bottom of which a short tube, B, proceeds, from which another short tube rises perpendicularly. The depth of the tube C is such as will be sufficient for the immersion of the pen. When ink is poured in at C, the bottle, being placed in an inclined position, is gradually filled up to the knob A: if the bottle be now placed in the position represented in the figure, the chamber A B being filled with the liquid, the air will be excluded from it, and the pressure tending to force the ink upward in the short tube C, will be equal to the weight of the column of ink, the height of which is equal to the depth of the ink in the bottle A B, and the base of which is equal to the section of the tube C. This will be manifest from the properties of hydrostatic pressure, established in hydrostatics. Now, the atmospheric pressure acts on the surface C with a force which would be capable of sustaining a column of ink many times the height of the bottle A B; consesequently, this pressure will effectually resist the escape of the ink from the mouth C, and will keep it suspended in the bottle A B. In this case the whole surface which is exposed to the effect of evaporation, is the surface of liquid in the tube C, and, consequently, an ink bottle of this kind may be left many months in a warm room and no perceptible diminution in the quantity of ink or change in its quality will take place. As the ink in the short tube C is consumed by use, its surface will fall to a level with the tube B. A small bubble of air will then insinuate itself through the tube B, and will rise to the top of the bottle A B; there it will exert an elastic pressure, which will cause the surface in C to rise a little higher, and this effect will be continually repeated until all the ink in the bottle has been used.

The only inconveniénce which has been attributed to these ink-bottles arises from sudden changes in the temperature to which they are exposed. When the external air, having been previously warm, becomes suddenly cold, the small quantity of air which is included in the bottle A not being cooled so fast as the external air, will exert an elastic pressure which will cause the ink to flow at C. This is an effect, however, which we have never observed, although we have seen these bottles much used.

If such an ink-bottle be placed upon a marble chimney-piece, or any other surface heated beyond the temperature of the air in the room, the air confined in the bottle will then become heated, and acquire increased elastic force, and in this case the ink will overflow.

The fountains for supplying water to bird-cages are constructed upon the same principle.

The pneumatic trough used in the chemical laboratories, and the gas-holders or gasometers used in gas works, depend on the atmospheric pressure. A vessel having its mouth upward, is completely filled with a liquid. The mouth is then stopped, a flat piece of glass, or a smooth plate of metal, pressed against it, and the vessel is inverted, the mouth being plunged in a cistern filled with the same liquid. If the height of the vessel in this case be less than the height of the column of the liquid which the atmospheric pressure would support, the vessel will continue to be completely filled with the liquid, even after the plate is removed from its mouth; for the atmospheric pressure, acting on the surface of the liquid in the cistern, will prevent the liquid contained in the vessel from falling out of it. Any one may satisfy himself of this fact. Take a wine-glass and fill it with water, and then, having applied a piece of card to its mouth so as to prevent the water from escaping, invert it, and plunge the mouth downward in a basin of water. Let the card be then removed, and let the glass be raised above the surface, still, however, keeping the edge of its mouth below the surface. It will be observed that the glass will still remain completely filled with water. Take a small quill, or a hollow piece of straw, and insert one end in the water, so that it will be immediately below the mouth of the glass, and at the same time blow gently through the other end, so as to introduce air in small quantities into the water immediately under the mouth of the glass. This air will ascend in bubbles, and will find its way to the highest part of the glass, and, remaining there, will expel the water from it; and this will continue so long as air is supplied, until all the water contained in the glass is expelled from it, and the glass is filled with air. If the process be further continued, the air will begin to escape under the edge of the glass, and rise in bubbles to the surface.

The pneumatic trough is a large cistern filled with mercury, in which is placed, below the surface of the liquid, a shelf to support a receiver. By plunging any vessel in the deeper part of the trough, it may be filled with mercury, and if it be slowly raised, keeping its mouth still below the surface of the liquid, it will still remain filled with mercury by the pressure of the atmosphere acting on the surface of the mercury in the trough. The mouth of the vessel may then be placed on the shelf, while the vessel itself is above the surface of the mercury.

The trough is represented in fig. 9, at A B. The shelf is placed in it at C; a receiver, R, is placed on the shelf, with its mouth downward, over an aperture, D, which communicates with a tube, by which gas may be introduced.

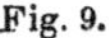
Fig. 9.

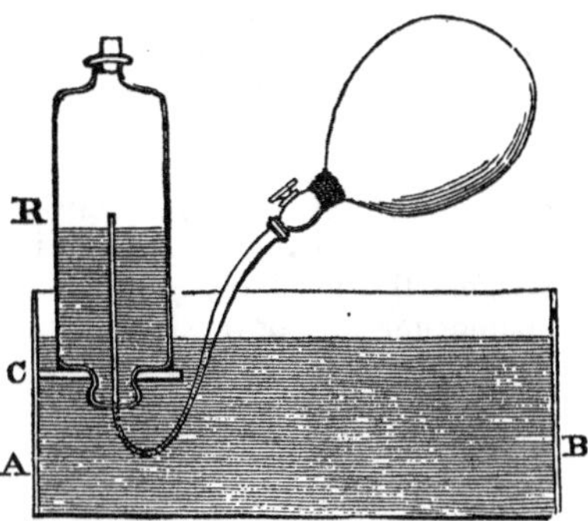

The gas, passing through the tube, rises in bubbles through the mercury in the receiver, and lodges at the top, and, by continuing this process, the whole of the mercury will at length be expelled from the receiver, and its place filled with the gas. In this manner gases of various kinds may be preserved out of contact with the atmosphere, and the same shelf may be furnished with several holes, and may support a number of different jars.

The gasometer used in gas-works is constructed on the same principle, only on a different scale. When used for great supplies of gas, such as are necessary for the illumination of towns, these vessels are constructed of a very large size, and are immersed in pits lined with cast-iron, and filled with water. It is clear that all which has been just explained will be equally applicable, whatever be the liquid used in the cistern, and for different gases it is necessary to use different liquids, since the contact with particular liquids will frequently affect the quality of the gas. The peculiar gurgling noise which is produced in decanting wine arises from the pressure of the atmosphere forcing air into the interior of the bottle. In the first instance, the neck of the bottle is completely filled with liquid, so as to stop the admission of air. When a part of the wine has flowed out, and an empty space is formed within the bottle, the atmospheric pressure forces in a bubble of air through the liquid in the neck, which, by rushing suddenly into the interior of the bottle, produces the sound alluded to. This effect is continually repeated so long as the neck of the bottle continues to be choked with the liquid. But as the contents of the bottle are discharged, the liquid, in flowing out, only partially fills the neck; and while a stream of wine passes out through the lower half of the neck, a stream of air passes in through the upper part. The flow in this case being continual and uninterrupted, no sound takes place.

The atmospheric pressure, acting on the surface of liquids, maintains air combined with them in a greater or lesser quantity, according to the nature of the liquid. If an open vessel, containing a liquid, be placed under a receiver, and the air be exhausted, the air combined with the liquid will be immediately set free, and will be observed to rise in bubbles to the top; this effect will be very perceptible if water be used, but still more so in the case of beer or ale.

When liquor is bottled, the air confined under the cork is condensed, and exerts upon the surface a pressure greater than that of the atmosphere. This has the effect of holding in combination with the liquor air which, under the atmospheric pressure only, would escape. If any air rise from the liquor after being bottled, it causes a still greater condensation, and an increased pressure above its surface.

If the nature of the liquor be such as to produce air in considerable quantity, this condensation will at length become so great as to force out the cork; or, failing to do that, break the bottle. This is found to happen frequently with beer, ale, or porter. The corks in such cases are tied down by cord or wire.

When the cork is drawn from a bottle containing liquor of this kind, the fixed air being released from the pressure of the air which was condensed under the cork, instantly makes its escape, and, rising in bubbles, produces effervescence and froth. Hence the bead observed on porter and similar liquors and the sparkling of champagne or cider.

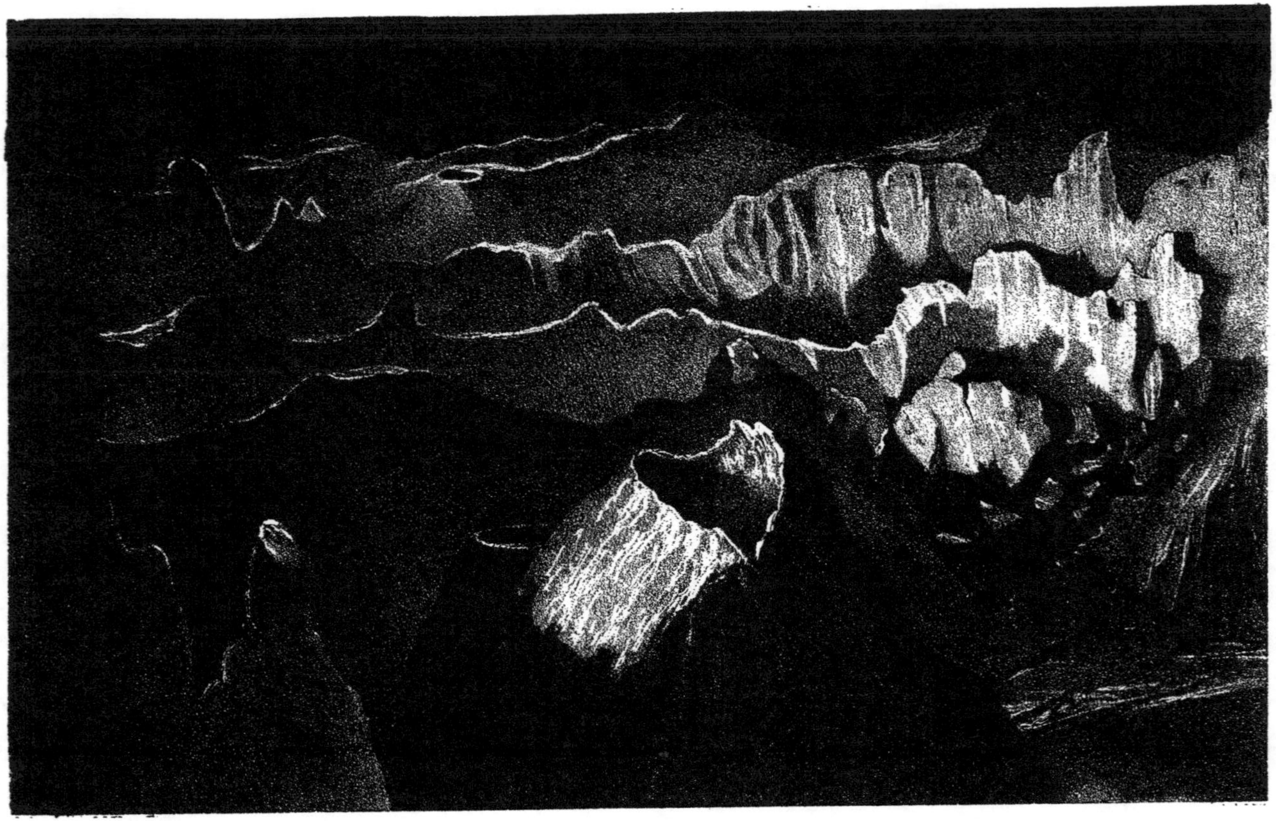

LUNAR CRATER.

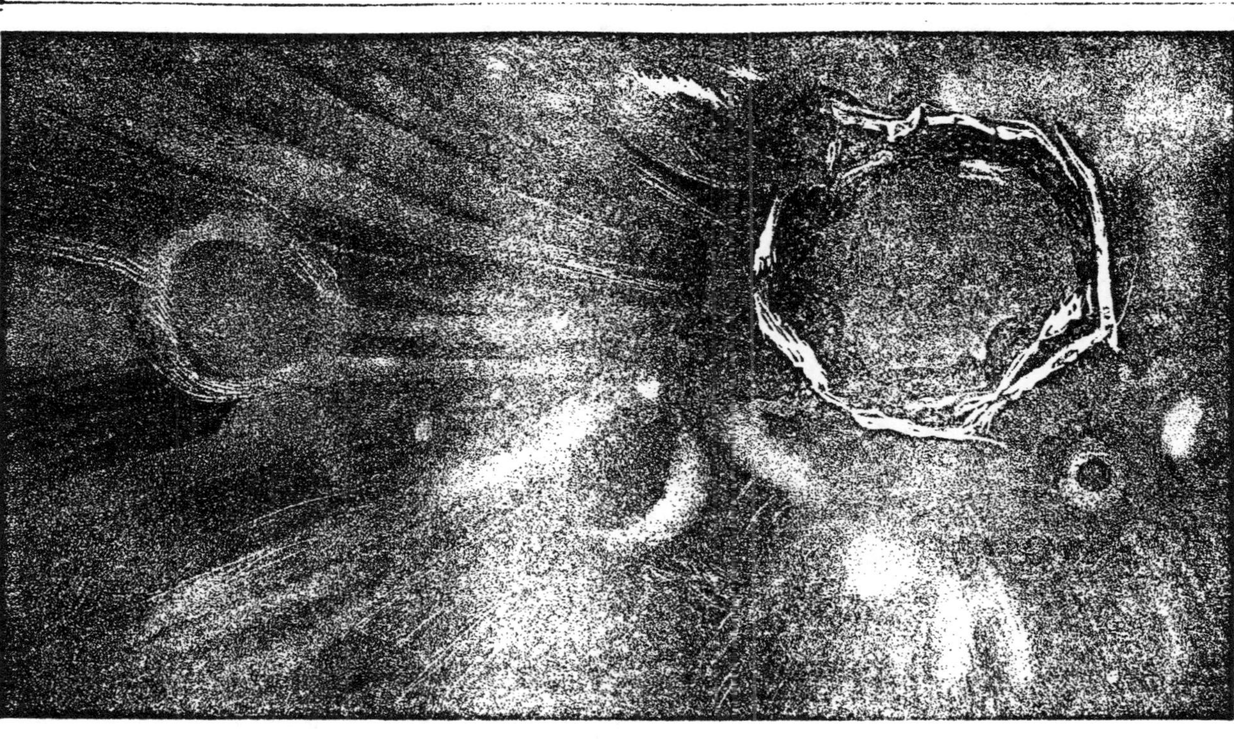

TYCHO AT FULL MOON

THE MOON.

Popular Interest attached to the Moon.—Its Distance.—Its Rotation.—Same Face always toward the Earth.—Its Phases.—Its changes of Position with regard to the Sun.—Has it an Atmosphere?—Optical Test to determine it.—Physical Qualities of Moonlight.—Is Moonlight Warm or Cold?—Does Water exist on the Moon?—Does the Moon influence the Weather?—Mode of determining this.—Physical condition of the Lunar Surface.—Absence of Air and Gases.—Absence of Liquids.—Appearance of the Earth as seen from the Moon.—Prevalence of Mountains upon it.—Their general Volcanic Character.—Appearance of the Mountain Tycho.—Heights of Lunar Mountains and Depths of Ravines.—Telescopic Views of the Moon by Beer and Madler.—Detached Views of the Lunar Surface.—Condition of a Lunar Crater deduced from Analogy.

THE MOON.

ALTHOUGH it be in mere magnitude, physically considered, one of the most insignificant bodies of the solar system, yet for various reasons the MOON has always been regarded by mankind with feelings of profound interest, and has been invested by the popular mind with various influences, affecting not only the physical condition of the globe, but also connected with the phenomena of the organized world. It has been as much an object of popular superstition as of scientific observation. These circumstances doubtless are in some degree owing to its striking appearance in the firmament, to the various changes of form to which it is subject, and above all to its proximity to the earth, and to the close alliance existing between it and our planet. It will not be uninteresting on the present occasion to collect and present in an intelligible form, the results of scientific research concerning this body.

THE DISTANCE OF THE MOON.

The distances of all objects in the heavens are ascertained by the same general principles as that by which the common surveyor determines the distance of inaccessible objects upon the earth. It need scarcely be said that a very small proportion of the terrestrial distances with which we are conversant are ascertained by the actual admeasurement of the space intervening between their extreme points. Other more easy and accurate methods are available, by which we can accurately measure the distance of objects inaccessible to us, by ascertaining the proportion between these distances and other spaces which are accessible and measurable by us. In this way it has been ascertained that the distance of the MOON is equal to about thirty times the diameter of our globe, or in round numbers a quarter of a million of miles.

MAGNITUDE OF THE MOON.

When the distance of a visible object is determined, its magnitude may easily be ascertained by comparing it directly with another object of known magnitude and a known distance. To illustrate this by its application to the MOON, let us take, for example, a cent-piece, which measures about an inch in diameter, and let it be placed between the eye and the moon at any distance from the eye. It will be found on the first trial that the coin will appear larger than the moon; it will, in fact, completely conceal the moon from the eye and produce what may be termed a total eclipse of that luminary. Let the coin be moved however further from the eye, and it will then appear smaller, and will apparently diminish in size as the distance from the eye is increased. Let it be removed until it becomes equal in apparent magnitude to the moon, so that it will exactly cover the disk of the moon, and neither more nor less. If its distance from the eye be then measured, it will be found to be about ten feet, or one hundred and twenty inches, or what is the same, two hundred and forty half inches. But it is known that the distance of the moon is about two hundred and forty thousand miles, and consequently it follows in this case, that one thousand miles in the moon's distance is exactly what half an inch is in the coin's distance. Now under the circumstances here supposed, the coin and the moon are similar objects of equal apparent magnitude. In fact the coin is another moon on a smaller *scale*, and we may use the coin to measure the moon's distance, provided we know the *scale*, exactly as we use the space upon a map of any known scale to measure a country. But it has been just stated that the *scale* is in this case half an inch to one thousand miles; since, then, the coin measures two half inches in diameter, the moon must measure two thousand miles in diameter. The moon is then a globe whose diameter is about one fourth of that of the earth. Its bulk is about one fiftieth of that of our globe, its weight a little less than one fiftieth, and its density something less than three fourths of the density of the earth.

ROTATION OF THE MOON.

While the moon moves around the earth in its monthly course, we find by observations of its appearance, made even without the aid of telescopes, that the same hemisphere is always turned toward us. We recognise this fact by observing that the same marks always remain in the same place upon it. Now, in order that a globe which revolves in a circle around a centre should turn continually the same hemisphere toward that centre, it is necessary that it should make one revolution upon its axis in the time it takes so to revolve. For let us suppose that the globe, in any one position, has the centre round which it revolves north of it, the hemisphere turned toward the centre is turned toward the north. After it makes a quarter of a revolution, the centre is to the east of it, and the hemisphere which was previously turned to the north must now be turned to the east. After it has made another quarter of a revolution the centre will be south of it, and it must be now turned to the south. In the same manner, after another quarter of a revolution, it must be turned to the west. As the same hemisphere is successively turned to all the points of the compass in one revolution, it is evident that the globe itself must make a single revolution on its axis in that time.

It appears, then, that the rotation of the moon upon its axis being equal to that of its revolution in its orbit, is 27 days, 7 hours, and 44 minutes. The intervals of light darkness to the inhabitants of the moon, if there were any, would then be altogether different from those provided in the planets; there would be about 13 days of continued light alternately with 13 days of continued darkness; the analogy, then, which prevails among the planets with regard to days and nights, and which forms a main argument in favor of the conclusion that they are inhabited globes like the earth, does not hold good in the case of the moon.

Although as a general proposition it be true that the same hemisphere of the moon is always turned toward the earth, yet there are small variations at the edge called librations, which it is necessary to notice. The axis of the moon is not exactly perpendicular to its orbit, but is inclined at a small angle. By reason of this inclination, the northern and southern poles of the moon lean alternately in a slight degree to and from the earth.

When the north pole leans toward the earth, we see a little more of that region, and a little less when it leans the contrary way. This variation in the northern and southern regions of the moon visible to us, is called the libration in latitude.

In order that in a strict sense the same hemisphere should be continually turned toward the earth, the time of rotation of the earth upon its axis must not only be equal the time of rotation in its orbit, which in fact it is, but its angular velocity on its axis in every part of its course, must be exactly equal to its angular velocity on its orbit. Now it happens that while its angular velocity on its axis is rigorously uniform throughout the month, its angular velocity in its orbit is subject to a slight variation; the consequence of this is that a little more of its eastern or western edge is seen at one time than at another. This is called the libration in longitude.

By the diurnal motion of the earth. we are carried with it round its axis; the stations from which we view the moon in the morning and the evening, or rather when it rises, and when it sets, are then different according to the latitude of the earth in which we are placed. By thus viewing it from different places, we see it under slightly different aspects. This is another cause of a variation, which we see in its eastern and western edges; this is called the diurnal libration.

PHASES OF THE MOON.

While the moon revolves round the earth, its illuminated hemisphere is always presented to the sun; it therefore takes various positions in reference to the earth. In the annexed diagram the effects of this are exhibited. Let S represent the sun, and T the earth; when the moon is at A, between the sun and the earth, its illuminated hemisphere being turned toward the sun, its dark hemisphere will be presented toward the earth; it will therefore be invisible. In this position the moon is said to be in conjunction. When it moves to the position B, the enlightened hemisphere being still presented to the sun, a small portion of it only is turned to the earth, and it appears as a thin crescent, as represented at *b*. When the moon takes the position of C, at right angles to the sun, it is said to be in quadrature; one half of the enlightened hemisphere only is then presented to the earth, and the moon appears halved, as represented at *c*. When it arrives at the position D, the greater part of the enlightened portion is turned to the earth, and it is gibbous, appearing as represented at *d*. When the moon comes in opposition to the sun, as seen at E, the enlightened hemisphere is turned full toward the earth, and the moon will appear full, unless it be obscured by the earth's shadow, which rarely happens. In the same manner it is shown that at F it is again gibbous; at G it is halved, and at H it is a crescent.

When the moon is full, being in opposition to the sun, it will necessarily be in the meridian at midnight, and will rise as the sun sets, and set as the sun rises; and thus, whenever the enlightened hemisphere of the moon is turned toward us, and when, therefore, it is the most capable of benefiting us, it is up in the firmament all night; whereas, when it is in conjunction, as at A, and the dark hemisphere is turned toward us, it would then be of no use to us, and is accordingly up during the day. The position at C is called the "first quarter," and at G the "last quarter." The position at B is called the first octant; D the second octant; F the third octant; and H the fourth octant. At the first and fourth octants it is a crescent, and at the second and third octants it is gibbous.

Fig. 1.

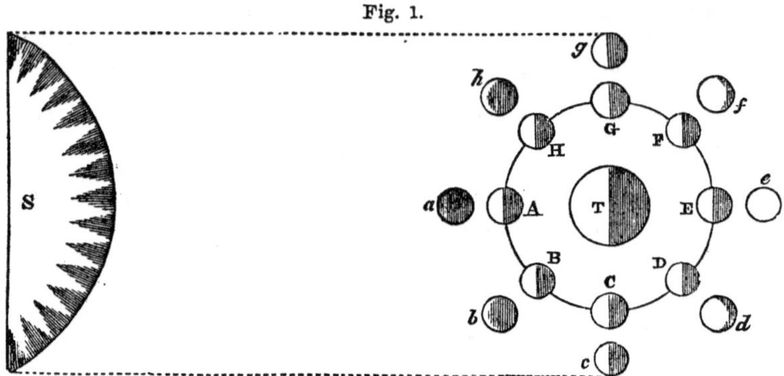

The apparent motion of the moon in the heavens is much more rapid than that of the sun; for while the sun makes a complete circuit of the ecliptic in 365 days, and therefore moves over it at about 1° per day, the moon makes the same circuit in little more than 27 days, and consequently must move at the rate of a little less than 14° per day. As the sun and moon appear to move in the same direction in the firmament, both proceeding from west to east, the moon will, after conjunction, depart from the sun toward the east at the rate of about 13° per day. If, then, the moon be in conjunction with the sun on any given day, it will be 13° east of it at the same time on the following day; 26° east of it after two days, and so on. If, then, the sun set with the moon on any evening, it will, at the moment of sunset on the following evening, be 13° east of it, and at sunset will appear as a thin crescent, at a considerable altitude; on the succeeding day it will be 26° east of the sun, and will be at a still greater altitude at sunset, and will be a broader crescent. After seven days, the moon will be removed 90° from the sun; it will be at or near the meridian at sunset. It will remain in the heavens for about six hours after sunset, and will be seen in the west as the half-moon. Each successive evening increasing its distance from the sun, and also increasing its breadth, it will be visible in the meridian at a later hour, and will consequently be longer apparent in the firmament during the night—it will then be gibbous. After about fourteen days, it will be 180° removed from the sun, and will be full, and consequently will rise when the sun sets, and set when the sun rises—being visible the entire night. After the elapse of three weeks, the distance of the moon from the sun being about 270°, it will not reach the meridian until nearly the hour of sunrise; it will then be visible during the last six hours of the night only. The moon will then be waning, and toward the close of the month will only be seen in the morning before sunrise, and will appear as a crescent.

HAS THE MOON AN ATMOSPHERE?

In order to determine whether or not the globe of the moon is surrounded with any gaseous envelope like the atmosphere of the earth, it is necessary first to consider what appearances such an appendage would present, seen at the moon's distance, and whether any such appearances are discoverable upon the moon.

According to ordinary and popular notions, it is difficult to separate the idea of an atmosphere from the existence of clouds; yet to produce clouds something more is necessary than air. The presence of water on the surface is indispensable, and if it be assumed that no water exist, then certainly the absence of clouds is no proof of the absence of an atmosphere. Be this as it may, however, it is certain that there are no clouds upon the moon, for if there were, we should immediately discover them, by the variable lights and shadows they would produce. If there is, then, an atmosphere upon the moon, it is one entirely unaccompanied by clouds.

One of the effects produced by a distant view of an atmosphere surrounding a globe, one hemisphere of which is illuminated by the sun, is, that the boundary, or line of separation between the hemisphere enlightened by the sun and the dark hemisphere, is not sudden and sharply defined, but is gradual—the light fading away by slow degrees into the darkness. This is an effect produced by a portion of the atmosphere which extends over the dark hemisphere being illuminated by the sun. Let A B (fig. 2) be a diameter of the moon separating the enlightened hemisphere A M B from the dark hemisphere A N B. Let C E D F be the upper surface of the atmosphere. Let S T be rays from the sun touching the moon at A B. It is evident that the portion of the atmosphere included between A T and C T, and that between B T and D T,

Fig. 2.

G

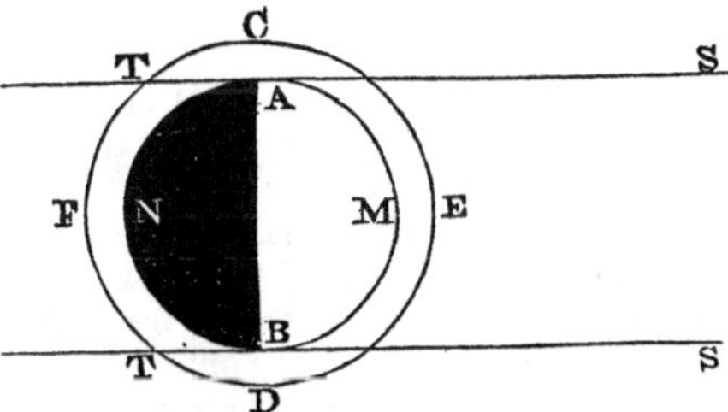

will be illuminated by the sun; and if the moon be viewed from a distant point G, then these latter portions of the atmosphere will be seen throwing a faint light on a portion of the dark hemisphere, which light will become gradually fainter till it dies away. This is the effect which on the earth is the cause of the morning and evening twilight.

Now, if such an effect as this were produced upon the moon, it would be discoverable by us with the naked eye, and still more certainly with the telescope. When the moon is a crescent, its concave edge is the boundary which separates the enlightened from the dark hemisphere. When it is in the quarters, the diameter of the semi-circle is also that boundary. In neither of these cases, however, do we ever discover the slightest indication of any such appearance as that which has just been described. There is no gradual fading away of the light into the darkness; on the contrary, the boundary, though serrated and irregular, is nevertheless perfectly well-defined and sudden.

All these circumstances conspire to raise a presumption that there does not exist upon the moon any atmosphere capable of reflecting light in any sensible degree.

But it may be contended that an atmosphere may still exist, though too attenuated to produce a sensible twilight. Astronomers, however, have resorted to another test of a much more decisive and delicate kind, the nature of which will be understood by explaining a simple principle of optics.

When a ray of light passes through a transparent medium, such as air, water, or glass, it is generally deflected from its rectilinear course, so as to form an angle. A simple and easily-executed experiment will render this intelligible. Let a visible object, such as a cent-piece, be placed at C, in the bottom of a bucket. Let the eye be placed at E, so that the side of the bucket, when empty, shall just conceal the coin from the eye, and so that the nearest point to the coin visible to the eye shall be at A, in the direction of the line E B A. Let the bucket be now filled with water, and the coin will become immediately visible; the reason of which is, that the ray of light C B proceeding from the coin is bent at an angle in passing from the water into the air, and reaches the eye by the angular course C B E. Thus it appears that the coin will be visible to the eye, notwithstanding the interposition of the opaque side of the bucket.

Fig. 3.

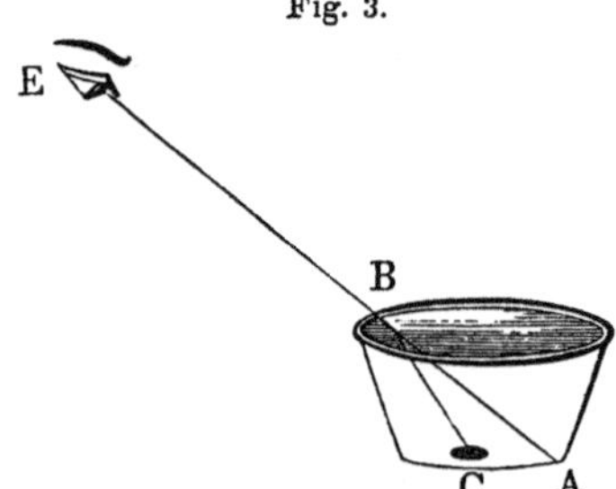

Let us see how this principle can be applied to the case of the moon's atmosphere, if such there be. Let M N (fig. 4) represent the disk of the moon. Let A B represent the atmosphere which surrounds it. Let C D and E F represent two lines touching the moon at M and N, and proceeding toward the earth. Let S T be two stars seen in the direction of these lines. If the moon had no atmosphere, these stars would appear to touch the edge of the moon at M and N, because the rays of light from them would pass directly along the lines S M D and T N F toward the earth; but if the moon have an atmosphere, then that atmosphere will possess the property which is common to all transparent media of refracting light, and, in virtue of such property, stars in such positions as Q and R, behind the edge of the moon, would be visible at the earth, for the ray Q M, in passing through the atmosphere, would be bent at an angle in the direction Q M P, and in like manner the ray R N would be bent at the angle R N O—so that the stars Q and R would be visible at P and O, notwithstanding the interposition of the edges of the moon. This effect is precisely the same as that in the example of the coin in the bucket; the ray from the star is bent over the edge of the moon so as to render the star visible notwithstanding the interposition of that edge just for the same reason and in the same manner as the ray from the coin is bent over the side of the bucket so as to render the coin visible notwithstanding the opacity of that side.

Fig. 4.

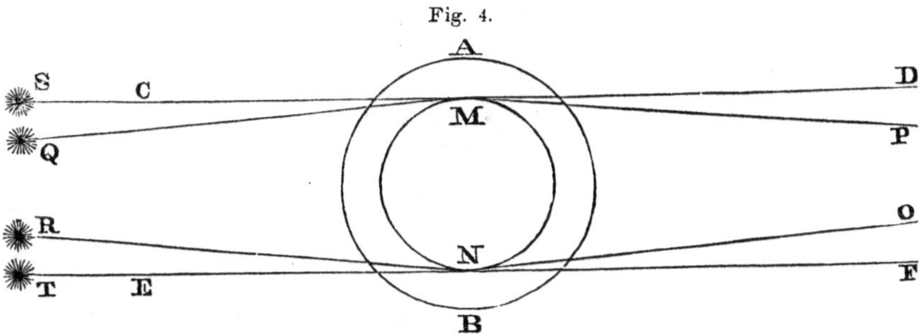

This reasoning leads to the conclusion that as the moon moves over the face of the firmament, stars will be continually visible at its edge which are really behind it if it have an atmosphere, and the extent to which this effect will take place will be in proportion to the density of the atmosphere.

The magnitude and motion of the moon and the relative positions of the stars are so accurately known that nothing is more easy, certain, and precise, than the observations which may be made with the view of ascertaining whether any stars are ever seen which are sensibly behind the edge of the moon. Such observations have been made by the most skilful astronomers, and no such effect has ever been detected. This species of observation is susceptible of such extreme accuracy, that it is certain that if an atmosphere existed upon the moon a thousand times less dense than our own, its presence must have been detected.

But what is an atmosphere a thousand times less dense than ours? Our atmosphere supports by its pressure a column of thirty inches of mercury in the barometer. One a thousand times less dense would not support so much as the thirtieth of an inch; in short, it may be considered as proved that there does not exist upon the moon an atmosphere as dense as is found under the receiver of the most perfect air-pump after that instrument has withdrawn from it the air to the utmost extent of its power. In fine, it may be considered as demonstrated that there is no air upon the moon.

THE PHYSICAL QUALITIES OF MOONLIGHT.

It has long been an object of inquiry among philosophers whether the light of the moon has any heat, but the most delicate experiments and observations have failed to detect this property in it.

A thermometer of extreme sensibility, called a differential thermometer, was the instrument applied to this inquiry. Let E and F be two thin glass bulbs connected by a rectangular glass tube E A B F partially filled with a liquid to the level. Let the bulbs E and F contain air. If the bulb F be exposed to any source of heat or cold different from E, the air within it will expand or contract, and the liquid in F B will fall or rise. This instrument has such extreme sensibility that it is capable of rendering manifest a change of temperature amounting to the five hundreth part of a degree. The light of the moon was collected into the focus of a concave mirror of such magnitude as would have been sufficient, if exposed to the sun's light, to evaporate gold or platinum. The bulb of the differential thermometer was placed in its focus so as to re-

Fig. 5.

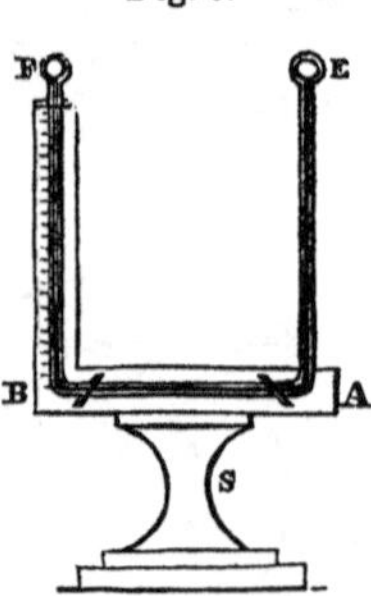

ceive upon it the concentrated rays of the moon. Yet no sensible effect was produced upon the thermometer. We must therefore conclude that the light of the moon does not possess the calorific property in any sensible degree.

This result will create less surprise when the comparative density of sunlight and moonlight are considered. It may be assumed without sensible error that the intensity of the sun's light on the surface of the moon and on the earth is the same, it follows from this, that supposing no light whatever to be absorbed by the moon, but the entire light of the sun to be reflected from its surface undiminished, the intensity of moonlight at the earth would bear to the intensity of sunlight the same proportion as the magnitude of the moon bears to the magnitude of the entire firmament, that is, the proportion very nearly of one to three hundred thousand; but there is no reflecting surface however perfect which does not absorb the light incident upon it in a very considerable degree, and the rugged surface of the moon must be a most imperfect reflector. It may then be considered as demonstrated that the intensity of moonlight is much more than three hundred thousand times more feeble than that of sunlight. We shall not, then, be surprised at the absence of its heating power.

But if the rays of the moon be not warm, the vulgar impression that they are cold is equally erroneous. We have seen that they produce no effect either way on the thermometer.

DOES WATER EXIST ON THE MOON?

We shall presently see that telescopic observation proves the non-existence of oceans, seas, or any other large reservoirs of water, on the surface of our satellite. This is not sufficient, however, to establish the total absence of water upon it, for besides its possible existence in the form of rivers and small lakes too minute to be discovered by the telescope, it might exist in the pores of organized and unorganized matter.

If, however, water, or any other liquid, existed upon the moon, it would be subject to the common process of evaporation, which would take place the more freely because of the absence of an atmosphere. It is evident, then, that the existence of liquids on the moon would necessarily be attended with the existence of an atmosphere surrounding the moon composed of the vapor of those liquids. It is difficult to imagine how such an atmosphere could exist without clouds, but its non-existence is conclusively proved by the fact that its presence cannot be detected by the optical test above-mentioned, by which the absence of an atmosphere is proved—an atmosphere of vapor, having in common with air and other transparent media the property of refraction, its effect on the stars will be similar, and consequently the same test which proves the absence of an atmosphere of air equally proves the absence of an atmosphere of vapor.

DOES THE MOON INFLUENCE THE WEATHER?

Among the many influences which the moon is supposed, by the world in general, to exercise upon our globe, one of those which have been most universally believed, in all ages and in all countries, is that which it is presumed to exert upon the changes of the weather. Although the particular details of this influence are sometimes pretended to be described, the only general principle, or rule, which prevails with the world in general is, that a change of weather may be looked for at the epochs of new and full moon: that is to say, if the weather be previously fair it will become foul, and if foul will become fair. Similar changes are also, sometimes, though not so confidently looked for, at the epochs of the quarters.

A question of this kind may be regarded either as a question of science, or a question of fact.

If it be regarded as a question of science, we are called upon to explain how and by what property of matter, or what law of nature or attraction the moon, at a distance of a quarter of a million of miles, combining its effects with the sun, at four hundred times that distance, can produce those alleged changes? To this it may be readily answered that no known law or principle has hitherto explained any such phenomena. The moon and sun must, doubtless, affect the ocean of air which surrounds the globe, as they affect the ocean of water—producing effects analogous to tides; but when the quantity of such an effect is estimated, it is proved to be utterly inappreciable, and such as could by no means account for the meteorological changes here adverted to.

But in conducting investigations of this kind we proceed altogether in the wrong direction, and begin at the wrong end when we commence with the investigation of the physical cause of the supposed phenomena. That method of conducting physical inquiries, which was bequeathed to us by the illustrious Bacon, and which has led to such an immense extension of our knowledge of the universe, imperiously requires that before we begin to seek for the causes of any phenomena, we must first prove beyond the possibility of doubt, the *reality* of these phenomena, and ascertain with the utmost precision, all the circumstances attending them. In other words, we are required to consider all inquiries of the kind now adverted to, as mere questions of *fact*, before we take them as questions of science.

What, then, let us see, is the present question? It is asserted that the moon produces such an influence on the weather as to cause it to change at the new and full moon, and at the quarters. But in this mode of stating the proposition, there are implicitly included two very distinct points, one of which is a simple matter of fact, and the other a point of physical science.

First.—It is asserted that at the epochs of a new and full moon, and at the quarters, there is generally a change of weather. This is a mere statement of alleged fact.

Second.—It is asserted that the phases of the moon, or in other words, the relative position of the moon and sun in regard to the earth is the cause of these changes.

Now it is evidently necessary to settle the first question before we trouble ourselves with the second, for if it should so happen that the first statement should prove to be destitute of foundation the second falls to the ground.

The question of fact, here before us, is one most easily settled. In many meteorological observations throughout Europe, a register of the weather in all respects, has been kept for a long period of time. Thus the height of the barometer, the condition of the thermometer, the hydrometer, and the rain gauge; the form and character of the clouds, the times of the falling of rain, hail, and snow, and in short, every particular respecting the weather has been duly registered, from day to day, and often from hour to hour.

The period of the lunar phases, it is needless to say, has also been registered, and it is, therefore, possible to compare one set of changes with the other.

This, in fine, has been done. We can imagine, placed in two parallel columns, in juxtaposition, the series of epochs of the new and full moons, and the quarters, and the corresponding conditions of the weather at these times, for fifty or one hundred years back, so that we may be enabled to examine, as a mere matter of fact, the conditions of the weather for one thousand or twelve hundred full and new moons and quarters. The result of such an examination has been, that no correspondence whatever has been found to exist between the two phenomena. Thus let us suppose that one hundred and twenty-five full moons be taken at random from the table; if the condition of the weather at these several epochs be examined it will be found, probably, that in sixty-three cases there was a change of weather, and in sixty-two there was not, so that under such circumstances the odd moon in this division of one hundred and twenty-five would favor the popular opinion; but if another random collection of one hundred and twenty-five full moons be taken, and similarly examined, it will probably be found that sixty-three are not attended by changes of weather, while sixty-two are. With its characteristic caprice the moon on this occasion opposes the popular opinion; in short, a full examination of the table shows that the condition of the weather as to change, or in any other respect, has, as a matter of fact, no correspondence whatsoever with the lunar phases.

Such, then, being the case, it would be idle to attempt to seek for a physical cause of an effect which is destitute of proof.

PHYSICAL CONDITION OF THE LUNAR SURFACE.

Curiosity will doubtless be awakened in a very lively manner regarding the physical condition of our moon: what part has the Maker of the solar system destined this body to play in the economy of his creation? Is it a globe teeming with life and organization like the earth? Is that orb, which rolls in silent, serene majesty in her silent course through the midnight firmament, the abode of life and intelligence? The beauty of her appearance, and the interest inseparable from this, naturally lead the mind to conjectures of this kind. Yet the circumstances which I have unfolded regarding the total absence of air and water, appear to exclude the possibility of any such supposition. How, may it be asked, can it be conceived that a globe can have upon it an organized world which is destitute of fluid matter in every form? How can growth, which implies gradual change, increase, and diminution, and all the various effects in which fluidity is an agent, go on there? How can they proceed upon such a solid, arid, unchangeable, crude mass? Let it be remembered what a multitude of purposes in our natural and social economy are subserved by the combination of the water and the atmosphere of our globe. None of these purposes can be fulfilled upon the moon. Perhaps, however, our notions on such questions may be cleared up to some extent by a careful examination of the facts that scientific research have collected together respecting the physical condition of the surface of our satellite.

If we examine the moon carefully, even without the aid of a telescope, we shall discover upon it distinct and definite lineaments of light and shadow. These features never change; there they remain, always in the same position upon the visible orb of the moon. Thus the features that occupy its centre now, have occupied the same position throughout all human record. We have already stated that the first and most obvious inference which this fact suggests, is that the same hemisphere of the moon is always presented toward the earth, and consequently, the other hemisphere is never seen, nor can we ever see it. This singular characteristic which attaches to the motion of the moon round the earth, seems to be a general characteristic of all other moons in the system. Sir William Herschel, by the aid of his powerful telescopes, ascertained that the moons of Jupiter revolve in the same manner, each presenting continually the same hemisphere to the planet. The cause of this peculiar motion has been attempted to be explained by the hypothesis that the hemisphere of the satellite which is turned toward the planet, is very elongated and protuberant, and it is the excess of its weight which makes it tend to direct itself always toward the primary, in obedience to the universal principle of attraction. Be this as it may, the effect is in the case of the moon, that our geographical knowledge is necessarily limited to that hemisphere which is turned toward us.

If the moon were inhabited, observers upon it would have an extraordinary spectacle presented to them by the earth. In their firmament the earth is an object with a diameter four times, and a disk sixteen times, greater than that which the moon presents to us. A spectator placed on the centre of the hemisphere of the moon which is toward us, would see the orb of the earth presenting the appearance of a gorgeous moon of immense magnitude, always in his zenith: it would never rise, nor set, nor change its position at all in the firmament; it would, however, undergo all the varieties of phases of the moon —when the moon appears to us full, it would be new, and when the moon appears new, it would be full; when the moon appears to us a crescent, it would be gibbous, and vice versâ.

But what is the condition and character of the surface of the moon? What are the lineaments of light and shade which we see upon it? There is no object outside the earth with which the telescope has afforded us such minute and satisfactory information.

If, when the moon is a crescent, we examine with a telescope, even of moderate power, the concave boundary which, is that part of the lunar surface where the enlightened hemisphere ends and the dark hemisphere begins, we shall find that this boundary is not an even and regular curve, which it undoubtedly would be if the surface of the globe of the moon were smooth and regular, or nearly so. If, for example, the lunar surface, resembled in its general characteristics that of our globe; granting the total absence of water, and that the entire surface is land, that land had the general characteristics of the continents of the globe of the earth; then I say, that the inner boundary of the lunar crescent would still be a regular curve, broken or interrupted only at particular points. Where great mountain ranges, like those of the Alps, the Andes, or the Himalaya, might chance to cross it, in such places these lofty peaks would project vastly-elongated shadows along the adjacent plain; for it will be remembered, that, being situated at the moment in question, at the boundary of the enlightened and darkened hemispheres, the shadows would be those of evening and morning; which are prodigiously longer than the objects themselves. The effects of these would be to cause gaps or irregularities in the general outline of the inner boundary of the crescent; with these rare exceptions, the inner boundary of the crescent produced by a globe like the earth would be an even and regular curve.

Such, however, is not the case with the inner boundary of the lunar crescent, even when viewed by the naked eye, and still less so when magnified by a telescope.

It is found, on the other hand, that this boundary is everywhere rugged and serrated, and brilliantly-illuminated points are seen in the dark parts of the moon, at some distance from the general boundary of the illuminated part, while dark shadows of considerable length appear to break into the illuminated surface. In short, there is a continued irregularity throughout the whole extent of the inner boundary of the lunar crescent. The inequalities thus apparent indicate singular geographical and geological characteristics of the lunar surface. Each of the bright points which are seen within the dark hemisphere are the peaks of lofty mountains tinted with the sun's light. They are in the condition with which all travellers on Alpine points are familiar; after the sun has set, and darkness has set in over the valleys at the foot of the chain, the sun's light still continues to illuminate the lofty peaks above. The dark streaks which break into the illuminated hemisphere of the moon are those of lofty mountains within that hemisphere which project their shadows toward the dark hemisphere.

It appears, then, that the surface of the moon is a continuity of mountainous regions. If we examine by means of a powerful telescope the full moon, we find those features rendered larger and more conspicuous, and greatly multiplied in number. What, it may be asked then, are those peculiar phenomena thus discovered upon the full moon? What is signified by the dark and what by the lighter parts? Elaborate telescopic research has shown us that the dark parts are generally cavities into which the light of the sun penetrates imperfectly, while the bright parts are eminences that catch the sun's light with great intensity. Toward the sides of the full moon, also, the dark portions are caused by the shadows of mountain peaks and ridges, which are more and more elongated the farther these points are removed from the centre of the full moon.

Within a recent period the moon has been subjected to extremely-elaborate telescopic examinations by Beer and Madler, who have published some very magnificent telescopic views of it. The telescopic map of the moon's surface, published by these eminent observers, measures three feet in diameter, and may truly be said to exceed in accuracy any chart of the globe of the earth.

The lunar mountains are of various formations and arrangements: peaks such as that of Teneriffe are common. Mountain ranges following straight or nearly straight courses are also discoverable; but the most frequent formation of the lunar mountains is that which resembles the crater of our volcano. It is estimated that three fifths of the portion of the moon visible to us is covered with caverns penetrating to a great depth, and surrounded by a circular wall of rock of a rugged and irregular character. These crater-formed cavities are very various in diameter, varying from 50 or 60 miles to a few hundred feet, and the number of them increases as the magnitude diminishes. The ridge surrounding these craters is generally precipitous and nearly vertical on the inside, but sloping more gradually on the outside. On descending to the bottom, it is often found to arrange itself in steps or terraces. "The bottom of the crater," says Professor Nichol, who has examined in detail the labors of Beer and Madler, "is very often convex, and low ridges of mountains run through it. We also find in it isolated conical peaks and smaller craters, whose heights, however, seldom reach the level of the base of the exterior wall. These curious objects are on some parts of the moon so crowded that they seem to have pressed on each other, and disturbed and even broken down each other's boundaries, so that through the mutual interference the most oddly-shaped caverns have arisen. It has often been observed that smaller craters are found on the walls of the crater, and in many instances we can discern that the wall has been shaken by force.

Among the singular remarkable appearances upon the moon, is that of a system of rays which appear to diverge from the crater-shaped ridges. One of the most remarkable of these is exhibited in the appearance of the mountain called *Tycho*. At the time of full moon, these appearances generally cast very broad, brilliant bands, issuing from all sides of the crater, and stretching to a greater or less distance, sometimes extending over a space of several hundred miles. Two characteristics of these singular bands necessarily attract notice. First, the light they throw is exactly of the same kind as that reflected from the edge of the crater itself, and from the lowest part of the chasm; so that we must suppose that the matter forming them had the same origin and source as the other portion of these mountainous formations. Secondly, it will be observed that they hold their course without being interrupted by other formations on the lunar surface. If, instead of a general rugged surface, the face of the moon had been one unbroken plane, the course of these radiating lines could not have been less disturbed, except that they accommodate themselves to the *contour* of the surface; if they meet a valley, they bend with it; if a precipitous mountain, they rise with it precipitously; and then pursue their previous path.

Before we dismiss the mountainous character of the moon's surface, it may be well to state that the heights of these mountains, and the depths, in many cases, of their cavities, have been pretty accurately ascertained by the measurement of their shadows. It is generally stated that they are higher than the mountain ranges of the earth. This, in a literal sense, is not true. The lunar mountains do not attain to the actual height of some of the highest of the terrestrial ranges; but, considering that the moon is a globe on a scale one fourth that of the earth, it may be truly stated that, according to the relative sizes of the globes, the lunar mountains are considerably higher than those of the earth.

It is not the mere height of these mountains that so forcibly commands attention; it is their universal prevalence.

At the early epochs of telescopic discoveries, when the moon was examined by telescopes of inferior power, extensive regions were observed upon it, which seemed to be level surfaces, and which were therefore mistaken for seas. These regions in the lunar surface have received names, every conspicuous mountain being designated by a peculiar title, names were also given to those apparent level portions, such as the Mare Imbrium, &c. As the power of the telescope was improved, it soon became apparent that regions supposed to be seas, were covered with asperities and inequalities, less indeed in elevation than other parts of the moon, but still considerable. Every augmentation of power which the telescope received, only adds fresh proof that there is no portion of the moon absolutely level, and consequently that there does not exist upon it, at least on the visible hemisphere, a collection of water.

The celebrated telescopic view of the moon produced by the labors of Beer and Madler, to which I have more than once referred, is exhibited on a reduced scale in the frontispiece of this volume. The mere inspection of that drawing will afford abundant evidence to corroborate the statements which have been here made; more especially, if it be remembered that minute portions of that view, where no inequalities are exhibited, will show innumerable inequalities if submitted to an examination with a still higher magnifying power.

I annex here two highly-magnified views of detached portions of the lunar surface, supplied by the observations of Madler. In these the prevalence of the crater form is especially conspicuous. The names of the more remarkable mountains are here inserted.

Fig. 6.

Fig. 7.

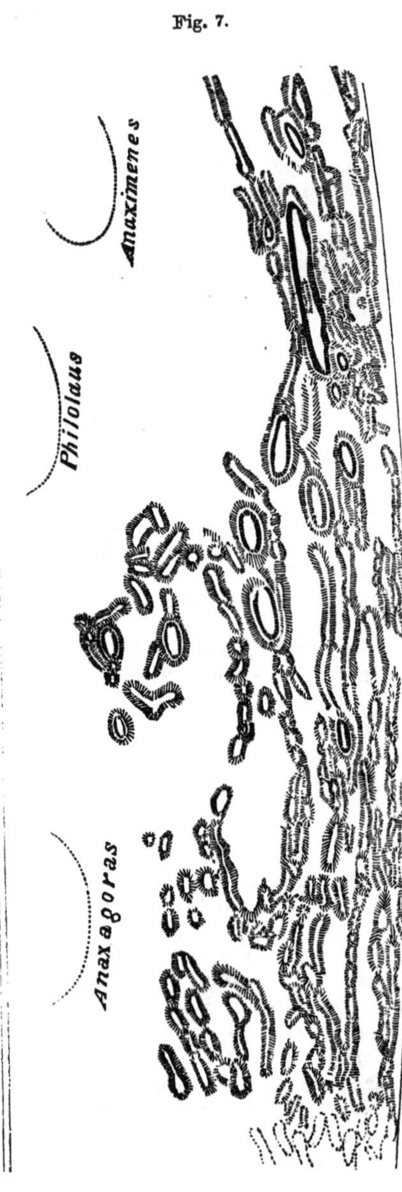

Astronomers have occasionally extended their speculations beyond the immediate and rigorous limits of observation, and had endeavored by analogy to afford us some idea of the actual condition of lunar surface. I annex here a drawing of a lunar crater, from the design of a French observer.

THE ORBIT OF THE MOON.

Although in its general form and character the path of the moon round the earth is, like that of the orbits of the planets and satellites in general, circular, yet, when it is submitted, to accurate observation we find that it is strictly an ellipse or oval, the centre of the earth occupying one of its *foci*. This fact can be ascertained by immediate observation upon the apparent magnitude of the moon. It will be easily comprehended that any change which the apparent magnitude of the moon as seen from the earth undergoes, must arise from corresponding changes in the moon's distance from us. Thus, if at one time the disk of the moon appears larger than at another time, as it cannot be supposed that the actual size of the moon itself could be changed, we can only ascribe the increase of the apparent magnitude to the diminution of its distance. Now we find by observation that such apparent changes are actually observed in its monthly course around the earth. The moon is subject to a continual and small, though perceptible change of apparent size. We find that it diminishes until it reaches a minimum, and then gradually increases until it reaches a maximum.

When the apparent magnitude of the moon is least, it is at its greatest distance from us, and when its apparent magnitude is greatest, it is at its least distance from us. The positions in which these distances lie, are directly opposite. Between these two positions the apparent size of the moon undergoes a regular and gradual change, increasing continually from its minimum to its maximum, and consequently between these positions, its distances must on the other hand gradually diminish from its maximum to its minimum. If we lay down on a chart or plan a delineation of the course or path thus determined, we shall find that it will represent an oval which differs however very little from a circle; the place of the earth being nearer to one end of the oval than the other.

The point of the moon's path in the heavens at which its magnitude appears the greatest, and when, therefore it is nearest the earth, is called its *perigee;* and the point where its apparent size is least, and where, therefore, its distance from the earth is greatest, is called its *apogee.* These two points are called the *moon's apsides.*

If the positions of these points in the heavens be observed accurately for a length of time, it will be found that they are subject to a regular change; that is to say, the place where the moon appears smallest, will every month shift its position; and a corresponding change will take place in the point where it appears largest. The movement of these points in the heavens is found to be in the same direction as the general movement of the planets; that is, from west to east, or progressive. This effect is called the progression of the moon apsides.

THE MOON'S NODES.

If the position of the moon's centre in the heavens be observed from day to day, it will be found that its path is a great circle, making an angle of about 5° with the ecliptic. This path consequently crosses the ecliptic at two points in opposite quarters of the heavens. These points are called the *moon's nodes.* Their positions are ascertained by observing from time to time the distance of the moon's centre from the ecliptic, which is called the moon's latitude; by watching its gradual diminution, and finding the point at which it becomes nothing; the moon's centre is then in the ecliptic and its position is the *node.* The node at which the moon passes from the south to the north of the ecliptic is called the *ascending node,* and that at which it passes from the north to the south is called the *descending node.*

If the positions of these nodes be observed from time to time, it will be found that they are not fixed; but that they change their positions in the ecliptic, moving upon that line in a direction contrary to that of the planets, or from east to west. This effect is called the *retrogression of the moon's nodes.*

HEAT.

Heat as a Branch of elementary Physics neglected.—Has as strong Claims as Light, Electricity, or Magnetism.—Is a universal Agent in Nature.—In Art.—In Science.—Astronomy.—Chemistry.—In every Situation of Life.—Applications of it in Clothing and artificial Warming and Cooling.—Lighting.—Admits of easy Explanation.—Dilatation.—Examples.—Thermometer.—Melting and Boiling Points.—Evaporation.—Specific Heat.—Heat produced by Compression.—Radiation.—Conduction.—Incandescence.

HEAT.

WHILE almost every other branch of physical science has been made the subject of systematic treatises without number, and some have been, as it were, set apart from the general mass of natural philosophy, and raised to the rank of distinct sciences by the badge of some characteristic title, *Heat* alone has been left to form a chapter of chemistry, or to receive a passing notice in treatises on general physics. Light has long enjoyed the exclusive attention of philosophers, and has been elevated to the dignity of a science, under the name of *Optics*. *Electricity* and *Magnetism* have also been thought worthy subjects for separate treatises, yet, can any one who has observed the part played by heat on the theatre of nature, doubt that its claims to attention are equal to those of light, and superior to those of electricity and magnetism. It is possible for organized matter to exist without light. Innumerable operations of nature proceed as regularly and as effectually in its absence as when it is present. The want of that sense which it is designed to affect in the animal economy, in no degree impairs the other powers of the body, nor in man does such a defect interfere in any way with the faculties of the mind. Light is, so to speak, an object rather of luxury than of positive necessity. Nature supplies it, therefore, not in unlimited abundance, nor at all times and places, but rather with that thrift and economy which she is wont to observe in dispensing the objects of our pleasures, compared with those which are necessary to our being. But heat, on the contrary, she has yielded in the most unbounded plenteousness. Heat is everywhere present. Every body that exists contains it in quantity without known limit. The most inert and rude masses are pregnant with it. Whatever we see, hear, smell, taste, or feel, is full of it. To its influence is due that endless variety of forms which are spread over and beautify the surface of the globe. Land, water, air, could not for a single instant exist as they do, in its absence; all would suddenly fall into one rude formless mass—solid and impenetrable. The air of heaven hardening into a crust would envelope the globe, and crush within an everlasting tomb all that it contains. Heat is the parent and the nurse of the endless beauties of organization. The mineral, the vegetable, the animal kingdoms, are its offspring. Every natural structure is either immediately produced by its agency, maintained by its influence, or intimately dependant on it. Withdraw heat, and instantly all life, motion, form, and beauty, will cease to exist, and it may be literally said, "Chaos has come again."

Nor is heat less instrumental in the processes of art, than in the operations of nature. All that art can effect on the productions of nature is to change their form or arrangement—to separate or to combine them. Bodies are moulded to forms which our wants or our tastes demand; compounds are decomposed, and their obnoxious or useless elements expelled, in obedience to our wishes. In all such processes heat is the agent. At its bidding the most obdurate masses soften like wax, and are fashioned to suit our most wayward caprices. Elements of bodies knit together by the most stubborn affinities—by forces which might well be deemed invincible—are torn asunder by this omnipotent solvent, and separately presented for the use or the pleasure of man, the great Master of Art.

If we turn from art to science, we find heat assisting or obstructing, as the case may be, but always modifying the objects of our inquiry. The common spectator, who, on a clear night, beholds the firmament, thinks he obtains a just notion of the position and arrangement of the brilliant objects with which it is so richly furnished. The more exact vision of the astronomer discovers, however, that he beholds this starry vault through a distorting medium; that, in fact, he views it through a great lens of air, by which every object is removed from its proper place; nay, more, that this distortion varies from night to night, and from hour to hour—varies with the varying heat of the atmosphere which produces it. Such distortion, and the variations to which it is subject, must then be accurately sustained, before any inferences can be made respecting the motion, position, magnitude, or distance of any object in the heavens; and ascertained it cannot be, unless the laws that govern the phenomena of heat be known.

But the very instruments which the same astronomer uses to assist his vision, and to note and measure the positions and mutual distances of the objects of his inquiry, are themselves eminently subject to the same distorting influence. The metal of which they are formed swells and contracts with every fluctuation in the heat to which it is exposed. A sunbeam, a blast of cold air—nay, the very heat of the astronomer's own body—must produce effects on the figure of the brazen arch by whose divided surface his measurements and his observations are effected. Such effects must therefore be known, and taken into account, ere he can hope to attain that accuracy which the delicacy of his investigations renders indispensably necessary.

The chemist, in all his proceedings, is beset with the effects of heat, aiding or impeding his researches. Now it promotes the disunion of combined elements, now fuses into one uniform mass the most heterogeneous materials. At one time he resorts to it as the means of arousing dormant affinities; at another he applies its powers to dissolve the strongest bonds of chemical attraction. Composition and decomposition are equally attended by its evolution and absorption; and often to such an extent as to produce tremendous explosions on the one hand, or cold, exceeding the rigors of the most severe polar winter, on the other.

But why repair to the observatory of the astronomer or to the laboratory of the chemist, for examples of a principle which is in never-ceasing operation around us! Sleeping or waking, at home or abroad, by night or by day, at rest or in motion, in the country or in the town, traversing the burning limits of the tropics, or exploring the rigors of the poles, we are ever under its influence. We are at once its slaves and its masters.

We are its slaves :—Without it we cannot for a moment live. Without its well-regulated quantity we cannot for a moment enjoy life. It rules our pleasures and our pains; it lays us on the sick bed, and raises us from it. It is our disease and our physician. In the ardor of summer we languish under its excess, and in the rigor of winter we shiver under its defect. Does it accumulate around us in undue quantity, we burn with fever; does it depart from us with unwonted rapidity, we shake with ague; or writhe under the pains of rheumatism, and the tribe of maladies which it leaves behind when it quits us.

We are its masters :—We subdue it to our will and dispose it to our purposes. Amid arctic snows we *confine it* around our persons, and prevent its escape by a clothing* impervious to it. Under a tropical sun we *exclude it* by like means. We extort it from water to obtain the luxury of ice in hot seasons, and we force it into water to warm our apartments† in cold ones. Do we traverse the seas—it lends wings to the ship, and bids defiance to the natural opponents, the winds and the tides. Do we traverse the land—it is harnessed to the chariot, and we outstrip the flight of the swiftest bird, and equal the fury of the tempest.‡

If we sleep, our chamber and our couch are furnished with contrivances for its due regulation. If we eat, our food owes its savor and its nutrition to heat. From this the fruit receives its ripeness, and by this the viands of the table are fitted for our use. The grateful infusion which forms our morning repast might remain for ever hidden in the leaf‖ of the tree, the berry§ of the plant, or the kernel¶ of the nut, if heat did not lend its power to extract them. The beverage that warms and cheers us, when relaxed by labor or overcome by fatigue, is distilled, brewed, or fermented, by the agency of heat. The productions of nature give up their sanative principles to this all-powerful agent; and hence the decoction or the pill is produced to restore health to the sinking patient.

When the sun hides his face and the heavens are veiled in darkness, whence do we obtain light? Heat confers light upon air, and the taper burns and the lamp blazes,** producing artificial day; guiding us in the pursuits of business or of pleasure, and thus adding to the sum of life, by rendering hours pleasant and useful which must otherwise have been lost in torpor or in sleep.

These, and a thousand other circumstances, prove how important a physical agent is that to the explication of whose effects the pages of the present discourse are devoted. But it is not alone the intrinsic importance of the subject, nor its connexion with every natural appearance that can attract observation or excite inquiry, which has induced us to examine it. It presents other advantages which merit peculiar consideration, with a view to popular instruction.

The phenomena all admit of being explained without the aid of abstruse reasoning, technical language, or mathematical symbols. The subject abounds

* Clothing, in general, is composed of non-conducting substances, which in cold weather prevents the heat produced by the body from escaping, and preserves its temperature; and in hot weather excludes the heat from the body, so as to prevent undue warmth.

† Buildings are warmed by hot water carried through the apartments in pipes.

‡ The swiftest flight of a carrier pigeon does not exceed the rate of twenty-six miles an hour. It is calculated that the velocity of a high wind is at the rate of about thirty to thirty-five miles an hour. The steam-carriages on the Manchester and Liverpool Railway have been known to travel about six-and-thirty miles an hour; and it is stated, in the evidence before a committee of the House of Commons, that steam-carriages have run on common roads at a speed exceeding forty miles an hour.

‖ The tea-tree.

§ Coffee.

¶ Chocolate.

** Flame is gas, or air, rendered so hot as to become luminous.

in examples of the most felicitous processes of induction, from which the general reader may obtain a view of that beautiful logic, the light of which Bacon first let in on the obscurity in which he found physics involved. And, finally, the whole range of our domestic experience presents a series of familiar and pointed illustrations of the principles to which it leads.

The first and most common effect of heat is to increase the size of the body to which it is imparted. This effect is called *dilatation*, or *expansion;* and the body so affected is said to expand, or be dilated. If heat be abstracted from a body, the contrary effect is produced, and the body contracts. These effects are produced in different degrees, and estimated by different methods, according as the bodies which suffer them are solids, liquids, or airs.

The dilatation of solids is very minute, even by considerable additions of heat; that of liquids is greater, but that of air is greatest of all.

The force with which a solid dilates is equal to that with which it would resist compression; and the force with which it contracts is equal to that with which it would resist extension. Such forces are, therefore, proportional to the strength of the solid, estimated with reference to the power with which they would resist compression or extension.

The force with which liquids dilate is equivalent to that with which they would resist compression; as liquids are nearly incompressible, this force is very considerable.

As air is capable of being compressed with facility, its dilatation by heat is easily resisted. If such dilatation be opposed by confining air within fixed bounds, then the effect of heat, instead of enlarging its dimensions, will be to increase its pressure on the surface by which it is confined.

The works of clocks and watches swell and contract with the vicissitudes of heat and cold to which they are exposed, When the pendulum of a clock or balance-wheel of a watch is thus enlarged by heat, it swings more slowly, and the rate is diminished. On the other hand, when it contracts by cold, its vibration is accelerated, and the rate is increased. Various contrivances have been resorted to to counteract these effects. When boiling water is poured into a thick glass, the unequal expansion of the glass will tear one part from another, and produce fracture. The same vessel contains a greater quantity of cold than of hot water.

If a kettle, completely filled with cold water, be placed on a fire, the water, when it begins to get warm, will swell, and spontaneously flow from the spout of the kettle until it ceases to expand.

If a bottle well corked be placed before the fire, especially if it contain fermented liquor in which air is fixed, the air confined in it will acquire increased pressure by the heat imparted to it, and its effort to expand will at length be so great that the cork will shoot from the bottle, or the bottle itself will burst.

Thus we perceive that the magnitude of a body depends on the quantity of heat which has been imparted to it, or abstracted from it; and as it must be in a state of continual variation, with respect to the heat which it contains, it follows that it must be in a state of continual variation with respect to its magnitude. We can, therefore, never pronounce on the magnitude of any body with exactness, unless we are at the same time informed of its situation with respect to heat. Every hour the bodies around us are swelling and contracting, and never for one moment retain the same dimensions; neither are these effects confined to their exterior dimensions, but extend to their most intimate component particles. These are in a constant state of motion, alternately approaching to and receding from one another, and changing their relative positions and distances. Thus, the particles of matter, sluggish and inert as they appear, are in a state of constant motion and apparent activity.

Since the magnitude of any body changes with the heat to which it is exposed, and since, when subject to the same calorific influence, it always has the same magnitude, these dilatations and contractions, which are the constant effects of heat, may be taken as the measure of the physical cause which produced them. The changes in magnitude which a body suffers by changes in the heat to which it is exposed, are called changes of *temperature;* and the actual state of a body at any moment, determined by a comparison of its magnitude with the heat to which it is exposed, is called its *temperature.* At the same temperature the same body always has the same magnitude; and when its magnitude increases, by being exposed to heat, its temperature is said to rise; and, on the contrary, when its magnitude is diminished, its temperature is said to fall. The variation of magnitude of any body is therefore taken as a measure of temperature; but as it would be inconvenient, in practice, to adopt different measures of temperature, one body is selected by the dilatation and contraction of which those of all other bodies are measured, and with this body a *thermometer*, or measure of temperature, is formed.

The substance most commonly used for this purpose is a liquid metal called *mercury* or *quicksilver.* Let a glass tube of very small bore, and terminating in a spherical bulb, be provided, and let the bulb and a part of the tube be filled with mercury. If the bulb be exposed to any source of heat, the liquid metal contained in it will expand, and, the bulb being no longer sufficiently capacious for it, the column in the tube will be pressed upward to afford room for the increased volume of the mercury. On the other hand, if the bulb be exposed to cold the mercury will contract, and the column in the tube will fall.

If we take another similar instrument, having a bulb of the same magnitude but a smaller tube, the same change of temperature will cause the mercury in the tube to rise through a certain space, and this space will be greater than in the former, in the same proportion as the bore of the tube is smaller, because in this case the actual dilatation of the mercury in both tubes is the same; but this dilatation will fill a more extensive space in the smaller tube. When the bulb, therefore, has the same magnitude, the thermometer will be more sensible the smaller the tube; or, in general, the less the magnitude of the tube, compared with that of the bulb, the greater will be the sensibility of the instrument.

It is evident, therefore, that the same change of temperature would produce very different effects on these two instruments, and the indications of the one could not be compared with those of the other. To render them comparable, it will be necessary to determine the effects which the same temperature will produce on both. Let the two instruments be immersed in pure snow in a melting state. The mercury will be observed to stop in each at a certain height; let these heights be marked on the scales attached to the tubes respectively. Now it will happen that at whatever time or place the instruments may be immersed in melting snow, the mercury will always fix itself at the points here marked. This, therefore, constitutes one of the fixed points of the thermometer, and is called the *freezing point.* Let the two instruments be now immersed in pure water in a boiling state, the height of the barometer being thirty inches at the time of the experiment. The mercury will rise in each to a certain point. Let this point be marked on the scale of each. It will be found that at whatever time or place the instruments are immersed in pure water, when boiling, provided the barometer stand at the same height of thirty inches, the mercury will rise in each to the point thus marked. This, therefore, forms another fixed point on the thermometric scale, and is called the *boiling point.*

The distance between these two points on the two thermometers in question, will be observed to be different. In the thermometer which has a tube with a smaller bore in proportion to its bulb, the distance will be greater than in the other, because the same volume of mercury which forms the dilatation of that liquid from the freezing to the boiling point fills a greater length of the smaller than of the large tube. It is plain, therefore, that since this given difference of temperature causes the column of mercury to rise through a greater space in the one than in the other, the one instrument is properly said to possess a greater sensibility than the other.

Let the intervals on the scale between the freezing and boiling points be now divided into 180 equal parts; and let this division be similarly continued below the freezing point to the place 0; and let each division upward from that be marked with the successive numbers, 1, 2, 3, &c. The freezing point will now be the 32d division, and the boiling point will be the 212th division. These divisions are called *degrees*, and the freezing point is, therefore, 32°, and the boiling temperature 212°.

It is evident, that although the degrees on these two instruments are different in magnitude, still the same temperature is marked by the same degree on each, and therefore their indications will correspond.

The manner of dividing and numbering the scale here described, is that which is commonly adopted in England, and is called Fahrenheit's scale. Other methods have been adopted in France and elsewhere, which will hereafter be described.

Let a mass of snow at the temperature of 0°, having a thermometer immersed in it, be exposed to an atmosphere of the temperature of 80°. As the snow gradually receives heat from the surrounding air, the thermometer immersed in it will be observed to rise until it attain the temperature of 32°. The snow will then immediately begin to be converted into water, and the thermometer will become stationary. During the process of liquefaction, and while the snow constantly receives heat from the surrounding air, the thermometer will still be fixed, nor will it begin to rise until the process of liquefaction is completed. Then, however, the thermometer will again begin to rise, and will continue to rise until it attain the same temperature as the surrounding air.

Heat, therefore, when supplied to the snow in a sufficient quantity, has the effect of causing it to pass from the solid to the liquid state, and while so employed, becomes incapable of affecting the thermometer. The heat thus consumed or absorbed in the process of liquefaction, is said to become *latent*, the meaning of which is, that it is in a state incapable of affecting the thermometer.

The property here described, with respect to snow is common to all solids. Every body in the solid state, if heat be imparted to it, will at length attain a temperature at which it will pass into the liquid state. This temperature is called its *point of fusion*, its *melting point* or its *fusing point;* and in passing into the liquid state, the thermometer will be maintained at the fixed temperature of fusion, and will not be affected by that heat which the body receives while undergoing the transition from the solid to the liquid state.

If water, at the temperature of 60°, be placed in a vessel on a fire having a thermometer immersed in it, the thermometer will be observed gradually to rise, and the water will become hotter, until the thermometer arrives at the temperature of 212°.

Other liquids are found to undergo a like effect. If exposed to heat, their temperatures will constantly rise, until they attain a certain limit, which is different in different liquid; but having attained this limit they will enter into a state of ebullition, and no addition of heat can impart to them a higher temperature. The temperature at which different liquids thus boil is called their *boiling point*.

The melting or freezing point and the boiling point constitute important physical characters, by which different substances are distinguished from each other.

When heat continues to be supplied to a liquid which is in the state of ebullition the liquid is gradually converted into vapor or steam, which is a form of body possessing the same physical characters as atmospheric air. The steam or vapor thus produced has the same temperature as the water from which it was raised, notwithstanding the great quantity of heat imparted to the water in its transition from the one state to the other. This quantity of heat is therefore *latent*.

The abstraction of heat produces a series of effects contrary to those just described. If heat be withdrawn from a liquid, its temperature will first be gradually lowered until it attain a certain point, at which it will pass into the solid state. This point is the same as that at which, being solid, it would pass into the liquid state. Thus water, gradually cooled from sixty degrees downward, will fall in its temperature until it attains the limit of thirty-two degrees; there it passes into the solid state and forms ice; and during this transition a large quantity of heat is dismissed, while the temperature is maintained at thirty-two degrees.

In like manner, if heat be withdrawn from steam or vapor, it no longer remains in the aëriform state, but resumes the liquid form. In this case it undergoes a very great diminution of bulk, a large volume of steam forming only a few drops of liquid. Hence the process by which vapor passes from the aëriform to the liquid state has been called *condensation*.

When a liquid boils vapor is generated in every part of its dimensions, and more abundantly in those parts which are nearest the source of heat; but liquids generate vapor from their surfaces at all temperatures. Thus, a vessel of water at the temperature of eighty degrees will dismiss from its surface a quantity of vapor, and if its temperature be retained at eighty degrees, it will continue to dismiss vapor from its surface at the same rate, until all the water in the vessel has disappeared. This process, by which vapor is produced at the surface of liquids at temperatures below their boiling point, is called *vaporization*.

The process of vaporization is generally going on at the surface of all collections of water, great or small, on every part of the globe; but it is in still more powerful operation when liquid juices are distributed through the pores, fibres, and interstices of animal and vegetable structures. In all these cases, the rate at which the liquid is converted into vapor is greatly modified by the pressure of the atmosphere. The pressure of that fluid retards vaporization, if its effects be compared with that which would take place in a vacuum; but, on the other hand, the current of air, continually carrying away the vapor, as fast as it is formed, in the space above the surface, gives room for the formation of fresh vapor, and accelerates the transition of the liquids to the vaporous state. The prooess of vaporization, thus modified by the atmosphere and its currents, so far as it affects the collections of water and liquids generally in various parts of the earth, is denominated *evaporation*.

The condensation of the vapor, thus drawn up and suspended in the atmosphere by various causes, tending to extricate the latent heat which gives to it the form of air, produces all the phenomena of dew, rain, hail, snow, &c., &c. A slight degree of cold converts the vapor suspended in the atmosphere into a liquid, and by the natural cohesion of its molecules it collects into spherules or drops, and falls in the form of rain. A greater degree of cold solidifies or congeals its minute particles, and they descend to the earth in flakes of snow. If, however, they are first formed into liquid spherules, and then solidified, hail is produced.

Thus there is a constant interchange of matter between the earth and its atmosphere—the atmosphere continually drawing up water in the form of vapor, and, when the heat which accomplishes this is diminished, precipitating it in the form of dew, rain, snow, or hail.

Different bodies are differently susceptible of the effects of heat. To produce a given change of temperature in some requires a greater supply of heat than in others. Thus, to raise water from the temperature of 50° to the temperature of 60° will require a fire of given intensity to act upon it about thirty times as long as to raise the same weight of mercury through the same range of temperature. In the same manner, if various other bodies be submitted to a like experiment, it will be found that to produce the same change of temperature on the same weights of each will require the action of the same fire for a different length of time.

The quantities of heat necessary to produce the same change of temperature in equal weights of different bodies are therefore called the *specific heats* of these bodies. If 1,000 express the specific heat of pure water, or the quantity of heat necessary to raise a given weight of pure water through 1°, then 33 will express the specific heat of mercury, or the quantity of heat necessary to raise the same weight of mercury through 1°; 70 will express the specific heat of tin, 80 of silver, 110 of iron, and so on. The specific heat furnishes another physical character by which bodies, whether simple or compound, of different kinds may be distinguished.

The specific heat of the same body is changeable with its density. In general, as the density is increased, the specific heat is diminished. Now, if the specific heat of a body be diminished, since a less quantity of heat will then raise it through 1° of temperature, the quantity of heat which it actually contains will make it hotter when it is rendered more dense, and colder when it is rendered more rare.

Hence we find that, when certain metals are hammered, so as to increase their density, they become hotter, and sometimes become red hot.

If air be squeezed into a small compass, it becomes so hot as to ignite tinder; and the discharge of an air-gun is said to be accompanied by a flash of light in the dark.

On the other hand, if air expand into an enlarged space, it becomes colder. Hence, in the upper regions of the atmosphere, where the air is not compressed, its temperature is much reduced, and the cold becomes so great as to cause, on high mountains, perpetual snow.

The specific heats of compounds frequently differ much from those of the components. If the specific heat of bodies be greatly diminished by their combination, then the quantity of heat which they contain will render the compound much hotter than the components before the combination took place. If, on the other hand, the specific heat of the compound be greater than that of the components, then the compound will be colder, because the heat which it contains will be insufficient to sustain the same temperature.

Hence we invariably find that chemical combination produces a change of temperature. In some cases cold is produced, but in most cases a considerable increase of temperature is the result.

Heat is propagated through space in two ways: First by radiation, which is apparently independent of the presence of matter, and, secondly, by conduction, a word which expresses the passage of heat from particle to particle of a mass of matter.

The principal properties of heat are so nearly identical with those of light, that the supposition that heat is obscure light is countenanced by strong probabilities. Heat proceeds in straight lines from the point whence it emanates, diverging in every direction. These lines are called *rays* of heat, and the process is called *radiation*. Heat radiates through certain bodies which are transparent to it, as glass is to light. It passes freely through air or gas; it also passes through a vacuum, and therefore its propagation by radiation does not depend on the presence of matter. Indeed, the great velocity with which it is propagated by radiation proves that it does not proceed by transmission from particle to particle.

The rays of heat are reflected and refracted according to the same laws as those of light. They are collected in foci by concave mirrors and convex lenses. These undergo polarization, both by reflection and refraction, in the same manner as rays of light. They are subject to all the complicated phenomena of double refraction by certain crystals, in the same manner exactly as rays of light.

Certain bodies possess imperfect transparency to heat: such bodies transmit a portion of the heat which impinges on them, and absorb the remainder, the portions which they absorb raising their temperature.

Surfaces also possess the power of reflecting heat in different degrees. They reflect a greater or less portion of the heat incident on them, absorbing the remainder. The power of transmission, absorption, and reflection, vary according to the nature of the body and state of its surface, with respect to smoothness, roughness, and color.

Rays of heat, like those of light, are differently refrangible, and the average refrangibility of calorific rays is less than that of luminous rays.

When a body at a high temperature, as the flame of a lamp or fire, is placed in contact with the surface of a solid, the particles immediately in contact with the source of heat receive an elevated temperature. These communicate heat to the contiguous particles, and these again to particles more remote. Thus the increased temperature is gradually transmitted through the dimensions of the body, until the whole mass in contact with the source of heat has attained the temperature of the body in contact with it.

Different substances exhibit different degrees of facility in transmitting heat through their dimensions in this manner. In some the temperature spreads with rapidity, and an equilibrium is soon established between the body receiving heat and the body imparting it. Such substances are said to be *good conductors* of heat. Metals in general are instances of this; earths and woods are bad conductors; and soft, porous, or spongy substances still worse.

When the temperature of a body has been raised to a certain extent by the application of any source of heat, it is observed to become luminous, so as to be visible in the absence of other light, and to render objects around it visible. Thus, a piece of iron, by the application of heat, will at first emit a dull, red light, and will become more luminous as the temperature is raised, until the red light is converted to a clear, white one, and the iron is said to be *white hot*. This process, by which a body becomes luminous by the increase of its temperature, is called *incandescence*. There is reason to believe that all solid bodies begin to be luminous when heated at the same temperature.

The degree of heat of incandescent bodies is distinguished by their color; the lowest incandescent heat is a *red heat*, next the *orange heat*, the *yellow heat*, and the greatest a *white heat*.

The heating powers of rays of light vary with their color, in general those of the lightest color having the most heating power. Thus yellow light has a greater calorific power then green, and green than blue.

Hence the absorption of heat from the same light depends on the color of the absorbing bodies. Those of a dark color absorb more heat than those of a light color, because the former reflect the least calorific rays, while the latter reflect the most.

There are several substances which, when heated to a certain temperature, acquire a strong affinity for oxygen gas; and when the elevation of temperature takes place in an atmosphere of oxygen, or in ordinary atmospheric air, the oxygen rapidly combines with the heated body, and in the combination so great a quantity of heat is evolved that light and flame are produced. This process is called *combustion.* Combustion is, therefore, a sudden chemical combination of some substance with oxygen, attended by the evolution of heat and light.

The flame of a candle or lamp is an instance of this. The substance in the wick, having its temperature raised in the first instance by the application of heat, forms a rapid combination with the oxygen of the atmosphere, and this combination is attended with the evolution of heat, which sustains the process of combustion.

Flame is, therefore, gaseous matter, rendered so hot as to be luminous. There are a few other substances besides oxygen by combination with which light and heat may be evolved, and which may therefore produce combustion. These are the substances called, in chemistry, *chlorine*, *iodine*, and *bromine*; but, as they are not of common occurrence, the phenomenon of combustion attending them may be regarded rather as a subject of scientific inquiry than of practical occurrence. All ordinary cases of combustion are examples of the combination of oxygen with a combustible.

I have thus, in a succinct and clear manner, laid before you the principal phenomena, and explained the most ordinary terms, which I shall have occasion to use in the discourses I intend to deliver on the subject of heat. These explanations will, I trust, greatly facilitate the comprehension of the laws and the narrative of the discoveries which I shall unfold to you.

THE ATLANTIC STEAM QUESTION.

The Project proposed in 1835.—Previous Condition of Steam Navigation in Europe.—Practicability of the Atlantic Voyage not denied or doubted.—Report of the Meeting of the British Association at Bristol.—Extract from the London Times.—Ocean Voyages for Steamers and Sailing Vessels compared.—Effect of the Westerly Winds in the Atlantic.—The British Post Office Contract necessary for the commercial Success of the Project.—Review of the Proceedings since 1837.—Cunard Line of Steamers.—The Support received by them from the British Post Office.—Total Failure of the Project to establish New York and Liverpool Steam-Liners.—Essay on the Question, "Has Atlantic Steam Navigation been Successful?" Published in the London Civil Engineer and Architect's Journal.

THE ATLANTIC STEAM QUESTION.

It is now (1845) just eight years since the project to establish a regular and permanent line of steam communication across the Atlantic was advanced in England, and the support of capitalists largely and urgently solicited for it. Previous to that date, however, the idea had been from time to time started, and the voyage had been made by the partial operation of steam power, nearly ten years before, by the steamship Savannah, across the Atlantic. The practicability of accomplishing a long voyage by the combination of the power of steam and sails had also been experimentally proved by the Enterprise, which had made the voyage from England to India, being occasionally propelled by steam. Generally, however, antecedent to the period I now refer to, steam power had never been regularly and permanently applied to navigation except to voyages of very limited length. A line of steamers had plied regularly between Falmouth and the Ionian islands, which afterward was extended to Alexandria, but this voyage was resolved into a succession of short stages, at each of which relays of fuel were obtained. The steamers usually touched at one of the ports of Spain, and invariably at Gibraltar and Malta. It was, therefore, to be expected that a project so novel and startling as to cross the wide expanse of the Atlantic, in the face of adverse winds almost as permanent as the Trades, should be entertained with caution by the prudent, and regarded with diffidence by the skeptical. Not, indeed, that any who had been conversant with the existing condition of the past history of steam navigation could entertain the least doubt of the abstract practicability of the project. A vessel having as her cargo a couple of steam-engines and some hundred tons of coals, would, *cæteris paribus*, be as capable of crossing the Atlantic as a vessel transporting the same weight of any other cargo. A steam-vessel of the usual form and construction would, it is true, labor under some comparative disadvantage, owing to the obstruction presented by her paddle-wheels and the paddle-boxes which cover them. Still, however, it would have been preposterous to suppose that these impediments could have rendered her passage to New York impracticable. Such a vessel merely transporting her machinery and fuel without working the one or consuming the other, would still make the voyage. That a steamship might be a tolerably good sailing vessel even in the state of advancement to which steam navigation had attained in the year 1837, was proved by the fact that the steam-frigate Medea, one of the most efficient steamers in the service of the Admiralty, accompanied the British fleet many thousand miles propelled by sails, and without working her engines at all. If, then, a steamship viewed merely as a sailing vessel, freighted with engines and coals, could traverse the Atlantic with certainty, how absurd must it have been to suppose that the abstract practicability of such a ship making the voyage to New York, with the aid of her machinery and fuel, as a propelling power, could for a moment be doubted, and how incredible ought it to appear that any individual possessing the most ordinary means of current information, to say nothing of an acquaintance with practical or theoretical mechanics, could ever have maintained that such a voyage was a physical impossibility.

Yet such a statement was not only widely circulated, but almost universally credited. It is publicly known that, at the time I now refer to, I was represented as having stated in a speech made by me at the annual meeting of the British Scientific Association, at Bristol, that such a voyage was a mechanical impossibility—that the project was chimerical—and that we might as well attempt to steam to the Moon as to New York. On the occasion referred to, a discussion took place at Bristol, in which I took a leading part. Projects had been started by two different and opposing interests: one advocated the establishment of a line of steamers between the west coast of Ireland and Boston, touching at Halifax; the other proposed a line direct between Bristol and New York. The project of the latter interest was at the moment the more rife. The keel of the Great Western was laid down. In the preceding year I had brought before the same society, at their meeting in Dublin, the former of these projects, and had strongly advocated it. On the occasion now referred to at Bristol, I again urged its advantages, and by comparison deprecated the project of a direct line between Bristol and New York. When I say I advocated one of these projects, it is needless to add that the popular rumor which unfortunately spread all over the world, that I had pronounced the Atlantic steam voyage impracticable, is utterly destitute of foundation. But that this disavowal of it may not rest alone upon my assertion, I annex here the report of what did actually pass at the Bristol meeting, extracted from the Times newspaper of the 27th of August, 1837.*

* "BRITISH ASSOCIATION—BRISTOL MEETING.

"SECTION OF MECHANICAL SCIENCE—THURSDAY, 25TH OF AUG., 1837.

"(Mr. Davies Gilbert in the chair.)

"Mr. Chatfield read a very long essay on Naval Architecture.

"Mr. Eungs gave a long account of the working of the Cornish steam-engines.

"The section became very impatient, and called for Dr. Lardner.

"Mr. Thomas Moore came into the room, and was received with much applause.

"STEAM COMMUNICATION WITH DISTANT PARTS.

"Dr. Lardner said he could not open the important business which had been appointed for this day, without expressing that, important as it unquestionably was, and involving as it did the interest of large branches of commerce, it should have interfered with another inquiry which, if less attractive for the moment, was in no respect inferior in its ultimate value. The very circumstance of the present and pressing interest which was felt upon this subject of steam communication to distant parts of the world—the fact that already considerable investment of capital had been made in such speculations—was a circumstance which would somewhat embarrass them in arriving at a safe and certain conclusion because it would be obvious that it would, more or less, engender in the minds of a considerable portion prejudices which would be liable to bias them unless they used a good deal of self-control, and brought with it the exercise of their own judgment. He would, therefore, beg of every one, and more especially of those who had a direct interest in the inquiry, to dismiss from their minds all previously-formed judgments about it, *and more especially upon this question, to be guarded against*

That journal sent a special reporter to Bristol, whose report of the discussion appeared the next day but one after it took place, and the general accuracy and fidelity of the reports which appear in that paper are sufficiently acknowledged.

In fact, a doubt had been neither entertained nor expressed by me as to the practicability of establishing a line of steam communication across the Atlantic, but I maintained that much difference of opinion might exist, and in fact such difference did exist, as to what manner of accomplishing that object might best insure certainty, safety, regularity, and profit, without which last element it was evident all others would be unavailing. I contended that, to establish such a line of communication, in the actual condition of steam navigation at that time, so as to combine commercial profit with permanence and regularity, would tax the powers of the steam-engine to the utmost extent of their existing limits, and that accordingly every precaution which skill and ingenuity could suggest in the construction and appointment of the vessels should be taken, and every available means of augmenting the pecuniary returns should be resorted to.

Steam navigation had till then been chiefly confined either to the crossing of narrow seas which separate adjacent countries, such as the Irish channel, the German ocean, the Baltic, the Mediterranean, or to coasting, or such as the voyages between port and port of the British islands and other parts of Europe, and those of the Mediterranean steamers between Falmouth, Gibraltar, Malta, and the Ionian isles.* For such navigation steamships have great and numerous advantages over sailing vessels, more especially for the transport of pas-

the conclusion of mere theory; for if there was one point in practice of a commercial nature which more than another required to be founded on experience, it was this one, of extending steam navigation to voyages of extraordinary length. He was aware that since the question had arisen in that city, it had been stated that his own opinion was averse to it; *that impression was totally wrong;* but he did feel, as steps had been taken to try this experiment, great caution should be used in the adoption of the means of carrying it into effect. Almost all depended on a first attempt: for a failure would much retard the ultimate consummation of their wishes. He believed those in the section who knew him, would readily acquit him of being forward to question the power of steam. He tendered the most unqualified allegiance to the sovereignty of steam, but he tendered the allegiance of a free and thinking subject to a constitutional monarch. He did not bow before the power of steam as an abject slave, and if he found a failure in the administration of that power he attributed it entirely to the ministers. (Cheers.)"

[The report then gives some calculations of the performances of Admiralty steamers, from which the speaker is represented as recommending the coast of Ireland as a point of final departure, in preference to making the voyage in one trip from the shores of England. The report concludes as follows] :—

"He would, therefore, counsel those who proposed to invest capital in this most interesting enterprise, to keep in mind certain points to which he would direct their attention. 1st, He would advise that the measured tonnage should correspond with the tonnage by displacement. 2d, To go to increased expense in using the best coals. 3d, He would earnestly impress upon them the expediency of adopting the paddle-wheels shown in the section yesterday. 4th, He advised the proportion of one-horse power to four tons as the best ratio of power to tonnage. 5th, He would impress upon them the expediency of giving more attention to the selection of engineers and stokers; it was a matter of the last importance and might produce a saving of thirty to forty per cent. With respect to the boilers he would recommend copper ones. Lastly, he would advise the coal boxes to be tanked. (Loud cheers.)

"Mr. Russell would confess he had listened with the greatest delight to the lucid and logical observations they had just heard. He would merely add one word—let them try this experiment with a view only to the enterprise itself, but on no account to try any new boilers or other experiments, but to have a combination of the most approved plans that had yet been adopted. (Cheers.)

"Mr. Brunel then pointed out some errors in the calculations made by Dr. Lardner, which would be in favor of the undertaking: he was convinced that nine or even ten miles an hour might be accomplished, and Dr. Lardner had formed his conclusions upon old vessels, and not from one in which everything was done on the most approved principles yet known, and thus reduced possibility to certainty. (Cheers.)

"Mr. Field said he had made the calculations for the Ordnance on the vessels to Corfu; they were taken upon an average which included the infancy of the undertaking.

"Dr. Lardner in reply said, that *he thought the voyage practicable; but he wished to point out that which would remove the possibility of a doubt,* because if the first attempt failed, it would cast a damp upon the enterprise and prevent a repetition of the attempt."

"This discussion has produced the greatest possible interest."

* The inland navigation of this continent required a form of boat so different, and was attended with such different conditions, as to have no analogy in the question here discussed.

sengers. In confined seas and in coasting, their superior safety was obvious; independent in a great degree of the wind, a steamer fears no lee-shore. If pressed by stress of weather, she has that within her which in most cases will carry her into the safe shelter of any neighboring port. Provided with convenient depots at short distances, she needs not to fill her tonnage with coals, and thereby limit the magnitude and power of her engines, or encroach upon the space which might be profitably occupied by passengers, or by objects of commerce. Supplied, therefore, by abundant mechanical power, she far outstrips all sailing vessels, and puts any such competition completely out of the question.

The steam-engine, however, like an animal, requires that its periods of labor should be of limited duration, and that repose should be allowed at reasonable intervals, during which the machinery should be looked over, cleaned, oiled, and put to rights. The service to which steam-vessels had been previously confined admitted of this, without interruption to the operation of the machinery. The frequent arrivals and the necessary time of remaining in port being generally more than sufficient for these purposes.

How different were the circumstances under which the Atlantic steamers were about to compete with sailing vessels. The dangers of confined seas and coasting navigation no longer menace the majestic ship, which in conscious security seems to triumph in the unlimited expanse of water around her, and to bound with gladness over the ocean swell. No threatening shore is present to call into requisition the peculiar powers of her mechanical rival, no shoals or sand-banks are encountered on which she may be driven by the disobedient wind, and from which her intractable helm and sails cannot save her, but among the intricacies of whose channels the powers of her rival can conduct her with unerring precision.

On the other hand designed expressly by her structure to encounter the tumultuous surface of the ocean, having the skill and experience of a hundred generations of men concentrated to confer on that structure security and defence from the perils of the deep, the sailing vessel has in the ocean storm some advantage as to safety, encumbered as the latter is by her machinery, by the unwieldly projecting masses of her paddle-boxes, and her chimney. The danger of fire and explosion in steamers is another circumstance which must operate more in favor of sailing ships in long voyages than in the service to which steamers had been confined until the epoch we now refer to. When such accidents occurred on board steamships, they were generally run into port or on shore, a source of safety of which the ocean steamers must of course be deprived.

On the occasion now alluded to, namely, in the public discussions which took place in the years 1836 and 1837, I urged all these circumstances and others to demonstrate the necessity, in attempting the grand enterprise contemplated, of calling into requisition every source of safety and efficiency which the most consummate mechanical and nautical skill could supply, and that, although novel expedients should be regarded with caution, still, that the exigency of the case would render it in the last degree imprudent not to give every fair trial to those pretensions compatible with security.

But independently of the considerations above stated, there were others not less imperatively demanding attention and consideration. To secure permanent success, safety, efficiency, and despatch, would not be enough. It was necessary besides that the enterprise should yield a fair profit on the capital it would absorb. I had had abundant professional experience in relation to steam navigation at that time, to be aware of the great magnitude of the expenditure which the proper maintenance of steamships like those necessary for the Atlantic voyage would require, to ensure for them the necessary expedition in their competition with the finest sailing vessels in the world, the Liverpool liners. It would be obviously necessary to supply them with a liberal amount of power in proportion to their tonnage; a very large portion of that tonnage would therefore be occupied by the machinery and fuel. It was therefore apparent that the freight of goods was a source of profit from which they would be almost excluded. Letters, packages, and a limited amount of light goods of such a kind as would bear a high rate of freight, were all that they could look to. Passengers must therefore be their chief source of revenue.

It was farther urged on this occasion by me, that the peculiar physical circumstances of the Atlantic would operate seriously against them in their competition with sailing vessels. It is well known that atmospheric currents prevail upon the Atlantic in these latitudes, blowing from west to east almost as permanently and regularly as that with which the trades blow between the tropics in the contrary direction. In fact these currents are nothing more than the reaction of the trades, by which the general atmosphere recovers its equilibrium. The effect of these currents on sailing vessels is, that while the average trip from Liverpool to New York is completed in 36 days, the average time from New York to Liverpool is under 20 days. Now it was very apparent before Atlantic steam navigation was established, that the steamers would be compelled in the trip from America to Europe to bring down their fares to a level with those of the sailing vessels, or nearly so, for in that trip their peculiar power would not give them such advantage in speed as would secure them, at high fares, the necessary preference. This was strongly urged by me at the time, and the event has verified my anticipations to the letter.

But still I contended that it was extremely doubtful, in the state in which the art of constructing steam-vessels then was, whether, with all the prudence and skill that could be exercised, a permanent and regular line of steamers running through the year between England and New York, or any other port of the United States, would be productive of that commercial profit which would be indispensable to sustain them, unless they should have some considerable revenue to fall back upon, especially in the winter part of the year, besides the utmost that could be expected from cargo and passengers. The source of such support was apparent, and I again and again at public meetings urged that the possession of the British Postoffice contract for conveying the mails, would form an indispensable element in the successful issue of the project; but to obtain this, it was understood that Halifax must be adopted as an intermediate station. The plan therefore that I advocated, both in Dublin, at the meeting of the British Association, in 1836, and subsequently in London, and other principal towns of England, and again at the meeting of the British Association at Bristol, where I have been charged with pronouncing the project impracticable, was to establish a line of steam communication between one of the western ports of Ireland and Boston, touching at Halifax, and thereby securing the contract for the conveyance of the British mails. I proposed that a railway should be constructed between the starting-point in the west of Ireland and Dublin, which, with the Dublin and Liverpool steamers, and the Liverpool, Birmingham, and London railway, would form one great continuous steam highway between the capitals of the new and the old world.

Such were the arguments urged and such the circumstances of the discussions, in which I chanced to have so prominent a share, in the United Kingdom, in the years 1836–'7. Now let us see what has been the result.

The line of Cunard steamers has been established, and has been kept in constant and regular operation for about five years. They have been subsidized by the British Postoffice by an annual stipend of increasing amount; first by $300,000 per annum, which, being found insufficient, has been raised to little less than half a million. They have been admirably built, supplied with the best machinery, manned and officered in the most efficient style, checked by the surveillance of the British government, and surrounded with every provision and precaution which can inspire confidence in the public throughout Europe, of their safety and efficiency; nevertheless, sustained, as they have been, by an endowment so magnificent as that of the Postoffice, and favored by the preference which such guarantees will always produce among the European public, it is understood that the enterprise is not inordinately profitable. I would not be understood here as implying that it is not attended with such results as will secure its continuance—I am persuaded to the contrary; but there are abundant manifestations that the competition of the packet-ships is felt by it with all its overwhelming advantages. Among these indications is the very manifest one that the Boston steamers are compelled to bring down the fare of the returning trip to the level of the liners.

But I am forgetting the projected line of New York steamers. Where is it? We heard it proclaimed trumpet-tongued throughout the land, in 1837, that the sun would not make two courses through the zodiac before a line of steamers would be running once or twice a month throughout the year, between Bristol or Liverpool and New York, which would put an everlasting extinguisher on the far-famed liners; and great was the indignation, bitter the scorn, and biting the irony, with which I was assailed, because I ventured to drop rather an unequivocal hint that I suspected that no such line would be in existence for some years to come, that is to say, if the postoffice line were to work in competition with them. Where then, I ask again and again, is this boasted line? The Great Western commenced her operations in 1838; she was supported by wealthy and enterprising capitalists; her triumphs were sung and shouted throughout the land: where are all the other steamers of the line? But although that company did not deem it prudent to enlarge their investment in this profitable speculation, others, without waiting the result of the experiment, ventured to do so, and some five or six steam-ships were successively placed on the New York line from Liverpool and London. Again and again, I ask, where are they? Echo answers, Where?

But the Great Western has continued, it will be said, to make the voyage with regularity, permanence, and profit. That she has done so with regularity, I will admit. That she has done so with permanence, I deny; for it is notorious that she has suspended her work during the winter season. To what extent she may have been profitable to her owners, will be judged from the fact publicly known, that they have more than once endeavored to get rid of her by public sale, and on a late occasion it was understood that a sale to the British government had been actually completed, but in consequence of some subsequent difference between the parties respecting the conditions on which it was made, the vessel remained on the hands of the original owners. Now, I will venture to ask, what is to be inferred by any unbiased observer of the facts connected with the great Atlantic question? Have the conditions under which the Cunard line of steamers have been established, been necessary or not for the permanent commercial success of the enterprise? We have before us two rival projects; the first started so far back as the year 1837, the second not commenced until 1840. The latter gradually increases the number of its vessels and the frequency of its voyages. At no season of the year does it suspend its operations—accommodating itself to the varying traffic at different seasons by the greater or less frequency of its trips. The second, commencing its operation in 1838, preceded by a loud flourish of trumpets, ends after seven years, as it begun, by running once a month during the summer season, a single steamship, having repeatedly in the interval endeavored to get rid of her. The inference appears to me so plain, that I feel almost compelled to apologise for enlarging on arguments so apparent. It is plain to my mind as the noontide light of the sun, that, in the shape and under the conditions in which it has been attempted between England and New York, the Atlantic steam project has utterly failed.

But in the interval which has elapsed since the Great Western projectors launched their ship, the art of steam navigation applied to sea voyages has been steadily and gradually improved, and the problem, consequently, is now offered to us under conditions different from those by which it was restricted in 1837. Whether ships may not now be constructed which, combining the principal advantages of sailing vessels and steamers, reducing the expense attending their machinery and its management, providing ample and available tonnage for merchandise, abridging in a very considerable degree the length of the voyage westward, and rendering the eastward trip more certain and regular, and to some extent shorter, are questions well entitled to the serious consideration of capitalists. I shall, however, on another occasion, have an opportunity of examining these questions in detail.

[The publishers of this volume, desirous to aid in disabusing the American public of the erroneous impression so long prevalent respecting the declaration imputed to Dr. Lardner, have inserted in the present volume the following essay, evidently proceeding from the pen of a writer of great skill and ability in practical science, which was published in the London Civil Engineer and Architect's Journal early in year 1842. From it the public in this country will see how this question and the share taken in it by Dr. Lardner are now regarded in Europe. In other respects the following essay will be read with much interest bring replete with sound information and practical views.]

HAS ATLANTIC STEAM NAVIGATION BEEN SUCCESSFUL?

ALTHOUGH practical men are usually ready to acquiesce in those deductions of the philosopher which relate to the establishment of abstract principles, they are too apt to resist any attempt to apply those principles to the analysis of the transactions of real life. General truths are usually treated as if they were individual fallacies; and a hypothesis, however just, requires to continue inert in order that it may remain uncensured. All men look upon general rules as being applicable to all cases except those in which their own antipathies or predilections happen to be enlisted, and however clear men's judgments may be upon indifferent topics, they appear incapable of apprehending the force of the plainest argument if establishing a conclusion adverse to their supposed interests. Hence the imperfect success of attempts to fix the current value of political or commercial measures by the aid of philosophical research. Some powerful vested interest is sure to step in to prove, "by most sufficient reasons," that the subject under inquiry is exempt from ordinary jurisdictions—that its peculiar features constitute it a case *sui generis*, which the said vested interest is by far the best qualified to illustrate. Truly, the public has much to be thankful for, from an intervention so discriminating and disinterested.

But the philosophers are sometimes censurable also. There is a philosophical as well as a popular infatuation, the former consisting in unwarrantable generalization, and the latter in irrational speciality. Things alike are yet things different; and although in the generic distribution of a subject it is impossible to take cognizance of minute differences, yet those differences must by no means be disregarded when an individual case is singled out for examination. Philosophers are too apt to pay exclusive regard to leading characteristics—to overlook those limitations and peculiarities which distinguish everything in nature from that which it most nearly resembles, and without an attention to which general rules cannot be rendered strictly applicable to the diversified cases which arise in practice.

The obvious remedy for these evils is for the practical man and the philosopher each to abate somewhat of his characteristic prejudice. Let the practical man trust a little more to reason, and the philosopher a little more to experience, and let the practical man take the proper steps to cure himself of that monomonia which the intermingling of considerations of private interest with philosophical investigation usually generates. He should adopt the synthetic rather than the analytic method of investigation, and should be more intent upon tracing resemblances than in multiplying differences. He should reason from principles to examples rather than from examples to principles, and should regard principles as the exponent of results rather than an attempt to raise results into an antagonism of principles. The philosopher should carefully examine whether the case he has undertaken to investigate be not an exception to a general law—or whether it may not possess such distinctive qualities as may materially modify the final result. He should ascertain the precise point at which the case under review diverges from other cases the most nearly coincident, and should assure himself he has overlooked no circumstance capable of influencing his conclusions. It is only by an observance of these rules that either practical or scientific men may hope to obtain results undistorted by prepossession, prejudice, or passion, and should hope to witness the adoption of these means of arriving at a correct conclusion in the investigation of the merits of Atlantic steam-voyaging, were it not an invariable attribute of keen disputations that the attainment of a correct conclusion is regarded as a matter altogether unimportant.

The clamor and confusion which marked the original discussions relative to Atlantic steam-voyaging have now happily subsided; but, although they made such an unceremonious noise, they have left no very distinct recollection as to what that noise was all about. In truth, it was not very easy to tell that even at the time; for so much of palpable absurdity was mixed up in the doctrines currently attributed to the most distinguished of the disputants, as to destroy in the minds of men unaffected with the steam *rabies*, all confidence in the genuineness of the imputed declarations. Men of penetration, indeed, regarded the representation that suppositions pregnant with absurdity were the sentiments avowed by eminent inquirers, as a sort of *ruse de guerre*, intended to shake the reputation of those whose arguments were unsusceptible of refutation. But the manœuvre was successful—the advocates of the Atlantic enterprise were "willing to swear anything for their client," and the faith of the multitude was equally comprehensive. Many of the absurdities so industriously disseminated as the sentiments of distinguished men, were really in some measure believed to be the veritable doctrines of those eminent persons, and of those who rejected such a supposition but a small proportion was aware of what the actual doctrines really were. We have been at some pains to supply this defect of information from authentic sources; it is our present purpose to state, 1st, the nature of the opinions really entertained upon the subject of Atlantic steam transit antecedently to its establishment; and 2dly, the present condition of the Atlantic enterprise, restricting the meaning of that term to the line of communication between Great Britain and New York, to which it was originally applied.

The discussion of the question of Atlantic steam transit first attracted the public attention during the meeting of the Bristol Association, held at Bristol, in 1836. One party alleged that the establishment of a line of steamers between Great Britain and New York, of sufficient size and power to enable them to perform the passage IN ONE TRIP, would inevitably be a most beneficial speculation. Another party, of which Dr. Lardner was the representative, contended that there were no good grounds for believing that the performance of the voyage IN ONE TRIP was practicable, with sufficient economy to render the enterprise successful; but if the voyage were resolved into suitable stages, the enterprise might then be brought under conditions which promised a fair prospect of a beneficial result. To understand clearly the force of the reasonings, we must first have a clear conception of the capabilities of steam navigation.

If any given steam-vessel, moved according to the ordinary practice, by the conjoined agency of steam and sails, be laden with coals to the extent of her capacity, she will in that state be capable of performing a voyage of a certain determinate length, with her engines acting for the whole time with their full power. Now it is well known that the same vessel is capable of making the same voyage by the agency of sails alone; for, although steam-vessels, when propelled by sails alone, without working their engines, may be inferior in speed or in nautical qualities to an ordinary ship, yet we know that they are capable of performing long voyages unassisted by steam, as has been abundantly proved by the voyages of the Madagascar and other steam-vessels to India, as well as by numerous government and other vessels. Between the performance of this voyage with the greatest expenditure of fuel which will in ordinary circumstances be made, when the engines are worked at their full power, and with the expenditure of no fuel at all, we may manifestly fix upon a given point where the expenditure of fuel during the voyage shall be precisely what we please. For we may either work the engines during the voyage for such a portion of the time as shall exactly consume the quantity of fuel we have fixed upon, or we may work the engines for the whole period of the voyage with such a diminished exertion of power as is capable of being produced by the quantity of fuel we propose to consume. We may, therefore, easily maintain the machinery of a steam-vessel in uninterrupted action for any length of voyage we think proper, provided only that the amount of power exerted by the engines be correspondingly diminished; or, what is the same thing, that the engines be, if worked at their full power, correspondingly small. The question, then, of the practicability of a steam voyage of any length whatever, resolves itself into the practicability of making ships very big and engines very little; a question which it can hardly be supposed any one could be so insane as to contest. Yet even this absurdity has been attributed to Dr. Lardner, who is represented to have said, at the Bristol or Liverpool meeting of the British Association, that for a steamer to reach America was a physical impossibility; and this, too, in the face of the well-known FACT, that the steamers Savannah, Curaçoa, &c., *had already* crossed the Atlantic, long antecedent to the date of the British meeting! And was a falsehood so preposterous believed? *It was—and is probably extensively believed to the present day!!* But it will be objected, "Dr. Lardner said that we might as well attempt to establish a steam communication with the moon as with America." If Dr. Lardner ever made use of any such expression, we presume he only meant to intimate that the Atlantic enterprise was in his opinion a visionary one. When we talk of a bubble speculation, we do not in general mean that the said speculation has reference to the manufacture of hollow aqueous spherules; or if we speak of sunset or sunrise, we are not usually interpreted as expressing our disbelief of the Copernican system; so, in like manner, if we institute an analogy between any given enterprise and a tunnel through the earth, or a railway to the moon, we are usually understood to express our belief that it is of a very hopeless character. Of physical impossibilities we rarely venture to speak—the subject is abstruse. We should not be warranted in saying that, in *rerum natura*, it was a physical impossibility to bore a tunnel through the earth, or, with the assistance of photography, to have a telegraphic communication with the moon, yet we are warranted in treating projects such as these as "trifles light as air," and in associating, by a common figure of speech, projects of which we would express our disapprobation with these unsubstantial fantasies. It is difficult to discover upon what principle Dr. Lardner is to be deprived of the use of the universally-employed language of metaphor, or why a doctrine is to be forced upon him which every man in his senses must utterly disavow. But it appears obvious to us that no very figurative acceptation of the expression attributed to Dr. Lardner is necessary, as will appear plain enough from the following considerations :—

The mere abstract practicability of performing voyages of any length whatever by steam-vessels is so palpable, that it cannot require another remark. But in practice other considerations arise. The vessels must be of a sufficient power to insure a rate of progress considerably superior to that of sailing vessels, and they must be so capacious that while furnishing sufficient stowage room for coals, they will render comfortable accommodations to passengers, and space for a moderate quantity of cargo. These questions being satisfactorily disposed of, another question of still greater consequence presents itself. Will vessels of the size indispensable for long steam voyages, of adequate power, capacity, and accommodation, for the navigation of the track of ocean between Great Britain and New York, in one unbroken voyage, PAY THE PROPRIETORS? The question of success or failure is sooner or later merged into the question of profit or loss.

The profit or loss of steam-voyaging is manifestly a function of a multitude of local and individual circumstances, which are incapable of reduction to any general form of expression. But, *cæteris paribus*, the longer the voyage is without the relays of fuel, the more remote becomes the prospect of a successful result. For, in proportion as the length of the voyage is increased, the size of the vessel suitable for the performance of that voyage must be increased, in a corresponding, though not in the same ratio; and the expense of maintaining steam-vessels of such power and tonnage as to be adapted to the performance of unusually long voyages is such, that scarcely any line of independent unprotected traffic is sufficient to sustain it. It may hence be safely assumed as a general principle, that in cases where the only sources of revenue are the profits upon freight and passengers, and the peculiarities of the voyage at the same time demand the employment of steam-vessels of similar size and power to those constructed for Atlantic voyaging, the success of the enterprise, that is, the continuance of a profitable and satisfactory issue, will be, to say the least of it, as is proper in a case judged *à priori*, exceedingly problematical.

The limitation which exists to ocean steam-voyaging is *expense*, not *impracticability*. This limitation is, in the present state of the art, immovable and inseparable; and the establishment of a steam communication with the moon is quite as feasible, as the profitable extension of steam-voyaging in the present state of the art, to cases to which it cannot profitably be extended. The attempt to surmount the difficulties by shutting our eyes to them, is not only futile, but is, in this case, productive of unmerited disfavor toward steam navigation. For the origination of enterprises which, from their nature, cannot be capable of yielding an adequate profit to render them permanent, destroys public confidence, and fearfully represses the spirit of commercial adventure. There is no achievement which ought to be more grateful to the public acceptation, than the analysis and exposition of such illusive enterprises; yet there is none which frequently obtains a more ungrateful requital. Persecution and calumniation appear to be the heritage of the public benefactor, and the same dark spirit which administered the cup to Socrates and Phocion, is not extinct at the present day. It is the part of philosophy to bear contumely without depression—nor ought the sensibilities of the philanthropist to be frozen by the breath of popular aspersion. If it be beneficent to attempt the dissipation of popular delusion, to continue that attempt unmoved by calumny, violence, and derision, is surely an approach to divinity. We trust that Dr. Lardner may long continue his patriotic endeavors to direct aright the national energies in any question similar to that which forms the subject of the present inquiry. Those energies, if suffered to run to waste, will produce a vegetation which may be fair for a season, but which will inevitably prove itself to be deadly and delusive. Like waters poured out upon the desert, they may cherish flowers pleasing to the eye, but bearing death in their exhalations—trees of luxuriant foliage and majestic stature, but hollow and poisonous within—fruit of tempting appearance, but turning in the grasp to bitterness and ashes.

With a view of assisting our readers to form a correct estimate of the true character of the Atlantic enterprise, we shall recapitulate some of the circumstances attending the discussion of that question. The asperity which characterized the discussion at Bristol, as well as the subsequent discussions at Liverpool and Newcastle, was a prominent feature of the inquiry; the more so, that it happily rarely attaches to statistical and philosophical investigation. The cause of this unbecoming heat has been attributed to the fact of considerable interest having been already enlisted, antecedently to those discussions, in the schemes which Dr. Lardner found himself constrained to condemn. The managers and directors of these several embryo projects, were, it is said, in conformity with our opening exposition of the besetting frailty of practical men, incensed at the application of Dr. Lardner's general conclusions respecting steam-voyaging to this particular case, which they contended ought to be, and was, an exception. It was considered that the clearness of Dr. Lardner's expositions, established a conclusion opposed to their interests, and involved an indirect reflection upon their capacity or disinterestedness, while engineers and other artificers were not without that bias in favor of the Atlantic enterprise which the anticipated fabrication of immense vessels might be expected to create. Though unable to cope with Dr. Lardner in argument, this united party reasonably concluded that Dr. Lardner was entirely wrong, because they were undoubtedly entirely right. They therefore attempted, and not without some temporary success, to undermine his reputation for practical sagacity, by attributing to him sentiments he never entertained, and then showing those sentiments to be altogether fallacious. When the phantoms thus arrayed as if they had been real entities had been valiantly slain, the victory was manifestly won, and was so adjudged by a "discriminating and enlightened public." That the popular voice should have adjudged to the advocates of the Atlantic scheme the superiority in the discussion of that question, is a circumstance which has been supposed to be partly due to the effect which *any* doctrine is capable of creating in the public mind if incessantly insisted on, but chiefly to the contemporaneous development of the most extravagant popular anticipations relative to steam agencies. This species of delusion has been not inappropriately termed the steam mania. During the severity of its paroxysms, projects the most preposterous were received with eagerness and applause, the country was drunk with expectation, and for a time appeared bereft of every atom of its accustomed discretion. In so distempered a state of the public mind, the project of Atlantic steam-voyaging could scarcely fail to attract numerous admirers. The magnitude and grandeur of the enterprise captivated the popular sympathies, while the implicit faith in the omnipotence of steam agencies, smoothed down all difficulties and surmounted all opposition. But, although enthusiasm may win a battle, it is only the material interests of mankind which can keep the field. Reason may be overborne for a season, but it is sure sooner or later to obtain the superiority. A few years of experience generally bring with them the subsidence of the most inveterate popular delusions. Men awake as if from a dream, and it is an honorable trait in the character of public opinion, that it has no resentments to perpetuate, but is desirous to atone for whatever injury its phrensy may have inflicted.

A very clever writer in the Quarterly Review, No. 123 (1838), undertakes to point out the magnificent prospects of Atlantic steam-voyaging, and the advantages direct and consequential which may be fairly expected from it. The period at which this article was written, shortly posterior to the accomplishment of the first voyages of the Great Western, was peculiarly favorable for lending weight to the reviewer's conclusions, and the writer is evidently a man of much general ability.

We shall proceed to make extracts from this article as an example of the arguments adduced in support of the advantage of the Atlantic scheme.

"The effect of this achievement is by no means easily to be described or foreseen. Even the Americans, with all their reputation as a self-possessed and considering people, have displayed unwonted raptures and antics on occasion of the first arrival of the Sirius and Great Western at New York, quite as much so as our Bristol neighbors on their return, and we are not sure that either party is to be blamed for it. We are not sure that the former are far out of their reckoning when they speak of this new epoch in the history of the world. We can enter into the feelings of the myriads who crowded the wharfs at New York when the English boats were hourly expected, when finally, after days of almost breathless watching (which to fearful spirits might well have afforded some pretext for disbelieving the new scheme, some excuse for casting even ridicule on it after all), at length, on the morning of St. George's day, the doubts, the fears, the scorn, were alike destined to be removed for ever from the mind of every living creature (even we dare say, but let us say it with due deference, from that of Dr. Lardner himself), for now appears a long dim train of distant smoke in a somewhat unaccustomed direction; it rises and lowers like a genius in the Arabian nights, portending something prodigious; by-and-by the black prow of a huge steamboat dashes round the point of some green island in the beautiful harbor,

"Against the wind, against the tide,
Steadying with upright keel."

It is not very easy to perceive what these doubts and fears really are, which the first voyage of the Sirius was destined to remove for ever. The doubts and fears of the possibility of a steamer being able to cross the Atlantic? Dr. Lardner can hardly be conceived to have entertained these doubts and fears, for one small reason among many others; the passage across the Atlantic had been accomplished by a steam-vessel about twenty years before. Are the doubts and fears meant to have exclusive reference to the profitable issue of the undertaking? How could the success of any enterprise in steam navigation be ascertained by a single trip?

"The British and American Steam Company, who have just launched at Blackwall a ship thirty-eight feet longer than any in her majesty's navy, notify to us moreover, that next year they mean to have boats like this running on each side, on the 1st and 16th of every month.* This is but one company, one which has not yet moved, we believe, for we understand the Sirius to have

* Where is the line which, by anticipation, was to annihilate the packet-ships?

been sent out by another, and the Great Western, it is well known, belongs to Bristol. Glasgow, too, will no doubt bestir herself, and above all, we must leave room for Liverpool. The sole marvel is, that Liverpool has waited so long, a secret only to be explained by the extent of interest there invested in the American liners. We see that a company is now started at that port who announce immediate operations."

To us it appears still more marvellous that the establishment of Atlantic steam-voyaging should have been accomplished by England *at all*, when America had, palpably, the greatest benefit to receive from the execution of that measure. The Americans would, it is alleged, have taken a share in the Atlantic enterprises had they not built their hopes upon a project which was to send a ship across the Atlantic by the instigation of a barrel of blue vitriol, but which failed. This circumstance is, however, insufficient to account for the torpidity of the Americans, where there is anything expected to be won. Had the expectation of a profitable result been as sanguine in the United States as for some time it was in England, it is the opinion of the best-informed persons that we should not have been left to enjoy the steam monopoly of the Atlantic. The fact appears to be that the Americans were better judges than we were of the amount of profit to be realized by the transport of passengers and light articles of merchandise across the Atlantic, arising in part from the experience they had had of Atlantic steam-voyaging before we began. "Scarce ten years had elapsed after Fulton first committed his little pinnace to the waters of the Hudson, ere the Savannah, a new steam-vessel of 300 tons, crossed from New York to Liverpool, and at several subsequent periods has the voyage been accomplished. The reason why Atlantic steam-voyaging has not grown up among the Americans, may be traced to the conviction that the adventure would not be productive of that honey of Hyblas, vulgarly called MONEY."*

The Quarterly proceeds: "What is to prevent a fair competition now? What account is to be made of a curve or two in a river with steamers 300 feet long, and a speed of fifteen miles an hour, as practical men, best versed in these matters, expect to see in a very few years? And, indeed, the American boats upon the Hudson having been running at much more than this rate for years." We confess we should like some verification of all this before we believe it. Our readers may try their penetration upon the following, which appears to us mere childishness :—

"We were speaking, however, of the first sensation the achievement has produced, and which we venture to predict will, at some future day, be a matter of no little historical curiosity. The New York editors seem scarcely able to contain themselves; 'Side by side with the old world at last,' says one—'Now then for the coronation,' cry half a dozen more—and then the files of European journals unrolled! Fifteen days from Bristol! &c., &c. A revolution this, such as the world rarely sees, even in our eventful age—a revolution thoroughly overturning the old systems of most of the business world at least—yet effected, as it were, instantaneously, and without one drop of blood!"

The following is a magnificent example of that figure of speech usually termed nonsense :—

"Some one has predicted, that presently, we shall have Covent Garden market stocked by the other continent. As to the floral department, there may be something in it, for aught we know, and indeed for some others too, for if the 'liners' could bring *the Duke* a present of fresh venison from his western admirers, we certainly get a clear vision here of divers good things to come. We say nothing, however, even of Yankee ice dropped in dog-days, at sunrise, upon every door-step in London as in Boston—not one word. '*Nil admirari*,'

* Thoughts on Steam Locomotion. Weale, 1840.

we repeat, is our motto; 'keep cool,' that is, ice or no ice—dog-days and all."

But, further: "It is only thirty years since Fulton ascended the Hudson with his boat. In 1810 there was no such thing in all England, and as late as 1820 there were only thirty-five. The most important improvements, also, have been *very* recently introduced, and without particularizing these, it is sufficient to say that the learned Dr. Dionysius Lardner's miscalculations on this subject of Atlantic navigation has evidently been caused by almost wholly overlooking these same improvements, even so far as some years past are concerned (and a year, in such a progress as this agent is making, is a matter not to be overlooked), or regarding them too much as mere speculations, not likely, or not yet fully proved to be capable of great practical effects (as they have already been), while as relates to what may yet be established, though now it is but experimental; or of what may be discovered of which nobody now dreams, the calculations in question have apparently left no lee-way for the ingenuity of our successors, or even our contemporaries. It was taken for granted that all had been done which could be done—that there were no 'hidden powers' hereafter to be brought to bear upon steam navigation, as well as upon other things, and to supersede steam itself, altogether. How grand a mistake this was, we need not say; let us beware of its being made again."

In reference to this statement, it is proper to observe that Dr. Lardner's deductions relative to the Atlantic enterprise were formed, as we shall presently have occasion to show, more in detail, from the performance of the Medea, and that the Medea was at that time the most perfect existing steam-vessel, in reference to the distance over which she might be propelled by a given quantity of fuel per horse-power.

In regard to the omission of "lee-way," in his computation, it is difficult to see upon what grounds the admission of such an element could be justified. Atlantic steam-voyaging, in the year 1836, either was or was not beneficially accomplishable. The point was evidently alone capable of being determined by a comparison of the difficulties of the enterprise with the existing capabilities of steam-voyaging; and how were the existing capabilities of steam navigation to be ascertained, except by a reference to the performances of the best existing steam-vessels? If Dr. Lardner did this, he did all he was called upon to do. He was not called upon to say that Atlantic steam-voyaging would be profitable in 1836 because the progress of improvement might, perhaps, render it so in ten years' time, or in ten months' time. It would have been highly unphilosophical to have based computations upon circumstances which were not really existent. No man can say, that in any branch of science or art, all has been done that can be done; but it is quite enough to adopt discoveries when they have been actually found out.

Once more: "It cannot be doubted, we think, that the passage of the Atlantic by steam will, even in the coming ten years, be brought to a state of (so to speak) artistical luxury and perfection of which those who have started the enterprise themselves little think." Alas! alas! how has this prediction been verified!

But we cannot enter upon a subject so agonizing as the loss of the President—the wounds are not yet cicatrized, but bleed afresh at the tenderest touch. The wail of the widow and the orphan—of the affianced bride, and the childless father—is yet sounding in our ears, and memory rekindles emotions which are only to be assuaged by time the comforter. The repetition of such calamities is now, Heaven be praised! unlikely. And, oh! what *can* be the reflections of those, if any such there be, by whom the one dire calamity has been directly or indirectly superinduced? Can anything be more reprehensible than that reckless precipitation which not merely sets at naught all considerations of failure and ruin, but tampers without compunction with the lives of the best and noblest of the land?

Having, in the preceding pages, adverted on several occasions to what Dr. Lardner did *not* say, we shall now attempt to show the nature of the opinions respecting the Atlantic enterprise he *really did* entertain. We are, fortunately, in possession of an authentic and well-known record upon this subject in the shape of an article written by Dr. Lardner for the Edinburgh Review, and which will be found in the 131st number (1837) of that publication. From this article we shall make considerable extracts.

"The imposing mechanical phenomena so rapidly and unexpectedly developed by the invention and improvement of the locomotive steam-engine, and its application to railways have, for years, so engrossed public attention, that other means for facilitating the operations of commerce and expediting the social intercourse of distant masses of people, less fascinating, perhaps, but not important, have been comparatively overlooked. The subject of water transport by steam has, from this cause, received less than its due share of attention. A reaction, however, appears to have been recently produced, and we have now a swarm of projectors much more largely supplied with zeal than knowledge, who, not content with advancing in the march of improvement with that calm deliberation and salutary caution so necessary to insure a permanently profitable issue for any great undertaking, would rush to their ends without ever informing themselves of the means at their disposal, and proceed, *per saltum*, from a channel trip to the circumnavigation of the globe.

"Within the last year considerable public attention has been directed to the question of the practicability and advantage of establishing a line of steam communication between Great Britain and the United States, and various projects have been started and companies formed for the construction of vessels for that purpose, several of which are already in a state of forwardness. At a meeting of the British Scientific Association, held at Bristol last September, one of the topics which engrossed a large share of interest was the question of the practicability of a steam-voyage across the Atlantic, raised in the mechanical section. The statement laid before that section by Dr. Lardner obtained such publicity, at the time, through the press, that it would be superfluous to recapitulate its arguments. The conclusions, however, to which he arrived, were briefly these: That *in the present state* of the steam-engine, as applied to nautical purposes, he regarded a *permanent* and *profitable* communication between Great Britain and New York by steam-vessels making the voyage IN ONE TRIP, as in a high degree improbable; that since the length of the voyage exceeds the present limits of steam-power, it would be desirable to resolve it into the shortest practicable stages, and therefore, that the most eligible point of departure would be the most western shores of the British Isles, and the first point of arrival the most eastern available port of the western continent; and that under such circumstances the length of the trip, though it would come fully up to the present limit of this application of steam-power, would not exceed it, and that we might reasonably look for such a degree of improvement in the efficiency of marine engines, as would render such an enterprise permanent and profitable."

Dr. Lardner then goes on to state that it had been objected to his conclusions that the data whence they were derived had been obtained from the performance of steam-vessels antecedently to 1834, whereas considerable improvement was alleged to have been effected in steam-machinery, which, by diminishing the consumption of fuel, was considered to have improved the prospects of Atlantic steam-voyaging. Of all the vessels then existing, the

Medea was universally allowed to be the one which was capable of being propelled over the greatest distance with a given quantity of coals per horse-power; she was therefore the most favorable actual standard by which prospects of the Atlantic enterprise could be measured, and was adopted as the basis of the present inquiry. Dr. Lardner then proceeds to show that the same conclusion respecting the Atlantic enterprise, which he had already deduced from the performances of vessels antecedently to 1834, was also deducible from the performances of the Medea and of other vessels between 1834 and 1837.

The misconception which has existed respecting Dr. Lardner's opinions upon this subject, and which nothing short of misrepresentation prepense was sufficient to have created, renders it here proper to repeat that the limits which exist to the achievement of steam-power are not imposed by any abstract impracticability of performing steam-voyages of any length whatever, but by the impracticability of *rendering those voyages sufficiently profitable to confer permanency upon enterprises in steam navigation.* The doctrine attributed to Dr. Lardner, that a steam-vessel (or any vessel) if only seaworthy, was incapable of proceeding from Great Britain to the coast of North America, *is so palpably absurd, that it scarcely deserves to be noticed.*

Dr. Lardner has however offered the following observations upon the subject, which we extract from the Monthly Chronicle, Vol. II., 1838:—

"A vessel having as her cargo a couple of steam-engines and some hundred tons of coal, would be, *cæteris paribus*, as capable of crossing the Atlantic as a vessel transporting the same weight of any other cargo. A steam-vessel, it is true, would labor under some comparative disadvantage, owing to the obstruction presented by her paddle-wheels and the paddle-boxes which cover them; still, however, it would be preposterous to suppose that these impediments would render impracticable her passage to New York. If, therefore, such vessel merely transported her machinery and fuel, without working the one or consuming the other, she would still make the passage. That a steam-vessel may be a tolerable good sailing-vessel, is proved by the fact that the steam-frigate Medea, one of the most efficient steamers in the service of the admiralty, accompanied the fleet many thousand miles propelled by sails, and without working her engines at all. If, then, a steamship, viewed merely as a sailing-vessel, freighted with engines and coals, can traverse the Atlantic with certainty, how absurd is it to suppose that the abstract practicability of such a ship making the voyage to New York with the aid of her machinery and fuel, can for a moment be doubted!

"In fact, *no doubt has been entertained or expressed as to the practicability of establishing a communication between these countries and New York, by a line of steam-vessels. But a difference of opinion has been entertained as to what mode of accomplishing the object may best insure certainty, safety, regularity, and profit, without which last element it is presumed the other objects could hardly be secured.*"

Returning from this digression to the Edinburgh Review, we find Dr. Lardner explaining the inconveniences to which extended steam-voyages are subject, arising from the incrustation of salt in the boilers, the deposition of soot in the flues, and other matters of that nature, to which we consider it unnecessary more particularly to refer. He then proceeds:—

"The several circumstances to which we have adverted, constitute difficulties having the general tendency to abridge the practical extent of an uninterrupted steam-voyage. There remains a still more serious impediment to the extension of steam navigation inherent in the very substance from which the engine at present derives its mechanical power—an impediment which places a definite and assignable limit, beyond which it is mechanically impossible to extend the voyage of a steamer (of ordinary construction). To form an estimate, therefore, of the major limit of the extent of a continuous steam-voyage, it will be necessary that we should examine, 1st, The proportion in which the capacity of the vessel may be distributed between the machinery, the fuel, and the objects of commercial transport; and 2d, The rate at which the fuel will be consumed in propelling the vessel over a given distance, regard being had to her tonnage and power.

"Assuming that a certain extent of the capacity of the vessel is appropriated to the mechanical means of propelling her, that portion will obviously be shared between the machinery and the fuel by which that machinery is moved.

"The proportion in which this space should be distributed between the machinery and the fuel will vary according to the length of the voyage. As the fuel may be replaced at the end of each trip, and as it is generally advantageous to give the vessel as powerful machinery as the extent of her capacity will admit, it is obviously expedient to reserve as limited a space as possible for the fuel, and to give a proportionably increased extent of room to the machinery. In the shortest class of voyages, therefore, a smaller supply of fuel being sufficient, a larger space must be appropriated to the machinery, and in proportion as the length of the voyage is increased, the quantity of space necessary for the fuel will be augmented, and that allotted to the machinery diminished. To this there must be an evident limit, inasmuch as the space for the machinery must be sufficiently extensive to contain engines of the power necessary to encounter the difficulties of the navigation and to insure an average rate of progress greater than that of sailing-vessels."

This limit, be it observed, is *one of expediency*—not of abstract *practicability*. To state the matter in other words—a certain determinate proportion must be observed between the power and tonnage, else the vessel will be incapable of carrying coals enough for the voyage, or her speed will be so defective as to give her no prominent advantage over sailing-vessels. And the adherence to this proportion involves the necessity of employing vessels of such magnitude as to be of too expensive maintenance for the profit of an ordinary trade. For, as in a symmetrical vessel the resistance increases nearly as the square of the increment of one dimension, and the capacity nearly as the cube of the increment of the same dimension, so it is in a certain point only in the divergence of those series where a result is attainable answerable to the conditions indispensable to Atlantic steamers. And that point is so high up in the series, the resistance and capacity are both so great as to indicate the necessity of employing those leviathan vessels whose voracious appetite is unappeased by the expenditure of all the proceeds of any merely commercial enterprise.

"To arrive at a practical conclusion as to the major limit of a probable steam-voyage under average circumstances of wind and water, it will be obviously necessary that we should obtain some probable approximative estimate of the impulsive virtue of a given quantity of coals of average quality. The consumption of coals, other circumstances being the same, will be proportional to the power of the engine, and it will therefore be sufficient to determine what is the average rate of hourly consumption for each horse-power in the machinery."

A table of the performances of a number of different vessels between 1834 and the date of the Bristol meeting, but which we consider it unnecessary to insert here, shows that the locomotive duty of the Medea was greater than that of any of the rest; the locomotive duty as defined by Dr. Lardner being "the distance over which a ton of coals per horse-power is capable of propelling a vessel."

Dr. Lardner proceeds: "To enable us to establish an analogy between the performances of these vessels and the circumstances under which a steamer would be placed in navigating the Atlantic, it will be necessary to explain some physical phenomena attending that ocean.

"The general atmospheric currents which prevail in directions near and parallel to the equator, from east to west, called the *trade-winds*, would have a tendency to produce a derangement in the atmospheric equilibrium, if not redressed by a contrary effect elsewhere. It is known that these remarkable winds are produced by the influence of the solar heat upon the atmospheric belt included between the tropics, combined with the diurnal motion of the earth from west to east. The heated air pressed upward by its buoyancy is replaced by currents from either hemisphere, which, carrying with them a less diurnal motion than that proper to the tropics, a relative atmospherical motion is produced in a direction contrary to that of the earth's rotation. Hence a nearly permanent wind is produced on each side of the line from east to west. As these currents approach the line, they gradually acquire the motion of the surface, which, combined with their mutually counteracting effect, produces those calms which prevail about the line, and which are only interrupted by the hurricanes, whirlwinds, and other violent atmospheric commotions, which are produced where the contrary tropical currents conflict before their force is sufficiently moderated.

"The stagnant atmosphere thus collected at the line, ascending by the effect of solar heat returns from the upper regions toward the poles, and coming upon the surface in either hemisphere, brings with it the diurnal motion of the equator, which being greater than that of the higher latitudes, prevailing winds are produced from the west. The agency of these causes is manifested in the westerly winds which prevail almost uniformly throughout the Atlantic between the shores of Europe and those of North America. There are other physical causes which mingle their effects with those to which we have just adverted. The extensive regions of North America covered with immense fresh-water lakes and primeval forests supply a current of cold air rushing into the warmer strata over the track of ocean between the Azores and the American coast. This current from the northwest consequently modifies the reaction of the trades, just explained; the result is wind blowing generally in the westerly direction, but varying between northwest and southwest, and sweeping across the face of the Atlantic throughout nearly the whole year.

"Atmospheric difficulties are not the only ones which the navigator has to encounter who crosses this extensive tract of water. The well known Gulf-stream is a great ocean-current issuing from the channel which separates Florida from the Bahama banks, taking first a direction little to the east of north, and becoming more and more westerly, until it approaches within a short distance of the tail of the great bank of Newfoundland, where it sets in due east to the Azores. The width of this current, at first one degree, gradually increases until it exceeds two degrees. Independently of the difficulty presented by the stream itself, the zone of the ocean marked out by it is characterized by weather so extremely unfavorable to navigation, that it is cautiously avoided by all outward-bound vessels. They invariably either take a course so far north as to be clear of its influence until they approach the western shores, where, by taking a southerly direction, they convert the westerly winds into favorable gales; or on the other hand, proceed first southward till they get beyond the lower limits of the Gulf-stream, and taking advantages of the trades, make the western coast. This latter, however, is a route never adopted by the best class of New York packets except they are reduced to a disabled state.

"The westerly winds which we have described as prevalent across the Atlantic, are accompanied by a heavy sea, which is subject to scarcely any subsidence or intermission. In land-locked seas, such as the Mediterranean, and the channels which intersect contiguous islands, the effect of the wind in raising the waters is rapid, and produces a short and chopping sea highly unfavorable to steamers; but these effects speedily subside, and, in the Mediterranean especially, they produce but a slight influence upon the average rate of vessels when that average is computed from long-continued performances. On the other hand, the long swell of the Atlantic is not so unfavorable during its operation, but its effects are incessant, and considerably more disadvantage to a steamer will be produced by its continuance than any which the occasional roughness of the more contracted seas to which we have referred could give rise to."

It is right to observe that a "short chopping sea" is a relative term having reference not merely to the nature of the waves, but the size of the vessel. That which is a long swell to a row-boat is a short unfavorable sea to a small vessel, and that which is a long swell to a small steamer, or even to a steamer of 500 or 600 tons, may be a short chopping sea to one of 2,000 tons. The swell of the Atlantic, therefore, may be of as prejudicial a quality to the large Atlantic steamers as that of the Mediterranean and of the channels is to the smaller vessels navigating those waters.

Another formidable objection to Atlantic steam-voyaging arises from the overwhelming force of the Atlantic storms. The shock of masses of water roused into a most violent commotion by the accumulated momentum of every wave in the whole three thousand miles of foaming waters is nearly irresistible, and is productive of the most injurious effects to vessels of large dimensions impelled by immense steam-power. We ourselves happened to see the Liverpool in dock after an exposure to one of these Atlantic storms, and she was really little better than a wreck. The straining she had undergone was inconceivable; the seams of the deck had opened greatly, a great part of the copper had been detached from the bottom of the vessel, in consequence of the irregular movement of the planking to which it had been nailed, and the oakum hung out of many of the seams in the exterior of the vessel, even below the water line, from which the great straining had displaced it. The "British Queen" it is well known has been similarly injured upon more than one occasion, and the frames of the engines of the Great Western have been all broken by the working of the ship. The wear and tear arising from this source is infinitely more to a long, large steamer, than to a compact, well-built ship; and the danger resulting from the same cause is most irresistible. The icebergs which are not unfrequent in the latitude of Newfoundland are another source of danger, and the dense fogs met with in the same regions are highly unfavorable to steam navigation; while the consequences of fire, a by no means uncommon visitation in steam-vessels, in the midst of the Atlantic, are appalling to contemplate. Several of these obstacles are manifestly irremovable, and are, therefore, only capable of being regarded as neutralizing to a certain extent, the benefit, if any, of the scheme. But others, and those the most formidable, are susceptible of diminution by the division of the voyage into suitable stages.

"Seeing, then, the unfavorable aspect under which the project of establishing an uninterrupted line of steam navigation between Great Britain and New York presents itself, let us consider whether by resolving the voyage into the shortest possible stages, the enterprise may be brought under more promising conditions. For this purpose it is obvious that the most western coast of the British Isles should be taken as the point of final departure. The west coast of Ireland would, therefore, be naturally selected, fringed as it is by numerous spacious and well-sheltered harbors. St. Johns, Newfoundland, is the most western port; but this harbor is attended with so many nautical difficulties that it could scarcely be regarded as accessible with that certainty which such a line of communication would require. Newfoundland presents an iron-bound coast; and even Nova Scotia should be avoided were it possible to extend the passage: but the distance from the west coast of Ireland to Halifax comes up to the extreme limit of a (profitably) practicable steam passage. *We greatly fear that any attempt to supersede the necessity of making Halifax a stage must prove* ABORTIVE;" that is to say, if commercial advantage be considered, and if the project be not regarded as a mere mechanical experiment.

In conclusion, Dr. Lardner observes: "Let us, however, not be misunderstood. That the passage from Liverpool to New York cannot be made in one run by a steamship, we do not maintain." But he declares his conviction that, as a *permanent, practical, profitable* thing, Atlantic steam-voyaging will not and cannot be, in the present state of the arts, successful, unsupported by some extrinsic aid from government. And this conclusion he is content to avow, notwithstanding its unpopularity.

"In confessing then, as we do, after the most careful and an anxious inquiry respecting this interesting question, our fears of the result of such an enterprise greatly preponderate over our hopes, we are sensible of expressing an unpopular opinion. It is the natural and fortunate tendency of the human mind to anticipate success, and we ourselves shared this feeling when we commenced the present investigation—we were wholly unaware to what point results since ascertained would lead us."

We shall offer no further remarks respecting Dr. Lardner's statements, which are well able to speak for themselves, but shall at once proceed to the second part of our subject, viz., the determination of the present condition of the enterprises for maintaining a steam communication between Great Britain and New York. This may, perhaps, best be shown by an enumeration of the several vessels which have been employed upon that line, and the mode of their respective disposition.

Vessel	Disposition	
Sirius	withdrawn.	
Royal William	withdrawn.	
Great Liverpool	transferred	Now maintaining steam communication with India, via the Red sea.
United States (now Oriental)	transferred	
British Queen	sold.	
President	lost.	
Great Western	for sale	Said to be.
Great iron steamer	unfinished	

The HALIFAX line, which carries out Dr. Lardner's recommendations to a certain extent, alone thrives; yet it has been questioned if even *it* could continue to keep the field without the aid it derives from the conveyance of the mails, unless it were to make the western coast of Ireland the point of final departure. The question might be worth considering by the proprietors of the Halifax packets, as well as by the West India Mail Packet Company, whether it would not be greatly to their advantage if all of their vessels were to make the western coast of Ireland their point of arrival and departure. But should the managers of those companies think differently, should the shareholders resolve, in spite of common sense and Dr. Lardner, to throw thousands upon thousands of pounds sterling into the gulf of DIRECT communication, they are quite welcome, for aught we care, to continue to indulge so reasonable a predilection.

There is one circumstance connected with the preceding table of the manner in which the vessels are employed in the Atlantic enterprise, which affords an example so striking of the coincidences between the deductions of philosophy and the results of experience, that, although it has no immediate reference to the present subject, we cannot permit this opportunity to pass without saying a word respecting it. Dr. Lardner, it is well known, did not confine his inquiries to Atlantic steam-voyaging; he also discussed the merits of steam communication with India, via the Red sea; and it may be satisfactory collaterally, to ascertain what his opinions were respecting that line of intercommunication. We shall find those opinions stated in his letter to Lord Melbourne, published in 1837, from which we extract the following passage:—

"It has been contended that the question should not be regarded as one to be determined merely upon a calculation of profit; that, on the contrary, it is one with which great political and social interests are interwoven so closely, that it ought to be adopted even though its entire cost should have to be defrayed by the nation. This principle has been implicitly admitted in the resolution of the select committee of 1834, and it has been explicitly avowed by the late governor-general, by several honorable members of the legislation and of your lordship's administration. But it is a principle which I think it unnecessary to discuss in the present case, because *there is no proposition, however self-evident, which carries to my mind a more clear conviction than I have that this measure, if efficiently carried into operation, will more than return its own expenses.*"

Here is an opinion diametrically opposite to that delivered respecting Atlantic voyaging. Let us inquire how far this conclusion is borne out by experience.

The "Great Liverpool" having in a single season earned a LOSS to her proprietors of six thousand sterling, upon the New York line, it was determined to withdraw her, and, with another new vessel built for Atlantic voyaging, now the Oriental, to open a communication with India, via the Red sea. The proprietors of the British Queen, who, we have been informed, have sustained a loss of about *sixty thousand pounds* in Atlantic steam transit, became competitors with the Great Liverpool and Oriental for the Alexandrian line, plainly showing that both of those, after a vast expenditure of money, had arrived at the very conclusion that Dr. Lardner held three or four years before. Has it never occurred to the proprietors of those vessels that they might have saved about £100,000 as well as vast responsibility, anxiety, risk, and discredit, if, at the commencement of the Atlantic discussions, they had prevented their passions from exercising their favorite calling, that of running away with their reason?

A recent meeting of the proprietary of the Peninsular and Oriental Steam Navigation Company enables us to state, that Oriental steam-voyaging has been highly successful; and this result has been attained with the same vessels and by the same management that were incapable of realizing anything but loss on the New York line. It is plain, from this result, that the Atlantic enterprise did not fail from mismanagement, even were we not assured as we are that Mr. Carleton and mismanagement are altogether incompatible. Can a coincidence such as this, between prediction and reality, be merely fortuitous?

Has the establishment of the several lines of steam communication between Great Britain and New York been productive of a permanently profitable issue? We leave the verdict to our readers, our part being merely to furnish such remarks and data as may conduce to the attainment of a just conclusion. Had we set out with a different resolution we might perhaps have given it as our opinion that the Atlantic scheme had proved itself a signal failure—that Dr. Lardner's views had been confirmed with singular exactness—that

> "Earth has its bubbles as the water hath,
> And this is of them."

But we originally said, as we now repeat, that we do not mean to divulge our own opinion.

One consummation, then, is devoutly to be wished, namely, that Dr. Lardner will soon return to this country to resume the wand which, like Prospero's, none but its master can wield. We can see no other antidote against that worst of Egyptian plagues, the swarms of vermin with which the track of practical philosophy is now overrun. We are death-sick of the reign of minute philosophers. If the choice rested with us, we would say, Give us back our wolves again—restore the dominion of barbarism—curse us with anything but the cant of philosophical imposture—the disgusting egotism of idiotic mountebanks. Dr. Lardner's return to England would be the death-warrant of all such quacks, which is of itself a sufficient reason to inspire the ardent desire that his return will not be much longer delayed.

GALVANISM.

Origin of the Discovery.—Galvani Professor at Bologna.—Accidental Effect on Frogs.—Ignorance of Galvani.—His Experiments on the Frog.—Accidental Discovery of the Effect of Metallic Contact.—Animal Electricity.—Galvani Opposed by Volta.—Volta's Theory of Contact Prevails.—Fabroni's Experiments.—Invention of the Voltaic Pile.—La Couronne de Tasses.—Napoleon's Invitation to Volta.—Physiological Effects of the Pile.—Anecdote of Napoleon.—Decomposition of Water.—Cruickshank's Experiments.—Davy commences his Researches.—Effect of Chemical Action discovered.—Ritter's Secondary Pile.—Calorific Effects of the Pile.—Hypothesis of Grotthus.—Davy's celebrated Bakerian Lecture.—Prize awarded him by the French Academy.—His Discovery of the Transferring Power of the Pile in Chemical Action.—His Electro-Chemical Theory.—Decomposition of Potash and Soda.—New Metals, Potassium and Sodium.—Discovery of Barium.—Strontium, Calcium, and Magnesium.—Rapid Discovery of the other new Metals.—Dry Piles.

GALVANISM.

THE investigation of the mechanical phenomena of material substances has been, in modern works, conducted by resolving these effects into two principal divisions; those in which the bodies exhibiting them are at rest, and those in which they are in motion. As applied to solid bodies, these divisions have been respectively denominated STATICS and DYNAMICS;* and, as applied to fluids, HYDROSTATICS and HYDRODYNAMICS. Electricity being assumed to be a physical agent, having the properties of an elastic fluid, and capable, like the grosser solids and fluids, of being maintained in a state of equilibrium by the mutual action and reaction of antagonist forces, or of moving in definite directions, and forming currents of greater or less intensity, the analysis of its effects would naturally be conducted by means of the same classification; and, accordingly, that division of the science in which the electric fluid is considered in a state of equilibrium or repose, and in which the physical conditions on which such equilibrium depends are investigated, would be denominated ELECTRO-STATICS, while that in which the effects of currents of electricity are considered, would be called ELECTRO-DYNAMICS.

REST being in its nature more simple than MOTION, and the cases of forces mutually destructive of each other's influence, and therefore productive of equilibrium, being more simple than those in which motion ensues from the combined action of forces differing from each other in various respects, it was natural that, in every part of physics, the principles of statics should be first established and understood. Such has been accordingly the course which the progress of discovery has taken in other branches of natural philosophy, and electricity is not an exception to it. All the phenomena which have been hitherto adverted to in this notice belong properly to ELECTRO-STATICS. In all of them the electric fluid is contemplated in a state of equilibrium; or if its motion be occasionally considered, it is only in sudden and momentary changes from one state of equilibrium to another. Thus, when a Leyden jar is char-

* The terms STEREO-STATICS and STEREO-DYNAMICS would be preferable.

ged, the positive electricity accumulated on the inner surface of the glass is maintained there, in spite of the tendency it has to escape in virtue of its self-expansive property, by the attraction of the negative electricity accumulated on the external surface. When a communication is made between the internal and external surfaces by a metallic wire, this state of equilibrium ceases; the positive fluid of the inner surface runs along the wire in one direction, and the negative fluid of the external surface runs along it in the other direction, until each neutralizes the other, and a new state of equilibrium is established by the actual combination of the two fluids. If this change occupied a sensible interval of time, and it were required to investigate the effects which would be produced during that interval either on the jar and wire, or on any bodies which might be within their influence, the question would properly belong to ELECTRO-DYNAMICS; but in fact the discharge, as it is called, or the transition from the one state of equilibrium to the other, is instantaneous, and the same may be said of all the phenomena which form the subject of the preceding pages.

In the commencement of this notice, the frequent influence of circumstances, apparently fortuitous, on the progress of discovery in the sciences, has been mentioned. It would be difficult, either in the history of the sciences or of the political growth of states, to find a more signal example of this than was offered by the discovery of that powerful instrument of physical investigation, the VOLTAIC PILE. "It may be proved," says M. Arago, "that this immortal discovery arose in the most immediate and direct manner from a slight cold with which a Bolognese lady was attacked in 1790, for which her physician prescribed the use of *frog-broth*."

Galvani was professor of anatomy at Bologna. At the period just mentioned, it happened that several frogs, divested of their skins, and prepared for cooking the broth prescribed for Madame Galvani, lay upon a table in the laboratory of the professor, near which at the moment stood an electrical machine. One of the professor's assistants, being employed in some process in which the machine was necessary, took sparks occasionally from the conductor, when Madame Galvani was astonished to see the limbs of the dead frogs convulsed with movements resembling vital action. She called the attention of her husband to the fact, who repeated the experiment, and found the motions reproduced as often as a spark was taken from the conductor. This was the first, but not the only or chief part played by chance in this great discovery.

Galvani was not familiar with electricity. Had he been so, he would have seen in the convulsions of the frog evidence of nothing more than a high electroscopic sensibility in the nerves of that animal, and an interesting example of the known principle of *electrical induction*. But luckily for the progress of science, he was more an anatomist than an electrician, and beheld with sentiments of unmixed wonder the manifestation of what he believed to be a new principle in the animal economy, and, fired with the notion of bringing to light the proximate cause of vitality, engaged with ardent enthusiasm in a course of experiments on the effects of electricity on the animal system. It is rarely that an example is found of the progress of science being favored by the ignorance of its professors.

Chance now again came upon the stage. In the course of his researches he had occasion to separate the legs, thighs, and lower part of the body of the frog from the remainder, so as to lay bare the lumbar nerves. Having the members of several frogs thus dissected, he passed copper hooks through part of the dorsal column which remained above the junction of the thighs, for the convenience of hanging them up till they might be required for the purposes of experiment. In this manner he happened to suspend several upon the iron balcony in front of his laboratory, when, to his inexpressible astonishment, the limbs were thrown into strong convulsions. No electrical machine was now present to exert any influence.

If the supply of capital facts be occasionally due to chance, or to the Being by whom what is miscalled chance is directed, it is to the operation of the faculties of exalted minds that the development of the laws of nature is due: if rude lumps of the natural ore of science be now and then thrown under the feet of philosophy, the discovery of the vein itself, its depth and direction, its quality and value, the separation of the precious metal it contains from its baser elements, the demonstration of its connexion with the phenomena of nature, and its adaptation to the uses of life, are all and severally the work of that noble faculty of intellect, that image of his own essence, which the Creator of the universe has impressed upon man, and which is never more worthily exercised than in the investigation of those laws of the material world, in all of which, whether they affect the vast bodies of the universe, or the imperceptible molecules of those around us, there is ever conspicuous a provident care for the wellbeing of his creatures.

In the convulsions of the frog, suspended by a copper wire on an iron rail, Galvani saw a *new fact*, and soon discovered that the circumstance on which it depended was the simultaneous contact of the metals with the nerves and muscles of the animal. He found that the effects were reproduced whenever the muscles touched the iron while the nerves touched the copper, but that contact with the copper alone did not produce them. He next placed the body of the animal upon a plate of iron, and touching the plate with one end of a copper wire, brought the other end into contact with the lumbar nerves. The convulsions followed as before. Galvani inferred from these and other similar experiments and observations, that the conditions under which the phenomenon was produced were, that a connexion should be made between the nerves of the animal and the muscles with which those nerves were united by a continued line or circuit composed of two different metals; and he explained this singular effect by assuming, hypothetically, that, in the animal economy, there exists a natural source of electricity; that, at the junction of the nerves and muscles, the natural electricity is decomposed; that the positive fluid goes to the nerve, and the negative to the muscle; that the nerve and muscle are therefore analogous to the internal and external coating of a charged Leyden jar; that the metallic connexion made between the nerve and the muscle in the experiments above-mentioned serves as a conductor between these opposite electricities; and that, on making the connexion, the same discharge takes place as in the Leyden experiment.

This theory fascinated for a time the physiologists. The phenomena of animal life had been ascribed to an hypothetical agent, which passed under the name of the "nervous fluid." The Galvanic theory consigned this term to the obsolete list; and electricity was now the great vital principle, by which the decrees of the understanding, and the dictates of the will, were conveyed from the organs of the brain to the obedient members of the body. Those who know how passionate is the love of a theory which appears to give a satisfactory account of effects otherwise mysterious, and how much more gratifying to the *amour-propre* it is to be able to connect effects with supposed causes, than to be compelled to view the former as the real limits of our knowledge, will understand the reluctance with which the Bolognese school and its distinguished leader would surrender a theory so dazzling as animal electricity; nevertheless it was doomed soon to fall under the irresistible assaults of physical truth directed against it by a giant intellect, which, though located in a little village of the Milanese, belonged to mankind.

Volta, professor of natural philosophy at Como, and subsequently at Pavia, had been already known for his researches in different parts of physics, but more especially in electricity. The Bolognese experiments naturally engaged his attention, and it was not long before his superior sagacity enabled him to perceive that the theory of Galvani was destitute of any sound foundation. Indeed, a single experiment was sufficient to overturn it, though not to carry conviction of its futility to the minds of its partisans. Volta applied the metals in contact with each other to the muscle alone, without touching the nerves, and the convulsions nevertheless ensued. The analogy of the muscle and nerve to the Leyden phial was no longer tenable. Volta transferred this analogy to the two metals, and contended that the mutual contact of two dissimilar metals must be regarded as the source of the electricity; that by the contact the natural electricity was decomposed, and the positive fluid passed to one metal, and the negative one to the other; and that the muscle merely played the part of a conductor in carrying off one of the fluids thus developed.

To this Galvani replied by showing that, when a single metal was used to connect the nerves and muscles the convulsions ensued, and that therefore the contact of dissimilar metals could not be the source of the electricity. Volta rejoined, that it was impossible to be assured of the perfect homogeneity of the metal, and that any the least heterogeneous matter contained in it would be sufficient for his hypothesis. Also, that when a single metal was used, the convulsions were uncertain, and never produced, except in cases where the organs were in the highest state of excitability; whereas, on the contrary, they happened invariably, and were long continued, when the connexion was made by two dissimilar metals.

Tenacious of this cherished theory to the last, Doctor Valli, a partisan of Galvani, confounded the advocates of the school of Pavia, by showing that, by merely bringing the muscles themselves into contact with the nerves, *without the intervention of any metal whatever*, the convulsions ensued. To this—the expiring effort of the Bolognese party—Volta readily and triumphantly replied, that the success of the experiments of Valli required two conditions: first, that the parts of the animal brought into contact should be as heterogeneous as possible; and, secondly, the interposition of a third substance between these organs. This, so far from overturning the theory of Volta, only gave it increased generality, showing, as it did, that electricity was developed, not alone by the contact of two dissimilar *metals*, but also by the contact of dissimilar substances not metallic.

From this time, the partisans of animal electricity gradually diminished, and no effort worth recording to revive Galvani's theory was made. Meanwhile, the hypothesis of Volta was, as yet, regarded only as the conjecture of a powerful and sagacious mind, requiring nevertheless much more cogent and direct experimental verification. This experimental proof he soon supplied.

The first analogy which Volta produced in support of his *theory of contact* was derived from the well-known experiment of Sulzer. If two pieces of dissimilar metal, such as lead and silver, be placed one above and the other below the tongue, no particular effect will be perceived so long as they are not in contact with each other; but if their outer edges be brought to touch each other, a peculiar taste will be felt. If the metals be applied in one order, the taste will be acidulous; if the order be inverted, it will be alkaline. Now, if the tongue be applied to the conductor of a common electrical machine, an acidulous or alkaline taste will be perceived, according as the conductor is electrified positively or negatively. Volta contended, therefore, that the identity of the cause should be inferred from the identity of the effects; that, as positive electricity produced an acid savor, and negative electricity an alkaline, on the conductor of the machine, the same effects on the organs of taste produced by the metals ought to be ascribed to the same cause.

However sufficient this analogy might seem to the understanding of Volta, it was insufficient for the rigid canons of the logic of modern physics, and he accordingly sought and obtained more direct and unequivocal proof of his hypothesis. Two disks, one of copper and the other of zinc, were attached to insulating handles, by means of which they were carefully brought into contact, and suddenly separated without friction. They were then presented severally to a powerful condensing electroscope. The usual indications of electricity were obtained, and it was shown that this electricity was positive on the zinc, and negative on the copper. By repeating the contact, and collecting the electricity by means of the condenser, sparks were produced, and the demonstration was complete.

That the contact of dissimilar metals was followed by the evolution of electricity, could therefore no longer be doubted. It will, however, hereafter appear that philosophers are not even yet agreed that the contact is the immediate or the only cause of the disengagement of electricity in such cases. Chemical agency is now known to be one of the sources of electricity ; and its operation is so subtle, often so imperceptible, and generally so inevitable, when heterogeneous molecules come into contact, that doubts have been entertained whether, in every case where electricity *seems* to proceed from contact, it has not really its origin in feeble and imperceptible chemical action.

Although the complete development of this last-mentioned idea belongs to a much more recent epoch in the progress of electrical discovery, yet the chemical origin of electricity did not altogether escape notice even at the period to which we now refer.

Of the numerous philosophers in every part of Europe who took part in the discussions, and varied and repeated the experiments connected with these questions, one of those to whom attention is more especially due was Fabroni, who, in the year 1792,* two years after the discovery of Galvani, communicated his researches to the Florentine Academy. In this paper is found the first suggestion of the chemical origin of Galvanic electricity.

Fabroni observes that in the mutual contact of heterogeneous metals there is a reciprocal action which favors chemical change ; that to this action must be ascribed many well-known phenomena, such as the more rapid oxydation of certain metals when combined, or in mere contact with other metals. According to him, a metal, like all chemical reagents, has a tendency to combination with another metal when they are brought into contact ; that this effect is only prevented by the superior force of cohesion which prevails among the particles of each. This cohesive force will, however, be lessened in its energy by the antagonism of the attraction of the molecules of the two metals toward each other, just in the same manner as it would be lessened by the action of heat. Being thus lessened, its opposition to the tendency which the particles of either metal have to combine with oxygen, taken either from the atmosphere, or obtained from the decomposition of water, would be proportionally diminished, and such oxydation would accordingly be promoted. In this way Fabroni accounted for the tendency of certain alloys of metal to oxydation, and for the well-known fact that iron nails, then used in attaching the copper sheathing to vessels, were rendered so liable to rust by their contact with the copper, that they became soon too small for the holes in which they were inserted. He supposed, therefore, that in the experiments of Galvani and Volta, in which the convulsions of the limbs of animals were produced, a chemical

* The date of the researches of this philosopher is generally, but erroneously, assigned to the year 1799.

change was made by the contact of one of these metals with the liquid matter always found on the parts of the animal body; and that the immediate cause of the convulsions was not, as supposed by Galvani, due to animal electricity, nor, as assumed by Volta, to a current of electricity emanating from the surface of contact of the two metals, but to the decomposition of the fluid upon the animal substance, and the transition of oxygen from a state of combination with it to combination with the metal. The electricity produced in the experiments Fabroni ascribed entirely to the chemical changes, it being then known that chemical processes were generally attended with sensible signs of electricity. He maintained that the convulsions were chiefly due to the chemical changes, and not to the electricity incidental to them, which, if it operated at all, he considered to do so in a secondary way.

The necessary limits of this notice will not allow of a further analysis of the researches of this philosopher; but if his original papers be referred to, it will be seen that he is entitled to the credit of having first distinctly demonstrated the chemical origin of Voltaic electricity.

In the year 1800, the attention of the scientific world was withdrawn from the controversy respecting the origin of Galvanic electricity, and all other matters of minor importance, and engrossed by one of those vast discoveries which constitute an epoch in the progress of knowledge, and give a new direction to the sciences. On the 20th of March, 1800, Volta addressed a letter to Sir Joseph Banks, then president of the Royal Society, in which he announced to him the discovery of the VOLTAIC PILE, one of the most powerful instruments for the investigation of the laws of nature, as exhibited in the mutual relations of the constituent parts of matter, which ever did honor to the science of any age, or any nation.

In order to complete the experimental analysis of the effects of Galvanic electricity, Volta felt the necessity of collecting it in much greater quantities than could be obtained in the processes which had then been adopted. According to his theory, when two plates of metal, zinc and copper for example, were brought into contact, two currents of electric fluid originated at their common surface, and moved from that point in opposite directions. The positive fluid passed along the zinc, and the negative along the copper. If the extremities of the two metals most remote from their mutual contact were connected by an arc of conducting matter, these contrary currents would flow along this arc, the positive fluid moving from the zinc toward the copper, and the negative from the copper toward the zinc; but the intensity of these currents was supposed to be so feeble that no ordinary electroscope, whatever might be its sensibility, would be affected by it. In order to bring into operation in this question those instruments which had been applied to common electricity, he therefore sought some expedient by which he could combine, and, as it were, *superpose* two or more currents, and thus multiply the intensity, until it should attain such an augmentation as to produce effects analogous to those which had been obtained by ordinary electricity.

With this object, he conceived the idea of placing alternately, one over the other, disks of different metals, such as zinc and copper. Let us suppose the lowest disk to be copper, having a disk of zinc upon it. On this disk of zinc let a second copper disk be placed, and over that a second disk of zinc, and so on. According to Volta's theory, currents of electricity would be established at each surface of contact of the two metals, the positive current running along the zinc, and the negative along the copper. With the arrangement above described, there would proceed from the first surface a negative downward, and a positive upward current; from the second a positive downward, and a negative upward current; from the third a negative downward, and a positive upward current, and so on: the downward current being negative, and the upward positive from the upper surface of each copper disk, and the upper current being negative and the downward positive from the lower surface of such disk. It is evident, therefore, that the downward currents would be alternately positive and negative; and the same would be the case with the upward currents. Now, since the surfaces of contact of the metals would be equal, these currents would have equal intensities, and accordingly each positive current would neutralize each negative current having the same direction. The result would be, that if the lowest and highest disk of the pile were of the same metal, all the currents neutralizing each other, the pile would evolve no electricity whatever; and if they were of different metals, all the downward currents, except one, would neutralize each other, and that one would be positive. The effect of the pile would therefore be the same as if it consisted of only two disks, one of copper, and the other of zinc.

Volta therefore saw the necessity of adopting some expedient by which all the currents in the same direction should be of the same kind; so that, for example, all the descending currents should be negative, and all the ascending currents positive. If this could be accomplished, the current issuing from the bottom of the pile would be a negative current as many times more intense than one proceeding from a single pair of disks as there were surfaces of contact supplying currents, and the same would be true of the positive current issuing from the top of the pile.

To effect this, it was necessary to destroy the Galvanic action at all those surfaces from which descending positive and ascending negative currents would proceed; that is, the lower surfaces of the copper disks and the upper surfaces of the zinc disks. But while this was effected, it was also essential that the progress of the descending negative and ascending positive currents should still be uninterrupted. The interposition of any substance which would have no sensible Galvanic action on either of the metals between each disk of copper and the disk of zinc immediately below it would attain one of these ends, since the action of all the surfaces in which ascending negative or descending positive currents could originate would thus be prevented. But in order to allow the free progress of the remaining currents in each direction, such substance must be a sufficiently free conductor of electricity. Volta selected, as the fittest means of fulfilling these conditions, disks of wet cloth. They would be free from any sensible Galvanic action on the metal, and their moisture would give them sufficient conducting power.

Having discovered the principles by which this species of electricity can be accumulated in quantity and strong currents obtained, he varied its form, and contrived the apparatus which is known by the name of *La Couronne de Tasses*. This arrangement, which Volta himself most commonly used in his experiments, consisted of a circle of cups filled with warm water, or a solution of sea-salt. He immersed in each cup a plate of zinc and one of silver, not in contact, and then established a metallic communication by means of wire between the zinc of one cup and the silver of the adjacent one. The positive fluid was found to proceed from the extreme zinc plate, and the negative from the extreme silver one, and a continuous current was obtained by connecting these by any conductors of electricity.

Profoundly impressed with the importance of the results likely to arise from the application of the powers of the pile in physical inquiries, and doubtless animated by the desire for which he was honorably distinguished to extend all possible encouragement and advantage to those engaged in the natural sciences, Napoleon, then first consul, and surrounded by the splendor of his southern triumphs, invited Volta to visit Paris; and there, at the Institute, before the *élite* of European philosophers, to explain personally his great invention, and expound his views as to its probable uses and powers as an instrument of scientific research. Volta accepted the proffered honor, and, in 1801, attended at three meetings of the Academy of Sciences, at which he explained his theory of contact, and developed his views respecting the *Voltaic*, or, as he called it, *electro-motive*, action of different metals upon each other. Among the audience at these memorable meetings was NAPOLEON himself, and none present appeared to appreciate more justly the vastness of the power which was on that occasion placed in the hands of the experimental philosopher.

When the report of the committee on the subject was read, the FIRST CONSUL proposed that the rules of the Academy, which produced some delay in conferring its honors, be suspended, and that the gold medal be immediately awarded to Volta, as a testimony of the gratitude of the philosophers of France for his discovery. This proposition being carried by acclamation, the hero of a hundred fields, who never did things by halves, and who was filled with a prophetic enthusiasm as to the powers of the pile, ordered two thousand crowns to be sent to Volta the same day from the public treasury, to defray the expenses of his journey.* He also founded an annual medal, of the value of three thousand francs, for the best experiment on the electric fluid, and a prize of sixty thousand francs to him who should give electricity or magnetism, by his researches, an impulse comparable to that which it received from the discoveries of Franklin and Volta.

The relation in which the Voltaic pile stood in reference to the Leyden jar and electrical machines now began to be perceived. In the latter apparatus a great quantity of electricity is accumulated on the surfaces of the jar, and held there in equilibrium, the positive fluid on one side of the glass, and the negative on the other. When the communication is made between the two surfaces, a torrent of the fluid precipitates itself instantaneously along the line of communication, and the electrical equilibrium is re-established in an interval of time so short as to be inappreciable. A sudden, instantaneous, and violent effect is produced on whatever bodies may be exposed to the transit of this electric fluid. On the other hand, the Voltaic pile is a generator of electricity, which supplies to its opposite poles the two fluids, the positive and the negative electricity, in a continued, gentle, and regulated current. It discharges it not suddenly or instantaneously, or with uncontrollable and irresistible violence, but with gentle, moderate, continued, and regulated action. What takes place in the Leyden jar in an interval so brief as to render observation of its progress, or examination of its successive effects, impossible, is with the pile spread over as long an interval as the observer may desire. Besides this, the effects themselves consequent on the two modes of action are different. That which in mechanical phenomena is effected by a violent blow or concussion, is not more different from the effects of a long-continued action of a uniform accelerating force or a constant pressure, than are the effects of the common electrical discharge from those of the currents of electricity propagated between the poles of the pile.

The physiological effects of electricity exhibited under these different forms, differ in a manner which might be anticipated from these modifications in the transmission of the electric fluid. If the wires proceeding from the opposite poles, and conducting the contrary currents of fluid, be taken in the hands, the sudden and violent shock of the Leyden jar is no longer felt. It is replaced by a continued convulsion in the arms and shoulders, which does not cease so long as the wires are held.

* Arago, Eloge de Volta, p. 42.

If a metallic plate, in connexion with the positive pole, be applied to the tongue, and another connected with the negative pole to any other part, a strong acidulous savor is perceived. If the plate applied to the tongue be connected with the negative pole, a strong alkaline savor is felt.

It is not the organs of taste only which are sensible to the influence of this instrument. The sense of sight is susceptible of its operation in a manner even more wonderful. Let a metallic surface connected with one of the poles be applied to the forehead, the cheek, the nose, the chin, or the throat; and, at the same time, let the patient take in his hand the wire connected with the other pole. Immediately a light will be perceived, even though the eyes be closed, the splendor and appearance of which will vary with the part of the face in contact with the metallic plate. By similar means, the perception of sound will be perceived in the ears.

The action of the pile on the animal body after the vital principle is destroyed is so well known, that it is scarcely necessary to mention it here. The trunk of a decapitated body will rise from its recumbent posture; the arms will move and strike objects near them; the legs will elevate themselves with a force súfficient to raise considerable weights; the breast will heave as if respiration were restored; and, in fine, all the vital actions will be manifested with terrific and revolting precision.

In the hands of the entomologist, the pile affords results not less interesting. The glow-worm, submitted to the electric current, shines with increased splendor; the grasshopper chirps, as if under the action of a stimulant.

The physiological action of the pile was strongly suggestive of a mysterious connexion between the electric fluid and the proximate principle of vitality. When some of these effects were exhibited to Napoleon, the emperor turned to Corvisart, his physician, and said, "Docteur, voilà l'image de la vie: la colonne vertébrale est la pile; le foie, le pôle negatif; la vessie, le pôle positif." †

The invention of the pile had been scarcely more than hinted at, when that course of electro-chemical investigations began which soon led to the magnificent discoveries of Davy, and the series of experimental researches which have been continued to the present time with results so remarkable by those who succeeded him. The first four pages only of the letter of Volta to Sir Joseph Banks were despatched on the 20th of March, 1800; and as these were not produced in public till the receipt of the remainder, the letter was not read at the Royal Society, or published, until the 26th of June following. The first portion of the letter, in which was described generally the formation of the pile, was shown in the latter end of April by Sir Joseph Banks to some scientific men, and among others to Sir Anthony (then Mr.) Carlisle, who was engaged at the time in certain physiological inquiries. Mr. W. Nicholson, the conductor of the scientific journal known as *Nicholson's Journal*, and Carlisle, constructed a pile of seventeen silver half-crown pieces alternated with equal disks of copper and cloth soaked in a weak solution of common salt, with which on the 30th of April they commenced their experiments. It happened that a

* Eloge, p. 33.

† This anecdote was told by Chaptel, who was present on the occasion, to Bequerel; and the latter relates it in the first volume of his work on electricity, published in 1834. The idea that electricity is the immediate principle of vitality has occurred to other minds. Sir John Herschel, in his Preliminary Discourse published in the Cabinet Cyclopedia in 1830, without any knowledge of the above anecdote, says (p. 343), "If the brain be an electric pile constantly in action, it may be conceived to discharge itself at regular intervals, when the tension of the electricity developed reaches a certain point, along the nerves which communicate with the heart, and thus to excite the pulsation of that organ. This idea is forcibly suggested by the view of that elegant apparatus, the dry pile of De Luc, in which the successive accumulations of electricity are carried off by a suspended ball, which is kept by the discharge in a state of regular pulsation for any length of time." A similar idea occurred to Dr. Arnott, and is mentioned in his Physics.

drop of water was used to make good the contact of the conducting wire with a plate to which the electricity was to be transmitted; Carlisle observed a disengagement of gas in this water, and Nicholson recognised the odor of hydrogen proceeding from it. In order to observe this effect with more advantage, a small glass tube, open at both ends, was stopped at one end by a cork, and being then filled with water was similarly stopped at the other end. Through both corks pieces of brass wire were inserted, the points of which were adjusted at a distance of an inch and three quarters asunder in the water. When these wires were put in communication with the opposite ends of the pile, bubbles of gas were evolved from the point of the negative wire, and the end of the positive wire became tarnished. The gas evolved appeared on examination to be hydrogen, and the tarnish was found to proceed from the oxydation of the positive wire. It was inferred that the process in which these effects were produced was the decomposition of water. This took place on the 2d of May, shortly after the receipt of the first portion of Volta's letter.

To ascertain whether the oxydation of the positive wire was an effect incidental to the experiment, or had an influence in producing the decomposition, Nicholson determined to try the effect of wires formed of metal more difficult of oxydation. Wires of platinum were accordingly inserted through the corks, and the experiment repeated. Bubbles of gas were now evolved from both wires. Two platinum wires were next inserted at the closed ends of two separate tubes, which, being open at the other ends and filled with water, were inserted in the same vessel of water. Being placed side by side close together, and the wires being continued to the lower ends of the tubes, so that the distance between their points was not more than two inches, their upper extremities were put in connexion with the ends of the pile. Gas was evolved from the points of both wires, and, ascending through the water, was collected separately in the two tubes. These gases being examined, proved to be hydrogen from the negative, and oxygen from the positive wire, nearly in the proportion known to constitute water.*

Thus was the decomposing power of the pile established within a few weeks after the first intimation of the invention of that instrument had been received in England, and before any description of it had been published. It seemed proper to give these details here, not only on account of the great importance of the discovery, but because it has been sought to depreciate the merit of it by ascribing it altogether to chance. It is probably impossible to exclude chance altogether from such investigations, but in this there was as little as is generally found.

When these experiments became known, Mr. W. Cruickshank, of Woolwich, repeated them, and obtained similar results; but observed that when the distilled water was tinged with litmus, the effects of an acid were produced at the positive, and those of an alkali at the negative wire. Led by this indication, he tried the effects of the wires on solutions of acetate of lead, sulphate of copper, and nitrate of silver. In each case he found the metallic base deposited at the negative pole, and the acid manifested at the positive pole. Muriate of ammonia and nitrate of magnesia were next decomposed, the acid as before going to the positive, and the alkali to the negative pole. These experiments of Mr. Cruickshank were made as early as June, 1800.†

In the September following, Mr. Cruickshank published the continuation of his researches,‡ in which he corroborated the results of his former experiments, showing more generally the tendency of oxygen and the acids in Voltaic decomposition to collect round the positive wire, and hydrogen, metals, alkalies, &c., round the negative pole.

* Nicholson's Journal, vol. iv., p. 179. 1800. † Ibid., p. 187. ‡ Ibid., p. 254.

The investigations of which the pile became the instrument now began to assume an importance which rendered it necessary to give it considerably augmented power, either by increasing its height or enlarging its component plates. In either case, inconveniences were encountered which imposed a practical limit on the increase of its power. When the number or magnitude of the metallic disks was considerable, the incumbent pressure discharged the liquid from the intermediate disks of cloth or card. The trouble of refilling it whenever its use was required, and of wetting the cloth or card, was very great. Mr. Cruickshank, adopting the principle of Volta's *couronne des tasses*, proposed, as a more convenient form for the apparatus, an arrangement consisting of a trough of baked wood, which is a non-conductor of electricity, divided by parallel partitions into a series of cells. Into these cells the liquid to be interposed between the successive pairs of metallic plates was poured. A series of rectangular plates of metal, alternately zinc and copper, were arranged so as to be parallel to each other, and at such a distance as to allow the partitions of the trough to pass between each pair of plates. This modification rendered the Voltaic apparatus capable of having its power increased without practical limit.

While these investigations were proceeding, Ritter, afterward so distinguished for his experimental researches, but then young and unknown, made various experiments at Jena on the effects of the pile; and, apparently without knowing what had been done in England, discovered this property of decomposing water and saline compounds, and of collecting oxygen and the acids at the positive, and hydrogen and the bases at the negative pole. He also showed that the decomposing power in the case of water could be transmitted through sulphuric acid, the oxygen being evolved from a portion of water on one side of the acid, while the hydrogen was produced from another separate portion of water on the other side of it.*

When the chemical powers of the pile became known in England, Sir Humphry (then Mr.) Davy was commencing those labors in chemical science which subsequently surrounded his name with so much lustre, and left traces of his genius in the history of scientific discovery which must remain as long as the knowledge of the laws of nature is valued by mankind. The circumstance attending the decompositions effected between the poles of the pile which caused the greatest surprise, was the production of one element of the compound at one pole, and the other element at the other pole, without any discoverable transfer of either of the disengaged elements between the wires. If the decomposition was conceived to take place at the positive wire, the constituent appearing at the negative wire must be presumed to travel through the fluid in the separated state from the positive to the negative point; and if it was conceived to take place at the negative wire, a similar transfer must be imagined in the opposite direction. Thus, if water be decomposed, and the decomposition be conceived to proceed at the positive wire where the oxygen is visibly evolved, the hydrogen from which that oxygen is separated must be supposed to travel through the water to the negative wire, and only to become visible when it meets the point of that wire; and if, on the other hand, the decomposition be imagined to take place at the negative wire where the hydrogen is visibly evolved, the oxygen must be supposed to pass invisibly through the water to the point of the positive wire, and there become visible. But what appeared still more unaccountable was, that in the experiment of Ritter it would seem that one or other of the elements of the water must have passed through the intervening sulphuric acid. So impossible did such an invisible

* Nicholson's Journal, vol. iv., p. 511.

transfer appear to Ritter, that at that time he regarded his experiment as proving that one portion of the water acted on was wholly converted into oxygen, and the other portion into hydrogen.*

This point was the first to attract the attention of Davy, and it occurred to him to try if decomposition could be produced in quantities of water contained in separate vessels united by a conducting substance, placing the positive wire in one vessel and the negative in the other. For this purpose, the positive and negative wires were immersed in two separate glasses of pure water. So long as the glasses remained unconnected, no effect was produced; but when Davy put a finger of the right hand in one glass and of the left hand in the other, decomposition was immediately manifested. The same experiment was afterward repeated, making the communication between the two glasses by a chain of three persons. If any material principle passed between the wires in these cases, it must have been transmitted through the bodies of the persons forming the line of communication between the glasses.

The use of the living animal body as a line of communication being inconvenient where experiments of long continuance were desired, Davy substituted fresh muscular animal fibre, the conducting power of which, though inferior to that of the living animal, was sufficient. When the two glasses were connected by this substance, decomposition accordingly went on as before, but more slowly.

To ascertain whether metallic communication between the liquid decomposed and the pile was essential, he now placed lines of muscular fibre between the ends of the pile and the glasses of water respectively, and at the same time connected the two glasses with each other by means of a metallic wire. He was surprised to find oxygen evolved in the *negative*, and hydrogen in the *positive* glass, contrary to what had occurred when the pile was connected with the glasses by wires. In none of these cases did he observe the disengagement of gas either from the muscular fibre or from the living hand immersed in the water.

In October, 1800, after many experiments on the chemical effects of the pile, Davy commenced an investigation of the relation which its power had to the chemical action of the liquid conductor on the more oxydable of its metallic elements. The influence of chemical decomposition in evolving the Voltaic electricity originally maintained by Fabroni, was again brought under inquiry by Colonel Haldane. Davy showed that at common temperatures zinc, connected with silver, suffers no oxydation in water which is well purged of air and free from acids; and that with such water as a liquid conductor, the pile is incapable of evolving any quantity of electricity which can be rendered sensible either by the shock or by the decomposition of water; but that if the water used as a liquid conductor hold in combination oxygen or acid, then oxydation of the zinc takes place, and electricity is sensibly evolved. In fine, he concluded that the power of the pile appeared to be, in great measure, proportional to the power of the liquid between the plates to oxydate the zinc.†

He inferred from these results that although the exact mode of operation could not be accounted for, the oxydation of the zinc in the pile, and the chemical changes connected with it, were *somehow the cause of its electrical effects.*

To ascertain whether a liquid solution capable of conducting the electric current between the positive and negative wires of a Voltaic pile, but not capable of producing any chemical action on its metallic elements, would, when used between its plates, evolve electricity, Davy constructed a pile in which the liquid was a solution of sulphuret of strontia. When the current from an active pile was transmitted through the liquid, the shock was as sensible as if the

* Nicholson's Journal, vol. iv., p. 512.

† Nicholson's Journal, vol. iv., p. 337.

communication had been made through water; but, on the other hand, solutions of the sulphurets were incapable of acting chemically on the zinc. If, therefore, chemical action on the zinc be a necessary condition to ensure the activity of the pile, such an arrangement must be inactive. Twenty-five pairs of silver and zinc plates, erected with cloths moistened in solution of sulphuret of strontia, produced no sensible action, though the moment the sides of the pile were moistened with nitrous acid, the ends gave shocks as powerful as those of a similar pile constructed in the usual manner.

The next question brought to the test of experiment was, whether the chemical action which takes place between the liquid and the plates of the pile is of the same kind as that which is manifested when water is decomposed by its extreme wires; that is, whether, when the oxygen is freed upon the surface of the zinc, the remaining constituent of the solution decomposed is also liberated at the surface of the zinc, as in ordinary oxydation; or is transmitted invisibly through the fluid to the surface of the silver, and there deposited, or otherwise liberated, as in the decomposition between the positive and negative wires. An arrangement of zinc and copper plates, in the form of the *couronne des tasses*, was formed, and charged with spring water. The general result of these experiments showed that the hydrogen liberated by the zinc was manifested not at the zinc, but at the silver surface; and, therefore, that the action in the cells is similar to the decomposition of water at the extreme wires of the pile. The phenomena were, however, rendered less decisive of the question by the modifications produced by the azote of the common air combined with the water, and also by saline matter which it held in solution, effects which were then imperfectly understood.

The inventor of the pile maintained that, among the metals, those which held the extreme places in the scale of electro-motive power were silver and zinc; and that, consequently, these metals, paired in a pile, would be more powerful, *cæteris paribus*, than any other. But as he also showed that pure charcoal was a good conductor of the electric current, and that the electromotive virtue depended on the different conducting powers of the metallic elements, it was consistent with analogy that charcoal, combined with another substance of different conducting power, would produce Voltaic action. Dr. Wells accordingly showed that a combination of charcoal and zinc produced sensible convulsions in the frog; and Davy, adopting this principle, constructed a *couronne des tasses*, consisting of a series of eight glasses, with small pieces of well-burned charcoal connected with zinc by pieces of silver wire, using a solution of red sulphate of iron as the liquid conductor. This series gave sensible shocks, and rapidly decomposed water. Compared with an equal and similar series of silver and zinc, its effects were much stronger. Hence he inferred that charcoal and zinc formed a combination equal, if not superior, to any of the metals.

Volta was understood to refer the electro-motive power of the metallic elements of the pile to the difference of their powers as conductors of electricity. The experiments of Davy induced him to connect the electro-motive power with the amount of chemical action on the more oxydable metal. These two principles might, nevertheless, be compatible, if it could be shown that the oxydation was dependant on, and proportional to, the difference of conducting power of the metals. To test this, it was only necessary to construct a pile with metals of nearly equal conducting power. With this view, Davy constructed a pile with gold and silver plates, these metals being supposed to differ very little in their power of conducting electricity, interposing disks of cloth moistened with dilute nitric acid. Voltaic action was produced. A similar pile, formed of plates of silver and copper, and a solution of nitrate of mercury, acted powerfully. The conducting powers of these several metals were then considered as nearly equal.*

In considering the various arrangements and combinations in which Voltaic action had been manifested, Davy observed, as a common character, that, in every case, one of the two metallic elements was oxydated, and the other not. Did the production of the electric current, then, depend merely on the presence of two metallic surfaces, one undergoing oxydation, separated by a conductor of electricity? and, if so, might not a Voltaic arrangement be made by one metal only, if its opposite surfaces were placed in contact with two different liquids, one of which would oxydate it, and the other transmit electricity without producing oxydation? To reduce this to the test of experiment with a single metallic plate would have been easy; but in constituting a series of pile, the two liquids, the oxydating and the non-oxydating, must be in contact, and subject to intermixture. To overcome this difficulty, different expedients were resorted to, with more or less success; but the most convenient and effectual method of attaining the desired end was suggested to Davy by Count Rumford. Let an oblong trough be formed, similar to that suggested by Cruickshank, as a substitute for the pile; and let grooves be made in it such as to allow of the insertion of a number of plates, by which the trough may be divided into a series of water-tight cells. Let plates of the metal of which the apparatus is to be constructed be made to fit these grooves; and let as many plates of glass or other non-conducting material, of the same form and magnitude, be provided. Let the metallic plates be inserted in alternate grooves of the trough, and the glass plates in the intermediate grooves, so as to divide the trough into a succession of separate cells, each cell having on one side metal, and on the other glass. Let such an arrangement be represented in fig. 1, where the metallic plates are represented at M, the intermediate plates being glass.

Fig. 1.

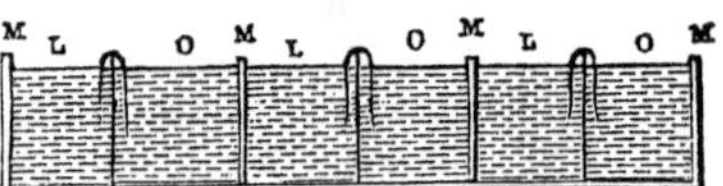

Let the alternate cells O be filled with the oxydating liquid, and the intermediate cells L with the liquid which conducts without oxydating. Let slips of moistened cloth be hung over the edge of each of the glass tubes, so that its ends shall dip into the liquids in the adjacent cells. This cloth, or rather the liquid it imbibes, will conduct the electric current from cell to cell, without permitting the intermixture of the liquids.

In the first arrangements made on this principle, the most oxydable metals, such as zinc, tin, and some others, were tried. The oxydating liquid O was dilute nitric acid, and the liquid L was water. In a combination consisting of twenty plates of metal, sensible but weak effects were produced on the organs of sense, and water was decomposed slowly by wires from the extremities. The wire from the end toward which the oxydating surfaces were directed evolved hydrogen, and the other oxygen.

To determine whether the evolution of the electric current was dependant on the production of oxydation, or would attend other chemical effects producible by the action of substances in solution upon metal, the oxydating liquid was now replaced by solutions of the sulphurets, and metallic plates were selected on which these solutions would exert a chemical action. Silver, copper, and lead, were tried in this way. Solution of sulphuret of potash was used in

* The relative conducting power of the metals has not even yet been satisfactorily established.

the cells O, and pure water in L. A series of eight metallic plates produced sensible effects. Copper was the most active of the metals tried, and lead the least so. In these cases, the terminal wires produced, in the usual manner, the decomposition of water, the wire from which hydrogen was evolved being that which was connected with the end of the series to which the surfaces of the metal not chemically acted on were presented.

It will be observed that in this case the direction of the electric current relatively to the surfaces of the metallic plates was the reverse of the former. When oxydation was produced, the oxydating sides of the plates looked toward the negative end of the series. Comparing these two effects, Davy was led by analogy to suspect that if the cells O were filled with an oxydating solution, while the cells L were filled with a solution of sulphuret, or any other which would produce a like chemical action, the combined effect of the currents proceeding from the two distinct chemical processes would be obtained. This was accordingly tried, and the results were as foreseen. The acid solution was placed in the cells O, and the sulphuret in the cells L. A series, consisting of three plates of copper or silver, arranged in this way, produced sensible effects; and twelve or thirteen decomposed water rapidly. The oxydating sides of the metal looked to the negative end of the series.

As it appeared from former experiments the charcoal possessed, as a Voltaic agent, the same properties as the metals, the next step in this course of experiments was naturally to try whether a Voltaic arrangement could not be constructed without any metallic element, by substituting charcoal for the metallic plates in the series above described. This was accomplished by means of an arrangement in the form of the *couronne des tasses*. Pieces of charcoal, made from very dense wood, were formed into arcs; and the liquids O and L were arranged in alternate glasses, as represented in fig. 2. The charcoal

Fig. 2.

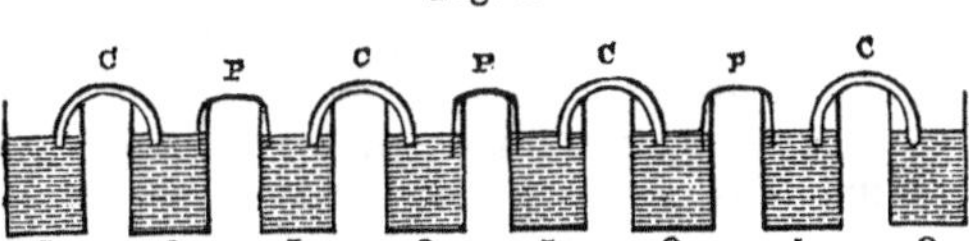

arcs C were placed so as to have one end immersed in each liquid, the intermediate glasses being connected by slips of bibulous paper P. When the liquid O was dilute acid, and L water, a series consisting of twenty pieces of charcoal gave sensible shocks, and decomposed water. This arrangement also acted, and with increased intensity, when the liquid O was sulphuric acid, and L was solution of sulphuret of potash.

The connexion of chemical change with the production of electricity in the pile, was too obvious not to attract the attention of other philosophers. Pepys in England, and MM. Biot and Frederic Cuvier in France, investigated the effect produced by the pile on the atmosphere in which it was placed. The former placed the pile in an atmosphere of oxygen, and found that in the course of a night 200 cubic inches of the gas had been absorbed. In an atmosphere of azote the pile had no action. MM. Biot and Cuvier also observed the quantity of oxygen absorbed, and inferred from their experiments that "although, strictly speaking, the evolution of electricity in the pile was produced by oxydation, the share which this had in producing the effects of the instrument bore no comparison with that which was due to the contact of the metals, the extremity of the series being in communication with the ground."

Dr. Wollaston and Gautherot, on the other hand, reproduced the principle advanced by Fabroni and Crève. Wollaston maintained that chemical action was not only the source of the electricity of the pile, but also of the common electrical machine. He showed that by conveying the electricity of the machine to gold wires terminated in extremely fine points the decomposition of water could be effected, and that the phenomenon was the same as when the decomposition was effected by Voltaic wires. He maintained that the friction of the rubber was attended with oxydation, and showed that the machine was ineffective in an atmosphere of dry hydrogen, or any other gas in which chemical action was not produced.

If an oblong slip of wet paper have its extremities in contact with the poles of a Voltaic pile, each half of the slip will be electrified; that which is in contact with the positive pole will be positively electrified, and that which is in contact with the negative pole will be negatively electrified. If it be removed from contact with the pile by a rod of glass, or other non-conductor, its electric state will continue. This means of producing electrical polarity was observed by Volta, and about the same time by Erhman.

This fact suggested to Ritter the idea of his *secondary pile*, which consisted of a series of disks of a single metal alternated with cloth or card, moistened in a liquid by which the metal would not be affected chemically. If such a pile have its extremities put in connexion by conducting substances with the poles of an insulated Voltaic pile, it will receive a charge of electricity in a manner similar to the band of wet paper, one half taking a positive and the other a negative charge; and after its connexion with the primary pile has been broken, it will retain the charge it has thus received. The secondary pile, while it retains its charge, produces the same physiological and chemical effects as the Voltaic apparatus.

The polarity which the band of wet paper and the secondary pile acquire by their temporary contact with the ends of a Voltaic apparatus, is a consequence of their imperfect conducting power. The electricity of each species appears to force its way through the imperfect conductor till the two opposite currents meet in the centre.

At the time of the discovery of the secondary piles, it was known that a piece of metallic wire, the ends of which had been placed in contact with the poles of a Voltaic pile, does not instantly recover its natural state when its contact with the pile is broken.

From the experiments of Davy and others, it appeared that if a communication was made between the poles of an insulated pile and two glasses of water, so that the water in the one would be charged with positive, and the other with negative electricity, a metallic wire connecting the two portions of water would evolve oxygen gas at one point, and hydrogen at the other. If, under such circumstances, the connexion of the glasses with the pile be suddenly broken, the action of the wire will nevertheless continue for some time, but its effects will be reversed; the point which before disengaged hydrogen will now disengage oxygen, and *vice versâ*. It appears, therefore, that the sudden suspension of the action of the pile has the effect of reversing the direction of the electric current which passes through the wire.*

The continuance of the electric state of a wire which had been used to connect the poles of a pile after its separation from the pile was also demonstrated by Oersted, who showed its effect on the organs of a frog.† The same effect was produced by a wire through which the current of a powerful electrical machine had been transmitted.

From the chemical effects of the pile, Davy turned his attention to its calorific powers. The means of experimental investigation placed at his disposal

* Histoire de Galvanism de Sue, tom. iii., p. 341.
† Journ. de Opim. de Van-Mons, No. iv., p. 68.

were enlarged by the apparatus of the laboratory of the Royal Institution, which was now under his direction. The Voltaic apparatus consisted of a series of 150 pairs of four-inch plates of zinc and copper, and a series of 50 pairs of zinc and silver of the same magnitude. The plates were cemented into four troughs of wood, according to the method proposed by Cruickshank. Another apparatus was provided, consisting of a series of twenty pairs of thirteen-inch plates of zinc and copper.

With the batteries of the smaller plates he repeated some of the experiments on the production of the spark, and the combustion of the metals which had already been made. When the poles consisted of two knobs of brass, the spark which attended the discharge was of dazzling brightness, and one eighth of an inch in apparent diameter. Between pieces of charcoal it had a vivid whiteness, and the charcoal remained red-hot for some time after the contact was broken, and threw off bright coruscations. The current passing through steel wire $\frac{1}{170}$th of an inch in diameter, rendered it white-hot, and caused it to burn with great splendor. Gold, silver, copper, tin, lead, and zinc, were also burnt. Platinum in thin slips was rendered white-hot and fused.

Fourcroy, Vauquelin, and Thénard, had investigated the different effects produced by enlarging the plates of a battery, and by increasing their number. They demonstrated that the power of the apparatus to heat and ignite metallic substances was augmented by enlarging the plates, without increasing their number; but that no increase of power to decompose water, or to produce the shock, ensued. The calorific power, therefore, appeared to depend, *cæteris paribus*, on the magnitude of the plates, while the chemical and physiological power depended on their number.

The battery of thirteen-inch plates was tried successively with pure water, a solution of common salt, and dilute nitric acid. With water its effects were feeble, with the solution of salt they were much more considerable, and were still more energetic with nitric acid. With the last, three inches of iron wire, $\frac{1}{170}$th of an inch in diameter, were rendered white hot, and two inches of the same wire were fused. The action of the water, feeble as it was, was ascribed to the air and saline matter it held in solution; and it was judged from analogy that water perfectly purged of air and free from all saline substances, would have no Voltaic action. A pile of thirty-six pairs of five-inch plates lost its activity in an atmosphere of azote and hydrogen in about two days; and its power was constantly restored by common air, and rendered more intense by oxygen gas.

When two pieces of well-burnt charcoal, or a piece of charcoal and a metallic wire, are connected with the apparatus and immersed in water, on completing the circuit, gas was abundantly evolved, and the points of the charcoal appeared red hot for some time after the contact was made. Sparks were also produced by means of charcoal points immersed in concentrated nitre and sulphuric acids. When two charcoal points acted in water, the gaseous products consisted of one eighth carbonic acid, one eighth oxygen, and one eighth inflammable gas, apparently hydrogen. The gases produced by a similar process from alcohol, ether, and dilute sulphuric acid, were also a mixture of oxygen and hydrogen. In all these cases it appeared that the gases proceeded chiefly from the decomposition of the water contained in the several solutions.

The effects of the ignition of charcoal in muriatic acid confined over mercury, were next tried. The charcoal being kept white hot for nearly two hours, the gas was very little reduced in volume, and the charcoal was not sensibly consumed. When the gas was examined, three fourths of it were absorbed by water, and the remainder was inflammable.*

* Davy's Works, vol. ii., p. 214. London, 1839.

Of the theories proposed at this early period of the experimental inquiry to explain chemical decomposition by the Voltaic apparatus, that of Grotthus was the earliest and most plausible. To simplify the view of this theory, we shall take as an example of its application the decomposition of water. Each molecule of water being composed of a molecule of oxygen and a molecule of hydrogen, their natural electricities are in equilibrium when not exposed to any disturbing force, each possessing equal quantities of the positive and negative fluids. The electricity of the positive wire acting by induction on the natural electricities of the contiguous molecule of water, attracts the negative and repels the positive fluid. It is further assumed in this theory, that oxygen has a natural attraction for negative, and hydrogen for positive electricity; therefore the positive wire in attracting the negative fluid of the contiguous molecule of water, and repelling its positive fluid, attracts its constituent molecule of oxygen, and repels its molecule of hydrogen. The particle of water, therefore, places itself with its oxygen next the positive wire, and its hydrogen on the opposite side. The positive electricity of the first particle of water thus accumulated on its hydrogen molecule, produces the same action on the succeeding molecule of water as the wire did upon the first molecule; and a similar arrangement of the second molecule of water is effected. This second molecule acts in like manner on the third, and so on. All the particles of water between the positive and negative wires thus assume a polar arrangement, and have their natural electricities decomposed; the negative poles and oxygen molecules looking toward the positive wire, and the positive poles and hydrogen molecules looking toward the negative wire. The attraction of the positive wire now separates the oxygen molecule of the contiguous particle of water from its hydrogen molecule, neutralizes its negative electricity, and either dismisses it in the gaseous form, or combines with it, according to the degree of the affinity of the metal of the wire for oxygen. The hydrogen molecule thus liberated effects in like manner the decomposition of the second particle of water, combining with its oxygen, and thus again forming water and dismissing its hydrogen. The latter acts in the same manner on the next particle of water, and so on. Thus, a series of decompositions and recompositions are supposed to be carried on through the fluid, until the process reaches the particle of water contiguous to the negative wire, and the molecule of hydrogen there disengaged gives up its positive electricity, by which an equal portion of negative electricity proceeding from the wire is neutralized, and the molecule of hydrogen escapes in the gaseous form. It is equally compatible with this theory to suppose the series of decompositions and recompositions to commence at the negative and terminate at the positive wire, or to commence simultaneously at both, and terminate at any intermediate point by the union of the last molecule of oxygen disengaged in the one series with the last molecule of hydrogen disengaged in the other.

Grotthus illustrated this ingenious hypothesis by comparing the supposed phenomena with the mechanical effects produced when a number of elastic balls—ivory balls for example—being suspended so that their centres shall be in the same straight line, and their surfaces mutually touch, either of the extreme balls of the series being raised and let fall against the adjacent one, the effect is propagated through the series, and the last ball alone recoils in consequence of the impact; and although the action and reaction are suffered by each ball of the series, and each is instrumental in transmitting the effect, no visible change takes place in any ball except the last, and the effect is continued by the alternate action of the extreme balls until the motion is gradually stopped by the resistance of the air, and other external causes.

The experiments of Davy, which have been already mentioned, were only the prelude to a brilliant series of discoveries, the commencement of which burst upon the scientific world in his Bakerian Lecture for the year 1806. As soon as the spendid results detailed in that paper became known in France, the members of the Institute, rising superior to the feelings of national animosity which at that time unhappily prevailed, unanimously conferred upon its distinguished author the prize which had been established by Napoleon for the best experiments on Voltaic electricity.*

The genius, address, and perseverance of him whose vocation is to investigate the laws of nature, are not always confined to the grateful labor of developing truths. The extirpation of error is a task which, while it demands the exercise of equally exalted powers, is never rewarded by that *eclat* which surrounds the discovery of natural harmonies before unobserved and unsuspected. In the commencement of the series of researches now referred to, Davy found it necessary to clear from his path certain difficulties, and, as he rightly conceived, errors, by which his progress was obstructed.

When the decomposing powers of the pile were first exhibited, the excitement attending a discovery so unlooked for prevented the details of the experiments from receiving all the attention to which they were entitled. When the circumstances attending the decomposition of water by the Voltaic wires were submitted to closer examination, it was found that indications of the presence of an acid always existed at the pole where oxygen was evolved, and those of an alkali at the other pole. In cases where the water submitted to decomposition might be supposed to hold saline matter in solution, such effects would create no surprise; but they were unequivocally manifested when the water used was distilled, and when there was every reason to think it chemically pure. Mr. Cruickshank explained this, by supposing the acid to be nitrous acid, proceeding from the combination of the azote of the common air held in solution by the water with the oxygen evolved at the positive wire; and the alkali to be ammonia, proceeding from the combination of the same principle with the hydrogen evolved at the negative wire. Desormes maintained that the acid was muriatic; and Brugnatelli that it was an acid *sui generis*, produced by the combination of positive electricity with one of the constituents of water, and called it *electric acid*. Some maintained that the constituents of the acid and alkali came over from the liquid used in the Voltaic apparatus in some undiscovered manner along the wires, and was thus deposited in the water; and others held that it was *generated* out of the elements of the water by Voltaic action. An article was published in the "Philosophical Magazine," † by

* It is stated in the Memoirs of Davy by Dr. Paris (p. 168), that the prize given to Davy was the *annual* medal, worth 3,000 francs, which was designed as a reward for the best experiments in electricity which should be made in each year. The same statement is made in a note by the editor in the fifth volume of Davy's Works (p. 56), edited by his brother, Dr. John Davy: "The minor prize of 3,000 francs, founded by Napoleon when first consul, for the most important result in electrical research during each year. was awarded by the Institute to the author for this paper: the principal prize of 60,000 francs, of which the preceding was only the interest, in the opinion of the best judges was rather due to him, as it was proposed to be given 'à celui, qui par ses expériences et ses découvertes, fera à faire à l'electricité et au galvanisme un pas comparable á cela qu'ont fait faire à ces sciences Franklin et Volta.' Thus the writer in the Quarterly Review already referred to remarks, 'It was only questioned by those who were capable of appreciating its importance, whether they acted with strict impartiality in assigning to him the annual interest only, when he appeared to have a fair claim to the principal.'"

On the other hand, the French writers on electricity claim the merit of having given Davy the higher prize: "Les grandes découvertes," says Becquerel (tom. i., p. 165), "dont Davy avait enrichi la science électro-chemique, le placaient hors de ligne avec les autres physiciens qui avaient parcouru la même carrière depuis Volta; aussi, l'Institut lui decerna-t-il le prix de 60,000f. qui avait été promis par Napoléon à l'auteur des plus grandes découvertes en électricité, comparables à celle de Volta et de Galvani." Whether Davy received the higher or the lower prize (we believe it was the lower), it is evident that the French scientific authorities *now* think he was entitled to the former.

† Vol. xxi., p. 279.

a Mr. Peel, of Cambridge, containing an account of an experiment in which the water that remained, after a large portion had been decomposed by the pile, yielded on evaporation muriate of soda, although the water used in the experiment had been distilled with every precaution necessary to free it from impurities. On inquiry being made at Cambridge, no person corresponding with the name and address of the professed author could be found; and the statement was concluded to be a mere attempt to practise on the credulity of the scientific world, when the surprise was revived by the publication of experiments actually made by Professor Pacchioni † of Pisa, in which the same result was attained as was stated in the pretended Cambridge experiment. Sylvester being led to the same conclusion, ascribed the supposed effects, in common with Pacchioni, to the oxydation of hydrogen, on the one hand in a higher, and on the other in a lower degree than that which forms water.

Such were the confusion and obscurity in which the community of science was involved on the subject of the Voltaic decomposition of water, when the question was taken up by Davy. In common with others, he had observed at an early period the presence of an acid and alkali in water under the process of decomposition; but states, that, so early as 1800, he concluded from his experiments that the acid proceeded from the animal and vegetable substances which he employed, and that the alkali arose from the corrosion of the glass vessels in which the experiment was conducted. Similar inferences were made by the Galvanic Society of Paris, by MM. Biot and Thénard, and by Dr. Wollaston; the last of whom removed one of the sources of these disturbing elements by the happy expedient of connecting the positive and negative portions of water by a piece of well-washed asbestos.

The investigation now undertaken by Davy was commenced by decomposing distilled water in two small cups of agate, P N (fig. 3), connected by a

Fig. 3.

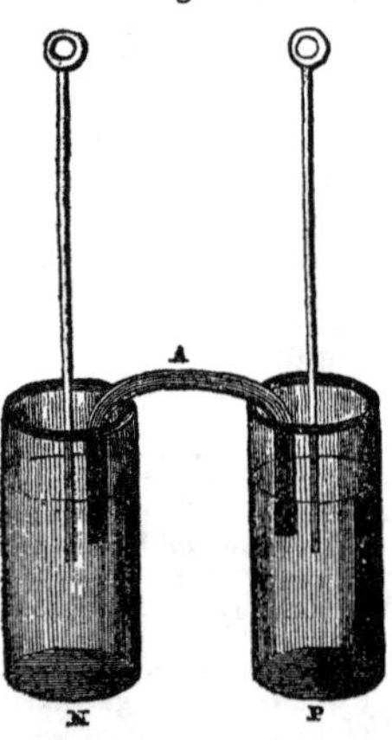

piece of white transparent amianthus, A. The wires of the Voltaic battery of 160 pairs of four-inch plates were connected with the water, the positive wire being immersed in the cup P, and the negative wire in N. After the process had been continued for forty-eight hours, the water in the cup P was found to redden litmus paper, and turmeric paper was affected by the water in N. It appeared, therefore, and further experiment confirmed the indication, that acid was present in the positive water, and alkali in the negative.

† Vol. xxii., p. 179.

This result, after all the precautions which had been taken, was quite unexpected, and, as may be imagined, gave not a little surprise to the experimenter. Still he did not for a moment entertain any of the speculations of the generation of these substances in the water. His next step was to repeat the experiment with glass instead of agate cups, using the *same* quantities of the *same* water, and exposing them for the *same* time to the action of the *same* battery. He argued, that if the cause lay in the water, the effects would be the same; but that if the *cups* had any share in producing them, they might be expected to be different. The result confirmed his anticipation. The alkali was produced in the cup N in quantity twenty times as great as with the agate cups, but there was no trace of the acid. The experiments were then repeated several times with the agate cups, when the acid and alkali reappeared in quantities, which, when compared with each other and with the result of the experiment with glass cups, left no doubt that the agate cups themselves had been the chief if not the only source of the acid, and, in a considerable degree, of the alkali also. Still it was impossible to ascribe the effects altogether to the material of the cups; and he was impressed with the suspicion that the *water itself*, notwithstanding its careful distillation, must have held more or less alkaline matter in solution. It was known that the usual tests would fail to indicate the presence of alkaline impurities when their proportion in water was under a certain limit; and the New river water, which he used, contained animal and vegetable impurities, which might furnish neutral salts capable of being carried over in the process of distillation.

The agate cups were now replaced by two conical cups of pure gold (fig. 4),

Fig. 4.

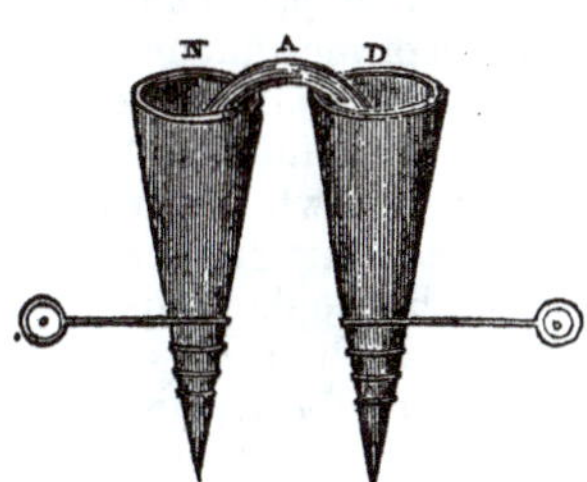

each containing about twenty-five grains of water. Distilled water in these was exposed to the action of a battery of 100 pairs of six-inch plates. In ten minutes indications of acid and alkali were formed in the cups D and N respectively. The process was continued for fourteen hours, during the whole of which time the acid increased in the cup D. The same increase was not, however, observed in the alkali in the cup N; on the contrary, it reached its maximum state in a short time, and continued without increase afterward. On heating the cup N, the alkali diminished, but could not be altogether dismissed.

These experiments being repeated with similar results, it became apparent that the source of the acid and alkali must exist in the water itself, and must either have arisen from saline matter remaining in solution in the water after distillation, or have been produced by the azote, which exists in minute portions in all water exposed to the air. The latter supposition would not be incompatible with the circumstance of the alkali speedily attaining a maximum, since the continued absorption of azote from the atmosphere by the water would be stopped when the latter would become charged with hydrogen.

The former supposition was adopted, and it was determined to submit the water which had been used in the last experiments to slow redistillation. A quart of this water was accordingly evaporated in a silver still at a temperature below 140°, and *a saline residuum was obtained weighing seven tenths of a grain.*

The gold cups were now again filled with the water thus purified, and exposed to the Voltaic action. After two hours the cup N failed to show any alkaline effect on turmeric paper. By very minute observation, its effect on the more delicate test of litmus was perceivable; but this disappeared by the application of heat, and was, therefore, ascribed to ammonia produced by the combination of the small quantity of azote contained in the water with the nascent hydrogen.

Finally, in order to insulate the results from the disturbing effects of the surrounding atmosphere, the gold cups containing the purified water were placed under the receiver of an air-pump, which was exhausted until the gauge stood at half an inch. Hydrogen gas was then introduced under the receiver, which, mixed with the very minute portion of atmospheric air which had remained, was again withdrawn by the pump. Pure hydrogen gas was now once more introduced around the cups, which being placed in connexion with the Voltaic apparatus, were suffered to remain under its action for twenty-four hours, at the end of which time neither of the portions of the water altered in the slightest degree the tint of litmus.

Thus were dispelled the speculations on the power of electricity to generate new principles in water; and by eliminating the disturbing action of other causes, the decomposing power of the pile upon a binary compound was presented in a manner fitted for theoretical investigation.

If chance occasionally deprives the philosopher of the merit of discovery by throwing facts under his feet, an ample field for the exercise of his sagacity remains in the due appreciation of the innumerable effects which are incidental to his experimental researches; to seize which as they arise, to pursue them through their consequences, to strip them of the Protean disguises which they borrow from other phenomena with which they become related, to expand them by comparison and generalization into comprehensive natural laws, is the province of the highest powers of philosophical inquiry. Never was this felicitous instinct more conspicuous than in the mind of Davy. No effect, however minute or accidental it might apparently be, presenting itself in his experiments, escaped his vigilance, if it offered the least clue to further discovery. In the course of the experiments just noticed, he found himself embarrassed by the disturbing action of the Voltaic wires on the material of the vessels containing the liquid, which was the immediate object of his attention. One material after another was put aside to get rid of this effect; but the *fact* was not overlooked or forgotten. It proved the germ of a vast discovery.

The negative wire effected a partial decomposition of the glass and agate cups, and brought a portion of their constituents into solution in the water contained in them. Might not a power, which thus subdued affinities so stubborn as those which produce the aggregation of substances so insoluble as agate and glass, be brought to bear on other similar bodies, and perchance resolve into their components substances now considered simple and elementary? As a first trial of the decomposition of insoluble or difficultly-soluble bodies, cups were formed of wax, resin, marble, argillaceous schist from Cornwall, serpentine from the Lizard, and graywacké. Being filled with purified water* in the same manner as in the experiments above described, decomposition was in all cases effected and saline matter evolved.

Pursuing this investigation, he successively decomposed by the same pro-

* By purified water in all the following experiments is to be understood water rendered chemically pure by the processes above described.

cess sulphate of lime, sulphate of strontia, fluate of lime, sulphate of baryta, and other insoluble salts, and in each case obtained the acid in the positive and the base in the negative cup. Certain mineral substances, such as basalt, zeolite, and vitreous lava from Ætna, were examined; and although the saline ingredients in some cases prevailed in extremely minute proportions, their presence was, nevertheless, distinctly manifested. The soluble compounds, such as sulphate and nitrate of potash, sulphate and phosphate of soda, were easily decomposed, and the results were the same.

The metallic salts deposited their metallic elements in crystals on the negative wire, round which the oxide was also deposited, while the acid was collected in the positive cup.

These, however, were only the first and least important of the consequences of the idea of extending the principle in virtue of which the Voltaic wire corroded the glass. We shall dismiss this for the present, to consider the next series of experiments in these researches, but shall resume the subject.

From many of his own experiments, and some described by Gautherot, Hisinger, Berzelius, and Ritter, it was apparent that the Voltaic influence was capable not only of decomposing compound bodies, but also of transferring, or, if the term may be permitted, *decanting* their constituents from one vessel to another. The series of experiments which follows next in order in these researches was directed to the examination of the limits of that power, and the effects attending it under conditions not before tried.

When the substance to be decomposed was insoluble, it was formed into a cup, as in the preceding experiments, and water contained in it was exposed to the Voltaic action. Thus let A, fig. 5, be an agate cup, and S a cup made of

Fig. 5.

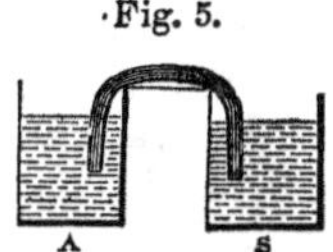

the substance to be submitted to Voltaic action. Let them each be filled with purified water, and connected by asbestos. If A be connected with the positive and S with the negative wire, it was expected that any acid constituent which may be in the substance of which S is formed would pass into A, which would become an acid solution, and appear by the application of the usual tests. If, on the other hand, A be connected with the negative and S with the positive wire, any alkali which may be in the substance of which S is formed was expected to pass into A, and to be manifested there by the common alkaline tests.

In the first case in which his method was tried, the cup S was formed of sulphate of lime. The cup A was connected with the negative and S with the positive wire. With a battery of 100 pair of plates, the water in A was in about four hours converted into a strong solution of lime, and the liquid in S was converted into sulphuric acid. When the cup A received the positive and S the negative wire, the effects were reversed. In that case, the water in A became sulphuric acid, and a solution of lime was found in S.

Other saline cups were submitted to the same process with like results; the water in the positive cup always receiving acid, and that in the negative cup alkali.

Two cups of glass were connected with the poles of the battery. One was filled with distilled water, and the other with a saline solution. In every case the salt was decomposed, the base passing into or remaining in the negative, and the acid in the positive cup.

The time required for these transmissions appeared to increase, *cæteris paribus*, as the space through which the decomposed elements were to be transmitted increased.

To determine whether the action of the metallic wires proceeding from the Voltaic battery was immediately engaged in the production of these decompositions, the next experiments were arranged so that the electric current should be transmitted to the solution to be decomposed through liquid conductors. For this purpose, three cups (P, I, and N, fig. 6) were provided; the extreme

Fig. 6.

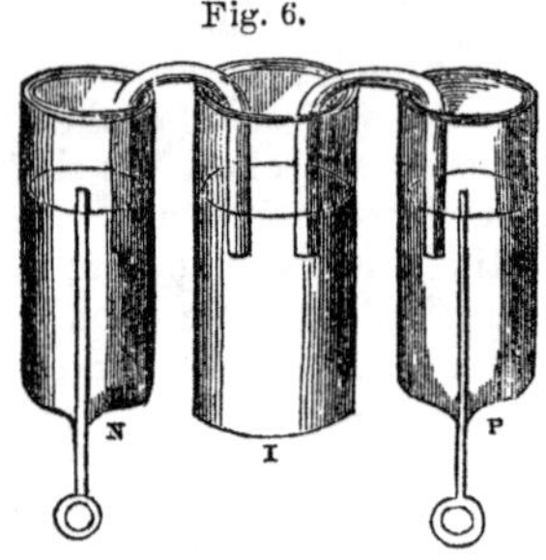

ones P and N receiving the positive and negative wires from the battery, and the cup I connected with each of them by amianthus. The cups P and N were filled with purified water, and the solution to be decomposed was put into the intermediate cup I. In every case the acid constituent of the solution was decanted into P, and the alkaline into N. Lest the amianthus siphons should have any mechanical effect on the transference of the solution between the cups, the cups P and N were so filled that the surfaces of the water in them were above that of the solution in I.

As it was now abundantly apparent that the elements of the decomposed substance were drawn from cup N through the interstices of the siphons, it was determined to try how far this decanting power could be carried by breaking the continuity of the siphons, and rendering it impossible for the decomposed element to reach its destination without passing through an intermediate liquid. For this purpose, the three cups being arranged as before, two of them, P and I, were filled with distilled water, the water in I being tinged with litmus; and the negative cup N was filled with a solution of the sulphate of potash. If the energy of the attraction of the positive wire for the acid constituent of the salt were sufficiently strong to cause it to pass from N to P, through the liquid in I, it was naturally expected that, on its route, its presence in I would be rendered manifest by the usual effect of reddening the litmus. The acid passed from N to P through I, but without being manifested in I by any redness of the solution.

When the saline solution was put in the positive cup P, and the purified water in the negative cup N, the water in I being tinged with turmeric, the alkali passed in like manner from P to N without producing any effect on the color of the liquid I.

As the transmission of acid or alkali by means of the electric current through water tinged with vegetable colors was effected without producing any sensible change in these delicate tests of their presence, it was conjectured that, while in this state of transition, or electrical progression, the chemical elements were deprived of their wonted properties, and that therefore they would equally pass through solutions of substances for which, under ordinary circumstances, they exhibit a strong affinity, that affinity being rendered dormant, or counteracted, by the predominating influence of the electrical attraction. To reduce this conjecture to the test of experiment, the water tinged with vegetable colors in the intermediate cup I was replaced by a weak solution of ammonia, purified water was put into the cup P, and a solution of the sulphate of potash in the cup N. The sulphuric acid, attracted by the positive wire, could only reach the cup P by passing through the solution of ammonia. With a battery of 150 pairs, the presence of the acid in P was manifested in five minutes by litmus paper. In half an hour, the solution in P became sour to the taste, and precipitated solution of nitrate of baryta. Thus the sulphuric acid passed through the solution of ammonia in I without producing upon it any chemical change. Solutions of lime, potash, and soda, were successively substituted, with similar results.

Muriate of soda and nitrate of potash were successively placed in the cup N, and the muriatic and nitric acids made to pass through concentrated alkaline menstrua in I without any chemical effects.

The neutral salts of lime, potash, soda, ammonia, and magnesia in solution, were successively placed in the cup P, distilled water in N, and sulphuric, nitric, and muriatic acids, successively in the intermediate cup I. The alkaline elements of the salts were thus drawn through the acids, and decanted into N, without undergoing any change themselves, or causing any change in the acids.

Strontia and baryta passed freely by a similar process through muriatic and nitric acids, and reciprocally these acids passed with equal facility through solutions of strontia and baryta. The uniformity of this series of phenomena was, however, broken when it was attempted to transmit the same alkalies through sulphuric acid, or to pass sulphuric acid through them. A new order of effects was here evolved.

A solution of sulphate of potash was placed in the cup N, distilled water in P, and a solution of baryta in I. The sulphate of potash was decomposed as before, and sulphuric acid passed from the negative cup on its route toward the positive wire; but its progress was arrested in the intermediate cup, where it was seized by the baryta and precipitated. It appeared, however, that this obstruction to the progress of the acid was not absolutely complete; for when the process was continued for several days, traces of acid were found in the positive cup. When a solution of strontia was substituted for the baryta in the intermediate cup, the effects were similar.

When the muriate of baryta was put in the positive cup, sulphuric acid in the intermediate cup I, and water in the negative cup N, no alkali passed to the cup N, all being arrested in I, where the sulphate of baryta was manifest, and muriatic acid remained in the cup P.

It appeared, therefore, that the exception to the transmission of the elements of bodies through menstrua for which they have an affinity, includes the cases in which the result of that affinity would be an insoluble compound. The sulphates of strontia and baryta are insoluble in water; and sulphuric acid cannot be transmitted, by the electric current, through strontia or baryta, nor the latter through the former.

The operation of these principles was very beautifully illustrated by the following experiment: The cups P and N were filled with solution of muriate of soda, and the cup I with solution of sulphate of silver. The cup P was connected with I by a slip of wet turmeric paper, and the cup N was connected with I by a slip of wet litmus paper. When the operation of the battery commenced, the presence of soda in a free state was manifested in the cup N, and muriatic acid in the cup P. The muriatic acid drawn from the cup N, through the litmus paper, was seen to form a dense precipitate in the cup I, and the soda passing through the turmeric paper from the cup P was observed in the cup I, forming a more diffused and lighter precipitate. But neither the acid in passing through the litmus paper, nor the alkali in passing through the turmeric paper, produced any change in the color of these tests.

When salts having metallic oxides as bases were placed in the cup P, acid solutions being put in I, the oxides passed through the acids; but their progress was much slower than that of the alkalies. When a solution of the green sulphate of iron was placed in P, and muriatic acid in I, the green oxide of iron began to appear in about ten hours on the amianthus connecting N and I; and it took three days to collect any considerable quantity of it in the cup N. The results were similar when solutions of sulphate of copper, nitrate of lead, and nitro-muriate of tin, were placed in the cup P.

The transmission of the constituents of salts through solutions of the neutral salts was next tried, and the results were what was anticipated. Saline solutions being placed in N and I, and purified water in P, the alkali of I first began to pass into N: then the alkali of P, after passing through I, reached N, and at the same time the acid of I passed into P. Ultimately the two acids were collected in P, and the two alkalies in N. As an example of this, the cup N was filled with a solution of the muriate of baryta, the cup I with sulphate of potash, and the cup P with pure water. A battery of 150 pairs brought sulphuric acid in five minutes, and muriatic acid in two hours, into P.

When the cup P was filled with a solution of sulphate of potash, I with muriate of baryta, and N with distilled water, the baryta appeared in the water in a few minutes; after an hour, the potash became sensible in it.

When the muriate of baryta was in P, the sulphate of potash in I, and water in N, the potash soon appeared in the water; but the baryta was arrested in the intermediate cup by the sulphuric acid, and sulphate of baryta was abundantly precipitated. In like manner, when sulphate of silver was placed in the cup I, muriate of baryta being in N, and water in P, sulphuric acid alone passed into P, and a precipitation took place in I.

The effects of the electric current on the principles of vegetable and animal substances was next tried. The fresh stalk of a polyanthus-leaf was used instead of the siphon of amianthus, to connect the two cups P and N (fig. 7), the

Fig. 7.

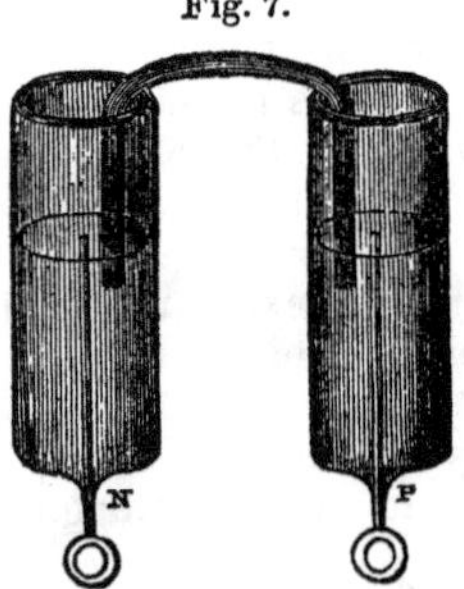

cup I being omitted. The cup P was filled with a solution of nitrate of strontia, and the cup N with purified water. The water soon became green, and showed the presence of alkali; and the solution in the cup P indicated the presence of free nitric acid. After ten minutes, the alkaline matter in N being examined, proved to be potash and lime, but no strontia had yet arrived in the cup. In half an hour, however, strontia appeared, and in four hours was abundant.

A piece of the muscular flesh of beef was used in like manner as a siphon connecting the two cups, P containing a solution of muriate of baryta, and N distilled water. Soda, ammonia, and lime, appeared first in the water, and after about an hour and a quarter the baryta began to arrive. Muriatic acid was abundantly liberated in the cup P.

It is nothing more than a general expression of the phenomena which have been just detailed to say, that hydrogen, alkaline matter, metals, and certain metallic oxides, are *attracted* toward the negative, and *repelled* from the positive pole of a Voltaic apparatus; and that oxygen and acid substances are affected with a similar attraction and repulsion in the contrary direction.

As to the actual process by which the transfer of the element decomposed takes place, either between the positive and negative wires in the solution under decomposition, or through the intermediate solution, no distinct opinion was expressed in the paper now noticed. Davy showed that it is natural to suppose that the repellent and attractive energies are conveyed *from one particle to another of the same kind*, and that locomotion (of these particles) takes place in consequence. He considered this to be proved by many facts. Thus when an acid was drawn from the negative to the positive cup through an alkaline solution contained in the intermediate cup, if the Voltaic action was for a moment suspended before the transfer of *all* the acid in the negative cup had been effected, traces of acid were always discoverable in the intermediate cup. It appears from this that the series of acid molecules, *while moving* between the ends of the amianthus siphons in the intermediate cup, do not enter into combination with the alkali; but if the motion be for a moment suspended, combination instantly takes place. In this case, therefore, it would not appear that any supposition of transmission by a series of decompositions and recompositions is compatible with the phenomena.

In the cases, however, of the decomposition of water (where the whole menstruum between the decomposing wires is water), and of solution of neutral salts (where also the menstruum is altogether composed of the same solution), he admits that there *may possibly* be a succession of decompositions and recompositions throughout the fluid. He admits, also, that the impossibility of transmitting through an acid or alkali any element which forms with it an insoluble compound, although the transmission is perfect when the compound is soluble, supports the hypothesis of a succession of compositions and decompositions taking place in every case. He maintains, that although in some cases insoluble substances are transmitted, the transmission is effected in a manner totally different from that which takes place in the more general case. The insoluble matter was, in these cases, carried over mechanically, either through the interstices of the siphons, or by means of "a thin stratum of pure water, where the solution had been decomposed at the surface by carbonic acid."

It appears from the tenor of the observations in this paper, "on the mode of decomposition and transition," that the mind of the author had not yet arrived at any opinion satisfactory to himself on this subject.

By the experiments of Volta it had been shown that different metals brought into contact were oppositely electrified after separation. Davy found that an acid and a metal being in contact, the former became negative, and the latter positive; but that when an alkali and a metal were in contact, the electrical effects were reversed. As a general fact it appeared, therefore, that positive electricity has a tendency to pass from acids to metals, and from metals to alkalies, and negative electricity to flow in the opposite direction. Different bodies were, therefore, regarded by Davy as having with relation to each other specific *electrical energies*. Acids have a negative and alkalies a positive energy, with relation to metals ; while metals have a positive energy with relation to acids, and a negative energy with relation to alkalies.

Various experiments of a delicate kind were made to establish this general principle. To avoid the disturbing effects which would be introduced by chemical action, the substances of each kind selected for experimental examination were in the solid and dry form. When oxalic, succinic, benzoic, or boracic acid, perfectly dry, either in powder or crystals, was touched upon a large surface with a disk of copper, zinc, or tin, insulated, the metal became positive, and the acid negative. Phosphoric acid and zinc gave a like result.

Metallic plates being brought in like manner in contact with lime, strontia, magnesia, or soda, became negative, the earths being positive. The attraction of potash for water was too strong to allow that alkali to be submitted to trial. Sulphur became positive after contact with a metallic plate, and the supposed exception to this in the case of lead was removed by showing that the substance rubbed against newly polished lead always became positive.

All these facts went to support the position, that the electrical relation of different substances, as shown by mere contact, was in harmony with the law according to which electricity was developed in the Voltaic apparatus, and with the phenomena of decomposition. To complete the experimental proof of this analogy, it would have been necessary to show that oxygen has a negative and hydrogen a positive electrical energy in relation to the metals. Not being able to accomplish this, recourse was had to the compounds of these substances. Sulphuretted hydrogen in water, used in the Voltaic arrangement of single metallic plates, plays the part of an alkali. To support by a like analogy the negative character of oxygen, he showed that oxymuriatic acid* (chlorine) was more powerfully negative in relation to metal than muriatic acid, even in a higher degree of concentration.

He assumed as a principle suggested by analogy and supported by experiment, that *two bodies which have contrary electrical energies in relation to a third body have contrary electrical energies in relation to each other ;* that is to say, two bodies, A and B, being successively brought into contact with a third C ; if A is found to be positive after separation and B negative, then it follows that if A and B be brought into mutual contact, A will be positive after separation and B negative. Lime and oxalic acid in a dry and solid state, the former being positive and the latter negative in relation to metals, were brought into contact, and the electricity collected after repeated contacts by a condensing electrometer. The lime was found to be positive and the acid negative.

Guided by the analogies suggested by such facts, Davy maintained, as a general principle, that oxygen and acid substances have a negative electrical energy in relation to hydrogen and alkaline substances ; and that in the decompositions and changes presented by the effects of electricity, the different bodies naturally possessed of chemical affinities appear to be incapable of entering into combination or of remaining in combination by virtue of these affinities when they are placed in a state of electricity, contrary to the natural relation of their electrical energies. Thus the acids in the positive part of the circuit separate themselves from the alkalies, oxygen from hydrogen, and so on ; and metals on the negative side do not unite with oxygen, and acids do not remain in union with their oxides ; and in this way the attractive and repellant agencies seem to be communicated from the metallic surfaces (the poles of the pile) throughout the whole of the menstruum.

* This substance was then supposed to be a compound.

In all cases in which bodies combine chemically, they are found to have contrary electrical energies. Examples are numerous. The bodies in the first of the following columns are all negative with respect to those which are opposite to them in the second: —

Oxygen	Zinc.	Gold	Mercury.
Oxygen	Silver.	Metals	Sulphur.
Copper	Zinc.	Acids	Alkalies.

The constituent particles of each of these substances when brought into contact, being naturally in opposite states of electricity, will, according to the common laws of electricity, attract each other. If they be solid bodies, the force of aggregation of these particles, which constitutes the character of their solidity, will resist their separation; but if the constituent particles be free to move and intermingle among each other, then the attraction due to their proper electricity will take effect, combination will ensue, the conditions of equilibrium of the electrical forces will be satisfied, and all signs of free electricity will cease.

In support of this hypothesis it is argued, that when, by artificial means, the elements of any compound are invested with electricity contrary to that which naturally belongs to them, such electricity exerting a force contrary to that which produces or maintains, or tends to produce or maintain their combination, that combination, if it exist, is dissolved, and if it tend to be effected, is prevented.

Thus zinc is one of the metals which have the strongest natural tendency to combine with oxygen. Let it be charged with negative electricity, and its oxydation becomes impossible, because, according to Davy's hypothesis, the positive electricity *naturally* belonging to its molecules is neutralized by the negative electricity *artificially* imparted to it. Again, silver is one of the metals which have the least tendency to unite with oxygen; but let silver be charged with positive electricity, and it oxydates easily. The positive electricity supplied artificially gives increased power to that which the particles possess, so as to augment their attraction for the negative particles of the oxygen.

The cases of bodies which have contrary electrical energies, either in relation to a third body or in relation to each other, are therefore simple, and easily apprehended. But two bodies may have electrical energies with respect to a third, the same in *kind*, but unequal in *degree*. Thus all acids are negative in relation to metals, but any two of them will be unequally so; and in like manner all alkalies are positive, but unequally positive in relation to metals. Sulphuric acid is *more negative* than muriatic acid in relation to lead, and potash is *more positive* than soda in relation to tin. Such bodies compared with each other may have the same or contrary electrical energies, or they may be neutral. Sulphur and the alkalies are positive in relation to the metals, but their electrical energies with respect to each other are contrary.

The evolution of heat and light, which commonly attends the restoration of electrical equilibrium between two bodies strongly charged with electricity by artificial means, is brought by Davy in further support of his theory. It is well known that heat and light also result from intense chemical action. When the electric current passes through bodies, the electricity being then incomparably more feeble in intensity than that which proceeds from the common machine, heat is evolved without light, and the degree of this heat is, *cæteris paribus*, augmented as the intensity of the electricity is increased. In the same manner in slow chemical combinations there is an increase of temperature without luminous appearance.

Heat, by producing fusion, and liberating the constituent particles of bodies from their natural aggregation, has been regarded as being conducive to their chemical combination. In the theory proposed by Davy it is, moreover, viewed as being otherwise instrumental in giving play to the affinities. That heat is one of the means of exalting the electrical energy of bodies, is apparent from its known effects on glass and tourmaline. But in the experiments now noticed, more distinct and specific evidence is adduced of its direct electric agency. A plate of sulphur was placed on an insulated plate of copper, and the temperature of the bodies being gradually elevated, their electrical state was examined at different stages of the experiment. At 56° the electricity was scarcely sensible to a condensing electrometer; at 100° it affected the gold leaves without the condenser, and increased in a still higher degree as the sulphur approached its point of fusion.

Since heat, therefore, increases the natural electrical energy of the component particles of bodies, it gives them, according to the theory of Davy, an increased tendency to combine chemically, if those energies be contrary.

Hence, when a spark, or other sufficient source of heat, is introduced into a mixture of oxygen and hydrogen, it renders the contiguous molecules of oxygen more strongly negative, and those of hydrogen more strongly positive. In virtue of their increased mutual attraction they combine, and in combining heat is evolved, which affecting other contiguous molecules causes further combination, and so on until the combination is complete.

According to this hypothesis, combination should be rapid, heat and light intense, and the compound neutral in its properties, whenever the electrical energies of the two constituents are strong and perfectly equal. But when they are very unequal, the effects would be less vivid, and the compound would have the acid or alkaline character, according as the energy of the negative or positive constituent is in excess.

The production of water from the combination of oxygen and hydrogen, and the formation of the metallic salts, are adduced as examples of strong and equal energies. Like examples are afforded by the nitrate, sulphate, and chlorate of potash and muriate of lime, which severally, when touched upon a large surface by plates of copper and zinc, gave no electrical signs. Subcarbonate of soda and borax, on the contrary, gave a slight negative charge, and alum and superphosphate of lime a feeble positive charge.

The next section of this remarkable paper professes to explain the author's views of the "mode of action" of the Voltaic pile. The absence of that perspicuous style of expression which so generally characterizes his writings, in this case justifies the supposition that his own perceptions on the subject of the theory he proposes were not at the time very clear or well defined. It must be recollected that Volta maintained that the source of electricity in the pile was the contact of the dissimilar metals, and that the intervening fluid merely acted the part of a conductor to carry away, in a continued stream, the positive electricity from each zinc surface, and the negative electricity from each copper surface. Fabroni and Crève, and afterward Wollaston and others, maintained that the source of the electricity was the chemical action between the zinc and the fluid, and that the intervening copper acted as a conductor to carry away, in a continued stream, the positive electricity from one side of the fluid, and the negative electricity from the other. Davy professed to reconcile these conflicting hypotheses by admitting, with Volta, that the opposite currents were propagated from the surface of contact of the zinc and copper; but that the liquid separating the pairs of plates *did not*, and *could not*, carry forward the currents, as Volta maintained, by their conducting power, but that they effected that object by the chemical action which took place between them and the zinc. This is our view of the theory proposed by Davy in the paper now referred to ; but, as has been already stated, the expressions are not so clear as to remove all doubt of his exact meaning.

Davy uses the term "electrical energy" apparently to express the same phenomenon which Volta called "electro-motive action," and which had been also called "Voltaic action." This term denotes the quantity of electricity evolved upon the two metals on either side of their common surface, according to Volta's theory of contact. The act of conveying forward through the series in each direction the electricity, positive and negative, thus propagated at the common surface, is called by Davy the "restoration of the electrical equilibrium which was disturbed by the electrical energy of the metals." Strictly speaking, there is no *restoration* whatever of electrical equilibrium during the action of the pile. The electric fluids are never in a state of repose. Two currents run in uninterrupted streams in opposite directions. When therefore Davy says that "the chemical changes" produced by the liquid interposed between the metallic elements of the pile are "the causes that tend to restore the equilibrium," he must, as we conceive, be understood to mean that these changes are "the causes by which the electric currents are propagated toward the poles of the pile."

Having premised these explanations, let us now consider the reasoning and the facts on which this theory of Davy has been based. He denies that the liquid elements of the pile can act as an ordinary conductor of electricity, the term conductor being used in the same sense as when applied to the metals and other solid conductors, because, with regard to electricities of such very low intensity, water (as well as liquids in general) is an insulating body. Besides, there is every reason to believe that, "if the fluid medium were a substance incapable of decomposition (by the metallic elements), the motion of the electricity would cease." When the liquid in a Voltaic arrangement of zinc and copper is a solution of muriate of soda, decomposition ensues. The oxygen and muriatic acid pass through the fluid from the copper toward the zinc, transporting or transported by the negative current; and the hydrogen and soda pass from the zinc toward the copper, transporting or transported by the positive current. Whether the author considered that the transfer of the electricity is effected by the locomotion of the decomposed elements through the fluid, or by a series of decompositions and recompositions, in which there is no motion of translation imparted to any of the elements resulting from the decomposition, and in which the electricities themselves are not transferred through the fluid, but rendered alternately free and latent as the successive decompositions and recompositions are effected, does not appear from the developments contained in this paper.

A pile of twenty-four pairs, in which the connecting fluid was water free from air, had no Voltaic power. To determine whether another liquid with superior conducting power, but still incapable of chemical action, would be affected, concentrated sulphuric acid was tried. No permanent current was produced. Solutions of neutral salts render the pile active at first; but when, by continued decomposition, the solution in contact with the zinc becomes acid, and that in contact with the copper alkali, the action ceases. Dilute acids being themselves easily decomposed, and promoting the decomposition of the water, dissolving the oxide of zinc as fast as it is formed, and evolving gases only on the copper side, are the most powerful and durable fluid elements for a pile. All these facts supply converging evidence upon the position that chemical action is essential to the vitality of the Voltaic apparatus.

Against the hypothesis that chemical change is the *primary* source of the action of the pile, it is contended that in a combination of zinc and copper plates with dilute *nitrous* acid, the side of the zinc exposed to the acid is positive; but in a Voltaic combination of zinc water and dilute *nitric* acid, the side of the zinc exposed to the acid is negative. The chemical action of the acid on the zinc being in both cases the same, it is argued that if the electric currents originated at the common surface of the zinc and acid, which they would do if chemical change were their primary source, the direction of the currents would be the same, instead of being contrary in the two cases.

As a further argument against the chemical theory of the pile, Davy maintained that in mere cases of chemical change, electricity is never exhibited; and endeavored to support this position by the examples of iron burned in oxygen, the deflagration of nitre and charcoal, the combination of solid potash and sulphuric acid, and other chemical actions. Subsequent investigation, however, has shown that this principle is not tenable, and that chemical change *is* attended with the evolution of electricity.

With Davy, as with Franklin, *application* ever trod closely on the heels of *discovery*. The same memoir which disclosed the brilliant series of discoveries of which we have here attempted to give a brief analysis, also indicated the vast applications of which they were susceptible, in the further investigations of the laws of nature, and in arts conducive to the economy of life. The detection of acid and alkaline matter in mineral, animal, and vegetable substances, and their separation from them, was sufficiently obvious. A piece of muscular fibre, through which the electric current was transmitted for five days, was rendered dry and hard. Potash, soda, ammonia, lime, and oxide of iron, were carried from it by the negative current; and the three mineral acids, with phosphoric acid, passed off with the positive current. From a laurel leaf the negative current carried green coloring matter, resin, alkali, and lime, and the positive current took vegetable prussic acid. Mint gave potash and lime with the negative, and an acid matter with the positive current. The flesh of the living hand, carefully washed in pure water, gave a mixture of muriatic, sulphuric, and phosphoric acids with the positive current, and fixed alkaline matter with the negative current. This fact accounts for the acid and alkaline tastes first observed by Sulzer given by metals in contact.

By converting the processes, the Voltaic currents may be made the means of introducing acids and alkaline or metallic principles, into the animal and vegetable system. This idea has since been realized in medical practice by some physicians.

In the experiments hitherto made, the acids and alkalies themselves were not decomposed. The history of scientific discovery affords no more remarkable example of that instinctive foresight which enables the philosopher to suspect the direction in which truth lies, and prompts him in the selection of subjects of inquiry, than is apparent in comparing Davy's present guesses with the result of his subsequent researches. "These facts," says he, "induce us to hope that this new mode of analysis may lead to the discovery of the *true* elements of bodies, if the materials acted on be employed in a certain state of concentration, and the electricity be sufficiently exalted. For if chemical union be of the nature which I have ventured to suppose, however strong the natural electrical energies of the elements of bodies may be, there is yet every probability of a limit to their strength: whereas the powers of our artificial instruments seem capable of indefinite increase."

How soon he led the way toward the realization of this magnificent conjecture will presently appear.

Sudden and violent derangements of the electrical equilibrium of the elements of our system are manifested in other cases besides the *glaring instances* offered by atmospheric phenomena. The electrical appearances which precede and attend earthquakes and volcanic eruptions admit of easy explanation on the electro-chemical theory. The slow and gradual changes observed by the geologist are indications of the more tranquil and incessant operations of electrical agency. Where strata of pyrites and coalblende occur; where the pure metals or the sulphurets are found in contact with each other, or with any conducting substances; and where different strata contain different saline menstrua, electricity must be evolved, and by its agency mineral formations would probably be influenced or produced.

These views, which have been recently confirmed by the observations of Mr. Fox on the electrical condition of the metallic veins in Cornwall, were illustrated by experiment. A mixed solution of muriates of iron, copper, tin, and cobalt, was placed in the positive cup P, and distilled water in the negative cup N, the cups being connected by asbestos. The four oxides passed through the asbestos to the cup N; a yellow metallic crust was formed on the negative wire, round the base of which the oxides collected in a mixed state. In another experiment the carbonate of copper was diffused in minute subdivision through water, and a negative wire placed in a small perforated cube of zeolite in the liquid. Green crystals collected upon the cube and adhered to it, the particles being incapable of penetrating it. By the multiplication of such instances, Davy conceived that the electrical power of decomposition and transference would afford a satisfactory explanation of some of the principal facts in geology, and his anticipations have since been to a considerable extent realized by the researches of Becquerel and others. "Natural electricity," says Davy in the conclusion of this memorable paper, "has hitherto been little investigated, except in the case of its evident and powerful concentration in the atmosphere. Its slow and silent operations in every part of the surface will probably be found more immediately and importantly connected with the order and economy of nature; and investigation on this subject can hardly fail to enlighten our philosophical systems of the earth, and may possibly place new powers within our reach."*

His theoretical ideas on the application of electrical decomposition to the solution of the phenomena of geology were seized with ardor by Guyton Morveau. That eminent chemist, like Davy, endeavored to exhibit on a small scale, by direct experiments, the processes which are continually going on in the crust of the earth. The native oxide of antimony he regarded as an example of slow transition from the state of a sulphuret to that of a pure oxide, by means of the decomposition of water by subterranean electricity. By careful examination of a specimen of this mineral, he observed that it still retained the structure of the crystallized sulphuret of antimony, and even preserved partially its metallic lustre, and inferred that a slow Voltaic action had changed its composition without disturbing the arrangement of its constituent parts. To support those ideas suggested to him in Davy's celebrated paper by direct experiment, he submitted a piece of sulphuret of antimony to the action of a powerful voltaic apparatus. An odor of sulphuretted hydrogen was soon perceivable; the liquid asumed a yellow color, and the sulphuret appeared of a darker tint, and iridescent, indicating incipient decomposition. The negative plate became black, and the positive one was coated with a light yellow incrustation, which proved to be the oxide of antimony. Thus it appeared that the sulphuret of antimony was capable of being transferred immediately into the oxide by the mere operation of the Voltaic forces. Other native sulphurets were tried in like manner, and gave similar results.†

During the twelve months next succeeding the date of the memoir above noticed, Davy devoted his labors, and directed all the powers of his genius, to the development of the consequences of the theoretical principles which he

* Philosophical Transactions, 1807.

† Annales de Chimie, tom. liii., p. 113.

had propounded, and to the realization of the ideas he had ventured to throw out respecting the resolution of natural substances, before regarded as simple, into their constituents. Never before did theory more surely lead to discovery; never was the prophetic instinct of a philosopher more speedily or more magnificently satisfied. His foreknowledge of the facts to be disclosed and the instruments for their disclosure, of the end to be attained and the means of attaining it, of the route to be followed and the goal to be reached, was distinctly expressed; and with the confidence inspired by clear perceptions and conscious power, he immediately advanced in the course he described, and attained the end he foresaw. The resolution of the alkalies and earths into their elements was the splendid result of his labors during the year 1807, and was consigned to the Bakerian lecture read before the Royal Society on the 19th of November in that year.

His first efforts were directed to potash, which was submitted in a state of solution to the electric current. The water only was decomposed, the alkali refusing to yield. In its dry state it would not transmit the current. In order to give it a conducting power, and at the same time exclude water, on which by preference the current appeared to act, the alkali was now placed in a platinum spoon, and exposed to the flame of a lamp directed upon it by a blast of oxygen. When reduced to the fluid state by such means, the potash transmitted the Voltaic current. When the metal of the spoon was positive, and the point of a platinum wire inserted in the fluid alkali negative, combustion attended by intense splendor was exhibited at the wire, and a column of flame arose from the point of contact of the wire with the alkali. When the spoon was negative, and the wire positive, a vivid light appeared on the former; aeriform globules rose through the liquid potash, which inflamed as soon as they escaped into the air.

It was conjectured that the constituent of the potash, attracted by the negative pole, was the matter which in these cases escaped in bubbles; and that its affinity for oxygen was so strong, that the moment it came in contact with the atmosphere it recombined with oxygen and produced combustion. The question, therefore, now was, how to arrest that element, and submit it to examination.

As the liquefaction of the alkali by heat appeared to entail, as a consequence the immediate recombination of its separated constituent, it was now attempted to give the necessary conducting power to the potash, by allowing it to imbibe from the atmosphere as much moisture as would give a conducting power to its surface. The alkali in this state was placed on a platinum disk, which was connected with the negative pole, while a wire connected with the positive pole was applied to its upper surface. *At the upper surface there was a disengagement of gas; at the lower surface small metallic globules appeared, like mercury, in their visible character.* Some of these burnt by contact with the air. Others had their metallic lustre tarnished, and finally covered with a white film, which defended them from the atmosphere, and preserved them in their metallic state.

The gas disengaged at the positive wire was oxygen, and the metal deposited was the base of the alkali, afterward called POTASSIUM.

Soda, when submitted to a like process, gave a similar result, and the metal educed from it was that which is now called SODIUM.

This capital discovery was made in October, 1807. Potassium was discovered on the 6th of that month, and sodium a few days after.

Sensitive friends of the great British chemist have been moved to vindicate the glory of this discovery from those who would tarnish it by ascribing to the accidental possession of the laboratory and apparatus of the Royal Institution of Great Britain a share in producing it. These generous survivors may tranquillize their fears. Possibly such vindication may be called for by a portion of the present generation having pretensions sufficient to raise them to the level of envy, but wanting those better qualities which would elevate them above it. Certainly no such apology will be needful with posterity.

The strong affinities of these new metals for one or other of the constituents of almost every body with which they were brought in contact, and of every menstruum or atmosphere with which they could be surrounded, was very embarrassing, and rendered the examination of their physical properties extremely difficult. It was found most convenient, either to preserve them in a tube protected from the contact of the air above recently distilled naphtha, or to allow them to combine with mercury so as to form an amalgam, and in that state to preserve them, separating them by heat when the pure metal was required.

The analogy suggested by the decomposition of the fixed alkalies naturally led to a like inquiry with respect to the earths which enjoy with the former common properties, and those which seemed most analogous to the alkalies. Baryta, strontia, lime, and magnesia, were tried by like methods, but without any satisfactory result. Being slightly moistened at their surfaces, they were exposed to the electric current transmitted by iron wire under naphtha. At the negative pole they assumed a darker color, and small particles appeared there, showing metallic lustre, and which gradually whitened by exposure to air. In the experiments on potassium it was found that when a mixture of potash and the oxide of mercury, tin, or lead, was exposed to the Voltaic current, decomposition ensued, and an amalgam of potassium was produced. The same method was accordingly tried with the alkaline earths. Mixtures of these substances with oxides of tin, lead, silver, and mercury, were exposed to the current. In these cases, a small quantity of a substance having the whiteness of silver was deposited at the negative pole, which was found to be an amalgam. Still the results were not conclusive or satisfactory.

The labors of Davy had attained this point when, in June, 1808, he received a letter from M. Berzilius, informing him that, assisted by Dr. Pontin, that chemist had succeeded in decomposing baryta and lime, by exposing them in contact with mercury to the current. Davy immediately repeated the experiment, and obtained the amalgam of the metallic base of baryta at the negative pole. This was accomplished by a battery of 500 pairs, weakly charged, acting on a surface of slightly moistened baryta through the medium of a globule of mercury. The mercury gradually became less fluid, and, after a few minutes, was found covered with a white film of baryta; and when the amalgam was thrown into water, the latter was decomposed, hydrogen was dismissed, mercury precipitated, and a solution of baryta formed. A like process gave a similar result with lime.

Having thus verified the results obtained by Berzelius, Davy extended the same method to strontia and magnesia. The former readily yielded; the latter was more intractable. By continuing the process, however, for a longer time, and keeping the earth continually moist, at last a combination of the basis with mercury was obtained, which slowly produced magnesia by absorption of oxygen from the air, or by decomposing water.

Thus were discovered Barium, Strontium, Calcium, and Magnesium, as an immediate consequence of the first great step made in this course of investigation by the discovery of potassium and sodium.

The next group of earths brought to trial consisted of alumina, silica, zirconia, and glucinia, which proved more refractory than any of the former. Driven in search of other methods of experimenting, he considered minutely their qualities in relation to other bodies, with a view to the discovery of analogies by which his researches might be conducted. From the absence of any tendency in alumina and silica to yield to the attraction of the electric current in the direction of either pole, he inferred the probability of their partaking of the nature of nutro-saline substances, and attempted their decomposition by processes suggested by that supposition. Failing in these, and observing that alumina and silica have both a strong affinity for potash and soda, and considering that such affinity could not proceed from the oxygen which might be one of their constituents, he inferred that it must be a quality of their metallic bases, and that it would, in that case, be probable that, if mixed with soda or potash, and exposed to the electric current, the base might be made to separate, and to attach itself to the base of the alkali. A mixture of silica and potash, in the proportion of one to six, was accordingly put in a platinum crucible, and reduced to a fluid state over a charcoal fire. The crucible was put in connexion with the positive pole of a battery of five hundred pairs, and a rod of platinum connected with the negative pole was brought in contact with the alkaline menstruum. The moment the end of the negative rod touched the liquid, globules rose through it to the surface, on which they swam about in a state of brilliant combustion. When the mixture cooled, the platinum bar was removed, and the alkali and salex which adhered to it detached; there remained upon it brilliant metallic scales, which, immediately on exposure, became covered with a white crust, and some of which burnt spontaneously. Being plunged in water, the end of the platinum produced effervescence, and an alkaline solution was formed, which, upon examination, was proved to contain silica. The same process applied to alumni gave a like result.

It was now determined to try the effect of the Voltaic current upon the earths, in contact with potassium itself. An amalgam of potassium, in contact with silica, was negatively electrified under naphtha. After being acted on for an hour, the amalgam was made to decompose water, and the alkali thus obtained was neutralized by acetous acid. A white precipitate was obtained having all the characters of silica.

The same process was applied, with the same results, to alumina, glucinia, and zirconia. It was inferred, therefore, that these earths were oxides of metals, to which respectively the names of SILICIUM, ALUMINIUM, GLUCINIUM, and ZIRCONIUM, were given.

Having established, by direct experiments, the fact that so many of the alkaline and earthy substances were oxides with metallic bases, it was consistent with sound physical logic to assume, as a general law, that "*the alkalies and earths are oxides of metals.*"

The question, how far the volatile alkali, ammonia, was to be regarded in relation to such a law, naturally presented itself. Without reference to this analogy, or offering any hypothesis to explain the fact, Seebeck had already shown that an amalgam could be obtained by the action of ammonia on mercury. This fact was reproduced by Berzelius and Pontin, and communicated by them, with various circumstances attending it, to Davy. Berzelius maintained that ammonia came within the scope of the general law, and that an idea which had been previously thrown out by Davy was justified by the phenomena which showed that ammonia was a *binary metallic base*. This question was then taken up by Davy, and the experiments of Berzelius repeated, but without arriving at any certain or clear result. Gay-Lussac and Thénard opposed the views of Davy and Berzelius; and a contest arose, for which, as it has little connexion with the progress of electrical science, we shall merely refer to the scientific periodical works in which it was carried on.*

It has been already observed, that the character of Davy's mind was to pass

* Annales de Chimie, tom. lxxii., p. 193., lxxv., 256–291.; Biblioth. Brit., June, 1809, p. 122.

directly from discovery to application. In the same memoir which contained the announcement of the subjugation of the alkalies and earths by the powers of the pile, is found his brilliant hypothesis to explain the phenomena of volcanoes and aerolites. The metallic bases of the alkalies and earths cannot exist at the surface of the earth in their simple or uncombined form, nor even alloyed with the more perfect metals, because of the intensity of their affinity for oxygen. But the same cause does not prevent their existence in the interior parts of the globe. Let the possibility of the existence of potassium, sodium, calcium, or any other metals of the same class in the inferior strata of the earth, either in a separate state or in combination with other metallic substances, be admitted; and it is only necessary to imagine their occasional exposure to the action of air or water, to obtain a satisfactory solution for volcanic eruptions. These highly combustible metallic principles, combining with oxygen, attended by violent combustion, are ejected from the bowels of the earth, and form the craters of volcanoes, the combination being an earthy matter exhibited after its ejection as lava. The formation of aerolites might proceed from the same causes, their luminous appearance and detonation being produced by the combustion attending the combination of the metals with oxygen as they enter the atmosphere.

With a view to test the validity of these ingenious hypotheses, Davy investigated carefully the phenomena of active volcanoes; and, not finding them to be in sufficient accordance with these, he relinquished his theory, without any of that regret which attends the failure of a favorite hypothesis, when the discovery of truth is an object secondary to the attainment of personal distinction.

The powers of decomposition and transfer by Voltaic electricity, so strikingly exhibited in the researches of Davy, directed the attention of physiologists and others once more to the investigation of the agency of electricity in the vegetable and animal economy. The experiments which had been made to show that the alkaline and earthy elements found in organized vegetable substances were evolved, by the process of vegetation, from air and water, had always been inconclusive and unsatisfactory; and Davy's experiments, in which it was shown that even in water carefully distilled there is still held in solution a portion of saline or metallic matter, together with the known fact, that air almost always holds in mechanical suspension solid matter of various kinds, finally overturned such hypotheses. All the substances developed in organized nature may be produced, by ordinary processes, from combination of known constituents. The compounds of iron, alkalies, and earthy bodies with mineral acids, abound in vegetable soil. The decomposition of basaltic, granitic, and other rocks, affords a constant supply of earthy, alkaline, and ferruginous matter to the superficial part of the earth. In the seeds of all plants which have been examined, nutro-saline compounds, containing potash, soda, or iron, have been found. It is easy to imagine that these principles pass from vegetables to animals.

The same analogies suggested to Dr. Wollaston the idea, that something like the decomposing and transmitting powers of the pile is the agent to which the animal secretions are due, especially as the existence of such agency in a considerable degree of intensity, in certain animals, was proved by the effects of the torpedo and Gymnotus electricus; and he considered that the universal prevalence of the same power, lower only in degree in other animals, was rendered highly probable by the extreme suddenness with which the nervous influence is propagated from one part of the living system to another. Although the electric power of decomposition and transfer has been experimentally demonstrated only in cases of comparatively high intensity of action, yet analogy countenanced the idea that very feeble electric energies would produce like effects more slowly, in proportion to their weakness. To illustrate this by immediate experiment, he tied a piece of clean bladder over one end of a glass tube three quarters of an inch in diameter, and two inches long, and filled it with water holding $\frac{1}{240}$ of its weight of salt in solution. Placing it on a shilling, he connected the silver with the surface of the water by a wire of zinc, and found that alkali was transmitted through the bladder to the silver by the attraction of the negative electricity. Decisive indications of this were obtained in five minutes. The efficacy of a power so feeble confirms the conjecture that similar agents may be instrumental in various animal secretions. The blood, which is alkaline, supplies the bladder with matter in which acid is strongly manifested; while an excess of alkali, above that contained in the blood, is manifested in bile. These effects would be explained by admitting a permanent state of positive electricity in the kidneys, and negative electricity in the liver. The coincidence of this view with the guesses of Napoleon, already mentioned, is curious and interesting.*

The last great discovery of Davy directed the attention of the philosophers of the continent to the same field of inquiry: and, much as had been expected from the powers of the pile when its illustrious inventor expounded its nature and properties to the assembled members of the Institute in 1801, it was now, from day to day, rendered more evident that these powers were inadequately estimated, and imperfectly understood, and that it was still destined to enrich every branch of physical science by the development of new and unlooked-for phenomena. Napoleon, in the magnificent spirit with which his encouragement of the sciences was always manifested, had presented to the laboratory of the Polytechnic School a Voltaic apparatus of immense magnitude and power. With this instrument MM. Gay-Lussac and Thénard undertook an experimental investigation of the powers of the pile, with the view of determining more especially the influence which the number of the metallic elements, and the nature of the liquid used to charge the pile, have on its chemical action. Assuming, as a modulus of the chemical energy of the pile, the quantity of gas evolved in the process of decomposition in a given time, they arrived at the following conclusions: 1. The decomposing energy depends conjointly on the conducting power of the liquid under decomposition, and on the nature of that which is used to charge the pile. 2. It is greater when the pile is charged with a mixture of acid and salt, than with salt alone. 3. The chemical effects are proportional to the force of the acids by which it is put in action: and, 4. They do not augment in the same ratio as the number of pairs of plates, but very nearly in the ratio of the cube root of that number.

That part of the electro-chemical theory of Davy in which the negative character natural to certain physical elements, and the positive to others, is assumed, was implicitly, if not expressly, included in the hypothesis of Grotthus. Without such a supposition, the series of decompositions and recompositions imagined by that philosopher could scarcely be admitted. The probable connexion of chemical attractions with electric forces had been also conjectured by Hube it his *Traité de Physique*, and Ritter obscurely expressed some ideas of the same kind. Immediately before the commencement of Davy's researches, Oersted, since so celebrated for his discoveries in electro-magnetism, promulgated a theory,† in which he maintained that all the phenomena of chemistry might be regarded as the result of two general forces common to all matter, and that the same forces produced those effects which were rendered sen-

* See Philosophical Magazine, vol. xxxiii., p. 1088.

† Recherches sur l'Identité des Forces Chimiques et Electriques. Traduit de l'Allemand. 1813.

sible in electric attractions and repulsions. This work, however, was exclusively of a speculative kind, unsupported by any experiments which could give force or validity to the theory it proposed.

The electro-chemical theory of Davy was the first which had ever professed to be based on clear and well-ascertained facts. It was laid down as a fundamental principle in this theory, that when two bodies, the particles of which are in opposite electrical states, and sufficiently exalted to enable their electric attraction to overcome the force of aggregation of their particles, are brought into contact, they will unite, and heat and light will be developed by the combination of the two electric fluids. When the combination is effected, all signs of electricity cease, as would necessarily ensue from the union of the two fluids, but by what power the aggregation of the new compound was maintained was not explained.

Berzelius and Ampère, who, of all the philosophers of the continent, evinced most justice and candor in their appreciation of Davy's merit, took up the electro-chemical theory, which was not pursued through its consequences by its author, owing probably to the natural disposition of his mind to investigate new facts rather than discuss the merits of hypotheses. Berzelius assumed that the constituent atoms of bodies were not only naturally electrical, as Davy had maintained, but that they possessed electric polarity, and that the intensities of their poles are unequal. He investigated, in the first place, the two questions, How electricity exists in bodies? and, How it is that some bodies are naturally negative, and others sometimes positive and sometimes negative?

A body never becomes electric, without manifesting the two opposite electric principles, either in different parts of it, or in the sphere of its action; when the two electricities appear separately in a continuous body, they are always found on opposite sides. The tourmaline and some other crystals offer an example of this. But, since the parts of a body possess the same properties as the body itself, it is necessary to admit that bodies are composed of atoms, each of which has an electric polarity, and its poles have unequal intensities. On this polarity depend the chemical phenomena, and its unequal intensity is the cause of the different force exercised by their affinities. Bodies are accordingly electro-positive or electro-negative in combining, according as the influence of the one or other of their atomic poles predominates.

The degree of polarity in this theory is influenced by the temperature. Thus many substances at common temperatures manifest but feeble electric polarity, which, at a red-heat, show a very strong one.

No combination can be effected unless the polarized molecules of one or both of the combining bodies have free mobility among each other, each being at liberty to turn on its own centre in any direction, so that the particles may present toward each other their contrary poles in obedience to their electric attraction. This condition renders it necessary that one or both of the combining bodies be in the fluid state.

The vulnerable point of this theory was found in the phenomena of aggregation. In what manner can the electric forces which it assumes produce the hardness, brittleness, ductility, and tenacity, of different species of solids, the viscidity of liquids, or the elasticity of gases?

Berzelius admits that these effects are not explicable by this hypothesis. M. Ampère attempted to solve this question,* by assuming that the atoms of bodies possessing each its proper electricity, in virtue of which they are united in combinations in the same manner as two leaves of paper oppositely electrified adhere to each other, also act by their electricity on the electricity of the

* Journal de Physique, 1821.

medium in which they exist, attracting the fluid of the contrary name, and repelling the fluid of the same name. The atoms are therefore considered as strictly analogous to the Leyden jar; the internal charge representing the natural electricity of the atom, and the external that which is drawn from the surrounding medium. If a combination is formed between an electro-positive and an electro-negative body, a discharge takes place; the atoms dismiss their external charge, and rush into union in virtue of the reciprocal attraction of their opposite natural electricities. The atmospheres of the atoms, as well as the atoms themselves, are combined; but, as the atoms cannot emerge from them, their electricities act on those of their atmospheres, exerting attractions and repulsions, so as to produce electrical phenomena the reverse of those which attended their combination.

The zinc plates of a Voltaic apparatus, being subject to continual oxydation, are at length so reduced in thickness, as to render it necessary to replace them by new ones. This gradual wear of the pile by use rendered it desirable to seek for means of constructing a pile composed of solid elements only; a project, however, which could only be entertained by those who conceived that chemical action was merely incidental, and not essential, to the development of Voltaic electricity. Although the high probability, if not the certainty, that chemical action is indispensable, must render abortive all attempts at the discovery of a *dry pile*, such researches have nevertheless been attended with some advantage.

The term *dry pile* was intended originally to express a Voltaic pile, of which all the elements were solid; and the advantages of such an instrument, if it could be discovered, were so apparent, that the attention of electricians was directed to it at an early period in the history of Voltaic discovery. If a pile composed of solid elements (thought they) could but be discovered, neither evaporation nor chemical action could take place; the electricity due to the contact of heterogeneous bodies, according to Volta's theory, would be continually evolved; and as the bodies evolving it would suffer no change, the quantity and intensity of the electricity supplied by the instrument would be absolutely uniform and invariable. In 1803, MM. Hachette and Desormes substituted starch for the liquid in the common pile; and, in 1809, De Luc invented a pile apparently free from any liquid element. This apparatus consisted of a column formed of alternate disks of zinc and paper gilt on one side, the gilt sides of the paper disks being all turned in one direction. This was in reality not a *dry pile;* the paper imbibed and retained moisture enough to give a feeble activity to the apparatus.

De Luc's pile was improved by Zamboni in 1812. He rejected the disks of zinc, and composed the pile of disks of paper only, one surface being tinned, and the other coated thinly with the peroxide of manganese, brushed with a mixture of flour and milk; or gilt or silver paper may be used, the metallic surface being wetted with a saturated solution of the sulphate of zinc, on which, when dry, the peroxide of manganese in powder, may be spread. Several leaves of paper thus prepared are placed one upon the other, and cut into the required form by a circular cutter. As many disks are thus formed by one operation as there are leaves of paper superposed; and these being afterward laid one upon the other, the pile is formed. This pile is usually placed in a hollow cylinder, of the same internal diameter. The paper disks are forced into close contact by pressure produced by screws.

Although, by the aid of a condenser, the electricity evolved in these piles may be rendered sensible, and sparks may even be obtained, the power is incomparably more feeble than that of the common pile, even in its most inefficient state. It is found that by increasing beyond a certain limit the number of disks composing these, their power is diminished. Their effects have been generally limited to those produced on the condenser; but, by diminishing considerably the number of disks, M. Pelletier has succeeded in decomposing water by these instruments. Their action, however, ceases after the lapse of a certain period, when the paper has lost all its humidity.

The sources of the disengagement of electricity in this pile are various and complicated. Besides what may arise from the contact of heterogeneous substances, chemical action intervenes in several ways. The organic matter acts upon the zinc as well as upon the peroxide of manganese, reducing the latter to a lower state of oxydation.

Zamboni examined the effects produced on the electricity of the pile by soaking the paper to which the tin leaf was pasted in different liquids, and found that, according as the state of the other side of the paper was changed, the poles of the pile were thrown to different ends. If the paper be soaked in oil, the poles are in a direction contrary to that which they assume when a coating of manganese is used. On the other hand, when the paper is soaked in honey, in an alkaline solution, a solution of the sulphate of zinc, or half curdled milk, the poles have the same position as when they are coated with manganese.

No sensible shock is received from a pile of two thousand pairs, although the tension at the poles is sufficient to produce a sensible effect on the proof plane, and a condenser applied to one of the poles will, in a few moments, give sparks an inch in length, and a Leyden battery may receive from it a charge.

The conducting power of the vapor suspended in the atmosphere, carrying away a portion of the electricity of these piles from their poles, produces a continual variation in the tension of the electricity at these points.

Zamboni found that the energy of the pile was greater in summer than in winter, whether measured by the tension of the electricity at the poles, or the rate at which the fluids were produced and propagated. M. Donné compared the tension with the height of the barometer, but could discover no relation between them. He found the tension the same in a vacuum as under the pressure of the atmosphere.

It is known that electricity may be developed on a plate of a single metal, by causing one surface of the plate to be acted on chemically, in a degree or manner different from the other surface. This may be effected by merely rendering one surface smooth and the other rough. This expedient is said to have been resorted to in the construction of a Voltaic battery with one metal, without any liquid element. From sixty to eighty plates of zinc, of four square inches of surface, are made clean and polished on one side, the other remaining rough as it comes from the mould. These are fixed in a wooden trough parallel to each other, their polished surfaces all turned toward the same end of the trough, and with an open space between the successive plates of from the tenth to the twentieth part of an inch. These intermediate spaces are filled by thin plates of atmospheric air. If one extremity of this apparatus be put in communication with the ground, and the other with an electroscope, the latter will receive a very sensible charge.

We can regard the dry pile in no other light than as an extended Voltaic series. The moisture, which is essential to its activity, is in the condition of anything but freedom of motion; so that the renewal of contact by the presence of fresh particles, which seems essential in all developments of electricity, exists in the lowest degree; and then again the feeble chemical actions existing between elements under circumstances so unfavorable, all conspire in producing the small quantity of electricity for which these instruments are remarkable; while the great length of series produces the high tension of the poles. It is only recently that chemical decomposition has been obtained by the dry pile. Mr. Gassiot prepaired 10,000 Zamboni's disks ; and by carefully directing the electricity through hydriodate of potassium on a slip of glass, he obtained the development of iodine on the wire connected with the oxide of manganese end of the series. He could not obtain heating effects on Harris's thermo-electroscope, unless he allowed the charge to pass in sparks.

The only uses to which dry piles have been hitherto applied are—1. To produce a continued motion, by an electrical pendulum suspended between the contrary poles of two such piles placed side by side, so that the positive pole of one and the negative pole of the other shall be at the summit. This motion will be continued as long as sufficient moisture is retained by the elements of the piles to sustain their activity ; but it will not be regular, since the development of electricity will be affected by variable atmospheric causes. 2. In condensing electrometers, to detect the presence of very small quantities of electricity on the inferior plate of the condenser.*

I shall conclude this notice of the progressive advancement of Voltaic electricity here. The phenomena and laws whose development followed the experimental researches which have been explained, will probably be noticed on a future occasion, when I shall offer a view of the actual state of Voltaic electricity, its relations with magnetism and heat.

* Becquerel, Traité de l'Electricité, tom. i., p. 166.

THE MOON AND THE WEATHER.

Ancient Prognostics of Aristotle, Theophrastus, Aratus, Theon, Pliny, Virgil.—Recent Predictions.—Theory of Lunar Attraction not in accordance with popular Opinion.—Changes of Weather compared with Changes of the Moon.—Prevalence of Rain compared with Lunar Phases.—Direction of the Wind.—Height of Barometer compared with Lunar Phases.—Erroneous Notions of Cycles of nineteen and nine Years.—Cycle of four and eight Years mentioned by Pliny.

THE MOON AND THE WEATHER.

THE physical laws which govern the phenomena of our atmosphere, and regulate the changes of the weather, have always been a favorite topic of speculation. As the principles of astronomical science supplied means of predicting, with the highest possible degree of certainty and precision, the motions and appearances of the heavenly bodies, it was not unnaturally expected that atmospherical phenomena might be brought under equally clear and certain rules. The connexion of the lunar motions with the tides was apparent, long before the mechanical influence by which the moon produced the rise and fall of the waters of the ocean was explained; and this gave countenance, at a very early period, to the idea that that body had an influence on the atmosphere, if not as certain and regular as on the waters, still sufficiently so to furnish probable grounds for conjecture as to certain periodical changes.

But even before analogies of this kind could have furnished much ground for reasoning, and when the heavenly bodies must have been regarded more as *signs* than *causes*, meteorological phenomena were connected with them by popular observation. The influence of climate on all the interests of a people in a pastoral, and subsequently in an agricultural state, is obvious; and accordingly we find weather prognostics coming down by tradition from the most remote antiquity. By a course, however, contrary to most other subjects of observation and inquiry, this was corrupted rather than improved with the progress of knowledge and civilization; and what was once a mere system of *signs* of a certain present state of the atmosphere, indicating certain approaching changes, was, by the craving of philosophy after the relations of cause and effect, converted into the most absurd system of *rules*, having no foundation in nature, never fulfilled by the phenomena except fortuitously, and maintaining their ascendency by the unbounded credulity of mankind.

In the writings of Aristotle, and, after him, in those of Theophrastus, Aratus, Theon, and others, although meteorology is treated as a part of astronomy, or astrology, it is easy to trace the simple views of the more ancient and less philosophical observers, and to perceive that the appearances referred to were by them regarded merely as signs, prognosticating (whether truly or not we shall see presently) approaching changes, and not at all as physical causes effecting these changes.

We shall limit ourselves to a few of the more remarkable and generally received ancient meteorological maxims, as examples of the whole.

In the work of Aratus, entitled Διοσημεῖα (*prognostics*), and in the Scholia of Theon, and elsewhere, the appearances of the moon in different phases are described as prognosticating the weather for a certain time to come :—

Σήματα δ' οὔτ' ἄρ' πᾶσιν ἐπ' ἤμασι πάντα τέτυκται.
"Αλλ' ὅσα μὲν τριτάτη τετραταίη τε πέληται,
Μέσφα διχαιομένης · διχάδος γέ μεν ἄχρις ἐπ' αὐτὴν
Σημαίνει διχόμηνον · ἀτὰρ πάλιν εκ διχομήνης
Ες διχά δα φθιμένην· ἔχεται δέ οἱ αυτίκα τετράς
Μηνος ἀποιχομενου. ΑΡΑΤ Διοσημεῖα.

Sin ortu quarto (namque is certissimus auctor),
Pura, neque obtusis per cœlum cornibus ibit,
Totus et ille dies, et qui nascentur ab illo,
Exactum ad mensem pluviâ ventisque carebunt.
VIRGIL, Georg., Lib. I., l. 432.

If the horns of the lunar crescent on the third day after new moon are sharply and clearly defined, the weather may be expected to be fair during the ensuing month.

Let us see how far this prognostic will stand the test of rational examination. The lunar crescent is produced by a peculiar relation of position which subsists between the aspects of the moon presented to the sun and earth. If only half the hemisphere which receives the sun's light be presented toward the earth, the moon is exactly halved ; if a quarter of the hemisphere be turned to the earth, the moon is crescent, and its age is then nearly four days. When its age is less than two days, therefore, less that one eighth of its illuminated hemisphere is presented to our planet, and consequently it appears a very thin crescent. It is evident that these effects, if seen through perfectly transparent space, could not alter with circumstances, and that, in the same position of the moon with respect to the earth and sun, the crescent must be at all times equally sharp and distinct. But when the moon is viewed (as it is by us) through an atmosphere that is from thirty to forty miles high—that atmosphere being liable to be more or less loaded with imperfectly transparent vapors—it will be seen with more or less distinctness, according to the varying transparency of the medium through which it is viewed. The fact, therefore, of the crescent appearing distinct and well defined, or obscurely, with the points of the horns blunted, is merely in consequence of our atmosphere being at one time more pure, clear, and transparent, than at another.

When the moon is under three days old, it is only visible for a short time after sunset, and therefore the phenomenon in question can only be observed in the evening, a little above the western horizon. This prognostic of Aratus may be thus translated : "When the atmosphere above the western horizon "soon after sunset on the third day of the moon is serene, the weather will be "fair for the remainder of the month ; but if it be loaded with vapors, the con- "trary event will ensue."

All the world, says Arago, will doubtless reject the prognostic when thus stated ; nevertheless, the words only in which it is expressed are changed, the meaning being absolutely the same.

But what shall be the import of this prognostic, if (as must frequently happen) the horns of the crescent, during the same evening, be at one time well, and at another ill defined ; at one time sharp and distinct, at another time blunt and confused ? Are we then to infer contradictory propositions ? Shall the prognostic be true for both or false for both ? Another prognostic of Aratus is, that if on the fourth day the moon project no shadow, we are to expect bad weather during the month.

As we have already observed, the light of the moon, or rather the light of the sun reflected from the moon, must in reality be the same, and would, in fact, always appear the same in like positions to an eye placed beyond the limits of our atmosphere. The presence or absence of shadow is merely an indication of a certain intensity of light, having reference to the sensibility of the human eye. That the moon in a certain phase should at one time produce, and at another time not produce a shadow, is, therefore, merely an indication that the atmosphere through which her light has passed is at one time more transparent than another. Now as the pure atmosphere has always the same degree of transparency, these varying effects can only proceed from the vapors which are mixed with it; and thus, as before, the moon in this case is only a *sign* of a certain state of the air at a particular time, and in a particular direction. The fourth day of the moon is selected, because on that day, if the atmosphere be very free from vapors, the light of the crescent is just sufficient to produce a shadow ; but if any considerable quantity of vapors be present in the atmosphere, even though they should not constitute what is called a cloud, they may impair its transparency so much as to deprive the faint light of the lunar crescent of the power of producing a shadow. Thus, as in the former case, the moon is here used as a meteorological instrument to ascertain the humidity of the air, and that only in the western direction, at or after sunset; so that when translated into its true meteorological language, this prognostic is equivalent to that to which we have just adverted.

Varro, as quoted by Pliny, gives the following meteorological maxim :—*Nascens Luna si cornua superior obatro surget, pluvias decrescens dabit ; si inferiore, ante plenilunium ; si in mediâ nigritia illa fuerit, imbrem in pleno.*

"If the new moon have its upper horn darkened, the declining moon will be attended with rain; if the new moon have its inferior horn darkened, there will be rain before the full moon ; and if the middle of the crescent be darkened, there will be rain at the full moon."

The obscurity here mentioned must, like those already alluded to, be produced by the atmospheric vapors, rendering the medium through which the crescent is beheld imperfectly transparent. If two lines be conceived to be drawn from the eye of the observer in the direction of the points of the horns, and an intermediate line toward the middle of the crescent, it will be evident that these lines will diverge from one another very slightly. Now the obscurity of either the upper or lower horn, or of the middle, the other parts being clear, would only indicate the presence of imperfectly transparent vapor in the direction of one of these lines, from which the others are free. To what, then, will this prognostic amount ? That if the highest of these lines happen to encounter, at any point of the space which it traverses, a sufficient quantity of vaporous matter to render the superior horn indistinct, rain may be expected toward the decline of the moon ; if a like portion of vapor be found in the direction of the middle line, from which the other two lines are free, rain may be expected at the full of the moon ; and if the obscure vapor be in the direction of the line to the lower horn, rain may be expected in the increase of the moon ! It is presumed that the absurdity of all this is sufficiently glaring, but it will be rendered more so if it be considered that, by the spectator changing his position through a distance of a few hundred yards, he may so place himself that the vapor which obscures the upper horn in one position, will obscure the middle in another, and the lower horn in the third. What then becomes of the prediction? Are we to infer that the same little portion of vapor suspended in the air will produce rain at three different times in the month, at three places situated a short distance asunder?

The truth is, that the ancient prognostics, whether derived from the moon, from the sun, or from the stars, were, in the first instance, used legitimately as mere indications of the state of the atmosphere by persons too simple-minded and uneducated to trouble themselves much with the philosophy of cause and effect; but when these appearances came into the hands of philosophers, they were at once elevated to the rank of physical causes, and their dominion extended in proportion to the dignity and importance thus conferred upon them. Such notions were in keeping with a philosophy which made the moon the boundary between corruption, change, and passiveness, on the one hand, and the active powers of nature on the other. "Thus," says Horsley, "the uncertain conclusions of an ill-conducted analogy, and false metaphysics, were mixed with a few simple precepts, derived from observation, which probably made the whole of the science of the prognostication in its earliest and purest state."

Although from age to age, the particular circumstances and appearances connected with the moon, by which the atmospheric vicissitudes were prognosticated, were changed, still the faith of mankind in general in her influence on the weather has never been shaken; and even the present day, when knowledge is so widely diffused, and physical science brought, as it were, to the doors of all who have the slightest pretension to education, this belief is almost universal. Many, it is true, may discard predictions which affect to define, from day to day, the state of the weather. There are few, however, who do not look for a change of the weather with a change of the moon. It is a belief nearly universal, that the epochs of a new and full moon are in the great majority of instances attended by a change of weather, and that the quarters, though not so certain, are still epochs when a change may be probably expected. Those who have least faith in the meteorological influence of the moon, extend their belief thus far.

There are two ways in which this question may be considered. It may be asked whether, by the known principles of physics, the moon can have any, and if any, what influence on our atmosphere? And whether that influence be such as would cause a change of weather at the epochs of the principal phases? Or, on the other hand, we may limit the inquiry to the mere matter of fact, and ask whether, by immediate observation, it has been found that the epochs of the chief lunar phases have been, in the majority of instances, attended by changes of weather? or, to put the question more generally, whether any *periodicity* of atmospheric phenomena is actually observed to correspond with the moon's phases.

It would seem at first view that neither of these inquiries could be attended with any doubt or difficulty; yet the case is quite otherwise. The former, involving as it does the whole theory of the moon's attraction on our atmosphere, modified by a multitude of disturbing causes, is a physical problem as difficult and complicated as could well be propounded. Indeed, it is one, taken in its most comprehensive form, which does not admit of solution in the present state of physical science. The latter being merely a question of fact and observation, is not attended, properly speaking, with ultimate difficulty, but it is one which would require a course of observation carefully and accurately conducted, continued for a series of years. Such observations when skilfully examined and discussed, would furnish grounds for safe and certain conclusions.

But such observations have not been carried to the necessary extent. If the question of fact were, whether there be any obvious and glaring correspondence of periodicity between the lunar phases and the atmospheric vicissitudes, it would be instantly answered in the negative. For although we do not possess sufficiently accurate and long-continued series of observations to decide the question whether the moon has any atmospheric influence, *however small*, we possess a sufficient body of ascertained facts to justify the conclusion that her influence is certainly not considerable, and that, whatever be its amount, it is probably in a great degree obliterated by the vast number of modifying and disturbing causes which are constantly in action.

Let us consider for a moment the theoretical question. If the moon can act upon our atmosphere by attraction, as she acts upon the waters of the ocean, she will produce *atmospheric tides*, similar to those of the waters. The greater mobility of air will cause those tides to be formed more rapidly than the water tides; and it may be, perhaps, assumed that the tides of the atmosphere will always be placed, either exactly, or very nearly under the moon. Thus, as there is *high water* twice daily, so would there be *high air* twice daily; and the times of this air tide would correspond with the moments of the transit of the moon over the meridian above and below the horizon.

The same causes, also, which at new and full moon, produce spring tides, and at the quarters, neap tides, would produce spring and neap atmospheric tides at the same epochs. At new and full moon, therefore, the air ought to be higher, daily, at noon and midnight than at any other times during the month; and, on the other hand, at the quarters it ought to be lower.

If, then, the barometer be observed twice daily, viz., at the times of the moon's transit over the meridian, above and below the horizon, it ought (so far as it will be affected by the sun and moon) to be the highest at new and full moon, and lowest at the quarters. Now as the rise of the barometer generally indicates fair weather, and its fall foul weather, the conclusion to which this would lead, would be, that the epochs of new and full moon should be generally fair, while at the quarters bad weather would generally prevail.

This, however, is not the popular opinion. The traditional maxim is that a *change* may be looked for at new and full moon; that is, if the weather be previously fair, it will become foul; if previously foul, fair.

M. Arago has made an ingenious attempt at the evaluation of the very minute effect of what we have called *atmospheric tides*. To comprehend his reasoning it will only be necessary to consider that, at a new and full moon, the sun and moon pass the meridian above and below the horizon together; and therefore, that *high air*, or atmospheric tides, must at these times take place at noon and midnight; *low air* would therefore occur about six, A. M., and six, P. M. Thus so far as the attraction of the moon affects the atmosphere, the barometer, which rises and falls as the atmosphere rises and falls, would be affected by an ascending movement for six hours before noon and midnight, and for six hours after these times. But, when the moon is in the quarters, being then one fourth of the heavens removed, before or behind the sun, it will pass the meridian, whether above or below the horizon, about six hours later or earlier than the sun. At the quarters, therefore, the atmospheric tides would occur about six, A. M., and six, P. M. Thus at the quarters the barometric column, so far as it is influenced by the moon's attraction, would be affected with a descending motion for about six hours after these times. It will be evident, that if we were in a condition to estimate the amount of these barometric movements, we should be at once in a condition to declare the amount of the lunar attraction on our atmosphere.

But these effects, if appreciable at all, are modified by at least one other influence, which has been the subject of certain and satisfactory observation. There is a daily fluctuation in the barometric column, called the *diurnal variation*, which has an obvious relation to the apparent diurnal motion of the sun, and which probably is caused by solar heat. It is observed that the barometric column falls daily, from nine in the morning till noon. In Europe, this effect is frequently obliterated by other disturbing causes; but it is always observable when a mean is taken of observations, continued for any considerable number of days. This diurnal variation will be combined with the effect of the lunar attraction in the results of the observations. Now at a new and full moon these causes produce contrary effects on the barometric column. During the three hours preceding noon, the lunar attraction has a tendency to impart to it an ascending movement; while, by reason of the diurnal variation, it would have at the same time a descending movement; the result would consequently be the *difference* of the two effects. If the diurnal variations were equal to the effects of the moon's attraction, the motions would neutralize each other, and the column would be stationary; but if they be unequal, the column will ascend or descend by their difference. At the quarters these two effects will conspire in producing a descending movement of the barometric column during those hours before noon, and the result of observation will be a descent equal to the *sum* of the two effects.

Observations, therefore, made at and before noon at the times of new and full moon, and at the quarters, ought to supply estimates of the sum and the difference of these two physical effects; and if such observations be continued for a sufficient length of time, a mean estimate may be obtained from which the effects of disturbing causes will be eliminated. M. Arago has applied this method of investigation to a series of observations conducted for twelve years in Paris, and he has found that the effect of the lunar attraction on the barometers produced between the high and low states of the atmosphere, corresponding to high and low water, cannot exceed the six hundredth part of an inch—a quantity too small to be appreciated by any meteorological instruments, and, certainly such as could produce no sensible effect on the atmosphere.

It is evident, then, that if the moon has any influence on our atmosphere, it does not proceed from any cause analogous to that which produces the tides of the ocean; and therefore, that the fact, that the moon does produce such tides can afford no countenance to her imputed meteorological influence.

But it may be said that although the moon may not affect the atmosphere by her gravitation, yet she may influence it by her light, or by electrical or magnetical emanations, or, in fine, by some occult physical causes not yet discovered by astronomers. This is an objection that, from its vagueness and indefiniteness, is difficult to be rebutted by any means which theory can furnish. It is known that the light of the moon concentrated in a point by the most powerful burning lenses, is incapable of producing the slightest sensible effect on the most susceptible thermometer, neither is it found to produce any effects of an electrical or magnetical kind. It may be assumed generally, that the effects commonly imputed to the moon, in producing change of weather at her principal phases, are so contradictory that it is impossible to imagine any physical causes which could account for them. If the new and full moon and the quarters are attended by changes of the weather, the cause producing this effect, under the same circumstances, has incompatible influences: if fair weather precede the phase, the supposed physical cause must be such as to be capable of converting it into foul weather; and if foul weather precede the phase, the same cause must convert it into fair weather. It will be admitted that it is hard to imagine any physical agent whatever, which, under precisely the same circumstances, shall prodnce upon the same body effects so opposite.

But let us dismiss the theoretical view of the question, and inquire as to the facts. Has it been found, *as a matter of fact*, that the epochs which mark the principal phases of the moon have been, in the majority of cases, attended with a change of weather? Before this question can satisfactorily be answered, it will be indispensable that the meaning of the phrase, *change of weather*, be distinctly understood. An observer who is predisposed to a belief in the influence of the lunar phases, will consider himself warranted in classing as a change of weather, every transition from a calm to a wind, whether feeble or forcible—every change from a clear and serene firmament to one ever so little clouded—from a firmament a little clouded to one quite covered over. He will consider the change from a day absolutely free from rain to one in which a few drops may chance to fall, as well entitled to be recorded as a change of weather as if the transition had been from a day absolutely fair to one of incessant rain. On the other hand, a disbeliever in the lunar influences will class all very slight changes as settled weather, and will only register as changes those of a very decisive character. These are difficulties hard to remove, but unless they be removed how is it possible to compare together, with any probability of arriving at the truth, the records of different observers? What value or importance are we to attach to the results of any such observations, unless the prejudices of the observer are admitted into our estimate?

Toaldo has given the result of a comparison of observations continued for forty-five years at Padua, in which changes of weather are recorded in juxtaposition with the lunar phases. Without detailing the particulars of these calculations, we may state at once the following results of them. He found that for every seven new moons the weather changed at six and was settled only at one; for every six full moons the weather changed at five and was settled at one; for every three epochs of the quarters there were two changes of weather.

He also examined the state of the weather in reference to the moon's distance from the earth, which is subject to some variation. The position of the moon when most distant from the earth is called *apogee*, and her position when nearest is called *perigee*. He found that of every six passages of the moon through *perigee* there were five changes of weather; and of every five through *apogee* there were four changes of weather. It is clear that if these results would bear the test of rigid examination, they would be decisive in favor of the popular notion of the influence of the lunar phases. But let us see in what manner Toaldo conducted his inquiry.

He was himself an avowed believer in the lunar influence, not merely upon the atmosphere, but even on the state of organized matter. In his memoir he has not informed us what atmospherical changes he has taken as changes of weather; and it is fair to presume that the bias of his mind would lead him to class the slightest vicissitudes under this head. But, further, Toaldo, in recording the changes of weather coinciding with the epochs of the phases, did not confine himself to changes which took place upon the particular day of the phase. On the pretext that time must be allowed for the physical cause to produce its effect, he took the results of several days. At the new and full moon he included in his enumeration all changes which took place two or three days before or two or three days after the day of new or full moon; while for the quarters he only included the day preceding and the day following the phases; and for epochs not coincident with the lunar phases he only counted the changes of weather which took place on the particular day in question.

It appears, then, that by the changes coinciding with a new and full moon recorded by Toaldo are understood any changes occurring within the space of from three to five days; for the changes recorded at the quarters are to be understood those which occurred within the space of two or three days; and for those not coinciding with the phases the changes which occurred on a particular day. It will not, we presume, require much mathematical sagacity to perceive that the results of such an inquiry must have been just what Toaldo found them to be; and that if instead of taking the epochs of the lunar phases he had taken any other periods whatsoever, and tried them by the same test, he would have arrived at the same results. Five days at the new and full moon would include rather more than a third of the entire lunar month; and thus a third of all the changes of weather which occurred in that period were ascribed by Toaldo to the lunar influence at these epochs.

Professor Pilgrim has examined a series of observations on the lunar phases as connected with the changes of weather, made at Vienna, and continued from 1763 to 1787—a period of 25 years—and he has found that, of every hundred cases of the phases, the proportion of the occurrence of changes to that of the settled state of the weather was as follows:—

	Changes.	Settled Weather.
New moon	58	42
Full moon	63	37
Quarter	63	37
Perigee	72	28
Apogee	64	36
New moon at perigee	80	20
New moon at apogee	64	36
Full moon at perigee	81	19
Full moon at apogee	68	32

Admitting these results, it would follow, contrary to popular belief and to the observations of Toaldo, that the new moon is the least active of the phases; and that the full moon and quarters are equally active; also that the influence of *perigee*, or the nearest position of the moon, is greater than than that of any of the phases, while the influence of *apogee*, or its greatest distance, is equal to that of the quarters and full moon, and greater than that of the new moon.

But Pilgrim's calculations are liable to objections similar to those to which Toaldo's are obnoxious. Like Toaldo, he included in his enumerations of changes, corresponding to the phases, changes which occurred the days preceding and following the phases: this being the case, the only wonder is that the proportion which he has found, especially for the new moon, is not more favorable to his hypothesis. But independently of this, Pilgrim's results are not entitled to any confidence: they bear internal evidence of their inaccuracy; and besides, the observations were not continued for a sufficient length of time to give a safe and certain conclusion.

In the years 1774 and 1775, Dr. Horsley directed his attention to the question, and published two papers in the *Philosophical Transactions* (to which we have already adverted), with a view to dispel the popular prejudice on the subject of lunar influences. Horsley's observations, however, were confined to so short a period of time (two years) that they could not be expected to afford any satisfactory results. He found that in the year 1774 there were only two changes of weather which corresponded with the new moon, and none with the full moon; and that in the year 1775 there were only four changes which corresponded with the new moon, and three with the full moon.

Dismissing, then, this popular notion of the correspondence of changes of the weather with the lunar phases, let us consider the question of lunar influences in a more general point of view, and see whether observation has supplied any ground for the supposition of any relation of periodicity between the moon and the weather. M. Schübler examined this question with considerable care so recently as 1830, and published the results of his observations, which, shortly after, were re-examined by M. Arago.

Schübler's calculations were founded on meteorological observations made at Munich, Stutgard, and Augsburg, for twenty-eight years.* His object was to ascertain whether any correspondence existed between the lunar phases and the quantity of rain which fell in different parts of the month. He defined a rainy day to be one in which a fall of rain or snow was recorded in the meteorological journals, provided it affected the rain gauge to an extent exceeding the six hundredth part of an inch. The following are the results of his observations of the number of wet days which occurred in each quarter of the month, and in each half of the month.

	Number of wet Days.					
	Wtihin 20 Years.	From 1809 to 1812.	From 1813 to 1816.	From 1817 to 1820.	From 1821 to 1824.	From 1825 to 1828.
From the new moon to the first quarter...	764	132	142	145	179	166
From the first quarter to the full moon....	845	145	169	173	180	178
From the full moon to the last quarter....	761	124	145	162	166	164
From the last quarter to the new moon...	696	110	139	135	153	159
During the increase of the moon.........	1609	277	311	318	359	344
During the decline of the moon..........	1457	237	284	297	319	323
Excess during the first interval..........	152	43	27	21	40	21

M. Schübler also calculated the number of rainy days which happened upon the days of the principal phases, including not merely days of new and full moons, and the quarters, but also the days of the octants intermediate between these. The following table includes the results at which he arrived; first for twenty years' observation and then for the whole period of twenty-eight years. He took at each phase the mean of two consecutive days, with a view to obliterate the effect of disturbing causes, and obtain a more regular series of numbers :—

	Number of wet Days.			
	During 20 Years.		During 28 Years.	
	On the Day.	Mean of 2 Days.	On the Day.	Mean of 2 Days.
On the day of the new moon..............................	105	109	148	148
On the succeeding day....................................	113		148	
On the day of the first octant............................	119	117	152	150
On the succeeding day....................................	115		148	
On the day of the first quarter..........................	111	112	156	153
On the succeeding day....................................	113		151	
On the day of the second octant.........................	124	126	164	165
On the succeeding day....................................	128		167	
On the day of the full moon..............................	116	115	162	161
On the succeeding day....................................	113		161	
On the day of the third octant............................	125	117	161	155
On the succeeding day....................................	109		150	
On the day of the last quarter............................	92	94	130	135
On the succeeding day....................................	96		140	
On the day of the fourth octant..........................	100	94	138	133
On the succeeding day....................................	88		139	

* At Munich, from 1781 to 1788 inclusive; at Stutgard, from 1809 to 1812 inclusive; and at Augsburg, from 1813 to 1828 inclusive.

These tables agree in indicating, with tolerable clearness, an increase of the number of rainy days from the new moon to the second octant, that is, from the day of the new moon to the eleventh day of the moon's age; afterward there is a gradual decrease, the minimum occurring between the last quarter and the fourth octant.

So far as these observations may be relied upon, it would follow, that in the places where they were made, out of every 10,000 rainy days the following are the number of those days which would happen at the different lunar phases:—

New moon	306
First octant	306
First quarter	325
Second octant	341
Full moon	337
Third octant	313
Last quarter	284
Fourth octant	290

Now as there are twenty-nine days and a half in the lunar month, if we suppose the fall of rain to be distributed equally through every part of the month, the total number of these 10,000 days which should happen on the eight days of the phases, would be found by a simple proportion; since it would bear to 10,000 the same proportion that 8 bears to $29\frac{1}{2}$: the number would therefore be 27.12. Whereas, it appears from the above table, that the actual number which fell upon these days were 25.02: it appears, therefore, that less than the proportional amount occurred upon them.

Pilgrim had already, in 1788, attempted to ascertain the influence of the lunar phases on the fall of rain; and he found that in every hundred cases there were 29 days of rain on the full moon, 26 at the new moon, and 25 at the quarters.

The preceding observations refer only to the number of wet days. Schübler, however, also directed his inquiries to the influence of the lunar phases, on the *quantity* of rain and on the clearness of the atmosphere. From observations continued for sixteen years at Augsburg, including 199 lunations, he obtained the following results:—

Epochs.	Number of clear days in 16 years.	Number of overcast days in 16 years.	Quantity of rain in 16 years in inches.
New moon	31	61	26·551
First quarter	38	57	24·597
Second octant	25	65	26·728
Full moon	26	61	24·686
Last quarter	41	53	19·536

In this table, by a clear day, is such days as exhibited a cloudless sky at seven in the morning, and at two and nine o'clock in the afternoon; those that were not clear at these hours, were counted as cloudy days. These results are in accordance with the former. It appears that the number of clear days is more frequent in the last quarter, which is an epoch at which, by the former method of inquiry, the number of rainy days was least; also the number of cloudy days is greatest at the second octant, which is a period at which the number of rainy days were found to be greatest; also the depth of rain agrees with this, being the greatest about the second octant, and least at the last quarter. Schübler extended his inquiries to the influence of the moon's distance on rain; and he found that, on examining 371 passages of the moon through the positions of her extreme limits of distance, during the seven days nearest to *perigee* it rained 1,169 times; and during the seven days nearest *apogee* it rained 1,096 times. Thus, *cæteris paribus,* the nearer is the moon to the earth the greater would be the chances for rain.

From observations of Pilgrim at Vienna (which, however, are much less to be depended on), it appears that the proportion of the prevalence of rain between *perigee* and *apogee* is that of nine to five—an improbable result.

From all that has been stated, it can scarcely be denied that there exists some permanent and regular correspondence between the prevalence of rain and the phases of the moon. What that exact correspondence is, remains for more extended and accurate observations to inform us; meanwhile, that rain falls more frequently about four days before full moon, and less frequently about four or five days before new moon than at other parts of the month, seems to be a conclusion attended, to say the least with some degree of probability.

Schübler also examined the question of a correspondence between the direction of the wind and the lunar phases, and found that winds from the south and southwest, became more and more frequent at those periods of the month at which rain was also observed to increase, and that such winds were more and more rare, while winds in the contrary direction occurred oftener toward those epochs of the month when least rain was observed to prevail. These results, it will be seen, are quite in accordance, and the question respecting the mode of action by which the periods of rain are produced, would be reduced to the question of the physical action by which the moon affects the currents of the atmosphere.

The connexion of barometric indications with atmospheric phenomena is so obvious, that the inquiry as to a correspondence between the lunar phases and the variations of the barometer, could scarcely escape the attention of meteorologists. M. Flaugergues accordingly made a series of observations at Viviers (in the department of Ardêche), in France, which were continued from 1808 to 1828, a period of twenty years, on the heights of the barometer in relation to the lunar phases: that the influence of the sun might be always the same, the observations were made at noon, and the heights of the barometer were reduced to what they would be at the temperature of melting ice. The following are the mean heights of the barometer, deduced from these observations:—

New moon	29·743
First octant	29·761
First quarter	29·740
Second octant	29·716
Full moon	29·736
Third octant	29·751
Last quarter	29·772
Fourth octant	29·744

Hence it appears that the height of the barometer is least about four days before full moon, and greatest six or seven before new moon. Now these are about the times at which the investigations of Schübler give the greatest and least quantity of rain: and, since the fall of the barometer generally indicates a tendency to rain, these results are in accordance. Although it must be admitted that the variation of the barometer is in this case so minute, that a sensible effect could hardly be expected from it, still, though minute, it is quite distinct and decided.

M. Flaugergues also observed the mean height of the barometer when the moon was at her greatest and least distance from the earth, and found that at perigee it was 29·713, and at apogee 29·753.

So, far, therefore, as this small difference can be supposed to indicate anything, it would indicate a prevalence to rain at perigee and at apogee, which is in accordance with the observations of Schübler.

"In spite, therefore," says M. Arago, "of the distance which separates Stutgard from Viviers, and in spite of the different methods pursued, and the difference of instruments used, MM. Flaugergues and Schübler have arrived at analogous results." It seems very difficult, therefore, at present, not to admit that the moon exercises upon our atmosphere an action very small, it is true, but which is nevertheless appreciable even with the instruments which meteorologists commonly use.

We have shown that the theory of the moon's attraction, applied to explain atmospheric tides similar to those of the ocean, would lead to the conclusion that the height of the barometer observed at noon, when the moon is in her quarters, would be less than its height at noon at new and full moon. Observation, however, shows the very reverse as a matter of fact. The observation of M. Flaugergues gives the mean height at the barometer quadratures 29·756, and at new and full moon 29·739; the height quadratures being in excess to the amount of 0·017. This result has been further confirmed by the more recent observations of M. Bouvard, at the Paris observatory: he has found the mean height of the barometer at the quarters 29·786, and at new and full moon 29·759; the excess at the quarters being 0·027.

Although, therefore, it cannot be denied that there exists a relation between the barometric column and the lunar phases, yet it is not the relation which the theory of atmospheric tides would indicate; and by whatever physical influence the effect may be produced, it is certainly not the gravitation of the moon affecting our atmosphere in a manner analogous to that by which she affects the waters of the ocean. Any physical effects which depend on the relative positions of the sun and moon, as seen from the earth, would necessarily occur in the same order throughout the year, when these two luminaries themselves have corresponding positions in the heavens on the same days of the year. At a very early period in the history of astronomical discovery, it was known that, after the lapse of nineteen years, the sun and moon assume on successive days of the year relative positions.

Thus, for example, if the moon were 90° behind the sun on a certain day of a certain month in the year 1800, it would be 90° behind the sun on the same day of the same month in the year 1819, and again in the year 1838, and so on; but on the same day of the same month in any intermediate year it would have a different relative position with respect to the sun. This cycle of nineteen years was known to the Greeks, and was called *the Metonic cycle*, from Meton, its reputed discoverer; and it has always been used as a convenient method of calculating eclipses and other phenomena depending on the relative positions of the sun and moon. In a solar eclipse, the sun and moon must occupy nearly the same position in the heavens; and in a lunar eclipse, nearly opposite positions: it is evident, therefore, that if an eclipse occur on any day in any given year, an eclipse of the same kind must occur on the corresponding day in every nineteenth succeeding year. The tides, depending as they do on the relative positions of the sun and moon, would be calculated with facility by means of the same cycle; and meteorologists who hold the doctrine that atmospheric vicissitudes depend solely or chiefly upon the relative aspects of the sun and moon, have favored the doctrines, that there is a general cycle of weather, the period of which corresponds with that which we have noticed. Thus they hold, that the general changes of weather succeed each other in the same, or almost the same order, throughout every successive period of nineteen years.

We shall not here object, on theoretical grounds, to the doctrine that the true amount of the Metonic cycle is not precisely nineteen years. But it is subject to a stronger objection founded on the principles which its supporters themselves rely upon. The attraction of bodies in virtue of their gravitation, increases in the same proportion as the square of the distance diminishes; and as we have already stated that the moon's distance from the earth is variable to an extent not inconsiderable, it is evident, that her influence on the atmosphere ought to be expected to depend much more on that variation of distance, than on her relative position with respect to the sun. Now, although the cycle of nineteen years corresponds with the changes of her relative position to the sun as *seen* from the earth, yet it has no correspondence whatever with the variation of her distance; and although, on each day of each succeeding period of nineteen years, she will have the same apparent position relatively to the sun, she will not have the same distance from the earth, and, therefore, will not exert the same attraction on our atmosphere. Seeing, then, that the theory of the moon's attraction does not lend its unqualified support to this assumed period of nineteen years as a cycle of weather, let us see how far fact and observation countenance such a meteorological period. M. Arago (to whom we are indebted for the most complete investigation of this question, and for the collection of the labors of others upon it) has successfully shown that observation affords no countenance or confirmation whatever to this hypothesis.

It has been said that the years 1701, 1720, 1739, and 1758, being corresponding years in successive intervals of nineteen years, show in the different months the same characters of weather. Now to try this fact, it will be necessary to adopt some distinct test of the characters of the seasons which has nothing in it arbitrary, and about which two observers cannot differ. For this purpose we shall take the highest and lowest temperature observed in each of the years, and the annual quantity of rain which fell in them respectively:—

Dates.	Temp. Max.	Temp. Min.	Rain, inches.
1701	90·5	27·5	22·7
1720	89·5	29·3	18·3
1739	92·7	28·6	20·4
1758	93·9	27·3	

Such is the kind of congruity on which the advocates for the Metonic cycle rely. If any four years were taken indiscriminately at any given places, the extremes of temperature and quantities of rain could scarcely be expected to exhibit greater differences. M. Arago had extended the comparison to other seasons separated by the same interval of nineteen years, or by multiples of nineteen years.

Years.	Max. Temp.	Min. Temp.	Annual quantity of rain in inches.
1725	88·2	24·6	18·6
1782	90·5	7·2	23·5
1709	87·1	5·8	23·2
1728	87·1	16·9	17·2
1710	83·1	7·3	16·9
1748	98·4	9·3	18·4
1711	85·3	14·9	26·8
1730	88·2	19·6	17·0
1733	90·5	28·2	19·6
1771	92.7	9·1	19·2
1734	89·4	23·0	18·7
1753	100·6	11.3	18·9

There are here no traces of correspondence in the extremes of temperature, or the quantities of rain. It is manifest that any season taken at hazard would not present greater discordances than are found in the above table.

The variation of the moon's distance from the earth (to which we have more than once adverted) is occasioned by the fact that her path round the earth is not circular, but oval—the position of the earth being nearer to the one end than the other. As the moon, therefore, approaches the furthermost extremity of her oval orbit, her distance from the earth continually increases until, arriving at that point, it becomes greatest; as she moves from that extremity of the orbit to the other end of the oval, her distance continually diminishes until arriving at the other end, it becomes least. These variations of distance are produced every revolution of the moon round the earth. Now, owing to a certain change of position, to which the moon's orbit is subject, the points which mark her greatest and least distances are subject to a slow, gradual, and regular change; so that the points in the heavens at which she reaches her greatest and least distances are different every revolution. After the lapse, however, of eight years and ten months, these points having traversed the whole circumference of the heavens, resume their former position very nearly; so that the actual times at which the moon is observed at the same distances from the earth, and also at the same points in the heavens, recur in a cycle, the length of which is about eight years and ten months.

So far, therefore, as the vicissitudes of the weather can be supposed to be influenced by this cause, their period should be such that, after the lapse of nine years, the corresponding states of the weather would be, as it were, two months in advance: thus the effect produced in December, 1800, would again be produced in October, 1809, in August, 1818, and so on.

If the purpose be to determine the cycle in which the lunar influence, so far as it depends on distance, would produce the same effects upon the same days of the year, the duration of the cycle would be six times eight years and ten months: for in six successive intervals of that period, there are exactly fifty-three years; but any less number of periods of eight years and ten months do not make a complete number of years. Therefore after a cycle of fifty-three years, the moon being on the same day of each successive year at the same distance from the earth, her influence, so far as depends on distances, will be the same, and will produce the same effect upon the weather.

Now we cannot better illustrate the loose and inaccurate manner in which scientific principles are applied by some meteorologists than by stating that this cycle of eight years and ten months has formed the theoretical grounds for a reputed meteorological period of nine years. It has been maintained that, through every successive interval of nine years, the changes of weather have a general correspondence: thus, if the state of the weather throughout the year 1800 be examined, it has been said to correspond with the weather throughout the years 1809, and 1818, &c.

That the changes in the positions of the points of the moon's greatest and least distance are insufficient in theory to account for such meteorological cycle as we have explained. But let us see how the fact stands.

Toaldo, whose meteorological researches we have adverted to, has stated, that at Padua, by resolving a long interval of time into successive periods of nine years, the quantities of rain collected in each of these periods were equal, but he adds this equality would disappear if the whole interval were resolved into groups of eight years, or into successive intervals of any other number of years. M. Arago, taking the Italian meteorologist at his word, and accepting without question, his own tables and data, has given the following estimate of the quantity of rain which had fallen in successive intervals of nine years:—

In the nine years commencing in		And ending inclusively in	Rain which had fallen at Padua.
1725	to	1733	325 English inches.
From 1734	to	1742	262 " "
From 1743	to	1751	320 " "
From 1752	to	1760	333 " "
From 1761	to	1769	320 " "
			Paris gives
From 1699	to	1707	160 French inches.
From 1708	to	1716	166 " "
From 1717	to	1725	131 " "
From 1726	to	1734	125 " "
From 1735	to	1743	139 " "
From 1744	to	1752	160 " "

The confidence to which Toaldo's reasoning and calculations are entitled, may be estimated by comparing the quantities of rain which fall in any other intervals, from which it will be seen that it is not subject to greater variation than that which exists among the above results.

M. Arago gives some amusing examples of the kind of speculation and reasoning in which meteorologists sometimes indulge. Some, he says, found the assumed cycle of nine years on the passage of Pliny, where he says that every fourth, and, more especially, every eighth year, the seasons undergo a kind of effervescence by the revolution of the hundredth moon. Admitting Pliny's maxim to be true, and supposing by the word effervescence we are to understand a regular recurrence every eight years of the changes of the weather which took place in the preceding eight years, what are we to conclude? Is not the question here, whether the vicissitudes of weather recur at intervals of nine years? and the celebrated Roman naturalist speaks of a period of only eight years.

From all that has been stated, it follows, then, conclusively, that the popular notions concerning the influence of the lunar phases on the weather have no foundation in the theory, and no correspondence with observed facts. That the moon, by her gravitation, exerts an attraction on our atmosphere cannot be doubted; but the effects which that attraction would produce upon the weather are not in accordance with observed phenomena; and, therefore, these effects are either too small in amount to be appreciable in the actual state of meteorological instruments, or they are obliterated by other more powerful causes, from which hitherto they have not been eliminated. It appears, however, by some series of observations, not yet confirmed or continued through a sufficient period of time, that a slight correspondence may be discovered between the periods of rain and the phases of the moon, indicating a very feeble influence, depending on the relative position of that luminary to the sun, but having no discoverable relation to the lunar attraction. This is not without interest as a subject of scientific inquiry, and is entitled to the attention of meteorologists; but its influence is so feeble that it is altogether destitute of popular interest as a weather prognostic. It may, therefore, be stated that, as far as observation combined with theory has afforded any means of knowledge, there are no grounds for the prognostications of weather erroneously supposed to be derived from the influence of the sun and moon.

Those who are impressed with the feeling that an opinion so universally entertained even in countries remote from each other, as that which presumes an influence of the moon over the changes of the weather, will do well to remember that against that opinion we have not here opposed mere theory. Nay, we have abandoned for the occasion the support that science might afford, and the light it might shed on the negative of this question, and have dealt with it as a mere question of fact. It matters little, so far as this question is concerned, in what manner the moon and sun may produce an effect on the weather, nor even whether they be active causes in producing such effect at all. The point, and the only point of importance is, whether, regarded as a mere *matter of fact*, any correspondence between the changes of the moon and those of the weather exists? And a short examination of the recorded facts proves that IT DOES NOT.

PERIODIC COMETS.

Encké's Comet.—Its Period and Orbit.—How its Motion shows the Existence of a resisting Medium.—This Result corroborated by the Theory of Light.—Newton's Conjectures respecting Comets.—Biéla's Comet.—Its Period and Orbit.—Lexell's Comet.—Causes of its Appearance and Disappearance.—Whiston's Comet.—His Theory.—Did this Comet produce the Deluge ?—Orbit of this Comet.

PERIODIC COMETS.

On another occasion, I gave at some length the history of Halley's comet, by far the most interesting of all the periodic comets yet discovered. I shall now bring under your notice the remaining bodies of this class.

A periodic comet, as the name implies, is one which is known to return at regular intervals to our system, and whose reappearance in the heavens can therefore be predicted. The paths of these bodies round the sun are eccentric ellipses, having the centre of the sun in one of their foci.

ENCKE'S COMET.

In the year 1818, a comet was observed at Marseilles, on the 26th of November, by M. Pons. In the following January, its path being calculated, M. Arago immediately recognised it as identical with one which had appeared in 1805. Subsequently, M. Encké of Berlin succeeded in calculating its entire orbit—inferring the invisible from the visible part—and found that its period round the sun was about twelve hundred days. This calculation was verified by the fact of its return in 1822, since which time the comet has gone by the name of *Encké's comet*, and returned regularly.

This comet exhibited the appearance of a mass of nebulous vapor, so transparent, even at its centre, that stars can be seen through it. It is round, or rather oval, in its form, and is too attenuated and feeble in its light to be discovered without the aid of a telescope. The annexed figure, 1, is that which is usually given as a representation of its telescopic appearance.

The orbit of Encké's comet is an oval, whose length is about double its breadth. At its nearest approach to the sun, the distance of the comet is about thirty-four millions of miles, which is about the distance of the planet Mercury When most remote from the sun, its distance is about four hundred and forty-three millions of miles, which is nearly four and a half times the earth's distance, and is little less than the distance of Jupiter. The orbit is inclined to

Fig. 1.

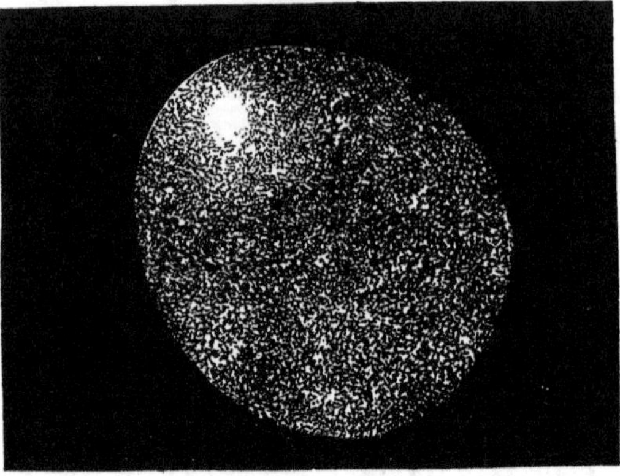

that of the earth at nearly thirteen degrees. This comet may be considered as a planet, revolving within the orbit of Jupiter, and nearly in the common plane of the solar system. Its motion is in the same direction as that of the planets.

In the calculations of Encké for the determination of the movement of this comet, the most scrupulous account was taken of the effects which the planets must produce upon it. Nevertheless, a small discrepancy was found to exist between its observed and computed returns; and what was still more remarkable, this discrepancy was of the same nature in every case, so that it is impossible to suppose that it could have arisen from any casual error of computation or of observation; since, had it so occurred, it would have affected the result irregularly. We must therefore conclude that this comet does not precisely retrace its course each revolution. It is found, however, that this irregularity, from whatever cause it may proceed, does not disturb the plane of the comet's path. It is, in fact, according to the observations and reasonings of Professor Encké, precisely the effect which would be produced if the space through which the comet moves was filled by a subtle fluid, offering a small resistance to the motion of the comet: just as our atmosphere resists the motion of any light body through it.

The existence of an extremely subtle ethereal fluid which fills the infinitude of space, has been adopted hypothetically to explain the phenomena of optics. In fact, light itself is, according to the undulatory theory, supposed to consist in vibrations transmitted through such a fluid, just as sound is known to consist in similar undulations transmitted through the atmosphere. Hitherto this assumed cause for light has been justly regarded as an ingenious hypothesis not proved, but which accounts for the various phenomena more fully and satisfactorily than the corpuscular theory, which, being open to the same objection, completely fails when applied to some phenomena of light which recent investigations have developed. If an effect similar to that which has been observed in Encké's comet should be discovered on the approaching return of Halley's comet, and still more, if it be observed on the next return of Biela's comet, the undulatory hypothesis will begin to assume the character of a *vera causa*; and that theory of light must, under such circumstances, be considered as established.

The effect on the return of a comet produced by this resistance, contrary to what might at first be expected, is to accelerate it, or to make the actual return anticipate the return as computed on the supposition that the comet moves in an unresisting medium. This difficulty will, however, be removed, if it be remembered that a resisting medium, by diminishing the velocity of the body in its orbit, diminishes the influence of the centrifugal force to resist solar attraction. The body, therefore, follows a path constantly nearer to the sun ; in other words, the orbit is in a progressive state of diminution. Now, the less the orbit is, the less time necessary to describe it ; and consequently the shorter the period of the successive returns of the body to the same position.

If the successive returns of the periodic comets should establish satisfactorily the existence of the luminous ether, it will follow that after the lapse of a certain time every comet will ultimately fall into the sun. In every succeeding revolution of the same comet, its path would fall a little within its former course, and it would describe a spiral line round the sun, continually approaching that body, until at length it would arrive close to its surface ; before this could happen, it would doubtless be wholly converted into a light gas by his heat, which would probably mingle with the solar atmosphere.

In the efforts by which the human mind labors after truth, it is curious to observe how often that desired object is stumbled upon by accident, or arrived at by reasoning which is false. One of Newton's conjectures respecting comets was, that they are "the aliment by which suns are sustained ;" and he therefore concluded that these bodies were in a state of progressive decline upon the suns, round which they respectively swept ; and that into these suns they from time to time fell. This opinion appears to have been cherished by Newton to the latest hours of his life : he not only consigned it to his immortal writings, but, at the age of eighty-three, a conversation took place between him and his nephew on this subject, which has come down to us. "I cannot say," said Newton, "when the comet of 1680 will fall into the sun : possibly after five or six revolutions ; but whenever that time shall arrive, the heat of the sun will be raised by it to such a point, that our globe will be burnt, and all the animals upon it will perish. The new stars observed by Hipparchus, Tycho, and Kepler, must have proceeded from such a cause, for it is impossible otherwise to explain their sudden splendor." His nephew then asked him, "why, when he stated in his writings that comets would fall into the sun, did he not also state those vast fires they must produce, as he supposed they had done in the stars ?"—"Because," replied the old man, "the conflagrations of the sun concern us a little more directly. I have said, however," added he, smiling, "enough to enable the world to collect my opinion."

It may be asked, if the existence of a resisting medium be admitted, whether the same ultimate fate must not await the planets ? To this inquiry it may be answered that, within the limits of past astronomical record, the ethereal medium, if it exist, has had no sensible effect on the motion of any planet. That it might have a perceptible effect upon comets, and yet not upon planets, will not be surprising, if the extreme lightness of the comets compared with their bulk be considered. The effect in the two cases may be compared to that of the atmosphere upon a piece of swan's down and upon a leaden bullet moving through it. It is certain that whatever may be the nature of this resisting medium, it will not, for many hundred years to come, produce the slightest perceptible effect upon the motions of the planets.

BIELA'S COMET.

On February 28, 1826, M. Biela, an Austrian officer, observed in Bohemia a comet, which was seen at Marseilles about the same time by M. Gambart. The path which it pursued was observed to be similar to that of comets which had appeared in 1772 and 1806. Finally, it was found that this body moved round the sun in an oval orbit, and that the time of its revolution was about six years and eight months. It has since returned at its predicted times; and has been adopted as a member of our system, under the name of Biela's comet.

The annexed diagram, fig. 2, exhibits the form and position of the orbit of this comet in relation to those of the principal planets, giving the successive positions it assumed during its appearance in 1832.

Fig. 2.

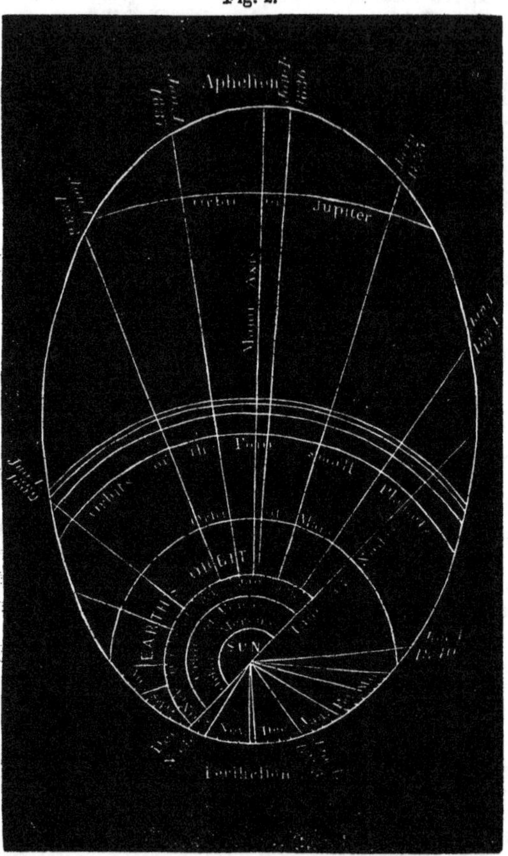

Biela's comet moves in an orbit whose plane is nearly the same with those of the planets. It is but slightly oval, the length being to the breadth in the proportion of about three to two. When nearest to the sun, its distance is nearly equal to that of the earth; and when most remote from the sun, its distance somewhat exceeds that of Jupiter. Thus it ranges through the solar system, between the orbits of Jupiter and the earth.

Notwithstanding the discovery of the periodic comets of Encké and Biela, still the comet of Halley maintains a paramount astronomical interest, and may be considered to stand alone in exhibiting those physical phenomena which seem to be the exclusive characteristics of the class to which it belongs. Although the comets of Encké and Biela are unquestionably objects of interest to the geometer and astronomer, yet their short periods, the limited space within which they are circumscribed in their motion, the small obliquity and eccentricity of their orbits, and consequently the very slight disturbance which they sustain from the attraction of the planets, render them, for all physical purposes, nothing more than new planets of inappreciable mass belonging to our system. Unlike other known comets, they do not rush from the invisible and inaccessible depths of space, and, after sweeping our system, depart to distances under the conception of which the imagination itself is confounded; they possess none of that grandeur which is connected with whatever appears to break through the fixed order of the universe. It is still reserved for the comet of Halley alone to exhibit a phenomenon, so far as we know, unique; to afford a splendid result of those powers of calculation by which we are enabled to follow it through the depths of space two thousand millions of miles beyond the extreme verge of the solar system; and, notwithstanding disturbances which render each succeeding period of its return different from the last, to foretell that return with precision.

LEXELL'S COMET.

In the month of June, 1770, Messier observed a comet, which was afterward sufficiently observed to render its course through the system calculable. It was found not to correspond with that of any comet previously known. It remained visible for an unusual length of time; and continued observations on it proved that it moved, not as comets were then generally found to move, in a parabola, or very elongated ellipse, but in an oval of very small dimensions.

Its orbit was calculated by the celebrated Lexell, and found to be an ellipse, of which the greater axis was only equal to three times the diameter of the earth's orbit, which showed that its periodical revolution round the sun would be completed in *five years and a half.*

With so short a period, the comet ought frequently to be seen. But here springs up a difficulty. This comet was never seen before, and has never been seen since! What, then, has become of it? and where and how did it exist before its discovery by Messier? Its appearance was too conspicuous and its light too vivid to allow of the supposition that it could have been present, yet not observed.

The law of gravitation discovered by Newton, and fully developed by his illustrious successors, enables us fully to explain this difficulty. We shall adopt the words of Arago:—

Why has not the comet been seen every five years and a half before 1770? Because the orbit was then totally different from that it has *since* pursued.

Why has not the comet been seen since 1770? For the reason that its passage to the point of perihelion in 1776 took place by day; and before the following return, the form of the orbit was so altered, that had the comet been visible from the earth it would not have been recognised.

Lexell had already remarked, according to his elements of 1770, that the comet ought to pass in the vicinity of Jupiter in 1767, less than the fifty-eighth part of his distance from the sun; that in 1779, when it returned to us, it would be, near the end of August, about five hundred times nearer that same planet than to the sun; so that then, notwithstanding the immense size of the solar globe, its attractive power on the comet was not the two hundredth part that of Jupiter. Thus it could not be doubted that the comet had experienced considerable perturbations in 1767 and 1779; but it is yet necessary to establish that these perturbations were *numerically* strong enough to explain the total want of observations, as well before as after the year 1770.

The formularies in the fourth volume of the *Mécanique Celéste* give the analytical solution of this problem : the actual elliptic orbit of a comet being known, what was its previous orbit ? What will it be hereafter, taking into account in both cases the perturbating effects caused by the planets of our system ?

Well, then, by putting these formularies into numbers—by substituting, for its component indeterminate letters, the particular elements of the comet of 1770—it will first be found that in 1767, previous to the approach of that body to Jupiter, the elliptic orbit which it described corresponds, not to five but to fifty years of revolution round the sun ; afterward, that in 1779, on its departure out of the attraction of the same planet, the orbit of the comet could not be completed in less than twenty years. From the same researches it results that, before 1767, during the whole progress of its revolutions, the shortest distance of the comet from the sun was one hundred and ninety-nine millions of leagues (five hundred and ninety-seven millions of miles), and that after 1779 the minimum of distance became one hundred and thirty-one millions of leagues (three hundred and ninety-three millions of miles). This was still too far removed for the comet to be perceptible from the earth.

However singular it may appear, we are, then, fully authorized to say of the comet of 1770, that the action of Jupiter brought it to us in 1767, and that the same action, producing an inverse effect, removed it from us in the year 1779.

WHISTON'S COMET.

A remarkable comet appeared in the year 1680, which has been rendered memorable by the attempt of Whiston to prove that it was periodic, and that on one of its former visits it was the proximate cause of the Mosaic deluge. Arago, in his essay on comets, has discussed fully the question raised by Whiston.

Whiston, says he, proposed to show not only in what manner a comet might have occasioned the deluge of Noah, but was desirous, moreover, that his explanation should agree minutely with all the circumstances of that great catastrophe as related in Genesis. Let us see how he has succeeded in his object.

The biblical deluge happened in the year 2349 before the Christian era, according to the modern Hebrew text ; or the year 2926, after the Samaritan text, the *Septuagint*, and *Josephus*. Is there, then, reason to suppose that at either of those periods a great comet had appeared ?

Among the comets observed by modern astronomers, that of 1680 may, from its brilliancy, without hesitation be placed in the first rank.

A great many historians, both native and foreign, mention *a very large comet, in similitude to the blaze of the sun, having an immense train*, which appeared in the year 1106. In ascending still higher, we find a very large and terrific comet designated by the Byzantine writers by the name of *Lampadias*, because it resembled a burning lamp, the appearance of which may be fixed in the year 531. All the world knows, in fine, that a comet appeared in the month of September, in the year of the death of Cæsar, during the games given by the emperor Augustus to the Roman people. That comet was very brilliant, as it became visible from the eleventh hour of the day, that is, about five o'clock in the evening, or *before sunset*. Its date is in the year 43 before our era.

Since we have not any exact observation of the comets of —43, or 531, or of 1106 ; since we cannot calculate their parabolic orbits ; since we want the only *criterion* which would enable us to decide with perfect certainty either the identity or dissemblance of two comets, let us at least remember that those of 1680, of 1106, of 531, and of —43, were very brilliant, and let us compare with each other the dates of these apparitions :—

From 1106 to 1680 we find....................................574 years.
" 531 " 1106 " " ....575 "
" —43 " 531 " " ....575 "

As we have not reckoned the months or portions of years, these periods may be regarded as equal to each other, and thence it becomes probable enough that the comet of the death of Cæsar, of 531, of 1106, and of 1680, have been only the reappearances of one and the same comet, which, after having run through its orbit—after having made its complete revolution in about five hundred and seventy-five years—became again visible from the earth. Then if the period of five hundred and seventy-five years is multiplied by four, we have twenty-three hundred, which, added to 43, the date of Cæsar's comet, gives, with the difference of only six years, the epoch of the deluge, resulting from the modern Hebrew text. In multiplying by five, the date of the *Septuagint* is found within eight years.

If we recollect the marked differences of the comet of 1759 in the period of its revolution round the sun, we shall acknowledge that Whiston might legitimately have felt authorized to suppose that the great comet of 1680, or of the death of Cæsar, was near the earth at the period of Noah's deluge, and that it had some part in that great phenomenon.

I shall not stop to explain minutely the series of transformations by which the earth, which, according to Whiston, was originally a comet, became the globe we now inhabit. I shall content myself by saying that he considers the nucleus of the earth as a hard and compact substance, which was the ancient nucleus of the comet; that the matters of various natures confusedly mixed, which composed the nebulosity, subsided more or less quickly, according to their specific gravities; that then the solid nucleus was at first surrounded by a dense and thick fluid; that the earthy matters precipitated themselves afterward, and formed a covering over the dense fluid—a kind of crust, which may be compared to the shell of an egg; that the water, in its turn, came to cover this solid crust; that in a considerable degree it became filtered through the fissures, and spread itself over the thick fluid; that, in fine, the gaseous matters remaining suspended, purified themselves gradually, and constituted our atmosphere.

Thus in this system the great biblical abyss is supposed to consist of a solid nucleus and of two concentric orbs. Of these orbs, that nearest to the centre is formed of a heavy fluid which first precipitated itself; the second is of water; it is, then, properly speaking, upon the last of these fluids that the exterior and solid crust of the earth reposes.

It is proper now to examine how, after that constitution of the globe to which at least many geologists could oppose more than one difficulty, Whiston explains the two principal events of the deluge described by Moses.

In the six hundredth year of Noah's life, says the book of Genesis, on the seventeenth day of the second month, the same day were *all the fountains of the great deep broken up, and the windows of heaven were opened.*

At the period of the deluge, the comet of 1680, says Whiston, was only nine or ten thousand miles from the earth: it attracted, therefore, the water from the great deep, as the moon at present attracts the waters of the ocean. Its action, on account of that great proximity, must have tended to produce an immense tide. The terrestrial shell could not resist the impetuosity of the inundation; it broke in at a great number of points, and the waters, then free, spread themselves over the continents. The reader will here recognise *the rupture of the fountains of the great deep.*

The ordinary rains of our days, even continued for forty days, would have produced but a small accumulation. In taking for daily rain that which falls at Paris annually, the produce of six weeks, far from covering the highest mountains, would scarcely have formed a depth of eighty feet. It is therefore necessary to refer to other sources *than the cataracts of heaven.* Whiston has found them in the nebulosity and tail of the comet.

According to him, the nebulosity reached the earth near the Gordian (Ararat) mountains. Those mountains intercepted the entire tail. The terrestrial atmosphere, thus charged with an immense quantity of aqueous particles, was sufficient to produce forty days' rain of such violence as the ordinary state of the globe can give us no idea.

Notwithstanding all its strangeness, I have exposed the theory of Whiston in detail, both on account of the celebrity which it has so long enjoyed, as well as because it appeared improper to treat with contempt the productions of the man whom Newton himself designed as his successor in the university of Cambridge; yet the following are objections which it seems his theory cannot resist.

Whiston having required an immense tide to explain the mystery of the biblical phenomena of the great deep, was not content to pass his comet extremely near the earth at the moment of the deluge: he has, moreover, given it a very great magnitude, in supposing it six times greater than the moon.

Such a supposition is completely gratuitous, and this is also its least fault; for it is not sufficient to account for the phenomena. If the moon really produces a tide on the waters of the ocean, it is because its angular diurnal motion is not very considerable; that in the space of some hours its distance from the earth scarcely varies; during a considerable time it remains vertically over almost the same points of the globe; the fluid which it attracts has therefore always time to yield to its action before it moves to a region where the force which emanates from it will be otherwise directed. But it was not the same with the comet of 1680. Near to the earth, its apparent angular motion must have been extremely rapid; in a few minutes it corresponded with a numerous series of points situated on terrestrial meridians very distant from each other. As to its rectilinear distance from the earth, it might, without doubt, have been very small, but only during a few instants. The union of these circumstances, it must be observed, was but little favorable to the production of a great tide.

I am very well aware that, to diminish these difficulties, it is sufficient to increase the comet—to make its mass not only six times the size of the moon, but thirty or forty times larger; but I reply that the comet of 1680 does not afford that latitude. On the 1st of November in that year it passed very near to the earth. (See figure 3, in which the orbit of this comet is represented.) It is shown that at the period of the deluge its distance was not less; then, as in 1680, it produced neither celestial cataracts, nor terrestrial tides, nor ruptures of the great deep; as, moreover, its train nor its hair did not inundate us, we may in all confidence say that Whiston's theory is a mere romance, unless, in abandoning the comet of 1680, we venture to attribute the same effect to another *much more* considerable star of the same description.

Whiston, as we have just seen, proposed to attribute to physical causes not only some deluge, but that of Moses, with all the circumstance related in the book of Genesis. His celebrated countryman, Halley, had viewed the problem in a less special manner.

There exists, says he, far from the sea, marine productions, even upon the highest mountains, which regions have been formerly under the sea. From what impulse has the ocean abandoned the limits in which, in our days, it with very slight oscillations remains constantly bounded? It is here that Halley calls to his aid, not like Whiston, a comet passing in our vicinity and causing

Fig. 3.

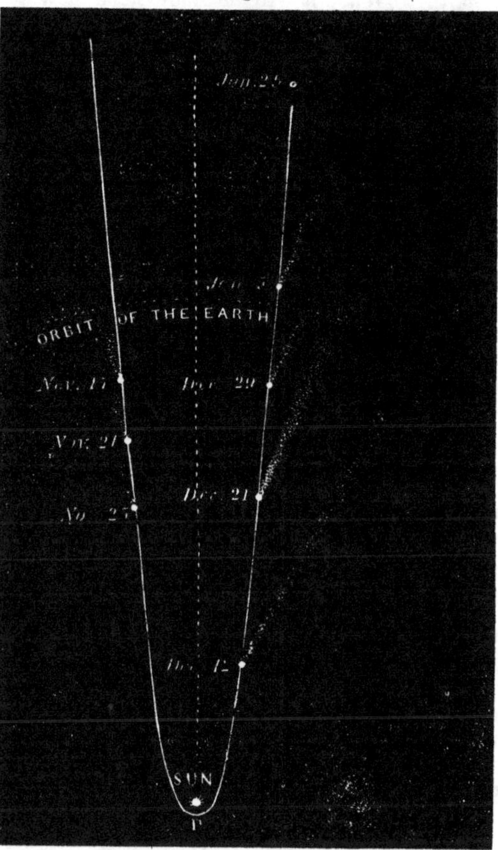

a very high tide, but a star of the same description, which, in its elliptic course about the sun, directly struck the earth. Let us examine closely what would be the effect of such an event.

Let us conceive a *solid body* proceeding in a straight line with a certain rapidity, and upon which from the outset another much smaller body *had been merely placed*. These two bodies, although not fastened together, will not separate in their progress, because the force which moves them will have gradually and from the commencement imparted equal velocities to them. But let us suppose that an insurmountable obstacle suddenly presents itself in the way of the first body, and stops it instantly; the fore part of the surface, the parts struck, are, strictly speaking, the only parts whose velocity is directly destroyed by the obstacle; but as all the other parts are intimately attached to the first—as, from our hypothesis, *the body is solid*—the whole of that body will stop.

It will not be so with the small body which we have *simply laid* upon the first. This we may stop without the other, to which nothing attaches it, unless it may be a slight degree of friction; and it will experience no effect—lose none of its celerity. By virtue of this acquired and undiminished velocity, the small body will separate itself from the large one, and will continue to move in the original direction until the moment when its own weight shall bring it to the earth. Hence it will be understood how a person is thrown forward when his horse, in falling down, suddenly stops; in what manner travellers seated on the imperial of a steam-carriage, moving with great velocity over an iron railroad, are launched into the air like so many projectiles when an accident instantaneously stops the motion of these ingenious contrivances. But is our earth anything else than a carriage, which, in its progress through regions of space, requires neither wheels nor railways? All we said, therefore, is directly applicable to it.

Our velocity round the sun is about twenty miles per second. If a comet of a sufficient mass in meeting the globe should, by a single shock, instantaneously stop its motion, the bodies placed upon its surface, such as animated beings, our carriages, furniture, utensils, all objects in short not implanted directly or indirectly in the soil, would fly off to the point of the earth shocked by the comet with the velocity with which they were in common originally endued—a velocity of twenty miles per second. The effects of such an event may be better conceived if I here remark that a twenty-four-pound shot has not even on its discharge from the gun a velocity of more than twelve hundred feet per second. All animated nature would certainly be destroyed in an instant.

As for the waters of the ocean—since they are moveable—as nothing fastens them to the solid portion of the earth—they would also be projected in mass toward the point of percussion. This terrific liquid mass would in its impetuous course overthrow every obstacle in its way. It would pass the summits of the highest mountains, and in its reflux would produce ravages scarcely less tremendous. The disorder which is occasionally observed in the strata of the different sorts of earth forming the crust of the globe is, it may be said, but a microscopic accident compared with the frightful chaos that would inevitably occur on a shock of a comet sufficiently powerful to stop the earth.

It is only necessary to diminish in some degree these prodigious effects to find what results would be experienced from the shock of a comet, which, without stopping our globe, should sensibly decrease its velocity. Certain it is, however, that the globe has never been stopped completely; for in such case, the central force not being counterbalanced, it must have fallen in a direct line toward the sun, where it would have arrived sixty-four and a half days after the shock.

The velocity of the earth and the magnitude of its orbit are so nearly connected, that one cannot change without at the same time producing a variation in the other. It is unknown whether the dimensions of the orbit have remained constant; nothing, then, proves that the velocity of the globe in the course of ages has not been more or less altered by a cometary concussion. At all events, it is incontestable that the inundations which would be produced by such an event do not explain the effects which the variations of the earth has undergone, now so well described by geologists.

A few words, again, before quitting this subject, on the consequences of cometary shock as respects its influence on the rotary movement of the earth.

The earth turns upon itself in twenty-hours from the west to the east. The axis of rotation is called the *axis of the world;* its extremities, the *poles;* and the circle equally distant from the two poles, the *equator.* The circle of the *equator* is about 25,000 miles in circumference.

Twenty-five thousand miles are in consequence the space through which a point on the equatorial region, solid or fluid, passes every twenty-four hours by the rotation of the globe. An observer situated above the earth and its atmosphere, would not be drawn into this movement, but would see all the parts of the equator pass below him with a velocity of about a thousand miles an hour. At the poles themselves this kind of movement does not exist; at intermediate latitudes it is less than at the equator.

The waters of the ocean, although they partake of this rapid motion, do not invade the surrounding country, for in every place the shore has precisely the same velocity as the water, and under all latitudes the continents and the seas that bathe them are in a *relative repose*. If this state of things were to change; if the waves at any given point were to continue their original velocity, while that of the adjacent land was suddenly to diminish, the ocean would at the same time overflow its limits.

In order to fix our ideas, let us imagine the oblique shock of a comet instantaneously to turn the whole solid part of the earth round its diameter at the point of Brest. That city having become the pole, the whole peninsula of Brittany would be in an almost perfect repose; but the ocean which washes its shores on the west would not be so; for as we have before observed on the occasion of the movement of translation, it would be only *resting* on the solid base of which its bed is formed. The waters would precipitate themselves in mass upon a shore which would no longer run before them with the former velocity of the parallel of Brest.

Behold, then, extensive parts of the continent inundated, lofty regions buried under the waves by cometary influence. But have the marine deposites which are actually discovered on the mountains been conveyed in this manner? By no means. These deposites are frequently horizontal, of great breadth, very thick, and very regular. The varied and often very small shells which compose them have preserved their crests, their most delicate points, their most brittle parts, unbroken. Every circumstance, then, dissipates the idea of a violent transposition; everything shows the deposites to have been formed on the spot. What now remains to complete the explanation without having recourse to an eruption of the sea? It must be admitted that the mountains and undulating grounds upon which they are based have risen up from below, like mushrooms; that they have grown up through the bosom of the waters. In 1694, Halley already cited this hypothesis as a *possible* explanation of the presence of marine productions upon the sides and on the summits of the highest mountains. This explanation was the *true* one; it is at present almost generally admitted. A comet which should perceptibly alter either the movement of rotation or the progress of translation of the earth would, without any doubt, occasion terrific convulsions in the shell of the globe; but, it must be repeated, these physical revolutions would differ in a thousand circumstances from those which are at present the objects of geological research.

The first glance of the matter of the present discourse may perhaps raise a question with some whether all comets must not be periodic; the difference among them being only that the periods of a few of them have been discovered, and those of the others still remain unascertained. It does not, however, follow at all that the comets move periodically round the sun. Newton showed that the law of gravitation would allow a body to move under the sun's attraction in any of those species of curves called conic sections; and that the particular species in which any body might happen to move would depend altogether on the velocity and direction in which such body might have originally been projected. There are three species of conic sections: the ellipse, the parabola, and the hyperbola. Now it is only the ellipse which would cause a periodical revolution round the sun. A body moving in either of the other curves would enter the system in some determinate direction, and leave it in another—never to return to it.

Although it is not certainly ascertained that any comets have moved in parabolas or hyperbolas, it seems probable, nevertheless, that such has been the case ; and we may therefore consider with propriety comets to consist of two classes : first, those which revolve round the sun in regular periods, reappearing in the system after equal intervals of time ; and secondly, those which enter it once, and depart from it, never to return.

RADIATION OF HEAT.

Radiation a Property of Heat.—Prismatic Spectrum.—Invisible Rays.—Two Hypotheses.—Invisible Rays alike in their Properties to luminous Rays.—Discoveries of Leslie.—Differential Thermometer.—Radiation, Reflection, and Absorption.—Effect of Screens.—Supposed Rays of Cold.—Common Phenomenon explained.—Theory of Dew.

RADIATION OF HEAT.

WHEN any physical effect is progressively transmitted or propagated in straight lines, especially if those lines proceed in various directions round the point whence the effect originates, the phenomenon is called *radiation*. The effect is said to be *radiated*, and the lines along which it is transmitted are called *rays*.

Several natural phenomena present examples of this, of which light is by far the most remarkable. Every point of a visible object emits rays of light which diverge in all possible directions from that point, and it is by these rays of light that the point itself becomes visible. These rays of light, in like manner, when they proceed from a luminous object, such as the sun, or the flame of a lamp, falling on other objects, illuminate them, and making the points of their surfaces become new centres of radiation, render them visible.

The secondary rays which they thus radiate by reflection meeting the eye, produce a corresponding sensation, which excites a consciousness of the presence of the object. Radiation is likewise a property of heat. A hot body, such as a ball of iron, raised to the temperature of 400°, placed in the middle of a chamber, will transmit heat in every direction round it. Now this heat may easily be proved not to be transmitted merely by means of the surrounding air, for in this case the effect would be an upward current of hot air, which would ascend by reason of its comparative lightness; on the other hand, the heat which proceeds from the ball is found to be transmitted downward, horizontally, and obliquely, and in every possible direction. It is likewise transmitted almost instantaneously, at least the time of its transmission is utterly inappreciable. A delicate thermometer, placed at any distance below the ball, will be immediately affected by it, and the proof that this is true radiation, is found in the fact that the rays may be intercepted by a screen composed of a material not pervious to heat. The rays may be proved to be transmitted in straight lines in exactly the same manner, and by the same reasoning, as is applied to rays of light.

But the radiation of heat, independently of any power of transmission which may reside in the air, is put beyond dispute by the fact that a thermometer suspended in the receiver of an air-pump, when it is exhausted, is affected by the solar rays directed upon it.

The effects of the radiation of hot bodies prove that rays of heat exist unaccompanied by light. On the other hand, the calorific property which constantly accompanies the solar rays, as well as the rays proceeding from flame, would indicate that heat is a necessary concomitant or property of light. It is ascertained also that the calorific principle exists with different degrees of energy in lights of different colors. Sir William Herschel, being engaged in telescopic observations on the sun, found that the colored glasses which he used to mitigate the brilliancy of that luminary, in order to enable the eye to bear its splendor, were cracked and broken in pieces by the heat which they absorbed from the light which acted on them. This led him to investigate the calorific properties of the different component parts of solar light; and the experiments which he instituted led to an important extension of the analysis of light originally discovered by Newton.

Let A, B, C, fig. 1, be a section of a glass prism cut at right angles to its length, and let S, S, be a ray of light admitted through a small aperture in a window-shutter, and striking the surface of the glass at S. It is a property of glass, which is explained in optics, that when light enters it in this manner, the ray is bent from its course, and instead of proceeding in the direction S, S′, as it would do, if it did not encounter the glass, it is deflected upward in an-

Fig. 1.

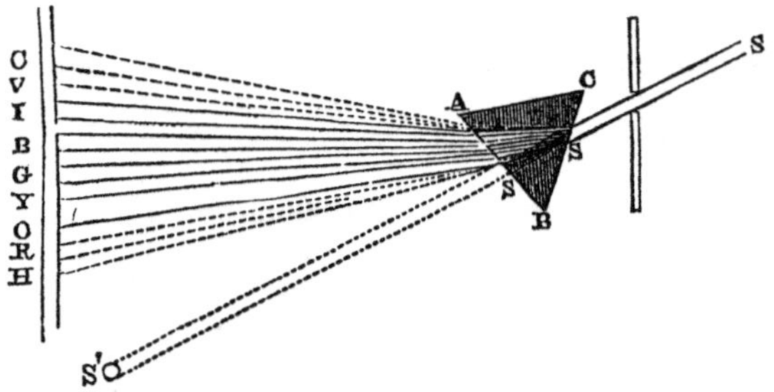

other direction, forming an angle with its original course. Now it is found that the ray thus bent upward does not continue to form one line of white light as before, but it spreads or diverges, and if received on the screen, instead of illuminating a single spot, as it would do if it were not intercepted by the prism, it covers an extended line on the screen from V to R, and the length of this line increases if the screen be moved from the prism, and decreases if the screen be moved toward the prism; a necessary consequence of the divergence of the rays issuing from the prism. It is also observed that this line of light thus produced on the screen, is not a uniform white light like the spot which would be produced on a screen held between A, B, C, and the window-shutter. On the other hand, an appearance is produced of a regular succession of brilliant colors, the highest color, V, being *violet*, the next below this, *indigo*, which is succeeded by *blue*, *green*, *yellow*, *orange*, and finally *red*, in regular succession, each color occupying a certain space on the line of light. This effect is commonly called the *prismatic spectrum*, and it depends upon two facts which are ascertained in optics, namely: first, that the ray of light, S, S, is compounded of several distinct rays, which differ from each other in color; secondly, that the glass of the prism A, B, C, is capable of refracting or bending out of their course these different-colored lights in different degrees. Thus it is capable of deflecting the violet light more than the indigo, the indigo more than the blue, and so on, each color in succession being more refrangible by the prism than that which occupies a lower place, and red being therefore the least refrangible component part of the solar beam.

Let us now suppose that the bulbs of a series of thermometers are placed in the different colored lights, from the violet to the red, in regular succession. The relative heating-powers of these different colors will be indicated by the effect which they produce on the several thermometers, the most powerful being that which raises the thermometer exposed to its influence highest. It is found that the thermometer whose bulb is covered with the violet light is less elevated than that which is exposed to the indigo. This again is less raised than that which is exposed to the blue, and the elevation of the several thermometers go on, thus regularly increasing; that which is acted upon by the red light standing at a greater elevation than any of the others. Hence we infer that the calorific power of the red light is greater than that of any other component part of the solar beam. It might at first view be supposed that the calorific power had some dependance on or connexion with the illuminating power of light, and that the light which was most brilliant would likewise be most hot. This, however, is not the fact; for the most brilliant part of the prismatic spectrum is found in the position of the yellow light, and the brilliancy gradually diminishes toward the extremity of the red, where the heat is found to be greatest.

It occurred to Sir William Herschel, that as hot bodies emit calorific rays which are not luminous, it was possible that non-luminous calorific rays might exist in solar light itself. To determine this point, he placed a thermometer in the space immediately below R, the red extremity of the spectrum. He accordingly found, as he had anticipated, that the thermometer still continued to be affected, and consequently that the presence of calorific rays, invisible and non-luminous, was manifested; but what was more singular, he found that the calorific power of these invisible rays was even greater than that of the luminous red rays, in fact, the maximum effect of the calorific rays was found at a point H, a little below R. From that point downward the calorific influence rapidly diminished, until it altogether disappeared. There are, therefore, a number of invisible rays proceeding from the prism, and occupying the space H, below R. These rays are refracted by the prism in the same manner as the luminous rays, but the refraction is less in quantity. These invisible rays also differ from each other in refrangibility, in the same manner as the luminous rays do, since they occupy a space of some extent below R. Those whose position is lowest being less refrangible than those nearer to the luminous rays.

Soon after these experiments of Sir William Herschel, the attention of several distinguished philosophers was attracted to the investigation of the properties of the prismatic spectrum, and among others the late Dr. Wollaston, Ritter, and Beckmann. It had been long known that the solar light produced an influence on certain chemical processes. Thus the chloride of silver, exposed to the direct rays of the sun, was known to acquire a black color. Chemical effects were also produced on the oxides of certain metals. It was shown by Scheele and others that these effects were produced by the rays of light which occupy the upper part of the spectrum, and not at all by the red rays. A feeble effect was produced by the green ray, and the chemical energy was increased by ascending toward the violet ray. The circumstance of Herschel having discovered invisible calorific rays under the lower extremity of the spectrum, and even finding the point of extreme energy in that space, suggested to these philosophers the inquiry, whether the chemical influence which was observed to increase in ascending toward the upper extremity, might not exist in the space above that point, where no luminous rays were apparent. They accordingly found, on exposing substances highly susceptible of this chemical influence in the several spaces occupying the upper part of the spectrum, and also in the space immediately above V, that the chemical action was continued, as they had anticipated, beyond the luminous rays; and as the maximum heating-power, was found below R, so the maximum chemical influence was found to be in the space above V, in ascending beyond that point the chemical influence rapidly diminished until it disappeared. It follows, therefore, that there are a number of chemical rays proceeding from the prism more refrangible than any luminous rays, and falling on the screen above the point V, in the space C. These chemical rays are found to be altogether destitute of the heating principle, or at least, their effects on a thermometer were inappreciable.

The experiments of Herschel were repeated by several other philosophers, with various success, some being unable to detect any calorific rays beyond luminous spectrum, others detecting their existence, but fixing the maximum calorific influence in the red rays, and others again agreeing in all respects with Herschel. Of these, the most valuable were experiments instituted by Berard, in the laboratory of Berthollet at Paris. This philosopher used a heliostat, which is an instrument constructed for the purpose of reflecting a ray of the sun constantly in one direction, notwithstanding the change of position of the sun by its diurnal motion. He thus obtained a perfectly steady and immoveable spectrum; and he repeated the experiment under much more favorable circumstances than those in which Herschel's investigations were conducted.

These experiments fully corroborated the results of former investigations, and put beyond all question the presence of invisible rays beyond both extremities of the spectrum, the one possessing the chemical, the other the calorific property. Berard, however, found the maximum calorific influence exactly at the extremity of the luminous spectrum, where the bulb of a thermometer was completely covered with red light. The only difference then which remained to be accounted for in the results of different experiments, was the point of maximum calorific power, and it was conjectured by Biot that this apparent discordance might be accounted for by the different materials of which the prisms were composed. This conjecture was subsequently verified by Seebeck, who proved that the position of greatest calorific intensity depended on the nature of the prism by which the rays are refracted. He found that a hollow prism, filled with water or alcohol, fixed the point of greatest calorific intensity in the yellow rays. If filled with a solution of corrosive sublimate, or with sulphuric acid, this point was found in the orange ray. When a prism of crown-glass was used, it was situated in the red ray, but when a prism of flint-glass was used, the point of greatest calorific intensity took the position which Herschel assigned to it, in the non-luminous space below the red ray. Thus all the apparent discordances in the experiment were satisfactorily accounted for. The results of these experiments have given rise to two distinct hypotheses respecting the constitution of solar light.

In one it is supposed that the solar ray, S, S, is composed of three distinct physical principles: the chemical, the luminous, and the calorific. Let us imagine a screen, M, N, fig. 2, placed between the prism and window-shutter, which is capable of intercepting the luminous and the calorific principle, but which allows the chemical rays to be transmitted. In that case, the prism will refract the chemical rays, and cause them to diverge and occupy a space on the screen between the point C, and C′, corresponding to the highest point above the luminous spectrum, where the chemical influence is found, and C′, the lowest point in the green light, where its presence is discoverable. Let

Fig. 2.

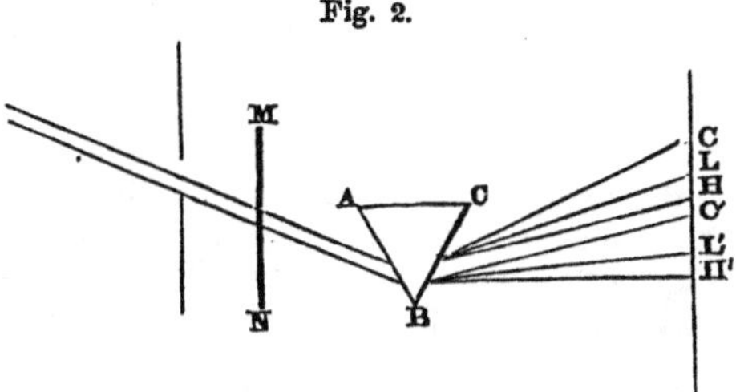

us next suppose the screen M, N, to allow the luminous rays to be likewise transmitted, these will be refracted by the prism, and will occupy the space L, L′, corresponding to that already described as limited by the violet and red lights. Finally, if the screen M, N, be removed, and all the rays allowed to pass through the prism, the calorific rays will occupy the space from H, to H′, these being the points where the thermometer, in ascending and descending, ceased to be affected. Thus, according to this supposition, three distinct spectra, if they may be so called, are formed: the chemical spectrum, the luminous spectrum, and the calorific spectrum. These spectra, to a certain extent, are superposed, or laid one upon another; but the chemical spectrum extends beyond the luminous, at the upper part, while the calorific spectrum extends beyond the luminous, at the lower end. Each spectrum consists of rays differently refrangible by the prism; and if the middle ray be considered as representing its mean refrangibility, it will follow that the mean refrangibility of the chemical rays is greater than that of the luminous rays, and the mean refrangibility of the luminous rays greater than that of the calorific rays. If prisms of different materials be used, the relative degree of mean refrangibility will be subject to change; thus, the liquid prism above-mentioned, will cause the mean refrangibility of the calorific rays to be more nearly equal to that of the luminous rays than the glass prism.

According to the other hypothesis, the solar beam consists of a number of rays, which differ from each other in their capability of being deflected by any refracting medium. When transmitted through a prism and received on a screen, the most refrangible passes to the highest point, and the least refrangible to the lowest point, those of intermediate degrees of refrangibility taking intermediate places. It is assumed that the rays which thus differ in refrangibility, have, also, different properties and qualities, and that they possess the same quality in different degrees. Thus rays of different refrangibility have different illuminating powers, and they possess the chemical agency with different degrees of energy. So far as the sensibility of thermometers enable us to discover the existence of the calorific principle, it extends from a certain point below R, to a certain point in the violet light, but the diminution of its temperature is observed to be gradual in approaching its limit, and it is consistent with analogy that it should exist, in a degree not discoverable by thermometers, beyond these points. Although, therefore, the thermometer does not indicate the calorific principle in the invisible chemical rays at the top of the spectrum, yet we cannot infer that these rays are altogether destitute of that principle, without assuming that the sensibility of thermometers has no limits. In like manner the chemical influence, so far as experiment determines its presence, ends somewhere in the green light, about the middle of the luminous spectrum, but the diminution of its influence to this point, is gradual; and it cannot be inferred with certainty, that it might not exist in less degree in the rays below this limit, and even in those invisible rays which are beyond the red ray, unless we assume that there are no tests of chemical influence of greater sensibility than those which have been used by the philosophers who instituted experiments on this subject.

The presence of the luminous quality is determined by its effect on the human eye, and the discovery of it must, therefore, be limited to the sensibility of that organ. To pronounce that there are no luminous rays beyond the limits of the visible spectrum, is to declare that the sensibility of the human eye is infinite. Now, it is notorious, not only that the sensibility of sight in different individuals is *different*, but even that the sensibility of the eye of the same person at different times, is susceptible of variation. If a person pass suddenly from a strongly-illuminated apartment into a chamber, the windows of which are closed, he will be immediately impressed with a sensation of utter darkness, and will be totally unable to discover any object in the room; but when he has remained some time in the darkened room, he will begin to be sensible of the presence of light, and will, at length, even discern distinct objects. In this case, the eye, while exposed to the intense light of the first chamber, accommodated its powers to the quantity of light to which it was exposed, and, by a provision of nature, limited its sensibility in proportion as the light was abundant. Passing suddenly into the darkened chamber, where a very small quantity of light was admitted through the crevices of the windows, the eye was incapable, in its actual state, of any perception of light, notwithstanding the undoubted presence of that physical principle; but when time was allowed for the organ to adapt itself to the new circumstances in which it was placed, its sensibility was increased, and a distinct perception of light obtained.

It is, therefore, perfectly certain, that the sensibility of the eye is variable in the same individual, and even changeable at will. It is likewise perfectly certain, that different individuals have different sensibilities of sight, one individual being capable of perceiving light which is not visible to another. Circumstances render it highly probable that many inferior animals have a sensation of light, under circumstances in which the human eye has no perception of it; and it is, therefore, consistent with analogy to admit, at least, the possibility, if not the probability, that the invisible rays which fall on the space beyond each extremity of the luminous spectrum, may be of the same nature as the other rays of light, although they are incapable of exciting the retina of the human eye in a sufficient degree to produce sensation. This, probably, will receive still further support and confirmation, if we can show that these invisible rays enjoy all the optical properties, save and except that of affecting the sight, which other luminous rays possess.

It has already appeared that the non-luminous calorific rays, H, fig. 2, are refracted by transparent media in different degrees; this refraction is also proved to be subject to the same laws as the refraction of luminous rays. Thus the sine of the angle of incidence bears a constant ratio to the sine of the angle of refraction, when the refracting medium is given, and refracting media of different kinds refract these rays in different degrees.

If the invisible calorific rays at H, fig. 3, be allowed to pass through a hole in the screen, and be received on the plane reflector M, they will be reflected in the direction M H, in the same manner as a ray of light would be under the same circumstances; that is, the rays M H′ and M H will be equally inclined to the plane of the reflector. If rays of heat be received on a concave reflector, they will be reflected to a focus in exactly the same manner as rays of light; and in a word, all the phenomena explained in optics, concerning the reflection of light by surfaces, whether plane or curved, are found to accompany the reflection of the non-luminous calorific rays. This is actually found to take place, whether the non luminous rays be those which are obtained by reflecting the solar light by the prism, or produced from a heated body.

Fig. 3.

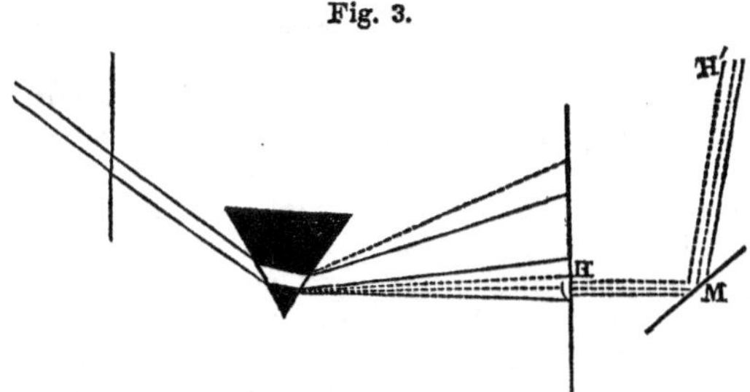

In the experiments of Berard, the question of the identity of the calorific and luminous rays was submitted to tests even more severe. There are certain crystallized bodies called double refracting crystals, which produce peculiar effects on the rays of light transmitted through them. Let A B, fig. 4, be the surface of a piece of Iceland spar, or carbonate of lime, which is one of this class of bodies, and let L L′ be a ray of light striking obliquely on the surface of this crystal; if the crystal were common glass this ray would be bent out of its course, and would pass through it in another direction; but, in the case of Iceland spar it is observed that the ray L L′ is divided into two distinct rays, which proceed in two different directions, L′ M, L′ M′, through the crystal. Let a non-luminous calorific ray, taken from the lower end of the spectrum, be in like manner transmitted to the surface of such a crystal, it will be found, that, in penetrating the crystal, it will be divided into two rays, and that these two rays will be deflected according to the same laws, exactly as a luminous ray is under the same circumstances.

Fig. 4.

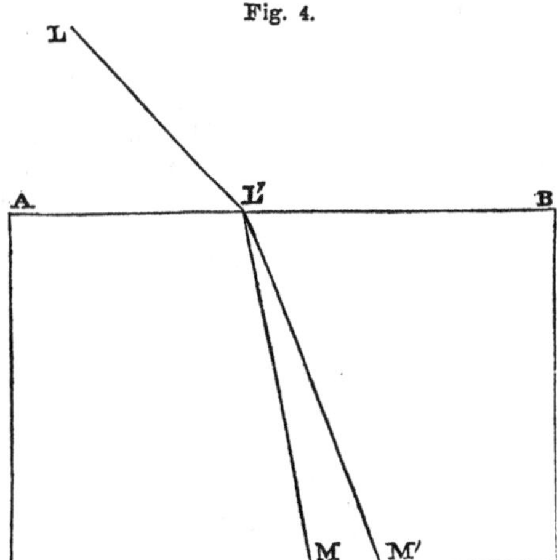

A luminous ray thus, after its transmission through a double refracting crystal, is observed to have received a peculiar physical modification, which is called polarization. In fact, a mirror, placed in a certain inclined position, above or below one of these two rays, is capable of reflecting them in the ordinary way; but if placed in the same oblique position, on either side of them, it becomes utterly incapable of reflecting them. The other ray possesses a similar quality, but the position of the non-reflecting side is reversed. Now, the two rays into which a non-luminous calorific ray, transmitted through such a crystal, is resolved, are found to possess precisely the same property—they are *polarized*.

A ray of light falling on a reflecting surface at a certain angle, the magnitude of which will depend on the nature of the surface, is found, when reflected in the ordinary way, to be polarized or put into the physical state just now mentioned, to result from the double refraction of a crystal. It is capable of being reflected by an oblique mirror placed above or below it, but it is incapable of being reflected by the same mirror, similarly placed, on either side. A non-luminous calorific ray, whether proceeding from the prism, or from a hot body reflected, is found to undergo the same effect, and to be also polarized.

In the experimental investigation of the phenomena attending the radiation of heat, it is necessary to distinguish the effect of radiated heat from the casual variation of the temperature of the air in the apartment in which the experiment may be conducted. The use of the thermometer would, in this case, be attended with material inconvenience, inasmuch as it would be extremely difficult to distinguish the effect of the heat radiated, from the casual change of temperature of the medium in which the thermometer is placed. A second thermometer, it is true, might be used in such experiments, the variations of which would show the change of temperature of the medium; but this second thermometer could never be placed exactly in the same position as the thermometer affected by the radiant heat: and it would not follow that the changes of temperature of two different parts of the same chamber would, necessarily, be exactly alike. An instrument, therefore, which is not affected by any change of temperature in the medium in which it is placed would be capable of giving much more accurate indications for such a purpose. Such an instrument was invented and applied by Sir John Leslie, in his experiments on radiant heat, the results of which have, so justly, placed that distinguished philosopher in the first rank of modern discoverers in physics.

The differential thermometer of Leslie consists of a small glass tube, fig. 5, at each extremity of which is placed two thin hollow bulbs, F E, of glass, and the tube is bent into the rectangular form, E A B F, and supported on a stand S, the bulbs being presented upward. This tube contains a small quantity of sulphuric acid, tinged red with carmine, to render it easily visible, filling the greater part of the legs and horizontal branch. To one of the legs, F B, a

Fig. 5.

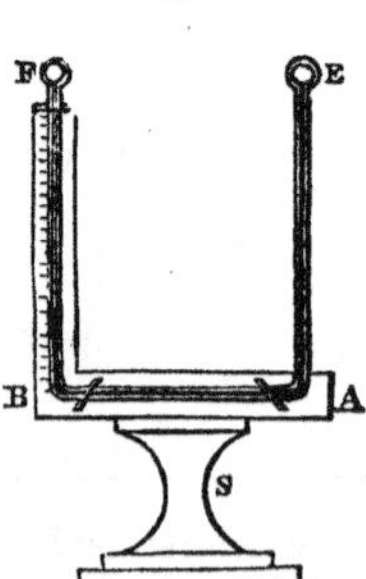

scale is attached, divided into 100°, and the liquid contained in the tube is so disposed, that it stands in the graduated leg opposite that point of the scale which is marked 0°, when both bulbs are exposed to the same temperature. The glass ball attached on the leg of the instrument which bears the scale, is called the *focal ball*. Dry air is contained in the balls above the sulphuric acid, which, not being vaporizable, does not affect the pressure of the air above it by its vapor.

If this instrument be brought into a warm room, the air contained in both bulbs is equally affected by the increase of temperature, and therefore no change takes place in the position of the liquid; and whatever changes the temperature of the apartment may undergo, for the same reason, produce no effect on the instrument. Suppose, however, that the focal ball F is submitted to the effect of heat, from which the ball E is free; then the air in F will acquire a greater degree of elasticity, while the air in E maintains its former pressure; the liquid in the leg F B will, therefore, be pressed downward, until the increased space obtained by the air in F, and the diminished space into which the air in E is pressed by the ascent of the liquid in A E is such, that the pressure of the air in the two balls, by diminishing that of the air in F and increasing that of the air in E, acquires a difference which is equal to the weight of the column by which the height of the liquid in A E exceeds the height of the liquid in B F. In fact, the least attention to the instrument will show, that the difference of the heights of the columns of liquid in the two vertical tubes, will represent the difference between their pressures of the air contained in the two bulbs. It is from this property of indicating, not the *absolute* temperatures, but the *difference* of the two adjacent points, that the instrument has received its name.

Let M M′, fig. 6, be two concave mirrors, placed face to face, at the distance of ten or twelve feet, having a certain form called *parabolic*, the property of which we shall now describe:—If the flame of a candle, or any other source of light, be placed at a point *f*, called the focus of the mirror M, the rays of light which proceed from it in every direction, and strike on the concave surface of the mirror M, will be reflected in parallel lines toward the mirror M′. When these parallel rays encounter the surface of the reflector M′, they will be again reflected by it, in lines which all converge to the same point *f′*, which is the focus of M′. Now, instead of a luminous flame, let amadou, gunpowder, or other matter easily inflammable, be placed in the focus *f*, and place a red-hot metallic ball in the other focus *f′*. In a few minutes the amadou or gunpowder will be inflamed or exploded by the heat radiated by the ball and collected at the point *f* by the reflectors M M′.

Fig. 6.

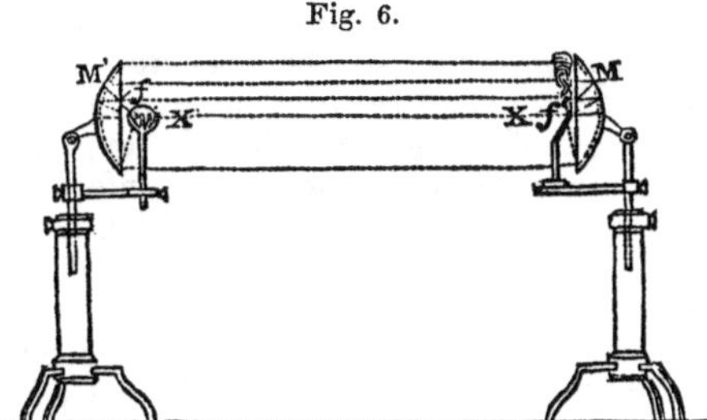

But to prove that the rays of non-luminous heat are similarly reflected, let the red-hot ball be removed, and a hollow ball of metal, filled with boiling water, be substituted for it at *f′*; let the focal ball of a differential thermometer be placed at f—instantly the liquid will be depressed in the leg of the thermometer, and the presence of the source of heat greater than that of the surrounding medium will be thus indicated. That this source of heat is derived from the vessel of hot water in the focus f' may be easily proved. Let this vessel be removed, and immediately the liquid in the thermometer will rise to its ordinary level; but it may be said that the effect is produced on the thermometer by the heat transmitted direct from f' to f. This, however, may be proved not to be the case; for let the hot water be placed as before at f', and let the mirror M be removed, the effect produced on the thermometer will immediately cease.

The rapidity with which the heat thus radiated from f' and reflected by the mirrors to f is propagated, may be shown by interposing between f and f' a screen, composed of any substance not pervious to calorific rays. When the screen is thus interposed, the liquid in the thermometer will recover its ordinary level; but the moment the screen is again withdrawn, the liquid instantly falls in the focal leg; and this takes place by whatever distance the two mirrors may be separated.

Of the two hypotheses already mentioned, which have been proposed for the explanation of the phenomena observed in the prismatic spectrum, that which supposes light to consist of three distinct principles seems to be attended with a variety of circumstances which throw improbability upon it. The three principles thus distinguished enjoy the same leading properties. They all obey, with the most minute precision, the ordinary laws of optics, and, in fact, possess every property of light except the most prominent and obvious one of affecting the sight. The other hypothesis, on the contrary, has the advantage of great simplicity; in it light is considered as compounded of a number of rays unequally refrangible, and possessing, consequently, different influences on other bodies, and on vision. The calorific and chemical properties which disappear alternately at the extremities of the spectrum, are considered as depending on, or connected with, the difference of refrangibility, and as becoming insensible under different variations in that property; it is very conceivable that the calorific power of rays may vary in some inverse proportion with respect to their refrangibility, while the energy of the chemical power may change in a contrary direction. In a word, since all the rays refracted by the prism agree in by far the greater number of their properties, and disagree only in some peculiar effects; and since even this disagreement may be considered more as apparent than real, and may arise from the want of sufficient sensibility in the tests by which these effects may be practically ascertained, it seems more philosophical to regard all the rays as of one species, than to adopt an hypothesis which classes things alike in all their leading qualities, under different denominations. It is not, however, necessary to assume either supposition, nor to adopt it as the basis of reasoning. Experiment is the sure and only guide in physics; and whether heat be obscure and imperceptible light, or a distinct physical agent, we shall regard it as a principle attended with certain sensible effects, capable of being ascertained by experiment or observation, and from such effects and such only, can legitimate inferences be drawn.

The heat which passes from a body by radiation has a tendency to cause its temperature to fall; and, the rate of this process of cooling, is proportionate to the difference between the temperature of the body and that of the surrounding medium, when this difference is not of very great amount. It follows, then, that a hot body at first, when its temperature greatly exceeds that of the surrounding air, cools rapidly; but as its temperature falls, and approaches nearer to equality with the temperature of the medium in which it is placed, the rate at which it cools gradually diminishes. This law of bodies cooling was first observed by Newton, and reduced to an exact mathematical expression, by which the rates of the cooling of bodies under given circumstances might be calculated with precision. Numerous experiments have been made on the rates at which bodies cool in media of lower temperatures, and become hot in media of higher temperatures; and the results of observation have been found to have a very exact conformity with those which are calculated on the Newtonian law, provided the difference of the temperature does not exceed a certain limit.

As radiation takes place altogether from the points of a body which are on or very near its surface, it may naturally be expected that the radiating power of bodies will mainly depend on the nature of their surfaces. This idea suggested to Sir John Leslie a series of experiments which led to some of the most remarkable discoveries ever made respecting the radiation of heat. In these experiments, cubical vessels, or *canisters*, of tin were employed, the side of which varied from three inches to ten. These vessels were filled with hot water and placed before a tin reflector, M, fig. 7, like those already described, in the focus *f* of which was placed the focal ball of a differential thermometer. The face of the canister *c* containing water being presented to the reflector, rays of heat proceeded directly from it, and striking on the reflector M were collected into the focus *f* on the ball of the thermometer. The depression of the liquid in the thermometer furnished a measure of the intensity of the heat radiated.

Fig. 7.

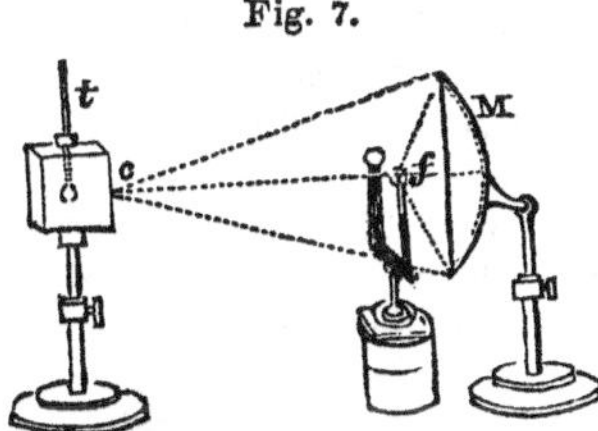

The first consequence of these experiments was a verification of the law aleady mentioned, that, other things being the same, the intensity of the radiation was always proportional to the difference between the temperature of the water and the temperature of the air. Thus suppose, the temperature of the air being 50°, that of the water 100°, that the thermometer fall 20°; then if the temperature of the air were the same, and the temperature of the water at 150°, the thermometer would fall 40°; and again, if the temperature of the water were 200°, the thermometer would fall 60°, and so on.

If, while the temperature of the water remains the same, the canister is placed successively at different distances from the reflector, it is found that the thermometer is differently affected; and that, as the distance of the radiating surface from the reflector is increased, the intensity of its effect is in the same proportion diminished. It was likewise ascertained, that if the magnitude of the radiating surface were increased, the distance remaining the same, the intensity of the radiation would be in the direct proportion of the magnitude of the radiating surface. From this it necessarily follows, that if the magnitude of the radiating surface be increased in the same proportion as the distance is increased, the intensity of the radiation will remain the same; for as much is gained by the increased magnitude of the radiating surface, as is lost by the increased distance; and accordingly it was found that the thermometer was equally affected by a surface of double magnitude at a double distance, and of triple magnitude at a triple distance.

We have hitherto supposed that the face of the canister is placed parallel to the reflector, so that the rays of heat take a direction perpendicular to the radiating surface; but if each point of the surface radiates heat in all possible directions, it will follow that the surface, when presented obliquely to the mirror, will still affect the thermometer. When the surface of the canister was presented thus obliquely, the effect produced on a thermometer was found to be the same as would be produced by a surface of less magnitude, in the proportion of the actual magnitude of the radiating surface to that of its projection. It follows, therefore, that the more inclined the radiating surface is to the direction of the radiation, the less will be the intensity of the radiation; but in general this intensity will be diminished, in the proportion of the actual magnitude of the radiating surface and the magnitude of its orthographical projection on the mirror.

We have hitherto supposed the nature of the radiating surface to remain unaltered. The effect of any change in this, however, may be easily ascertained by covering the side of the canister with the different substances the effect of which is required. Thus, let the four sides of the canister be coated with different substances—one with lampblack, another with isinglass, another with china ink, and a fourth left uncovered, and therefore presenting a surface of polished tin. The vessel being now filled with hot water, all the surfaces will acquire the same temperature, and may be successively presented to the reflector at the same distance; they will be observed to produce different effects on the thermometer. If the lampblack depresses the liquid 100°, the china ink will depress it 88°, the isinglass 80°, and the tin 12°. The great difference in the radiating power produced by the different nature of the surfaces will be hence very apparent.

The inquiries of Professor Leslie were directed to this point with great effect, and he found that various substances possessed very different radiating powers. In general, metallic bodies proved to be the most feeble radiators. The following table exhibits the relative power of radiation of different substances, as exhibited in these experiments:—

Substance	Power	Substance	Power
Lampblack	100	Isinglass	80
Water, by estimate	100	Plumbago	75
Writing-paper	98	Tarnished lead	45
Rosin	96	Mercury	20
Sealing-wax	95	Clean lead	19
Crown glass	90	Iron polished	15
China ink	88	Tin-plate	12
Ice	85	Gold, silver, copper	12
Minium	80		

When the substance forming the radiating surface remains of the same nature, its radiating power is subject to considerable elevation, according to its state with respect to smoothness, or roughness. In general, the more polished and smooth a surface is, the more feeble will be its power of radiation. Anything which tarnishes the surface of metal also increases its radiating power. In the preceding table, tarnished lead radiated 45°, while clean lead radiated only 19°. If the surface of a body be rendered rough by mechanical means, such as scratching with a file, or with sand-paper, the radiating power is increased.

Leslie also proved that the particles forming the surface of a body are not the only ones which radiate, but that radiation proceeds from particles at a certain small depth within the surface. He determined this curious point by covering one side of a vessel containing hot water with a thin coating of jelly, and putting on another side four times the quantity. In each case, when dried, the jelly formed an extremely thin film on the surface. Now, although the nature of these two surfaces was precisely the same with respect to material and smoothness, they were found to radiate very differently; the thinner film depressed the thermometer 38°, while the thicker depressed it 54°. The increased radiation must in this case be attributed to the increased quantity of radiating material. The increase of radiation was found to continue until the coating amounted to the thickness of about 1000th part of an inch, after which no further increase took place. It might, therefore, be inferred that, in the case of the surface of jelly, such as that here submitted to experiment, the particles radiate heat from a depth below the surface equal to the 1000th part of an inch.

A similar effect was found with other substances. In the case of metals, no increase was observed when leaf metal of gold, silver, and copper, was used; but on using glass, enamelled with gold, a slight increase of radiating power was produced, as compared with the ordinary radiating power.

In these experiments the heat radiated undergoes three distinct physical effects: 1. The radiation from the surface of the canister; 2. The reflection from the surface of the reflector; 3. Absorption by the glass surface of the focal ball, for without such absorption the air included could not be affected. Now, of these three effects, we have hitherto examined but one, viz., the radiating power. Let us consider what circumstances affect the power of reflecting heat, and the power of absorbing it.

The reflector used in the experiments already described was formed of polished tin. If, instead of this, a reflector of glass be used, it will be found that the thermometer will be affected in a much less degree, whence we infer that glass is a worse reflector than metal. If the surface of the reflector be coated with lampblack, all reflection whatever is destroyed, and no effect is produced on the thermometer. Thus it appears that, as different surfaces have different radiating powers, so also they have different reflecting powers; but to determine the reflecting power of different surfaces with great exactness, Leslie received the rays proceeding from the reflector M, fig. 8, on a flat reflecting sur-

Fig. 8.

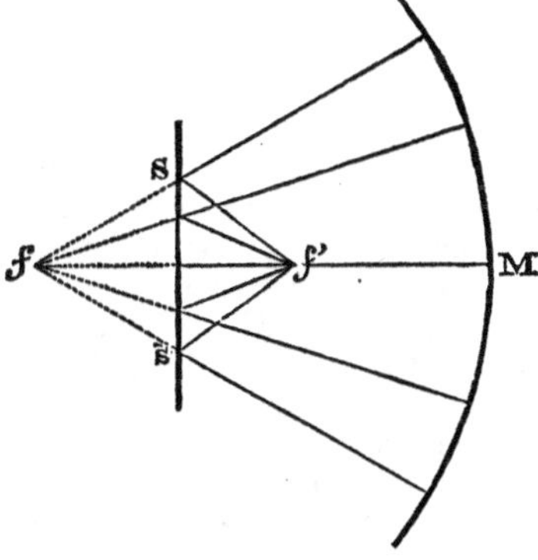

face, S, before they came to a focus; and by the laws of reflection they were reflected to another focus, *f*, as far before the reflecting surface S as the focus *f*, to which they would have proceeded is behind it. The reflecting power of the surface S will, therefore, be determined by the intensity of the heat in the focus *f'*, compared with the intensity which it would have had in the focus *f*, had the rays been allowed to converge to that point. By experiments conducted in this way, and exposing the surfaces of different substances to receive the rays, as at S, Leslie determined the reflecting powers of several bodies as follow:—

Brass	100	Lead	60
Silver	90	Tin-foil, softened with mercury	10
Tin-foil	85	Glass	10
Block tin	80	Glass, coated with wax or oil	5
Steel	70		

If these results be compared with the table of radiating powers in page 476, it will be found that, generally, those substances which are the best radiators are the worst reflectors, and vice versa. In fact, in proportion as the radiating power is increased, the reflecting power is diminished. This analogy is further confirmed by the fact, that the reflecting power is increased by every increase in smoothness or polish of the reflecting surface; while, on the contrary, this cause, as we have seen, diminishes its radiating power. The effect of coating the reflector with a thin film of jelly or other substance has, in conformity with the same analogy, exactly a contrary effect to that which such a coating produced on radiation. It was found that, as the thickness of the coating increased to a certain limit, the intensity of the radiation was likewise increased. On the other hand, in the case of reflection, the intensity of the reflection is diminished in proportion as the thickness of the coating is increased.

Let us now consider the effect produced on the focal ball, which will lead us to determine the different powers of absorption which different bodies possess. In all the experiments to which we have hitherto alluded, the focal ball has presented a polished surface of glass, and the effect produced on a thermometer, other things being the same, has depended on the absorptive power of the glass over the heat incident upon it. When radiant heat strikes on the surface of different substances, we have seen that a portion of it is reflected, and that this portion varies according to the nature of the substance and according to the state of the surface. It is clear that all that portion of the incident heat which is not reflected must be absorbed; and we are led, therefore, by analogy to the inference that, in proportion as the reflecting power of a surface is great, its absorptive power is small, and vice versa.

To bring this inference to the test of experiment, let the ball of a thermometer be coated with tin-foil, which was found to be one of the best reflectors. If the side of the vessel coated with lampblack, while the focal ball is covered with tin-foil, be now presented to the reflector, the thermometer will only indicate 20°, whereas it indicates 100° when the surface of the ball was uncovered. If the bright side of a canister be presented to the reflector when the focal ball is uncovered, the thermometer indicates 12°; but, if the focal ball be covered with tin-foil, it will indicate only 2½°. Thus we see that the anticipation of theory is confirmed. If the surface of the tin-foil be rubbed with sand-paper, so as to render it rough, and therefore to diminish its reflecting power, its absorbing power will be increased, and the effects on the thermometer will be likewise augmented. Like experiments performed on other bodies lead to the general conclusion, that the absorptive power of bodies increases as the reflecting power decreases.

Since the radiating power of a surface is inversely as its reflecting power, it follows, also, that the power of absorption is always in the same proportion as the power of radiation. In reference to their power of transmitting light, bodies are denominated *transparent* or *opaque*. A body which is pervious to light is said to be *transparent*, and one which does not allow light to pass through it is said to be *opaque*. Transparency is also a quality which bodies possess in different degrees: some, such as glass, water, or air, being almost perfectly transparent, while others, such as paper, horn, &c., are imperfectly so. Analogy leads us to inquire whether bodies are also pervious to heat.

In the preceding experiments, rays of heat passed through the atmosphere, which is therefore, transparent to heat. It appears from the experiments of Leslie and others, which have been since instituted, that all gases are pervious to the rays of heat, and equally so; for the radiation of a given surface is the same in whatever gas it takes place.

Gases, therefore, as they have perfect or nearly perfect transparencies for the rays of light, have the same quality in reference to the rays of heat. A hot body placed behind a solid or a liquid is found, however, not to radiate sensibly through them. But the most direct method of determining the transparency of bodies for the rays of heat, is to interpose a *screen* between the radiating body and the reflector, in the experiment already described, and to observe the effect produced on the thermometer by this circumstance. Leslie's investigation respecting the property of transparency to heat of different bodies, form a very remarkable part of that philosopher's discoveries.

Different substances are pervious by heat in different degrees. A screen of thin deal board, placed between the canister, *c*, and the focal ball, *f*, figure 7, produced a diminution in the effect on the thermometer, but did not destroy that effect altogether. The heat transmitted through the board varied with its thickness, slowly diminishing as its thickness increased. The radiation of the surface of the lampblack, which, while unobstructed, produced an effect of 100° on the thermometer, produced an effect of 20° when a deal board the eighth of an inch thick was interposed. It produced an effect of 15° when the thickness was three eighths of an inch, and an effect of 9° when the board was an inch thick. A plane of glass interposed reduced the effect of the radiation by the surface of lampblack from 100° to 20°.

The distance of the screen from the canister was also found to produce a considerable effect on its transparency. When placed near the canister, a considerable quantity of heat was transmitted; but if the distance was increased, the quantity of heat transmitted diminished. A pane of glass at the distance of two inches reduced the effect of radiation from 100° to 20°. As its distance from the radiating surface was slowly increased, the effect on the thermometer was gradually diminished; and at the distance of one foot from the radiating surface all effect of radiation was destroyed.

It appeared that the metals, even when reduced to an extreme degree of tenuity, were absolutely opaque to heat. A screen of tinfoil absolutely intercepted all radiation. The thinnest gold leaves, 300,000 of which, piled one upon another would not measure an inch, also absolutely stopped the rays of heat. White paper is partially opaque.

It appears, generally, that the bodies which intercept heat most effectually are those which radiate heat worst, and *vice versa*. This, indeed, might easily have been anticipated from what has been already proved of reflection. The screens which are the best reflectors are the worst radiators, and must evidently be also most powerful in intercepting heat; for if they reflect much they can transmit but little. Some other effects, which Leslie observed in his experiments with screens, may also be accounted for by the same circumstance. He took two panes of glass and coated one side of each with tinfoil. He then placed their uncovered sides in close contact, so as to form one double pane, both surfaces of which were covered with tinfoil. When this was interposed as a screen before the radiating surface, all effect on the thermometer was destroyed, and all the radiant heat intercepted. This is easily accounted for by the perfect power of reflection which the coating of tinfoil possesses. The heat incident on the surface of tinfoil is nearly all reflected; and, consequently, no sensible quantity is transmitted. He next placed the two panes with their coated surfaces in contact, the uncovered surfaces being outside. A part of the radiant heat was now transmitted, and the effect on the thermometer was observed to be 18°. Thus about one fifth of the radiant heat incident on the screen was transmitted. In fact, nearly as much heat was thus transmitted by the two panes of glass with the tinfoil between them, as would have been transmitted by a pane of uncovered glass. From this result it would appear that the tinfoil loses its power of reflecting heat when the rays of heat have previously passed through a medium of glass instead of a medium of air; and that, instead of reflecting them, it transmits them.

The idea of investigating the effects which different temperatures in a radiant body produce on the power of the radiated heat to penetrate screens of different substances, does not seem to have suggested itself to Sir John Leslie. Later experiments, instituted by M. de la Roche, prove that the power of calorific rays to penetrate bodies increases with the temperature of the radiator. This heat radiating from a surface at a certain temperature, fails to penetrate glass, except in a very limited degree; but if the radiating body be considerably elevated in its temperature, then the rays penetrate the glass in much greater quantities. In fact, the degree of transparency of glass relatively to the rays of heat would seem to depend on the temperature of the radiating body, and to increase with that temperature.

The results of the preceding experiments, and, indeed, all the phenomena connected with the radiation of heat, are satisfactorily explained by *the theory of exchanges*, first proposed by Prevost of Geneva. According to this theory, every point at and near the surfaces of bodies is regarded as a centre from which rays of heat diverge in all directions. The surfaces also reflect rays of heat incident upon them, in a greater or less degree, rays of heat striking on a body, and reflected or radiated by the other bodies around. Thus every body, so far as regards heat, is constantly under the operation of three distinct processes—it radiates, reflects, and absorbs: it follows, from this, that between bodies which are placed in each other's neighborhood, there must be a constant interchange of heat. The heat which is radiated by one body strikes on others; part of it is absorbed by them, and is retained within their dimensions, so as to raise their temperature, while another part is reflected, and strikes on other bodies, where it is subject to like effects. The body which radiates heat in this manner is, at the same time, receiving on its surface rays of heat which proceed from other bodies in its neighborhood; and these rays of heat are subject to the same effects on its surface as the rays which, proceeding from it, encounter on the surface of other bodies—they are partly absorbed and partly reflected.

If a body raised to a high temperature be placed in the neighborhood of other bodies at a lower temperature, it will radiate a greater quantity of heat than the bodies which surround it; consequently the heat which it receives from them will be less than the heat which it transmits to them. They will receive more heat than they give, and it will give more heat than it receives; the temperature, therefore, of the hot body, will gradually fall, while the temperature of the surrounding bodies will gradually rise. This will continue until the temperatures of the bodies are equalized. Then the heat radiated by each of them will be exactly equal to the heat absorbed, and the temperature will remain stationary.

It has appeared from the result of direct experiments, that the bodies which are the best radiators are also the best absorbers of heat. This would follow as a necessary consequence of the theory which has been just explained. If a body which is a powerful radiator were at the same time a bad absorber, the consequence would be that it would radiate heat faster than it would absorb it;

consequently its temperature would continually fall, and this depression of temperature would continue without any limit. Now this is not supported by observation. It therefore follows, as a necessary consequence, that the power of radiation in every body must be equal to its power of absorption.

It has likewise appeared that the best reflectors are the worst radiators. This effect might likewise be foreseen on the principle of the theory just explained. A good reflector is a body which reflects the principal part of the rays of heat which strike upon it. Now the heat which is incident on a body must be either reflected or absorbed, and whatever portion of it is not reflected must be absorbed. If, therefore, a great part be reflected, a proportionally small part remains to be absorbed; consequently it follows, that in the same proportion as a body is a good reflector it must be a bad absorber; and, *vice versa*, if it be a bad reflector, it must in proportion be a good absorber. But it necessarily follows, if a body be a powerful absorber of heat, that it must also be a powerful radiator of heat, for otherwise its temperature would rise infinitely by the heat which it absorbs accumulating in it, and not being carried off by radiation. A good reflector, therefore, will be a bad radiator, and *vice versa*. In the experiments of Leslie with the concave reflector, our attention was only directed to the radiation of the hot surface, and we considered only the rays which, proceeding from it, were collected on the bulb of a thermometer by the concave reflector. It might appear to follow, from an extension of this experiment, that bodies *radiate cold* as well as heat. Let one of the cubical vessels used by Leslie in his experiment be filled with snow, and placed before a reflector. Immediately the focal ball of the differential thermometer placed in the focus will exhibit a rapid depression of temperature. Are we, therefore, to suppose in this case that *rays of cold* proceed from sides of the vessel, and are collected on the ball of the thermometer? On the contrary, it has appeared from previous investigation, that no body is perfectly destitute of heat, and that snow itself, as well as mixtures much colder than it, are capable of imparting heat to other bodies, and therefore possess heat in them. The surface, therefore, of a vessel containing snow, in this case radiates heat, and these rays of heat are collected on the bulb of the thermometer in the same manner as when that vessel was filled with boiling water. The bulb of the thermometer, however, itself, like all other bodies, radiates heat, and this heat is reflected by the concave reflector toward the surface of the vessel containing the snow. The two bodies, therefore, are radiating heat toward each other; but the bulb of the thermometer having the higher temperature, radiates more heat than it receives, while the surface of the vessel containing the snow receives more heat than it radiates. The thermometer, therefore, gradually falls in its temperature, while the vessel containing the snow gradually rises.

In the experiment with the concave reflector already described, the hot body placed in one focus, and the bulb of the thermometer placed in the other, are both radiators and absorbers of heat; the hot body radiates heat to the bulb, and the bulb radiates heat to it. The hot body absorbs the heat which is radiated by the bulb, and the bulb absorbs the heat radiated by the hot body. But the hot body, radiating more heat than the bulb, necessarily absorbs less, consequently the temperature of this body gradually falls, while that of the bulb of the thermometer rises. Let us now suppose that instead of a hot body, a globe of snow be placed in the focus of the reflector, the bulb of the thermometer having a higher temperature, will radiate more heat than it receives from the snow, and it will become a hot body relatively to the snow. Since, therefore, it radiates more heat than it absorbs, its temperature will fall until it becomes equal to that of the snow; the interchange of heat being then equal, no further alteration in temperature will take place.

Numerous facts of ordinary occurrence, and many interesting natural phenomena, admit of easy and satisfactory explanation on the principle of the above theory of radiation.

Vessels intended to contain a liquid at a higher temperature than the surrounding medium, and to keep that liquid as long as possible at the higher temperature should be constructed of materials which are the worst radiators of heat. Thus, tea-urns and tea-pots are not adapted for their purpose when constructed of black porcelain. A black porcelain tea-pot is the worst conceivable material for that vessel, for both its material and color are good radiators of heat, and the liquid contained in it cools with the greatest possible rapidity. On the other hand, a bright metal tea-pot is best adapted for the purpose, because it is the worst radiator of heat, and therefore cools as slowly as possible. A polished silver or brass tea-urn is better adapted to retain the heat of the water than one of a dull brown color, such as is most commonly used in England.

A tin kettle retains the heat of water boiled in it more effectually if it is kept clean and polished, than if it be allowed to collect the smoke and soot, to which it is exposed from the action of the fire. When coated with this, its surface becomes rough and black, and is a powerful radiator of heat.

A set of polished fire-irons may remain for a long time in front of a hot fire without receiving from it any increase of temperature beyond that of the chamber, because the heat radiated by the fire is all reflected by the polished surface of the irons, and none of it is absorbed; but if a set of rough, unpolished irons, were similarly placed, they would speedily become hot, so that they could not be used without inconvenience. The polish of fire-irons is, therefore, not merely a matter of ornament, but of use and convenience. The rough, unpolished poker, sometimes used in a kitchen, soon becomes so hot that it cannot be held without pain.

A close stove, intended to warm an apartment, should not have a polished surface, for in that case it is one of the worst radiators of heat, and nothing could be contrived more unfit for the purpose to which it is applied. On the other hand, a rough unpolished surface of cast-iron is favorable to radiation, and a fire in such a stove will always produce a more powerful effect.

A metal helmet and cuiras, worn by some regiments of cavalry, is a cooler dress than might be at first imagined. The polished metal being a nearly perfect reflector of heat, throws off the rays of the sun, and is incapable of being raised to an inconvenient temperature. Its temperature is much less increased by the influence of the sun than that of common clothing.

The polished surfaces of different parts of the steam-engine, especially of the cylinder, is not matter of mere ornament, but of essential utility. A rough metal surface would be a much better radiator of heat than the polished surface, and if rust were collected on it, its radiating power would be still further increased, and the steam contained in it would be more exposed to condensation by loss of heat.

It may be frequently observed that a deposition of moisture has taken place on the interior surface of the panes of glass of a chamber-window, on a morning which succeeds a cold night. The temperature of the external air during the night being colder than the atmosphere of the chamber, it communicates its temperature to the external surface of the glass, and this is transmitted to the interior surface, which is exposed to the atmosphere of the room. This atmosphere is always more or less charged with vapor, and the cold of the external surface of the glass acting on the air in contact with it, reduces its temperature below the point of saturation, and a condensation of vapor takes place on the surface of the panes, which is observed by a copious deposition of moisture in the morning. If the temperature of the external air be at or below the freezing point, this deposition will form a rough coating of ice on the pane. Let a small piece of tin-foil be fixed on a part of the *exterior* surface of one pane of the window in the evening, and let another piece of tin-foil be fixed on a part of the *interior* surface of another pane. In the morning it will be found that that part of the interior surface which is opposite to the external foil will be nearly free from ice, while every other part of the same pane will be thickly covered with it. On the contrary, it will be found that the surface of the internal tin-foil will be more thickly covered with ice than any other part of the glass. These effects are easily explained by the principle of radiation. When the tin-foil is placed on the exterior surface, it reflects the heat which strikes on the exterior surface, and protects that part of the glass which is covered from its action. The heat radiated from the objects in the room striking on the surface of the glass, penetrates it, and encountering the tin-foil attached to the exterior surface, is reflected by it through the dimensions of the glass, and its escape into the exterior atmosphere is intercepted; the portion of the glass, therefore, covered by the tin-foil, is in this case subject to the action of the heat radiated from the chamber, but protected from the action of the external heat. The temperature of that part of the glass is therefore less depressed by the effects of the external atmosphere than the temperature of those parts which are not covered by the tin-foil. Now, glass being, as will appear hereafter, a bad conductor of heat, the temperature of that part opposite to the tin-foil does not immediately affect the remainder of the pane, and consequently we find that while the remainder of the interior surface of the pane is thickly covered with ice, the portion opposite the tin-foil is comparatively free from it. On the contrary, when the tin-foil is placed on the internal surface, it reflects powerfully the heat radiated from the objects in the room, while it admits through the dimensions of the glass, the heat proceeding from the external atmosphere. The portion of the glass, therefore, covered by the tin-foil, becomes colder than any other part of the pane, and the tin-foil itself receives the same temperature, which is not reduced by the effect of the radiation of objects in the room, because the tin-foil itself is a good reflector of heat, and a bad absorber. Hence the tin-foil presents a colder surface to the atmosphere of the room than any other part of the surface of the pane, and consequently receives a more abundant deposition of ice.

If a body, which is a good radiator of heat, be exposed in a situation where other good radiators are not present, it will have a tendency to fall in its temperature below the temperature of the surrounding medium; because, in this case, while it loses heat by its own radiation, its absorbing power is not satisfied by a corresponding supply of heat from other objects. A clear sky, in the absence of the sun, has scarcely any sensible radiation of heat; if, therefore, a good radiator be exposed to the aspect of an unclouded firmament at night, it will lose heat considerably by its own radiation, and will receive no corresponding portion from the radiation of the firmament to repair this loss, and its temperature consequently will fall.

A curious experiment made by Dufay affords a striking illustration of this fact. He exposed a glass cup, placed in a silver basin, to the atmosphere during a cold night, and he found in the morning a copious deposition of moisture on the glass, while the silver vessel remained perfectly dry. He next reversed the experiment, and exposed a silver cup in a glass basin. The result was the same: the glass was still covered with moisture, and the metal free from it. Now metal is a bad radiator of heat, and consequently has a tendency to preserve its temperature. Glass is a much better radiator, and has therefore a tendency to lose its temperature. These vessels being exposed to the aspect of a clear sky, received no considerable rays of heat to supply the loss sustained by their radiation. This loss in the metal was inconsiderable, and therefore it maintained its temperature nearly or altogether equal to that of the air; the glass, however, radiating more abundantly, and absorbing little, suffers a depression of temperature. The glass, therefore, presented a cold surface to the air contiguous to it, and reduced the temperature of that air, until it attained that temperature at which it was below a state of saturation with respect to the vapor with which it was charged; a deposition of vapor, therefore, took place on the glass.

This discovery of Dufay remained a barren fact until the attention of Dr. Wells was directed to the subject. The result of his inquiries was the discovery of the cause of the phenomena of dew, and affords one of the most beautiful instances of inductive reasoning which any part of the history of physical discovery has presented. Dr. Wells argued that, as a clear and cloudless sky radiates little or no heat toward the surface of the earth, all objects placed on the surface which are good radiators must necessarily fall in temperature during the night, if they be in a situation in which they are not exposed to the radiation of other objects in their neighborhood. Grass and other products of vegetation are, in general, good radiators of heat. The vegetation which covers the surface of the ground in an open, champaign country, on a clear night, will therefore undergo a depression of temperature, because it will absorb less heat than it radiates. This fact was ascertained by direct experiment, both by Dr. Wells and Mr. Six. A thermometer, laid on a grass plot on a clear night, was observed to sink even so much as 20° below another thermometer suspended at some height above the ground. The vegetables, which thus acquire a lower temperature than the atmosphere, reduce the air immediately contiguous to them to a temperature below saturation, and a proportionally copious condensation of vapor takes place, and a deposition of dew is formed on the leaves and flowers of all vegetables. In fact, every object, in proportion as it is a good radiator, receives a deposition of moisture. On the other hand, objects which are bad radiators are observed to be free from it. Blades of grass sustain large, pellucid dew-drops, while the naked soil in their neighborhood is free from them.

In the close and sheltered streets of cities the deposition of dew is very rarely observed, because there the objects are necessarily exposed to each other's radiation, and an interchange of heat takes place which maintains them at a temperature uniform with that of the air. A deposition of dew, in this case, can only take place when the natural temperature of the air falls below its point of saturation.

In an obscure, cloudy night no deposition of dew takes place, because in this case, although the vegetable productions radiate heat as powerfully as before, yet the clouds are also radiators, and they transmit heat, which, being absorbed by the vegetables, their temperature is prevented from sinking much below that of the atmosphere.

METEORIC STONES & SHOOTING STARS.

Inductive Method.—Appearances accompanying Meteorites.—Theories to explain them.—Examination of these Theories.—Shooting Stars.—November and August Meteors.—Orbits and Distances.—Heights.—Ch.adni's Hypothesis.

METEORIC STONES & SHOOTING STARS.

When we reflect upon the length of time which has elapsed since just methods of investigating nature were first formally taught by Bacon, we can not fail to be struck with surprise at witnessing the frequency with which those inestimable precepts are neglected and overlooked. There appears to be a disposition inherent in the mind—springing probably from that arrogance and vanity, which are invariably the offspring of ignorance—that induces a disposition, in every case, precipitately to rush to the formation of theories and the assumption of causes, omitting, or postponing, the far more important though less ambitious duty of analyzing phenomena. It is true that these observations are less applicable to that order of minds which have been disciplined in the severe schools of the old and long-established universities, where the works of Bacon, and the mathematical classics of Newton and Laplace, are studied with a zeal and perseverance which do not fail to infuse their spirit into the minds of their aspiring successors. But in the much larger class of half-disciplined or self-taught aspirants to scientific rank, the disposition we refer to frequently exists, and to a proportionate extent retards their progress, and impairs the value of their labors.

The public teacher should, therefore, omit no proper opportunity of inculcating the true spirit of the inductive philosophy, which, in our day, has afforded so rich a harvest of discovery. I shall avail myself of the opportunity which the consideration of aerolites offers, to afford you an example of the rigorous observance of the canons of Bacon's philosophy in the investigation of nature.

Every one possessed of the smallest amount of the current information of the day, imagines that he knows what meteoric stones are. He knows that they fall from the air, and that they are accompanied by fire and noise. With this amount of information he unhesitatingly sets about to conjecture their origin, and to get up a theory to explain them. As might be expected, the theory produced under such circumstances is always crude and absurd, and falls to pieces upon the slightest comparison with the phenomena.

When any new and unexplained phenomenon offers itself to our inquiry, the first duty of the investigator is to inform himself, with the most scrupulous accuracy, of all the circumstances, however minute, which accompany it; and if past observation can not answer all circumstantial inquiries which his understanding may suggest as necessary, he must patiently wait the recurrence of a like phenomenon, and diligently observe it. When he shall have thus collected all the circumstances that can be imagined to throw light on its origin, he will then, and not until then, be in a condition to justify an inquiry into its cause.

Let us see, then, what circumstances attending the appearance of meteorites past observation has supplied.

It is agreed by all observers, in every part of the earth, that these meteors manifest themselves by the appearance of a stream of light, passing with great velocity through the firmament; after which an explosion usually takes place, so loud that windows and doors, and even buildings themselves, are sometimes shaken as if by an earthquake.

The phenomenon is sometimes called *ball-lightning*, a term which is liable to the objection that it implies an analogy, or identity of origin, between these meteors and common lightning; which not only is not proved, but is attended with no probability.

The luminous appearance and subsequent explosion attending these meteors was long known; the fact, however, that heavy substances, now called meteoric stones, were projected upon the surface of the earth at the same time, was not clearly proved or generally admitted until the present century. Abundant evidence, however, has been supplied, by the vigilance and zeal of contemporaneous philosophers, of the reality of these deposites. Chladni, in his work on this subject, has supplied an extensive chronological catalogue of the meteoric stones whose falls have been recorded in different parts of the earth, which supplies examples of these phenomena occurring in various parts of the world several times in each year of the present century.

The fact, then, may be regarded as conclusively established, that masses of stony matter, of various size and magnitude, and often of very considerable weight, are frequently seen passing athwart the heavens, with great apparent velocity, which are afterward precipitated upon the earth with extraordinary force.

The second circumstance I shall mention as worthy of attention is, that these bodies rarely strike the surface of the earth in a direction either vertical or nearly so. They generally, on the other hand, come in a direction very oblique to the plane of the horizon. It may be asked, how the direction in which they strike the earth can be ascertained unless they are seen, which rarely happens at the moment of their fall. To this I answer, that their direction is rendered manifest by the manner in which they penetrate the surface of the ground—which they always do, and to a depth more or less considerable.

The velocity of their motion when they encounter the earth, is another circumstance of much importance. This velocity is discoverable by observation on their movement while visible, as well as by inferring the force with which they struck the ground from the depth to which they penetrated.

It is accordingly found by means of such observations, that the velocities of these bodies belong to the kind of motions which characterize the bodies of the solar system, and such as are never witnessed upon the surface of the earth. They are velocities which could not be imagined to be imparted by the earth's gravitation to any masses attracted from points within the limits of the atmosphere.

On examining the physical condition, and analyzing the constituents of the masses thus precipitated, several circumstances worthy to be noted are presented. It is found that their surfaces are generally black, having a burnt appearance; but the most remarkable circumstance attending them is, that at whatever time, or in whatever part of the earth they may have fallen, they generally consist of the same constituent parts, and always very nearly in the same proportion. Their ingredients are silex, magnesia, sulphur, iron, nickel, and chromium. There is occasionally, but not invariably, a trace of charcoal.

It is important to observe here, that the iron and nickel found in these bodies are always in the metallic form—a state in which they are never known to exist naturally on the surface of the earth. These metals, when found in the earth, are invariably combined with oxygen, and it is their oxides only which have a place among natural terrestrial substances. The iron and nickel used in the arts are obtained by the decomposition of the ores in the process of metallurgy.

The distances from the earth at which these meteors pass when they are visible has been ascertained with a tolerable degree of approximation, by observing the length and position of their visible course at the same time from two distant places. It has been found by these means that they are frequently visible at the height of from 30 to 40 miles. This is generally considered as the limit of the height of the atmosphere.

Such are the circumstances attending the exhibition of these meteors, which have been collected from careful and accurate information. Let us now turn our attention to the different methods by which it has been attempted to explain them. Three different hypotheses, or theories, have been proposed for this purpose.

First.—It is supposed that the matter composing them has been drawn up from the surface of the earth in a state of infinitely minute subdivision, as vapor is drawn from liquids; that, being collected in clouds in the higher regions of the atmosphere, it is there agglomerated and consolidated in masses, and falls by its gravity to the surface of the earth; being occasionally drawn from the vertical direction which would be imparted to it by gravity, by the effect of atmospheric currents, and thus occasionally striking the earth obliquely. We shall call this the *atmospheric hypothesis.*

Secondly.—It is supposed that meteoric stones are ejected from volcanoes, with sufficient force to carry them to great elevations in the atmosphere, in falling from which they acquire the velocity and force with which they strike the earth. The oblique direction with which they strike the ground is explained by the supposition that they may be projected from the volcanoes at corresponding obliquities, and that, by the principles of projectiles, they must strike the earth at nearly the same inclination as that with which they have been ejected. This we shall call the *volcanic hypothesis.*

Thirdly.—It has been supposed that these bodies are not either terrestrial or atmospheric, but belonging to the solar system; and that their origin is the same as that which has produced the small planets which have been discovered moving between the orbits of Mars and Jupiter.

This theory supposes that, at some former epoch, the solar system possessed a planet which revolved round the sun at the distance of two hundred and fifty millions of miles; a supposition which is rendered highly probable, if not morally certain, by reasons which are fully detailed in my discourse on the new planets. The catastrophe by which this former planet was broken into pieces is supposed to have been produced, either by internal explosion (from some cause similar to that which produces on the earth volcanoes and earthquakes), or by the collision of a comet. It is supposed that the new planets are not the only fragments which resulted, but that innumerable smaller pieces may have been scattered about the system, which, owing to their extreme minuteness, may have been subject to disturbing causes that have occasionally brought them so near the earth, that they have been drawn by its attraction within the limits of the atmosphere, and have ultimately, by the resistance of that fluid, fallen upon the earth. We shall call this the *planetary hypothesis*.

Fourthly.—It has been suggested by LAPLACE, that meteoric stones may be substances ejected from lunar volcanoes, either now or formerly in active operation. He has proved that no very improbable amount of mechanical force would be sufficient to produce such an effect, since there is no atmosphere around the moon, or, at least, none that could be sufficient to offer a sensible resistance to the motion of a solid body. The force, therefore, that would be required is only that which would be sufficient to overcome the moon's attraction, which is found by calculation to be about four times the force with which a ball is expelled from a cannon with the ordinary charge of gunpowder. A body projected toward the earth, with the velocity of about eight thousand feet per second from the lunar surface, would rise to such a height that it would arrive at a point between the earth and moon where the attraction of the earth would predominate and prevent its return. It would, consequently, continue to move toward the earth with accelerated speed, and, arriving within the limits of the atmosphere, would necessarily reach the surface. We shall call this the *lunar hypothesis*.

Fifthly.—It has been supposed that meteoric stones, showers of dust, and other similar meteorological phenomena, proceed from chaotic matter which prevails in the spaces within which the planets move, and which is generally but irregularly diffused throughout the universe, producing in the heavens the appearances called nebulæ. This matter is supposed to lie irregularly in the space through which the earth annually passes and its neighborhood; that it is occasionally brought by the attraction of the earth within the limits of the atmosphere, and thus descends to the surface. This we shall call the *nebular hypothesis*.

Such are the various theories which have been offered to explain the phenomena attending meteoric stones. The evolution of light which attends their rapid progress through space has been accounted for in all of them in the same manner. It is supposed that, in the rapid motion with which the body proceeds, the air which lies in its path is so extremely condensed, as either to become itself luminous, or to acquire so intense a heat as to render the stone incandescent, or, perhaps, to produce upon it even a superficial combustion, the signs of which are exhibited in the blackness which marks the surface of these bodies. This reasoning is attempted to be supported by the well-known experiment of the fire-syringe. In that instrument a solid piston is fitted in a cylinder, so as to be air-tight, carrying a piece of amadou or other easily combustible matter, at its end. When the piston is suddenly forced down, so as to produce an instantaneous and severe compression of the air under it, the amadou takes fire, and, if the cylinder be glass, a flash of light is visible through it. It has therefore been contended, that in this experiment the air under the piston has acquired, by compression, such a temperature as renders it luminous.

More recent experiments, however, made in France (an account of which has fallen in my way), throw doubt upon the validity of this inference. It is said that the unctuous matter commonly used to lubricate the piston in the fire-syringe is, in fact, the source of the ignition; for that, when experiments were made with pistons not so lubricated, the flash of light was not produced. It is, therefore, considered not to be satisfactorily proved, that air by mere mechanical compression can ever become luminous. Still, however, it might be contended that, even though the air were not to become luminous, it might, nevertheless, be raised to such a temperature by compression as, by contact with the meteorite, might render the latter luminous; but, even admitting the possibility of this supposition, as applied to the air contiguous to the earth, or even at any moderate elevation, an almost insuperable difficulty arises from the vast height at which meteorites have been visible. By barometric experiments and observations made on the duration of the morning and evening twilight, it may be considered as proved, that beyond the elevation of thirty miles there exists no atmosphere possessing any sensible mechanical properties. We may safely conclude that at such elevations the air, if any really exists there, must be so infinitely attenuated as to be divested of all sensible resistance or inertia. The space there must, for example, be a more absolute vacuum than any which could be produced under the receiver of the most perfect philosophical air-pump; how, then, can we imagine such a compression of that fluid to be produced, as would be necessary to evolve the enormous temperature requisite to render luminous the matter composing meteoric stones? still less to become luminous itself.

In short, it must be admitted that none of these theories afford a satisfactory explanation of the luminous appearances which accompany these meteors. Let us, however, examine these theories respectively, and see how far they will bear a further comparison with the actual circumstances of the phenomena.

The atmospheric hypothesis is subject to objections so unanswerable, that it may be considered as altogether set aside. In order to suppose it probable that aërolites could be formed in the atmosphere, we must show that their constituent elements can exist there. We know that hail and snow can be formed in the air, because it can be proved that aqueous vapor is suspended there, and that a temperature is sometimes produced there so low as to convert that vapor, first, into a liquid, and then into the solid form of snow or hail. But the most rigorous analysis has never detected in the atmosphere any of the constituents of meteoric stones, nor is there any proof that the constituent principles of the air could dissolve, evaporate, or sublimate such substances. Nor can it be said that, although the atmosphere which immediately surrounds us may not have such properties, yet, that at the great elevations in which meteorites are formed, the air may consist of different constituents, for, besides the fact that it has been ascertained by direct analysis that the atmosphere, at all elevations to which man has ever yet attained, consists of exactly the same constituents, in exactly the same proportions, there is a general law, which prevails among all gaseous substances, that when different gases are superposed they will, notwithstanding their different degrees of levity, ultimately mingle so as to form a uniform mass; thus, if we could imagine for a moment a stratum of air to exist near the top of the atmosphere, having constituents different from those around us, such stratum would gradually intermingle with the strata below it, until the whole would acquire a uniform quality. It is, therefore, physically impossible that there can exist in any elevated region of the air any substances capable of dissolving or sublimating the matter of meteoric stones.

To these objections we may add others. Although it may be admitted, as Arago argues, that the constituent principles of aërolites should really exist in the atmosphere at all heights, and that they only escape analysis because of their extreme minuteness, it would still be necessary to explain with such feeble and such dispersed elements a sudden precipitation, yielding stones of several hundred weight, such as those preserved at Ensenheim, in Alsace, or 3,000 or 4,000 stones of various dimensions, like those which were separated and shot off by the Laigle meteor. It would be necessary to assign the cause that combines the scattered molecules, and forms them into a single mass. It is not affinity, for the elements composing aërolites are not in a state of combination, but simply agglomerated and held together in juxtaposition. And yet, if they are not subjected to any force, these little globules ought to fall separately as they are formed. It is in vain to object that they might be suspended, for more or less time, by a cause analogous to that which, according to the ingenious opinion of Volta, balances the particles of hail between two clouds, so as to give them time to enlarge by the addition of new layers of ice. The fact still remains, that these latter have never been seen to amount to several hundred weight, though the elements that form hail are much more abundant in the air than those of aërolites are supposed to be. Besides, in Volta's theory, the suspension of hail in the atmosphere is attributed to the reciprocal action of electric clouds, a cause which can not be in like manner adapted to the formation of aërolites, since the meteors that carry them sometimes burst in the clearest weather.

But even granting all this, and admitting the formation of aërolites in the atmosphere by some unknown agency, how shall we account for the circumstances attending their collision with the surface of the earth? According to this theory, they would move to the surface of the earth by the operation of terrestrial gravity alone, and would meet the earth with a velocity due to the height from which they fell. Now the actual velocities with which they are known to strike the earth could never be acquired under the mere agency of terrestrial gravity, through any height within the ordinary limits of the air.

But, if the velocity of the meteorites be incompatible with this theory, their direction is still more so. Their obliquity could never be produced by any conceivable atmospheric current.

We may, therefore, safely pronounce the atmospheric theory to be incompatible with the ascertained circumstances of the phenomena, and to require admissions inconsistent with the established principles of physics.

The volcanic theory is subject to objections as decisive as that we have first examined. The nature of the substances ejected from terrestrial volcanoes is well known, and we do not find among them the substances which form the constituents of meteorites; besides this, it is found that meteoric stones fall on parts of the earth so remote from volcanoes, and at times so distant from any known extensive eruptions, that it is impossible to admit the supposition that they have proceeded from this cause. For these and other reasons, needless to dwell on, the volcanic hypothesis is set aside.

The planetary hypothesis is subject to less difficulty, and is much more in harmony with the phenomena. The velocity and direction of meteoric stones when they strike the earth are quite in accordance with this theory, and the existence in them of constituents like metallic iron and nickel, which have no natural existence on the earth, is also explicable; but these circumstances are equally accounted for by all the extra terrestrial theories, and afford, therefore, no more countenance to the planetary than to the lunar or nebular hypothesis. On the other hand, a serious difficulty is presented in the uniform analysis of the meteorites. How can it be supposed that all the various fragments of a broken planet should consist of the same constituents in the very same proportion? If the earth were split in pieces by any cause internal or external, would its fragments be so uniform in its constituents? Assuredly not. We should find fragments of very heterogeneous character. One would consist of a mass of sandstone, another a lump of granite; here would be an agglomerate of one kind, there of another. It is, therefore, in the highest degree improbable that the fragments of another planet should be uniform in their constituents, and this improbability is rendered greater by the fact that the meteorites are composed of heterogeneous materials, mechanically agglomerated, and not of a uniform substance, composed of different elements, united like those of water or air.

Until, therefore, the advocates of the planetary hypothesis can remove these difficulties, that theory cannot be admitted.

The lunar hypothesis appears to be compatible, generally, with the circumstances of aërolites. It explains satisfactorily enough the force and direction of their collision with the earth. If it be admitted that they proceed from the same lunar volcano, or that all lunar volcanoes eject the same kind of substances, the similarity of their constituents will be explained; in short, all that is necessary to raise the lunar hypothesis to the rank of a theory is to prove the fact that there really do exist volcanoes in the moon. Now although observation has supplied circumstances which give some probability to that idea, yet it is still very far from being clearly established. Telescopic examination of the lunar surface, has certainly and clearly established the fact that it is covered in every part that is visible with mountains, having all the external forms and characters of terrestrial volcanoes. The craters are not only distinctly visible, but we have been enabled to ascertain the existence of the *cones* within them. Sir John Herschel, who has had the advantage of observing with the most powerful reflecting telescopes, has declared that the generality of the lunar mountains present a striking uniformity and singularity of aspect. They are wonderfully numerous, occupying by far the larger portion of the surface, and almost universally of an exactly circular or cup-shaped form, foreshortened, however, into ellipses toward the limb; but the larger have for the most part flat bottoms within, from which rises centrally a small, steep, conical hill. They offer, in short, in its highest perfection, the true *volcanic* character, as it may be seen in the crater of Vesuvius, and in a map of the volcanic districts of the Campi Phlegræi or the Puy de Dôme. And in some of the principal ones, decisive marks of volcanic stratification, arising from successive deposites of ejected matter, may be clearly traced with powerful telescopes. What is, moreover, extremely singular in the geology of the moon is, that although nothing having the character of seas can be traced (for the dusky spots which are commonly called seas, when closely examined, present appearances incompatible with the supposition of deep water), yet there are large regions perfectly level, and apparently of a decidedly alluvial character.

But this condition of things may have resulted from volcanic action, which took place at an epoch long antecedent to the commencement of the present condition of our globe, and it may be required to establish the fact of the present existence of active volcanoes on the moon.

To this it may be answered, *first*, that if active volcanoes existed at any remote period, the substances ejected from them may have been ever since revolving in the space around the earth, and that they may now, from time to time, become entangled in the earth's atmosphere and descend to the surface.

Secondly, it may be replied that we do possess indications of the present existence of lunar volcanoes, inasmuch as bright, luminous spots have been detected by various astronomers at different times and places, on the occasion of total eclipses of the sun, on the surface of the moon, then dark, and that it is impossible, on the one hand, to deny the existence of what has been witnessed by so many competent observers, and that no other supposition has been offered to explain such luminous spots, except one, which from its extreme improbability cannot be seriously entertained, namely, that which supposes the sun to have been rendered visible by holes through the moon.

Thus, then, stands the lunar theory of meteorites. It is exempt from most of the difficulties and objections that attend the other hypotheses, but nevertheless, until it be actually established beyond all question that there are, or have been, active volcanoes on the moon, and that substances ejected from these have actually fallen upon the earth, the lunar theory of meteorites cannot be pronounced to be established according to the rigid rules of inductive philosophy.

The nebular hypothesis can scarcely be regarded in a more definite point of view than as a conjecture. We have no observation to prove what the nature of the nebulous matter is, nor whether it is solid, liquid, or gaseous. We know that as it exists in the stellar regions it is self-luminous; but there is no indication of such a quality in any matter existing in the solar system. It may also be contended that if it exist within the solar system in the quantity contemplated in this hypothesis, we might expect it to be visible, if not by its own light, at least by the reflected light of the sun.

From the exposition I have here given it will be perceived that the origin of meteoric stones is still involved in much obscurity. We may, perhaps, pronounce with some degree of confidence that they are not of terrestrial origin, nor generated in the atmosphere, and that strictly speaking they are cosmical.

But we are not yet in possession of all the information which observation may supply respecting them. It is not yet clearly ascertained whether they are identical with the appearances so often exhibited in the heavens, called *shooting stars*, nor has the cause of this latter meteor been explained. A great impediment to the correct information of these phenomena, arises from the fact that their exhibition in the heavens is not preceded by any circumstance which can prepare the observer for them, and their continuance is seldom long enough to afford opportunity for correct observations. We are, therefore, compelled to collect from scattered sources, and loose records, much of the information which is available respecting them.

One of the most interesting narratives of this kind on record is that of a meteor which appeared in America, on the 13th of November, 1833. It was published in the American Journal of Science, and is entitled to especial notice. The following is an abstract of this narrative:—

The meteors began to attract notice by their frequency as early as 9 o'clock on the preceding evening (November 12); the exhibition became strikingly brilliant about 11 o'clock, but most splendid of all about 4 o'clock, and continued with but little intermission until darkness merged in the light of day. A few large fire-balls were seen even after the sun had risen. The entire extent of the exhibition is not ascertained, but it covered no inconsiderable portion of the earth's surface. It has been traced from the longitude of 61° in the Atlantic ocean, to longitude of 100° in central Mexico, and from the North American lakes to the southern side of the island of Jamaica. Everywhere within these limits, the first appearance was that of fire-works of the most imposing grandeur, covering the entire vault of heaven with myriads of fire-balls resembling sky-rockets. On more attentive inspection, it was seen that the meteors exhibited three distinct varieties; the first consisting of *phosphoric lines*, apparently described by a point; the second of large fire-balls, that at intervals darted along the sky, leaving numerous trains, which occasionally remained in view for a number of minutes, and in some cases for half an hour or more; the third, of undefined, luminous bodies, which remained nearly stationary for a long time.

One of the most remarkable circumstances attending this display was, that the meteors all seemed to emanate from one and the same point. They set out at different distances from this point, and proceeded with immense velocity, describing, in some instances, an arc of 30° or 40° in less than four seconds. At Poland, on the Ohio, a meteor (of the third variety) was distinctly visible in the northeast for more than an hour. At Charleston, South Carolina, another of extraordinary size was seen to course the heavens for a great length of time, and then was heard to explode with the noise of a cannon. The point from which the meteors seemed to emanate, was observed by those who fixed its position among the stars to be in the constellation Leo; and what is very remarkable, this point was *stationary* among the stars during the whole period of observation; that is to say, it did not move along with the earth in its diurnal rotation eastward, but accompanied the stars in their apparent progress westward. It is not certain whether the meteors were, in general, accompanied by any peculiar sound. A few observers reported that they heard a hissing noise, like the rushing of a sky-rocket, and slight explosions, like the bursting of the same bodies. Nor does it appear that any substance reached the ground which could be clearly established to be a residuum or deposite from the meteors. A remarkable change of weather from warm to cold, accompanied the meteoric shower, or immediately followed it, in all parts of the United States.

From these circumstances and other particulars recorded, it has been inferred that had these meteors appeared to emanate from a point not in the direction of the earth's rotation, they had not their origin in the atmosphere. By comparing observations made upon them in different latitudes, it was calculated that their distance from the surface of the earth must have been above 2,000 miles. Assuming this result, which is, however, only an approximation, the velocity with which they would enter the atmosphere may be computed.

A body falling from the height of 2,000 miles would acquire by the attraction of gravity, at 50 miles from the earth, where it might be supposed to enter the atmosphere, a velocity of four miles per second, being ten times the velocity of a cannon-ball. It is contended, therefore, that on entering the atmosphere they would produce a sudden compression of air, and corresponding evolution of heat. That the heat thus produced would render the bodies incandescent, and if they were combustible, would set them on fire. It is argued that the quantity of heat which would be extricated from the air by such compression would exceed that of the hottest furnace; but that if the velocity arising from the earth's motion were added to the proper velocity of the body itself, which it must be, if these motions are contrary, there would then be an effective velocity of fourteen, instead of four miles per second, and a still greater amount of heat would be produced. It is argued that these meteors must have been constituted of very light materials; for if their quantity of matter had been considerable, with so great a velocity they would have had sufficient momentum to reach the earth, and the most disastrous consequences might have ensued. From the apparent magnitude of many of the meteors, and their probable distance, it was conjectured that they were bodies of a very large size, although it was impossible to ascertain their magnitude with any certainty. It was supposed that they were only stopped in the atmosphere, and prevented from reaching the earth by transferring their motion to columns of air, large volumes of which they would suddenly and violently displace. It was considered remarkable that the state of the weather, and the condition of the seasons following this meteoric shower, were just such as might have been anticipated from these disturbing circumstances of the atmospheric equilibrium. Such were the speculations to which this remarkable phenomenon gave rise.

Whatever be the origin of the phenomena of shooting stars, it cannot fail to be interesting to learn the principal circumstances which observation has collected respecting them.

Their apparent magnitudes are very various. Sometimes they are not brighter or larger than the smallest star visible to the naked eye, and at other times they surpass in splendor the most brilliant of the planets. Sometimes the globular form can be distinctly recognised upon them, and they are not distinguishable from the meteors called fire-balls.

Shooting stars seem to prevail equally in every climate and in every state of the weather. They are occasionally seen at all seasons of the year, but more frequently in summer or at the end of the autumn. They appear usually to be followed by a luminous train of intensely white light.

A question will immediately arise, whether this be a real continued physical line of light, or whether it must not rather be ascribed to the same cause which makes us see a complete circle of light when a lighted stick revolves rapidly in a circle. In that case the circle of light is not real, the effect being an optical illusion. The membrane of the eye which is affected by light has been ascertained to preserve the impression made upon it for about one tenth of a second after the cause which produced that impression has ceased to act. We, consequently, continue to see a visible object in any position for a tenth of a second after it has left that position. If, then, a luminous object move over a certain space in one tenth of a second, the eye will see it at the same time in every part of that space, and consequently, that space will appear one continuous line of light.

If, therefore, the luminous train which is visible after a shooting star, extends through a space over which the star moved in one tenth of a second, it is then possible that such luminous train may be illusory, being a mere optical effect of the rapid motion of the star. But if it be longer than this, or if it be visible in one place for more than the tenth of a second after the star has moved from that place, then it cannot be explained on this principle and must be admitted to be an actual train of light. Now it is stated by observers of these meteors, that the trains are sometimes seen for several minutes. In the case of actual fire-balls, Dr. Olbers observed trains which continued visible for six or seven minutes, and Brandes in one instance estimated that fifteen minutes elapsed between the extinction of the fire-ball and the disappearance of the luminous train. In general the trains have the same hollow, cylindrical appearance as the tails of comets, their inner part appearing to be void of luminous matter, and a further resemblance to comets is exhibited in the curved form, which they sometimes assume.

Various and discordant have been the explanations offered of these luminous trains. Some have ascribed them to an oily sulphurous vapor existing in the atmosphere, which, being disposed in thin layers and becoming inflamed would exhibit the appearance of a brilliant spark passing rapidly from point to point. Beccaria and Vassali considered them to be lines of electrical sparks, an hypothesis, however, which has been abandoned. Lavoisier, Volta, and others, explain these meteors by supposing that hydrogen gas accumulated, by its lightness, in the higher regions of the atmosphere, was inflamed. But the general law of gases, which gives them a tendency to mingle, notwithstanding the effect of their specific gravities, puts aside this hypothesis.

In the year 1798 an investigation of the heights of shooting stars was undertaken by Brandes, at Leipsig, and Benzenberg, at Dasseldorf. Having selected a base line (about nine miles in length), they placed themselves at its extremities, on appointed nights, and observed all the shooting stars which appeared, tracing their courses through the heavens on a celestial map, and noting the instants of their appearances and extinctions by chronometers previously compared. The difference of the paths traced on the heavens afforded data for the determination of the parallaxes, and consequently the heights and the lengths of the orbits. On six evenings, between September and November, the whole number of shooting stars seen by both observers was 402: of these, 22 were identified as having been observed by each in such a manner that the altitude of the meteor above the ground at the instant of extinction could be computed. The least of the altitudes was about 6 English miles. Of the whole, there were 7 under 45 miles; 9 between 45 and 90; 6 above 90; and the highest was above 140 miles. There were only two observed so completely as to afford data for determining the velocity. The first gave 25 miles, and the second from 17 to 21 miles, in a second. The most remarkable result was, that one of them, certainly, was observed not to *fall*, but to move in a direction away from the earth.

By these observations a precise idea was first obtained of the altitudes, distances, and velocities, of these singular meteors. A similar but more extended plan of observation was organized by Brandes, in 1823, and carried into effect at Breslau and the neighboring towns, by a considerable number of persons, observing at the same time on concerted nights. Between April and October about 1800 shooting stars were noted at the different places—out of which number 62 were found which had been observed simultaneously at more than one station, in such a manner that their respective altitudes could be determined, and 36 others of which the observations furnished data for estimating the entire orbits. Of these 98, the heights (at the time of extinction) of 4 were computed to be under 15 English miles; of 13, between 15 and 30 miles; of 22, between 30 and 45; of 33, between 45 and 70; of 13, between 70 and 90; and of 11, above 90 miles. Of these last, two had an altitude of about 140 miles, one of 220 miles, one of 280, and there was one of which the height was estimated to exceed 460 miles.

On the 36 computed orbits, in 26 instances the motion was downward, in one case horizontal, and in the remaining nine more or less upward. The velocities were between 18 and 36 miles in a second. The trajectories were frequently not straight lines, but incurvated, sometimes in the horizontal and sometimes in the vertical direction, and sometimes they were of a serpentine form. The predominating direction of the motion of the meteors from northeast to southwest, contrary to that of the earth in its orbit, was very remarkable, and is important in reference to their physical theory.

A similar set of observations was made in Belgium, in 1824, under the direction of M. Quetelet, the results of which are published in the *Annuaire de Bruxelles* for 1837. M. Quetelet was chiefly solicitous to determine the velocity of the meteors. He obtained six corresponding observations, from which this element could be deduced, and the result varied from 10 to 25 English miles in a second. The mean of the six results gave a velocity of nearly 17 miles per second, a little less than that of the earth in its orbit.

Another set of corresponding observations was made in Switzerland, on the 10th of August, 1838, a circumstantial account of which is given by M. Wartmann in *Quetelet's Correspondence Mathematique* for July, 1839. M. Wartmann and five other observers, provided with celestial charts, stationed themselves at the observatory of Geneva, and the corresponding observations were made at Planchettes, a village about sixty miles to the northeast of that city.

In the space of seven and a half hours the number of meteors observed by the six observers at Geneva was 381, and during five and a half hours the number observed at Planchettes by two observers, was 104. All the circumstances of the phenomena—the place of the apparition and disappearance of each meteor, the time it continued visible, its brightness relatively to the fixed stars, whether accompanied with a train, &c.—were carefully noted, and the trajectories described by the meteors, were very different, varying from 8° to 70° of angular space. The velocities appeared also to differ considerably; but the average velocity was supposed by M. Wartmann to be 25° per second. It was found, from the comparison of the simultaneous observations, that the average height above the ground was about 550 miles; and hence the relative velocity was computed to be about 240 miles in a second. But as the greater number moved in a direction opposite to that of the earth in its orbit, the relative velocity must be diminished by the earth's velocity (about 19 miles in a second), this still leaves upward of 220 miles per second for the absolute velocity of the meteor, which is more than 11 times the orbitual velocity of the earth, seven and a half times that of the planet Mercury, and probably greater than that of many of the comets at their perihelion.

Such are the principal facts which have yet been established respecting the heights, velocities, and orbits, of the shooting stars: and it is from these, chiefly, that we are enabled to form any probable conjectures respecting their origin. And since it is now established that no difference is observable between the larger shooting stars and small fire-balls, both having similar altitudes and velocities, and presenting absolutely the same appearances, we may assume them to be of the same nature, and that whatever has been proved respecting fire-balls will apply equally to the larger shooting stars. Whether the meteoric appearances to which the latter term is applied may not include objects of totally different natures, is a question admitting a doubt. It is possible that among the shooting stars there may be objects which are merely electric sparks, or which have their origin in spontaneously-inflammable gases, known or unknown, existing in the atmosphere ; but the greater part of them must be considered as identical with fire-balls.

The lunar hypothesis advanced by Laplace, Berzelius, and others, to explain meteoric stones, appears to be attended with serious difficulties, if, indeed, it be not altogether incompatible with the phenomena of shooting stars. In order to enter our atmosphere with a velocity of 20 miles in a second, it may be shown that, if they come from the moon, they must have been projected from the lunar surface with a velocity of about 120,000 feet in a second, which may be regarded as almost impossible.

It thus appears that those shooting stars and fire-balls which have the planetary velocity of from 20 to 40 miles in a second, cannot, with any probability, be regarded as having their origin in the moon. Whether any individual bodies, moving with a smaller velocity, may have a lunar origin, is a question which cannot be decisively answered. "To me," says Dr. Olbers, "it does not appear at all probable ; and I regard the moon, in its present circumstances, as an extremely peaceable neighbor, which, from its want of water and atmosphere, is no longer capable of any strong explosions."

The hypothesis first suggested by Chladni is that which appears to have met with most favor, having been adopted by Arago and other eminent astronomers of the present day to explain the November phenomena. It consists in supposing that, independently of the great planets, there exist in the planetary regions myriads of small bodies which circulate about the sun, generally in groups of zones, and that some of these zones intersect the ecliptic, and are, consequently, encountered by the earth in its annual revolution. The principal difficulties attending this theory are the following:—

First, that bodies moving in groups in the circumstances supposed, must necessarily move in the same direction, and consequently they become visible from one point and move toward the opposite. Now although the observations seem to show that the predominating direction is from northeast to southwest, yet shooting stars are observed on the same nights to emanate from all points of the heavens, and to move in all possible directions. Secondly, their average velocity (especially as determined by Wartmann), greatly exceeds that which any body circulating about the sun can have at the distance of the earth. Thirdly, from their appearance, and the luminous train which they generally leave behind them, and which often remains visible for several seconds, sometimes for whole minutes, and also from their being situated within the earth's shadow, and at heights far exceeding those at which the atmosphere can be supposed capable of supporting combustion, it is manifest that their light is not reflected from the sun, they must therefore be self-luminous, which is contrary to every analogy of the solar system. Fourthly, if masses of solid matter approached so near the earth as many of the shooting-stars do, some of them would inevitably be attracted to it, but of the thousands of shooting-stars which have been observed, there is no authenticated instance of any one having actually reached the earth. Fifthly, instead of the meteors being attracted to the earth, some of them are observed actually to rise upward and to describe orbits which are convex toward the earth, a circumstance of which, on the present hypothesis, it seems difficult to give any rational explanation.

From the difficulties attending every hypothesis which has hitherto been proposed, it may be inferred how very little real knowledge has yet been obtained respecting the nature of the shooting-stars. It is certain that they appear at great altitudes above the earth, and that they move with prodigious velocity, but everything else respecting them is involved in profound mystery. From the whole of the facts, M. Wartmann thinks that the most rational conclusion we can adopt is, that the meteors probably owe their origin to the disengagement of electricity, or of some analogous matter, which takes place in the celestial regions on every occasion in which the conditions necessary for the production of the phenomena are renewed.

The presumption in favor of the cosmical origin of the shooting stars are chiefly founded on their periodical recurrence at certain epochs of the year, and the extraordinary displays of the phenomena in various years on the nights of the 12th or 13th of November.

We shall here merely state the principal circumstances accompanying those of 1799, which put the notion of a *lunar* origin entirely out of the question.

On the morning of the 12th of November, 1799, before sunrise, Humboldt and Bonpland, then on the coast of Mexico, were witnesses to a remarkable exhibition of shooting stars and fire-balls. They filled the part of the heavens extending from due east to about 30° toward the north and south. They rose from the horizon between the east and northeast points, described arcs of unequal magnitude, and fell toward the south; some of them rose to the height of 40°, all above 25° or 30°. Many of them appeared to explode, but the larger number disappeared without emitting sparks; some had a nucleus apparently equal to Jupiter. This most remarkable spectacle was seen at the same time in Camana, on the borders of Brazil, in French Guiana, in the channel of Bahama, on the continent of North America, in Labrador, and in Greenland, and even at Carlsruhe, Halle, and other places in Germany, many shooting stars were seen on the same day. At Nain and Hoffenthal in Labrador, and at Neuhernhut and Lichtenau in Greenland, the meteors seem to have appeared the nearest to the earth. At Nain they fell toward all points of the horizon, and some of them had a diameter which the spectators estimated at half an ell. (See Humboldt's Recueil des Voyages, &c., Vol. II.)

A not less stupendous exhibition took place in North America on the night of the 12th of November, 1833. In 1834 similar phenomena occurred on the night of the 13th of November; but on this occasion the meteors were of a smaller size. In 1835, 1836, and 1838, shooting stars were observed on the night of November 13, in different parts of the world, but though diligently looked for on the same nights in 1839 and 1840, they do not appear to have been more numerous than on other nights about the same season of the year.

The second great meteoric epoch is the 10th of August, first pointed out by M. Quetelet, and although no displays similar to those of the November period have been witnessed on this night, there are more instances of the recurrence of the phenomena. In the last three years (1838, 1839, 1840), shooting stars were observed in great numbers both on the 9th and 10th; but they appear in general to be unusually abundant during the first two weeks of August. The other periods which have been remarked, are the 18th of October, the 23d or 24th of April, the 6th and 7th of December, the nights from the 15th to the 20th of June, and the 2d of January.

Halley first suggested the idea that the shooting stars may be observed as signals for determining differences of latitude by simultaneous observations, and Maskelyne in 1783 published a paper on the subject, in which he calls the attention of astronomers to the phenomena, and distinctly points out this application. The idea was revived by Benzenberg in 1802, but so long as they were regarded merely as casual phenomena, it could scarcely be hoped that they would be of much use in this respect to practical astronomy. As soon, however, as their periodicity became probable, the phenomena acquired a new interest, and some recent attempts to determine longitudes in this manner have proved that the method is not to be disregarded.

The probability of the conjecture that the causes of the meteoric phenomena observed in the months of August and November is to be found in the fact that the particular regions of the solar system through which the earth passes at these seasons, are the seats of an unusual quantity of the matter composing these meteors, must in a great degree depend on the extent to which it can be proved by observation that such meteors do really prevail at each of those periods of the year.

With a view of testing this, I have collected together, from various sources, the dates of the most remarkable atmospheric appearances of this class from the eighth century to the present time. In the following table, the day of the month when it has been recorded, is placed in the column under the month, and in the line with the year of the occurrence. Where an asterisk occurs under the month, the particular night has not been recorded, but the appearance has merely been mentioned as having occurred.

Years.	Jan.	Feb.	March.	April.	May.	June.	July.	Aug.	Sept.	Oct.	Nov.	Dec.
763	....	....	*									
902	....	....	.....	.....	.....	.....	.....	.....	.....	*		
1029	....	....	.....	.....	.....	.....	.....	*				
1092	....	....	.....	25								
1202	....	....	.....	.....	.....	.....	.....	.....	.....	19		
1741	....	....	.....	.....	.....	.....	.....	.....	.....	.....	.....	25
1777	....	....	.....	.....	.....	17						
1779	....	....	.....	.....	.....	.....	.....	9				
1781	....	....	.....	.....	.....	.....	.....	8				
1784	....	....	.....	.....	.....	.....	27	9				
1785	....	....	.....	.....	.....	.....	27					
1798	....	....	.....	.....	.....	.....	.....	.....	.....	.....	.....	7
1799	....	....	.....	.....	.....	.....	.....	9	.....	.....	11	
1803	...	....	.....	22								
1805	....	....	.....	.....	.....	.....	.....	.....	.....	23		
1806	....	....	.....	.....	.....	.....	.....	10				
1811	....	....	18	.....	.....	.....	.....	10				
1812	....	....	.....	.....	.....	.....	.....	.....	.....	.....	?	
1813	....	....	.....	.....	.....	.....	.....	11	.....	.....	8	
1815	....	....	.....	.....	.....	.....	.....	10				
1818	....	....	.....	.....	.....	.....	.....	14	.....	.....	19	
1819	....	....	.....	.....	.....	.....	.....	6				
1819	....	....	.....	.....	.....	.....	.....	13				
1820	....	....	.....	.....	.....	.....	.....	9	2	.....	12	
1822	....	....	.....	.....	.....	.....	.....	.....	10	.....	12	
1823	....	....	.....	.....	.....	.....	.....	15				
1823	....	....	.....	.....	.....	.....	.....	10				
1824	....	....	.....	.....	.....	.....	.....	14				
1826	....	....	.....	.....	.....	.....	.....	14	.....	.....	6	
1826	....	....	.....	.....	.....	.....	.....	10				
1827	....	....	.....	.....	.....	.....	.....	14				
1828	....	....	.....	.....	.....	.....	.....	10				
1829	....	....	.....	.....	.....	.....	.....	14				
1830	....	....	.....	.....	.....	.....	.....	.....	.....	.....	12	
1831	....	....	.....	.....	.....	.....	.....	.....	.....	.....	13	
1832	....	....	.....	.....	.....	.....	.....	.....	.....	.....	13	
1833	....	....	.....	.....	.....	.....	.....	10	.....	.....	13	
1834	....	....	.....	.....	.....	.....	.....	10	.....	.....	13	
1835	....	....	.....	.....	.....	.....	.....	10	.....	.....	13	
1836	....	....	.....	.....	.....	.....	.....	8	.....	....	13	
1836	....	....	.....	.....	.....	.....	.....	10				
1837	....	....	.....	.....	.....	.....	.....	10				

There are here recorded fifty-two nights on which these appearances prevail to such a degree as to attract particular notice. Of these, twenty-six occurred between the 8th and 15th of August, and thirteen the 6th and 19th of November. Thus three fourths of the nights recorded correspond to the epochs to which we have referred.

We have not seen any sufficiently precise account of the number of these phenomena which were observed in November, 1837, and in July, 1838. Fewer were noticed in Paris in November, 1837, than were expected; but on the night between the 15th and 16th, seventeen were seen at that place by M. Arago, within a minute and a half. At Jamble, in the department of the Seine and Loire, thirty-nine were observed on the night between the 14th and 15th; and ten were observed at Marseilles on the night between the 12th and 13th; six were observed on the same night at Geneva, and four at Montpellier.

Some disappointment was produced in 1837, by the circumstance of an unusually small number being seen on the night between the 12th and 13th, arising from an erroneous impression that that was the night on which their periodical return should be expected. It will be seen, however, from the preceding table, that these appearances have not at all been confined to the night of the 12th; but independently of this, the night of the 12th at Paris was so bright, that stars of the second magnitude were not visible, and consequently meteors—even supposing them to have existed of similar or of inferior brightness—could not have been observed. It should also be considered, that their non-appearance at any particular place, is no proof of their non-existence in our atmosphere. They may be produced during the day, or they may be produced in a part of the atmosphere not visible from the place in question. Thus, in 1833, when they were a general object of terror to the people of America, they attracted but little attention in Europe. On the other hand, they sometimes appear contemporaneously in the atmosphere on opposite sides of the globe. In 1837, they were observed from the French ship *Bonite*, on the other side of the globe, while on the same day in Europe, a vast number appeared.

On the night of the 12th of November, 1836, Sir John Herschel observed these phenomena at the cape of Good Hope. Their number was not very considerable, but their motion had a marked regularity; they appeared to diverge from a centre or focus, which preserved a fixed position with respect to the horizon, but had no such fixed relation to the objects on the firmament. This point, or centre, to which their common directions converged, was a point of about thirty degrees above the horizon, and sixty degrees west of north.

On the night of the 9th of August, 1837, M. Wartmann observed these phenomena at Geneva; between nine o'clock, P. M., and midnight, eighty-two were seen in different parts of the heavens. They were most frequent about ten o'clock, and then appeared to emanate from a centre or focus situated between the star *B*, in the constellation of Bootes, and the star *A*, in the constellation of the Dragon. At a quarter past ten, twenty-seven were seen, and were remarkable for their bright bluish light. Other observers in the same neighborhood and on the same night, counted one hundred and forty-nine in one part of the heavens, between a quarter before nine and half past eleven o'clock.

Of these hundred and forty-nine meteors, three had the appearance of round disks, or globes, of a ruddy red color, measuring from 4 to 5 minutes in diameter, being about one sixth part of the moon's diameter. Twenty-six were more brilliant than the planet Venus, and of resplendent whiteness; the remainder had the appearance of stars from the first to the third magnitude, their colors varying between blue, yellow, and orange.

On the night of the 11th of November, 1832, M. Tharand, a retired officer at Limoges, stated that workmen who were employed in laying the foundation of the bridge over the river Vienne, observed the firmament brilliant with meteors, which at first only amused them, but after some hours the number and splendor of these luminous appearances were so greatly augmented, that the people were seized with panics, and so great was their terror, that they abandoned their labor and flew to their families, exclaiming that the end of the world had arrived. On the next day these people were interrogated on the subject, and their accounts varied according to the different impressions which had been produced on their imaginations. Some declared that they saw streams of blue fire; others that they beheld bars of red iron crossing each other in all directions; others that they beheld an immense quantity of flying rockets. All agreed that the phenomena were diffused over every part of the firmament; that they commenced at eleven o'clock, and continued till four the next morning.

THE EARTH.

A difficult Subject of Investigation.—Form of the Earth.—How proved Globular.—Its Magnitude.—Its annual Motion.—Elliptic Form of its Orbit.—Proofs of its annual Motion from the Theory of Gravitation.—From the Motion of Light.—The Earth's diurnal Motion.—Inequalities of Day and Night.—Weight of the Earth.—Maskelyne's Experiment.—Cavendish's Experiment.—Their Accordance.—Density of the Earth.—The Seasons.—Calorific Effect of the Sun's Rays.—Why the longest is not the hottest Day.—Why the shortest Day is not the coldest.—The hottest Season takes place when the Sun is farthest from the Earth.—Proofs of the diurnal Rotation.—Spheroidal Form of the Earth proved by Theory and by Observation.

THE EARTH.

LOCKE somewhere observes, with his usual felicity of illustration, that the " mind, like the eye, while it makes us see and perceive all other things, can never turn its view with advantage upon itself." We encounter something similar to this in our researches through the universe; for of all the objects which compose it, one of the most difficult with which to obtain a complete and accurate knowledge is the planet which we inhabit. The cause of this is our proximity to it, and intimate connexion with it. We are confined upon its surface, from which we cannot separate ourselves. We cannot obtain a bird's-eye view of it, nor at any one time behold more than an insignificant portion of its surface. We have the same difficulty in obtaining an acquaintance with it that a microscopic animalcule would have in acquiring a perfect knowledge of the form and dimensions of a terrestrial globe twelve inches in diameter, on the surface of which it creeps.

Still, by a variety of indirect methods supplied by the ingenuity of scientific research, we have been enabled to ascertain its form, and dimensions, and physical constitution, with a considerable degree of accuracy.

FORM OF THE EARTH.

The first impression produced upon the eye of an observer, who has not carried his inquiries further, is, that the surface of the earth is a flat plane, interrupted only by the inequalities of the land. A little careful observation, however, upon the many phenomena which are easily accessible to every observer, will correct this erroneous impression.

1. It is well known that if a voyage were made upon the earth, continually preserving one and the same direction, or doing so as nearly as circumstances will permit, we should at length arrive at the place from which we departed. If the earth were an indefinite plane, this could not happen. It is evident, then, that whatever be the exact form of the earth, it is a body which is on

every side limited, and one which must therefore have such a surface that a traveller or navigator can completely surround it in one continuous course.

Let us see, however, whether we may not obtain evidence more distinct as to its form. If we stand on the deck of a ship at sea, and out of sight of land, the view being bounded only by sea and sky, and look at the horizon when a ship approaches, we shall at first see its topmast rising out of the water like a pole. As it gradually comes nearer to us, more of the mast will become visible, and the sails will be seen—cut off, however, horizontally, by the line at which the water and sky unite. Upon the nearer approach of the ship, the hull will at length become visible. Now, since this takes place on all sides around us, it will follow that when the ship is at a distance, there must be *something* interposed between the eye and it which intercepts the view of it; but as the surface of the water is generally uniform, and not subject to sudden and occasional inequalities like that of the land, we can only imagine its general form to be convex, and that its convexity is interposed between the eye and the object so as to intercept the view.

Since the same effects are observed from whatever direction the ship may approach, it will follow that the same convexity must prevail on every side.

If we admit the earth to be globular, or nearly so, and the surface of the water to partake of this figure, 1, the manner in which a ship becomes visible on approaching the eye will be easily and simply explained.

Fig. 1.

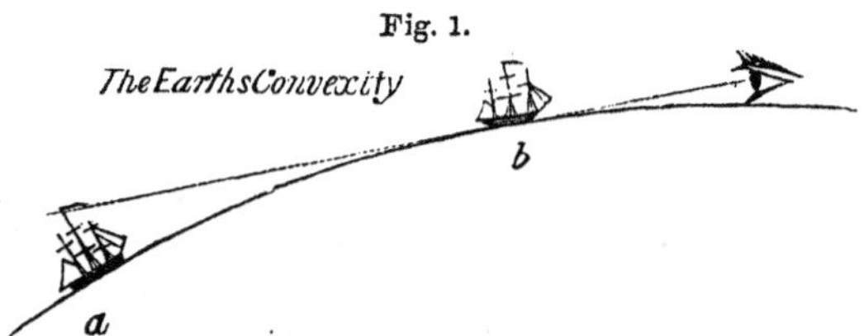

In the position *a*, in the annexed figure, the convexity of the globe being between the ship and the eye, the view of it is intercepted; but as the ship approaches toward *b*, the masts first and then the sails and rigging rise above the line of sight and come into view, and lastly the hull will be seen.

If, on the contrary, the surface extending from the eye to the ship were a plane, the ship would be rendered invisible only by reason of its distance; whereas it is ascertained that a ship frequently is invisible at a distance at which it must be seen but for the interposition of some other object; this may be tested, and in fact is frequently tested at sea by mounting to the masthead, whence the seaman being enabled to overlook the convexity, sees vessels which are invisible from the deck, athough, strictly speaking, he is nearer to those vessels on the deck than at the masthead.

When the mariner, after completing a long voyage, discovers by his observations and reckonings that he is approaching the desired coast, he ascends to the topmast and looks out for the appearance of mountains or other elevated land, and he invariably sees them from that point long before they are visible from the deck. He afterward sees them from the deck long before the general level of the country will be observed by him. All these are natural and necessary consequences of the convexity of the surface of the ocean. The same effects would be seen in any part of a continent which is sufficiently free from mountains and other inequalities.

But we have a still more conclusive and convincing proof of the general form of the earth even than those which have been explained. When the moon passes directly behind the earth, so that the shadow which the earth projects behind it in the direction opposite to the sun shall fall upon the moon, we invariably find that shadow to be, not as is commonly said, circular, but such exactly as one globe would project upon the surface of another globe. Now, as this takes place always, in whatever position the earth may be, and while the earth is revolving rapidly with its diurnal motion upon its axis, it follows that the earth must either be an exact globe or so little different from a globe that its deviation from that figure is undiscoverable in its shadow.

We may, then, consider it demonstrated that the earth may be practically regarded as globular in its form. We shall hereafter see that it slightly departs from the spherical figure, but our present purpose will be best answered by regarding it as a globe.

The objection will doubtless occur to many minds that the inequality which exists on the surface of that portion of the globe that is covered by land, especially the loftier ridges of mountains, such as the Andes, the Alps, the Himalaya, and others, are incompatible with the idea of a globular figure. If the term globular figure were used in the strictest geometrical sense, this objection doubtless would have great force. But let us see the real extent of this presumed deviation from the globular form. The highest mountain on the surface of the globe does not exceed five miles above the general level of the sea. The entire diameter of the globe, as we shall presently see, is eight thousand miles. The proportion, then, which the highest summit of the loftiest mountains bears to the entire diameter of the globe will be that of five to eight thousand, or one to sixteen hundred. If we take an ordinary terrestrial globe of sixteen inches in diameter, each inch upon the globe will correspond to five hundred miles upon the earth, and the sixteen hundredth part of its diameter, or the hundredth part of an inch, will correspond to five miles. If, then, we take a narrow strip of paper, so thin that it would take one hundred leaves to make an inch in thickness, and paste such a strip on the surface of the globe, the thickness of the strip would represent upon the sixteen-inch globe the height of the loftiest mountain on the earth. We are then to consider that the highest mountain-ranges on the earth deprive it of its globular figure only in the same degree and to the same extent as a sixteen-inch globe would be deprived of its globular figure by a strip of paper pasted upon it the hundredth part of an inch thick.

It is supposed that the greatest depth of the ocean which covers any portion of the globe does not exceed the greatest height of the mountains upon the land. If this be true, the ocean upon the earth might be represented by a film of liquid laid with a camel's-hair pencil upon the surface of a sixteen-inch globe.

It is apparent, therefore, that depths and heights which appear to the common observer to be stupendous, are nothing when considered with reference to the magnitude of the earth; and that, so far as they are concerned, we may practically regard the earth as a true globe.

THE MAGNITUDE OF THE EARTH.

Having ascertained satisfactorily the figure of the earth, our next inquiry must be as to its magnitude; and since it is a globe, all that we are required to know is the length of its diameter.

If a line were described surrounding the globe, so as to form a circle upon it, the centre of which should be at the centre of the globe, such a circle is called a *great circle* of the earth. Now if we know the length of the circumference of such a circle, we could easily calculate the length of its diameter, for the proportion of the circumference to the diameter is exactly known. But we could calculate the circumference if we knew the length of one degree upon it, since we know that the circumference consists of three hundred and sixty degrees; we should therefore only have to multiply the length of one degree by three hundred and sixty to obtain the circumference, and should thence calculate the diameter.

On another occasion, in our discourse upon latitudes and longitudes, it was shown how the latitude of a place can be ascertained. Now, let us suppose two places selected which are upon the same meridian of the earth, and therefore have the same longitude, and which are not very far removed from each other. Let them, moreover, be selected so that the distance between them can be easily and accurately measured. Now let the latitude of these two places be exactly determined, and let us suppose that the difference between these two latitudes is found to be one degree and a half; and suppose also that on measuring the distance between them, that distance is found to be one hundred and four miles and thirty-five hundredths. We should thence infer that such must be the length of one degree and a half of the earth's surface, and that consequently the length of one degree would be two thirds of this, or sixty-nine and a half miles. Having thus found the length of a degree, we should have to multiply it by three hundred and sixty, by which we should obtain the circumference of the earth. This would give twenty-five thousand and twenty miles, and we should then find by the usual mode of calculation the diameter of the earth, which would prove to be a little under eight thousand miles.

We have made these calculations chiefly with a view of rendering the principles of the investigation intelligible. The more exact dimensions of the earth will be explained hereafter.

We conclude, then, that the earth is a globe eight thousand miles in diameter.

ANNUAL MOTION OF THE EARTH.

We have on other occasions shown that the distance of the earth from the sun may be expressed in round numbers by one hundred millions of miles. It is more exactly ninety-five millions of miles.

We have also considered in general the path of the earth in its annual course round the sun to be a circle, in the centre of which the centre of the sun is placed. This is nearly but not exactly true. That the path of the earth is not a circle with the sun in its centre, has been ascertained by the following observations.

In astronomical telescopes there are placed by a particular arrangement, within the eye-pieces, certain very fine threads or wires, which are extended parallel to each other across the field of view. These wires are so constructed that, by a simple mechanical contrivance, they may be moved toward each other, preserving, however, their parallelism. The mechanism which so moves them is made to measure exactly the distance between them.

When such a telescope is presented to the sun or moon, the wires may always be so adjusted, by turning a screw, that one of them shall touch the upper and the other the lower limb of the disk, as represented in the annexed diagram, fig. 2, where S represents the disk of the sun, and A B and C D the wires.

Now let us suppose that a telescope is pointed to the sun, and the wires so adjusted that they shall exactly touch the upper and lower limbs. Let the observer then watch from day to day the appearance of the sun and the position of the wires: he will find that, after a certain time, the wires will no longer

Fig. 2.

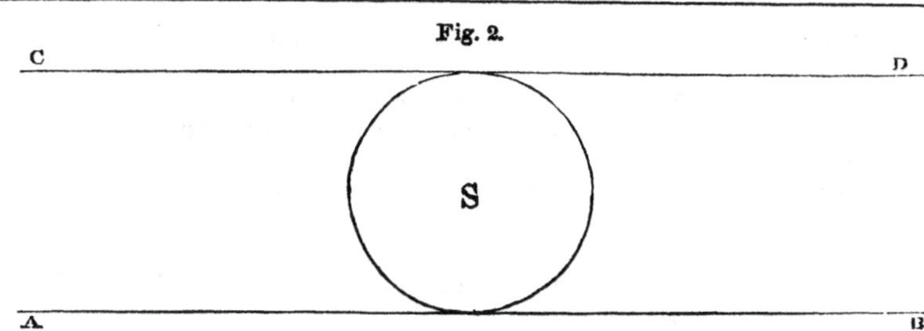

touch the sun, but will perhaps fall a little within it, as represented in the annexed figure, 3.

Fig. 3.

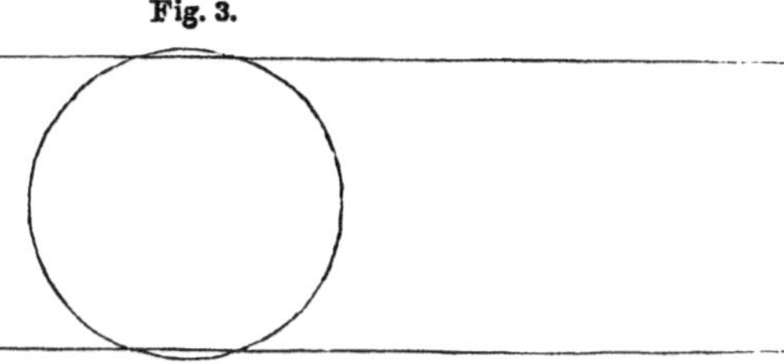

And after a further lapse of time, he will find, on the other hand, that they fall a little without it, as in the following figure, 4.

Fig. 4.

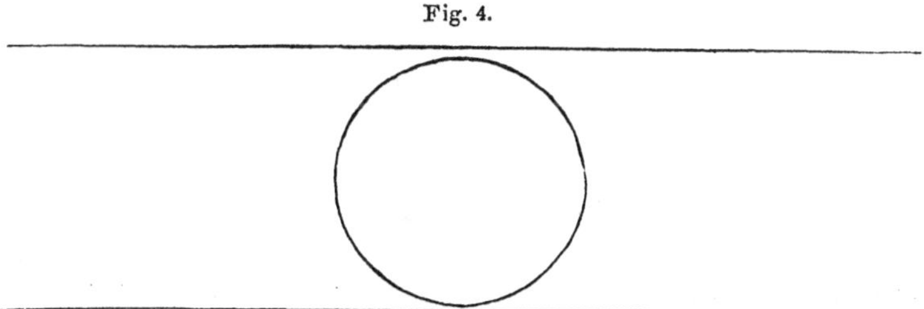

Now, as the wires throughout such a series of observations are maintained always in the same position, it follows that the disk of the sun must appear smaller at one time, and larger at another—that, in fact, the apparent magnitude of the sun must be variable. It is true that this variation is confined within very small limits, but still it is distinctly perceptible. What, then, it may be asked, must be its cause? Is it possible to imagine that the sun *really undergoes a change in its size?* This idea would, under any circumstances, be absurd; but when we have ascertained, as we may do, that the change of apparent magnitude of the sun is regular and periodical—that for one half of the year it continually diminishes until it attains a minimum, and then for the next half year it increases until it attains a maximum—such a supposition as that of a real periodical change in the globe of the sun, becomes altogether incredible.

If, then, an actual change in the magnitude of the sun be impossible, there is but one other conceivable cause for the change in its apparent magnitude—which is, a corresponding change in the earth's distance from it. If the earth at one time be more remote than at another, the sun will appear proportionally smaller. This is an easy and obvious explanation of the changes of appearance that are observed, and it has been demonstrated accordingly to be the true one.

On examining the change of the apparent diameter of the sun, it is found that it is least on the 1st of July, and greatest on the 31st of December ; that from December to July, it regularly decreases ; and from July to December, it regularly increases. By observing the rate of its variation through these intervals, it will be found that the path of the earth around the sun is an ellipse, having the sun in one of the *foci*.

In the annexed figure, 5, if S represent the place of the sun, A will represent that of the earth when at that place called *perihelion*, or that point where it is nearest the sun; and B its position at *aphelion*, or the point where it is most distant from the sun. The elliptic path of the earth is represented by the figure A D B O ; C being its centre, and S its focus.

Fig. 5.

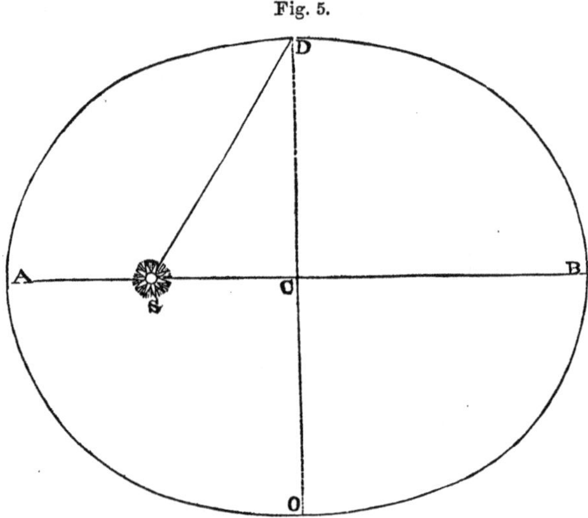

It is proper to observe here that the earth's orbit departs infinitely less from the circular shape than the oval exhibited in the annexed diagram. In fact, the real figure of the orbit of the earth is so slightly oval, and so little different from a circle, that if it were delineated on paper in its true proportions, the eye could not discover its difference from a circle ; actual instrumental measure alone could detect it. If the greatest distance of the earth from the sun were expressed by 1,000, its least distance would be expressed by 983.

It is worthy of observation that the earth is most remote from the sun at midsummer, and nearest to it at midwinter.

It was not until the date of the revival of letters that the annual motion of the earth was admitted. The apparent stability of our globe was, until that epoch, generally maintained ; and even now, when so universal is the assent given to this fundamental principle of astronomy, it may still perhaps be useful briefly to state the leading arguments by which it is established.

When the sun is observed in the firmament, it appears to move among the stars from west to east, following a course in the heavens which has been called the ECLIPTIC ; and at the end of a year its centre returns, after a complete circuit of the heavens, to the point from which it set out. This is an effect which would be produced by a real motion of the sun round the earth in a year. By such a motion, being placed in the centre and at rest, we should see the sun progressively moving round us; we should project his disk among the stars, and the apparent motion would be to us what it is. But it is most necessary to reflect that the very same effect would be produced without a single change of circumstance, if, instead of the earth being at rest and the sun moving round it, the sun were at rest, and the earth were carried annually round it. Such a motion of the earth would cause the sun to be successively seen at all points of the ecliptic at which it is seen throughout the year; and, in short, would give to the sun exactly the same apparent motion which it appears to us to have. It is therefore evident that the annual motion of the sun will be explained with equal clearness, and would be equally produced or caused, either by its own motion round the earth, or by the annual motion of the earth round it. There is nothing in the appearance of the sun itself which would give a preference or confer a greater probability on either of these suppositions rather than the other. If we are to choose between them, we must therefore seek the grounds of choice in some other circumstances.

But the long-continued and deeply-rooted opinion that the sun and not the earth moves, must have had some natural and intelligible grounds. These grounds undoubtedly arose from impressions that if the earth moved, we should in some way or other be sensible of its motion; more especially if that motion had the enormous velocity which must be imputed to the earth if it be granted that it moves round the sun at all.

But, on the other hand, it must be considered that we are conscious of motion through the senses only by observing the relative change of position of some external sensible objects. We see the mutual distance and relative position of two or more visible objects change, and we infer immediately that some one or other of them must have moved. We can be rendered sensible of the motion of the room we occupy, or of the ground upon which we stand, only by some derangement of the position of these relative to our own body. But if we could conceive all the objects that surround us moving with perfect uniformity in a fixed direction, and that our own bodies should participate in the motion, we should then have no evidence by which we could ascertain the existence of that motion at all. This will be clear to every one by considering the effect produced when we are in the cabin of a boat which is drawn uniformly on smooth water. If we cannot look at the banks of the river or canal, we then shall be entirely unconscious that the boat is moving; but if we are enabled to look out from a window from which we can see the banks, the first impression will be that the banks are moving in the contrary direction to the boat, and it is only by reason and reflection that this impression will be corrected. If we are in the cabin of a steamboat from which we cannot look abroad, the only motion of which we are conscious is the tremulous motion produced by the working of the machinery, and we are only conscious of this because it changes in a slight degree, and momentarily, the relative position of the frame of the boat and our own bodies. But we are even then unconscious of the progressive motion of the boat.

It will, then, be easily conceived that the motion of the globe of the earth through space being perfectly smooth and uniform, we can have no sensible means of knowing it, except the same which we possess in the case of a boat moving smoothly along a river: that is, by looking abroad at some external objects which do not participate in the motion imputed to the earth. Now, when we do look abroad at such objects, we find that they appear to move—exactly as stationary objects would appear to move, seen from a moveable station like the earth. It is plain, then, even if it be true that the earth really has the annual motion round the sun which is contended for, that we cannot expect to be conscious of this motion from anything which can be observed on our own bodies or those which surround us on the surface of the earth: we must look for it elsewhere.

But it will be contended that the apparent motion of the sun, even upon the argument just stated, may equally be explained by the motion of the earth round the sun, or the motion of the sun round the earth; and that therefore this appearance can still prove nothing positively on this question. We have, however, other proofs, of a very decisive character.

Newton showed that it was a general law of nature, and part, in fact, of the principle of gravitation, that any two globes placed at a distance from each other, if they are in the first instance quiescent and free, must move with an accelerated motion to their common centre of gravity, where they will meet and coalesce; but if they be projected in a direction not passing through this centre of gravity, they will both of them revolve in orbits around that point periodically. And in fact the same will be the case with any number of globes whatsoever, and consequently would be applicable to the solar system itself.

Now, the centre of gravity of the solar system, owing to the immense predominance of the mass of the sun over all the rest of the bodies composing it put together, is situated *within the sun, and near its centre.* All the bodies of the system, and the earth among them, must therefore, according to this law, revolve periodically round that point.

But as the principle of gravitation itself may by some be considered as based upon some previous admission of the motion of the planets, it may be desirable to obtain a still more direct and positive manifestation of the annual motion of the earth. Fortunately, the discovery which has been developed by the labors of astronomical observers have put us in possession of a decisive test, which has been considered as setting at rest for ever the question of the earth's annual motion. If the earth were moved round the sun—as it certainly must be if the sun is not moved round it—an effect would be produced upon the apparent position of the fixed stars, owing to the combination of the motion of light with the motion of the globe. Light is propagated from the stars in straight lines with a velocity of about two hundred thousand miles per second. The earth, if it moves at all, moves with a velocity of about twenty miles per second; and with this velocity, the eye of the observer upon the earth strikes the light in the direction of the earth's motion, while the light itself comes in another direction. The direction in which the observer will see the star will be determined by the combined effect of the velocity of light and the velocity of the earth, inasmuch as the impact of the light upon the eye will be the result of these two motions; thus, if the earth moved with a velocity equal to that of light, the star would be seen forty-five degrees in advance of its real position. If the earth moved with a less velocity, it would be seen less in advance of its true position in proportion to the relative velocity of the earth and light.

Now, the velocity of the earth being incomparably smaller than that of light, the star ought to be seen in advance of its true position to an extent which is proportionate to this small ratio, and the deviation of the star or planet's true position should also be in the direction of the earth's motion. This effect, moreover, should be found to be produced upon all stars and planets visible in the firmament; modified, however, in a certain complicated manner, according to their position with respect to the orbit of the earth.

The observations of Bradley and subsequent astronomers detected these effects; and as they are everywhere produced upon the countless myriads of objects that glitter upon the firmament, and everywhere produced in the manner and degree exactly in which they ought to be produced by the earth's annual motion, an unanswerable demonstration is obtained of the reality of that motion.

We have seen that the observation of the sun establishes demonstratively this alternative—either that the earth revolves round the sun annually, or that the sun revolves round the earth annually. There is no other motion which would be consistent with the phenomena. Now, the effect on the stars called the aberration of light, just explained, proves that of the sides of this alternative, that which must be adopted is the motion of the earth.

There is an instinct of the human mind which leads it to anticipate discoveries. The grounds on which the annual motion of the earth and the stationary position of the sun are demonstrated, are modern. The theory of gravitation dates only from the era illustrated by Newton. The discovery of the aberration of light is still more recent; and yet the first suggestion of the annual motion of the earth, and the stationary position of the sun, dates as far back as the era of Pythagoras. It is true that this hypothesis did not obtain general assent until it was urged by the sagacity of Copernicus, and reinforced by the eloquence and talents of Galileo and Kepler. But still it affords an example of one of those wonderful anticipations of human intellect which leads us irresistibly back to the impression that the mind is itself an emanation of the Divine spirit which was breathed into our nostrils when He who created us gave us the breath of life, and made us a living soul.

THE EARTH'S DIURNAL MOTION.

While the earth revolves annually round the sun, it has a motion of rotation at the same time upon a certain diameter as an axis which is inclined from the perpendicular to its orbit at an angle of 23°, 28′. During the annual motion of the earth this diameter keeps continually parallel to the same direction, and the earth completes its revolution upon it in twenty-three hours and fifty-six minutes. In consequence of the combination of this motion of rotation of the earth upon its axis with its annual motion round the sun, we are supplied with the alternations of day and night, and the succession of seasons.

When the globe of the earth is in such a position that its north pole leans toward the sun, the greater portion of its northern hemisphere is enlightened, and the greater portion of the southern hemisphere is dark. This position is represented in the annexed figure, 6, where C is the north pole, and D the

Fig. 6.

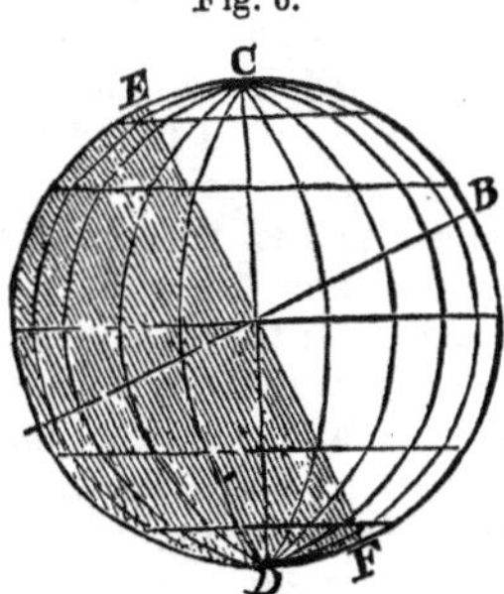

south pole. As the earth revolves upon its axis, the parallels of the equator are unequally divided by the circles of light and darkness: the greater segment of each of them being illuminated, and the lesser segment dark. The days are therefore longer than the nights in the northern hemisphere. The reverse is the case with the southern hemisphere, for there the greater segments of the parallels are dark, and the lesser segments enlightened ; the days are therefore shorter than the nights. Upon the equator, however, at B, the circle of the earth is equally divided, and the days and nights are equal. When the south pole leans toward the sun, which it does exactly at the opposite point of the earth's annual orbit, circumstances are reversed : then the days are longer than the nights in the southern hemisphere, and the nights are longer than the days in the northern hemisphere. At the intermediate point of the earth's annual path, figure 7, when the axis assumes a position perpendicular to the

Fig. 7.

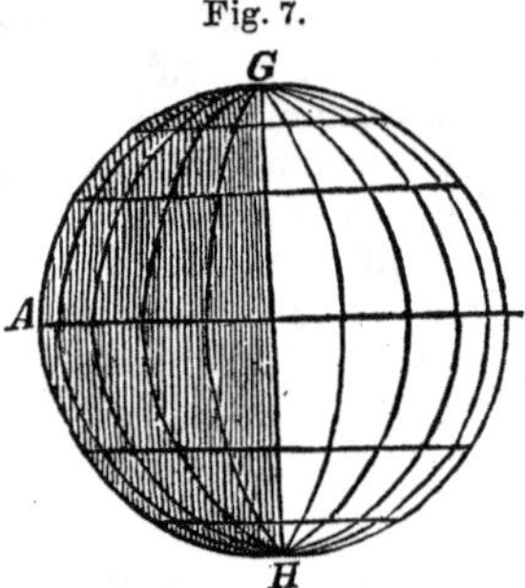

direction of the sun, then the circle of light and darkness passes through the poles ; all parallels in every part of the earth are equally divided, and there is consequently equal day and night all over the globe.

In the annexed perspective diagram, fig. 8, these four positions of the earth are exhibited in such a manner as to be clearly intelligible.

On the day of the 21st of June, the north pole is turned in the direction of the sun ; on the 21st of December, the south pole is turned in that direction. On the days of the equinoxes, the axis of the earth is at right angles to the direction of the sun, and it is equal day and night everywhere on the earth.

The annual variation of the position of the sun with reference to the equator, or the changes of its declination, are explained by these motions. The summer solstice—the time when the sun's distance from the equator is the greatest—takes place when the north pole leans toward the sun ; and the winter solstice—or the time when the sun's distance south of the equator is greatest—takes place when the south pole leans toward the sun.

In virtue of these motions, it follows that the sun is twice a year vertical at all places between the tropics ; and at the tropics themselves it is vertical once a year. In all higher latitudes the point at which the sun passes the meridian daily alternately approaches to and recedes from the zenith. From the 21st of December until the 21st of June, the point continually approaches the zenith. It comes nearest to the zenith on the 21st of June ; and from that day until the 21st of December, it continually recedes from the zenith, and attains its lowest position on the latter day. The difference, therefore, between the meridional altitudes of the sun on the days of the summer and winter solstices at all places will be twice twenty-three degrees and twenty-eight minutes, or forty-six degrees and fifty-six minutes. In all places beyond the tropics in the northern hemisphere, therefore, the sun rises at noon on the 21st of June, forty-six degrees and fifty-six minutes higher than it rises on the 21st of December. These are the limits of meridional altitude which determine the influence of the sun in different places.

Fig. 8.

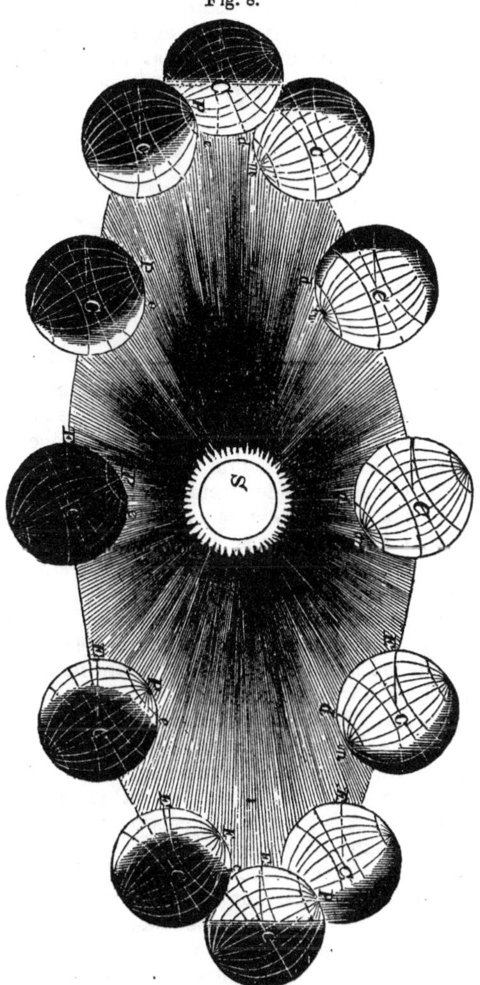

WEIGHT OF THE EARTH.

It was at a recent epoch in the progress of knowledge that the problem to ascertain the weight of the globe of the earth, or the actual quantity of matter it contains relative to some known standard, was solved.

The researches of Newton had established the general fact that the weights of bodies were the exponents of their masses or quantities of matter, and that the weights themselves were nothing more than the attractions which the bodies in question suffered from other bodies near them.

Toward the end of the last century, two philosophers of great eminence in England—the celebrated Cavendish and Dr. Maskelyne—achieved the solution of this problem by different methods; and the accordance of the results which they obtained is the best test of their accuracy and truth.

The method of Dr. Maskelyne consisted in comparing the attraction which the entire globe of the earth would exert in a body near it, with that which a mass of matter of known weight, such as a mountain, would exert upon the same body. The mode of executing that memorable experiment was as follows: Let A B, fig. 9, represent a small portion of the earth's surface,

Fig. 9.

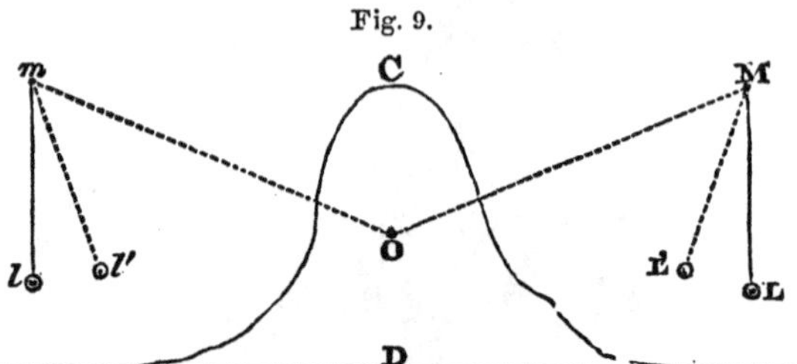

which may be regarded as a plane; let C D represent a mountain, and let O be supposed to be its centre of gravity. The entire attraction of the mass of the mountain will then be exerted as if it were concentrated on the point O. The direction of the earth's attraction will be perpendicular to the plane A B. Now, let L be a weight suspended from any point; M L forming what is called a plumb-line. If the weight L were solicited by no force except the earth's attraction, the string by which it is suspended would take a position at right angles to the plane A B; but as this plumb-line is suspended near the mountain C D, it will be attracted by the gravitation of the mass of the mountain, which will be exerted in the direction M O toward the centre of gravity of the mountain. If we could imagine the globe of the earth on which the mountain rests removed, and the mountain alone to remain near the plumb-line, then the weight L would be drawn in the direction M O, and the string M L suspending it would take that direction; for in that case, the only force by which L would be attracted would be the gravitation of the mountain, which takes place in the direction M O. If, on the other hand, the mountain were removed, and the earth alone left to affect the plumb-line, it would take the usual direction, M L, perpendicular to A B; but in the case actually supposed, the weight L is solicited at the same time by both attractions—by the attraction of the globe of the earth drawing it perpendicularly to A B, and by the attraction of the mountain drawing it in the direction M O. By the common principles of mechanics, the weight L will in this case take a direction M L′, intermediate between M L and M O, leaning toward the mountain but very slightly, inasmuch as the attraction of the mountain is incomparably less than that of the earth.

Now, if we could exactly ascertain the degree in which the plumb-line is deflected from its true vertical position by the attraction of the mountain, that deviation or deflection will enable us immediately to estimate the proportion which the attraction of the mountain bears to the whole attraction of the earth, and that proportion would be the same as that which the weight of the mountain or the mass of matter contained in it bears to the mass of matter contained in the globe of the earth. But where the deviation of the plumb-line is so small, and where any ordinary test of its deviation would be affected by the same cause as the plumb-line itself, there would be a difficulty in determining it.

If the plumb-line were undisturbed by the mountain, its direction ought to point to a star in the zenith of the place of the observer; but being disturbed by the attraction of the mountain, it will point to a star at one side of the zenith—say, for example, to the east of it.

Let us suppose now that another plumb-line is suspended similarly on the opposite side of the mountain, to *m l:* it is evident that the attraction of the mountain will draw the plumb-line in this case in a direction opposite to that in which it draws the former. Both plummets will be drawn toward the mountain; and if the string suspending one be made to point a little to the eastward of the zenith, the string suspending the other will be made to point a little to the westward of it.

By due attention to this circumstance, we shall easily find the real deviation of the plumb-line from the zenith. Let the points in the heavens to which the two plumb-lines are respectively directed be accurately observed: one of these points will be as much to the eastward as the other will be westward of the true zenith. If we take half the space between them, that will be the deviation of the direction of the plumb-line from the zenith, or, in other words, it will be the actual deviation of the plumb-line from the true vertical direction.

We have then the amount of the deflection, and can therefore calculate the proportion which the mass of the earth bears to the mass of the mountain. If, then, we knew the mass of the mountain, we should necessarily know the mass of the earth.

The mountain on which Dr. Maskelyne tried this celebrated experiment was Schehallien, in Wales. The geological structure of this mountain was known, and the magnitude and nature of its stratification had been ascertained. The weight, therefore, of the materials that composed it was easily calculated, and thus the weight of the mountain obtained.

By computing thence, by means of the experiments just described, the weight of the earth, it was found to be about five times the weight of its own bulk of water.

The method adopted by Cavendish for solving this problem depended on a different mechanical principle. It is well known that the vibrations of the common pendulum, used as a measure of time in clocks, are produced by the attraction of the globe of the earth on the matter composing the ball or disk. If that attraction were greater, its vibration would be more rapid; if it were less, it would be slower; in short, the rate of vibration of the pendulum is the exponent of the energy of force by which it is moved.

If we suppose, then, two globes, containing different quantities of attractive matter, and near these globes two pendulums to be placed, each pendulum being kept in a state of vibration by their attraction: by noting the rates of vibration of these two pendulums, we should be enabled to compare the relative quantities of matter in the two globes. In making this comparison, however, there are several circumstances which should be attended to, which need not be particularly adverted to here. Cavendish adopted this principle as the basis of his method for determining the weight of the earth. He took a large globe of metal, of known weight, and suspended near it in a horizontal position a fine vertical needle, the point of suspension corresponding with its centre of gravity. The effect of the earth's attraction was thus neutralized. Its susceptibility of vibration in a horizontal plane depended upon the torsion of the filament by which it was suspended. The ball of this pendulum was then directed to the centre of the metallic globe, and the pendulum was put in vibration near it, subject to the same mechanical condition as those by which a common pendulum is affected near the surface of the earth. By observing the rate of vibration of this horizontal pendulum, and comparing it with the rate of vibration of the ordinary pendulum subject to the earth's attraction, Cavendish was enabled to obtain the numerical proportion which the earth's attraction bore to the attraction of the metallic globe which he used in his experiments. Having computed thence the weight of the earth, he arrived at a conclusion nearly the same as that to which Dr. Maskelyne had previously arrived by a different method. It was thus finally established that the weight of the globe of the earth is about five and a half times greater than the weight of its own bulk of water.

It follows from this that the mean density of the earth is five and a half times greater than the density of water. We are, however, carefully to remember that this conclusion affects the *mean* density of the earth only. Now, as the density immediately at its surface is not nearly so great as this, it follows that the density of those parts nearer to its centre must be much greater.

THE SEASONS.

The succession of spring, summer, autumn, and winter, and the variations of temperature of the seasons—so far as these variations depend on the position of the sun—will now require to be explained.

The influence of the sun in heating a portion of the earth's surface, will depend partly on its altitude above the horizon. The greater that altitude is, the more perpendicular the rays will fall, and the greater will be their calorific effect.

To explain this, let us suppose A B C and D, fig. 10, to represent a beam of

Fig. 10.

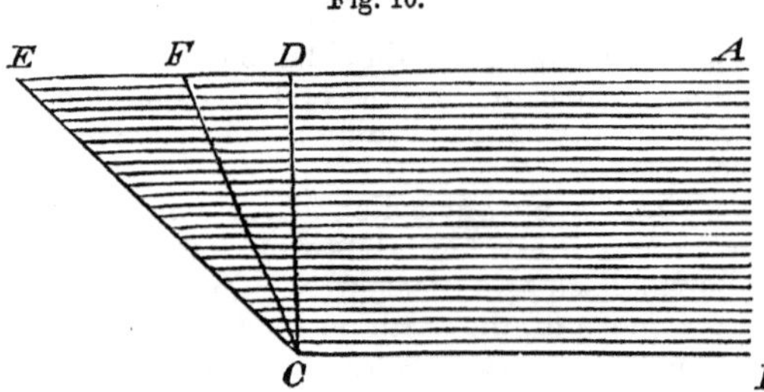

the solar light; let C D represent a portion of the earth's surface, upon which the beam would fall perpendicularly; and let C E represent that portion on which it would fall obliquely; the same number of rays will strike the surfaces C D and C E; but the surface C E being obviously greater than C D, the rays will necessarily fall more densely on the latter: and as the heating power must be in proportion to the density of the rays, it follows that C D will be heated more than C E in just the same proportion as C E is greater than C D. But if we would compare two surfaces on neither of which the sun's rays fall perpendicularly, let us take C E and C F. They fall on C E with more obliquity than on C F; but C E is evidently greater than C F, and therefore the rays being diffused over a larger surface, are less dense, and therefore less effective in heating.

The calorific effect, of the sun's rays on a surface more oblique to their direction than another, will then be proportionably less.

If the sun be in the zenith, its rays will strike the surface perpendicularly, and the heating effect will therefore be greater than when the sun is in any other position.

The greater the altitude to which the sun rises, the less obliquely will be the direction in which its rays will strike the surface at noon, and the more effective will be their heating power. So far, then, as the heating power depends on the altitude of the sun, it will be increased with every increase of its meridian altitude.

Hence it is that the heat of summer increases as we approach the equator. The lower the latitude is, the greater will be the height to which the sun will rise. The meridian altitude of the sun at the summer solstice being everywhere forty-six degrees and fifty-six minutes more than at the winter solstice, the heating effect will be proportionately greater.

But this is not the only cause which produces the greatly superior heat of summer as compared with winter, especially in the higher latitudes. The heating effect of the sun depends not alone on its altitude at midday; it also depends on the length of time which it is above the horizon and below it. While the sun is above the horizon, it is continually imparting heat to the air and to the surface of the earth; and while it is below the horizon, the heat is continually being dissipated. The longer, therefore—other things being the same—the sun is above the horizon, and the shorter time it is below it, the greater will be the amount of heat imparted to the earth every twenty-four hours. Let us suppose that between sunrise and sunset, the sun, by its calorific effect, imparts a certain amount of heat to the atmosphere and the surface of the earth, and that from sunset to sunrise a certain amount of this heat is lost: the result of the action of the sun will be found by deducting the latter from the former.

Thus, then, it appears that the influence of the sun upon the seasons depends as much upon the length of the days and nights as upon its altitude; but it so happens that one of these circumstances depends upon the other. The greater the sun's meridional altitude is, the longer will be the days, and the shorter the nights; and the less it is, the longer will be the nights, and the shorter the days. Thus both circumstances always conspire in producing the increased temperature of summer, and the diminished temperature of winter.

A difficulty is sometimes felt when the operation of these causes is considered, in understanding how it happens that, notwithstanding what has been stated, the 21st of June—when the sun rises the highest, when the days are longest and the nights shortest—is not the hottest day, but that on the contrary, the dog-days, as they are called, which comprise the hottest weather of the year, occur in August; and in the same manner, the 21st of December—when the height to which the sun rises is least, the days shortest, and the nights longest—is not usually the coldest day, but that, on the other hand, the most inclement weather occurs at a later period.

To explain this, so far as it depends on the position of the sun and the length of the days and nights, we are to consider the following circumstances:—

As midsummer approaches, the gradual increase of the temperature of the weather has been explained thus: The days being considerably longer than the nights, the quantity of heat imparted by the sun during the day is greater than the quantity lost during the night; and the entire result during the twenty-four hours gives an increase of heat. As this augmentation takes place after each successive day and night, the general temperature continues to increase. On the 21st of June, when the day is longest, and the night is shortest, and the sun rises highest, this augmentation reaches its maximum; but the temperature of the weather does not therefore cease to increase. After the 21st of June, there continues to be still a daily augmentation of heat, for the sun still continues to impart more heat during the day than is lost during the night. The temperature of the weather will therefore only cease to increase when, by the diminished length of the day, the increased length of the night, and the diminished meridional altitude of the sun, the heat imparted during the day is just balanced by the heat lost during the night. There will be, then, no further increase of temperature, and the heat of the weather will have attained its maximum.

But it might occur to a superficial observer that this reasoning would lead to the conclusion that the weather would continue to increase in its temperature until the length of the days would become equal to the length of the nights, and such would be the case if the loss of heat per hour during the night were equal to that gain of heat per hour during the day. But such is not the case; the loss is more rapid than the gain, and the consequence is that the hottest day usually comes within the month of July, but always long before the day of the autumnal equinox.

The same reasoning will explain why the coldest weather does not usually occur on the 21st of December, when the day is shortest and the night longest, and when the sun attains the lowest meridional altitude. The decrease of the temperature of the weather depends upon the loss of heat during the night being greater than the gain during the day; and until, by the increased length of the day and the diminished length of the night, these effects are balanced, the coldest weather will not be attained.

These observations must be understood as applying only so far as the temperature of the weather is affected by the sun, and by the length of the days and nights. There are a variety of other local and geographical causes which interfere with these effects, and vary them at different times and places.

On referring to the annual motion of the earth round the sun, it appears that the position of the sun within the elliptic orbit of the earth is such that the earth is nearest to the sun about the 1st of January, and most distant from it about the 1st of July. As the calorific power of the sun's rays increases as the distance from the earth diminishes, in even a higher proportion than the change of distances, it might be expected that the effect of the sun in heating the earth on the 1st of January would be considerably greater than on the 1st of July. If this were admitted, it would follow that the annual motion of the earth in its elliptic orbit would have a tendency to diminish the cold of the winter in the northern hemisphere, and mitigate the heat of summer, so as to a certain extent to equalize the seasons; and on the contrary, in the southern hemisphere, where the 1st of January is in the middle of summer and the 1st of July the middle of winter, its effects would be to aggravate the cold in winter and the heat in summer. The investigations, however, which have been made in the physics of heat, have shown that that principle is governed by laws which counteract such effects. Like the operation of all other physical agencies, the sun's calorific power requires a definite time to produce a given effect, and the heat received by the earth at any part of its orbit will depend conjointly on its distance from the sun and the length of time it takes to traverse that portion of its orbit. In fact, it has been ascertained that the heating power depends as much on the rate at which the sun changes its longitude as upon the earth's distance from it. Now it happens that in consequence of the laws of the planetary motions, discovered by Kepler, and explained by Newton, when the earth is most remote from the sun, its velocity is least, and consequently the hourly changes of longitude of the sun will be proportionally less. Thus it appears that what the heating power loses by augmented distance, it gains by diminished velocity; and again, when the earth is nearest to the sun, what it gains by diminished distance, it loses by increased speed. There is thus a complete compensation produced in the heating effect of the sun by the diminished velocity of the earth which accompanies its increased distance.

The place of aphelion, or the point where the earth is most distant from the sun, and the place of perihelion, or the point where it is nearest to the sun, are ascertained by observing when and where the sun's diameter is least and greatest.

The diurnal rotation of the earth on its axis is a fact which all the world are now so habituated to admit, and are taught so early, that few even think of the necessity of asking for any demonstration of it; and yet for thousands of years this fundamental fact of astronomy was not only not admitted, but any one who would have had the temerity to have asserted it, would have been deemed a fit candidate for an asylum for insane persons. Such is the wonderful force of habit.

Let us, however, suppose ourselves ignorant of this fact, and that for the first time we should be told that the place we dwell on and the ground on which we walk is carried round the diameter passing through the poles of the globe once in twenty-four hours; that if we happen to be on or near the equator, we are thus whirled round at the rate of a thousand miles an hour, and that at the latitude of forty to fifty degrees we should be transported at about half that speed: it is surely conceivable that such an assertion heard for the first time would excite very naturally astonishment and incredulity; and although habit has taught us to assent to it, reason must still suggest the question, "What arguments have induced mankind to instil into the minds of the young this principle as an indubitable fact?"

We direct our view to the firmament, and we see all the objects upon it rise in the east and set in the west, the sun among the number. The stars preserve their relative positions; and, in short, all objects which appear in the firmament move as though the motions did not belong to them, but as if the whole firmament was carried round the earth every twenty-four hours with a common motion, carrying all the bodies which appear upon it with that motion.

Now, there are two suppositions, either of which will with equal precision explain this appearance; and there is no other possible way, save these two, by which it can be explained.

It may either be produced—as at the first view it appears to be—by the whole universe turning with a common motion every twenty-four hours round the globe of the earth, or by the globe of the earth itself turning on its axis once every twenty-four hours. How long mankind embraced by preference the former supposition, will be rendered apparent by the very etymology of the term universe* itself. Yet, to our apprehension, informed as we are of the magnitudes, distances, and general structure, not of the solar system only, but of the stellar universe, how eminently absurd does not such a supposition appear! It would compel us to admit, not only that the stupendous globe of the sun, nearly a million and a half times greater than that of the earth, revolves every twenty-four hours round the earth at a distance of one hundred millions of miles, but also that the planets, including Jupiter, fourteen hundred times, and Saturn, one thousand times greater than the earth, the one at four hundred millions of miles and the other at nine hundred millions of miles from the earth, have also this inconceivable motion. But this is not all: we should be forced to admit not only that the entire solar system whirls round the earth once a day, but we should have to impute the same diurnal rotation to the countless myriads of stars placed in regions of the universe so distant that light takes several hundred years to come from them to the earth, moving at the rate of two hundred thousand miles per second; these stars, moreover, being suns, many of them more stupendous than our own! It will be readily admitted that such suppositions are invested with a degree of improbability amounting to

* *Universe*, from UNUS, *one*; and VERSUM, A THING TURNED: signifying *to turn with one common motion.*

moral impossibility. It may, however, be asked how they could have been entertained by the world for so long a succession of ages. The answer is, that so long as the rotation of the universe round the earth was admitted, mankind was ignorant of its vast dimensions and of the comparative insignificance of the earth, with which every person of ordinary education is now more or less familiar. The discovery of this has been reserved for modern times, and consequently the absurdity of the supposition that the earth is at rest and the universe revolving daily round it was not apparent, as it now is.

The first demonstration which we have to offer of the motion of the earth upon its axis, is what is called, in the language of schools, a *disjunctive syllogism.*

1. Either the earth must turn diurnally on its axis, or the universe must turn diurnally round it.

2. But it is absurd to suppose that the whole universe should turn diurnally round the earth.

Conclusion. The earth must therefore turn diurnally on its axis.

Although this negative demonstration be sufficiently conclusive to satisfy the understanding, it has always been considered desirable that we should obtain some positive and direct evidence that the earth really has this diurnal motion. Now, an experiment has been suggested and actually executed, by which a mechanical effect produced by the diurnal motion is actually exhibited. Let us suppose a lofty tower erected on the surface of the earth; the top of the tower would, of course, be more distant than its base from the centre of the earth; consequently it is evident that if the earth had a diurnal motion, the top of the tower, in virtue of that motion, would describe a greater circle than the bottom, and consequently would move from west to east with a greater velocity. Let us suppose, then, a heavy body, such as a leaden bullet, held on the top of the tower; that body would participate in the velocity from west to east which the top of the tower has by the earth's diurnal motion. If the bullet were then disengaged and allowed to fall to the base of the tower, it would still retain the velocity which it had at the top of the tower, and in fact it would have a *downward* motion and an *eastward* motion at the same time. In virtue of the downward motion, it would fall to the ground at the base of the tower; but in virtue of the eastward motion, it would fall as far to the eastward as the top of the tower would have moved *more than the bottom* in the time of its fall.

Now it must be remembered that the motion of the base of the tower eastward by the diurnal motion of the earth is less than that of the top of the tower, and consequently in the time the ball would take to fall from the top of the tower to the ground, the base of the tower would not be as far eastward as the top would move; and consequently the ball ought to be expected to fall eastward of the foot of the tower at a distance equal to the difference between the space through which the top and the base would have moved in the time of the fall.

But if the tower and the earth on which it was built had not this diurnal motion, but were at rest, then the ball ought to fall exactly at the foot of the tower, or vertically under the point from which it was disengaged. Thus, then, we have a positive experiment, the result of which, if rightly executed and accurately observed, must discover to us the fact of the earth's motion, if such motion existed.

The experiment has been made; the question has been asked; nature has been submitted to cross-examination by science: and the secret has been extorted from her. The ball has fallen, not at the point vertically uner the place where it was disengaged, but eastward of that place to the extent and in the degree which it ought to do in virtue of the earth's diurnal motion.

SPHEROIDAL FORM OF THE EARTH.

Although the earth be said to be a globe in the ordinary sense of the term, and when extreme accuracy is not sought, yet, strictly speaking, it deviates from the globular form. It has been ascertained that its figure is that which in geometry is called an *oblate spheroid.* To acquire a notion of this form, we have only to imagine an oval, such as A B C D, fig. 11, to revolve upon its short axis B D. The figure it would produce by such a revolution would be an oblate spheroid. It will differ from that of a sphere, inasmuch as the polar diameter B D will be shorter than the equatorial diameter A C.

Fig. 11.

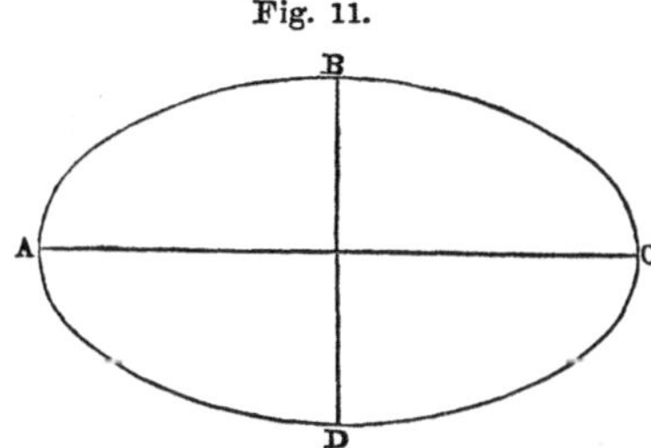

A familiar example of this figure is presented by a *turnip*, or in a less exaggerated form by an *orange.*

The degree in which the earth has this peculiar form is, however, so very slight, that if we made a model of it in a lathe, the eye could not discover that it was not a true globe. Its oblateness could only be detected by accurate measurement, or by causing it to revolve in different positions in the lathe, and applying to it a tool fixed on a rest. In fact, the equatorial diameter of the earth is to the polar diameter in the proportion of three hundred and one to three hundred; or, in other words, the diameter of the equator exceeds the length of the polar axis by one part in three hundred. If, then, we take in round numbers the polar diameter to be eight thousand miles, we shall find the equatorial diameter to be eight thousand and twenty-six miles; thus the parts of the earth's surface at the equator are twenty-six miles further from the centre of the earth than the parts near the poles.

Such being understood to be the real figure of our globe, it will be asked how it has been ascertained to be so. This question may be examined in either of two ways—either as one of *theory* or one of *fact.* We may show, that, from the known laws of mechanics, a globe like the earth revolving on an axis in twenty-four hours, *must become* an oblate spheroid of the above dimensions; or we may show by measurements made on different parts of the earth's surface, that it *is*, in fact, such a spheroid, whatever cause may have imparted that figure to it.

It is well known that when any particle of matter revolves in a circle, it has a tendency to recede from the centre of the circle, in virtue of what is called centrifugal force. Now all points on the surface of the earth revolve very rapidly in circles by reason of the diurnal motion of the globe. Any point, for example, on the equator, revolves in a circumference of twenty-five thousand miles in twenty-four hours. A point at a higher latitude revolves in the same time in a less circle; and the circles of diurnal revolution become gradually less and less as we approach the poles. Since, then, the centrifugal force depends conjointly on the magnitude of the circle of revolution and the velocity of the motion, it follows that it will be less and less as we approach the poles, and greater and greater as we approach the equator.

This force, however, exists at all latitudes, in a greater or less degree of energy, and it is everywhere directed from the centre of the circle of diurnal rotation. Let N O S, figure 12, be the earth, and E Q the equator.

Fig. 12.

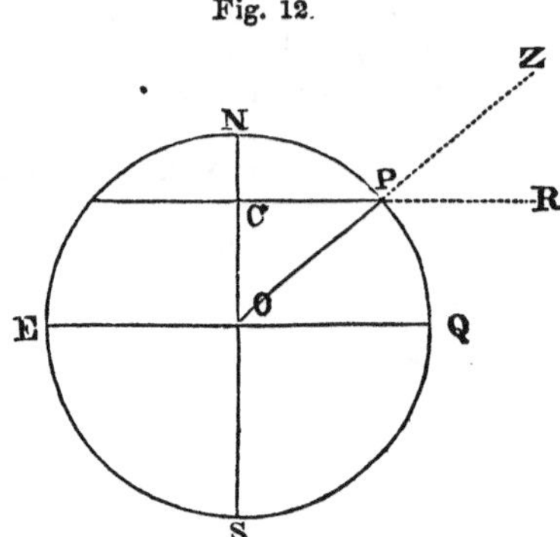

Let P be a point on the surface of the earth anywhere between the equator and poles. Since P is carried by the diurnal motion round the centre C, it will have a tendency to fly from the centre in the direction P R. This tendency will be partially counteracted by its gravity, which acts in the direction P O. But since P O is not directed immediately against P R, the result will be that a particle of matter P thus acted on will move toward Q. To counteract this tendency, there must be such a protuberance at Q as will place an acclivity before P so steep as to prevent its ascent. Without such a protuberance, all the fluid and loose matter on the globe would run toward the line.

It appears, then, that the effect of the earth's revolution would be to cause all loose matter placed on the surface of the earth in either hemisphere to move toward the equator; and that if the earth were a perfect globe, there would be no power to resist this tendency, and the effect would consequently be actually produced.

Let us, then, suppose an exact globe, partially covered with land and water, revolving on an axis in twenty-four hours; the land or solid matter composing it would be affected by the centrifugal force, like all other matter, but the cohesive principle which gives it solidity would prevent a derangement of its structure or change of position by such a cause, and the effect of the centrifugal force would therefore be confined to the fluid matter, which, in obedience to the tendency above described, would flow from either hemisphere toward the regions about the equator, where it would be gradually heaped up so as to form a convex protuberance around the line between the tropics, and to give to the earth, so far as the fluid matter upon it is concerned, the form of an oblate spheroid. But this movement of the fluid would cease as soon as the equatorial protuberance should attain a certain limit; for we may regard such a protuberance as a sort of mountain piled round the equator, down the sides of which there would be a tendency to fall, in obedience to gravitation, as would be the case down any other declivity.

The particles of fluid placed upon the side of this protuberance would be affected by two opposite forces: that which would result from the rotation would have a tendency to move them toward the line—that is, ascending the acclivity—while their gravity, on the other hand, would have a tendency to make them descend, or to move them from the acclivity. When the protuberance would attain the limit at which these two tendencies would become equal, so that the descending force of gravity should be equal to the ascending force proceeding from the rotation, the particles of the fluid would be at rest, and would neither approach the line nor recede from it. It is within the province of mathematical physics to calculate what the limit of this protuberance would be which would produce this state of equilibrium, and the result of such calculations has given us a form which corresponds nearly to that which the earth is actually found to have.

But it may be objected that such reasoning would apply only to fluid matter upon the earth, whereas the oblate form is known to belong to its solid as well as its fluid surface.

This circumstance has been explained in two ways. 1. It is said that the earth in its original formation was altogether fluid; that in that fluid state it received its diurnal rotation, and consequently took the form corresponding with that rotation which we have just explained; that, by cooling down, the fluid matter partially hardened into a solid matter, leaving the liquid ocean covering about two thirds of the globe.

But if this original fluid state of the globe be denied or doubted, and if it be maintained that the globe received its revolution upon its axis when it was composed as it is, partly of land and partly of water, it is nevertheless contended that its present figure is explicable. If a true globe, diversified by land and by water, received a diurnal rotation like that of ours, the water would in the first instance flow toward the equator, and the geographical condition of the globe would be, two polar continents, separated by an extensive equatorial ocean. But after the lapse of ages, the ocean, washing continually upon the shores of the continents, would cause the constant abrasion of their solid matter, which, in the form of mud and sand, would mix with the liquid of the ocean, and would obey all its tendencies. In fact, in process of time the land by decadence and abrasion would obey the same principles which would affect a fluid; and the earth would at length, though after a long lapse of time, assume the form of fluid equilibrium. The present distribution of land and water which characterizes it has arisen from causes belonging more properly to geology than astronomy.

Such is the theoretical reasoning applicable to the form of the earth. We are still, however, required by the rigorous principles of inductive philosophy to ascertain, as a matter of fact, independent of all theory, the actual figure of the globe. This has accordingly been done.

The section of an oblate spheroid made by a plane passing through the poles, is an oval, the longer axis of which is in the equator. It will be evident upon mere inspection that the curvature of the earth having such a form, would increase as we approach the equator, and diminish as we approach the poles; that is to say, a piece of a meridian taken near the equator would be part of a less circle than a similar piece taken near the poles. This is equivalent to stating that a degree of latitude near the equator would be shorter than a degree of latitude near the poles.

Thus, then, the question of the figure of the earth is in fact resolved into the measurement of a degree of latitude at different parts of the globe.

Such measurement has accordingly been executed with great precision, and it has been found, as was anticipated, that the degrees of latitude become shorter as we approach the equator, and longer as we approach the poles. A comparison of their lengths has given the degree that characterizes the oblateness of the earth.

But this is not the only test by which the figure of the earth has been ascertained. If the earth were a true globe revolving on its axis in twenty-four hours, the effect of its revolution would cause gravity to diminish on approaching the equator, and increase on approaching the poles; for the centrifugal force due to the rotation increasing toward the equator would cause a greater diminution of gravity there than toward the poles, where it lessens. Now, it is possible to calculate the effect of such centrifugal force upon the earth if it had the figure of a true globe. The effect of this diminution of gravity will be ascertained with great exactness by observing the vibration of a pendulum in different parts of the earth. It has been already explained that the motion of a pendulum is produced by the gravity of the earth acting upon the ball of the pendulous body, and that the greater the attraction of gravity, the more rapid will be the vibration; and *vice versa*. We carry, then, a pendulum alternately toward the equator and toward the poles, and find invariably that its vibration is slower when taken toward the equator, and more rapid when taken toward the poles. But we find that this variation in its vibration does not correspond to that which it ought to have if the earth were an exact globe. It is just the variation which ought to take place if the earth were an oblate spheroid, of the form already described.

Thus we have two independent tests of the figure of the earth, which give accordant results.

LUNAR INFLUENCES.

The Red Moon.—Supposed Effect of the Moon on the Movement of Sap in Plants.—Prejudice respecting the time for felling Timber.—Extent of this Prejudice.—Its Prevalence among Transatlantic People.—Prejudices respecting Effects on Grain.—On Wine.—On the Complexion.—On Putrefaction.—On Wounds.—On the Size of Oysters and Shellfish.—On the Marrow of Animals.—On the Weight of the Human Body.—On the Time of Births.—On the Hatching of Eggs.—On Human Maladies.—On Insanity.—On Fevers.—On Epidemics.—Case of Vallisnieri.—Case of Bacon.—On Cutaneous Diseases, Convulsions, Paralysis, Epilepsy, &c.—Observations of Dr. Olbers.

LUNAR INFLUENCES.

On a former occasion I examined the question respecting the supposed influence of the moon upon the weather, and demonstrated that so far as actual observation has hitherto afforded grounds for reasoning, there is no discoverable correspondence between the lunar changes and the vicissitudes of rain and drought which can justify or in any degree countenance the popular belief so generally entertained as to dependance of change of weather upon the changes of the moon.

But meteorological phenomena are not the only effects imputed to our satellite; that body, like comets, is made responsible for a vast variety of interferences with organized nature. The circulation of the juices of vegetables, the qualities of grain, the fate of the vintage, are all laid to its account; and timber must be felled, the harvest cut down and gathered in, and the juice of the grape expressed, at times and under circumstances regulated by the aspects of the moon, if excellence be hoped for in these products of the soil.

According to popular belief, our satellite also presides over human maladies; and the phenomena of the sick chamber are governed by the lunar phases; nay, the very marrow of our bones, and the weight of our bodies, suffer increase or diminution by its influence. Nor is its imputed power confined to physical or organic effects; it notoriously governs mental derangement.

If these opinions respecting lunar influence were limited to particular countries, they would be less entitled to serious consideration; but it is a curious fact that many of them prevail and have prevailed in quarters of the earth so distant and unconnected, that it is difficult to imagine the same error to have proceeded from the same source. At all events, the extent of their prevalence alone renders them a fit subject for serious investigation; and I propose at present to lay before you some of the principal facts and arguments bearing on these points, for the collection of which we are mainly indebted to the industry and research of M. Arago.

A large volume would be necessary to analyze all the popular opinions which refer to the supposed lunar influences. We shall confine ourselves therefore to the principal of them, and shortly examine how far they can be reconciled with the established principles of astronomy and physics.

The Red Moon.—It is believed generally, especially in the neighborhood of Paris, that in certain months of the year, the moon exerts a great influence upon the phenomena of vegetation. Gardeners give the name of *Red Moon* to that moon which is full between the middle of April and the close of May. According to them the light of the moon at that season exercises an injurious influence upon the young shoots of plants. They say that when the sky is clear the leaves and buds exposed to the lunar light redden and are killed as if by frost, at a time when the thermometer exposed to the atmosphere stands at many degrees above the freezing point. They say also that if a clouded sky intercepts the moon's light it prevents these injurious consequences to the plants, although the circumstances of temperature are the same in both cases.

Any person who is acquainted with the beautiful theory of dew, which we owe to Dr. Wells, will find no difficulty in accounting for these effects erroneously imputed to the moon. If the heavens be clear and unclouded, all substances on the surface of the earth which are strong and powerful radiators of heat, lose temperature by radiation, while the unclouded sky returns no heat to them to restore what they have lost. Such bodies, therefore, under these circumstances, become colder than the surrounding air, and may even, if they be liquid, be frozen. Ice, in fact, is produced, in warm climates, by similar means. But if the firmament be enveloped in clouds, the clouds having the quality of radiating heat, will restore by their radiation, to substances upon the surface of the earth, as much heat as such substances lose by radiation; the temperature, therefore, of such bodies will be maintained at a point equal to that of the air surrounding them.

Now the leaves and flowers of plants are strong and powerful radiators of heat; when the sky is clear they therefore lose temperature and may be frozen; if, on the other hand, the sky be clouded, their temperature is maintained for the reasons above stated.

The moon, therefore, has no connexion whatever with this effect; and it is certain that plants would suffer under the same circumstances whether the moon is above or below the horizon. It equally is quite true that if the moon be above the horizon, the plants cannot suffer unless it be visible; because a *clear sky* is indispensable as much to the production of the injury to the plants as to the visibility of the moon; and, on the other hand, the same clouds which veil the moon and intercept her light give back to the plants that warmth which prevents the injury here adverted to. The popular opinion is therefore right as to the *effect*, but wrong as to the *cause;* and its error will be at once discovered by showing that on a clear night, when the moon is new, and, therefore, not visible, the plants may nevertheless suffer.

Time for felling Timber.—There is an opinion generally entertained that timber should be felled only during the decline of the moon; for if it be cut down during its increase, it will not be of a good or durable quality. This impression prevails in various countries. It is acted upon in England, and is made the ground of legislation in France. The forest laws of the latter country interdict the cutting of timber during the increase of the moon. M. Auguste de Saint Hilaire states, that he found the same opinion prevalent in Brazil. Signor Francisco Pinto, an eminent agriculturist in the province of Espirito Santo, assured him as the result of his experience, that the wood which was not felled at the full of the moon was immediately attacked by worms and very soon rotted.

In the extensive forests of Germany, the same opinion is entertained and acted upon with the most undoubting confidence in its truth. Sauer, a superintendent of some of these districts, assigns what he believes to be its physical cause. According to him the increase of the moon causes the sap to ascend in the timber; and, on the other hand, the decrease of the moon causes its descent. If the timber, therefore, be cut during the decrease of the moon it will be cut in a dry state, the sap having retired; and the wood, therefore, will be compact, solid, and durable. But if it be cut during the increase of the moon, it will be felled with the sap in it, and will therefore be more spongy, more easily attacked by worms, more difficult to season, and more readily split and warped by changes of temperature.

Admitting for a moment the reality of this supposition concerning the motion of the sap, it would follow that the proper time for felling the timber would be the new moon, that being the epoch at which the descent of the sap would have been made, and the ascent not yet commenced. But can there be imagined in the whole range of natural science, a physical relation more extraordinary and unaccountable than this supposed correspondence between the movement of the sap and the phases of the moon? Assuredly theory affords not the slightest countenance to such a supposition; but let us inquire as to the fact whether it be really the case that the quality of timber depends upon the state of the moon at the time it is felled.

M. Duhamel Monceau, a celebrated French agriculturist, has made direct and positive experiments for the purpose of testing this question; and has clearly and conclusively shown that the qualities of timber felled in different parts of the lunar month are the same. M. Duhamel felled a great many trees of the same age, growing from the same soil, and exposed to the same aspect, and never found any difference in the quality of the timber when he compared those which were felled in the decline of the moon with those which were felled during its increase; in general they have afforded timber of the same quality. He adds, however, that by a circumstance, which was doubtless fortuitous, a slight difference was manifested in favor of timber which had been felled between the new and full moon—contrary to popular opinion.

Supposed Lunar Influence on Vegetables.—It is an aphorism received by all gardeners and agriculturists in Europe, that vegetables, plants, and trees, which are expected to flourish and grow with vigor, should be planted, grafted, and pruned, during the increase of the moon. This opinion is altogether erroneous. The increase or decrease of the moon has no appreciable influence on the phenomena of vegetation; and the experiments and observations of several French agriculturists, and especially of M. Duhamel du Monceau (already alluded to) have clearly established this.

Montanari has attempted, like M. Sauer, to assign the physical cause for this imaginary effect. During the day, he says, the solar heat augments the quantity of sap which circulates in plants by increasing the magnitude of the tube through which the sap moves; while the cold of the night produces the opposite effect by contracting these tubes. Now, at the moment of sunset, if the moon be increasing, it will be above the horizon, and the warmth of its light would prolong the circulation of the sap; but, during its decline, it will not rise for a considerable time after sunset, and the plants will be suddenly exposed to the unmitigated cold of the night, by which a sudden contraction of leaves and tubes will be produced, and the circulation of the sap as suddenly obstructed.

If we admit the lunar rays to possess any sensible calorific power, this reasoning might be allowed; but it will have very little force when it is considered that the extreme change of temperature which can be produced by the lunar light, does not amount to the thousandth part of a degree of the thermometer.

It is a curious circumstance that this erroneous prejudice prevails on the American continent. M. Auguste de Saint Hiliare states, that in Brazil cultivators plant during the decline of the moon, all vegetable whose roots are used as food, and, on the contrary, they plant during the increasing moon, the sugar-cane, maize, rice, beans, &c., and those which bear the food upon their stocks and branches. Experiments, however, were made and reported by M. de Chauvalon, at Martinique, on vegetables of both kinds planted at different times in the lunar month, and no appreciable difference in their qualities was discovered.

There are some traces of a principle in the rule adopted by the South American agronomes, according to which they treat the two classes of plants distinguished by the production of fruit on their roots or on their branches differently; but there are none in the European aphorisms. The directions of Pliny are still more specific: he prescribes the time of the full moon for sowing beans, and that of the new moon for lentils. "Truly," says M. Arago, "we have need of a robust faith to admit without proof that the moon, at the distance of 240,000 miles, shall in one position act advantageously upon the vegetation of beans, and that in the opposite position, and at the same distance, she shall be propitious to lentils."

Supposed Lunar Influence on Grain.—Pliny states that if we would collect grain for the purpose of immediate sale, we should do so at the full of the moon; because, during the moon's increase the grain augments remarkably in magnitude: but if we would collect the grain to preserve it, we should choose the new moon, or the decline of the moon.

So far as it is consistent with observation that more rain falls during the increase of the moon than during its decline, there may be some reason for this maxim; but Pliny, or those from whom we receive the maxim, can barely have credit for grounds so rational: besides which, the difference in the quantity of rain which falls during the two periods is too insignificant to produce the effects here adverted to.

Supposed Lunar Influence on Wine-making.—It is a maxim of wine-growers, that wine which has been made in two moons is never of a good quality, and cannot be clear. Toaldo, the celebrated Italian meteorologist, whose mind appears to have been predisposed for the reception of lunar prejudice, attempts to justify this maxim. "The vinous fermentation," he says, "can only be carried on in two moons when it begins immediately before the new moon; and, consequently, that this being a time when the enlightened side of the moon is turned for the most part from the earth, our atmosphere is deprived of the heat of the lunar rays; that therefore the temperature of the air is lowered, and the fermentation is less active.

To this we need only answer, that the moon's rays do not affect the temperature of the air to the extent of one thousandth part of a degree of the thermometer, and that the difference of temperatures of any two neighboring places in which the process of making the wine of the same soil and vintage might be conducted, must be a thousand times greater at any given moment of time, and yet no one ever imagines that such a circumstance can affect the quality of the wine.

It is a maxim of Italian wine merchants, that wine ought never to be transferred from one vessel to another in the month of January or March, unless in the decline of the moon, under penalty of seeing it spoiled.

Toaldo has not favored us with any physical reason for this maxim; but it is remarkable that Pliny, on the authority of Hyginus, recommends precisely the opposite course. We may presume that from such contrary rules, it may reasonably be inferred that the moon has no influence whatever in this case.

Among the maxims of Pliny we find that grapes should be dried by night at new moon, and by day at full moon.

When the moon is new it is below the horizon during the night, and above it during the day; and when it is full it is above the horizon during the night, and below it during the day. The maxim of Pliny, therefore, is equivalent to a condition requiring that the grapes should be dried when the moon is below the horizon. It is evident that the absence of the moon is not required in this case in consequence of any effect which her light might produce if she were present; for when the moon is new she affords no light, even when in the firmanent, the illuminated side being turned from the earth. If the maxim be founded upon any reason, it must, therefore, either be on some influence which the moon is supposed to produce when present, independent of her light (the absence of which influence is desired), or it may be that she may be supposed to transmit some effect through the solid mass of the earth when on the other side of it which she is incapable of producing without its intervention. The maxim is probably as absurd and groundless as the other effects imputed to the moon.

Supposed Lunar Influence on the Complexion.—It is a prevalent popular notion in some parts of Europe, that the moon's light is attended with the effect of darkening the complexion.

That light has an effect upon the color of material substances is a fact well known in physics and in the arts. The process of bleaching by exposure to the sun is an obvious example of this class of facts. Vegetables and flowers which grow in a situation excluded from the light of the sun are different in color from those which have been exposed to its influence. The most striking instance, however, of the effect of certain rays of solar light in blackening a light colored substance, is afforded by chloride of silver, which is a white substance, but which immediately becomes black when acted upon by the rays near the red extremity of the spectrum. This substance, however, highly susceptible as it is of having its color affected by light, is, nevertheless, found not to be changed in any sensible degree when exposed to the light of the moon, even when that light is condensed by the most powerful burning lenses. It would seem, therefore, that as far as any analogy can be derived from the qualities of this substance, the popular impression of the influence of the moon's rays in blackening the skin receives no support.

M. Arago (who generally inclines to favor rather than oppose prevailing popular opinions), appears to think it possible that some effect may be produced upon the skin exposed on clear nights, explicable on the same principle as that by which we have explained the effects erroneously imputed to what is called the *red moon.* The skin being, in common with the leaves and flowers of vegetables, a good radiator of heat, will, when exposed on a clear night, for the same reasons, sustain a loss of temperature. Although this will be to a certain extent restored by the sources of animal heat, still it may be contended that the cooling produced by radiation is not altogether without effect. It is well known that a person who sleeps exposed in the open air on a night when the dew falls, is liable to suffer from severe cold, although the atmosphere around him never falls below a moderate temperature; and although no actual deposition of dew may take place upon his skin. This effect must arise from the constant lowering of temperature of the skin by radiation. In military campaigns the effects of bivouacking at night appear to be generally admitted to darken the complexion.*

* Le hâle de bivouac is an effect quite recognised. Hâle is a term which expresses a state of the air which makes an impression upon the complexion, rendering tanned and burnt.

There is a proverb which is used in certain parts of France as a warning against night promenades:—

> "Que lou sol y la sereine
> Fau gerie la gent Mouraine."

It is remarkable that this proverb is current in places where the red moon is not noticed.

Supposed Lunar Influence on Putrefaction.—Pliny and Plutarch have transmitted it as a maxim, that the light of the moon facilitates the putrefaction of animal substances, and covers them with moisture. The same opinion prevails in the West Indies, and in South America. An impression is prevalent, also, that certain kinds of fruit exposed to moonlight lose their flavor and become soft and flabby; and that if a wounded mule be exposed to the light of the moon during the night, the wound will become irritated, and frequently become incurable.

Such effects, if real, may be explained upon the same principles as those by which we have already explained the effects imputed to the red moon. Animal substances exposed to a clear sky at night, are liable to receive a deposition of dew, which humidity has a tendency to accelerate putrefaction. But this effect will be produced if the sky be clear, whether the moon be above the horizon or not. The moon, therefore, in this case, is a witness and not an agent; and we must acquit her of the misdeeds imputed to her.

Supposed Lunar Influence on Shell-fish.—It is a very ancient remark, that oysters and other shell-fish become larger during the increase than during the decline of the moon. This maxim is mentioned by the poet Lucilius, by Aulus Gellius, and others; and the members of the academy *del Cimento* appear to have tacitly admitted it, since they endeavor to give an explanation of it. The fact, however, has been carefully examined by Rohault, who has compared shell-fish taken at all periods of the lunar month, and found that they exhibit no difference of quality.

Supposed Lunar Influence on the Marrow of Animals.—An opinion is prevalent among butchers that the marrow found in the bones of animals varies in quantity according to the phase of the moon in which they are slaughtered. This question has also been examined by Rohault, who made a series of observations which were continued for twenty years with a view to test it; and the result was that it was proved completely destitute of foundation.

Supposed Lunar Influence on the Weight of the Human Body.—Sanctorius, whose name is celebrated in physics for the invention of the thermometer, held it as a principle that a healthy man gained two pounds weight at the beginning of every lunar month, which he lost toward its completion. This opinion appears to be founded on experiments made upon himself; and affords another instance of a fortuitous coincidence hastily generalized. The error would have been corrected if he had continued his observations a sufficient length of time.

Supposed Lunar Influence on Births.—It is a prevalent opinion that births occur more frequently in the decline of the moon than in her increase. This opinion has been tested by comparing the number of births with the periods of the lunar phases; but the attention directed to statistics as well in this country as abroad, will soon lead to the decision of this question.*

Supposed Lunar Influence on Incubation.—It is a maxim handed down by Pliny, that eggs should be put to cover when the moon is new. In France it is a maxim generally adopted, that the fowls are better and more successfully reared when they break the shell at the full of the moon. The experiments and

* Other sexual phenomena, such as the period of gestation, vulgarly supposed to have some relation to the lunar month, have no relation whatever to that period.

observations of M. Girou de Buzareingues have given countenance to this opinion. But such observations require to be multiplied before the maxim can be considered as established. M. Girou inclines to the opinion that during the dark nights about new moon the hens sit so undisturbed that they either kill their young or check their development by too much heat; while in moonlight nights, being more restless, this effect is not produced.

Supposed Lunar Influence on Mental Derangement and other Human Maladies. —The influence on the phenomena of human maladies imputed to the moon is very ancient. Hippocrates had so strong a faith in the influence of celestial objects upon animated beings, that he expressly recommends no physician to be trusted who is ignorant of astronomy. Galen, following Hippocrates, maintained the same opinion, especially of the influence of the moon. Hence in diseases the lunar periods were said to correspond with the succession of the sufferings of the patients. The critical days or *crises* (as they were afterward called), were the seventh, fourteenth, and twenty-first of the disease, corresponding to the intervals between the moon's principal phases. While the doctrine of alchymists prevailed, the human body was considered as a microcosm; the heart representing the sun, the brain the moon. The planets had each its proper influence: Jupiter presided over the lungs, Mars over the liver, Saturn over the spleen, Venus over the kidneys, and Mercury over the organs of generation. Of these grotesque notions there is now no relic, except the term *lunacy*, which still designates unsoundness of mind. But even this term may in some degree be said to be banished from the terminology of medicine, and it has taken refuge in that receptacle of all antiquated absurdities of phraseology—the law. Lunatic, we believe, is still the term for the subject who is incapable of managing his own affairs.

Although the ancient faith in the connexion between the phases of the moon and the phenomena of insanity appears in a great degree to be abandoned, yet it is not altogether without its votaries; nor have we been able to ascertain that any series of observations conducted on scientific principles, has ever been made on the phenomena of insanity, with a view to disprove this connexion. We have even met with intelligent and well-educated physicians who still maintain that the paroxysms of insane patients are more violent when the moon is full than at other times.

Mathiolus Faber gives an instance of a maniac who at the very moment of an eclipse of the moon, became furious, seized upon a sword, and fell upon every one around him. Ramazzini relates that, in the epidemic fever which spread over Italy in the year 1693, patients died in an unusual number on the 21st of January, at the moment of a lunar eclipse.

Without disputing this fact (to ascertain which, however, it would be necessary to have statistical returns of the daily deaths), it may be objected that the patients who thus died in such numbers at the moment of the eclipse, might have had their imaginations highly excited, and their fears wrought upon by the approach of that event, if popular opinion invested it with danger. That such an impression was not unlikely to prevail is evident from the facts which have been recorded.

At no very distant period from that time, in August, 1654, it is related that patients in considerable numbers were by order of the physicians shut up in chambers well closed, warmed, and perfumed, with a view to escape the injurious influence of the solar eclipse, which happened at that time; and such was the consternation of persons of all classes, that the numbers who flocked to confession were so great that the ecclesiastics found it impossible to administer that rite. An amusing anecdote is related of a village curate near Paris, who, with a view to ease the minds of his flock, and to gain the necessary time to get through his business, seriously assured them that the eclipse was postponed for a fortnight.

Two of the most remarkable examples recorded of the supposed influence of the moon on the human body, are those of Vallisnieri and Bacon. Vallisnieri declares that being at Padua recovering from a tedious illness, he suffered on the 12th of May, 1706, during the eclipse of the sun, unusual weakness and shivering. Lunar eclipses never happened without making Bacon faint; and he did not recover his senses till the moon recovered her light.

That these two striking examples should be admitted in proof of the existence of lunar influence, it would be necessary, says M. Arago, to establish the fact that feebleness and pusillanimity of character are never connected with high qualities of mind.

Menuret considered that cutaneous maladies had a manifest connexion with the lunar phases. He says that he himself observed in the year 1760, a patient afflicted with a scald head (*teigne*), who, during the decline of the moon, suffered from a gradual increase of the malady, which continued until the epoch of the new moon, when it had covered the face and breast, and produced insufferable itching. As the moon increased, these symptoms disappeared by degrees; the face became free from the eruption; but the same effects were reproduced after the full of the moon. These periods of the disease continued for three months.

Menuret also stated that he witnessed a similar correspondence between the lunar phases and the distemper of the itch; but the circumstances were the reverse of those in the former case; the malady obtaining its maximum at the full of the moon, and its minimum at the new moon.

Without disputing the accuracy of these statements, or throwing any suspicion on the good faith of the physician who has made them, we may observe that such facts prove nothing except the fortuitous coincidence. If the relation of cause and effect had existed between the lunar phases and the phenomena of these distempers the same cause would have continued to produce the same effect in like circumstances; and we should not be left to depend for the proof of lunar influence on the statements of isolated cases, occurring under the observation of a physician who was himself a believer.

Maurice Hoffman relates a case which came under his own practice, of a young woman, the daughter of an epileptic patient. The abdomen of this girl became inflated every month as the moon increased, and regularly resumed its natural form with the decline of the moon.

Now if this statement of Hoffman were accompanied by all the necessary details, and if, also, we were assured that this strange effect continued to be produced for any considerable length of time, the relation of cause and effect between the phases of the moon and the malady of the girl could not legitimately be denied; but receiving the statement in so vague a form, and not being assured that the effect continued to be produced beyond a few months, the legitimate conclusion at which we must arrive is, that this is another example of fortuitous coincidence, and may be classed with the fulfilment of dreams, prodigies, &c., &c.

As may naturally be expected, nervous diseases are those which have presented the most frequent indications of a relation with the lunar phases. The celebrated Mead was a strong believer, not only in the lunar influence, but in the influence of all the heavenly bodies on all the human. He cites the case of a child who always went into convulsions at the moment of full moon. Pyson, another believer, cites another case of a paralytic patient whose disease was brought on by the new moon. Menuret records the case of an epileptic patient whose fits returned with the full moon. The transactions of learned societies abound with examples of giddiness, malignant fever, somnambulism, &c., having in their paroxysms more or less corresponded with the lunar phases. Gall states, as a matter having fallen under his own observation, that patients suffering under weakness of intellect, had two periods in the month of peculiar excitement; and in a work published in London so recently as 1829, we are assured that these epochs are between the new and full moon.

Against all these instances of the supposed effect of lunar influence, we have little direct proof to offer. To establish a negative is not easy. Yet it were to be wished that in some of our great asylums for insane patients, a register should be preserved of the exact times of the access of all the remarkable paroxysms; a subsequent comparison of this with the age of the moon at the time of their occurrence would furnish the ground for legitimate and safe conclusions. We are not aware of any scientific physician who has expressly directed his attention to this question, except Dr. Olbers of Bremen, celebrated for his discovery of the planets Pallas and Vesta. He states that in the course of a long medical practice, he was never able to discover the slightest trace of any connexion between the phenomena of disease and the phases of the moon. In the spirit of true philosophy, M. Arago, nevertheless, recommends caution in deciding against this influence. The nervous system, says he, is in many instances an instrument infinitely more delicate than the most subtle apparatus of modern physics. Who does not know that the olfactory nerves inform us of the presence of odoriferous matter in air, the traces of which the most refined physical analysis would fail to detect? The mechanism of the eye is highly affected by that lunar light which, even condensed with all the power of the largest burning lenses, fails to affect by its heat the most susceptible thermometers, or, by its chemical influence, the chloride of silver; yet a small portion of this light introduced through a pin-hole will be sufficient to produce an instantaneous contraction of the pupil; nevertheless the integuments of this membrane, so sensible to light, appear to be completely inert when otherwise affected. The pupil remains unmoved, whether we scrape it with the point of a needle, moisten it with liquid acids, or impart to its surface electric sparks. The retina itself, which sympathizes with the pupil, is insensible to the influence of the most active mechanical agents. Phenomena so mysterious should teach us with what reserve we should reason on analogies drawn from experiments made upon inanimate substances, to the far different and more difficult case of organized matter endowed with life.

In conclusion, then, it appears that of all the various influences popularly supposed to be exerted on the surface of the earth, few have any foundation in fact. The precession of the equinoxes, the accumulated effect of which rendered necessary the alteration of the calendar, which produced the distinction between the old and new style, is a consequence of the moon's attraction combined with that of the sun upon the protuberant matter around the equatorial parts of the earth; and the nutation of the earth's axis, and the consequent periodical change of the obliquity of the ecliptic, is an effect due to the same cause. I have on another occasion shown that the tides of the ocean are real effects also arising from the combined attractions of the moon and sun, but chiefly of the former.

The precession of the equinoxes is a progressive annual change in the position of those points on the firmament where the centre of the sun crosses the equator on the 21st of March and the 21st of September. It has been ascertained by observation, and verified by theory, that these points move annually on the ecliptic with a slow motion in a contrary direction to the apparent motion of the sun; in consequence of which the sun, after each revolution of the ecliptic, meets these points *before* that revolution has been completed; consequently the sun's centre returns to the same equinoctial point before it makes one complete revolution of the heavens: hence has arisen the distinction between a sidereal year, which is the actual time the earth takes to make a complete revolution round the sun, and an equinoctial or civil year, which is the period between the successive returns of the centre of the sun to the same equinoctial point, and is the interval within which the periodical vicissitudes of the seasons are completed

PHYSICAL CONSTITUTION OF COMETS.

Orbitual Motion of Comets.—Their Number.—Their Light.—Explanation of this.—Theory of Herschel.—Constitution of Comets.—Nebulosity.—Nucleus.—Tail.—Comets of 1811—1680—1769—1744—1843—1844.

PHYSICAL CONSTITUTION OF COMETS.

Of all the objects which attract attention in the heavens, none have excited feelings of greater awe, or awakened sentiments of more intense curiosity, than comets. What are these bodies? or are they bodies at all? What is their character and constitution? Whence do they derive their light? Do they belong to our system? Whence have they come, and whither do they go? Are they, as was long believed, of the same class as the aurora borealis? Although much still remains to be discovered before full, clear, and definite answers can be given to these and similar questions, yet much that is interesting has been ascertained by the labors chiefly of contemporary astronomers. We shall, on the present occasion, present what is certainly known in as brief a space as possible.

ORBITUAL MOTIONS OF COMETS.

Comets are attached to the solar system by the tie of gravitation, and in their motions round the sun are governed by the same law of attraction, as that which operates on the planets. Since they are susceptible of gravitation, they must therefore be material.

In their motions, however, they present circumstances strikingly different from those which characterize the planets. The law of gravitation determines nothing regarding the orbit of a body in moving round the sun, except that it be one or other of those curves called *conic sections*, and that the place of the sun shall be the *focus* of the curve. Subject to this restriction, the orbit of a revolving body may be very various in *magnitude, form, position*, and *direction*. The orbits of the planets are, nevertheless, all very nearly of the same *form*, being all nearly *circular*, and all in the same *position*, being all very nearly in the *plane of the ecliptic;* and they all move in the same direction, being that of the annual motion of the earth. The comets observe none of these characteristics in their orbitual motions. Their orbits vary indefinitely in form. None are circular, or even nearly so. Some are ovals of various eccentricity. Some are either parabolas, or ellipses of such extreme eccentricity as to be undistinguishable from parabolas by any observations we have been enabled to make upon them. Others, again, seem to move in hyperbolas.

The magnitudes of the planetary orbits increase regularly, according to a certain harmonious proportion. No order or regularity is discoverable among the magnitudes of the cometary orbits.

The orbits of comets are not confined to the plane of the ecliptic: they are found to be at every possible angle with it from 0° to 90°. Arago has examined the position of the orbits of a great number of comets, and has found that an equal number move at every inclination with the ecliptic.

Unlike planets, comets do not move in one uniform direction round the sun. Some move in the same direction as the earth, and some in the opposite direction. There are about as many retrogade as direct.

Such are the chief circumstances which distinguish the motions of the comets from those of the planets.

NUMBER OF COMETS.

The determination of the number of comets connected with our system is a question which, although not admitting of a demonstrative solution, may be solved upon grounds of a high degree of probability; and it is one of so much interest, that we are induced here to lay before our readers the views of M. Arago and others on this point.

The total number of distinct comets, whose paths during the visible parts of their course had been ascertained up to the year 1832, was one hundred and thirty-seven. In order to discover whether bodies of this nature prevail more in any particular regions of space than in others—whether, like the planets, they crowd into a particular plane, or are distributed through the universe without any preference of any one region to any other—it was necessary to examine and compare the paths of these hundred and thirty-seven bodies. After a close examination of the planes of their orbits with respect to that of the earth, it appears that the numbers inclined at various angles, from 0° to 90°, is pretty nearly the same. Thus, at angles between 80° and 90° there are fifteen comets; while at angles between 10° and 20° there are thirteen; and between 30° and 40° there are seventeen. Again, the points where they pass through the plane of the earth's orbit are found to be uniformly distributed in every direction around the sun. The points where they pass nearest to the sun are likewise distributed uniformly round that body. Their least distances from the sun also vary in such a manner as leads to the supposition of their uniform distribution through space. Thus, if we suppose a globe, of which the sun is the centre, to pass through the orbit of Mercury, so as to enclose the space round the sun, extending a distance on every side equal to the distance of Mercury, thirty of the ascertained comets, when at their least distance from the sun, pass within that globe. Between that globe and a similar one through the orbit of Venus, forty-four comets pass under like circumstances. Between the latter globe and a like one through the orbit of the earth, thirty-four pass. Between the globe through the orbit of the earth and one through the orbit of Mars, twenty-three pass; and between the latter and a globe through the orbit of Jupiter, six pass. No comet has ever been visible beyond the orbit of Jupiter. It must be here observed, that beyond the orbit of Mars it is extremely difficult to discern comets; and this may account for the comparatively small number of ascertained comets which do not come nearer to the sun than that limit. A comparison of the above numbers with the spaces included between these successive imaginary globes, and with the relative facility or difficulty of discerning comets in the different situations thus assigned, leads to a demonstration that, so far as these hundred and thirty-seven observed comets can be considered as an indication of the general distribution of comets through space, that distribution ought to be regarded as uniform ; that is, an equal number of comets have their least distances included in equal portions of space.

Adopting, then, this conclusion, M. Arago reasons in the following manner: The number of ascertained comets which, at their least distances, pass within the orbit of Mercury is thirty. Now, our most remote planet, Herschel, is forty-nine times more distant from the sun than Mercury; consequently, a globe, of which the sun is the centre, and whose surface would pass through the orbit of Herschel, would include a space greater than a similar globe through the orbit of Mercury, in the proportion of the cube of forty-nine to one. Assuming the uniform distribution of comets, it will follow that, for every comet included in a globe through the orbit of Mercury when at its least distance, there will be a hundred and seventeen thousand six hundred and forty-nine comets similarly included within the globe through the orbit of Herschel. But as there are thirty ascertained to be within the former globe, there will, therefore, be three millions five hundred and twenty-nine thousand four hundred and seventy within the orbit of Herschel.

Thus it appears that, supposing no comet ranging within the limits of Mercury has escaped observation, that portion of space enclosed within the globe through Herschel must be swept by at least three millions and a half of comets. But there can be no doubt that many more than thirty comets pass within the globe through Mercury; for it would be contrary to all probability to assume that, notwithstanding the many causes obstructing the discovery of comets, and the short time during which we have possessed instruments adequate to such an inquiry, we should have discovered *all* the comets ranging within that limit. It is, therefore, more probable that *seven millions* of comets are enclosed within the known limits of the system than the lesser number! Such is the astounding conclusion to which M. Arago's reasoning leads.

LIGHT OF COMETS.

The light of comets is an effect of which astronomers have hitherto given no satisfactory account. If any of these bodies had been observed to have exhibited phases like those of the moon and the inferior planets, the fact of their being opaque bodies, illuminated by the sun, would be at once established. But the existence of such phases must necessarily depend upon the comet itself being a solid mass. A mere mass of cloud or vapor, though not self-luminous, but rendered visible by borrowed light, would still exhibit no effect of this kind: its imperfect opacity would allow the solar light to affect its constituent parts throughout its entire depth—so that, like a thin fleecy cloud, it would appear not superficially illuminated, but receiving and reflecting light through all its dimensions. With respect to comets, therefore, the doubt which has existed is, whether the light which proceeds from them, and by which they become visible, is a light of their own, or is the light of the sun shining upon them, and reflected to our eyes like light from a cloud. For a long period this question was sought to be determined by the discovery of phases. M. Arago then proceeded to apply to the question a very elegant mode of investigation, depending on a property* by which reflected light may be distinguished

* Polarization.

from direct light, and the existence of which property there are sufficient optical means of detecting. He has, however, more recently furnished us with, as we conceive, much more simple and satisfactory means of putting the question finally at rest; if, indeed, it be not already decided.

It is an established property of self-shining bodies, that at all distances from the eye they have the same apparent splendor. Thus the sun, as seen from the planet Herschel, *seems* as bright as when seen from the earth. It is true that he is much smaller, but still equally bright. The smallest brilliant may be as bright as the largest diamond. We must not here be understood to imply that he affords the same light; that is quite another effect. What is intended to be conveyed, will perhaps be best understood by considering the effect of viewing the sun through a pin-hole made in a card. The card being placed at a small distance from the eye, it is evident that the eye will view only a small portion of the sun's disk, limited by the magnitude of the pin-hole; but that portion, *so far as it goes*, will be as bright as it would be were the card removed. Now, the effect here produced, by limiting the portion of the sun's disk which the eye is permitted to see, is precisely the same as if the eye were carried to so great a distance from the sun, that its apparent magnitude would be reduced to equality with that portion of its disk which is seen through the hole in the card.*

Now, applying this principle to the question of cometary light, it will follow that, if a comet shines by light of its own, and not by light received from the sun, it will, like all other self-luminous bodies, have the same apparent brightness at all distances. It will, therefore, cease to be visible; not from want of sufficient apparent brightness, but from want of sufficient visual magnitude. Now, it may be shown that the limit of visual magnitude which would cause the disappearance of a self-luminous body is so extreme, that it would be totally inapplicable to this case. By varying the magnitude of the object-glass of a telescope (which may be easily done), with which such a body is viewed, in proportion to the magnifying power of the eye-glass, it is always possible to make the image of the same apparent brightness; that is, supposing the object itself to maintain a uniform splendor. Consequently, if a body submitted to this species of observation, cease to be visible even by a telescope, it will follow, that it must disappear either by a very extreme diminution of visual magnitude, or by the loss of its own intrinsic splendor. Now, to apply this test to the question of comets. Let us ask in what manner they disappear? Is their disappearance the consequence of an excessive diminution of visual magnitude? or is it to be attributed to the diminished quantity of light which they transmit? Every astronomer will immediately reply that the latter only can cause the disappearance. The greater number of comets, including the most brilliant and remarkable one of 1680 more especially, have obviously disappeared by the gradual enfeeblement of their light. They were, as it were, extinguished. At the very time they ceased to be visible, they possessed considerable visual magnitude. But such a mode of disappearance is incompatible with the character of a self-luminous body, unless we suppose that, from some physical cause, it gradually loses its luminosity.

But in answer to this is adduced the observed fact, that the dimensions of comets are enlarged as they recede from the sun; that the luminous matter, thus existing in a less condensed state, will shine with a proportionably enfeebled splendor; and that at length, by the dilation of the body, the light becomes so dilute, that it is incapable of affecting the retina so as to produce sensation.

* This property is demonstrable by mathematical reasoning.

In answer to this objection, M. Arago has submitted to examination the rate at which comets increase their dimensions as they recede from the sun, according to Valz; and calculates the corresponding diminution of intrinsic splendor which would arise from such a cause. The question then is, whether, by such a diminution of splendor, the brightest comets would be invisible beyond the orbit of Jupiter? This question he proposes to decide by the following experimental test, to be applied to some future comet.

Let a telescope be selected having a large opening and low magnifying power, by the aid of which the comet may be observed in every part of its visible course. Let the body be observed with this instrument at some determinate distance from the sun, such as, for example, the distance of Venus. M. Arago shows how, by applying different magnifying powers to the telescope under these circumstances, the image of the comet may be made to assume different degrees of brightness. He shows, also, how the magnifying power may be regulated, so as to exhibit the image of the comet with just that degree of brightness with which it would appear at any given increased distance to the lowest magnifying power; on the supposition of its being a self-shining body, losing brightness by reason of the enlargement of its dimensions. In this way, he shows that the actual brightness which the comet *ought to have* at any given distance from the sun, when looked at with any given magnifying power, may be *predicted*. He proposes, then, that, this observation being previously made, the comet should be observed subsequently at the proposed distances. If it appear with that degree of brightness which it ought to have in correspondence with such previous observations, then there will be a presumption that it shines with its own light. But if, as is probable, and perhaps nearly certain, the splendor of the comet at increased distances will be greatly less than it ought to be, and that it will be wholly invisible at distances at which it ought to be seen, then there will be conclusive proof that it is a body not self-luminous, but one which derives its light from the sun; and that its disappearance, when removed to any considerable distance from that luminary, arises from the extreme faintness of the light which its attenuated matter reflects.

It will, of course, be perceived, that the enlargement of the volume of the comet will produce a diluting effect upon its reflected light, as much as it would if it shone with direct light; and this furnishes an additional reason for its rapid disappearance as it recedes from the sun.

It will doubtless excite surprise, that the dimensions of a comet should be enlarged as it recedes from the source of heat. It has been often observed in astronomical inquiries, that the effects, which at first view seem most improbable, are nevertheless those which frequently prove to be true; and so it is in this case. It was long believed that comets enlarged as they approached the sun; and this supposed effect was naturally and probably ascribed to the heat of the sun expanding their dimensions. But more recent and exact observations have shown the very reverse to be the fact. Comets increase their volume as they recede from the sun; and this is a law to which there appears to be no well-ascertained exception. This singular and unexpected phenomenon has been attempted to be accounted for in several ways. Valz ascribed it to the pressure of the solar atmosphere acting upon the comet; that atmosphere, being more dense near the sun, compressed the comet and diminished its dimensions; and, at a greater distance, being relieved from this coercion, the body swelled to its natural bulk. A very ingenious train of reasoning was produced in support of this theory. The density of the solar atmosphere and the elasticity of the comet being assumed to being such as they might naturally be supposed, the variations of the comet's bulk were deduced by strict reasoning, and showed a surprising coincidence with the observed change in the dimensions. But this theory is tainted by a fatal error. It proceeds upon the supposition that the comet, in the one hand, is formed of an elastic gas or vapor; and, on the other, that it is impervious to the solar atmosphere through which it moves. To establish the theory, it would be necessary to suppose that the elastic fluid composing the comet should be surrounded by a *nappe* or envelope as elastic as the fluid composing the comet, and yet wholly impenetrable by the solar atmosphere.

Several solutions of this phenomenon have been proposed by Sir John Herschel:* one is, that the comet consists of a cloud of particles, which either have no mutual cohesion, or none capable of resisting their solar gravitation; that, therefore, these particles move round the sun as *separate and independent planets*, each describing an ellipsis or parabola, as the case may be. If this be admitted, it is demonstrable on geometrical principles, and, indeed, it follows as a necessary consequence of the principle of gravitation, that the particles thus independently moving, must converge as they approach the sun, so as to occupy a more limited space, and to become condensed; and that on receding from the sun, they will again diverge and occupy increased dimensions.

Herschel insists on this the more, because he conceives it has the character of a *vera causa*. The fact is, the hypothetical part of it consists, not in the assumed effect of the gravitation of the particles of the comet, but in the assumption that the mutual cohesion or mutual gravitation of these particles is a quantity evanescent in comparison with their separate gravitation toward the sun. This can scarcely be ranked as anything but a supposition assumed to account for the phenomena.

Another theory proposed by Sir John Herschel, which indeed is not altogether incompatible with the simultaneous operation of the former cause, is, that the nebulous portion of the comet, or that portion which reflects the sun's rays, is of the nature of a fog, or a collection of discrete particles of a vaporizable fluid floating in a transparent medium; similar, for example, to the cloud of vapor which appears at some distance from the spout of a boiling kettle. Now, since these molecules, during the comet's approach to the sun, absorb its rays and become heated, a portion of them will be constantly passing from the liquid to the gaseous or invisible state. As this change must commence from without, and must be propagated inward, the effect will be a diminution of the comet's *visible* bulk. On the other hand, as it retreats from the sun, it will lose by radiation the heat thus acquired; which, in conformity with the general analogy of radiant heat, will escape chiefly from the unevaporated or nebulous mass within. The dimensions of this will therefore begin and continue to increase by the precipitation immediately above it of fresh nebula; just as we see fogs in cold and still nights forming on the surface of the earth, and gradually extending upward as the heat near the surface is dissipated. The comet would thus appear to enlarge rapidly in its visible dimensions, at the moment that its real volume is in fact slowly shrinking by the general abstraction of heat from the mass.

"This process," says Sir John Herschel, "might go on in the entire absence of any solid or fluid nucleus; but supposing such a nucleus to exist, and to have acquired a considerable increase of temperature in the vicinity of the sun, evaporation from its surface would afford a constant and copious supply of vapor, which, rising into its atmosphere, and condensing it at its exterior parts, would tend yet more to dilate the visible limits of the nebula. Some such process would naturally enough account for the appearances which have been

* Memoirs Royal Astron. Soc., vol. vi., p. 104.

noticed in the head of certain comets, where a stratum void of nebula has been observed, interposed, as it were, between the denser portion of the head, or nucleus, and the coma. It is analogous to the meteorological phenomenon of a definite *vapor plane*, so commonly observed; and in certain cases, may admit of two or more alternations of nebula and clear atmosphere."

Sir John offers a third supposition to account for the effects, by attributing them to the ethereal medium surrounding the sun.

"Fourier," says he, "has rendered it not improbable, that the region in which the earth circulates has a temperature of its own greatly superior to what may be presumed to be the absolute zero, and even to some artificial degrees of cold. I have shown, I think, satisfactorily, that if this be the case, such temperature cannot be due simply to the radiation of the stars, but must arise from some other cause, such as the contact of an ether, possessing itself a determinate temperature, and tending, like all known fluids, to communicate this temperature to bodies immersed in it. Now if we suppose the temperature of the ether to increase as we approach the sun, which seems a natural, and indeed a necessary consequence, of regarding it as endued with the ordinary relations of fluids to heat, we are furnished with an obvious explanation of the phenomenon in question. A body of such extreme tenuity as a comet, may be presumed to take very readily the temperature of the ether in which it is plunged; and the vicissitude of warmth and cold thus experienced, may alternately convert into transparent vapor, and reprecipitate the nebulous substance, just as we see an increase of atmospheric temperature dissipate the fog, not by abstracting or annihilating its aqueous particles, but by causing them to assume the elastic and transparent state which they lose, and again appear in fog when the temperature sinks."

CONSTITUTION OF THE COMETS.

The word comet is derived from a Greek word signifying *hair*, and hence the name implies a hairy star. The *nebulosity*, or a sort of illuminated haze which always appears around these bodies, is that from which the name was probably taken.

The *head* of the comet is the brightest part of the centre, usually supposed to be a nucleus something like that of a planet; but this is so enveloped in the hair, or nebulosity, that it has never yet been satisfactorily ascertained whether it be solid matter.

A luminous train, varying in length, is frequently, though not always, attached to these objects. It has been generally called the *tail*. Sometimes comets have more than one of these appendages.

THE NEBULOSITY.

As the brightness of the nebulosity gradually fades away toward the edges, there is sometimes a difficulty in measuring its bulk. Its form is generally globular, and its light is often so faint that the comet can only be discovered by telescopes. The diameter of the nebulous mass has been found to vary from 6,000 miles upward. The comets of 1795, 1797, 1798, and 1804, were surrounded by a nebulosity which measured less than 7,000 miles in diameter.

That many comets have no solid matter in the centre of the nebulosity is proved by the fact that the smallest stars are often visible through them; even the ancients, without the aid of the telescope, ascertained this fact. Seneca reported that stars were discoverable through comets, although he does not distinctly state through what part of the comet they were seen. Sir William

Herschel, however, distinctly saw a star of the 16th magnitude through the very centre of the head of the comet which appeared in the year 1795. Prof. Struve, on the 28th of Nov., 1828, saw a star of the 11th magnitude, so small as to be invisible to the naked eye, through the centre of Enckè's comet.

The parts of the nebulosity which immediately surround the nucleus appear to be much less luminous than the more distant parts, as if the nebulous atmosphere became less dense and more transparent near its surface. At some distance from its centre the luminous effect suddenly increases so as to assume the appearance of rings of light around the nucleus; sometimes two, three, or more, such concentric rings have been perceived surrounding comets, separated by dark intervals.

It must be understood, that the arrangement which produces the appearance of these concentric rings, is, in reality, a succession of spherical shells of vapor or nebulous matter, which alternately increases and decreases in density, forming an atmosphere of various densities around the comet. This has been illustrated by Arago by comparing it to successive layers of clouds of different heights surrounding our globe. To perfect the analogy we have only to imagine three transparent spherical shells, still retaining the peculiar optical quality which distinguishes them from the pure air by which they are separated.

The memorable comet of 1811 was enveloped by a nebulosity the thickness of which measured 30,000 miles above the surface or nucleus of the comet.

The thickness of the nebulosity of the comet of 1807 was 36,000 miles; that of 1799 was 24,000 miles.

In comets which have a tail, the rings we have now adverted to are not complete; they terminate at the edges of the tail, and are open through the space where the tail abuts upon the head.

THE NUCLEUS.

Some difference of opinion prevails among observers whether comets really have nuclei at all. When, however, they are supposed to have them, they are generally admitted to be small, and of doubtful magnitude. The following measurements are given by Arago as having been ascertained, or, at least, assumed :—

The comet of 1798 had a nucleus whose diameter was 30 miles; that of 1805, 35 miles; the comet of 1799, 450 miles; the comet of 1807, 650 miles; and the second comet of 1811, about 3,000 miles.

Those who deny the existence of solid matter within the nebulosity of comets, maintain that even the most brilliant and most conspicuous of those bodies, and those which have presented the strongest resemblance to planets, are completely transparent. It might be supposed that a fact so simple as this, in this age of astronomical activity, could not remain doubtful; but it must be considered, that the combination of circumstances which alone would test the truth of this doctrine, is of rare occurrence. It would be necessary that the centre of the head of the comet, although very small, should pass critically over a star, in order to ascertain whether such star is visible through it. With comets having extensive nebulosity without nuclei, this has sometimes occurred; but we have not had such satisfactory examples in the more rare instances of those which have distinct nuclei. The following examples are, however, adduced :—

On the 23d of October, 1774, Montaigne, at Limoges, saw a star of the 6th magnitude through the nucleus of a small comet; but, unfortunately, he has not stated through *what part* of the nucleus he saw it, and the power of the telescope he used was too limited to entitle his observations to much consideration.

On the 1st of April, 1796, Dr. Olbers, at Bremen, saw a star of the sixth or seventh magnitude, and although it was covered by a comet, he found that its light was not perceptibly diminished. The observer in this case did not feel sure that the nucleus was between the eye and the star.

MESSIER, when observing a comet in 1774, saw a small telescopic star beside it, and having looked at it again after the lapse of some hours, he observed a second star near the first. He explained this by the supposition that at the moment of his first observation the nucleus of the comet concealed the second star.

WARTMANN states that on the night of the 28th November, 1828, a star of the 8th magnitude was completely eclipsed by Enckè's comet. Here again, however, it is objected that Wartmann's telescope was too feeble to be trusted in such an observation.

In the absence of a more decisive test of the occultation of a star by the nucleus, it has been maintained that the existence of a solid nucleus may be fairly inferred from the great splendor which has attended the appearance of some comets. A mere mass of vapor could not, it is contended, reflect such brilliant light. The following are the examples adduced by Arago:—

In the year 43 before Christ, a comet appeared which was said to be visible to the naked eye by daylight. It was the comet which the Romans considered to be the soul of Cæsar transferred to the heavens after his assassination.

In the year 1402 two remarkable comets were recorded. The first was so brilliant that the light of the sun at noon, at the end of March, did not prevent its nucleus, or even its tail, from being seen. The second appeared in the month of June, and was visible also for a considerable time before sunset.

In the year 1532, the people of Milan were alarmed by the appearance of a star which was visible in the broad daylight. At that time Venus was not in a position to be visible, and consequently it is inferred that this star must have been a comet.

The comet of 1577 was discovered on the 13th of November by Tycho Brache, from his observatory on the isle of Huene, in the sound, before sunset.

On the 1st of February, 1744, Chizeaux observed a comet more brilliant than the brightest star in the heavens, which soon became equal in splendor to Jupiter, and in the beginning of March it was visible in the presence of the sun. By selecting a proper position for observation, on the 1st of March it was seen at one o'clock in the afternoon without a telescope.

Such is the amount of evidence which observation has supplied respecting the existence of a solid nucleus within the nebulosity of comets. The most that can be said of it is, that it presents a plausible argument, giving some probability, but no positive certainty, that comets have visited our system which have solid nuclei, but, meanwhile, this can only be maintained with respect to few; most of those which have been seen, and all to which very accurate observations have been directed, have afforded evidence of being mere masses of semi-transparent vapor.

THE TAIL.

Although by far the great majority of comets are not attended by tails, yet that appendage, in the popular mind, is more inseparable from the idea of a comet than any other attribute of these bodies. This circumstance probably proceeds from its singular and striking appearance, and from the fact that most comets visible to the naked eye have had tails. In the year 1531, on the occasion of one of the visits of Halley's comet to the solar system, Pierre Apian observed that the comet generally presented its tail in the direction from the sun. This principle was hastily generalized, and is even at present too generally adopted. It is true that in most cases the tail extends itself from that part of the comet which is most remote from the sun; but its direction rarely corresponds with the direction of a shadow of the comet. Sometimes it has happened that the tail forms with the line drawn to the sun a considerable angle, and cases have occurred when it was actually at right angles to the direction of the sun.

Another character which has been observed to attach to the tails of comets, which, however, is not invariable, is, that they incline constantly toward the region last quitted by the comet, as if, in its progress through space, it were subject to the action of some resisting medium, so that the nebulous matter with which it is invested, suffering more resistance than the solid nucleus, remains behind it and forms the tail.

The tail sometimes appears to have a curved form. The comet of 1744 formed almost a quadrant. It is supposed that the convexity of the curve, if it exists, is turned in the direction from which the comet moves. It is proper to state, however, that these circumstances regarding the tail have not been clearly and satisfactorily ascertained.

The tails of comets are not of uniform breadth or diameter; they appear to diverge from the comet, enlarging in breadth and diminishing in brightness as their distance from the comet increases. The middle of the tail usually presents a dark stripe, which divides it longitudinally into two distinct parts. It was long supposed that this dark stripe was the shadow of the body of the comet, and this explanation might be accepted if the tail was always turned from the sun; but we find the dark stripe equally exists when the tail, being turned sideward, is exposed to the effect of the sun's light.

This appearance is usually explained by the supposition that the tail is a hollow, conical shell of vapor, the external surface of which possesses a certain thickness. When we view it, we look through a considerable thickness of vapor at the edges, and through a comparatively small quantity at the middle. Thus, upon the supposition of a hollow cone, the greatest brightness would appear at the sides, and the existence of a dark space in the middle would be perfectly accounted for.

The tails of comets are not always single; some have appeared at different times with several separate tails. The comet of 1744, which appeared on the 7th or 8th of March, had six tails, each about 4° in breadth, and from 30° to 44° in length. Their sides were well defined and tolerably bright, and the spaces between them were as dark as the other parts of the heavens.

The tails of comets have frequently appeared, not only of immense real length, but extending over considerable spaces of the heavens. It will be easily understood that the apparent length depends conjointly upon the real length of the tail and the position in which it is presented to the eye. If the line of vision be at right angles to it, its length will appear as great as it can do at its existing distance; if it appear oblique to the eye, it will be foreshortened more or less, according to the angle of obliquity. The real length of the tail is easily calculated when the apparent length is observed and the angle of known obliquity. The following results of actual observation and calculation have been given by Arago.

The comet of 1811 exhibited a tail which extended over 23° of the heavens. It was observed by Herschel and Schröeter, the latter of whom deduced from his calculations the following results: That the central globe of light or nucleus was 50,000 miles in diameter, or about six and a half times the diameter of the earth. The nebulosity was extremely rarified in comparison with nucleus, resembling a faint, whitish light, scattered in separate portions. It was separated into two, one immediately encompassing the nucleus, the other of a more faint and grayish light, sweeping round it at a distance and forming its double tail. The *head-veil*, as he called it, surrounded the nucleus at a distance equal to its breadth, and seemed as unconnected with the nucleus as the ring of Saturn is with its body. The diameter of this ring measured nearly a million of miles, being greater than the diameter of the sun. Between the 4th and 6th of December a great change took place in its appearance, the rarefied nebulous matter, which had for three months been so unusually repelled from the nucleus on every side, was again attracted to it.

The double tail of this comet was exceedingly faint when compared with its nucleus. On the 16th of October a small tail instantaneously issued from it, then vanished, and suddenly reappeared, when its length was nearly two millions and a half of miles.

Herschel's estimate of the magnitude of the nucleus is much less than that of Schrŏeter; he calculates that, on the 15th of October, the tail measured one hundred millions of miles, and was, consequently, greater than the entire distance of the sun from the earth. He estimated its breadth on the 12th of October at fifteen millions of miles.

Attempts have been made to calculate on probable grounds the elliptic orbit of this comet. Bessel computed that its period is three thousand three hundred and eighty-three years, and other astronomers make it more than four thousand years. A sketch of the comet of 1811 is annexed.

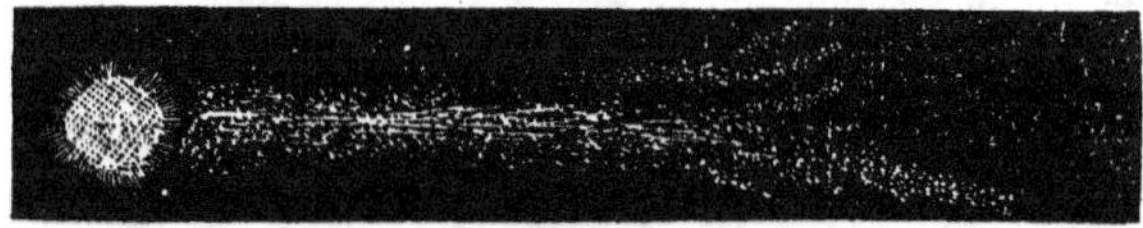

The comet of 1680 exhibited a tail measuring 68°, of a curved form; of which a traditional sketch is annexed.

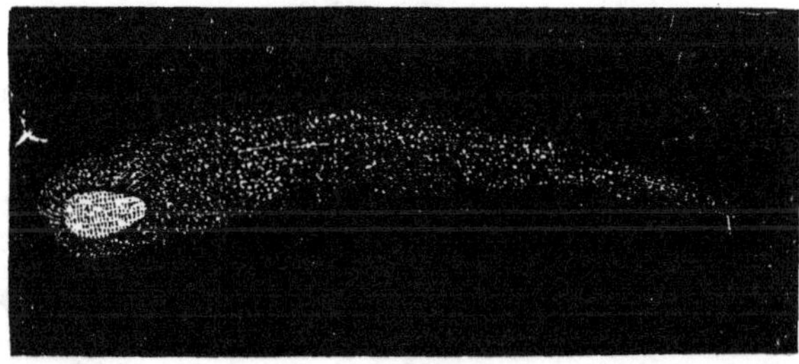

The comet of 1680, which was observed by all the European astronomers of that day, exhibited a tail which extended over 90° of the heavens at its perihelion; its distance from the surface of the sun was not more than one sixth of the sun's diameter; and it was calculated in that position to have a velocity of more than 120,000 miles an hour. When the head of this comet was seen at the zenith, its tail reached the horizon. The actual length of the tail was calculated to be one hundred and twenty-three millions of miles; so that if the head of this comet were at the sun, the tail would extend thirty millions of miles beyond the earth's orbit.

In 1769 a comet appeared, the tail of which spread over a space of 97° of the heavens, and its actual length was fifty millions of miles. Different estimates have been given of the length of the tails of the comet of 1744.

Arago assigns their length at about ten millions of miles, others have estimated it at twenty-three millions of miles. The following description of it is taken from the memoirs of the Academy of Sciences for 1744. It was first seen at Lausanne, in Switzerland, December 13, 1743: from that period it increased in brightness and magnitude as it approached nearer the sun. On the evening of January 23, 1744, it appeared exceedingly bright and distinct, and the diameter of its nucleus was nearly equal to that of Jupiter. Its tail then extended above 16° from its body, and was supposed to be about twenty-three millions of miles in length. On the 11th of February the nucleus, which had before been always round, appeared oblong in the direction of the tail, and seemed divided into two parts by a black stroke in the middle. One of the parts had a sort of beard brighter than the tail: this beard was surrounded by two unequal dark strokes that separated the beard from the hair of the comet. These odd phenomena disappeared the next day, and nothing was seen but irregular obscure spaces, like smoke, in the middle of the tail, and the head resumed its natural form. On the 15th of February the tail was divided into two branches—the eastern, about 8° long, the western, 24.° On the 23d the tail began to be bent. It showed no tail till it was as near the sun as the orbit of Mars, and it increased in length as it approached that luminary. At its greatest length it was computed to equal a third part of the distance of the earth from the sun. This was one of the most brilliant comets that had appeared since that of 1680. Its tail was visible for a long time after its body was hid under the horizon. It extended 20 or 30 degrees above the horizon two hours before sunrise.

In the month of March, 1843, a comet appeared in the heavens exhibiting a great extent of tail, but very faintly luminous. Its course was calculated from the observations made upon it, but no satisfactory grounds were obtained by which it might be identified with any former body of the same kind. The form of the tail was remarkable, inasmuch as its edges were parallel and not divergent. The length of the tail was calculated from the observations, and said to amount to above one hundred millions of miles. This comet was rendered memorable by the fact of its having passed at its perihelion so close to the sun that Arago believed it must have grazed its surface. A sketch of this comet is annexed on the opposite page.

The following observations of Professor Nichol on this comet will be read with interest:—

" Early in the year 1843, an object appeared in the heavens that must have astonished many worlds besides ours. Situated in the region below the constellation Orion, it had the appearance of a long auroral streak, visible immediately after sunset, and evidently pursuing a course through our system. Unfavorable weather concealed it from me until the 25th of March, when it presented the dim and strange appearance I have shown in the frontispiece. The beginning or head of this streak, although never observed here, was often seen in southerly latitudes, where it appeared like a very small star with an enormous misty envelope; beyond which that immense tail streamed through the sky. There is no reason to believe that this nucleus was in reality a star, but only a denser portion of the nebulous substance of which the whole object was composed; for with other apparitions of the same kind, whose brighter parts looked like a star, the application of a very small telescopic power has always been enough to dissipate the illusion, and to resolve what seemed their solid region into a thin vapor.

' This extraordinary visiter was measured, and the nature of its path detected; and certainly the results of these inquiries caused us to look on it with still greater wonder. The diameter or breadth of its nucleus was rather more than a hundred thousand miles; and the tail streaming from it, which in some

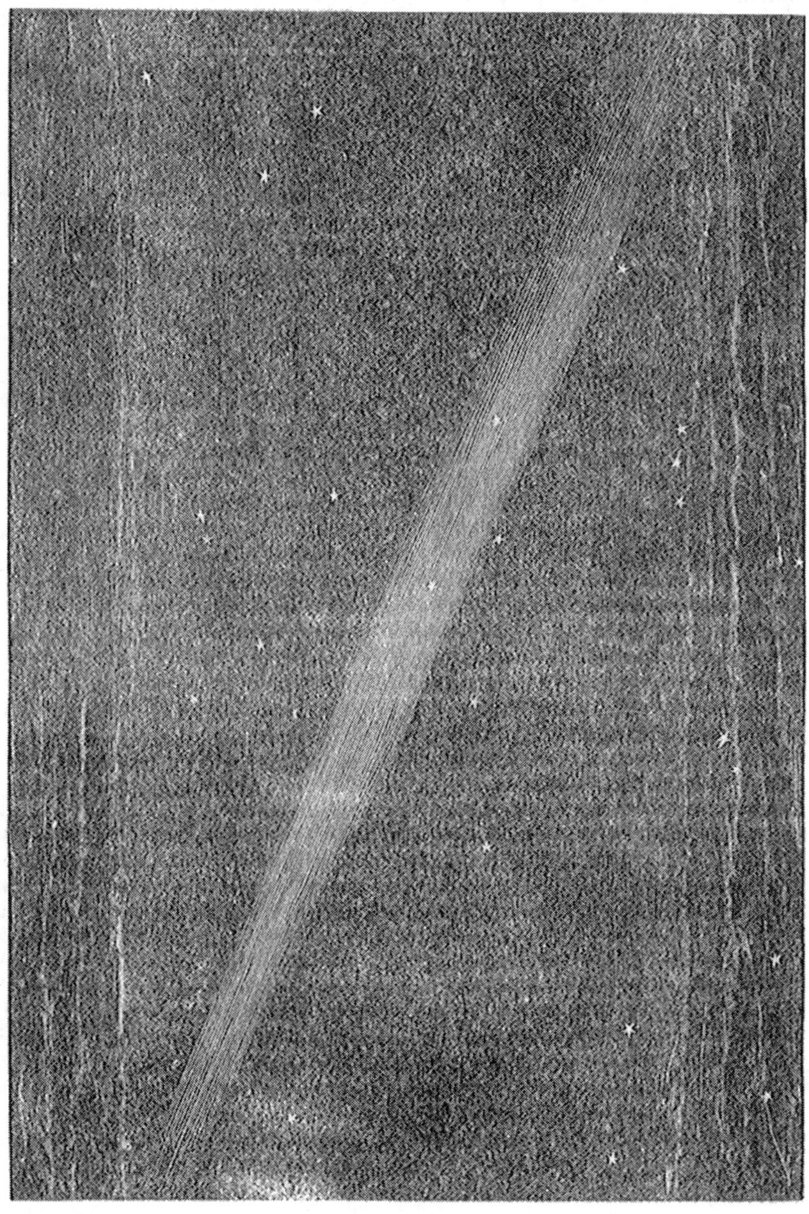

parts was thirty times as broad, stretched through the celestial spaces to the enormous distance of one hundred and seventy millions of miles, or about the whole size of the orbit of the earth. Nor were its motions less singular. Unlike any globe connected with the sun, it did not move in a continuous curve, which, like the circle or ellipse, re-enters into itself, and thus constitutes, to the body that has adopted it, a fixed, however eccentric home; but spying our luminary afar off, as it lay amid those outer abysses, it approached along the arm of a hyperbola, rushed across the orderly orbits of our system into closest neighborhood with the sun, being at that time apart from him only by a seventh part of our distance from the moon, and, defying his attraction, by force of its own enormous velocity, which then was nothing less, in one part of its mass, than one third of the velocity of light, it entered on the other divergent arm of its course, and sped toward new immensities.

"It was when retiring that this unexpected visitant was seen for a brief period in Europe. In the course of its approach it must have passed between us and the sun, causing a cometic eclipse, and, in so far, an interception of his heating rays; but that occurred during our night.

"And now, what is to be made of this extraordinary apparition? what is its nature? what its relations to our system? and what new revelation does it bring concerning the structure of the universe? Its relations with our system appear to have been few and transitory; and in this it resembles the probable millions of such masses, that have, since observation began, crossed the planetary orbits toward the sun, and, after bending round him, gone in pursuit of some other fixed star. No more than three are known to belong, properly speaking, to the scheme dependant on our luminary—Encke's, Biela's, and Halley's; but though these do revolve around him in fixed periods, the circumstance must be regarded in the light of an accident, their orbits being wholly unlike any other, and having little assurance of stability; for as they cross the planetary paths, every one of them may yet undergo the fate of Lexell's, which, by the action of Jupiter, was first twisted from its diverging orbit into a comparatively short ellipse; and then, after making two consecutive revolutions around the sun, so that it might have begun to deem itself a denizen, was, by the same planet twisted back again, and sent off, never to revisit us, away to the chill abysses! Strange objects, with homes so undefined—flying from star to star—twisting and winding through tortuous courses, until, perhaps, no depth of that infinite has been untraversed! What, then, is it your destiny to tell us? To what new page of that infinite book are you an index? We missed, indeed, only very narrowly, an opportunity of information which might have been not the most convenient; for the earth escaped being involved in the huge tail of our recent visiter, merely *by being fourteen days behind it.* For one, I should have had no apprehension, even in that case, of the realization of geological romances, viz., of our equator being turned to the pole, and the pole to the equator—the ocean, meanwhile, leaping from its ancient bed. But if that mist, thin though it was, had, with its next to inconceivable swiftness, brushed across our globe, certainly strange tumults must have occurred in the atmosphere; and probably no agreeable modification of the breathing medium of organic beings. Right, certainly, to be most curious about comets; but prudent, withal, to inquire concerning them from a greater distance than that: although one night in November, 1837, I cannot be persuaded that the earth did not venture on a similar, but comparatively small experiment. It was when our globe passed from the peaceful vacant spaces into that mysterious meteor region. The sky became inflamed and red as blood; coruscations, like auroras, darted across it; not as usual, streaming from one district, but shifting constantly, and sweeping the whole heavens."

In the year 1844* two comets appeared, the first of which was seen in the month of July. It was described to have a bright white color—that its tail was turned from the earth so as not to be visible to us. Stars of very small magnitude were visible through its body, and its light was so strong that it was said to be easily detected in the heavens, in Europe, during the bright sunsets of July. A drawing of this comet, obtained at the Royal Observatory, Greenwich, is annexed.

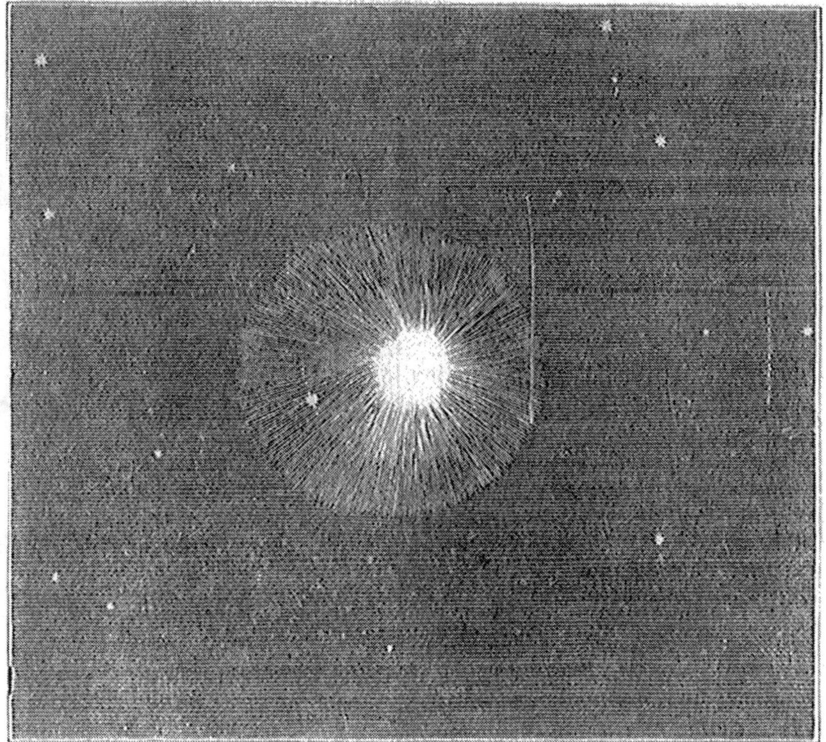

The second comet of 1844 was seen in the month of September. It was observed at Kensington, by Sir James South, on the evening of the 15th. In the course of that month a drawing was obtained of it by the assistance of Sir

* The following note is annexed to the last edition of Nichol's Solar System, relative to one of the comets of 1843:—

"As this volume is leaving the press, intelligence has been received of a new comet being added to our system. Its orbit has been determined by the illustrious Gauss, and its period is nearly seven years.

"The importance of this fact cannot well be overrated; for, along with Encke's and Biela's, it must advance our knowledge of some of the mysterious points connected with the constitution of the planetary scheme. We are yet ignorant whether this body has merely not been observed till now, or whether, like Lexell's, it has been constrained into a new orbit by the action of some planets."

James South and the use of his instruments. We subjoin a copy of this drawing.

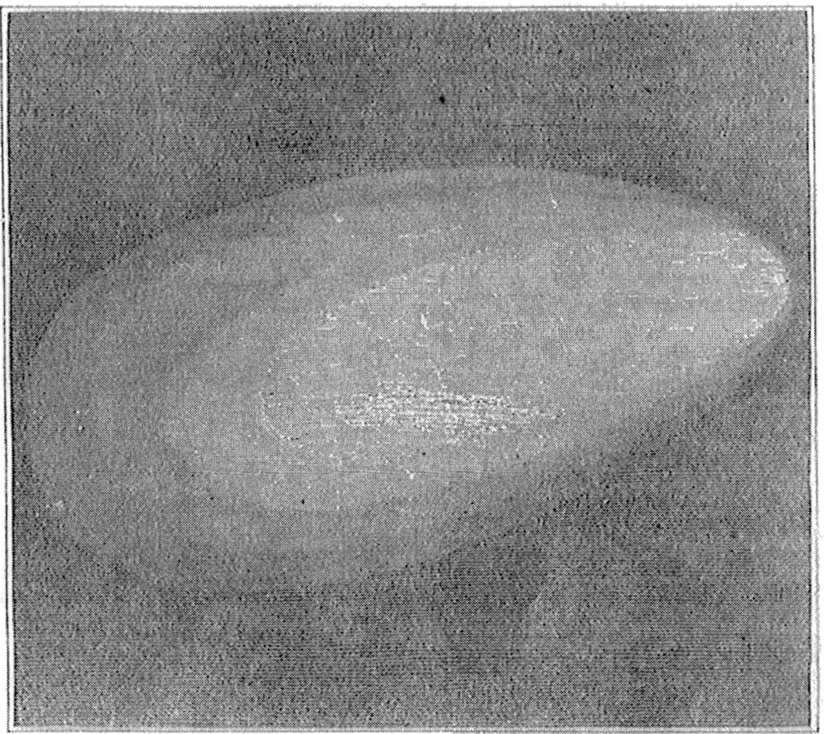

This comet appeared to have a brilliant and well-defined nucleus five seconds in diameter, and a broad luminous tail of about two degrees in length.

THUNDER-STORMS.

The Deficiency of our present Knowledge.—*Of common Thunder-Clouds.*—Character and Electric Charge of Clouds.—Discharge between vicinal Clouds.—Conditions for such Discharge.—Discharge between the Clouds and the Earth.—Mutual Attraction or Repulsion of Electrized Clouds.—Characters of the upper and of the lower Surface of Clouds.—Negative Testimony respecting Thunder from an isolated Cloud.—Cases of Lightning from an isolated Cloud.—A fresh Case related by M. Duperrey.—Obvious Inferences from the above Cases.—*Of Volcanic Thunder-Clouds.*—Lightning from the Ashes, Smoke, and Vapor of Volcanoes.—Theoretical Ideas of its Origin.—*Of the Height of Stormy Clouds.*—Mode of Observation.—Ascending Flashes of Lightning.—Minor Limits of the Height of Storm-Clouds.—Inefficiency of many recorded Observations.—Table of Observations as collected by Arago.—Flash of Lightning from a Cloud upward.—*Of Lightning.*—Varieties of Lightning.—Zigzag Lightning.—Forked Lightning.—Deficiency in our Vocabulary of Terms.—Sheet Lightning.—Table of Instances of Ball-Lightning.—Mr. Harris's Explanation of Ball-Lightning.—*On the Speed of Lightning.*—Theory of Vision illustrated by a rotating Disk.—Wheatstone's Experiments.—Observations of the Velocity of Lightning.—*Silent Lightning.*—Heat Lightning.—Thunder Bursts.—*Of Luminous Clouds.*—Clouds themselves faintly Luminous.—Possession of the Quality in various Degrees.—Clouds visibly Luminous.—Various Observations of luminous Clouds.—Sabine's Observations.—*Of Thunder.*—Rolling of Thunder.—Duration and Intensity of rolling Thunder.—Violent Thunder from Ball-Lightning.—Interval between Lightning and Thunder.—A case in which they were almost simultaneous.—Thunder without Lightning.—Noise attendant on Earthquakes.—*Of the Attempts to explain the Phenomena of Thunder and Lightning.*—Identity of Lightning and Electricity.—Whether ponderable Matter, or a Propagation of Undulations.—Difficulties of the Undulatory Hypothesis.—Ball-Lightning and the Inferences to which it leads.—Bituminous Matter accompanying a Case of Lightning Discharge.—Explanations of silent Lightnings.—Observations of silent Lightnings.—Difficulties in the Explanation of silent Lightnings.—Arago's Suggestion for Observations.—Lightning hidden by dense Clouds.—Place of the Sound of Thunder.—Greatest Distance at which Thunder is heard.—Case of Distance beyond which it was Inaudible.—Distance at which other Sounds have been heard.—Effects of Heat, Cold, Wind, &c.—On the Transmission of Sound.—Thunder heard when no Cloud was Visible.—Hypothesis of the Cause of Thunder from the Creation of a Vacuum.—Contractions and Dilatations of the Air assigned as the Cause.—Pouillet's Theory of Decompositions and Recompositions.—Influence of Echo in causing the Roll.—Duration of an Echo.—Duration of the Roll of Thunder at Sea.—Dr. Robison's Explanation of the Roll.—Application of the Theory to Zigzag Lightning.—Inefficiency of the Theory.—Means of obtaining a Minor Limit of the Length of a Flash.

THUNDER-STORMS.

Since the epoch of the memorable experiments of Franklin, meteorologists, in all parts of the world where physical science is cultivated, have observed with increased interest the phenomena of thunder-storms. Although a great body of facts have been, by such means, accumulated, the general conclusions deducible from them are few; nor are even these few invariably sustained by that consistency, and harmony of effects which are necessary, to command universal assent. Indeed, the facts themselves, on which, alone, any safe and certain generalization could be based, were isolated, and scattered through the memoirs of the various scientific bodies to which their observers had originally consigned them; and many of the most important and valuable observations remained in unpublished memoranda, or were incidentally mentioned in the narratives of voyagers and travellers, where they were little likely to attract the attention of those who, alone, are capable of estimating their value, until, by the indefatigable zeal of M. Arago they were collected, arranged, and compared, and presented to the world, invested with all those charms of style which render the productions of that philosopher so universally attractive.* It is natural that the impatient student should desire to be supplied with clear and comprehensive principles, and be relieved from the tedious details of particular observations and experiments; that facts should be laid before him in extensive groups and classes, so as to suggest easy and obvious generalizations. It is equally natural that the authors of elementary and general treatises should desire, in every case, to present the scientific truths in concise and general propositions, connected together by distinct logical relations. The temptation to yield to this disposition by presenting all physical problems as completely resolved, and all elementary questions as completely exhausted—of laying down sweeping conclusions and general principles, on matters which are, in fact, surrounded with difficulty and doubt—is most hurtful to the progress

* See Notice sur le Tonnerre dans l'Annuaire du Bureau des Longitudes pour l'An 1838.

of science, and a great impediment to the development of truth. To no part of physical science do these observations apply with more force than to the subject of the present discourse. That the phenomena of thunder and lightning proceed from sudden and violent derangements of the electrical equilibrium of the atmosphere or the clouds which float in it, may be regarded as certain; and that the laws which are observed to prevail among electrical phenomena offer various analogies which afford explanations more or less plausible and probable, for some of the facts observed in thunder-storms, may be admitted. But that any comprehensive and general principles have been established from which the various atmospheric phenomena in which thunder and lightning are exhibited, can be deduced in the same manner, and with the same clearness and certainty, as the effects of common electricity have been deduced from the theory of Dufaye, Summer, and Poisson, cannot be maintained. Under such circumstances, both author and reader must patiently submit to the investigation of facts separated from theory or hypothesis; and when these facts have been clearly and fully stated, such general consequences as they justify may be easily deduced from them, and the apparent discordances which, by comparison, may be apparent among them, will afford grounds for further observation and inquiry to those who devote their labor to such researches.

COMMON THUNDER-CLOUDS.

It is generally agreed that the formation of clouds is due to the partial condensation, in the upper regions of the air, of the vapors which have exhaled from the surface of the earth. This condensation may be effected by any cause which produces a diminution of temperature, and is, probably, in most cases, the consequence of the mixture of two currents of air, charged with vapor, and having different temperatures. The positive electricity which rises into the atmosphere with the vapor, and which augments in intensity, as the height increases, to the greatest elevation to which observation is extended, is collected in the clouds thus formed; and when the globules or vesicles composing the cloud have collected together in sufficiently close proximity, the cloud takes the nature of one continued conductor and the free electricity accumulates on its surface in the same manner as on the conductor of an electrical machine. The existence of positively-electrified clouds is, therefore, easily conceived.

If the electroscopic observations which indicate negatively-electrified clouds be rightly interpreted, and the existence of such clouds be admitted, several hypotheses have been proposed to explain them.

If a cloud in its natural state, or feebly charged with positive electricity, approach another cloud strongly charged with the same electricity, the latter will exercise upon it an inductive action, by which its natural electricities will be decomposed, the positive electricity being repelled to the most remote part, and the negative fluid being accumulated at the nearest part. If, under these circumstances, the most remote part be in contact with the earth, as it might be, with the summit of a mountain, for example, the positive electricity will escape to the earth, and the cloud will remain charged with negative electricity. If any cause disengage this cloud from contact with the earth, it will float in the atmosphere and afford an example of a negatively-electrified cloud.

If two clouds, one or both of which are charged with electricity, approach each other, the same phenomena must be evolved as when two conductors, one or both of which are similarly charged, come together. If it happen (a circumstance against which the chances are infinite), that the quantities of free electricity with which they are charged have the same relation as they would have when the clouds are in contact, then their approach and subsequent contact will cause no change in their electrical state save what would be due to inductive action. Their charges after contact will be the same as before, no electricity passing from either to the other. But if their electrical charges have not this particular relation, then a new distribution of electricity will be the consequence of their mutual approach; that which has less positive electricity than the condition of contact requires will receive the deficiency from the other, and this change will be effected by an explosion before the actual contact of the clouds, in the same manner as the electrical equilibrium of two conductors is established by the transmission of the spark before contact. The distance at which the explosion will take place, and its force, will depend on many circumstances, such as the difference between the actual charges of the clouds, and the charges due to contact, the form of the clouds, and the state of the intervening atmosphere.

It is evident, therefore, that an electrical explosion may take place between two clouds, whether they are both similarly electrified, or oppositely electrified, or one be electrified and the other in its natural state.

As the ground is, *in general*, negatively, and the clouds positively electrified, a discharge will take place between the clouds and the earth when the former approach the earth within such a distance that the force of the electricity shall overcome the resistance of the surrounding air.

Since free electricity accumulates in great intensity at prominent points of a conducting body, the negative electricity of the earth may be expected to be most intense at mountain summits. Clouds being, in general, charged with positive electricity, an attraction will, consequently, be exerted upon them which, conspiring with the attraction of gravitation, will draw them round such summits.

The mutual approach of two clouds oppositely electrified is promoted by the attraction due to their electricities: but when two clouds are similarly electrified they will repel each other and their approach must be due to contrary currents of air passing through strata of the atmosphere at different elevations, by which the clouds are brought one under the other.

Beccaria, who observed at Turin, in Piedmont, in a country eminently favorable for such observations, being almost surrounded by lofty ranges, has recorded, with great precision, the appearances of the clouds precursive of a storm. The observations of this philosopher being limited to the lower surface of the clouds, M. Arago has obtained some accounts of the superior surface, from the military engineers employed in the trigonometrical survey, and who, being placed at elevated stations on the Pyrenees, were enabled to observe the superior surface of the strata of clouds situated below them. From the reports of these officers, and especially those of MM. Peytier aud Hossard, it appears that there is no correspondence between the upper and lower surface of a stratum of thunder-clouds; that when the inferior surface is perfectly even and level, the superior surface will be broken into ridges and protuberances, rising upward to great altitudes, like the surface of the earth in an alpine district. In times of great heat, such strata were observed suddenly to send upward lofty vertical cones, which, stretching into higher regions of the air, established, by their conducting power, an electrical communication between strata of the atmosphere at very different heights. This appearance was generally observed to precede a thunder-storm.

Franklin, Saussure, and most other meteorologists, have agreed that thunder never proceeds from a solitary, isolated cloud. Franklin states, that if a thunder-cloud be at any considerable distance from the zenith of the observer, so as to be viewed obliquely, it will be apparent that there are, in every such case, a series of two or more clouds, situate at different elevations, one below the other; and that sometimes the lowest of the series is not far removed from the surface of the earth.

Saussure states that he never witnessed lightning to proceed from a solitary cloud. In observations on the *Col de Géant*, when a single cloud, however dense and dark it might be, was seen upon the summit, no thunder was ever heard to issue from it; but whenever two strata of two such clouds were formed, one below the other, or if clouds ascended from the plain and approached that collected round the summit, the encounter was attended by a storm of thunder, hail, and rain.

Such is the negative testimony of Franklin and Saussure against the fact of thunder proceeding from solitary clouds. Franklin is even more circumstantial than Saussure, and maintains that thunder never proceeds from any save a cloud of great magnitude, below which are placed a series of smaller clouds, identical in fact, with the adscititious clouds of Beccaria.

Negative evidence is, however, not conclusive against a fact, unless the witness be actually present at the time and place of its alleged occurrence. Had the eminent philosophers above mentioned consulted the records of science, their persuasion of the impossibility of thunder issuing from a single cloud would have been shaken. It is related in a memoir of the academician *Marcorelle* of Toulouse, that on the 12th of September, 1747, the heavens being generally cloudless, a single small cloud was seen, from which thunder rolled and lightning issued, by which a female by name Bordenare was killed.

In his meteorological observations made at Denainvilliers, Duhamel de Monceau relates that on the 30th of July, 1764, at half past five, A. M., in bright sunshine and a clear sky, there appeared a small dark solitary cloud, from which thunder and lightning proceeded, by which an elm-tree near the château was stricken.

Similar observations of lightning having issued, followed by thunder, from solitary clouds, have been recorded by Bergman and by Captain Hossard, already mentioned.

M. Duperrey, who commanded the French corvette *Uranie*, relates that being in the straits of Bombay, in November, 1818, he saw a small white cloud in a clear sky, from which lightning issued in all directions. It ascended slowly in the heavens in a direction opposed to the wind, and was at a great distance from all other clouds, which appeared to be fixed upon the horizon. This cloud was round in its form, and did not exceed the apparent magnitude of the sun. Zigzag lightning issued from it, followed by thunder which resembled the irregular discharge of musketry from a battalion commanded to fire at pleasure. This phenomenon lasted for about thirty seconds, and the cloud completely disappeared with the last detonations.

Such are the evidences on the question whether the presence and proximity of a plurality of clouds be essential to the development of the phenomena of thunder and lightning. The analogies offered by common electricity favor the supposition that two or more clouds are essential; and for this very reason the greater should be the caution for receiving the testimony of observers. It is difficult for those whose minds are prepossessed by theory to observe and record facts and appearances as they are; there is a disposition sometimes—perhaps often—to see them as it is supposed they *ought to be*, and consequently the testimony of the ignorant is frequently more deserving of attention than that of the better informed. Be this as it may, the subject is one well worthy of attention, and all persons, who happen to be located in regions where these phenomena prevail, will have it in their power to contribute to the real advancement of science, by carefully and accurately noting down what passes above them, more effectually than those who with greater pretensions attempt to build up theories, which, at best, can have no other object than as means of classifying facts and guiding observers to the fittest objects of examination.

OF VOLCANIC THUNDER-CLOUDS.

The clouds of ashes, smoke, and vapor, which issue from volcanoes, exhibit the phenomena of thunder and lightning. All observers, ancient and modern, concur in their evidence on this question. *Pliny the younger*, in his celebrated letters to Tacitus, speaks of the lightning that issued from the clouds in the eruption of Vesuvius, in the year 79 of the Christian era, in which his uncle, *Pliny the naturalist*, lost his life. *Della Torre* gives the same evidence respecting the eruption of 1182 ; and *Bracini* states that the column of smoke which issued from the same volcano in the eruption of 1631, and which spread in the atmosphere to a distance of forty leagues, was attended by lightning, by which many persons and animals were killed. The lightning in all these accounts is described as being tortuous and serpentine. The same description is given by *Giovanni Valetta* of the appearance of the eruption of 1707.

The inhabitants of the foot of the mountain assured Sir William Hamilton that, in the eruption of 1767, there were more terrified at the lightning which fell among them than at the burning lava and other fearful circumstances attending tho eruption.

Sir William Hamilton states, that in the eruption of 1779 there issued from the crater of Vesuvius, together with the red-hot fluid lava, constant puffs of black smoke, intersected by serpentine lightning, which appeared at the moment it escaped from the crater.

In 1779 the lightning was not attended by audible thunder. It was otherwise in the eruption of the 16th of June, 1794, of which an account has been supplied by the same observer. During the latter eruption, the loudest and most-continued claps of thunder were heard. The lightning was in this case productive of the usual effects. Houses stricken by it were destroyed, and the clouds of ashes, from which these lightnings issued, were carried by the wind as far as Tarentum, a distance of one hundred leagues from Vesuvius, where the lightning struck a building and destroyed a part of it. The ashes of which this cloud was composed were as fine as common snuff.

According to Seneca, a great eruption of Etna, in his own time, was accompanied by similar effects, and the same phenomena are recorded by the Abbé Francesco Ferrara of the eruption of 1755.

When the island called *Sabrina*, in the neighborhood of the Azores (which has since disappeared), rose from the sea in 1811, columns of intensely black smoke, composed of dust and ashes, ascended from the bosom of the deep, and were intersected in their darkest and most opaque parts by vivid lightnings.

The same appearances were observed in the small volcano which, in July, 1831, appeared between Sicily and Pantellaria.

It would be natural to ascribe the electricity of volcanic clouds to the aqueous vapor which is ejected, mixed with the dust, ashes, and lava, in great quantities from the crater; but this supposition is not so free from difficulties as to be admitted without some hesitation. In the eruption of Vesuvius, in 1794, it is hard to conceive that the vapor should be carried uncondensed from Vesuvius to Tarentum; nor was there anything in the appearances on that occasion which indicated the presence of any other substance in the cloud save a fine dust; yet the lightning struck a building at that place. According to the narrative of M. Tellard, who witnessed the phenomenon, columns of black smoke rose from the ocean before the island of *Sabrina* was formed. In this case, any aqueous vapor which might have been ejected from the submarine crater must have been condensed before the column reached the surface of the sea, and the smoke which rose into the atmosphere must have, therefore, been free from vapor; yet this smoke or cloud of volcanic dust was intersected by lightning.

OF THE HEIGHT OF STORMY CLOUDS.

The distance of the clouds from which lightning proceeds is estimated by observing the interval of time which elapses between the moment at which the flash is seen and that at which the thunder is heard. It has been demonstrated by certain astronomical observations, that light is propagated through space at the rate of about two hundred thousand miles in a second of time. This space being greater in a vast proportion than the greatest distance at which any thunder cloud can be placed from the observer, it may be assumed that the moment at which the lightning is seen is practically coincident with the moment at which it emanates from the cloud. It has, however, been also proved that sound is propagated through the air at about eleven hundred feet per second. This rate is subject to some small variations, depending on the temperature of the air, but for our present purpose it may be taken at its mean value. If, then, the number of seconds be observed, which elapse between the moment a flash of lightning is seen and the moment the thunder consequent upon it is heard, and eleven hundred feet be allowed for each second in that interval, the distance of the place whence the lightning issues from the observer will be determined. Thus, if five seconds elapse, the distance will be five thousand five hundred feet; for six seconds, it will be six thousand six hundred feet, and so on.

If the cloud be vertically over the observer, this distance will be equal to its actual height above the level of the observer. If it be not vertical, then its angular elevation must be observed, and the height above the level of the observer will be obtained by multiplying the computed distance by the trigonometrical *sine* of the angular elevation.

The height of thunder-clouds is also attempted to be determined, by observing the effects produced upon objects in elevated situations stricken by the lightning which issues from them. If it be admitted that lightning always *descends* from the clouds toward the earth, then it may be inferred that the place where such effects are manifested must be lower than the position of the cloud from which the lightning proceeds; but, if it shall appear that lightnings sometimes dart *upward*, nothing respecting the height of the cloud can be inferred from such effects. Among those effects which lightning produces when it strikes the earth is the superficial vitrification of rocks. Such effects have been observed on the summits of some of the highest mountains of South America by Humboldt, on the summit of Mont-Blanc by Saussure, and on the Pyrenees by Ramond.

In cases where no means have been taken by those who witnessed thunder-storms to determine the height of the clouds from which they proceed, the situations of the observers themselves afford a minor limit of the value of that height. Bouguer and La Condamine were assailed by a thunder-storm on one of the summits of the Cordilleras, in Peru. Saussure and his son encountered violent storms on the *Col du Géant* and *Mont-Blanc*. MM. Peytier and Hossard witnessed thunder-storms on the *Pic de Troumouse*, the *Pic de Baletous*, and the *Tuc de Maupas*, in the Pyrenees.

Such are the principal observations collected by M. Arago, made in mountainous localities. The comparison of the results of these with the heights of thunder clouds, computed from observations made in flat countries and at sea, would supply means of determining whether the development of storms is affected by the density of the air in which the clouds float, or by their proximity to the surface of the earth. Thus, if it should appear that, in clouds at the same height above the level of the sea, storms are developed more frequently when these clouds are in the neighborhood of mountains, and therefore at a comparatively small distance from the surface of the earth, it would follow, with a probability proportionate to the number and character of the facts observed, that the earth exerts an influence on clouds charged with electricity independently of the atmosphere in which these clouds float.

The height of thunder-clouds observed in a flat country, or at sea, are obtained by the method first mentioned, that is, by observing the interval between the flash and the thunder, and measuring or estimating the angular elevation of the cloud. Unfortunately, the latter element of the computation has been very frequently neglected by observers, the sole object having been apparently to determine the *distance* of the cloud from their station, and not its vertical height. In some cases it appears, incidentally, that the cloud from which lightning issued was in the neighborhood of the zenith, and consequently the distance may be taken as equivalent to the height. In some few the angular elevation has been observed and recorded, and consequently the vertical height of the cloud may be computed.

The following results of the labors of various observers have been collected by M. Arago:—

Place.	Observer.	Date.	Height of thunder-stricken rock above the level of the sea.	Vertical height of thunder-cloud above the level of the sea.	Observations.
			Feet.	Feet.	
Tolucca, in Mexico	Humboldt	-	15,154		
Summit of Mont Blanc	Saussure	-	15,777		
Mont Perdu (Pyrenees)	Ramond	-	11,185		
Pic du Midi (Pyr.)	-	-	9,627		
Pinchincha, (Cord.)	Bouguer and La Condamine	-	-	15,967	Storm mentioned by Bouguer in his work on the figure of the earth.
Col du Géant	Saussure	5th July, 1788	-	11,382	The thunder in this storm succeeded the lightning without any sensible interval.
Mont Blanc	-	-	-	14,760	
Pic de Troumouse (Pyr.)	Peytier and Hossard	1826	-	9,840	
Pic de Baletous (Pyr.)	-	-	-	10,496	
Tuc de Maupas (Pyr.)	-	1827	-	10,824	
Paris	De L'Isle	6th June, 1712	-	25,500	
Tobolsk (Siberia)	Chappe	2d July, 1761	-	10,955	
		13th July, 1761	-	11,382	
Berlin	Lambert	25th May, 1773	-	6,232	
		17th June, 1773	-	5,248	
Pondicherry	Legentil	28th Oct., 1769	-	10,824	
Tobolsk	Chappe	1761	From	700 to	2,600

The height of thunder-clouds determined by other data being in some cases greater than the heights of rocks vitrified by lightning, there is nothing in the comparison of the results exhibited in the preceding table, to justify the supposition that the vitrifications observed by Humboldt, Saussure, and Ramon, did not proceed from lightning which issued from clouds at a greater elevation. But, on the other hand, facts are not wanting to show that this inference cannot be certainly made. There is a church in Styria erected on a summit of a lofty peak called *Mount Saint Ursula*. *Jean-Baptiste Werloschnigg*, a medical practitioner, who happened to visit this church on the first of May, 1700, observed a stratum of dense black clouds to be formed below him at about half the elevation of the place where he stood. These clouds soon became the seat of a violent thunder-storm. Meanwhile the heavens remained perfectly clear, the sun shining with unusual splendor. No one thought for a moment of danger; nevertheless, a flash of lightning, ascending from the cloud, struck the church, and killed seven persons who were in company with Werloschnigg.

It is, therefore, clearly established that lightning may issue upward from thunder-clouds.

LIGHTNING.

Lightnings are resolved by M. Arago into three classes: *First*, the *zigzag*, which present the appearance of narrow, well-defined threads or lines of light, following a course which is clearly enough expressed by their name. In color they vary, being often white, sometimes purple, blue, or violet. *Second*, those lightnings which appear diffused over extensive surfaces, and which are commonly called *sheet-lightning*. In color these also vary, being often an intense red, but occasionally white, blue, or violet. This lightning has an appearance of a momentary light seen through a plate of glass rendered semi-transparent by having its surface ground. *Third*, lightning which moves through the air at a comparatively slow rate, appearing like a luminous ball or sphere, or like a globe of fire. Let us call this *ball-lightning*.

The almost incredible velocity, as will hereafter appear, of lightning of the first class, would hardly seem compatible with the sudden and extreme changes of direction to which its motion is subject. This frequent reversion of direction has been more especially observed in the lightning which traverses volcanic clouds. Minute and circumstantial accounts of such appearances have been supplied by Sir William Hamilton and others, who have observed the eruptions of Vesuvius. In the eruption of 1707, described by Sorrentino, the lightnings which issued from the crater traversed the cloud of ashes as far as the cape Pausillippo, where the cloud terminated. After attaining that point the lightning retraced its course, and struck the summit of the volcano.

Sir William Hamilton states, that in the eruption of 1779 the lightning was generally confined in its play to the cloud of ashes which extended toward Naples; that in traversing that cloud from the crater to its limits, it seemed to menace the city with destruction; but it, nevertheless, after reaching the limit of the cloud, returned toward the crater, where it rejoined the ascending column whence it originally issued.

Zigzag lightning seldom flashes between two clouds. It is generally manifested between a cloud and some terrestrial object.

It has been supposed that the extremity of the lightning of the first class has a barbed form, like the point of an arrow. Of this there is no sufficient evidence. It is, however, sufficiently ascertained that it is often attended by the effect which has given it the name of *forked lightning*. Thus, when a single luminous line issuing from a cloud has traversed a certain distance it will sometimes divide itself into two lines, which, diverging at an angle more or less considerable, will strike distant objects. In some cases it has been seen to separate into three perfectly distinct lines. The former may be called *bi-cuspidated*, and the latter *tri-cuspidated lightning*.

Well-ascertained examples of these phenomena are rare; the occasional occurrence is not, however, the less certain. The abbé Richard states that he witnessed a flash of lightning which left the cloud in a single line of light, and at some distance from the earth dividing into two, and each part struck a separate object.

Nicholson states, that, in a storm which broke over the west end of London, on the 19th of June, 1781, being at Battersea, he saw distinctly several flashes of bi-cuspidated lightning.

The Abbe FERRARA relates that on the 18th of June, 1763, he witnessed tri-cuspidated lightnings in the clouds which issued from the southern side of Etna during an eruption.

The German meteorologist, KAMTZ, states that he witnessed on one occasion, and one only, tri-cuspidated lightning.

If the simultaneous destruction of two or more objects in the same locality by lightning could be taken as conclusive evidence of a corresponding sub-division of a single flash, numerous examples might be given of multi-cuspidated lightning. Such grounds are, however, too conjectural to be admitted as the basis of any safe conclusions.

It is a general opinion that cuspidated lightnings, or lightnings of the first class, are those only by which terrestrial objects are stricken.*

The lightnings of the second class, or *sheet-lightnings*, are inferior in the intensity, and generally different in the color of their light, from those of the first class. These distinctions are very apparent whenever the space over which sheet-lightning is diffused is intersected by flashes of cuspidated lightning. Sheet-lightning sometimes appears to illuminate the edges only of the clouds; occasionally, however, it seems to issue from the interior of their mass. The common expression that the clouds appear *to open*, is strongly indicative of its appearance.

Sheet-lightning is that which is the most frequent, and every one is familiar with its appearance, many having never seen, or never noticed any other. In common thunder-storms it appears in a thousand cases for one in which cuspidated, or ball-lightning, is exhibited.

The flashes of sheet-lightning often appear in very rapid succession, and continue, with interruptions, for many hours. In extreme heat, these flashes succeed each other as rapidly as the flapping of the wings of a small bird, and present a flickering appearance in the clouds which they illuminate. The thunder by which they are accompanied is generally low and distant.

Lightning of the third class, or ball-lightning, is still more rare in its appearance than the zig-zag, or cuspidated lightning. The following instances of this meteor have been collected by M. Arago:—

* If the reader has attentively considered the preceding paragraphs, and what has been elsewhere written on this subject, he will be sensible of the deficiency in the vocabulary of the English language as regards the effects necessary to be expressed. There are three distinct terms in the French language, *Le Tonnerre*, *L'Eclair*, and *La Foudre*. The first expresses the sound proceeding from the clouds which usually follows the flash of light, and is properly translated by *thunder*. The second expresses the light which precedes the thunder, and the third expresses the actual *matter*, the *physical substance*, whatever it may be, which strikes terrestrial objects, and produces those effects which are so well known. In English there is, properly speaking, no term corresponding to *La Foudre*. The terms *thunder* and *lightning* are indifferently used to express the same effect as when we say *thunder-struck* and *struck with lightning*. In French there is also the useful and necessary verb *foudroyer*, of which there is no better English synonyme than *to strike with lightning*. The term thunder-bolt corresponds to *La Foudre*, but it is scarcely admissible into the nomenclature of science. The *electric fluid*, which is sometimes used to avoid the term *thunder-bolt*, is faulty, inasmuch as an effect familiar to all mankind in all ages, ought not to be expressed by a term having immediate reference to modern physical science.

Place.	Time.	Observer.	Appearances.	Effects.
Couesnon, near Brest.	April 14–15, 1718.	M. Deslandes.	Three globes of fire three and a half feet in diameter.	They destroyed a church.
Horn.	March, 1720.	- - - -	A globe of fire struck the earth and rebounded.	After the rebound struck the dome of a tower and set fire to it.
Northamptonshire.	July 3d, 1725.	Rev. Jos. Wasse.	A globe of fire the apparent size of the moon, accompanied by a hissing noise.	
Northamptonshire.	July 3d, 1725.	- - - -	A globe of fire as large as the head of a man, which broke into four pieces near the church.	
Dorking, Surrey.	July 16, 1750.	- - - -	Large balls of fire which, breaking into a prodigious number of fragments, were dispersed in all directions.	A house near which they b'ke was struck by them.
Ludgoan, Cornwall.	Dec. 1752.	Borlase.	Several balls of fire projected from the clouds to the earth.	
Schemnitz, Hungary.	Jan. 1770.	- - - -	A globe of fire as large as a barrel *(tonneau)*.	It struck the tower of the church.
Isle of France.	1770.	Legentil.	Three globes of fire issued from low clouds, and suddenly disappeared without any explosion.	
Steeple Aston, Wiltshire.	1772.	- - - -	A globe of fire oscillated for a long time in the air over the village, on which it fell vertically.	It destroyed the houses on which it fell.
Wakefield.	Mar. 1, 1774.	Nicholson.	Meteors like falling stars fell from the higher of two clouds to the lower.	
Eastbourne, Sussex.	Sept. 1780.	Jas. Adair.	Several balls of fire fell from a large black cloud into the sea.	Two serv'ts were killed in the house of the observer at the same moment.
Villers la Garenne.	Aug. 18, 1792.	Haller.	A globe of fire passed over the village.	It str'ck the house of Haller.
Portsmouth.	Feb. 14, 1809.	- - - -	Three successive balls of fire fell from the clouds in a short interval of time.	They struck three times the ship Warren Hastings in the harbor, passing down the masts each time.
Cheltenham.	April, 1814.	Howard.	A globe of fire fell from the clouds.	It struck a mill which it destroyed.
Vesuvius.	1779 and 1794	Sir W. Hamilton.	Luminous globes appeared in the volcanic clouds, which burst like shells from a mortar, projecting on every side zig-zag flashes.	
Chapel Royal, Madrid.	- - - -	- - - -	Two balls of fire bounded like elastic balls in the chapel and burst in pieces.	The royal palace was struck with lightning.
Samford, Courtenay, Devonshire.	Oct. 7, 1711.	- - - -	A voluminous globe of fire fell among persons assembled under the porch of the church during a storm. At the same moment four smaller globes burst within the church and filled it with a sulphureous smoke.	One of the towers of the church was destroyed by the lightning.
Steeple Aston, Wiltshire.	1772.	Reverend Messrs. Wainhouse and Pitcairne.	In the same storm, the observers being in a room in the vestry, saw suddenly appear before them at a foot distance, and about their own height, a ball of fire about the size of a closed hand, surrounded by a	Pitcairne was dangerously wounded;—his body, clothes, shoes, and his watch, showed the usual marks of being struck

Place.	Time.	Observer.	Appearances.	Effects.
			black smoke. It burst with a noise like that of the simultaneous discharge of several pieces of ordnance. A sulphureous vapor was diffused through the house. Lights of various colors, and having various oscillatory motions, were seen to play through the room.	by lightning. He stated that he saw the globe of fire in the room for one or two seconds after he was sensible of having been struck.
Petersburg.	1752.	Sokoloff.	On the occasion of the death of Richmann, a ball of fire passed from the conductor to his body.	Richmann was killed.
Newcastle on Tyne.	1809.	David Sutton.	In a thunder-storm the lightning descended the chimney of the house of the observer, and after an explosion, several persons assembled in a room, saw at the door of the room a globe of fire, which, after remaining sometime immovable, advanced to the middle of the room, where it burst into several fragments with an explosion like that of a rocket.	
At sea, 35° 40′ lat. S., 52 lon. E.	July 13, 1798.		A globe of fire fell from the clouds upon the ship *Good Hope*, which burst with a violent explosion.	It killed one sailor and severely wounded another.

Before the concurrent force of this evidence all doubt as to the reality of ball-lightning must disappear.

But while on the one hand we are compelled to admit that such phenomena do occur, and that they are true electrical effects, on the other hand we are no less compelled to trace in them the characters of a different kind of electrical discharge from the ordinary lightning flash. Professor Faraday divides the forms of discharge into the spark, the brush, and the *glow*. The *glow* is most readily obtained in the rarefied air of a *partially* exhausted receiver; and differs from the brush in being due to a constant renewal of discharge instead of an intermitting action. Now Mr. Snow Harris suggests in his recent *Treatise on Thunder Storms*, p. 38, that the ball discharge in question possesses many features of resemblance to the glow; and in addition it possesses *motion*. The latter fact is readily accounted for, inasmuch as the cloud which causes the discharge is always progressing. The transition from the *glow* to the spark, or flash, is easily explained; for when the cloud passes over any terrestrial object by which the resistance to discharge is reduced within the striking distance, disruptive discharge must take place; the glow remaining only so long as the resistance opposed the actual flash. Such a ball discharge is described as having approached the ship "Montague," and to have exploded on the topmast; and this is just what Mr. Harris's theory would lead us to expect. And there is reason to believe that many of the cases before us are not to be classed among the effects of lightning. We shall again advert to this.

ON THE SPEED OF LIGHTNING.

The solution of this problem is due to Wheatstone, and like some other results of physical inquiry, such as the abstraction of lightning from the clouds, which was effected by a boy's kite, and the iridescent effect due to the varying magnitudes of luminous undulations, which were derived from observations on soap-bubbles blown from a tobacco-pipe, it is found in the plaything of a child. Every one knows that if the end of a lighted stick be whirled rapidly round in a circle or other curve, it will present the appearance of a continued line of light, the lighted end, which occupies, *in succession*, every point of the curve, appearing to the eye to be *continually present* at all its points.

Fig. 1.

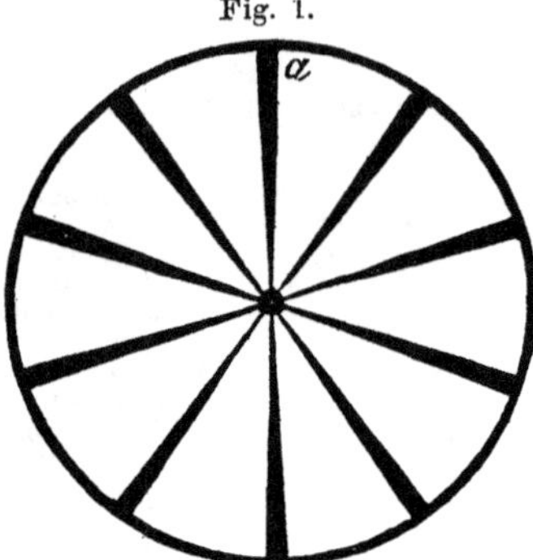

To develope the principle on which this fact rests, let fig. 1 represent a wheel with ten thin spokes or radii, dividing its circumference in ten equal parts, and of some strong bright color, such as red. Let this wheel be put in communication with clock-work, so as to be made to revolve uniformly at any required rate. This wheel, having its face vertical, and turning on a horizontal axis; let a screen be placed before it, so as to conceal it from view, and in this screen let an oblong opening be made, corresponding in magnitude and position to that spoke of the wheel which is in the vertical position and presented from the centre upward. Let the screen, with such an aperture, be represented in fig. 2.

Fig. 2.

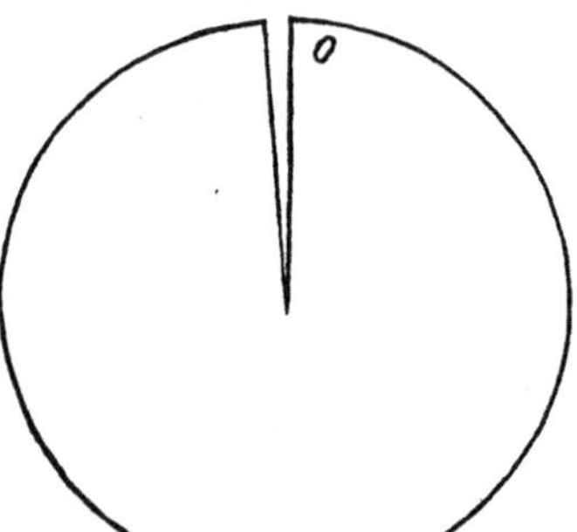

As the wheel revolves its spokes pass the opening *o*, in succession, and if the motion of the wheel be not very rapid, a person placed before the screen will perceive the spokes appear and disappear in regular and uniform succession at the opening. If the velocity of the wheel be gradually increased, the succession of appearances and disappearances will be rendered, by degrees, indistinct, until, at length, a velocity will be attained which will cause a spoke to be continually seen at the opening *o*, in the same manner as if the wheel were at rest, and the spoke *a* were placed behind the aperture. Now, since it is certain that in this case the presence of the spokes at the aperture is successive, and that the intervals which the spokes are absent bear to the intervals of their presence, the proportion of the breadth of the spokes to the breadth of the spaces between them, it necessarily follows that the *eye perceives a spoke at the aperture during the intervals when no spoke is present there.*

This circumstance is accounted for by considering the manner in which vision is effected by means of the mechanism of the eye. The light proceeding from a visible object, entering the pupil, strikes the retina and produces in it a certain vibration, which vibration is the immediate cause of the perception of the object from which the light has been transmitted. After the object has ceased to transmit light to the eye, this vibration continues for a certain time, just as the vibration of a musical string continues for a certain interval after the bow which put it into vibration has been withdrawn; and, as the vibration of the string continued, after the bow is withdrawn, produces the perception of a proportionately prolonged sound, so the vibration of the retina, after the visible object has been withdrawn, produces a proportionately prolonged perception of its presence. In fact, there is no *damper* in the mechanism of the eye to stop the effect of the action of light at the instant that action ceases. It is, therefore, an interesting physiological problem to determine how long after that visible object is withdrawn, and the action of light ceases, the effect on the retina remains, and the object continues to be seen. This problem is beautifully solved by the apparatus above described. The velocity of the wheel being gradually augmented until the spoke appears to be continually present at the opening, it has been found that *this effect is produced when the wheel performs one complete revolution in a second of time.* Since the space round the centre of the wheel is equally divided by the ten spokes, it follows that in this case the interval between the arrival of two successive spokes at the opening is one tenth of a second, and this must, therefore, be the duration of the impression of an object on the retina after it has been withdrawn. If the duration were *less* than this the colored spoke would not *appear* continually at the aperture *o* when the wheel revolves in one second, but would alternately appear and disappear. If it were *greater*, a less velocity than one revolution per second would be sufficient to cause its continuous appearance.

Since there is nothing in what has been stated to render it necessary that the aperture, through which the spokes are seen, should be in the vertical, rather than any other position, it follows that in whatever position, round the centre, that aperture be placed, a spoke will appear to be continually behind it, so long as the wheel revolves at a rate of not less than one revolution per second.

If, therefore, there be two or more such apertures made in the screen, a spoke will appear constantly behind each of them. In fine, if there be an infinite number of such apertures round the centre, or, in other words, if the screen be altogether removed, spokes will be seen in every direction round the centre without any open spaces between them, or what is the same, the wheel will appear as a circular disk of uniform red, no spokes being distinguishable.

We have here supposed that the wheel is continually illuminated. It is necessary now to inquire how long light must shine upon it in order that, revolving once per second, it may appear as a plane disk without spaces between the spokes. If the light fall upon it only for an instant, that is, an infinitely short time, then the wheel will be distinctly seen, for the tenth of a second, in the position which it had when the light fell upon it. The spokes will be as distinctly visible as if the wheel were at rest. But if the light continue to fall upon the wheel during the tenth of a second, then each spoke will continue to be illuminated from the position it has the moment the light first falls upon it, until it arrives at the position which the preceding spoke had at that moment. Each spoke will, therefore, act upon the eye while it passes through the space between two successive spokes, and will, therefore, be seen at every point of that space; and as the perception it causes at any point will continue while the spoke passes through the whole of that space, it follows that the wheel will appear to the eye as a flat, circular disk uniformly illuminated.

If, however, the light continue to fall on the wheel during an interval *less* than the tenth of a second, suppose, for example, the twentieth of a second, then each spoke will be illuminated while passing through half the interval between two successive spokes, and the wheel will present the appearance of a circle divided into ten equal sectors, half of each sector being visible and half invisible. If the duration of the light be any other part of the tenth of a second, the wheel will, for the same reason, present the appearance of a circle divided into ten equal sectors, a portion of each sector being visible, bearing to the remaining portion, invisible, the same ratio as the duration of the light bears to the difference between that duration and the tenth of a second.

Such an instrument will, therefore, serve as the means of estimating the duration of any light which continues to illuminate the wheel for a period of time not exceeding the tenth of a second; and it is evident that, by varying the number of spokes and the velocity of the wheel, the duration of any light may be measured when its amount is greater or less than the tenth of a second.

Such is the instrument which has been applied by its inventor to measure the duration of a flash of lightning, and, also, of the electric spark. A wheel consisting of a hundred spokes, dividing the space round the centre into as many equal sectors, was exposed to the light of lightning during a thunder-storm. By clock-work, it was made to revolve ten times per second, making, therefore, one revolution in the tenth of a second, and moving through the interval between two spokes in the thousandth part of a second. If the duration of the light by which this wheel was illuminated amounted to the thousandth part of a second, it would appear as a complete illuminated disk without spokes. If it amounted to half a thousandth of a second, it would appear as a circle divided into a hundred equal sectors, half of each sector being visible and half invisible. If the duration of the light were instantaneous, it would appear as a wheel with a hundred spokes stationary, in the particular position it had at the moment the light fell upon it.

Now, such a wheel, being thus exposed to the flashes of lightning, in a storm, it was found that when illuminated it always appeared stationary, though revolving ten times in a second. The spokes were seen distinctly, with no more than their proper thickness. It, therefore, follows that the duration of the light of the flashes did not amount to so great a fraction of the thousandth part of a second as was capable of being appreciated by estimating the apparent width of the spokes when seen by the light of the flashes. The duration of the flashes must then have been a very small fraction of the thousandth part of a second.

But the duration of a flash is the time which the lightning takes to move through that part of space which it traverses while it is visible. Hence it follows, that whatever be the extent of such a distance, it is traversed in a very minute fraction of the thousandth of a second.

This method of observation has only been applied to lightning of the first and second kind, no opportunity having yet been found to apply it to ball-lightning.

SILENT LIGHTNING.

When the heavens are perfectly serene in hot weather, lightnings are frequently observed to continue flashing in the atmosphere for many hours unaccompanied by thunder. These have been called *heat lightnings*. Such appearances are not confined, as has been supposed, to those parts of the atmosphere which are near the horizon; on the contrary, their light extends frequently over the whole visible firmament.

Lightning, unaccompanied by thunder, appears much more rarely when the heavens are clouded. Sufficient evidence, however, of this phenomenon in different parts of the globe has been collected by M. Arago.

Thibalt de Chanvalon, in his meteorological observations, records its occurrence on two days in July, 1751, at Martinique. Such lightning is very common at the Antilles. Dorta mentions the same phenomena at Rio Janeiro, in a paper published in the memoirs of the Academy of Sciences of Lisbon, in the years 1783, 1784, 1785, and 1787, during which time he witnessed one hundred and seventy days on which lightnings were seen unaccompanied by thunder.

Lind witnessed at Patna, in India, latitude N. 25° 37′, in the year 1826, on seventy-three days lightning without thunder; but neither Lind nor Dorta state whether the heavens were clear or clouded. The probability is, that where the occurrence of the phenomenon was so frequent, they were sometimes clouded.

De Luc, the younger, mentions a great storm which took place at Geneva on the 1st of August, 1791, during which very vivid lightnings were seen without any audible thunder. Some of the flashes on this occasion were so strong that the loudest claps of thunder would have been expected to follow them. In the same storm, however, other flashes were accompanied by loud thunder.

Dalton states that, in Kendal, on the 15th of August, 1791, at nine o'clock in the evening, he witnessed in a storm vivid and continual flashes of lightning, but heard only *some* thunder which was distant.

At Philadelphia, in the month of July, in the year 1841, and in New York, in the following month, I witnessed frequent *thunder-bursts* (as they are there called), in which in a clouded sky I saw a constant succession of flashes of lightning, which sometimes continued for several hours, accompanied by very short, occasional showers of rain. On these occasions thunder was sometimes not heard at all, and sometimes it was only heard after long intervals of silence, and seemed from its sound to be distant. The lightnings, nevertheless, were vivid, and illuminated the heavens to the zenith. They appeared generally like a light behind the clouds, the edges of which were strongly illuminated, the centres more faintly. These lightnings sometimes succeeded each other so rapidly that they had a *fluttering* appearance, like the motion of the wings of a small bird; and this fluttering of light would be often continued for three or four seconds. These trembling lightnings would succeed each other at intervals of some minutes.

OF LUMINOUS CLOUDS.

In the darkest nights of winter, at the hour of midnight, when the influence of the solar light is altogether withdrawn from the atmosphere, and in the absence of moonlight, a sufficient quantity of light is always diffused to render objects around us faintly visible, and to enable us to walk without hesitation in any open country. If the firmament be serene and cloudless, this light is ascribed to the stars. But let the heavens be overcast, let the stars be hidden by an unbroken mass of the most dense clouds, and still a sufficiency of light will be diffused in the open country to prevent any of the difficulty and inconvenience which would attend any attempt to walk in a dark cave, or in an apartment with closed windows. It cannot, then, be doubted that, in the most clouded nights of deep winter, light, proceeding from some source, is diffused through the air. If this light be supposed to be that of the stars penetrating the clouds, it is necessary to admit that the light of the stars in a *clear night* is greater, in the same proportion as the splendor of the unclouded noonday sun exceeds the light when the firmament is covered with dense clouds. No one having the least powers of observation can admit such an assumption; and if it be not admitted, there remains no other explanation of the nocturnal light of a clouded sky, except in the admission that *the clouds themselves are faintly luminous.*

If the supposition of the self-luminous property of clouds be entertained, the probability that, under varied circumstances of form, density, mutual position, temperature, and many other conditions, which will easily suggest themselves to every mind, clouds may be endowed with this quality in various degrees. The probability, therefore, of the hypothesis which we have just proposed to account for nocturnal light, will be strengthened, if it can be shown that, on particular occasions, clouds have been observed unequivocally and in much higher degrees luminous.

In a memoir of Rozier, dated 15th of August, 1781, that philosopher states that, being at Bézieres on that day, in the evening, at a quarter before eight o'clock, the sun having gone down, and the firmament being overcast, thunder was heard. At five minutes past eight, it being then complete night, the storm having attained its height, Rozier observed a luminous point above the brow of a hill fronting his house, which gradually augmented in magnitude until it assumed the form and appearance of a phosphoric zone, subtending at his eye an angle of about sixty degrees measured horizontally, and having the apparent height of a few feet. Above this luminous zone was a dark space equal to its own breadth, and over that space appeared another horizontal zone, of the same breadth, and about half the apparent length. The middle of each of these zones exhibited a uniform brightness, but the edges were irregular. Lightning issued three times from the edges of the inferior zone, but no thunder was audible. The duration of this extraordinary phenomenon was nearly a quarter of an hour.

Nicholson relates that, on the 30th of July, 1797, at about five o'clock in the morning, he observed the heavens covered with dense clouds, which moved rapidly to the west-southwest. Lightnings played constantly at northwest and southwest, which, after an interval of twelve seconds, were succeeded by loud claps of thunder. The lower parts of the clouds, which were undulated and checkered, exhibited a red light which was very vivid. At one moment, houses placed in front of that which he inhabited had the appearance which would have been produced by viewing them through a deep-blue glass; at that time, on looking at the clouds, they appeared to emit a blue light.

Beccaria states that the clouds over his observatory at Turin frequently diffused in all directions a strong reddish light, which was sometimes so intense as to enable him to read a page printed in ordinary type. This nocturnal light was especially observed in winter, between successive snow-showers.

The selfsame luminous quality has been observed in fogs. The dry fog of 1783 was described by M. Verdueil, a physician of Lausanne, as having diffused at night a light sufficiently strong to render distant objects visible, and this light was equally spread in all directions. It resembled the light of the moon seen through clouds.

De Luc states that, returning home to his lodgings in the neighborhood of London, on a winter night, when the atmosphere was clear, and not cold, he saw a band of clouds intersecting the southern meridian, about thirty or forty degrees from the zenith, and extending on either side nearly to the eastern and western horizons. The brightness of this cloud resembled that of a thin cloud concealing the moon, and was sufficient to render the stars in its neighborhood invisible.

Dr. Robinson, professor of Astronomy at Armagh, states, in a letter to M. Arago, that, during the voyage of Major Sabine in Scotland, undertaken to observe the lines of equal magnetic intensity, that officer, being at anchor in Lough Scarig, in the Isle of Sky, observed a cloud which constantly enveloped the summit of one of the naked and lofty mountains which surround that island. This cloud, which resulted from the precipitation of the vapor brought by the constant west winds from the Atlantic, was self-luminous at night, not occasionally, but permanently. Major Sabine saw frequently issue from it jets of light resembling those of the aurora. He rejects, however, the supposition that these jets were produced by real auroras near the horizon, and which were concealed from direct observation by the mountain. He regarded all these phenomena of continued and intermitting light as originating in some physical property of the cloud itself.

OF THUNDER.

Thunder, as every one knows, is a certain noise, proceeding apparently from the clouds, which usually follows, after a greater or less interval, the appearance of a flash of lightning. Of all natural phenomena, those which occupy the meteorologist present the greatest difficulties, when it is necessary to convey a precise notion of them to those who may not immediately have witnessed them. It is, doubtless, to this difficulty that we must ascribe the practice of meteorological writers of resorting to similes and other like illustrations in their descriptions.

Thunder is described by some as a sound resembling the acute noise produced when stiff paper is torn, or when a strong silk cloth is suddenly torn, or when a heavy wagon is rolled rapidly over a rough, stony road. It is imitated with much effect in theatres by shaking a piece of sheet-iron about four feet long and two feet broad. This is held in the hand at one of its corners, and the varieties of thunder may be imitated by skilfully varying the movement of the hand.

Thunder is sometimes heard as a clear, single, distinct sound, like the report of a gun, unattended by any reverberation. More frequently the sound is deep, or, in a musical sense, *grave*, and consists, not of a single sound, but of that rapid succession of sounds, first increasing and afterward diminishing in intensity, which has been expressed by the term *rolling*.

The difficulty of expressing and recording in *words* the exact nature of such phenomena has limited to a small number the observations on which any safe reasoning can be based.

The duration of the rolling of thunder was observed and recorded by De L'Isle, in Paris, in the year 1712. On one occasion it was observed to endure for forty-five seconds. On other occasions, during the same storm (17th June), the roll continued from thirty-four to forty-one seconds. On the 3d, 8th, and 28th of July, the roll continued on different occasions from thirty-five to thirty-nine seconds.

De L'Isle also observed the varying intensity of the sound in each roll. In some cases the clap is loudest at the commencement, and afterward declines gradually until it ceases to be heard. Sometimes it commences with a low and barely audible sound, which augments in force until it attains a maximum loudness, after which it diminishes gradually in intensity until it becomes inaudible. These changes were carefully observed and recorded on several occasions by De L'Isle. The following examples will serve to illustrate the phenomenon:—

1712	*Seconds.*	
17th of June,	0	Lightning flashed.
	3	Thunder feebly audible.
	12	Thunder loudest.
	19	Thunder became gradually inaudible.
21st of July,	0	Lightning flashed.
	16	Thunder feebly heard.
	20	Thunder loudest.
	32	Thunder became gradually inaudible.
8th of July,	0	Lightning flashed.
	11	Thunder feebly heard.
	12	Thunder loudest.
	38	Loudest thunder began to decrease in force.
	47	Thunder became gradually inaudible.
8th of July,	0	Lightning flashed.
	11	Thunder feebly heard.
	12	Thunder became loudest.
	38	Thunder began to decrease in loudness.
	47	Thunder became gradually inaudible.
8th of July,	0	Lightning flashed.
	10	Thunder feebly heard.
	13	Thunder became loud.
	20	Thunder broke with redoubled force.
	35	Thunder began to lose its force.
	39	Thunder became gradually inaudible.

It appears from these observations that the durations of the loudest part of each roll varied from twenty to thirty seconds.

The degree of loudness is also very various. On the 2d of March, 1769, the tower of the church at Buckland Brewer was struck by lightning, followed by a clap of thunder described by an ear-witness as equal to the simultaneous report of one hundred pieces of cannon.

The most violent thunder sometimes follows ball-lightning. When the ship Montague was struck, on the 4th of November, 1749, the captain (Chalmers) declared that the sound produced by the explosion was equal to the simultaneous discharge of several hundred pieces of ordnance, but that it did not last above half a second.

The interval of time which elapses between the flash of lightning and the thunder which succeeds it is an important element in the theoretical investigation of the atmospheric conditions which produce these phenomena. It is especially useful to ascertain the major and minor limits of this interval. The observations of this kind collected by M. Arago are arranged in the following table:—

Places.	Time.	Observer.	Intervals.
			Seconds.
Petersburgh.	2d May, 1712	De L'Isle.	42
—	—	—	48
—	—	—	48
—	6th June, 1712	—	47
—	—	—	48
—	—	—	48
—	—	—	49
—	30th April, 1712	—	72
Tobolsk.	2d July, 1761	—	42
—	—	—	45
—	—	—	47
—	10th July, 1761	—	46
—	—	—	2
—	—	De L'Isle.	3
—	—	—	4
—	—	—	5

M. Arago states, as the general impression on his memory, that he has often observed the thunder follow the flash after an interval so brief as half a second.

In the early part of June, 1841, being in the reading-room of the *Athenæum* at Philadelphia, I witnessed a vivid flash of lightning which was succeeded by the loudest clap of thunder I ever recollect to have heard. The interval was, by my estimation, a very small fraction of a second. An ordinary observer would have said that the flash and the sound were simultaneous

The occurrence of thunder not preceded by lightning has not been proved by evidence as clear and satisfactory as that by which the existence of silent lightnings have been established. No example is found of it in any of the meteorological registers kept at observatories in Europe. *Thibault de Chanvalon*, already quoted, mentions in the register of his observations made at *Martinique*, that in October, 1751, there were two days on which thunder was heard without the appearance of lightning; and that on one day in November there were three loud claps of thunder without lightning.

On the 19th of March, the vessel in which *Bruce* the traveller had embarked on the Red sea, near Cosseir encountered a clap of thunder so violent as to strike the seamen with terror. There was no lightning.

The occurrence of thunder when the firmament is cloudless has been doubted. SENEBIER speaks of thunder on clear days as a known fact, but does not state whether such was the result of his own observations. VOLNEY states, that on the 12th of July, 1788, at six o'clock in the morning, the sky being unclouded, he heard at *Pont Chartrain*, a place four leagues from *Versailles*, four or five claps of thunder. At a quarter past seven clouds began to rise in the southwest, and in some minutes the heavens were covered. Soon afterward hailstones fell as large as a man's fist.

The noise which often attends earthquakes is similar to thunder, and by an acoustic deception not yet clearly explained, it is heard as if it proceeded from the upper regions of the air. Observations, therefore, of supposed thunder with a clear sky, in places subject to earthquakes, cannot safely be received as evidence of real thunder.

THE ATTEMPTS TO EXPLAIN THE PHENOMENA OF THUNDER AND LIGHTNING.

Although the investigations of Franklin removed all doubts respecting the identity of lightning and artificial electricity, still, in the great variety of atmospheric phenomena developed in the disturbances of electrical equilibrium which are produced on so grand a scale in the vast regions of the air, much remained and still remains unexplained. Succeeding philosophers have accomplished little more than exhibiting, by direct experiments, and by the comparison of numerous observations, analogies which throw more or less light on the relations between the appearances which are exhibited in the atmosphere and those general laws which have been deduced from experiments made on artificial electricity.

The luminous appearances which attend the electrical discharges in the atmosphere, and which characterize the different kinds of lightning, must be regarded as explicable on the same principles as those of artificial electricity; and the various hypotheses and conjectures, more or less plausible, which have been proposed to account for the one must equally be brought to bear on the other.

To regard the principle which darts through space with the enormous velocity which the observations of Professor Wheatstone have shown lightning to be endowed with, as ponderable matter, is extremely difficult. If it be ponderable matter it must follow the path of projectiles, and, consequently, its course must be curved with a concavity turned toward the earth, except when it follows the vertical direction. In the zigzag path of cuspidated lightning there is nothing analogous to this. On the other hand, such rapid and rectilinear motions are quite consonant with the supposition of a system of undulations propagated through a highly elastic medium, and are in all respects analogous to the actual phenomena of light. The bi-cuspidated lightning finds its obvious type in the double refraction of crystallized media, and the heterogeneous matter suspended in different strata of the air through which the lightning is transmitted completes the parallel.

The undulatory hypothesis is, nevertheless, beset with its own difficulties. How can the pulsations of an imponderable ether be reconciled with the mechanical effects of lightning? The analogy to the phenomena of light fails when it is considered that, notwithstanding its velocity of 200,000 miles per second, light has never acquired in its motion, even when condensed by the largest burning reflector, sufficient momentum to affect in any sensible degree the lightest substance suspended in vacuo by a filament of spider's web, while, on the contrary, the electric fluid, issuing from the clouds, splits rocks, overturns the most massive structures, destroys gigantic trees, and projects to a distance enormous weights.

But of all the forms under which the results of electrical explosions in the air present themselves, the most inexplicable is that of *ball-lightning*. Observation seems to countenance the supposition that these globes of fire are real agglomerations of ponderable matter formed in the regions of the air by some unexplained process. Where such formations are made; whence proceed their ponderable constituents; what is their nature; what sustains them in the air; and what causes finally precipitate them; are questions before which science is mute.

The constituents of the atmosphere are oxygen and azote, in the proportion of four parts by weight of the former to fourteen of the latter. If the electric spark be transmitted through a mixture of these two gases confined in a glass tube, a portion of the oxygen will combine chemically with a portion of the azote, and nitric acid will be formed. What the electric spark does in such a mixture the transmission of the electric fluid accomplishes in the atmosphere, and nitric acid is formed, distinct traces of which are discoverable in the rain which falls in thunder-storms. If, then, this power of determining the chemical combination of these constituents of the air be undeniable in this case, we cannot reject the possibility of other combinations being effected by the same agency. Besides oxygen and azote, the proper constituents of pure atmosperic air, there are various foreign substances occasionally suspended in it, of which the chief but not the only one is the vapor of water. Carbonic acid exists in it in variable quantity but it is nowhere totally absent. SAUSSURE found it in air collected at the top of Mont Blanc. FUSINIERI states that he constantly found sulphur, iron, and its different oxides, in fissures through which lightning has forced its way.

If such analogies be considered to have any weight, it is not impossible to imagine the constituents of solids to be suspended in the atmosphere in a vaporous sublimated state, and to coalesce and enter into combination by the transmission through them by a strong discharge of electricity. But as a matter of *fact* is it *proved* that ponderable masses in a state of ignition have actually fallen from the clouds? The following evidence is produced by M. Arago on this question:—

Boyle states that in July, 1681, the British ship Albemarle was struck with lightning off Cape Cod. A mass of burning bituminous matter fell in the boat suspended at the stern of the vessel, which diffused an odor like that of gunpowder. It was consumed in the place where it fell, after ineffectual efforts to extinguish it by water, or to throw it out of the boat with rods of wood.

Silent lightnings, whether they appear in a clear or clouded sky, are usually explained by the supposition that they are the reflection of lightnings which issue from clouds below the horizon, and so distant that the thunder which accompanies them cannot be heard. It has been, on the other hand, objected, that the splendor of lightning is not sufficiently intense to cause a reflection so bright as the silent lightnings, and that a reflection inferior in brightness to lightning itself in the same proportion as twilight is to the brightness of the sun, would not be visible. To this objection M. Arago replies by the following facts:—

CASSINI and LACAILLE, when engaged in making a series of experiments on the velocity of sound, in the year 1739, saw the light produced by the discharge of a piece of ordnance placed at the base of the lighthouse of *Cette*, although at the station they occupied both the town and the lighthouse were concealed by intervening hills.

In 1803 M. ZACH gave signals on the *Brocken* (a mountain of the *Harz* range), by exploding six or seven ounces of gunpowder. The light produced by this was seen by observers stationed on Mount *Kellenberg*, at a distance of nearly three leagues from the *Brocken*. Since a direct view would have been rendered impossible by the convexity of the earth, the light must have been seen by reflection.

The flashes of artillery discharged at the base of the *Hôtel des Invalides*, at Paris, are visible in the gardens of the *Luxembourg*, near the *Rue d'Enfer*, although the highest point of the dome of the hotel is invisible from that place.

If, then, the feeble effect produced by the explosion of a few ounces of gunpowder be sufficient to be so apparent by reflection, may it not be expected that the more resplendent illumination produced by lightning would be infinitely more vivid?

That this mode of explaining *silent lightning* may not take the character of mere conjecture, it will be necessary to show that distant lightnings are actually visible when the thunder which accompanies them is inaudible. Two unexceptionable observations are adduced for this purpose.

On the night between the 10th and 11th of July, 1783, the weather being calm and the sky unclouded, Saussure, stationed at the *Hospice* of the *Grimsel*, looking in the direction of Geneva, saw on the horizon some streaks of clouds from which lightning issued, but no thunder was heard. It was afterward ascertained that at the moment this occurred a storm broke over Geneva the most terrific that the people of that country ever witnessed.

On the 21st of July, 1813, Mr. LUKE HOWARD, observed at *Tottenham*, near *London*, in a clear sky, lightning, such as is called heat-lightning, appear toward the southeast. It was afterward ascertained that a violent storm at that moment raged in France, which extended from *Calais* to *Dunkirk*. This lightning, above fifty leagues distant, was visible in the atmosphere of London.

It must then be admitted as proved, that silent lightnings *may be* and *sometimes are* produced by the reflection in the atmosphere of lightning of which the thunder is too distant to be heard. But it does not therefore follow that such appearances *must be* and *always are* produced by that cause. On the contrary, heat-lightnings frequently present appearances, to explain which it would be almost impossible to admit the hypothesis of distant storms. Thus it frequently happens that when the whole visible firmament is unclouded, these lightnings will play for entire nights on every side of the horizon, and will extend even to the zenith. If distant storms were admitted to explain such phenomena, it would be necessary to suppose that portion of the atmosphere visible from a single place clear and serene, yet surrounded on every side by a ring of clouds, throughout which storms rage. The improbability of such an hypothesis is apparent.

M. Arago proposed for the decision of this question, the same expedient which he suggested a few years ago, in his essay on comets, to determine whether their tails were self-luminous, or derived their light from the sun. There are certain crystals endowed with optical properties, in virtue of which, objects viewed through them are seen under different appearances according as those objects are self-luminous or illuminated by light derived from other objects. He proposes that the silent lightnings shall be observed through such crystals, and the question whether they be actual lightnings, unattended by thunder, or only reflections of distant lightnings, be thus decided.

Thunder unaccompanied by lightning, is explained by M. Arago, by supposing two strata of clouds at different heights, of which the superior stratum is the seat of the thunder-storm, and of which the inferior stratum is sufficiently dense to be impervious to the light which precedes the thunder. Nevertheless, the density of the inferior cloud will not at all impede the transmission of sound through it, and the thunder will consequently be heard while the lightning is invisible.

The method of computing the distance of stormy clouds by observing the interval which elapses between the flash and the thunder, is based upon the assumption that the sound is produced *in the cloud*. It has been however maintained by some persons, that when the electric discharge takes place between a cloud and the earth, the lightning issues from the earth to the cloud. According to the hypothesis of a single electric fluid, this would always be the case when the cloud is negatively electrified. As a test of this, M. Arago proposes to observe the interval between the appearance of the lightning and the perception of the thunder under circumstances in which the distance of the cloud is known *by other means* within a given limit. If the distance obtained by computation from observing the interval between the light and the sound be manifestly less than the known minor limit of the distance of the cloud, it must then follow that the seat of the sound is *not the cloud*, but is some place in the atmosphere less distant, which would necessarily be the case if the lightning issued upward from the earth. This method of observation might be practised in the neighborhood of any lofty tower or steeple, or near a hill, or by means of a small balloon confined by a cord to a given height. If the cloud were observed to be considerably *above* any such objects and yet the computed distance of the seat of the sound considerably *below* them, the conclusion just stated would be justified.

From the observations which have been recorded of the time between the flash and the thunder, it appears that although in one instance this interval amounted to seventy-two seconds, it usually does not exceed forty-eight seconds. It follows, then, that the greatest distance from which the atmospheric explosions which produce thunder are heard at about *ten miles*. If the single recorded observation of an interval of seventy-two seconds can be relied on, it would follow that in that particular case thunder was heard at the distance of *fifteen miles*.

Evidence still more direct and convincing can be adduced that beyond the distance of eight or ten miles thunder is inaudible.

When the steeple of Lestwithiel in Cornwall was struck by lightning, on the 25th of January, 1757, and almost entirely destroyed, the thunder was terrific; yet Smeaton the engineer, who was then within thirty miles of the place, heard no thunder. Muschenbroeck states that thunder at the Hague is inaudible at Leyden and at Rotterdam, the distance of the former being ten and the latter twelve miles. There are also examples of violent storms breaking over Amsterdam which were inaudible at Leyden, the distance being about twenty miles.

To deduce right conclusions from these facts it will be necessary to consider the distances at which other sounds, generally much less intense than thunder, are heard. Cannon discharged at Florence are heard at Leghorn, a distance of fifty miles; at Leghorn, are heard at Porto Ferraio, the same distance. The cannonade at the siege, was audible at Leghorn, a distance of about ninety miles. It may be added that the great bell of St. Paul's cathedral in London, is said to be audible at Windsor, a distance of about twenty-four miles.

The conditions of the atmosphere, which affect the transmission of sound, are imperfectly understood, and it is therefore the more necessary to accumulate well-ascertained facts, to form a safe basis for general reasoning. It is generally believed that sounds are heard more distinctly and at greater distances in winter, especially in frost, than in summer. This popular impression has been corroborated in the narrative of those who have made voyages to the polar regions. Parry states that he frequently heard distinctly at the distance of a mile, men conversing in their ordinary voice. On the 11th of February, 1820, he heard a man singing to himself (and therefore probably ir ther a low tone), at more than a mile distant.

Durham observes that new-fallen snow impedes the transmission of sound, and that fogs also deaden its force. This latter effect, however, is not invariable. In a November fog, in 1812, Mr. Howard heard distinctly at five miles from London, the noise of the carriages rolling over the streets.

Humboldt has proved that sounds are audible at greater distances by night than by day; and from the circumstances under which his observations were made, it would appear that the silence of night could not be assumed as an explanation of this.

It seems to be established that an adverse wind is an impediment to the transmission of sound; but according to the observations of M. F. Delaroche, a favorable wind *does not assist it*.

Volney, at Pontchartrain, heard four or five claps of thunder. Looking carefully round him, he could see no clouds either in the heavens or near the earth. Now since thunder has never been heard at a greater distance than fifteen miles, and since an object to be invisible at that distance with a well-defined horizon must have an elevation less than about one hundred feet, it follows either that the thunder heard by Volney on that occasion was produced in the clear atmosphere, or that it proceeded from a cloud not more than thirty-three yards from the ground, at a distance of about fifteen miles from the observer.

It has been elsewhere stated that the explanation proposed and universally received as accounting for the phenomena, is a sudden displacement of the air, produced by the electrical discharges, in which lightning is evolved. Since all sound must proceed from an agitation of the air, and since lightning and electricity are identified, this explanation consists of little more than a statement of the facts. A more rigorous account, however, must be exacted from those who would propound an adequate theory of thunder.

Some have explained the origin of thunder, by supposing that the electric fluid, in passing with great velocity through the air, leaves behind it a vacuum; that the air rushing suddenly into this vacuum produces a detonation like that which takes place in the common experiment in which a vacuum being produced under a bladder extended tightly over the mouth of a receiver, the bladder is broken by the pressure of the external air. To make this explanation valid, it would be necessary to show *how* the vacuum is produced, or that it *is, in fact*, produced, otherwise the explanation is reduced to a mere conjecture.

It is also explained by supposing that the electric fluid in passing through the air, compresses successively the air lying before it, whence there results a displacement of those masses of air which are contiguous, and consequently a series of contractions and dilatations, which, extending to a distance, produce long-continued reverberations.

M. Pouillet rejects these hypotheses as insufficient to explain the phenomenon. He considers that if such were the cause of thunder, the passage of a cannon-ball through the air ought to produce a like effect. M. Pouillet maintains that when an electric discharge takes place between two bodies charged with opposite electricities, the fluid does not actually pass from the one body to the other, but that the effect is produced by a series of decompositions and recompositions of the natural electricities of the molecules of the intervening medium, precisely similar to that which takes place in a liquid solution in which the poles of the Voltaic arrangement are immersed. He argues that there must thence result vibrations more or less violent in the ponderable matter of that medium, which would be sufficient to explain the sound.

The rolling of thunder has by some been ascribed to the effect of *echo*. That echo has *in some cases* a share in the production of the phenomena cannot be doubted b[illegible] one who has ever witnessed an Alpine storm. A multitude of causes a[illegible] the loudness, the reverberation, and the continuity of the peals, are quite apparent. The question is whether echo is the only cause of the *rolling thunder*.

It has been shown that the duration of the thunder-roll amounts sometimes to forty-five seconds. Whether the echoes of any sound ever have such duration, can only be determined by observation. The example of the often-reiterated echo at a certain island on the lake of Killarney, is known to all travellers. Mr. Scoresby observed on a particular occasion its duration, and found it about thirty seconds. The original sound is usually produced by the discharge of a small piece of cannon.

It would seem that on the occasion of Mr. Scoresby's observations, a pistol was used. It is argued by M. Arago, that if a cannon had been used, the duration would have been much greater, and probably equal to the continuance of the longest roll of thunder.

During the experiments made to determine the velocity of sound in June, 1822, MM. Humboldt, Bouvard, Gay-Lussac, and Emile de Laplace, heard the echo of a cannon discharged near them during twenty-five seconds.

Mariners state that thunder heard at sea is marked by rolling as long continued as on land, although none of those causes which are generally supposed to produce echoes, such as walls, rocks, wood, hills, or mountains, are present. Unless the surface of the clouds reflects sounds, no means of producing an echo can exist under such circumstances. Although it might seem that the clouds would be as little capable of reflecting sound as the air itself, there appears to be some reason to judge otherwise. Muschenbröeck states, as the result of his own observations, that a cannon, which, being discharged when the heavens are unclouded, produced only a single report, had its sounds several times reverberated when discharged in the same place under a clouded sky. In the course of the experiments made in 1822, to determine the velocity of sound already referred to, the same observation was made.

In the posthumous works of Hooke, published in 1706, an explanation was proposed for the rolling of thunder, which was more recently reproduced with more full developments by Dr. Robinson in the *Encyclopædia Britannica*, and which seems more adequate, and open to fewer objections, than any other hypothesis yet suggested. The sound is supposed to be developed by the lightning in passing through the air, and consequently separate sounds are produced at every point through which the lightning passes. As the object of the hypothesis is to explain the *rolling* or *succession* of sounds, and not the sound itself, it is immaterial what the manner of producing the sound may be.

Let us first suppose that the lightning were to move in a circle, of which the observer is the centre. The velocity of the lightning is so extreme that, for the purposes of this explanation, it may be assumed to be at the same moment in every part of the circle. Explosions will, therefore, be produced simultaneously at every point in the circumference of the circle, and, as all these sounds have the same distance to traverse in coming to the observer, they will arrive at his ear at the same instant; the effect would, therefore, be a single sound, having a force due to the combined effects of all the sounds produced in the circumference of a circle. To apply this reasoning to the actual case of thunder, let it be supposed that two small clouds oppositely electrified are situated near each other, and at the same height in the zenith of the observer. The clouds may be considered as placed in the surface of a sphere, in the centre of which the observer stands. If the electric discharge takes place between the clouds, the thunder would be heard by the observer as a single clap, without any roll or reverberation.

Let us next suppose the lightning to move in any line which is not part of a circle or sphere, with the observer in the centre; let its course be a straight line, for example, such as A B, the observer being at O. From O, suppose a

Fig. 3.

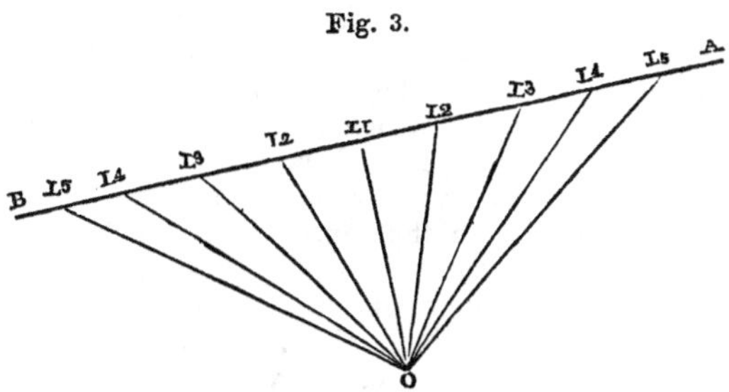

perpendicular, O L¹, drawn to A B, and let two lines, O L², the length of which shall exceed O L¹ by one hundred and ten feet, be inflected from O on

A B, one on each side of O L^1; let other two lines, O L^3, exceeding O L^2 by one hundred and ten feet, be also inflected on A B, and in the same manner let a series of lines, such as O L^2, O L^3, O L^4, be successively inflected on A B, each line exceeding that which precedes it by one hundred and ten feet. If we suppose sounds to be simultaneously produced at the points L^1, L^2, L^3, that which is produced at L^1 will be first heard by the observer. Since sound moves at the rate of eleven hundred feet per second, it will take the tenth of a second to move through one hundred and ten feet; therefore the two sounds emitted at L^2 will arrive together at the ear of the observer a tenth of a second after the sound at L^1 has been heard. In the same manner, the two sounds emitted at L^3 will arrive after another tenth of a second, and so on. Thus every ten sounds of the series, though simultaneously produced, would take a second in being heard, and would be recognised by the ear as a distinct, though rapid succession of ten sounds.

If it be admitted, then, that the electric fluid, in passing through the air with the great velocity it is proved to have by the experiments of Professor Wheatstone, produces sonorous vibrations of this kind in the air, the rolling of thunder would be a necessary consequence.

According to this manner of viewing the phenomena, the thunder would be loudest which proceeds from L^1, the nearest point to the observer, and would gradually be enfeebled for points more and more distant from L^1. Therefore the roll would always be loudest at the commencement, and would gradually diminish in force until it becomes inaudible. This is not in accordance with the actual phenomena.

But the preceding explanation proceeds on the supposition that the lightning moves continually in the same straight line. Let us see what the effects of a zigzag course would be, such as that represented by the line A, B. Taking

Fig. 4.

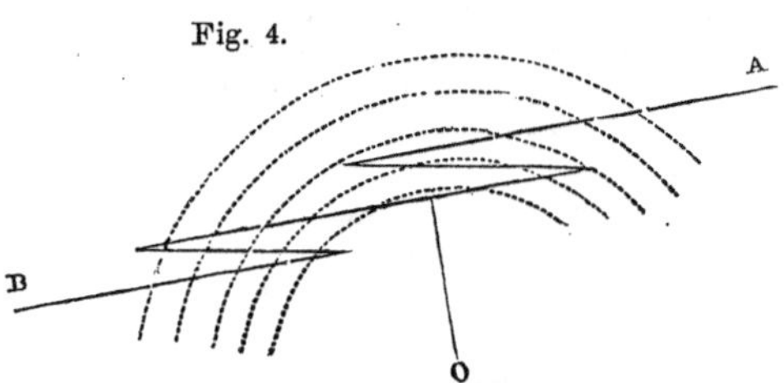

the place of the observer, O, as a common centre, let a series of circular arcs be drawn with radii increasing in magnitude each successive distance exceeding the last by one hundred and ten feet. These arcs will intersect the zigzag course of the lightning in several points more or less in number, according to the position of the directions of the lightning, and the magnitude of the radius of the circle. The first sound which will reach the observer will be that produced at the points where the least of the circles meets the lightning, and the succeeding sounds will correspond to those emitted at the point of intersection of the succeeding circles with the course of the lightning. It is easy to conceive, that the mutual position of the zigzag lightning and the observer may be such that the number of points of intersection of the circles with the lightning may alternately augment and diminish in a manner corresponding to any supposable variations in the intensity of the rolling of the thunder.

It is evident that, independently of the infinite varieties of sound capable of being explained by this hypothesis applied to zigzag lightnings, the changes are not less various for lightning which preserves a single course, the same flash, according to its direction with respect to the observer, being susceptible of an infinite variety of sonorous effects.

An objection to this fascinating hypothesis occurs to me, which appears to have escaped the attention of its advocates, and which, nevertheless, is entitled to consideration. I have supposed, for the sake of illustration, in the preceding developments that a succession of distinct sounds are emitted at points of a space the difference of whose distance from the observer is one hundred and ten feet, and therefore these sounds succeed each other at intervals of a tenth of a second. Any other difference of distance would equally serve the purposes of illustration, the interval between the successive detonations being determined by it according to the known velocity of sound. But it does not appear to me that there is anything in the physical effects to warrant the supposition of a series of separate sounds emitted at points of space more or less distant from each other. The electric fluid rushes through space, producing *the same effect at every point.* The analogy on which Dr. Robinson bases the explanation (to a file of soldiers, placed at certain distances asunder, who discharge their muskets at the same instant, but are, nevertheless, heard in succession) does not seem to be in accordance with the phenomena. The passage of the electric fluid through the air would be more aptly illustrated by a bow drawn over the string of a violin, or the current of air driven by the mouth through a wind instrument, or by a bellows through an organ-pipe. There would, according to such analogy, be one sustained sound, instead of a succession or series of distinct sounds. It is true that, in the gravest note on an organ, and even in those produced on certain wind instruments (the trombone, for example), and on the strings on the double base, the *vibrations* are distinguishable; but these vibrations do not seem to have any analogy to the series of sounds which form the rolling of thunder.

If this hypothesis, nevertheless, be admitted to explain the rolling of thunder, the *duration* of the rolling will become an important element in determining the minor limit of the space through which the lightning passes. Supposing that no line drawn from the observer to the course of the lightning is perpendicular to it, it will follow that one extremity of the course is nearer than any other point of it to the observer, and the other extremity more remote. The difference between the distance of these extreme points would be the length of the flash, if its direction was immediately toward or from the observer; and if it have any other direction, this difference will be *less than* the length of the flash. The duration of the roll of the thunder being the time sound would take to move over the difference between the greatest and the least distance, this difference may be computed, and thence a minor limit of the length of the flash may be obtained.

From the observations of De L'Isle, it appears that the rolling of thunder, observed by him in 1712, lasted in some instances forty-five seconds. Allowing eleven hundred feet for each second, this would amount to forty-nine thousand five hundred feet, or very near *ten miles.* The length of the flash must, therefore, have *exceeded* this distance.

I have, in these explanations, assumed that the loudest sound is that which proceeds from the *nearest* focus of sound to the observer. The loudness of a sound, however, depends partly on the temperature and hygrometric condition of the air at the place where the sound is developed. It might happen that these conditions, varying in different parts of the air where the sounds are produced, would render more remote sounds sometimes louder than nearer ones.

One of the circumstances in the natural exhibition of lightning, which seems not so satisfactorily explicable as most of the others, is the frequent repetition of the flashes from the same cloud, which often follow each other in rapid succession, contrary to what takes place in metallic conductors in which the electric equilibrium is restored in a single discharge, or nearly so. The most obvious way of explaining this is by supposing that the vapor composing thunder clouds being a much less perfect conductor than metal, and the cloud being often of extensive magnitude, possibly measuring miles in length or breadth, the equilibrium cannot be restored, except by successive discharges, according as the fluid dispersed over or through the cloud can collect at or near the striking point.

THE LATITUDES AND LONGITUDES.

Definition of the Equator and Poles.—Northern and Southern Hemispheres.—Latitude of a Place.—Parallel of Latitude.—Meridian of a Place.—Longitude of a Place.—Standard Meridian.—Methods of determining Latitude and Longitude various.—To find the Latitude.—Methods applicable in Observatories.—At Sea.—Hadley's Sextant.—To determine the Longitude.—How to find the Time of Day at Land.—At Sea.—Use of Chronometers.—Lunar Method of finding the Longitude.—Apparatus provided at Greenwich for giving the exact Time to Ships leaving the Port of London.—Method of determining Longitude by Moon-Culminating Stars.

THE LATITUDES AND LONGITUDES.

Before it is possible to acquire a distinct knowledge of the position or distances of any bodies in the universe outside the surface of the earth, it is first indispensable that we, who have to make these calculations, should distinctly ascertain our own position in reference to the bodies we observe. But as our position is subject to continual change, as well by reason of the diurnal rotation of the earth upon its axis, on the surface of which we are carried round, as the annual motion of the globe in its orbit round the sun, we are obliged as a necessary preliminary to analyze with accuracy all the circumstances of these motions. But even before we are in a condition to accomplish this, there is another preliminary step not less indispensable, which is to ascertain our own position on the surface of the globe we inhabit.

This is not so easy a matter as at the first view it might seem to be. The earth we dwell on is a globe of stupendous magnitude. The range of our vision around any situation which we may occupy upon the surface of this globe is small. In the most unobstructed situation we can obtain—that which is presented us at sea, when out of sight of land, on the clearest day—our observation is circumscribed by a radius of a few miles. The portion of the surface which we see at one and the same time, forms in reality so small a patch of the globe of the earth, that it is only by indirect reasoning that we can recognise upon it any character save that of a flat plane. How, then, are we to know in what part of the terrestrial globe that small patch of surface is situated?

To answer this question, it is evidently necessary first to settle some fixed points or lines to which we may refer various places, and by which we may express their positions. The points which have been usually selected for this purpose are the *poles* and the *equator*. The poles are those points on the surface of the earth where the axis on which it performs its diurnal rotation terminates, and they are distinguished as is well known by the names of the *north* and *south* poles.

If we imagine a circle surrounding the surface of the globe in such a manner as to divide it into two hemispheres, having in the midst of one the north pole, and in the midst of the other the south pole, such a circle is called the *equator*, and is so called from equally dividing the globe. Every point in this circle will be at the same distance from the poles, and if we imagine the globe to be cut by a plane through the poles, that plane will be at right angles to this circle, and the section it forms will be what is called a terrestrial meridian. The arc of this meridian between either pole and the equator will be one quarter of its entire circumference, and will therefore be 90°. The equator is, therefore, everywhere 90° from each of the poles.

The hemispheres into which the equator divides the earth are called the *northern* and *southern hemispheres*. That which includes the north pole, being the northern, and that which includes the south pole, the southern.

The position of a place in either hemisphere with reference to the equator is expressed by stating the number of degrees of a terrestrial meridian included between the place and the equator. This is called the *latitude* of the place; which is the distance of the place from the equator expressed in degrees of the meridian. Thus, if a place be midway between the pole and the equator, its latitude is 45°. If it be distant from the equator by two thirds of the entire distance from the equator to the pole, its latitude will be 60° and so on.

The latitude is said to be northern and southern, according as the place is in the northern or southern hemisphere.

But it is evident that the latitude alone will be insufficient for the determination of the position of a place. If we state that a certain place is 45° north of the equator, it will be impossible to ascertain certainly the place in question, inasmuch as there is a circle of points on the earth, all of which are 45° north of the equator. If we suppose a line drawn on the surface of the northern hemisphere parallel to the equator, at the distance from the equator of 45°, every point of such line or circle will be equally characterized by the latitude of 45° north.

Such a circle is called a *parallel of latitude*, and it is therefore apparent that wherever such a parallel may be drawn upon the earth, all the places upon it will have the same latitude.

The latitude is, then, insufficient to determine the position of any place. How, then, it may be asked, can the exact position of any place be expressed?

Let us suppose that a meridian is arbitrarily selected, passing through some particular place, such as the Capitol at Washington. We may conceive another meridian drawn upon the earth east or west of that, so that the two meridians shall include between them an arc of the equator, consisting of a definite number of degrees; say, for example, that it shall consist of 20°; then such a meridian will be defined by stating that it is 20° east or west of the *meridian of Washington*. All that can be settled by such a statement is the position of the meridian in which the place lies with reference to the arbitrarily chosen meridian of Washington. This relative position of the two meridians is called the *longitude of the place*. As the meridian from which the longitude is measured is altogether arbitrary, there being no physical or geographical reason why one meridian should be chosen rather than another, each nation has naturally selected as the zero of longitude the meridian of some noted place in its precincts. In England, the Royal Observatory at Greenwich has been the place selected, and accordingly in all English works on geography, political and physical, longitudes are invariably expressed in reference to the meridian of Greenwich. It will, therefore, be most convenient for us here chiefly to refer to that meridian.

When these explanations are clearly understood, we shall be in a condition, distinctly and definitely, to express the position of a place upon the surface of the globe of the earth. If we state its latitude and its longitude, we can fix at once, and unequivocally, the position of a place. Thus, let us suppose that its latitude is 50° north, its longitude 30° east of Greenwich; its position will be found by imagining a line parallel to the equator drawn upon the northern hemisphere at a distance of 50° from the equator; then, supposing a meridian drawn through Greenwich, intersecting this parallel, and another drawn so as to cross the equator at a point 30° east of the former; the place in question will be upon the line parallel to the equator first drawn, inasmuch as it will be 50° north of the equator, and it will be also in the meridian last drawn, inasmuch as it will be 30° east of Greenwich. Since, then, it will be at the same time in both these lines, it will necessarily be at the point where they cross each other at the east of the standard meridian of Greenwich.

Thus, then, we have succeeded at least in establishing standards of position and a nomenclature by which the exact position of a place on the surface of the globe can be expressed. But we have still another much more important and difficult question to settle. How are we to discover in what part of the globe any place is which we may occupy at a given time; in other words, how are we to discover its latitude and its longitude? These are questions, especially the latter, attended with some difficulty, and which have been solved by different methods, applicable in different cases, according to the circumstances under which the position of the place is sought, and the purpose for which such position is to be determined.

At any place on land where the geographical position is once determined, it may be recorded, so as to be permanently known for the future without a repetition of the process for determining it; but it is otherwise at sea. On the trackless surface of the deep all marks of events and operations are immediately obliterated, and a new investigation must be instituted in every case when the position of any point is to be determined. The mariner must, therefore, be supplied not only with the means of determining the position of his ship at all times, but with means the application of which is practicable under the peculiar circumstances in which he is placed. The instruments he uses must not only be portable, but must be such as may admit of being manipulated, subject to the disturbances and the vicissitudes of the sea. The object of his observations must be such as are almost always in his view. It is evident, then, that the problem, as applicable on land, is wholly different in its circumstances and conditions from that which is applied on the deep. But even on land the problem presents itself under various circumstances and conditions. In the fixed observatory, where the philosopher is supplied with instruments of the greatest magnitude, of the most refined accuracy, and the most absolute stability, methods have been used which are susceptible of the last conceivable degree of accuracy, and accordingly the position of those points on the globe where such observatories have been erected, are usually determined with the greatest degree of precision. Such points on the globe serve, therefore, as a sort of geographical landmarks, relative to which the position of all surrounding places may be determined.

The circumstances under which the scientific traveller and geographer makes his observations, with a view to the general determination of the points of a country, are less favorable to accuracy than those available to the astronomer, but still are more susceptible of precision than those which can be placed at the disposal of the mariner. It is, however, the business and the duty of those who devote their lives to the advancement of the sciences, to supply to each class of observers those instruments and methods of inquiry which are capable, respectively of giving results which, in the circumstances of the case, have the great-est attainable accuracy.

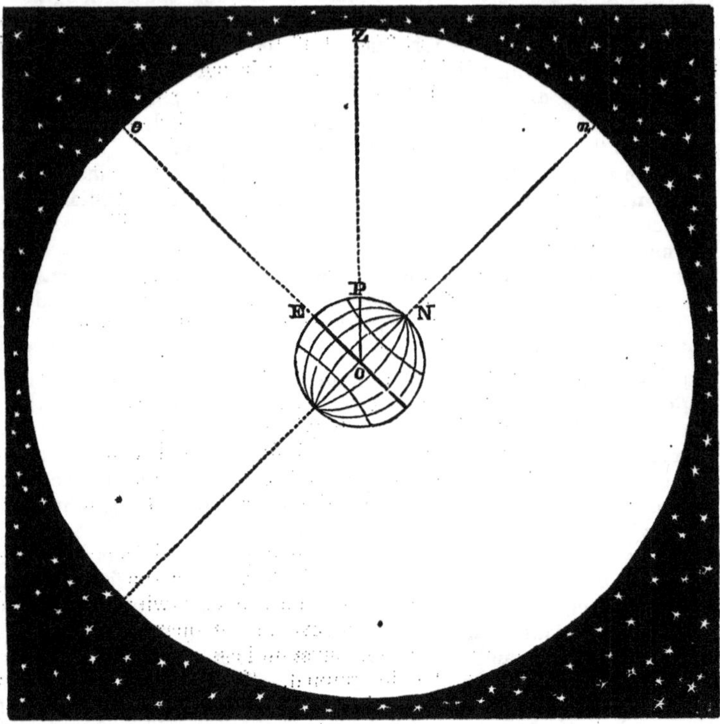

TO FIND THE LATITUDE.

Let us suppose the globe of the earth to be represented at O, and let N be its north pole, and E its equator; let P be a place upon it, whose latitude, that is, whose distance from the equator is to be determined. Let *n* Z *e* represent the firmament surrounding the globe at an indefinite distance. The point *n*, immediately over the north pole, and which is in fact, the continuation of the line O N will be the place of the north pole in the heavens, very near to which is a star, called the Polar star. The point *e*, in the continuation of the line O E, will be that which is directly over the equator and will be that point in the heavens, representing the position of the equator and the point Z, in the continuation of the line O P, the point of the heavens which is directly over the observer at the place P, will be that which is called his zenith. This point is that to which a plumb line would direct itself.

Now the points *n*, Z, and *e*, are the points in the firmament which correspond with the points N, P, and E, upon the earth, and it is evident that whatever arcs of the terrestrial meridian N P E are included between these points, similar arcs of the celestial meridian must be included between the points *n* Z *e*. If, then, P E were 40°, Z *e* must also be 40°, just as *n e* is 90°, while N E is also 90°.

In short, the zenith of any place in the heavens is the point in the firmament which corresponds with the position of the place on the globe, and the distance of the zenith in the heavens of one place, from the zenith of another must necessarily be the same in degrees as the distance between two places on earth. Thus *n* is the zenith of P; *e* is the zenith of E; *n* is the same number of degrees from *e* as P is from E. This being clearly understood, it is evident that if we can, by any means ascertain by observations, the distance from Z to *n*, we can infer at once the distance from P to N, and hence, can discover the distance from P to E, or the latitude of the place.

It is apparent, then, if we can observe the distance of the zenith of any place from the celestial pole, that will give us the distance in degrees of the place itself from the terrestrial pole, and by subtracting that from 90°, we shall obtain the distance of the place itself from the equator, or what is the same, its latitude. As an example of this, let us suppose that in measuring the distance from Z to *n* we find it to be 50°; we infer, therefore, that since the distance of the zenith from the pole is 50°, the distance of the place from the terrestrial pole is also 50°. But since the terrestrial pole is 90° from the equator, it follows that the distance of the place from the equator must be 40°, and it is north or south, according as the zenith of the place is in the northern or southern hemisphere of the firmament.

Thus, then, it appears that the latitude of a place can always be found, provided we can measure the distance of its zenith from the celestial pole; and this, of course, can always be done by the use of proper instruments, provided that the zenith and the pole can be distinctly seen. Now the direction of the zenith can always be determined by the plumb line; but although the pole star is very near the pole, it is not exactly at it; there is, in fact, no star exactly at the pole, and there being no visible object there, it is impossible to measure directly its distance from the zenith. This difficulty is eluded by measuring the distance of the zenith from some star, or other celestial object, whose distance from the pole happens to be known: for example, suppose that there were a star directly between the zenith and pole, whose distance from the pole was known to be 10°. Then if we find by observing the distance of the zenith from this star was 40°, we should immediately infer the distance of the zenith from the pole to be 50°.

It is in fact, then, by this device that the latitude is always ascertained. By various observations made by astronomers, the positions of most of the stars and other celestial objects, with respect to the poles, are known and recorded; and when we desire to determine the latitude of any place, we measure the distance of the zenith of that place from some celestial object whose position with respect to the pole is known, and thence infer the position of the place with respect to the terrestrial pole; and from that deduce at once the latitude.

But our purpose would be equally served if we were supplied with the position of any visible object with reference to the celestial equator. Thus, if we know the distance of the centre of the sun from the celestial equator, we shall readily be able to find the latitude; for it would only be necessary when the sun is in, or very near the meridian, that is, at or near noon, to measure the distance of the zenith of the place from the centre of the sun. This would be done by measuring the distance of the zenith, first from the upper, and then from the lower limb of the sun. The distance from the centre would be the mean between these.

Let us suppose, for example, that the sun being between the zenith of the equator, we find that the distance from the zenith to the centre of the sun is 20°, and that we also ascertain from the table of the position of the sun, that the distance of the centre of the sun at that time from the equator, is also 20°, we should infer at once that the distance of the zenith from the equator must be 40°, and that such, therefore, must be the latitude of the place.

This method of ascertaining the latitude is, perhaps, the most easily practicable. The observations may be performed daily, at noon, when the sun is visible: and in all almanacs, the distance of the centre of the sun from the equator, which is called the sun's declination, is registered. The instrument by which the observations are executed on land are, usually, a quadrant furnished with a telescope moving upon its centre. One radius of the quadrant is placed in the direction of the plumb line, and therefore points to the zenith. The telescope moves round the centre until it is directed to the object whose distance from the zenith is to be observed. The angle between the telescope and the vertical radius of the quadrant will then be the same as the distance of the object from the zenith.

In astronomical observatories methods of observation have been applied susceptible of much greater accuracy. Stars upon the meridian can thereby be used with great advantage. The distance of these stars from the pole are accurately known, and the astronomer selects for his observation those conspicuous stars which pass very near to his zenith. He observes the arc of the celestial meridian between his zenith and these stars. And from the magnitude of the arc and the distance of the star of the celestial pole, he discovers the distance of the zenith from the pole and thence the latitude.

The principal source of accuracy in this method is, that the distance between the zenith and the star being very small, is capable of more exact measurement, for reasons connected with the structure of the astronomical instrument, than could be attained in the measurement of greater angles.

In observations made at sea, it is not practicable, however, to use the plumb line, and indeed, even for the purposes of geographers it is not always convenient. An admirable instrument has been invented equally applicable to observations by land or by water, called Hadley's sextant, by means of which the observations can be made with reference to the horizon, independent of the zenith, and therefore independent of the plumb line.

It is not our purpose here to enter into a description of the principles and structure of this celebrated and most useful instrument. It will be sufficient for the present purpose to state that it is capable of being applied to the measurement of the angular distances between any two visible objects with a very great degree of precision, and that it may be used with facility, even when the position of the observer is subject to all the unsteadiness incidental to the condition of the mariner.

When this instrument is used, instead of observing the distance of any object from the zenith, we observe its distance from the horizon, which will answer the same purpose, inasmuch as that whenever the distance of an object from the horizon is known, its distance from the zenith can be found, since the distance from the zenith to the horizon being 90°, if we subtract the distance of the object from that, the remainder will be the distance of the object from the zenith.

At sea we have generally, indeed almost always, a well-defined horizon. If the mariner desires to measure the altitude of an object, he has only to measure the distance of the object from the horizon in a direction perpendicular to it, and this he is enabled to do with a little practice, with admirable facility and precision, with Hadley's sextant.

Let us see, then, how the mariner is thus enabled daily to determine the latitude of his ship.

As noon approaches, the sky being sufficiently clear to render the disk of the sun visible, he applies the instrument and measures the altitude of the lower and upper limbs of the sun from the verge of the horizon. The mean of these will be the altitude of the sun's centre. If this altitude be taken from 90°, the remainder will be the distance of the sun's centre from the zenith. He finds in his almanac the distance of the centre of the sun on that day from the equator, and hence he at once, as already explained, obtains the distance of his zenith from the equator; that is, the latitude of the ship.

There are several minute circumstances observed in the practice of this problem, which do not affect its general spirit, and the introduction of which here would be unsuitable to the object of these discourses; we therefore omit them.

Thus we see that, whether by sea or by land—whether in the observatory of the astronomer, traversing the sands of the desert, or the forests of America, or voyaging over the trackless and unimpressible surface of the ocean—we are in every case by science supplied with suitable and practicable means by which we can ascertain the distance of the place where we are, north or south, east or west on the globe.

TO DETERMINE THE LONGITUDE.

In expressing and determining the latitude of a place, we have fixed points and lines on the firmament to refer to—such as the celestial pole and equator; and to find it, nothing more is necessary than to ascertain the position of the zenith of the place with reference to these. But with respect to the longitude, the case is very different; it is impossible even to express the longitude without involving a reference to two places at least—that of which we wish to determine the longitude, and that which is selected as the starting point from which all longitudes are to be measured. If we could observe in the firmament the two points which at the same time form the zeniths of the two places, then the difference of their longitudes could be found by noting the times at which these two points would cross the meridian of the place whose longitude is to be determined.

To comprehend fully the spirit of the celebrated problem of finding the longitude, we must imagine the globe of the earth turning on its axis, having around it the starry firmament. Let us suppose A B to be the northern hemisphere of the globe, *p* being the pole, and let F E represent the firmament. Let P be a place whose zenith is the point on the firmament marked by Z. If we suppose the globe to turn upon its axis in the direction of Q P N, P will, by its rotation, be carried to the right of Z, and the same point Z will become successively the zenith of the points R Q; and, in fact, every point in the circumference of the earth will successively come under the point Z, which will be, therefore, in regular succession, their zenith points. In twenty-four hours, or, more accurately, in twenty-three hours and fifty-six minutes, the globe will make its complete revolution; therefore three hundred and sixty degrees of the earth will successively pass under the same point of the firmament.

By knowing exactly the time of rotation of the earth, and having ascertained that its diurnal motion is uniform, we can ascertain by simple arithmetic what extent of its surface will pass, in a given time, under any point of the firmament. Thus if we say in round numbers that the whole circumference corresponds to twenty-four hours, it will follow that fifteen degrees will move under the point Z each hour, or one degree in four minutes.

If we suppose Z to represent the place of the sun, then it will be noon, or twelve o'clock, at the place which is immediately under Z; that is, at P. If R be fifteen degrees west of P, then it will arrive under Z one hour after P; consequently, when it is noon at P it is eleven o'clock at a place fifteen degrees to the west of P; and, for the same reason, it is ten o'clock at a place thirty degrees to the west of P, and so on.

Again: if O be a place fifteen degrees to the east of P, O must have been under Z an hour before P reached it. It will be noon, therefore, at O, an hour before it is noon at P; therefore, when it is noon at P it is one o'clock at O. In the same manner, and for like reasons, if N be a place thirty degrees east of P, N will pass under Z two hours before P; and therefore when P passes under Z it will be two o'clock at N.

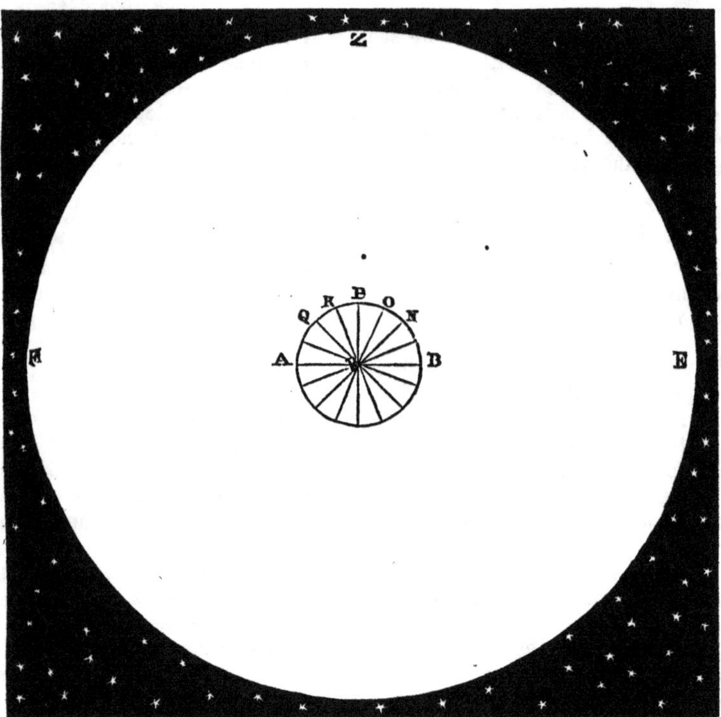

It will be apparent from these explanations, that, in general, the hour of the day at different places upon the earth, at the same time, will depend upon their relative position east or west of each other. If one place be east of another, the hour at that place will be later with respect to noon than the hour at the other; and the extent to which it is later will depend on the distance which one place is east of the other. In calculating this difference of time from the difference of position east or west, we may take fifteen degrees to correspond with an hour, as already explained.

But this distance of one place east or west of another, expressed in degrees, is, in fact, the difference of their longitudes; and if one of the two places in question be that from which the longitudes are measured, the determination of the longitude of a place would resolve itself into the discovery of the hour of the day in the place whose longitude we want to find, and also at the place from which the longitudes are measured.

Thus, for example, let us suppose that we ascertain the hour of the day in New York, and find that it is 2 o'clock in the afternoon, and that we have a means by which we can discover, at the same time, what the hour of the day is at Greenwich, and that by these means we know that it is 56 minutes past 6 o'clock. We know, then, that the time is 4 hours 56 minutes earlier at New York than at Greenwich, and consequently we infer that New York must be west of Greenwich by a longitude which corresponds to 4 hours 56 minutes. Now 4 hours correspond to 60°, and 56 minutes correspond to 14° ; therefore it follows, that the longitude of New York must be 74° west of Greenwich. We can, then, always discover the longitude of any place, provided we can ascertain, at any moment, the hour of the day at the place in question, and know, at the same time, what the hour of the day is in that place from which the longitude is measured.*

There are simple methods of observation and calculation by which the hour of the day in the place where we are can be determined, with more or less accuracy, according to the circumstances of our position. If we are on land, and supplied with a proper transit instrument, we can, by its means, observe the moment at which the centre of the sun's disk passes the meridian. Thus, as the moment of noon arrives, by observing it, we can set a good clock, which will inform us of every other hour of the day. But even in the absence of a clock we can determine the hour of the day at any moment at which the sun is visible, by observing its altitude, having previously ascertained the latitude of the place at which we are.

If we are at sea, where we cannot command a transit instrument, nor use it if we could, the latitude of the place of the ship is first determined, and then the hour is found by observing the altitude of the sun at any convenient time in the afternoon or forenoon. The hour being once found, the time can be kept by a chronometer for any number of hours afterward. Thus it appears, under all circumstances, whether by sea or by land, there is no practical difficulty in determining what o'clock it is where we are. This at once reduces the problem of the longitude to the simple discovery of the hour of the day, at any given time, at the place from which the longitudes are reckoned.

The first and most obvious method of accomplishing this which would occur to the mind, would be to carry a good chronometer from the place from which the longitude is reckoned. Supposing this chronometer subject to no error, it will continue to inform you of the hour of the day at that place. Thus, suppose that on leaving London the mariner takes with him a chronometer set according to the time at Greenwich, and with it makes his voyage to New York; the chronometer will continue to inform him what the time is from hour to hour at Greenwich. When he arrives at New York, he will find that when the chronometer points to 12 o'clock, or noon, it will be early in the morning; and if he ascertains the hour exactly, he will find that it will be 4 minutes after 7 o'clock. He will therefore know that the time at New York is 4 hours 56 minutes earlier than at Greenwich, and, consequently, that New York must be 74° west of Greenwich. It is for these reasons that the perfection of chronometers has always been considered so essential to the progress of navigation. Every ship that makes a long voyage ought to be supplied with one, at least, of these instruments; but as they are liable to accident, and as even the best of them cannot be rendered perfect, it is usual with ships that are well provided for long voyages to carry more than one chronometer.

Although the art of constructing time-keepers has been brought to a high degree of perfection by the skill of modern artisans, these instruments are even yet, and probably will ever continue to be, too imperfect to be implicitly and exclu-

* There are several corrections to be attended to in the practical working of the methods of determining latitude and longitude which I have purposely omitted, as they do not affect the spirit of the method, which is all I would here convey.

sively relied upon. If we only required their indications for short spaces of time, such as a few days, or even weeks, we might perhaps place a secure reliance upon them; especially if the voyager were provided with more than one instrument of this kind. But in voyages or journeys which occupy months, we cannot rely on the indications of these instruments, even when most liberally provided and most perfectly constructed.

In the absence, then, of a chronometer, how, it will be asked, can the longitude of a place be ascertained at all. The first method that will occur to the mind, will be that of some conspicuous signal which can be seen at the same time at the two places, whose difference of longitude is to be determined. For this we require two observers; but it is perhaps the method of all others, susceptible of the greatest accuracy. Let us suppose that on some elevated position between two distant places, such as New York and Boston, a sudden and conspicuous light is produced, such as the celebrated Drummond light, which might be exhibited on the top of a high mountain so as to be visible a great distance. Let this signal be exhibited at any required moment, so as to render it suddenly visible at the two places. Let the observers at these places note precisely the hour of the day or night at which the light is seen. By comparing afterward, these times, their difference will at once give us the difference of the longitude at the two places.

But this method is evidently applicable only on a limited scale, and under peculiar circumstances; it is altogether unavailable to the mariner. Now the astronomer supplies him with a chronometer of unerring precision; a chronometer which can never go down, nor fall into disrepair; a chronometer which is exempt from the accidents of the deep; which is undisturbed by the agitation of the vessel; which will at all times be present and available to him wherever he may wander over the trackless and unexplored regions of the ocean. Such a chronometer has been found; made by an Artisan who cannot err, and into whose works imperfection can never enter. Such a chronometer is supplied by the firmament itself. The unwearied labors of modern astronomers have converted the face of the heavens into a clock, and have taught the mariner to read its complicated but infallible indications. We may regard for this purpose the firmament as the dial-plate of a chronometer on an immense scale. The constellations and the fixed stars upon it, which for countless ages are subject to no change in position, serve as the hour and minute-marks. The sun, the moon, the planets, and the satellites, which move continually over the surface of this splendid piece of mechanism, play the parts of the hands of the clock. The positions of these bodies from day to day and from hour to hour, and every change of their positions, are accurately foreknown and exactly registered in a book published some two or three years in advance, called the "Nautical Almanac," and circulated for the benefit of mariners. In this work, the navigator is told what the hour is or will be at Greenwich for every variety of position which the sun, moon, and planets, shall have from time to time upon the heavens. But of all objects in the heavens, that which is best suited for this species of observation is the moon, and hence this method of determining the longitude at sea has been distinguished by the appellation of the *lunar method.* By the use of Hadley's sextant, which we have already alluded to, it is easy, whenever the heavens are clear, to observe the angular distance of the moon either from the sun or from the most conspicuous stars or planets. The motion of the moon in the firmament is so rapid that its change of position is perceptible, even by such observations as can be made on board a ship from hour to hour.

How, then, it may be asked, can such observations be made subservient to the discovery of the longitude of a ship? Nothing can be more simple. The navigator requires only to know what is the hour at Greenwich at the time he makes his observation. This he discovers in the following manner: He observes with the sextant the distance of the moon from the sun, or from some of the most conspicuous stars; he then, after certain preliminary calculations not necessary to detail here, examines in the Nautical Almanac, where he learns what the hour is at Greenwich, when it has these particular distances from the sun or the stars. Knowing this, and knowing the hour where he is, the difference of the longitude of a ship and the observatory at Greenwich is known to him.

Although the moon be of all the celestial objects the best adapted for this observation, it is not the only one which has been resorted to. It may be in a position so near the sun that it cannot be conveniently observed; in its absence, the navigator may resort to planets which may happen to be visible. These may be used in the same manner and according to the same principles as the moon, but they do not afford a result susceptible of the same accuracy, inasmuch as their motions being slower, he cannot be so certain of their exact positions.

The advantage which the lunar method of determining the longitude has for the purpose of the mariner is, that it is always available, when the sky is unclouded. There are, however, other methods which are applicable occasionally, both by sea and by land, which ought not to be omitted here; among these the most frequent, and consequently the most generally available, is the eclipses of Jupiter's satellites. Whenever that planet is sufficiently removed from the sun to be visible after night-fall, his moons may be seen with an ordinary telescope; indeed, they were discovered at so early a period in the progressive improvement of the telescope, that they must have been first observed with a very inferior instrument of that kind. The periodic time of the first of these satellites, or that which is nearest to Jupiter, being only about 42 hours, and its position and motion being such that it cannot pass behind Jupiter without going through his shadow, its eclipse must regularly recur every 42 hours. The times of the eclipses at Greenwich are registered in the Nautical Almanac, and if they are observed at a distant place, the time at which they occur may be compared with the time at which they would be seen at Greenwich, and the longitude of the place consequently known. In fact these eclipses may be regarded as signals which can be seen at the same time from the two places; the only difference between them and common signals being that their occurrence can be certainly and accurately predicted. It is proper however to observe, that although this method is eminently useful to the geographical traveller, it can scarcely be said to be available in navigation.

There are other celestial phenomena of occasional occurrence which may also be used for determination of longitudes. Such are solar eclipses, but more especially the occultation of stars by the dark edge of the moon. This latter phenomena is one which admits of very great precision.

In connexion, with the subject of this discourse, it may not be uninteresting or unprofitable to explain the expedient by which the British government enable all navigators leaving the Thames to take with them the precise Greenwich time, which, as we have shown, is necessary for the determination of the longitude of the ship in the absence of the opportunity or ability of practising the lunar method. For a great number of years, the establishment of an easy and certain method of accomplishing this was regarded as an object of great national importance by the English public. At length the object was accomplished by the expedient now in use, and which we are about to explain.

The Royal Observatory of England is built on the summit of an elevated ridge that overhangs the town of Greenwich, on the right bank of the Thames, and forms a conspicuous object from the river. The towers of the observatory are at all times visible from ships sailing down the river. It was, therefore, decided that a signal should be given at the instant of one o'clock in the afternoon of each day; by observing which, navigators within view of the observatory could correct their chronometers. The signal adopted for this purpose was the sudden fall of a large black ball, placed upon a pole raised from the top of one of the towers of the observatory.

Before elevating the ball, at five minutes before one o'clock, a signal is made of the intention to do so by raising it half-mast high. Observers are then instructed to prepare their chronometers; and as the descent of the ball occupies several seconds, they should confine their attention to observing the moment when the ball leaves the top, as it is that alone which indicates the hour.

The use of this signal is not merely confined to the indication of the mean time at Greenwich for navigators going down the river. By observing the drop of the ball, repeated day after day, mariners who are in the river will be enabled to ascertain the daily rate of their chronometers. Thus, if a clock were found to show the time of 3 min. 5 sec. after 1 o'clock at the moment of dropping the ball one day, it will appear that the clock is 3 min. 5 sec. faster than the mean Greenwich solar time. On the following day, if you again observe the descent of the ball, and find that the clock shows 3 min. 7 sec. after 1 o'clock, you find that it gains 2 seconds per day. Thus you are enabled, not only to ascertain the actual error of the chronometer, but also predict the manner in which that error will be augmented or diminished for the future.

In noticing the different methods which have been proposed for determining the longitude, I ought not to omit one which has been recently resorted to with considerable advantage, and which is called the method of determining the longitude by *moon-culminating stars*. In the practice of this method a star is chosen which culminates or passes the meridian nearly at the same time with the moon, and which differs so little in declination with the moon, that it may be seen at the same time in the field of view of the telescope. The transit of the star and that of the moon's limb, is observed at both stations, and the difference of the time at the two stations noted. This difference being dependant on the moon's change of position on the firmament, in passing from the meridian of one station to the meridian of the other, will enable the observers to determine the time which the centre of the moon takes to pass from the one meridian to the other, which will give the difference of the longitudes.

The spirit of this method is derived from the great accuracy of the knowledge we have acquired of the moon's motions, and the precision with which we can observe its transits over the meridians. In the practice of this method, it is indispensable that the moon and star should differ so little in declination that the position of the telescope will not require to be changed to observe their respective transits. Although the method has been called that of moon-culminating stars, the only reason why the moon and star should be required to pass the meridian nearly together is, that the same errors may, as far as possible, affect both transits, and if so no effect would be produced on the ultimate result.

THEORY OF COLORS.

Refraction of a Ray of Light.—At plane Surfaces.—By a Prism.—The Prismatic Spectrum.—The Decomposition of Light.—Newton's Discoveries.—Colors of the Spectrum.—Brewster's Discovery of three Colors.—How three Colors can produce the Spectrum.—Colors of natural Bodies.—How they are produced.

THEORY OF COLORS.

When a ray of light meets the surface of a transparent medium, such as water or glass, in a line perpendicular to that surface, it will pass through without changing its course; but, if it meet the surface at any oblique angle, it will be bent into another direction, which will depend on the direction of the incident ray, and the relative densities of the media, between which the ray passes. Generally, when it passes from a less dense into a more dense medium, it is bent toward the perpendicular drawn to the surface of the medium at the point of incidence of the ray. In this deflection it does not leave the plane passing through the incident ray, and that perpendicular.

Fig. 1.

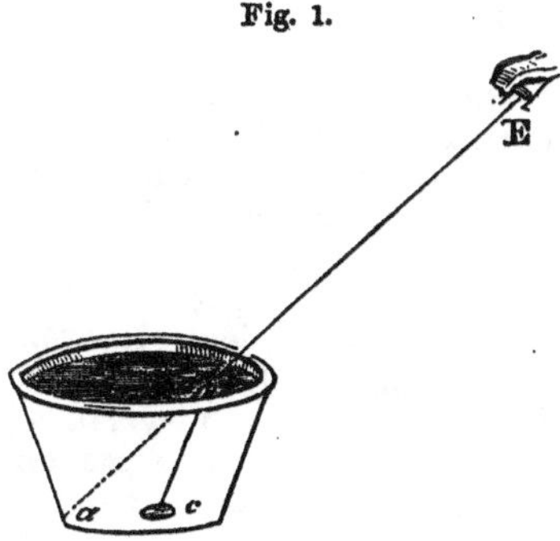

To render this more clear, let *c*, fig. 1, be any visible object placed on the bottom of a vessel of water. Let *c n* be a ray of light passing from that object to the surface of the water, that ray after leaving the surface of the water and passing into the air will not continue in the direction *c n*, but will take another direction, *n* E, so that an eye placed at E would see the object in the direction E *n*.

This deflection which a ray of light suffers in passing from one transparent medium into another, having a different density, is called refraction.

REFRACTION AT PLANE SURFACES.

Let S S′, fig. 2, represent the surface which separates two transparent media, P O being less dense than P O′. Let A P be a ray of light falling at P, and let O O′ be perpendicular to S S′. After passing into the denser medium the ray will follow the course P A′, making with the perpendicular P O, a less angle than A P O.

Fig. 2.

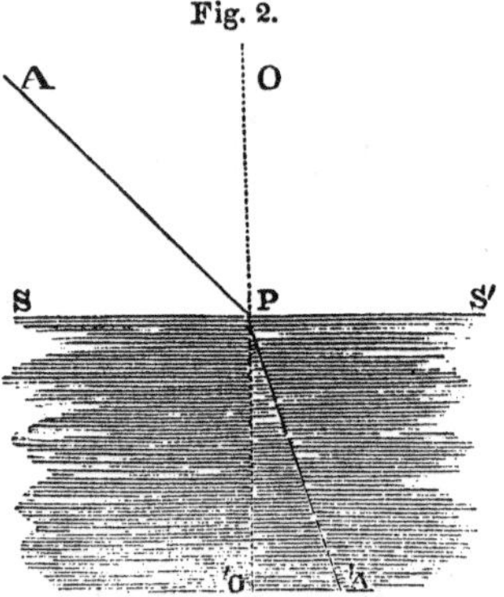

If, on the other hand, the ray passed from A′ to P, it would follow the course P A in the less dense medium. This law of refraction is usually expressed thus: when light passes from a rare into a dense medium, as from air to water, or from water to glass, it is always deflected *toward* the perpendicular to the reflecting surface, and when it passes from a denser medium into a rarer, as from glass to water, or from water to air, it is bent *from* the perpendicular.

The extent of this deflection has been determined by a general law, which, expressed in the language of geometry, is, that the sine of the angle of incidence bears to the sine of the angle of refraction, a fixed ratio when the media are given.

From this it follows that the deflection of light by refraction will always be increased with the obliquity of the incident rays.

It is also found that the degree of refraction will be greater the greater the difference of the density of the media is. Thus the refraction is greater when a ray passes from air into glass than when it passes from air into water; it is, also, greater when it passes from glass into air than from glass into water.

In his celebrated optical investigations, Newton found that the solar beam was composed of different kinds of light, which, besides differing in color, also differ in refrangibility, that is to say, if they fall at the same angle on any reflecting surface, they will not pass in the same direction through it, but will follow different directions, according to their different susceptibilities of being refracted.

The kind of experiment by which this remarkable fact was ascertained is as follows:—

Suppose a beam of light proceeding from the sun to enter a hole in a window-shutter and to fall obliquely on the surface of a triangular piece of glass, called a prism, at D. The parts of that ray in passing through the prism will diverge from each other, and falling upon the second surface of the prism, at F, will issue from it still more divergent. If the prism had not been interposed, a circle of light would be formed upon a white screen at E N, which would correspond with the magnitude of the opening in the window-shutter. But when the light is made to pass through the prism an oblong spectrum will be formed on the screen, the breadth of which will correspond with E N, but which will have considerable length. This spectrum will exhibit a series of colors, the lowest of which will be red, and the highest violet. They will succeed each other in the following order, proceeding upward: red, orange, yellow, green, blue, indigo, and violet. These colors will not, however, have distinct boundaries, but will pass gradually, by insensible tints, one into another, so that it will be impossible to say exactly where the red ends and the orange begins, and so of the others.

Fig. 3.

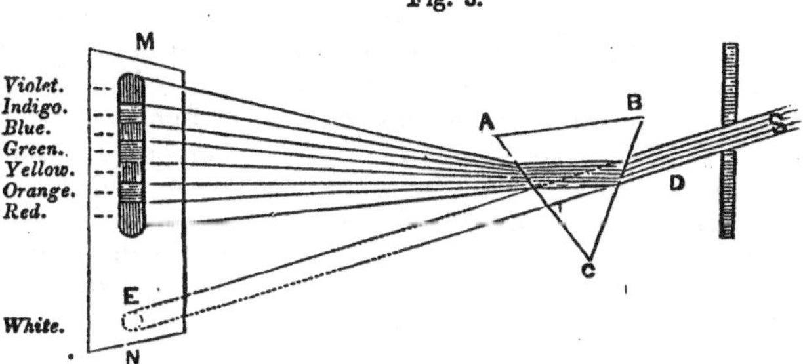

This remarkable phenomenon was explained by Newton by showing that the solar light was composed of a number of different kinds of light, which were capable of being refracted in different degrees by the prism, those lights which were least refrangible passing to the lower extremity, and those that were most refrangible to the upper extremity of the spectrum. By inspecting the figure it will be evident that the red light is less deflected from its straight course than the orange; the orange less than the yellow; the yellow less than the green, and so on. Newton, therefore, inferred that there were lights of seven distinct kinds, having seven different degrees of refrangibility, and seven different colors.

This conclusion, however, has been subject to much modification by subsequent optical investigators.

It is found that rays of light of the same color differ slightly in refrangibility, and the investigations of Brewster, and others, appear to justify the conclusion, that the solar light, instead of consisting of seven elementary colors, is only composed of three.

At so early a period as the year 1775, it was suspected that the conclusion of Newton, that the spectrum was divisible into seven different simple constituent lights, was fallacious. Mayer maintained that there were but three elementary colors, red, yellow, and blue, and at a later epoch, Dr. Young suggested that all colors were compounded of red, green, and violet.

Let us, however, for a moment contemplate the actual result of the prismatic experiment of Newton, and let us separate, carefully, that which is matter of observation in it, from that which is, properly speaking, matter of hypothesis or theory.

In passing through the prism, and being, thereby, submitted to a considerable refracting action, a single beam of light is spread out into a fan of rays as represented in fig. 3. This fan-like form is produced by the fact that some of the rays which compose the beam are more strongly refracted by the prism than others, and the divergence of the fan depends upon the difference between the extent of the deflection of the most refrangible, and the least refrangible rays. The angle of divergence of the fan has been called the dispersion of the original beam by the prism.

When the rays, thus dispersed, in virtue of their different susceptibility of refraction, are received upon a white screen, they exhibit a streak of surface illuminated by a series of different tints of color, which, in their general character, are conformable to the distinction assigned to them by Newton; but accurate examination shows that there are no distinguishable boundaries between the successive tints; that throughout the limits of the red the degree of redness varies, that it insensibly melts away into the beginning of the orange, which, increasing to a point where its intensity is greatest, again gradually melts away insensibly into the yellow, and so on, the successive colors and tints of color fading imperceptibly into each other. Now there is nothing in these circumstances to afford any rigid justification of the seven elementary colors assigned by Newton, and when we consider, what is not disputed by Newton himself, that the commingling or blending together of lights of different colors will produce intermediate tints, it follows that there are an infinite variety of ways in which the constituent colors of light might be imagined to be arranged which would equally produce the phenomenon of the prismatic spectrum.

This problem has, accordingly, been taken up in our own times by Sir David Brewster, with all the advantages which the increased knowledge and experience of the age, and improved methods of inquiry, could afford. He has shown, by innumerable experiments on the transmission of light through colored media, and on artificial lights, produced by combustion, of various circumstances, that the pure and elementary simple lights are one or other of the three colors, red, yellow, and blue; that the light of each of these colors, respectively, is composed of constituent rays which are differently refrangible, so that if a beam of any one of these lights were transmitted through a prism, an oblong spectrum would be produced, of one uniform color, corresponding to that of the light itself. Thus if we suppose a beam of red light transmitted through a prism in the same manner as the original beam of white light, fig. 3, was transmitted, then we should obtain an oblong spectrum, similar in form and length to that which we originally obtained, but all of one tint. It would be all red, although the redness would be greatest at one particular point, and would decrease from that point toward each extremity, and gradually fade away. These circumstances may be represented by the diagram, fig. 4.

Let L M represent the screen, and let L represent the lower and M the upper end of the spectrum; let N be the point at which the redness is most intense, it will gradually diminish from N to M and from N to L. Let us suppose that we draw a curved line, L P′ P P″ M, so that the lines or distances N P′, N P, N P″, &c., shall, respectively, represent the intensities of the light at the several points N′ N″, &c. Such a figure will exhibit, geometrically, the gradation of tints from the point N, where the red is brightest, upward and downward to the points where it fades away. It is found by experiment that the point where it is brightest is near the lower extremity of the spectrum.

In like manner, if a beam of pure yellow light be transmitted through the prism, a similar yellow spectrum will be produced, which may be represented in a similar manner, the point of greatest brightness, however, being at a higher point in the spectrum, represented in figure 5, by similar letters.

Finally, let us suppose a beam of blue light transmitted through the prism in

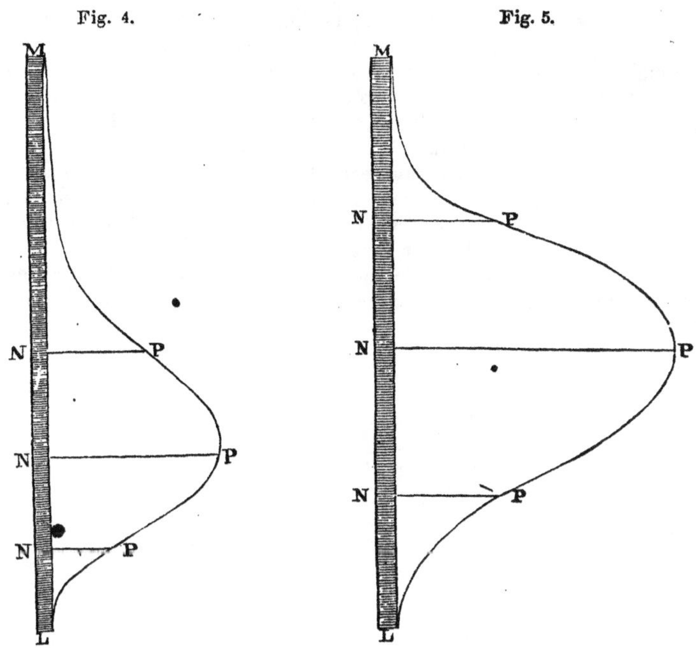

like manner. Its point of maximum brilliancy will be still higher than that of the yellow, as represented in fig. 6.

Fig. 6.

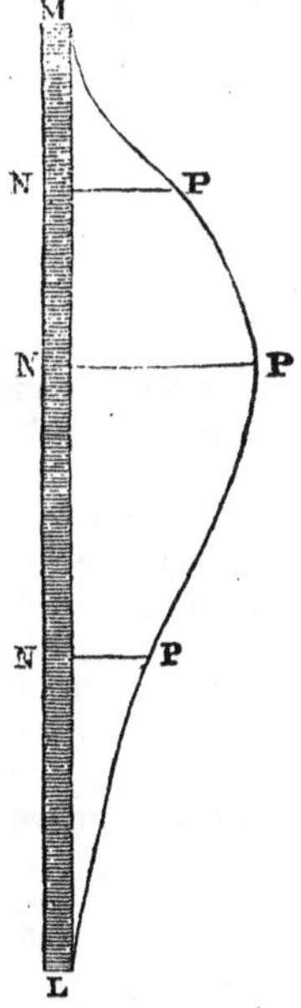

Now, if we suppose a beam of white light, like the natural light of the sun, which is composed of these three constituent elementary lights, to be transmitted through the prism, we ought to expect these three spectra of the elementary colors, red, yellow, and blue, to be simultaneously produced, the maximum of each being at the place already assigned to it. The combination of these is represented in the diagram, fig. 7, and the tint of color at each point of the spectrum will be that which would result from the corresponding mixture of colors. Thus at R N, where the red is most intense, a portion of blue, represented by N *b*, and of yellow, represented by N *a*, are mixed with it, and the resulting tint will be that which will be produced by the mixture; in like manner at Y N, where the yellow is most intense, a portion of blue, represented by N *b'* and a portion of yellow, represented by N *a'*, will be mingled with it.

Fig. 7.

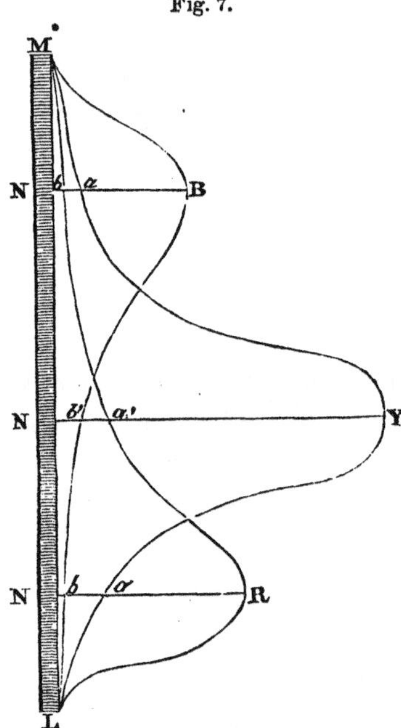

In the same manner, throughout the whole extent of the three uniform spectra thus intermingled the tints of color will correspond to the intensities of the spectra at the same point.

In this manner the succession of colors exhibited by the prismatic spectrum is explained. The orange, for example, is only the intermixture of a considerable quantity of red and yellow, qualified by a small quantity of blue. The green, in the same manner, is a mixture of a considerable quantity of blue and yellow, qualified by a very small quantity of red.

There is a certain proportion in which these three elementary colors may be mixed together so as to produce white. If any one of them, the red, for example, be in excess above this proportion, the other two observing it, the resulting color will be a red diluted with white. If, on the other hand, there be a deficiency of the proper proportion of red, the tint will be green diluted with white, produced by the excess of blue and yellow.

In general, if we take the actual proportion in which these three elementary colors are combined, and assuming that which is least intense among them, combine with it the proportion of the other two, which is necessary to produce white, the resulting tint will be such as would be produced by the balance of the remaining colors diluted by the resulting white.

By following out this reasoning, it will be seen how the infinite variety of tints of color may be produced by the simple component colors, red, yellow, and blue, existing in different degrees of intensity.

The color called black is produced by the absence of all light, and is, in fact, a name for absolute darkness. If it were possible to find a substance absolutely incapable of reflecting any light to the eye, or what is the same, of absorbing all the light which falls upon it, such substance would appear absolutely black. But as no substance in nature is, on the one hand, capable of reflecting all the light which falls upon it, so, on the other hand, no substance in nature is capable of absorbing all the light that falls upon it. If we take the blackest known substance and throw upon it strongly-condensed light, it will become distinctly visible to the eye by a small portion of light which it will reflect, which will make it appear of a gray color, or faint white. It appears, then, that objects which are popularly termed black, are, in fact, faintly white. A true black would be an object having no color at all.

Experiments made on finely-divided substances have proved that there is no substance absolutely opaque. The most dense substances known, and those that are, apparently, most impervious to light, are found, when cut into leaves or filaments sufficiently thin, to be transparent; but the light which goes through them is always of a tint contrary to that which they reflect. Thus if an object appears to the eye to be of a yellow color, we know that the reason is that it reflects to the eye yellow light. What, then, becomes, it may be asked, of the red and the blue components of the solar light which falls upon it? If we obtain a shaving of the body sufficiently thin, and look behind it, we shall find that it will appear of a color composed of the red and blue; that is, it transmits through it the colors which it fails to reflect.

Hence it has been inferred that the absorption of light which takes place in colored bodies is effected, not immediately on their surface, but at some definite depth within their dimensions, and that such portion of the compound solar light that falls upon it, as is not reflected, passes successively through lamina, one within another, each of which absorbs a portion of it, until, at length, it is altogether lost.

As heat is, by some means not clearly known to us, connected with light, we have, in these circumstances, a clear explanation of the fact, that more heat is absorbed by bodies of a dark color than by those of a light color. In general the lighter the color the greater the proportion is of the reflected light, and the darker the color the less the proportion is. The greater the proportion of light that is absorbed the greater will be the proportion of the heat which attends that light. Hence it follows that, as dark colors absorb more heat than light ones, and as black absorbs the most of all, dark colors are, in general, warm, and black the most so. If two pieces of cloth be thrown upon snow, one black and the other white, the black will sink through it, melting the snow under it, before the other penetrates into it perceptibly.

Hence, dark-colored cloths are most suitable in cold weather, and light-colored in warm weather.

After all that has been explained, it will be scarcely necessary to say that the sense in which color is commonly understood to be a quality of bodies, is incorrect, and, strictly speaking, it is true, although it may sound paradoxical to say that leaves are not green, and that the sky is not blue. The green and the blue colors belong, properly speaking, not to the objects which appear to the eye to be green or blue, but to the light which they reflect from their surfaces. A red object is one which reflects red light and absorbs all other colors, a blue object one which reflects blue light and absorbs other tints, and so on. The color of a body, then, or more properly, the cause which produces the color, is the quality possessed by its particles to reflect certain lights and absorb others.

That the color which seems to belong to a body is not really inherent in the body, or inseparable from it, is proved by showing that we can give any color that may be desired to a body by exposing it to light of that peculiar tint. Thus if a piece of blue cloth be illuminated by a beam of pure red light, it will appear red; or, if by yellow light, it will appear yellow; but neither the yellow, nor the red, will be as vivid as the color it would exhibit if illuminated by blue light.

THE VISIBLE STARS.

What occupies the Space beyond the Limits of the Solar System.—Wide Vacuity between this System and the Stars.—Indications of this observable in the Motions of the Planets.—Indications in the Motions of the Comets.—The immense Distance of the Stars proved by the Earth's annual Motion.—Observations made at Greenwich.—Bessel's Discovery of the Parallax.—The consequent Distance of the Stars.—Illustrations of the Magnitude of this Distance.—The different Orders and Magnitudes of the Stars.—How accounted for.—Why those of the lowest Magnitude are most Numerous.—The real Magnitude of the Stars.—The Telescope unable to Magnify them.—Dr. Wollaston's Investigations of the comparative Brightness and Magnitude of the Stars in Relation to the Sun.—Their stupendous Magnitude.—Application of this to the Dog-star.

THE VISIBLE STARS.

On former occasions we have taken a survey of the group of inhabited globes which, in company with the earth, revolve around the sun. We have examined their motions and estimated their magnitudes and distances. Passing successively from planet to planet, the mind has been oppressed by the stupendous dimensions offered to its contemplation. Jupiter, a globe 1,400 times the bulk of the earth, revolving at a distance of five hundred millions of miles from the sun; the Saturnian system, with its globe a thousand times larger than the earth—its system of revolving rings, and its suite of seven moons—sweeping round the sun in a vast orbit at a distance of a thousand millions of miles, and having a year thirty times the length of ours, diversified by similar seasons, but varied by seven different kinds of months; and, finally, having attained the extreme limit of the system, the planet Herschel is found, moving at such a distance from the sun that that luminary is reduced to a star, with moons too distant to allow of their number being satisfactorily ascertained, and probably other illuminating apparatus, the discovery of which is reserved to future observers. Such are the objects, such the distances, and such the motions, here presented to us. But the aspirations of the inquisitive spirit of man rest not here contented. Taking its station at this extreme verge of the system, and throwing its searching glance toward the interminable realms of space which extend beyond those limits, it still asks—What lies there? Has the Infinite circumscribed the exercise of his creative power within the precincts of the solar system—and has he left the unfathomable depths of space that stretch beyond it a wide solitude? Has He whose dwelling is immensity, and whose presence is everywhere and eternal, remained inactive throughout regions in the universe compared with which the solar system itself shrinks into a point?

Even though scientific research should have left us without definite information on these questions, the light which has been shed on the Divine character, as well by reason as by revelation, would have filled us with the assurance that there is no region of space however remote, which does not teem with evidences of the exalted power, the inexhaustible wisdom, and the untiring goodness of the Most High.

But science has not so deserted us. It has not failed to afford us much interesting and elevating information regarding those distant regions of space. The sagacity and activity of modern astronomers have supplied us with much interesting information respecting regions of the universe the extent of which is so great that even the whole dimensions of the solar system supply no modulus sufficiently great to enable us to express their magnitude. It will not, then, be unprofitable or unpleasing, on the present occasion, to carry our inquiries into those realms of space that stretch beyond the limits of our own system, and to inquire into the condition of the physical creation there.

We are furnished with a variety of evidence, establishing, incontestably, the fact, that around our system to a vast distance on every side there exists an unoccupied space; that the solar system stands alone in the midst of a vast solitude. What are the proofs of this? Newton has demonstrated in his investigations respecting the law of gravitation, that all masses of matter exercise upon each other mutual attraction; in virtue of which, the presence of any mass in the neighborhood of another is betrayed, even though we should not see it, by the effects which it produces on the condition and motion of the other. The group of globes constituting the solar system, exercise upon each other this influence; and although, from the enormous preponderance of its mass above all the rest, the sun seems to annihilate the separate influence of the planets and satellites upon each other, yet, by rigorous examination of the motions of these bodies, we are able to detect the effects of their reciprocal influences. The motion of each body of the system is the combined result of the attraction of the sun and the other bodies of the system upon it. A rigorous analysis of the motions of the planets has exhibited all these effects, and in these motions we can distinctly see the gravitating influences of the various bodies of the system. Now, if there exists beyond the limits of the system, and within a distance not so great as to render the attraction of gravitation imperceptible, any mass of matter, such as another sun like our own, such a mass would undoubtedly exercise a gravitating force upon the various bodies of the solar system. It would cause each of them to move in a manner different from what it would have moved if no such body existed.

Thus it appears that, even though the presence of a mass of matter in our neighborhood should escape direct observation, its presence would be invariably betrayed by the effects which its gravitation would necessarily produce upon the planets. No such effects, however, are discoverable. The planets move as they would move if the solar system were independent of any external disturbing attraction. These motions, which are accurately observed, are such, and such only, as can be accounted for by the attraction of the sun and the reciprocal attraction of the other bodies of the system. The inevitable inference from this is, that there does not exist any mass of matter in the neighborhood of the solar system within any distance which permits such a mass to exercise upon it any discoverable gravitating influence, and that, if any body analogous to our sun exists in the universe, it must be placed at a distance from our system inconceivably great—so great, indeed, that the whole magnitude of our system will shrink into a point compared with it.

But we have other indications of this condition of things. The solar system is supplied with *feelers*, which it is enabled to throw out into the regions surrounding it to vast distances, and these are endowed with the highest conceivable susceptibility, which would cause them to betray to us the presence in these regions even of masses of matter of very limited dimensions. These feelers are the COMETS, and in particular that called Halley's comet. This body emerges from the system periodically, and makes an excursion into the surrounding regions to a distance of little less than two thousand millions of miles beyond the limits of our system, and returns at regular intervals to the sun. It is a body of extreme levity and tenuity compared even with the smallest planetary masses; it is, therefore, eminently susceptible of the effects of gravitation proceeding from a body external to it.

We have shown, on another occasion, that when this body, once in seventy-five years, departs from our system to make its vast excursion through distant regions of space, the eye of science pursues it along its path, watches its movements, and follows its course. That course is calculated upon the supposition that it is subject to no attraction through the entire range of its orbit except those of the sun and planets, and the calculations of its return are based upon that supposition. The time and the place of each of its successive returns to our system have been foretold on these suppositions; and we have found that its returns have corresponded faithfully with such predictions. It is certain, then, that, in its range through space, this body has not passed in the neighborhood of any mass of matter capable of exercising an observable attraction upon it. In fact, it moves exactly as it would move if no material object existed in the creation save those of the solar system itself. It follows, therefore, that all other objects must be too distant from our system to produce any discoverable attraction even on so light a body as this.

Yet when, on any clear night, we contemplate the firmament, and behold the countless multitudes of objects that sparkle upon it, and remember what a comparatively small number are comprised among those of the solar system, and even of these how few are visible at any one time, we are naturally impelled to the inquiry, Where in the universe are these vast numbers of objects placed?

Very little reflection and reasoning, applied to the consideration of our own position and to the appearances of the heavens, will convince us that the objects that chiefly appear in the firmament must be at almost immeasurable distances from our system. The earth in its annual course round the sun moves in a circle, the diameter of which is about two hundred millions of miles. We, who observe the heavens, are transported upon the globe round that vast circle. The station from which we observe the universe at one period of the year is, then, two hundred millions of miles from the station to which we are transported at another period of the year. Thus, if we view the heavens on the night of the 1st of January and note their aspect, and view them again on the night of the 1st of July, we know that the two stations from which we take these two surveys are separated by a space of two hundred millions of miles.

Now it is a fact within the familiar experience of every one, that the relative position of objects will depend upon the point from which they are viewed. If we stand upon the bank of a river, along the margin of which a multitude of ships are stationed, and view the masts of the vessels, they will have among each other a certain relative arrangement. If we change our position, however, through the space of a few hundred yards, the relative position of these masts will not be the same as before. Two which before lay in line will now be seen separate, and two which before were separated are now brought into line. Two, one of which was to the right of the other, are now reversed; that which was to the right, is at the left, and vice versa; nor are these changes produced by any change of position of the ships themselves, for they are moored in stationary positions. The changes of appearance are the result of *our own change of position*, and the greater that change of position is, the greater will be the relative change of these appearances. Let us suppose, however, that we are moved to a much greater distance from the shipping; a very slight change in our position will produce much less effect upon the relative position of the masts; perhaps it will require a very considerable change of position to produce a perceivable change upon them. In fine, in proportion as our distance from the masts is increased, so in proportion will it require a greater change in our own position to produce the same apparent change in the position of the masts.

Thus it is with all visible objects. When a multitude of stationary objects are viewed at a distance, their relative position will depend upon the position of the observer, and if the station of the observer be changed, a change in the relative position of the objects must be expected; and if no perceptible change is produced, it must be inferred that the distance of the object is incomparably greater than the change of position of the observer.

Let us now apply these reflections to the case of the earth and the stars. The stars are analogous to the masts of the ships, and the earth is the station on which the observer is placed, and which is changeable in its position by reason of its annual motion. It would, doubtless, be expected that the magnitude of the globe, being eight thousand miles in diameter, would produce a change of position of the observer sufficient to cause a change in the relative position of the stars, but we find that such is not the case. The stars, viewed from opposite sides of the globe of the earth, present exactly the same appearance; we must, therefore, infer that the diameter of the globe of the earth is absolutely nothing compared to their distance.

But the astronomer has still a much larger modulus to fall back upon. He reflects, as has been already observed, that he is enabled to view the stars from two stations, separated from each other, not by eight thousand miles, the diameter of the earth, but by two hundred millions of miles, that of the earth's orbit. He, therefore, views the heavens on the first of January, and views them again on the first of July, yet he finds, to his amazement, that the aspect is the same. He thinks that this cannot be—that so great a change of position in himself cannot fail to make some change in the apparent position of the stars;—that, although their general aspect is the same, yet when submitted to exact examination a change must assuredly be detected. He accordingly resorts to the use of instruments of observation capable of measuring the relative positions of the stars with the last conceivable precision, and he is more than ever confounded by the fact, that still no discoverable change of position is found.

For a long period of time this result seemed inexplicable, and, accordingly, it formed the greatest difficulty with astronomers in admitting the annual motion of the earth. The alternative offered was this: it was necessary, either to fall back upon the Ptolemaic system, in which the earth was stationary, or to suppose that the immense change of position of the earth in the course of half a year, which we have already mentioned, could produce no discoverable change of appearance in the stars; a fact which involves the inference that the diameter of the earth's orbit, which measures two hundred millions of miles, must be a mere point compared with the distance of the nearest stars. Such an idea appeared so preposterous and inconceivable, that for a long period of time many preferred to embrace the Ptolemaic hypothesis, beset as it was with difficulties and contradictions.

Since, however, the annual motion of the earth must now be regarded as a proved fact, we are driven to the inference, deduced from the absence of all change of relative apparent position in the stars, that the distances of these objects from our system is, in the common popular sense of the word, infinitely great compared with the dimensions of our system, and this inference is in perfect accordance with the other indications of the wide vacuity that surrounds the system.

In such a state of things, it will easily be imagined that astronomers have diligently directed their observations to the discovery of some change of apparent position, however small, produced upon the stars by the earth's motion. As those stars most likely to be affected by the motion of the earth are those which are nearest to the system, and therefore probably which are brightest and largest, it has been to such chiefly that this kind of observation has been directed. Since it was certain, that if any observable effect was produced by the earth's motion at all it must be extremely small, the nicest and most difficult means of observation were those alone from which the discovery could be expected. Among the many expedients used for the detection of such effects, we shall select as an example one which was adopted at the Royal Observatory at Greenwich. A telescope of great length was attached to the side of a pier of solid masonry erected upon a foundation of rock. This instrument was screwed into such a position that particular stars as they crossed the meridian would necessarily pass within its field of view. Micrometric wires were in the usual manner placed in its eye-piece, so that the exact point at which the stars passed the meridian each night could be observed and recorded with the greatest precision. The instrument being thus fixed and immoveable, the transits of the stars were noted each night, and the exact places where they passed the meridian recorded. This kind of observation was carried on through the year, and if the earth's change of position, by reason of its annual motion, should produce any effect upon the apparent position of the stars, it was anticipated that such effect would be discovered by these means. After, however, making all allowance for the usual causes which we knew to affect the apparent position of the stars, such as refraction or aberration, no change of position was discovered which could be assigned to the earth's motion.

Within the last few years, however, Professor Bessel has directed his scientific labors to this inquiry, and has succeeded in detecting a small effect on one of the stars in the constellation of the Swan. In a communication, made in 1838 by that astronomer to Sir John Herschel, he says: "After so many unsuccessful attempts to determine the parallax of a fixed star, I thought it worth while to try what might be accomplished by means of the accuracy which my great Fraunhoffer heliometer gives to the observations. I undertook to make this investigation upon the star 61 Cygni; which, by reason of its great proper motion, is perhaps the best of all, which affords the advantage of being a double star, and on that account may be observed with greater accuracy, and which is so near the pole that, with the exception of a small part of the year, it can always be observed at night at a sufficient altitude."

These observations were continued for four years, and the result was the discovery that the position of the star in question was affected by the earth's motion to the extent of a little less than *one third of a second.* From this may be calculated the distance of the star from the solar system.

To render intelligible the spirit of the method by which the distance of the stars may be inferred from their discovered parallax, let us suppose two lines drawn from a star to opposite ends of a diameter of the earth's orbit, or to two positions which the earth occupies after an interval of six months. The angle formed by these two lines is, in fact, the amount of the apparent change of position of the star by reason of the earth's motion, and it is technically called the *parallax.* We may in this case consider the diameter of the orbit as a portion of an enormous circle, the centre of which is at the star, and the radius of which is the distance of the star from the earth. It is known, in geometry, that an arc of a circle which measures one second is in length the 206,265th part of the radius, and if it measures one third of a second, it will, of course, be the 618,795th part of the radius.

Professor Bessel found that the angle contained by those two lines, drawn from the star in question to the opposite sides of the orbit, contained an angle amounting to two thirds of a second, and, consequently, that the angle included by the lines between the sun and the earth would form one third of a second. From this it would follow, that the distance from the star, being the radius of a circle, of which the distance between the earth and sun is an arc of one third of a second, will be 618,795 times the length of the earth's distance from the sun.

Taking round numbers, then, it will follow from this observation that the distance of this star is 600,000 times greater than the distance of the earth from the sun. But the distance of the earth from the sun being 100 millions of miles, it will follow that the distance of the star must be sixty millions of millions of miles.

Such is the nearest approximation that observation has supplied for the space that separates the solar system from other bodies of the universe.

Minds unaccustomed to the contemplation of great numbers and magnitudes are overwhelmed in their efforts to conceive such distances; and even astronomers have been compelled to resort to extraordinary expedients to express and conceive clearly such spaces.

On another occasion we have shown that light moves through space at the rate of 200,000 miles per second. This motion of light has accordingly been adopted as the most convenient modulus for expressing the distances of the stars; and we are accustomed to express them by saying how long light would take to move over them. If, then, sixty millions of millions of miles be divided by 200,000 we shall obtain the number of seconds which light would take to come from the nearest star to the solar system; and if this number of seconds be, in the usual manner, reduced to years, it will be found that light would take about ten years to travel from the nearest star to the earth. Such is, then, the space that divides us from them.

To conceive this prodigious distance more clearly still, it has been calculated that a cannon-ball, which moves with a velocity of 500 miles an hour, would take to travel from the nearest star to the earth, an interval of 14,255,418 years. Again: it has been computed that a steam-carriage starting from the earth, and moving toward the star at the rate of 20 miles an hour, would take to reach the star, 356,385,466 years; a period of time 61,000 times greater than the whole interval since the creation of the world, according to Mosaic chronology.

But this is only the interval that separates our system from the *nearest* stars. Analogy and all the grounds of probability lead to the conclusion that corresponding intervals separate the stars from each other. We shall hereafter see that the stars are, in fact, suns like our own, or, what is the same, that our sun is a star; and it is consistent and natural to suppose our sun is no farther removed from the stars than the stars are from each other.

Among the multitude of stars which we behold in the firmament we find a great variety of splendor. Those which are the brightest and largest, and which are said to be of the *first magnitude*, are few; the next in order of brightness, which are called of the *second magnitude*, are more numerous; and as they decrease in brightness their number rapidly increases.

The number of stars of the first magnitude does not exceed twenty; those of the second, fifty; those of the third, two hundred; and so on, the number of the smallest being incapable of estimation.

The stars which are capable of being seen by the naked eye are usually resolved into seven orders of magnitudes—the first being the brightest and largest, while those of the seventh magnitude are the smallest that the eye can distinctly see.

Are we to suppose, then, that this relative brightness which we perceive really arises from any difference of intrinsic splendor between the objects themselves, or does it, as it may equally do, arise from their difference of distance? Are the stars of the seventh magnitude so much less bright and conspicuous than those of the first magnitude because they are really smaller orbs placed at the same distance, or because, being intrinsically equal in splendor, the distance of those of the seventh magnitude is so much greater than the distance of those of the first magnitude that they are diminished in their apparent brightness? We know that by the laws of optics the brightness of a luminous object diminishes in a very rapid proportion as the distance increases. Thus at double the distance the brightness will be four times less, at triple the distance it will be nine times less, at a hundred times the distance it will be ten thousand times less, and so on.

It is evident, then, that the great variety of brightness which prevails among the stars may be indifferently explained, either by supposing them objects of different intrinsic brightness and magnitude, placed at the same distance, or objects generally of the same order of magnitude placed at a great diversity of distances.

Of these two suppositions, the latter is infinitely the most probable and natural; it has, therefore, been usually adopted: and we accordingly consider the stars to derive their variety of brightness almost entirely from the positions assigned to them in the universe being at various distances from us.

Taking the stars generally to be intrinsically the same in brightness, various theories have been proposed as to the positions which would explain their appearances; and the most natural and probable is, that their distances from each other are generally equal, or nearly so, and correspond with the distance of our sun from the nearest of them. In this way the fact that a small number of stars only appear of the first magnitude, and that the number increases very rapidly as the magnitude diminishes, is easily rendered intelligible.

If we imagine a person standing in the midst of a wood, surrounded by trees on every side and at every distance, those which immediately surround him will be few in number, and by proximity will appear large. The trunks or stumps of those which occupy a circuit beyond the former will be more numerous, the circuit being wider, and will appear smaller, because their distance is greater. Beyond these again, occupying a still wider circuit, will appear a proportionally augmented number, whose apparent magnitude will again be diminished by increased distance; and thus the trees which occupy wider and wider circuits at greater and greater distances will be more and more numerous, and will appear continually smaller. It is the same with the stars; we are placed in the midst of an immense cluster of suns surrounding us on every side at inconceivable distances. Those few which are placed immediately about our system appear bright and large, and we call them *stars of the first magnitude.* Those which lie in the circuit beyond, and occupying a wider range, are more numerous and less bright; and we call them stars of the second magnitude. And there is thus a progression increasing in number and distance and diminishing in brightness, until we attain a distance so great that the stars are barely visible to the naked eye. This is the limit of vision. It is the range of the universe which the eye in its natural condition is destined to behold; but an eye has been given us more potent still, and of infinitely wider range,—the eye of the mind. The telescope, a creature of the understanding, has conferred upon the bodily eye an infinitely augmented range, and, as we shall presently see, has enabled us to penetrate into realms of the universe, which, without its aid, would never have been known to us. But let us pause for the present and dwell for a moment upon that range of space which comes within the scope of natural vision.

Sir William Herschel, to whose researches we are indebted for a large portion of the knowledge which we possess respecting the fixed stars, has investigated the probable progression of distances which regulate the stars visible to the naked eye, and has shown reasonable grounds for concluding that the smallest visible star is at a distance about twelve times greater than stars of the first magnitude. He supposes that the intermediate stars between the smallest that can be seen by the naked eye, and stars like the dogstar, which, from their brightness, must be presumed to be nearest to us, are ranged at intermediate distances. It would therefore follow that if we assume the distance of the nearest star according to the results of Bessel's observations, to be a space that light would move over it in 10 years, the distance of the smallest star perceivable by unassisted vision must be such that light would take 120 years to move over! If, then, we imagine a sphere surrounding us, the radius of which is equal to the space that light moves over in 120 years, that sphere is the range of natural and unassisted vision, and is that portion of the universe which men are privileged to contemplate unaided by art.

MAGNITUDE OF THE STARS.

The extent of the stellar universe visible to the naked eye, and the arrangement of stars in it and their relative distances, have just been explained. But a natural curiosity will be awakened to discover not merely the position and arrangement of those bodies, but to ascertain what is their nature, and what parts they play on the great theatre of creation? Are they analogous to our planets? Are they inhabited globes, warmed and illuminated by neighboring suns? Or on the other hand, are they themselves suns, dispensing light and life to systems of surrounding worlds.

When a telescope is directed to a star, the effect produced is strikingly different from that which we find when it is applied to a planet. A planet, to the naked eye, with one or two exceptions, appears like a common star. The telescope, however, immediately presents it to us with a distinct circular disk similar to that which the moon offers to the naked eye, and in the case of some of the planets a powerful telescope will render them apparently even larger than the moon. But the effect is very different indeed when the same instrument is directed even to the brightest star. We find that instead of magnifying, it actually diminishes. There is an optical illusion produced, when we behold a star, which makes it appear to us to be surrounded with a radiation which causes it to be represented when drawn on paper, by a dot with rays diverging on every side from it. The effect of the telescope is to cut off this radiation, and present to us the star as a mere *lucid point*, having no sensible magnitude; nor can any augmented telescopic power which has yet been resorted to produce any other effect. Telescopic powers amounting to six thousand were occasionally used by Sir William Herschel, and he stated that with these the apparent magnitude of the stars seemed *less*, if possible, than with lower powers.

We have other proofs of the fact that the stars have no sensible disks, among which may be mentioned the remarkable effect called the occultation of a star by the dark edge of the moon. When the moon is a crescent or in the quarters, as it moves over the firmament, its dark edge successively approaches to or recedes from the stars. And from time to time it happens that it passes between the stars and the eye. If a star had a sensible disk in this case, the edge of the moon would gradually cover it, and the star, instead of being instantaneously extinguished, would gradually disappear. This is found not to be the case; the star preserves all its lustre until the moment it comes into contact with the dark edge of the moon's disk, and then it is instantly extinguished, without the slightest appearance of diminution of its brightness. This effect also presents a striking proof of the non-existence of an atmosphere round the moon.

It may be asked then, if such be the case, if none of the stars, great or small, have any discoverable magnitude at all; with what meaning can we speak of stars of the first, second, or other orders of magnitude? The term magnitude thus applied, was used before the invention of the telescope, when the stars, having been observed only with the naked eye, were really supposed to have different magnitudes. We must accept the term now used to express not the comparative magnitude, but the comparative brightness of the stars. Thus a star of the first magnitude, means of the greatest apparent brightness; a star of the second magnitude means that which is in the next degree of splendor, and so on. But what are we to infer from this singular fact, that no magnifying power, however great, will exhibit to us a star with any sensible magnitude? must we admit that the optical instrument loses its magnifying power when applied to the stars, while it retains it with every other visible object? Such a consequence would be eminently absurd. We are therefore driven to an inference regarding the magnitude of stars as astonishing and almost as incredible as that which was forced upon us respecting their distances. We saw that the entire magnitude of the annual orbit of the earth, stupendous as it is, was nothing compared to the distance of one of those bodies, and consequently if that orbit were filled by a sun whose magnitude would therefore be infinitely greater than that of ours, such a sun would not appear to an observer at the nearest star of greater magnitude than one third of a second; consequently would have no magnitude sensible to the eye, and would appear as a mere lucid point to an observer at the star! We are then prepared for the inference respecting the fixed stars which the telescopic observations already mentioned leads to. The telescope of Sir William Herschel, to which he applied a power of six thousand, did undoubtedly magnify the stars six thousand times, but even then their apparent magnitude was inappreciable. We are then to infer that the distance of these wonderful bodies is so enormous compared with their actual magnitude, that their apparent diameter, seen from our system, is above six thousand times less than any which the eye is capable of perceiving.

Under such circumstances it might appear hopeless to attempt to discover the probable magnitude and brightness of the stars as compared with any standard known to us. Yet this problem, however hopeless it may seem, has yielded to the ardor of astronomical inquiry.

Dr. Wollaston instituted a series of observations and calculations, which terminated in an estimate of the magnitude and brightness of the fixed stars as compared with our sun.

There are optical instruments called *photometers*, the use and application of which is to ascertain the comparative brightness of luminous objects. By such instruments we can take any two visible luminous objects and compare them so as to be enabled to say what is the numerical ratio of the lights which they afford. Thus a common candle and a gas-lamp may be tried, and we should be enabled immediately to say how many candles would be necessary to give light equal to that of the lamp.

By instruments of this species Dr. Wollaston prosecuted investigations, the object of which was to ascertain the numerical proportion between the light afforded by the sun and that afforded by the stars. Let us take, for example, the case of *Sirius*, or the dogstar. He found by such means, that the light received by us from Sirius was 20,000,000,000 of times less than that received from the sun. This, be it observed, was a result not of theory or speculation, but of immediate observation and measurement. Having ascertained this, his next object was to compute the distance to which our sun would have to be removed in order that it should assume an appearance like that of the dogstar. Although this might at the first view appear a difficult problem, it was by no means so. We know by the principles of optics, that if the sun were removed to twice its present distance it splendor would be four times less; at three times its present distance it would be nine times less; at ten times the distance it would be one hundred times less, and so on.

We have, therefore, a simple arithmetical rule of calculation, by the application of which we can say in what proportion the brightness of the sun would be reduced by any proposed increase of distance, or what increase of distance would be necessary to produce any proposed diminution of brightness. If this rule be applied to determine how much further the sun should be removed from us than it now is, in order that it should be reduced to the appearance of the dogstar, it will be found that the requisite increase of distance would be in proportion of about 150,000 to 1. If, then, the sun were removed to 150,000 times its present distance it would be seen by us as a second dogstar.

Now it will be apparent, that if we had reason to know that the dogstar is at a distance of 150,000 times greater than that of the sun, it would immediately follow that the dogstar must be a sun equal to our own, because then it would be inferred that the sun, if placed where the dogstar is, would have exactly the same splendor and magnitude.

But if, on the other hand, we had reason to know that the real distance of the dogstar is greater than 150,000 times that of the sun, then it would follow that the dogstar at a greater distance would have the same splendor as the sun at a less distance; and, consequently, the inevitable inference would be that the dogstar must be larger and more splendid than the sun.

The discovery of Bessel having led to the conclusion that the distance of the nearest stars is at least 600,000 times greater than that of the sun, it follows that these objects, at that distance, are as large and bright as the sun would be at a distance four times less. This being admitted, it immediately follows that the stars, or at least many of them, *must be objects transcendentally greater and brighter than the sun.*

At the time of the observations of Dr. Wollaston it was not supposed that the distances of the stars were as great as they are now known to be; and Dr. Wollaston, adopting a much less distance than the truth, felt himself warranted in the inference that the dogstar must be a sun equal at least to fourteen of ours. Had he known what has since been inferred from the observations of Professor Bessel, how much more stupendous would he not have inferred the stars to be!

But still, it may be asked, what are those wondrous objects? Are they planets shining with reflected light? or are they themselves native fountains of light, like our sun? It is easy to perceive that no reflected light could be intense enough to be visible at distances so enormous; independent of which, the splendor of the stars as seen through powerful telescopes is such as to satisfy us that they must be suns. Sir William Herschel stated that when his great telescope was directed to the region of the heavens through which the star Sirius passed, the appearance exhibited on the approach of that star was like that of the eastern firmament on the approach of sunrise; and that when the glorious object itself entered the field of view, although it appeared as a mere lucid point, having no sensible magnitude, its light was so overpowering that he was compelled to protect his eye with a colored glass. It is needless to say that such splendor could not proceed from an opaque globe shining with borrowed light at a distance of sixty millions of millions of miles.

To persons not familiar with optical researches it may appear incomprehensible that a star presenting, even with the telescope, no disk of sensible magnitude, could, nevertheless, appear so splendid. There is, however, a law of light, clearly established in optics, which will probably remove this difficulty. It is demonstrated that the apparent brightness of an object is not diminished by its removal from the eye, although the quantity of light which it gives is decreased in a high proportion. This statement may appear at first paradoxical; let us, however explain it.

If the sun, for example, were removed to twice its present distance it would appear to the eye with half its present diameter; yet, in its diminished size, the apparent brightness of its surface would be the same as that with which we behold it at the lesser distance. To illustrate this, let us suppose that a small circular opening is made in a card, and that the card is presented to the sun, so that a portion of the sun's disk only shall be seen through it, but that that portion shall be circular; the opening will present to the eye the appearance of a sun of less magnitude than the real one, but of equal brightness. Let the card then be held at such a distance from the eye that the circular portion of the sun's disk visible through it shall have a diameter equal to half of the entire disk. A sun will thus be seen of equal brightness with the true sun, but of only half the linear diameter, and one fourth the superficial magnitude.

From this illustration it will be easily perceived that one object may be smaller than another in apparent magnitude, and that it may give less light, but, nevertheless, be equally bright.

This being clearly understood, it remains to be shown, that if the sun were removed to double its present distance it would exhibit a surface to the eye as bright, though only half of the diameter. To comprehend this, let it be remembered that the light which proceeds from the smaller sun seen from double the distance, issues from the entire surface of the sun, while the light which would proceed from an equal portion of the sun's disk seen at its present distance, would only proceed from one fourth of the entire area of the disk. The actual quantity of light, therefore, which issues from the small sun, seen from the larger distance, is greater, in the proportion of 4 to 1, than that which proceeds from the small portion of the larger sun, seen at the lesser distance. It follows, then, that the actual quantity of light by which the object is rendered visible at the greater distance, is four times more than that by which the equivalent part of the nearer object is rendered visible at the lesser distance; but in consequence of the distance being less in the latter case, the intensity of the lesser quantity of light is four times greater. In short, it follows that as the object recedes from the eye the quantity of light which proceeds from a given portion of the visual area is increased in the same proportion as the square of the distance, while the intensity of the light is diminished in exactly the same proportion. What is, therefore, lost in intensity by increased distance, is gained in quantity; and the effect is, that the splendor of the object is not changed by distance, but only its apparent magnitude.

The apparent diameter of the sun is very nearly 2,000 seconds of a degree. If it were removed to 2,000 times its present distance it would present a diameter of one second; but it would appear as bright as a small portion of the present disk would appear having an apparent diameter 2,000 times less than its present apparent diameter; or if a pin-hole be made in a card, and a portion of the sun seen through it, which would subtend to the eye at an angle of one second, the appearance of such portion would be, as to brightness as well as to magnitude, that which the sun would have at 2,000 times its present distance.

Since, then, the brightness of the stars, in the proper sense of the term *brightness*, is not diminished by increased distance, we shall be the less surprised at their being visible, notwithstanding that they present no sensible disk even when magnified by the most powerful telescope.

It may again be asked how it can be said that the brightness of a star is not diminished by distance, when it is maintained that the splendor of the dog-star compared with one of the seventh magnitude, is owing to the greatness of the distance of the latter. To this we reply, according to the proper term brightness the dogstar is not brighter than an equal star of the seventh magnitude. It is a more splendid object as viewed by the eye, because it transmits more light to the eye, but its intrinsic splendor may be the same. The sun as seen from the earth and as seen from the planet Herschel, has the same *intrinsic brightness*, but its apparent magnitude at Herschel 200 times less.

WATER-SPOUTS AND WHIRLWINDS.

Character and Effects of Water-Spouts.—Difference between Water and Land Spouts.—Land-Spout at Montpellier.—Land-Spout at Esclades.—Columns of Sand on the Steppes of South America.—Meteor at Carcassonne.—Meteor at Dreux and Mantes.—Land-Spout at Ossonval.—Meteor witnessed and described by M. Peltier.—Conversion of a Storm into a Land-Spout.—M. Peltier's Tables of Water-Spouts and Land-Spouts.—Analysis of the above Tables.—Water-Spouts seen by Captain Beechy.—Experimental Illustration of the Phenomena.—Illustration of the gyratory Motion of Water-Spouts.—M. Peltier's Deductions concerning Water-Spouts.—Action of charged Clouds on light Bodies.—Noise attending Water and Land Spouts.—Transition from direct to gyratory Motion.—Effect of Induction on watery Surfaces.—Disappearance of Pools, &c.

WATER-SPOUTS AND WHIRLWINDS.

Water-spouts apparently consist of dense masses of aqueous vapor, presenting, often a gyratory and progressive motion, and resembling in form a conical cloud, the base of which is presented upward, and the vertex of which generally rests upon the ground, but sometimes assumes the contrary position. This phenomenon is attended with a sound like that of a wagon rolling upon a rough pavement.

Violent mechanical effects sometimes attend these meteors. Large trees torn up by the roots, stripped of their leaves, and exhibiting all the appearances of having been struck by lightning, are projected to great distances. Houses are often thrown down, unroofed, and otherwise injured or destroyed, when they lie in the course of a water-spout. Rain, hail, and frequently globes of fire, like the ball-lightning already mentioned, accompany these meteors, which are manifested equally at sea and on land.

Although the electrical effects which attend this meteor prove that it is closely connected with atmospheric electricity, yet, as no theory has hitherto been proposed which affords a satisfactory and adequate explanation of the phenomena, it is the more necessary to state, with as much clearness and precision as possible, independently of all hypotheses, the exact circumstances which have been found to attend them in the various parts of the globe where they have been observed. They are called water-spouts or land-spouts, according as they take place over the surface of the water or the land.

In the history of the Academy of Sciences is the following narrative :—

" On the 2d of November, 1729, about 8 o'clock in the morning, at Montpellier, a small and very obscure cloud was seen, in a very elevated position, in the direction of the southeast, whence the wind then blew. It advanced toward the town with a noise at first low, but which augmented as it approached: it gradually descended toward the ground, and a light was perceived to issue from it, like that which accompanies the smoke of a great fire. After the passage of this cloud, a strong odor of sulphur was perceived, like that which is diffused in places that have been struck by lightning. This cloud had a very rapid motion, and formed round it a whirlwind, which extended to a distance of above a hundred yards round, the force of which was so prodigious that it tore up trees by the roots, carried away the roofs of houses, overturned buildings, and scattered their ruins to a distance of nearly 500 yards. After having moved along half a league, with a width of above 200 yards, it was dissipated, followed by heavy rain, but not accompanied by thunder or lightning."

In the *Journal de Physique* for November, 1780, is the following description of one of these meteors, which took place at five o'clock in the evening, near Carcassonne:—

"This meteor originated upon the borders of the Aude. It commenced by pouring down a great quantity of water; it then projected upward, to a great height, quantities of sand. It unroofed eighty houses, and scattered over the country the sheaves of corn which it carried away. It tore up by the roots large oaks, and transported to a distance of fifty yards their branches, projecting them in a direction contrary to that of its own motion. It broke the doors, windows, and furniture of a chateau; it destroyed the pavement in the middle of a room, without deranging china cups which were placed there; it broke the frame of a looking-glass which was placed upon a chimney-piece, and scattered the fragments upon the chairs of the room, leaving the glass, however, in its place uninjured."

In the *Memoirs of the Academy of Toulouse*, vol. v., is the following description of a land-spout, which, on the 15th of June, 1785, devastated the neighborhood of Esclades, about four leagues from Narbonne:—

"The night before this terrible visitation was very fine, the sun rose unobscured by a single cloud, and the morning air was calm and pure. At half-past six o'clock the heat became very great, and continued to increase till seven o'clock, when it was excessive. At that time there appeared in the west a small cloud, which, gradually augmenting, extended in an hour over the whole horizon. The thermometer of Réaumur stood at 29°,* and the barometer at 28 inches. There was a light wind from the west. Such being the state of the atmosphere at two o'clock in the afternoon, a kind of smoky and blustering (*bruyante*) column was formed in the west, which passed between Esclades and Mont Brun. In its course it swept away earth and sand, tore up trees, and ravaged everything which came before it. This lasted for about five minutes. At about five miles from Esclades it became stationary for about five minutes, after which it returned upon its steps: the noise which it made resembled the continual roaring of thunder. It burst upon Esclades in a terrific shower of hail. This hail was succeeded by a rain so abundant that the country was inundated. During this shower, which lasted three quarters of an hour, lightning fell in several places. The thermometer rose to 32°.†

"The barometer rose a quarter of an inch, and the wind was very violent. After the meteor disappeared the weather became cool, and the barometer fell an inch and a quarter."

Humboldt states that, in the Steppes of South America, the plain or table land presents an extraordinary spectacle, which he describes as follows:—

"The sand rises in the middle of a rarefied whirlwind, probably charged with electricity, like a vapor, or a cloud in the form of a funnel, the point of which slides upon the ground, and resembling the blustering water-spout so much feared by the experienced navigator. On the roads in Europe, we see something which approaches the singular appearance of these whirlwinds of sand; but they are especially observed in the sandy deserts situate in Peru, between Coquimbo and Amotape. It is worthy of remark, that these partial cur-

* Equal to 100 degrees Fahr.

† Equal to 104 degrees Fahr.

rents of air which encounter each other are only perceived when the atmosphere is entirely calm—the ocean of air, therefore, like the ocean of water, encountering each other only in a dead calm."*

The *Courier* of the 19th of September, 1826, published the following narrative of a meteor which ravaged the arrondissement of Carcassonne on the 26th of August preceding :—

"The wind was from the south, and the heat of the morning was suffocating. About noon, the clouds accumulated in the west, and a violent wind arose. A thick black cloud appeared, suspended over a piece of land near the château of La Counette. In the direction of Fombraise, the clouds were seen to encounter each other, and, after the collision, to descend very low, as if they were attracted by the earth. The thunder grumbled on every side with a dull rolling noise; domestic animals fled to their sheds. Suddenly a frightful explosion (*craquement*) was heard in the west; the air, violently agitated, was drawn with extreme velocity toward the black cloud above mentioned: the moment they encountered was signalized by a loud detonation, and the appearance of an enormous column of fire, which, sweeping over the field, tore up everything in its way. A young man of 17 was carried away by this whirlwind, raised in the air, and dashed against a rock, by which his head was split; 14 sheep were carried away, and fell senseless.

"This column of air and fire overturned walls, displaced enormous rocks, tore up by the roots the largest trees, broke into the château by two openings, tore up and overturned the stones of the *porte cochère*, broke the gate, twisted all the iron work, broke through a window, entered the saloon on the first floor, broke through its ceiling, entered the second floor, passed to the roof, and, in fine, reduced to ruin these three stories. The ladies, who were in the saloon on the first floor, saw a globe of fire enter it, and owed their safety only to an enormous beam which formed an arch to support the wood-work. A vortex of air, entering by the window above the kitchen, broke through a partition, raised the floor, broke the furniture, overturned the beds, opened the closets without disturbing their contents, penetrated a thick wall and projected its ruins to a great distance, broke the timber-work of the château, tore up by the roots an enormous oak five feet in circumference, crushed two small houses, carried away wagons, which it precipitated into a ravine, uprooted several enormous walnut-trees, ravaged the vines, leaving in the earth deep trenches, and impregnating the air with a strong odor of sulphur. This meteor disappeared in the direction of Forcenas, and was succeeded by very heavy rain. The heavens then became serene, and a wind arose from the east."

In 1823, this meteor made great ravages in the neighborhood of Dreux and Mantes in France.

"In the village of *Marchefroid*, fifty-three houses were destroyed in the space of one minute, yet the storm was scarcely heard, and the appearance of the water-spout was only preceded by a little hail. A child three years old, who stood beside its mother in a court-yard, was killed upon the spot. On examining its body, no wounds were found upon it except a hole of a certain depth in the neck. Entire roofs were carried away either in the direction in which the meteor moved, or in the contrary direction. The four walls of a garden were thrown down in a regular manner, all falling on the outside of the garden: their fall was marked by great regularity. After the meteor passed away, the temperature did not seem changed, and the sun immediately reappeared."

On the 6th of July, 1822, a land-spout was formed in the plain of Ossonval, near the village of that name, in the department of the Pas de Calais.

* Tableau de la Nature, tom i., pp. 43 and 177.

Clouds coming from different directions and collecting over the plain, ultimately formed a single cloud which covered the heavens: immediately afterward a cone descended from this cloud, presenting its vertex downward, and having its base in the cloud. This meteor, driven by the wind, beat down a barn, tore and carried away the tops of the largest trees, overturned twenty-five to thirty of them, and strewed them in different directions, proving that the meteor had a revolving motion. It carried away and crushed other trees from sixty to seventy feet high. Globes of fire and sulphureous vapor were seen from time to time to issue from its centre. This meteor, in its rapid course, was attended with a sound like that of a heavy carriage rolling on a paved road.

It then penetrated into the valley of *Wetternester* and *Lambre ;* in the former of these villages, only eight habitations of forty were uninjured: the meteor left everywhere traces of its passage.

On the 18th of June, 1839, the neighborhood of Chatenay, in the department of Seine et Oise, was visited by a meteor, which happened to be witnessed by MM. Peltier, Bouchard, and Becquerel. The following narrative of it is abridged from the account given of it by M. Peltier :—

In the morning, a storm was formed to the south of *Chatenay*, and about ten o'clock it took the direction of the valley between the hills of *Ecouen* and *Chatenay*. The clouds, which were high, after extending above the extremity of the village, came to a stand, the thunder muttered, and the first cloud followed the ordinary route, when, toward noon, a second storm coming also from the south, advanced toward the same plain and the same hills. Arriving near the extremity of the plain over *Fontenay*, in presence of the first storm which, by its elevation, it overtopped, a pause took place, doubtless while the two storms were presenting themselves to each other by means of their clouds charged with the same electricity, and repelling each other.

To this time, thunder which was heard proceeded from the second cloud, when suddenly one of the inferior clouds descending, fell into communication with the earth, and the thunder seemed to cease. A prodigious attraction was manifested ; all light bodies and all the dust which covered the surface of the ground, was raised toward the point of the cloud : a continual rolling noise succeeded ; little clouds were fluttering and whirling round the inverted cone, and rising and falling rapidly. Trees, placed to the southeast of the meteor, were struck on their northwest side which faced it, the other side remaining in its usual state. The sides which were struck exhibited strong marks of the meteor, while the other parts preserved their sap and their vegetable life. The meteor descended the valley to the extremity of *Fontenay*, toward a row of trees planted along the bed of a stream which was then without water, though still humid. After having broken and uprooted these, it traversed the valley, and advanced toward other plantations which it also destroyed. There, having arrived at the point vertically under the limits of the first cloud, it paused, and the latter, which was hitherto stationary, began to be agitated and to retreat toward the valley west of *Chatenay*, and, overthrowing all that it encountered in its way, it passed to the park of the chateau of *Chatenay*, which it completely desolated. The walls were overturned, and the roofs and chimneys of the buildings carried away. Trees were transported several hundred yards ; windows, rafters, tiles were thrown to a distance of upward of 500 yards.

The meteor having ravaged that place, descended a mountain toward the north, and paused over a fish pond, where it overthrew and parched the trees, killed all the fish, and proceeded slowly along an alley of willows. Here it lost a great portion of its extent and violence. It then proceeded still more slowly over a neighboring plain, and after advancing three quarters of a mile, it divided itself into two portions near a clump of trees, one part rising into the clouds, while the other part sunk into the ground and disappeared.

All the trees struck by this meteor had their sap completely evaporated, the ligneous part being as much dried as if it had been exposed in a stove at the temperature of 300°. The immense quantity of vapor suddenly formed by the sap, having no means of escape from the interstices of the wood, split the tree in the longitudinal direction. All the trees presented marks of this effect.

By observing the progress of this phenomenon, the transformation of a common storm into a land-spout will be apparent. Two stormy clouds moved toward the same vertical line in which they settled at different altitudes. Being charged with the same electricity, the lower cloud descends toward the ground, and is put in electrical communication with the ground by whirlwinds of dust and by trees. This communication once established, the noise of the thunder immediately ceases, the discharge taking place by the continuous conductor formed by the clouds which have descended and the trees upon the plain. These last, traversed by the electricity, have their sap dried up and their trunks split; finally, flashes of light, balls of fire, and sparks appear, and a sulphureous odor remains in the houses for several days, the curtains of which are everywhere scorched.

In his voyage to the Pacific Captain Beechey witnessed water-spouts off Clermont Tonnerre, lat. 19° south, long. 137° west, of which he has given the drawings, from which figs. 1 and 2 have been taken.

Fig. 1.

Colonel Reid, in his work on storms, has given the following extract from a letter addressed to him by Captain Beechey, containing a circumstantial account of water-spouts, witnessed by him in the same voyage: "The day had been very sultry, and in the afternoon a long arch of heavy cumuli and nimbi rose slowly above the southern horizon; while watching its movements a water-spout began to form, at a spot on the under side of the arch, that was darker than the rest of the line. A thin cone (fig. 3), first appeared, which gradually became elongated, and was shortly joined by several others which went on increasing in length and bulk until the columns had reached about halfway down to the horizon. The sea beneath had hitherto been undisturbed; but when the columns united it became perceptibly agitated, and almost immedi-

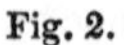
Fig. 2.

Fig. 3.

ately became whirled in the air with a rapid gyration and formed a vast basin, from the centre of which the gradually lengthening column appeared to drink fresh supplies of water (fig. 4).

Fig. 4.

"The column had extended to about two thirds of the way toward the sea, and nearly connected itself with the basin, when a heavy shower of rain fell from the right of the arch, and shortly after another fell from the opposite side. This discharge appeared to have an effect on the water-spout, which now began to retire.

"The sea, on the contrary, was perceptibly more agitated, and for several minutes the basin continued to increase in size, although the column was considerably diminished (fig. 5).

Fig. 5.

"In a few minutes more the column had entirely disappeared. The sea, however, still continued agitated, and did not subside for three minutes after all the disturbing causes from above had vanished. The phenomenon was unaccompanied by thunder or lightning, although the showers of rain which fell so suddenly seemed to be occasioned by some such disturbance."

M. Peltier has attempted to illustrate the electrical origin of these phenomena by producing them artificially. With this view he has represented the cloud in which the meteor originates by a globe of metal kept constantly charged with electricity by a machine. The inequalities of the cloud he represented by points raised on the surface of a globe. By means of the influence which this globe exercised upon water, vapors, and dust, he was able to produce a depression of the liquid, and the vortical or gyratory motion, and some other effects similar to those observed in the meteor.

All these effects disappeared when the globe was divested of points. In this case, instead of a depression, an elevation was produced; the vapors rose under the smooth ball, but showed little agitation. When the points were restored, the vapor was increased in more than a threefold proportion.

The globules of vapor, being electrified at a distance by the points, were repelled in all directions, and made to whirl, more or less, according to the degree of the electric charge.

There are other electrical experiments made with other views, which M. Peltier brings to bear on the illustration of water-spouts.

A plate of copper, not insulated, being placed under a sphere, a little light ball is placed between them. When the sphere is electrified, the ball plays alternately upward and downward between the sphere and the plate; but if, instead of the ball, elongated or flat bodies be interposed, so as to present only a long and narrow strip of gold leaf, the alternate motion just described is transformed into a vortical motion, which ultimately becomes one of rapid rotation between the sphere and the plate. Such are the gyratory motions which M. Peltier conceives to arise from electrical radiation.

The consequences which he deduces from these and similar facts are as follows:—

1. All the immediate phenomena observed in water-spouts are due to electricity: they are the results of secondary phenomena, which almost always accompany them. The latter vary with the locality and the state of the atmosphere.

2. Their general effects are due either to statical or dynamical electricity: most generally they proceed from both.

3. The statical effects are phenomena of attraction and repulsion.

4. The attraction of an electrical cloud is accompanied by a rush of air toward this cloud, whence result currents directed from the exterior to the interior, and proceeding from all surrounding points. It is manifested also by the projection of the vapor of water, of liquid water itself, and of bodies that it raises or tears, according to the force with which it acts.

5. The progress of its attractive power is plainly marked both on sea and land. On sea it appears by the boiling of the waters, and the smoky appearance which is raised from them, as represented in figures 1 and 2. On land its course is rendered manifest by its effects upon the air, the ground, and all loose bodies which it encounters.

6. The attraction of the clouds is also manifest by the greatly increased evaporation of the waters, and the consequent fall of their temperature. The repulsion is manifested by currents of the air which issue from the electric cloud, and only exist in its neighborhood. At a little distance from it a dead calm prevails. These double currents undergo various modifications, produced by the localities and various qualities of the ground.

7. The repulsion is also manifested by the cone which is formed in the sea, in the very centre of the smoky vapors, an effect which can be easily reproduced experimentally.

8. If an inductive action take place between two clouds charged with opposite electricities, placed at a certain distance asunder, a portion of their vapor will resume the state of common vapor; this will lower the temperature of the neighboring parts, which may descend even below the freezing point; then the vapor of water crystallizes in snowy flakes, which act immediately after their formation, like other light bodies. The portion thus transformed into snow, and which is charged with the electricity of the inferior cloud, is attracted by the superior cloud, then there is a neutralization of electricity, a fall of temperature, and so on.

9. Finally, the electrical tension of the superior cloud facilitates the evaporation of the liquid which moistens the snowy globule, or which already covers the ice.

The electrified clouds, acting by induction upon the ground, are attracted to it. The clouds thus approach the earth in a greater or less quantity, depending on the energy of the attraction, and their specific gravity.

When the tension of the clouds and their density differ little from those of the inferior strata of air, or when superior clouds, having the same electricity, act upon the inferior by repulsion, the latter may approach the earth sufficiently to be discharged without explosion by the intervention of other clouds which touch it.

It happens, often, that all the bodies placed upon the surface of the earth under these clouds, which have the form of an inverted cone, serve as conductors in various degrees, according to their constituent matter, their form, their extent, and the magnitude of their contact with the ground. Light and small bodies, oppositely electrified, are attracted and raised toward the cloud; when their electricity is neutralized they fall again upon the earth, where, being once more charged with electricity, they reascend, and so on. It is thus that an immense cloud of dust is formed under the cone. If the bodies are attached to the earth, like trees or buildings, they are instantaneously charged with an immense quantity of electricity. The earth, which is contiguous to them, partakes of this electricity, yields to the attraction of the cloud, and the trees, buildings, or other objects upon it, are torn up and transported afar. It is in this manner that bodies which are strongly attached to the earth are torn from it, while others in their immediate neighborhood are undisturbed. All these effects are subject to infinite variation, according to the conducting powers of the bodies, and of the parts of the earth to which they are attached.

If the great lightness of the clouds prevents them from falling sufficiently low to be in electrical communication with the ground, then the electricity will be discharged at a distance, attended by the flash of lightning and the roll of thunder. The electric tension will gradually diminish, rain will ensue, and the cloud will rise.

The sound which sometimes accompanies this phenomenon is attributed, by M. Peltier, to a number of small partial explosions, which take place between the cloud and ground. They are louder in the case of water-spouts which traverse the land, because of the imperfectness of the conductors presented to them; they lose their intensity over the sea because water is a better conductor.

Considering the progress of the air under the different attractions and repulsions to which it is submitted, and the contrary and unequal currents encountering different obstacles, M. Peltier endeavors to explain how the direct motion impressed on the air is changed into a gyratory motion more or less decided. It results from this, that the same meteor may present at different moments an example of direct and gyratory motion.

When the meteor is presented over water, its inductive action gives to the water near the surface an opposite electricity, and a consequent attraction ensues. If the contrary fluids do not unite by explosion, the surface of the water will swell upward at the several points of attraction, and the moment a discharge takes place, and the contrary fluids unite by explosion, this elevation subsides.

If, however, the electrified cloud is formed with points or prominences, which favor the escape of the electric fluid, the water becomes charged with the fluid descending from the cloud, and, being similarly electrified, is repelled by the cloud, and therefore depressed. Currents result from this in the water, which soon acquire a vortical motion.

On similar principles, M. Peltier explains the rapid disappearance of pools, or small collections of water, the entire mass being electrified by induction, and raised like trees and other objects.

The discharge of electricity through water may kill the fish contained in it; but the mere transmission of an electric current through the liquid without explosion will not have this effect, unless a considerable elevation of temperature takes place. An electric discharge passing near water, but not through it, may kill animals in it, by the effect of the lateral shock. By these principles, many of the observed effects of water-spouts are explained.

When by induction the electrical tension of the ground and objects upon it is elevated, the fluid with which it becomes charged will have a tendency to escape by all pointed conductors, and to issue upward toward the cloud. If the conductor be imperfect, an elevation of temperature will attend these upward currents, the effects of which will be apparent in the conductors by which they escape. Trees, plants, and vegetables, conducting the electric fluid imperfectly by means of their sap, are dried up by this temperature; and wher the elevation takes place suddenly, the vapor into which the sap is convertec splits the wood.

Such is a general outline of the theory of M. Peltier, by which the phenomena attending water-spouts and whirlwinds are explained.

www.ingramcontent.com/pod-product-compliance
Lightning Source LLC
LaVergne TN
LVHW021104110826
845150LV00001B/161

* 9 7 8 1 4 2 5 5 6 5 2 3 7 *